Enron Ascending

Political Capitalism: A Tetralogy

Book 1 Capitalism at Work: Business, Government, and Energy

Book 2 Edison to Enron: Energy Markets and Political Strategies

Book 3 Enron Ascending: The Forgotten Years, 1984–1996

Book 4 Contra-Capitalism: Enron and the Post-Enron World (Forthcoming in 2020)

Enron Ascending
The Forgotten Years, 1984–1996

Robert L. Bradley Jr.

Scrivener

WILEY

This edition first published 2018 by John Wiley & Sons, Inc., 111 River Street, Hoboken, NJ 07030, USA and Scrivener Publishing LLC, 100 Cummings Center, Suite 541J, Beverly, MA 01915, USA.
© 2018 Scrivener Publishing LLC.
For more information about Scrivener publications, please visit www.scrivenerpublishing.com.

Wiley Global Headquarters
111 River Street, Hoboken, NJ 07030, USA

For details of our global editorial offices, customer services, and more information about Wiley products visit us at www.wiley.com.

Limit of Liability/Disclaimer of Warranty
While the publisher and author have used their best efforts in preparing this work, they make no representations or warranties with respect to the accuracy or completeness of the contents of this work and specifically disclaim all warranties, including without limitation any implied warranties of merchantability or fitness for a particular purpose. No warranty may be created or extended by sales representatives, written sales materials, or promotional statements for this work. The fact that an organization, website, or product is referred to in this work as a citation and/or potential source of further information does not mean that the publisher and author endorse the information or services the organization, website, or product may provide or recommendations it may make. This work is sold with the understanding that the publisher is not engaged in rendering professional services. The advice and strategies contained herein may not be suitable for your situation. You should consult with a specialist where appropriate. Neither the publisher nor author shall be liable for any loss of profit or any other commercial damages, including but not limited to special, incidental, consequential, or other damages. Further, readers should be aware that websites listed in this work may have changed or disappeared between when this work was written and when it is read.

Library of Congress Cataloging-in-Publication Data:

Names: Bradley, Robert L., 1955- author.
Title: Enron ascending : the forgotten years, 1984-1996 / Robert L. Bradley Jr.
Description: Hoboken, NJ : John Wiley & Sons, Inc., 2018. | Includes
   bibliographical references and index. |
Identifiers: LCCN 2018002976 (print) | LCCN 2018010698 (ebook) | ISBN
   9781119494201 (epub) | ISBN 9781119494232 (pdf) | ISBN 9781119493709
   (oBook) | ISBN 9781118549575 (cloth) | ISBN 9781119556169 (dust jacket)
Subjects: LCSH: Enron Corp--History. | Energy industries--United
   States--History.
Classification: LCC HD9502.U54 (ebook) | LCC HD9502.U54 E5727 2018 (print) |
   DDC 333.790973--dc23
LC record available at https://lccn.loc.gov/2018002976

Cover images: Provided by the author
Cover design by: Russell Richardson

Set in size of 10pt and Palatino by Exeter Premedia Services Private Ltd., Chennai, India.

10 9 8 7 6 5 4 3 2 1

In Memory of Two Mentors

Murray N. Rothbard

Donald C. Lavoie

"We still have much to learn about and learn from Enron's remarkable history to understand its meaning for twenty-first-century American capitalism."

—Malcolm S. Salter, emeritus professor, Harvard Business School; author of *Innovation Corrupted: The Origins and Legacy of Enron's Collapse.*

Contents

Preface

Enron is well on its way to becoming the most intensively dissected company in the history of American business." So wrote Bethany McLean and Peter Elkind in their 2003 account, *The Smartest Guys in the Room*. Today, Enron stands as *the* most-analyzed corporate scandal in modern history, with countless books, journal articles, and reports about an iconic company gone rogue.

Imprudent investments coupled with financial and accounting legerdemain constitute the well-documented *why* of Enron's artificial boom and decisive bust. But the *why behind the why*—the attitudes and strategies that produced risky and deceptive practices—has been less chronicled and little understood.

Simplistic criticisms have abounded. "Fish rot at the head" declared one popular Enron book. "Shocking incompetence, unjustified arrogance, compromised ethics, and an utter contempt for the market's judgment" found another. "Thoughtless and incompetent leadership" and "careless and lazy management" concluded the most professorial study of Enron to date.

Hubris, amorality, and greed were certainly present at Ken Lay's company. But accusations of incompetence, lethargy, and thoughtlessness fall short. Enron brimmed with smart, dedicated, focused decision makers who tirelessly sought to create a new kind of company. How and why did so much talent and effort go astray? Why was "innovation corrupted," as a Harvard Business School professor asked.

Was it capitalism run amok? A species of market failure? Or was it, directly or indirectly, a *non*market failure, an unintended consequence of interventionist public policies and a contra-capitalist ethos by, respectively, government and executives?

More specifically, did prevalent government involvement with natural gas, coal, oil, and electricity before and during Enron's life shape the leadership and strategies atop the once storied company? Did special features of America's

ix

mixed economy invite financial deceit and other delinquencies at the grand experiment called Enron?

If so, why did bad practices come to dominate Ken Lay's Enron rather than, say, Lee Raymond's Exxon (later Exxon Mobil) or Charles Koch's Koch Industries? What was so different about Enron? What was the role of the company's founder and beginning-to-end chairman, the Great Man of his industry, and, as much as anybody, Mr. Houston?

These questions have been inadequately explored for several reasons. First, many journalists lacked deep familiarity with Enron and the energy industry. Second, employee-book retrospectives (a dozen or so), which might have offered deeper insight, tended to be provincial and personal narratives. Third, most analyses were preoccupied with Enron's last years and missed how earlier developments made the end all but predictable, absent a major (even radical) course correction. Above all, though, most accounts failed to appreciate the political dimension of Enron's profit centers and the pervasively contra-capitalist mentality of Enron's leadership.

Lacking technical depth and theoretical breadth, mainstream history became misleading history, especially when placing Enron in its social-economic-historical-political context. Ironically, commentators fell back on Enron's own misleading self-narrative about its free-market reverence.

The company, and no one more than Ken Lay, time and again pledged allegiance to free enterprise, deregulation, privatization, and competition. Come the implosion, that rhetoric was taken at face value. If Enron was capitalism, then capitalism was prone to flim-flam and deception, even fraud—and *failure*. Conclusion: More, tighter, smarter regulation was and will be needed; privatization must be checked, especially in undeveloped countries; and business-funded lobbying must be constricted, if not banned. Only then can the government intervention that might have prevented Enron prevent future ones.

This narrative stubbornly persists. The fall of the company remains a modern-day allegory for the perils of free enterprise and the capitalist spirit. Business students and professors purport to draw lessons about the need for regulatory oversight. Pundits, politicians, and intellectuals continue to make ideological points by using the company's name as a metaphor for unfettered profit seeking. The result is that, even after the 15th anniversary of Enron's bankruptcy (December 2, 2016), the company still lacks the detailed, chronological, you-are-there history needed for fuller interpretation and better insight.

A complete history must focus on Enron's beginning and maturation—and even its antecedents. What the company actually did—not merely what it said it was doing—must be established. Painstaking analyses must document how the company's principals, and no one more than Ken Lay, acted, interacted, reacted, and failed to act during his company's solvent life (approximately 17 years).

But more than better documentation is required. The real lessons of Enron require a reliable, integrated worldview spanning the social sciences. Earlier interpretations, albeit presented as just-the-facts, rested explicitly or subtly on the worldview of American Progressivism: Whatever capitalists do is capitalism. The result was a contradictory and unintelligible picture of a supposedly free-enterprise firm profiting heavily from its political influence. This book, and the tetralogy *Political Capitalism* of which it is a part, endeavors to resolve that contradiction.

Capitalism at Work (Book 1) explicated the classical-liberal worldview; *Edison to Enron* (Book 2) detailed the back story of Enron's industry and Ken Lay's early career. Drawing on those previous works, this book (and the one to come) will trace the false prosperity and spectacular demise of Enron to the company's violations of classical-liberal principles in epistemology, ethics, business, and politics.

Contra-capitalism is most easily recognized in the pursuit of special government favor, a practice that came to define Enron. Its deepest roots, however, lie in transgressions of the "bourgeois morality" (or Smilesian virtue, as Book 1 termed it) that has always constituted the foundation of commercial capitalism. Such contra-capitalist transgressions may be essentially personal—such as self-deceit, imprudence, recklessness, and prodigality. Or they may be intracorporate vices that violate the rules for honest cooperation and best-practices leadership.

The false representation of achievements and difficulties, *philosophic fraud*, was Enron's greatest corporate sin. But mixing personal and professional relationships, serving multiple masters, substituting image making for profit making, and CEO worship were others. Such contra-capitalism is explained in the Introduction and identified throughout this book to show that Enron, in spirit and in practice, was radically antithetical to classical liberalism.

Classical liberals applauded the fact that the market, not regulators, exposed and ruined Enron. True, but the broader point and the deeper moral of the story is this: *Enron and Ken Lay, as they were and became, would not have existed in a truly capitalist culture.* The ambitious and talented Lay took a political company to the top of a politicized industry within a politicized economy, fooling nearly everyone about the firm's economic sustainability and goodness.

————

The first draft of history, emanating from news analyses and resulting books about Enron, reached three major conclusions: one correct, one partially so, and one wrong. Affirming, completing, and rectifying those takeaways is the task of the present book—and the finale to follow.

The first conclusion—*Enron should have failed*—is sound. Ken Lay and Jeff Skilling reversed cause and effect by arguing that Enron had been undermined by bad press and short sellers of ENE stock. Enron was not "a great company," as Skilling and Lay each maintained. And Enron certainly was not "a strong, profitable, growing company even into the fourth quarter of 2001," as Lay avowed until his death. Enron was a hollow enterprise that had precious few assets to offset liabilities when liquidated after its 2001 bankruptcy.

Enron was able to deceive outsiders, and even itself, for far too long. The company's few critics and short sellers were brilliantly right, in retrospect, working from traces of smoke to find fire. If anything, Enron should have failed *sooner.* Many years of apparent success, Ken Lay's mighty persona, political correctness, new-economy hyperbole, and financial trickery kept the mirage shimmering for years longer than otherwise would have been the case.

The half-true conclusion is that a successful, sustainable Enron was sunk by the loss of Richard Kinder and the ascension of Jeff Skilling as 1996 turned into 1997. "It was one of the saddest days for Enron when Rich Kinder left," an Enron board member reminisced. "Sometime around 1996–1997, Enron crossed the line," a book author wrote. "Richard Kinder's departure as the financial conscience of the company seemed to be a critical step in this transformation."

Enron employees echoed the same sentiment. "I think that your book and other people's books are going to come back and say, Enron's downfall started on January 1, 1997," stated Jim Barnhart, a beloved, long-time Florida Gas Company/Enron executive who retired in that year.

Although true in important respects, the reality is that Enron was *badly off track by 1996.* Tipping points can be identified in 1987 (the Valhalla crisis), in 1989 (earnings acceleration), in 1992 (mark-to-model accounting), and in 1996 (financial gaming), not only in the more recognized episodes in 1997 forward, associated with CFO Andy Fastow. Outside the rock-solid interstate pipelines, as well as the industry-leading exploration and production unit, both of which had very different corporate cultures from their parent, Enron's major divisions were listing, and important new initiatives were unproven and problematic.

Ironically, troubles at Enron were partly the *result* of its might-have-been savior. In the leadership triumvirate of Ken Lay, Rich Kinder, and Jeff Skilling, tough-guy Kinder was the chief operating officer who wielded the hammer and ensured accountability from the business units. But Lay had helped make Kinder successful and rich, and Kinder had been notably compromised in the process. Indeed, he kowtowed to Ken Lay. The boss's shortcomings—a lack of focus and a perilous appetite for hazard—left Kinder with messes and complicity. From an oil-trading scandal to short-sighted accounting practices to Lay-family nepotism to inflated public relations to political forays, the CEO called the shots, and the COO was in places that he did not want to be.

Kinder's flaws went beyond acquiescence. Because he was Enron's top lawyer, the Valhalla trading debacle was partly his gamble and whitewash too. Kinder was personally unrelenting in his efforts to make promised earnings, quarter to quarter, year to year. He jumped at quick fixes that violated the economics of net present value to meet corporate and key-executive performance goals and, not coincidentally, put himself over the top financially. Until his time was up in 1996, the chief operating officer presided over misleading financial engineering, practices that would worsen.

Kinder developed flawed compensation systems, including a system for international projects that rewarded closings, not successful operation. He signed off on naked risks and okayed investments that resulted in large write-offs. A large buildup of off-balance-sheet debt occurred under his purview. Imprudence and artifice existed alongside Kinder's constructive actions of instilling accountability and practicing tough love.

The belief that Kinder would have saved Enron rests less on what he did at the company than on what he accomplished afterward. Having declared personal bankruptcy earlier in his life, Kinder relearned at Enron how high-sounding ventures by smart people could go awry. This lesson, and the end of his subservience to Ken Lay, served him well. Kinder and fellow HNG-ex William Morgan founded Kinder-Morgan on a hard-asset, midstream model that achieved a multibillion-dollar valuation by the time of Enron's demise. (They began by purchasing assets Enron no longer wanted.) This *anti*-Enron company, located across the street from the Enron Building, resulted from a fortuitous exit by a company builder (Kinder) who became, entrepreneurially and managerially, the anti-Lay.

Meanwhile, the new team of Skilling and Lay substituted hype, hope, and hurrah for midcourse corrections and allowed the company's bad divisions to overwhelm the good. Enron chose not to bid aggressively for new pipelines or focus on new domestic infrastructure projects at the core, betting instead on trendy ventures with postulated higher rates of return. The divergent paths taken by Enron and by Kinder-Morgan gave rise to an alternative history—*if only Kinder had stayed*—that is far from certain.

The third major conclusion, concerning the role of ideology in shaping Enron's business strategy, demands wholesale revision. The question to be answered is: Was the "systemic failure" involved in Enron's collapse—implicating all the private and government gatekeepers and guardians of business—attributable primarily to free-market incentives and capitalist attitudes or to an outlook favoring government intervention (regulation, tax preferences, subsidies), as well as deceit and cornercutting?

The mainstream view is that capitalism failed. Didn't Enron egregiously exploit the rules meant to protect the public? Didn't Ken Lay pay homage to deregulation and free markets during his entire Enron tenure? Wasn't Jeff Skilling the epitome of Social Darwinian capitalism? Didn't the final result—tens of thousands of innocents financially compromised—reveal the downside of modern capitalism? Amid the wreckage, even the *Wall Street Journal* editorialized that Enron was "a problem for anyone who believes in markets." More regulation and better enforcement, Progressives concluded, must protect against free-market debacles. Post-Enron legislation, supported by both political parties, reflected this view.

But one must look *beyond Enron's promarket image to actual behavior and true motivation*. It is here that a far different view emerges.

Enron is a problem for anyone who believes in the modern mixed economy. Ken Lay's business model leveraged government-sponsored commercial opportunities in myriad and sustained ways that ultimately came at the expense of competitors, investors, taxpayers, and consumers. In contrast to such business/political scandals as Crédit Mobilier and Teapot Dome, however, Enron's acts of political enrichment were legal. In the mixed economy, moreover, they were often politically correct, achievements to be heralded in the media and in Enron's own annual reports.

Enron is also a problem for anyone who believes in the highly regulated economy. The company became a master of gaming complex tax codes and regulatory rules. Indeed, Enron came to embody those sharp practices and philosophic frauds so long decried by classical-liberal thinkers and free-market entrepreneurs. Yet, as with Enron's lobbying, these manipulations were almost all legal. And those that were not were typically mere infractions of accounting minutiae.

What allowed Enron to prosper greatly through its dissimulations, and for so long, was nothing but the government's regulatory role, which Enron's brightest gamed into profits. Because of the moral hazard created by Progressivism's bureaucratic oversight, private-sector gatekeepers failed to discover and denounce the company's violations of moral and commercial best practices, as they surely would have in more of a self-reliant, buyer-beware market.

A revisionist view of Enron must also focus on the modus operandi of Ken Lay, a big-picture PhD economist with much regulatory experience inside and outside federal agencies. After becoming CEO of Enron-predecessor Houston Natural Gas Corporation, Lay quickly remade his new company into a federally regulated entity. From innocent beginnings, he gradually came to abandon centuries-old maxims of business prudence, in a vain quest to make Enron into the world's leading energy company and, later, the world's leading company.

Highly ambitious and über-optimistic, Enron's chairman was running from a past and superaccelerating into the future. What appeared to be a real-life Horatio Alger story would end up as an American tragedy, the subject of Book 4 (covering Enron from 1997 through bankruptcy and the criminal prosecutions). Jeff Skilling's release from prison will constitute a final data point for my history of Enron and this tetralogy on political capitalism inspired by the rise and fall of Ken Lay's enterprise.

———

The current project began as a three-part book: *Political Capitalism: Insull, Enron, and Beyond*. Then each part—worldview, backstory, and Enron proper—expanded to become its own book, reflecting the unanticipated richness of each subject on a stand-alone basis.

Book 1, *Capitalism at Work: Business, Government, and Energy* (2009), applied the classical-liberal worldview to Enron and the US mixed economy in which the company thrived. My foray into business strategy, history, philosophy, economics, and political economy documented how leading capitalist thinkers identified and emphasized economically sustainable commercial practices.

Adam Smith, Samuel Smiles, and Ayn Rand each warned against the behaviors that came to define Enron. In our day, classical-liberal entrepreneur Charles Koch has codified an integrative business philosophy in his books *The Science of Success* (2007) and *Good Profit* (2015) that is quite opposite to Enron's modus operandi.

No less important than the history of ideas is the history of institutions. Book 2, *Edison to Enron: Energy Markets and Political Strategies* (2011), explored the antecedents of Enron in terms of predecessor companies and individuals, including Ken Lay himself. The rhyme-in-history stories of John Henry Kirby and Samuel Insull offer parallels to that of Ken Lay, bankruptcy and all. The lessons of history, particularly the rise and fall of seemingly bedrock individuals and firms, show that history unknown, unlearned, forgotten, or simply unappreciated is valuable knowledge foregone.

The present book begins my analysis of Enron proper and its aftermath. But for several reasons this book turned into two—and the trilogy into a tetralogy.

First was the sheer complexity of Ken Lay's always-charging, always-changing Enron, which was a collection of companies having separate management, business plans, and incentive structures. Those companies were in exploration and production (Enron Oil & Gas); interstate gas transmission (Florida Gas Transmission, Transwestern Pipeline, Northern Natural Gas, among others); natural gas marketing (Enron Capital & Trade Resources, and predecessors); and international infrastructure (Enron International). Gas liquids and other Enron ventures, such as those in renewable energy, had their own histories as well.

Enron repeatedly spun off units into public companies, one of which was brought back as a wholly owned subsidiary. Monetizing assets to fund the next big thing was important in Enron's quest to become North America's leading integrated natural gas company, then the world's first natural gas major, then the world's leading energy company. (Enron's final vision, to become the world's leading company, is part of the forthcoming Book 4.)

Second, Enron was bound up with external events that were much bigger than the company itself. In business and in public policy forums, Ken Lay became the spokesman for natural gas against coal on one side and oil on the other. Lay also became the closest thing to a Mr. Houston by the mid-1990s, using his personal wealth and his company's vast resources to support numerous philanthropies and to drive ballot initiatives that he considered important to Enron and its hometown.

Third, reliable and scholarly history must capture the context and purpose of events, not only their sequence. Enron was not a place or thing or event; it was a process of decision making, with each stage unfolding into the next. Contextual, *insider*, purpose-centered history—as opposed to mere external storytelling—requires a detailed you-are-there approach to understand what might otherwise be bewildering, even to Enron scholars.

Finally, pre-1997 Enron is a story unto itself. The events and lessons of the "forgotten years" stand on their own without the complications of later history. The past is prologue to the last five (solvent) years of Enron. Still, the process has two natural segments: 1984–96 and 1997–2001.

————

Enron is one of the most important stories in American business—and certainly in the domestic energy industry, where Ken Lay's saga joins those of John D. Rockefeller (1881–1911) and Samuel Insull (1892–1932). Rockefeller was Mr. Petroleum; Insull was "The Chief" of electricity. Ken Lay was Mr. Natural Gas and reaching for more.

When I began this project some 20 years ago as a bright-eyed Enron employee, I believed that Lay would achieve, or at least approach, his rarefied goals and be a notable success story. What I did not know—what this book documents—is that many of the seeds of failure and tragedy had already been sown.

Acknowledgments

The present history owes much to my 16-year career at Enron (1985–2001), the first part of which was at Transwestern Pipeline, an interstate transmission system delivering natural gas from Texas and New Mexico to California. There, I learned firsthand about rates and terms of service under rules set by the Federal Energy Regulatory Commission and FERC's changeover to mandatory open-access transmission from the prior regulatory regime. I also learned about California's extensive energy and environmental controls—administered by the California Public Utilities Commission, the California Energy Commission, the California Air Resources Board, and the South Coast Air Quality Management District.

My second phase at Enron was in a corporate-level position created just for me. As Director of Public Policy Analysis, I was involved in different legislative and regulatory issues and in preparing executive presentations, primarily for Ken Lay. In the debates over renewable energy and climate, I was Enron's lone libertarian. As such, I was outnumbered by my conventional-wisdom colleagues, who on cue from the chairman pursued politically derived profits (a practice that economists call *rent-seeking*). Nevertheless, my voice was heard by a respectful Lay, who at least professed to believe in free markets.

Practically from the beginning, I took notes and retained materials with a company history in mind. I first proposed such a book to Enron's then chief of staff, Ed Segner, in a memo dated February 12, 1992. In 2000, when the corporate vision was about to about to become "The world's leading company," I began interviewing key figures for a sanctioned corporate history. Joining me as codirector of the project was the University of Houston's Cullen Professor of History and Business Joseph Pratt, the leading energy-industry chronicler of his generation in the tradition of Henrietta Larson and the Harvard University–led Business History Foundation. Alas, the Enron Oral History Project terminated with the implosion of the company in late 2001.

That research, as well as much other primary material collected from inside the company, is utilized throughout this book. Unless otherwise noted, copies of the referenced illustrations, promotional materials, interoffice memos, corporate documents, interviews, and emails between me and Enron executives are "in the author's possession" and will eventually be deposited in a publicly available archive. As with Book 2, source notes (approximately 5,300); a complete bibliography (comprising approximately 1,000 entries), and 39 Internet appendixes are posted online at www.politicalcapitalism.org. Also available at that web address are fuller versions of this book's three indexes: Name Index, Business Index, Political Economy Index. Because the online versions include a third level of analysis, they can be used for more precise searching.

My rare opportunity to apply a multidisciplinary classical-liberal worldview to Enron has been the result of many generous, patient people. My thanks begin with the board of directors of the Institute for Energy Research and IER president Thomas J. Pyle. The philanthropy of classical-liberal entrepreneur Charles Koch, as well as the encouragement of my parents, the late Robert L. Bradley and Margaret Bradley, allowed me to take the intellectual road less traveled.

I also wish to acknowledge some of my intellectual debts. Early in my career, two esteemed classical-liberal scholars took a special interest in me when I was long on enthusiasm and short on expertise, not to mention published work. Donald Lavoie taught me the value of scholarship in which opposing views are deeply understood, charitably interpreted, and thoroughly evaluated. Murray Rothbard imparted the importance of a multidisciplinary worldview to produce reliable history. My 1977 summer with both in Menlo Park, California, will always be a highlight of my personal and intellectual life.

Liberty Fund colloquia, under the direction of Doug Den Uyl, have proved invaluable to my intellectual development. They built upon my earlier study of the science of liberty at seminars of the Institute for Humane Studies, now housed at George Mason University.

Economist Robert Michaels of California State–Fullerton, as well as Richard Bilas and Tom Tanton of the California Energy Commission, were great educators and proliberty allies in the most energy-unfree state in the union. I also remember many friends and teachers I met through business at the California utilities, including Larry Flexer of Southern California Gas Company and Manuel Alvarez of Southern California Edison Corporation.

Critical readers of various sections of the manuscript who (re)lived the Enron years with me include Jim Alexander, Gerald Bennett, Ron Burns, John Esslinger, Mark Frevert, Steve Harvey, Forrest Hoglund, Stan Horton, Vince Kaminski, Rebecca Mark-Jusbasche, Dan McCarty, Mike Muckleroy, Cindy Olson, Lee Papayoti, Ken Rice, Geoff Roberts, Mark Schroeder, Clark Smith, Bruce Stram,

Terry Thorn, George Wasaff, and Sherron Watkins. Dozens more at Enron consented to personal interviews that are now part of the historical record.

Becky Cantrell gave me a treasure trove of internal memoranda during our last days together at Enron. My colleague Jeff Gray understood the company's problems in real time and educated his more tenured colleagues (including me). John Olson reviewed parts of the manuscript and imparted his story of a professional analyst questioning authority, including the emperors of Enron. John Jennrich, the premier energy journalist of his era, kindly reviewed chapters and hunted down research material for this book.

Roger Donway, a scholar's scholar, provided primary research, helped me develop the notion of contra-capitalist business management, and carefully edited the entire volume. Jean Spitzner provided the expert graphics herein. Copy editor Evelyn Pyle made sure that all was in editorial order.

The quest to pen timeless history is a long, painstaking process. My publisher and friend Martin Scrivener has been the most patient and encouraging publisher an author could have. On his watch, one book turned into three and prospectively four. I am proud to have the imprimatur of Scrivener Publishing, in conjunction with John Wiley & Sons, on this book.

Any shortcomings in this effort are my responsibility alone. I will post corrections, criticisms, and elaborations from readers at my website: www.politicalcapitalism.org/Book3/Revisions.html. To this end, I invite readers to send information to me at robbradley58@gmail.com.

Robert L. Bradley Jr.
March 2018

Introduction: The Process of Enron

Enron always lived dangerously. The peril began in 1984 just months after Ken Lay took charge of predecessor company Houston Natural Gas (HNG) and grew until Enron's bankruptcy in December 2001. What kept Enron in harm's way during those 17 years was less unfavorable industry conditions than Lay's conviction that extraordinary growth, tied to a grand narrative, would create an ever more dominant company.

In year 1, Ken Lay paid top dollar (and more) for two interstate pipelines, then engineered a merger based on his side's exaggerated projection of profit. By mid-1985, the originally cash-rich HNG had become debt-laden HNG/Inter-North, a company with (in Lay's words) "no margin for error."

Enron would skate on thin ice in the next years, even dodging one near-death experience. But the CEO, empowered and emboldened, was looking for the type of growth that required new businesses—*and new practices.*

Into the 1990s, Enron's earnings streak was the talk of the industry. But the Lay Way included a number of distinct, aggressive behaviors. Enron was entering into very large commitments that relied on educated guess and hope, not mitigated risk. Quick fixes to enlarge current earnings sacrificed the future. Important pockets of profit turned on political favor at home and on unstable, anticapitalist regimes abroad.

Still more, Enron's fastest-growing division reported earnings that were subjectively derived, not objectively accrued. Abuse was just ahead.

Enron became hooked on outsized earnings growth, quarter to quarter, year after year. ENE was a *momentum stock*, with Lay assuring everyone about the future. Employees, heavily vested in ENE, were thinking big and fast—just as the CEO wanted.

When the inevitable slowdowns and reversals came, Enron resorted to financial machinations and half-truth disclosures to keep the narrative going. This misfeasance brought short-term relief but also a weakened future. Dodging new trouble invited still more imprudent actions and sharp practices. Such was the *process of Enron*,[1] by which deviations from best practices grew, corrupting the company's engines and controls, even as the overall structure soared higher.[2]

Enron Ascending documents this process as manifest in the half-dozen major businesses that operated under Enron parentage between 1984 and 1996. Three market-oriented divisions—natural gas transmission, exploration and production, and gas liquids—were marked by prudence, probity, and productiveness. Not coincidentally, they had also been the core at HNG and at InterNorth. But Enron's other three divisions (natural gas and power marketing, power development, renewables and clean fuels) were government-enabled and prone to imprudence and hyperbole—the very antithesis of good business identified by classical liberals since the days of Adam Smith.

————

This introduction-cum-summary highlights the major themes and key facts from the large body of business history to come. Two major conclusions emerge.

First, Enron's ultimate fate arose naturally from the practices of its first dozen years. In particular, the Valhalla oil-trading scandal in 1987 (chapter 4) has been well analyzed by others as an adumbration of Enron's fate. But this book identifies and connects many more deviations from best practices—often small, but some large—in order to highlight the process by which early decisions and flaws evolved to put and keep Enron in peril.

The *why* of Enron's collapse is found in the company's post-1996 injudicious investments and accounting legerdemain, the exposure of which brought on bankruptcy in late 2001—and wonderment that it did not happen sooner.

This leaves the *why behind the why*, the far less understood business strategy and personal motivations that inspired the all-too-frequent missteps and mistruths prior to 1997. Viewed chronologically, with each sector of the company

————

1. See also "Enron as a Process," in the Epilogue, pp. 667–68, and Internet appendix I.1, "Business History Scholarship: Some Methodological Notes," at www.politicalcapitalism.org/Book3/Introduction/Appendix1.html.

2. Enron's bankruptcy filing listed $49.8 billion in assets and $31.2 billion in liabilities, which did not include off-balance-sheet financing and contingent liabilities. In the final accounting, Enron's liabilities exceeded assets and lawsuit recoveries by a factor of five: $63 billion vs. $12 billion.

examined in detail, *the process of Enron* becomes apparent prior to 1997, not just afterwards.

What explains the process within Enron, the related institutional failures outside Enron, and the utter surprise of it all for so many constituencies? The answer is found in this book's second conclusion: Ken Lay's enterprise was *the least-capitalistic megacompany in modern US history,* creating its own model along the way. This characteristic is the common denominator that elucidates a saga which otherwise appears abrupt, unfathomable, and even irrational.

No prior analysis has made this connection. Progressives interpreted Enron as the supreme embodiment of unchecked capitalism and institutionalized greed. Exaggeration, deceit, ill-gotten riches, and cronyism marked Ken Lay's enterprise. Their prescription: less economic freedom and more public-interested government regulation to protect citizens from selfish, destructive market behaviors.

Probusiness analysts, conservative or libertarian, on the other hand, dismissed Enron as just the proverbial bad apple. Apologies were in order, not major regulatory reform. The market, after all, had punished the guilty and gained many valuable lessons in the process.

In short, Enron was symptomatic of the economic system to the Left but unrepresentative of capitalism to the Right.

Both positions have validity. Enron was symptomatic of our culture and political economy yet had little to do with capitalism. Reconciling these viewpoints requires a new term—even an entirely new lexicon. The syndrome of symptoms embodied in Enron's life and death was *contra-capitalism,* a nonideological pattern of behaviors systematically antithetical to the moral, economic, and political precepts of classical liberalism.

Contra-Capitalism

Best-practices capitalism has its opposite in behaviors that characteristically fail to result in mutually beneficial exchange and wealth production. But without a concept to denote such behaviors, proponents of free-market capitalism were flummoxed by Ken Lay's enterprise. Embarrassed, the editorial board of the *Wall Street Journal* could only opine that Enron was "a problem for anyone who believes in markets." At the Cato Institute, chairman Willian Niskanen went into damage control, raising money, assembling scholars, and publishing articles and books to better decipher this new reputational threat to capitalism.

For Progressives, Enron-as-capitalism was a welcome game changer after two decades of increasing appreciation for markets. Just months after one of the most traumatic events in US history, Paul Krugman wrote in the *New York Times*: "I predict in the years ahead Enron, not September 11, will come to be seen as the greater turning point in U.S. society." Other staunch critics of capitalism predicted the decline of free-market advocacy and pronounced the need for universal, mandated ethics training for business students in order to moderate the allegedly antisocial motivations of capitalists.

What made the Progressives' case seem obvious is that Enron's principals were not ideological foes of capitalism. Ken Lay and Jeff Skilling proclaimed their belief in free markets and spoke often about the virtues of competition, deregulation, liberalization, and privatization. Government—not markets—was their stated foe, even the butt of derision. ("Imperfect markets," Lay liked to say, "are often better than perfect regulation.")

But actions speak louder than words. The bad behaviors of Enron—market deception, gamed accounting, engineered finance, government largesse, and general hubris—have long been recognized by procapitalists as inconsistent with the ethics, economics, and politics of the free market. Until now, however, such deviancy was dismissed as atypical, not pronounced and interrelated enough to constitute an *ism*.

Enron *was* culturally symptomatic. It was not one man's Ponzi scheme, like Bernie Madoff's investment fund. Nor was Ken Lay just hopelessly over his head, like WorldCom's Bernie Ebbers. Enron was revered inside the business community and lionized outside it. Ken Lay had a doctorate in economics, and Jeff Skilling graduated at the top of his class at the Harvard Business School. Enron was peopled by the best and brightest, almost all highly educated.

Contra-capitalist management has three characteristics. Most obviously, the pursuit of corporate profit through government-sanctioned coercion (*rent-seeking*) is contra-capitalistic because it makes exchange involuntary, if only for taxpayers subsidizing a particular business practice. In a free market, government neutrally enables production and trade by prohibiting force and fraud. Absent physical coercion or false representation under the rule of law, transactions are voluntary, and win-win outcomes are fostered.

More subtly, as this history will document, Enron relied on government in ways that went far beyond simple corporate welfare. In his late 20s and early 30s as a government bureaucrat, if not before in his study of political economy, Ken Lay learned how companies could profit from regulatory changes intended to serve the public interest.

Contra-capitalism also includes reliance on legal (nonprosecutable) dishonesty, which breaches the counterparty's ability to enter into beneficial exchange. Short of *criminal fraud* under the rule of law, *philosophic fraud* denotes those (nonprosecutable) behaviors that are merely devious, unethical, or delusory—all at the expense of fair dealing and mutually advantageous outcomes. In a peculiarly odious twist on philosophic fraud, Enron devised (legal) financial structures so mind-numbingly complex as to be impenetrable, leaving investors to rely on its (trumped-up) reputation.

Third, and most subtly, contra-capitalism subsumes violations of bourgeois moral virtues (for example: prudence, caution, humility, forethought, and frugality) that tend to foster profitable, sustainable production and trade.[3] But as classical liberal Samuel Smiles insisted back in the 19th century, virtue also includes the character traits of courtesy, politeness, and reverence, which came to be in short supply at mighty Enron.

Although the term *contra-capitalist* was not coined in *Capitalism at Work* (Book 1 of this series), its first three chapters sketched out the philosophic foundations of capitalism and highlighted Enron's innumerable violations of that long tradition. Enron's modus operandi was contrasted with that of Market-Based Management, an organizational philosophy codified by the classical-liberal entrepreneur Charles Koch. His *The Science of Success* (2007) and *Good Profit* (2015) showed how the traditional virtues and principles of the free market applied to the firm. Business practices within contra-capitalism (the mirror opposite of Koch's Market-Based Management) systematically violate the traditional virtues and principles behind free-market prosperity and a flourishing civil society.

The present book documents how many employees and divisions, taking their cue from the top, contributed to Enron's cascading problems and, eventually, calamitous end. Market-violating practices and bad profits overwhelmed the good. Led by Ken Lay and Jeff Skilling, contra-capitalists extraordinaire, Enron became a uniquely *contra-capitalist enterprise.*

———

Enron's contra-capitalism reflected ideas that dominated late-20th-century business and society, although Ken Lay brought its practice to unprecedented heights. Lay did not embark on a contra-capitalist strategy (such practices had not been isolated or defined). Lay's training and outsized ambition simply led him in a contra-capitalist direction. A politicized industry (energy) and America's political economy offered that path—or slippery slope, as it would turn out.

Ascendant philosophies buttressed some of Enron's uniquely aggressive practices. Ideas have consequences, and prevailing doctrines of political economy and political correctness were keenly noted by a move-on-all-fronts CEO.[4] Ironically, anticapitalist academics and politicians who promoted such doctrines

———

3. These attributes have gray areas and may be reevaluated with experience (a later draft of history). For example, a reckless and imprudent business gamble might later be judged bold and brave simply because it succeeded. Only detailed case studies can decide whether prudence or imprudence dominated a decision before it was made and whether favorable outcomes resulted from entrepreneurial alertness or sheer luck.

4. In the energy-policy field, Enron was the beau at the ball for anti–fossil fuel environmentalists and politicians pushing the narrative of problematic global warming and the need for government subsidization of wind and solar power (to displace fossil fuels). And as described in Book 1 (Bradley, *Capitalism at Work*, pp. 309–12), Enron was also wed to the doctrine of corporate social responsibility.

as Pragmatism, Progressivism, and Postmodernism helped create the very entity they would later falsely denounce as capitalism.[5]

Although it may seem implausible to argue that Enron's business-management practices had direct philosophic affinity with the academy's anticapitalist theories, consider that Enron, until the end, was beloved by much of America's left-wing intelligentsia. And today, that same intelligentsia reviles the very company that is most unlike Enron, the one most based on classical-liberal management.[6]

Primrose Paths, Slippery Slopes

Enron's contra-capitalism—what would be later condemned as "ethical drift" and "defining deviancy down"—was not born whole but *evolved*. In fits and starts, Ken Lay's struggle to grow Enron rapidly yet maintain investor confidence pitted sound business practices against contra-capitalist ones: sophisticated risk avoidance against imprudent risk taking, honest accounting against earnings manipulation, and wealth creation against rent-seeking.

This is not to say that all Enron's well-made decisions succeeded or that all its contra-capitalist undertakings failed. Business is not so simple. During Enron's forgotten years of 1984–1996, however, the company's contra-capitalist practices were present and growing, a process that would accelerate and become unstoppable in the following years.

Enron lived on the edge. But for thousands of employees, of whom I was one, there was more excitement than foreboding in the service of a Great Man of Industry. Chairman Lay seemed to be escaping business as usual in a traditionally run industry to make ours into more than just another Fortune 500 company. New strategies, even wholly new ways of doing business, seemed to outdistance the competition, time and again, to put Enron in a league of its own.

What was Lay's new, superior business model? Not asset redeployment; that was the norm in the 1980s for Enron's upstream and midstream rivals in a buyer's market for natural gas. Natural gas integration was part of the plan, but federal regulation limited the synergies between Enron's wide-ranging gas transmission and its national marketing network. Attracting and retaining superior management was certainly key, but competitors were noticeably picking off Enron's talent by 1988. Simply being bolder than the competition did win extraordinary profits, but it produced major write-offs too.

---

5. For a review of these doctrines, see Internet appendix I.2, "Pragmatism, Progressivism, Postmodernism," at www.politicalcapitalism.org/Book3/Introduction/Appendix2.html.

6. That company is Koch Industries Inc. under the leadership of philosopher, entrepreneur, and philanthropist Charles Koch.

Something else was required to turn the normalized returns of competitive markets into double-digit, multiyear uninterrupted growth. Enron's answer was a strategy that circumvented market rigors and norms in unprecedented ways.

That is not to indict Ken Lay as an iniquitous executive. In fact, he had many endearing and admirable qualities. But his business practices were, unfortunately, a reflection of his times, carried to an extreme by his extraordinary, hurried ambition. In place of nefarious intent, this CEO became entrapped by the process of Enron, a tyranny of small decisions and path dependence, whereby imprudence took Enron from health to precariousness to ruination, much to Lay's surprise.

Process analysis explains how Enron's life implied the nature of its death. It says, in outline, that Ken Lay, a child of the 20th century's mixed economy and pragmatism, failed to see how *personal* circumvention of traditional bourgeois morality was linked to *legal* circumventions of accounting, regulatory, and tax codes, as well as to profits achieved by *politically* bypassing the free market.

Ultimately, Lay failed to envision how a business heavily based on imprudence, deceit, and political cronyism was unsustainable, if pushed too far and too fast. Tracing and explicating Enron's embrace of such contra-capitalism is the normative purpose of this book.

––––

This book details Enron's birth, adolescence, and maturation—a period that lasted roughly from 1984 to 1996. The genuine achievements that led most observers to believe that Enron was historically great are detailed. So too are the risky, rash, and even reckless actions whereby Enron pushed itself ever faster toward the goal of supreme eminence. It is here that an exposé emerges of the contra-capitalist ethos that pervaded Enron in attitude, interpersonal relations, legal interpretation, and political strategy.

Enron's beginning was not necessarily more contra-capitalist than other natural gas firms of the 1980s, certainly including Lay's prior company, Transco Energy.[7] That is why this Introduction emphasizes *process*, whereby relatively small violations of bourgeois morality and best-practices management laid down precedents for the catastrophic sins that occurred after 1996. These well-chronicled misdeeds had precedents, even during the Richard Kinder era—a revelation that is part of this book's historical revisionism.

––––

7. Transco, under chairman Jack Bowen, advocated a national energy plan, similar to Jimmy Carter's, that included oil tariffs; forced conservation (conservationism), coupled with government synthetic-fuel subsidies; and a legislative fix for the company's natural gas take-or-pay liabilities. Bowen was also instrumental in forming the Gas Research Institute, which was funded by a federally authorized national surcharge to interstate-transmission rates.

By the mid-1990s, Enron was not above misleading people to boost its narrative of recent and prospective growth, a practice begun several years earlier with its subjective estimates of current profit from long-term contracts. During one quarter of 1996, as discussed in chapter 11, Enron stared at a $190 million shortfall from its promised quarterly profit, owing to severe trading losses in its prized unit. (Enron was taking large positions—something it told investors it was not doing—which sometimes lost.) Having never missed a quarterly target, ENE could plunge on such bad news.

At the last minute, Enron's high-powered accountants, most hired in the early 1990s, declared that assets held in a co-owned investment vehicle were not core assets but assets being held for resale. A switch from historical basis to "fair value" (mark-to-market) basis generated the needed (paper) profits. Perception maintained by Lay, Kinder, and Skilling; crisis averted.

Conflicts of Interest

Creating and exploiting *conflicts of interest* was another contra-capitalist practice within the process of Enron. The index in Malcolm Salter's scholarly tome on Enron includes 15 such entries.

Serving two masters instead of one climaxed when Enron's board of directors waived a conflict-of-interest provision for CFO Andy Fastow, allowing him to manage special-purpose entities (SPEs) buying assets from Enron.[8] On at least 13 occasions, the Enron employees with whom Fastow was negotiating were his underlings as CFO.

Then again, these major deviations had precedent during Enron's forgotten years. One conflict emanated from the Omaha-based InterNorth side following the 1985 merger when Arthur Andersen was retained as auditor in order to keep its Omaha office open. HNG's auditor was dismissed, leaving Andersen for both auditing and consulting for the combined company. But perhaps the earliest conflict of interest began when the new CEO steered HNG's travel business to his sister's firm, of which he was part owner.

The conflict-of-interest precedents grew when Lay allowed employee-turned-consultant John Wing to be on both sides of Enron's cogeneration deals. Fastow's waiver also repeated the experience, qualitatively speaking, of Enron spin-off Enron Global Power & Pipelines (EPP), in which the public as minority owner was represented by Enron-controlled management. (This 1994–96 experiment was terminated when EPP rejoined Enron.) There was also Andy Fastow's opaque, even blatantly dishonest, partnership in early 1997 that allowed Enron to skirt regulatory requirements with its purchase and resale of wind power facilities.

---

8. See Internet appendix I.3, "Enron Special-Purpose Entities: From 1991 to 1996, and Beyond," at www.politicalcapitalism.org/Book3/Introduction/Appendix3.html.

In short, what happened at Enron during its last years of boom and bust flowed—logically, predictably, almost inevitably—from the company's beginnings and growth. It is here that this corporate *Bildungsroman* elucidates the cause-and-effect processes that led up to the oft-mentioned but inadequately explained "post-1997 drift from innovation to reckless gambling to deceptive management."

Chairman Lay

"An institution is the lengthened shadow of one man." That was certainly the case at Enron. The company that became Enron began in mid-1984 when the erstwhile president and COO of Transco Energy Company arrived at 1200 Travis Street in downtown Houston as chairman and CEO of Houston Natural Gas Corporation. Kenneth Lee Lay remade the company in his first months and then orchestrated a reverse merger to create HNG/InterNorth in 1985. The next year, the nation's largest and most-integrated natural gas company was renamed Enron.

Enron is the story of its founder and leader—and wonder boy of his industry. Ken Lay was chairman from June 1984 until January 2002, when Enron was in receivership. He ceded his president's title to John "Mick" Seidl in 1986, retook it upon Seidl's departure in early 1989, and ceded it for good to three consecutive individuals: Rich Kinder (1990–96), Jeff Skilling (1997–2001), and Mark Frevert (2001).[9] Lay was CEO until Enron's last 10 months as an operating company, when Jeff Skilling and then Greg Whalley briefly held the title.[10]

More than Enron's visionary, Ken Lay was an *industry* visionary, championing natural gas as the premium fuel compared to coal and oil in the all-important electric-generation market. (He briefly held a natural gas vision for transportation also.) Lay was highly likable, empathetic, and God-like to his employees. He was measured and diplomatic in public arenas. He was revered by his board of directors, highly respected by the media, and a go-to person for

---

9. Before becoming president in 1990, Kinder was arguably number three at Enron from his top legal-administrative position. Kinder's titles at Enron were senior vice president and general counsel (1985–86); executive vice president, law and administration (1986–87); executive vice president and chief of staff (1987–88); vice-chairman (December 1988–October 1990); and president (October 1990–December 1996). He joined the board upon his election as vice-chairman.

10. Vice-chairs at Enron were Rich Kinder (1988–90), John Urquhart (1991–98), Ken Harrison (1997–2000), Rebecca Mark (1998–2000), Joseph Sutton (1999–2000), and J. Clifford Baxter (2000–2001). Each was a member of Enron's board of directors. Except for Kinder, none could be considered a true number three at Enron with this title. In the late 1990s, in fact, this position became known as the "ejection seat" for expendable executives at Enron.

many external constituencies—all this until Enron's death spiral began in the summer of 2001.

Others were certainly important in Enron's tumult, beginning with Jeff Skilling and including, through 1996, Rich Kinder. Lou Pai, Rebecca Mark, and particularly Andy Fastow were key figures, followed by Richard Causey, Ken Rice, and Kevin Hannon. But Lay enabled these individuals and set the tone and expectations for all. He was both the head and the figurehead of Enron.

Highly ambitious. Always in spin mode. Washington expert and insider. Media driven. An "inveterate collector of relationships." Primed to make a phone call, write a check, or give a speech. Friend of Republicans, Democrats, environmentalists, academics, think tanks, charities, churches, schools, minorities. Folksy or intellectual ("the voice of God with a sense of humor"). Ken Lay was a private-sector politician, a politico CEO, with local, state, national, and even international reach.

To his few but perceptive critics, however, this friend of everyone was something else: a *chameleon*, or what Ayn Rand called a *second hander*.[11]

———

Why did it all happen at Enron? The quick answer is Ken Lay, who was the right person at the right time given the political opportunities and incentives for all energy CEOs in Enron's era. But leadership makes a company. By background and upbringing, Ken Lay was driven to seek the pinnacle of success for himself and his firm—and to gain it rapidly, not eventually. By temperament and training, big-picture, Washington-wise Ken Lay was not at all the free-market apostle of his proclamations ("I believe in God, and I believe in free markets"), declarations that came to be taken at face value by the press. ("He was widely known as a free-market advocate and an outspoken lobbyist for deregulation.")

On the contrary, Lay was a *political* capitalist who never hesitated to exploit extramarket advantage if it was available—or to create such an advantage if it was not. This PhD economist with a penchant for the written and spoken word was a politician-CEO who deployed good-sounding rationalizations (competition, national security, diversity, consumer benefits, empowerment, momentum, success) to promote less-than-free competition and tolerate behavior that fell short of prudence and veracity.[12]

"The constant theme in Mr. Lay's career over the last three decades is his understanding of the symbiotic relationship between business and politics and his willingness to aggressively play the game," read a *New York Times*

———

11. See *Capitalism at Work*, pp. 8–11, 13, 68, 302, 321.

12. Traditional business analysis focuses on performance-management systems and financial results. This interpretation of Enron also looks at the political (nonmarket) opportunities that allowed Ken Lay and Jeff Skilling to reach and, for a time, thrive atop the business world.

retrospective following Enron's collapse. Books on Enron, too, have noted Lay's free-market, procompetition image was at odds with Enron's active politics.[13] But far more than a side matter, political capitalism was the "constant theme" of Ken Lay's career.

Appetite for Risk

Ken Lay began with a financially strong company in a weak market. But the status quo was unacceptable to him, notwithstanding the fact that HNG stockholders needed to be made whole after previous management's rebuff of a rich tender offer. HNG would need to meld with other companies in order to retain its independence and lead the industry.

In his first six months, the acquisition of two major pipelines by HNG's new CEO doubled the size of the company—and doubled the debt-to-capitalization ratio to 59 percent. Just months later, the InterNorth merger doubled the size of the company again, leaving a debt-to-capitalization ratio of 73 percent, twice what is considered prudent.

These moves were all about size and reach—with little change in market valuation. The promise of higher profitability was undercut by increased debt service. With lower credit ratings, Lay's colossus became dependent on high-interest junk bonds, pioneered by Drexel Burnham Lambert's Michael Milken. (Jim Alexander, a Drexel employee later with Enron, remembered how "we helped refinance Enron's huge amounts of debt that were about to go into technical default.") This put the operating units on the firing line to cover debt service, while shouldering Lay's first-class overhead.

The resulting Enron, impressive in terms of assets and storyline, was financially weak. In their first 19 months together, HNG and InterNorth lost more than $100 million, a far cry from the $420 million in net income that the two companies collectively made in premerger 1984. Precarious debt of 70 percent of total company capitalization at year-end 1987 resulted in higher interest rates than better-capitalized companies paid.

In many ways, the fate of an oil-trading unit symbolized the company's early years. Enron Oil Corporation (EOC), located in Valhalla, New York, was prized for requiring little capital while producing high earnings. Clear evidence of misfeasance at EOC was met only by finger shaking from Ken Lay, who was willing to live dangerously in order to (in his mind) keep the cash coming.

Soon enough, that unit's earnings proved to be fictitious, requiring a major write-off in 1987. This "canary in the coal mine," in terms of Enron's ultimate fate, began with "sirens and denials," followed by "crisis and cleanup," and ended in the unit's dissolution (chapter 4). Had Valhalla's losses been greater, as

---

13. See, for example, McLean and Elkind, *The Smartest Guys in the Room*, pp. 88–89; Fox, *Enron*, pp. 110–12; Bryce, *Pipe Dreams*, p. 5.

they very nearly were, Ken Lay's career at Enron might have ended 15 years earlier—and less tragically than it did.

Confidence, Optimism, Hubris

The risk-taking über-optimist had a chip on his shoulder. Ken Lay had started behind the eight ball in rural Missouri and again as the new CEO of a cash-rich, prospect-poor Fortune 500 company. (HNG's market capitalization at year-end 1984 was below that in each of the previous three years.) But never did he feel cornered; quite the opposite. Lay excelled as a child, as a teenager, and in college. He was coordinated, musical, competitive, smart, and affable. He knew he was more talented than just about anyone else who might have grown up in more affluent circumstances or was physically bigger.

At a series of jobs, begun at a very young age, and then in every classroom, he was tops. Ken Lay was elected president of his fraternity at the University of Missouri, became a protégé of the school's top economics professor (Pinkney Walker), and graduated Phi Beta Kappa. He was a 4.0 with street smarts, a classmate said.[14] And it just went up from there at his corporate stops, as described in *Edison to Enron* (Book 2).

Early in his career, Ken Lay became attracted to the extraordinary in business management and to *getting there first*. Peter Drucker's *The Age of Discontinuity* (1968), a text used by Professor Lay teaching graduate economics at George Washington University, spoke of the corporation's need for major change in the coming era. Revolutionary change was to be Enron's mantra; incremental improvement was the stuff of those firms Lay was determined to leap. To that end, he would spend much time in political venues seeking Big Change, delegating things back at the ranch. With Rich Kinder as COO, this all seemed to work.

Lay's reputation grew and grew. By the time he headed Enron, Lay had emerged as Mr. Natural Gas (the first ever) with national recognition. "Ken in those early years earned a nickname," remembered John Jennrich, the founding editor of *Natural Gas Week*. "And that was just simply, Saint Ken.... He was just so clearly far and away ahead of people."

Overconfidence with a dose of hubris spawned different combinations of imprudence and philosophic fraud. But when did Enron deviancies begin? One beginning would be in 1985 during the merger negotiation with InterNorth when Lay stretched his already elongated profit projections to get a higher price for HNG—and gave his "personal assurances" that 15 percent annual growth was makeable. (It would not be, by the widest of margins.)

----

14. A chronology of Lay's life is provided on pp. 677–88.

It certainly was present in the spring of 1987, after Arthur Andersen reported trading improprieties at Enron Oil Company to the Audit Committee of the Enron board, and Lay responded: "I have decided not to terminate these people. I need their earnings." It was also in force in the aftermath of Valhalla, when Lay's explanation of Enron's close call erased the background of warnings and controversy—a cleansing so thorough that some involved employees feared for their future and hid files at home.

A Harvard Business School case study described Ken Lay as "an intense competitor who set goals with 'a lot of stretch in them.'" Annual compounded earnings growth of 15 percent was just that. Lay's first such goal—made to get InterNorth to pay an inflated $70 per share for HNG stock—was hubristic. Compared to premerger earnings of $1.2 billion for HNG and InterNorth as separate companies between 1982 and 1984, the next three years' earnings as one entity were slightly in the red until a federal-income-tax reduction produced a retroactive $450 million gain. Pricey debt had more than tripled the assets of the company, with meager profitability, although cash flow was stronger. But Ken Lay, confident always, kept the mood right and expectations high for a turnaround.

Lay's overambition also included *going first class*, a disdain for watching expenses closely, at least at the corporate level. "You cannot cut your costs to prosperity," Lay would say. (Forrest Hoglund, across the street at EOG, disagreed.) Facilities and business norms had to be first class for his best and brightest. Strict cost control was beneath Enron, at the top anyway. Less innovative companies had to do that. To Lay, Enron chased dollars rather than pinched pennies.

Yet there was cost cutting in the tough years of 1985 and 1986. And in fourth-quarter 1988, expenses were pared when the management of Gas Pipeline Group and Corporate merged to make Ken Lay and Rich Kinder pipeliners, at least nominally.[15] But after this, there would be nary an all-employee cost-containment initiative from Ken Lay until Enron neared its demise.

Getting Governmental

Ambition, and overambition, included *getting political*. It began innocently: adding highly regulated interstate gas pipelines to HNG's lightly regulated intrastate gas system, hitherto its bread and butter. Enron was not seeking something for nothing via politics, however. It accepted the mixed-economy structure within which it could profitably create value for its counterparties

---

15. See chapter 5, pp. 243–44. After the late-1988 reorganization, things improved, whereupon Lay became increasingly removed from the day-to-day operations of Enron, entrusting that to COO Kinder.

(gas producers on one side, gas buyers on the other). In fact, Enron worked to *lighten* regulation and improve service in the interstate gas-transmission market during the entire period.

Mandatory open-access (MOA) rules were somewhat similar. In principle, it was a form of infrastructure socialism, forcing companies to provide the use of their property to other companies on equal terms. But obligatory transmission access for gas had been driven more by economist reformers than by industry rent-seekers, which, historically speaking, was more the exception than the rule.

Ken Lay simply embraced the inevitable—and welcomed a new profit center for Enron, *wholesale gas marketing* (as he had at Transco with Transco Energy Marketing Company). The pipelines would and did adapt to their diminished role as pure transporters, not buyers and sellers of gas as before. MOA for electricity, at both wholesale and retail, on the other hand, coming later, was Enron driven as well as reformer driven.

But gas-fired cogeneration projects by independents (nonutilities, such as Enron) were rent-seeking—or rent-reaping. The political basis had not involved Ken Lay's lobbying, either in his Enron or prior career. It was a 1978 federal law, championed by renewable interests, that required utilities to buy the generated power at an "avoided cost," which also applied to new, efficient gas technology. The government intervention enabled a windfall for the talented, particularly the crack team Lay attracted to Enron.

There was more, much more. Beginning in 1988, the global-warming issue became central to Enron's messaging to substitute natural gas for coal and for oil, a start that would lead "green" Enron into solar power, wind power, environmental services, and emissions trading. In the early-to-mid 1990s, Enron burst upon the developing world to build power plants on the strength of tax-payer-aided financing from US and foreign entities. And otherwise market-driven Enron Oil & Gas Company took a political detour into tight-sands gas production in the early 1990s to capitalize on a bountiful tax credit, itself the product of deft lobbying by parent Enron.

Lay Unleashed

Ken Lay had a boss—nominally. Enron's board of directors was composed of accomplished individuals in a range of professions, from academia (three PhDs, other than Lay), business, and even medicine. Several were current and former Enron employees, and some were handpicked by Lay based on years of personal affiliation and friendship. Only a few directors were inherited by Lay from the original HNG and InterNorth boards, some very strong and independent, at least initially.

As it would turn out, Enron's board hardly stood at arm's length from Ken Lay, as accomplished as the members might have been in their own professions. Inadequate separation and control is a problem at many institutions. But, as

Malcolm Salter emphasized, it was a fatal characteristic at Enron, assuming that director independence would have better checked Lay's contra-capitalist management.

In theory and practice, the interests of management *should* be aligned with the interests of shareholders. But a principal/agent problem emerges when management compensation and perks are not in line with value creation, as graded by consumers and affirmed by investors. The board of directors is responsible for ensuring a reasonable alignment of the interests of management and employees (agents) with the interests of owners (principals).

How did this gatekeeping role by Enron's board become compromised? Why did such a distinguished dozen or so directors allow Enron to violate best-business practices, including time-honored conflicts-of-interest guidelines? How did the board ultimately lose control of the company?

Courting the board with princely fees and company favors was part of Lay's largesse. But the bigger reason, certainly in Enron's earlier life, was that the board considered Lay not only one of them but also *superior*.

Ken Lay became recognized as the top young talent of his industry by the early 1980s. The new 38-year-old president of Transco Companies, serving under industry leader Jack Bowen, had never disappointed. "Transco's Ken Lay Credited as Natural Gas Innovator," read a *Houston Chronicle* headline in 1983. So, when HNG lured Lay to be its new CEO in mid-1984, praise was effusive. "[We wanted] good, aggressive management, and we think we've found it now," one board member told the *Wall Street Journal*. "We didn't dream it would be such a significant upgrade," raved another many years later.

Such confidence only grew, despite some ups and downs in the business. It was easy to trust Ken Lay. After all, he had always met his promises and made everyone richer, beginning with HNG shareholders in 1985 and continuing with stockholders who saw ENE quadruple in value between the mid-1980s and 1996.

————

Ken Lay, nominally, welcomed tough, arm's-length oversight. "My operating philosophy regarding boards," he stated in 1994, "is that a strong company requires a strong and independent board of directors." And how did it work at Enron? "Occasionally, individual directors or even the entire board might disagree with my particular opinion on an issue or strategy," he stated. "But we are always able to openly and candidly discuss and resolve our differences and move forward."

The Great Man, however, had a board with *too much* confidence in him. "I'm here to support management," stated Robert Jaedicke, the Stanford Graduate School of Business accounting professor and dean who headed Enron's audit committee from 1985 to 2002. "I'm here to support Ken Lay." Jaedicke did just that, from Valhalla through Fastow's LJM ventures. This was well before the

73-year-old, who also held a half-dozen other directorships at large US corporations, found himself voting in favor of Enron's bankruptcy filing in fourth-quarter 2001.

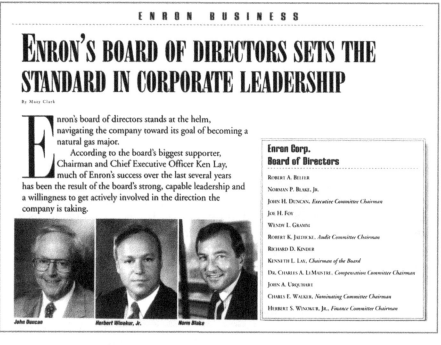

ENRON BUSINESS

ENRON'S BOARD OF DIRECTORS SETS THE STANDARD IN CORPORATE LEADERSHIP

By Mary Clark

Enron's board of directors stands at the helm, navigating the company toward its goal of becoming a natural gas major.

According to the board's biggest supporter, Chairman and Chief Executive Officer Ken Lay, much of Enron's success over the last several years has been the result of the board's strong, capable leadership and a willingness to get actively involved in the direction the company is taking.

Enron Corp.
Board of Directors

ROBERT A. BELFER
NORMAN P. BLAKE, JR.
JOHN H. DUNCAN, *Executive Committee Chairman*
JOE H. FOY
WENDY L. GRAMM
ROBERT K. JAEDICKE, *Audit Committee Chairman*
RICHARD D. KINDER
KENNETH L. LAY, *Chairman of the Board*
DR. CHARLES A. LEMAISTRE, *Compensation Committee Chairman*
JOHN A. URQUHART
CHARLS E. WALKER, *Nominating Committee Chairman*
HERBERT S. WINOKUR, JR., *Finance Committee Chairman*

John Duncan   Herbert Winokur, Jr.   Norm Blake

Figure I.1 Enron's nominally strong board of directors had too much allegiance to Ken Lay, in part because of Enron's largesse toward them. John Duncan, executive chairman from beginning to end, was particularly smitten with Enron's and Lay's apparent success.

In retrospect, Enron's board failed both to monitor Lay and to prevent "a pattern of deceptive behavior that unfolded in incremental steps over time." Enron's otherwise "principled and responsible leaders in the worlds of business, education, medical research, and public service" exhibited "passive behavior as both decision makers and overseers." Harvard's Salter (the source of the previous quotations) identified the problem as the board's "long-standing personal relationship and emotional bonds with Ken Lay."

Tragedy in the Making

"Whom the gods wish to destroy, they first call promising." Ken Lay's tragic flaw was an overambition born of prior success and future promise. In the final analysis, Lay failed to "overcome success." His life had always been exemplary, supremely so. A top-notch education was intertwined with early career triumphs. To those, he added a remarkable proclivity to move up rapidly when-ever opportunities opened or could be created.

He had been president of Continental Resources Company for just two years when he answered the call to become president of Transco. He had been presi-dent at Transco for just three years when he answered the call to become CEO of Houston Natural Gas at age 42. Speaking of reaching the pinnacle, Ken's wife, Linda, told a friend: "It's fun to be the king." The sky appeared to be the limit for a restless powerbroker. But wisdom had an adage: *The higher you fly, the farther you fall.*

Although the Texas-centric natural gas company was a strong Fortune 500 company, Ken Lay wanted a national, and international, presence. Natural gas might not be big enough either, in time. The industry intellect saw his potential as a philosopher-king for the whole field of energy, if not beyond, dealing with the great political-economic issues of the day. Transco had given him a good taste of that.

But Lay was going to need a bigger boat. He sought new businesses and the very best talent both on top and throughout the organization. He particularly prized convention breakers who would identify opportunities and unleash change. The business/government, government/business mixed economy offered a wide-open path for escaping the status quo.

This vision was the origin of Enron's contra-capitalism.

Earnings Issues

Big bets and problematic investments, alongside good and solid undertakings, were characteristic of Enron in its early years and middle-age. Expensive junk-bond financing was necessary in the 1980s, and Enron was rated low invest-ment grade by the three major US rating agencies in the 1990s.[16] Downgrades had to be avoided to retain counterparty credit for trading, a silent but deadly risk for Enron.

"Kenneth L. Lay, Houston Natural Gas Corp's chairman and chief executive officer," the *Wall Street Journal* noted in 1984, "is a man in a hurry." He would not slow down. *By year-end 1987, roughly $500 million—one-eighth of Enron's $4 billion debt—was attributable to Lay's aggressiveness in achieving size and independence.* Three major components were:

1. *Interstate pipeline premiums (1984):* The purchases of Transwestern Pipeline Company and Florida Gas Transmission Company were between $100 and $200 million (10–20 percent of the purchase price) above competing bids.

---

16. These ratings remained unchanged until 2001: Moody's at Baa2 (set 1989), Fitch BBB+ (set 1993), and Standard & Poor's BBB+ (set 1995).

Although Ken Lay doubled the size of HNG, he also doubled the company's debt ratio, "with negative credit implications."[17]

2. *InterNorth overpayment (1985):* Lay had InterNorth overpay for HNG by *at least* $5 per share, or $150 million. While getting the best price was arguably Lay's short-run fiduciary duty, basic market ethics should have precluded using trumped-up (and thus unmeetable) earnings projections, which hurt InterNorth investors and left Enron with postmerger debt of $4.6 billion, a precarious 73 percent of the company's total capitalization.[18]

3. *Jacobs buyout (1987):* As the last act from the InterNorth merger, Lay bought out "corporate raider" Irwin Jacobs and Leucadia at a $200 million shareholder cost, leaving Enron's debt load uncomfortably high even after large asset sales that year.[19]

Ever confident, at least in public, Lay believed that his "superstars" were smarter than the competition, not to mention the regulators at the Federal Energy Regulatory Commission (FERC) and other agencies. It was part of the CEO's unshakable belief in himself and a higher power that good times would cover the bad and leave Enron better off than if the company had chosen the status quo—or just a more prudent path. It would not change with future acquisitions either, which were all rich and many misguided.

Icarus Projects

Risk management was proclaimed as a core competency, but Enron imprudently took on nonhedged (really nonhedgable) risk to *get there first*. Moving fast and loose resulted in large write-offs during the Lay/Kinder era.[20] Period losses or even charges to earnings could have been more if Enron had employed mark-to-market accounting as aggressively in the down direction as in the up.

Absent the physical assets of a true energy major, Enron could scarcely have afforded any greater losses than those incurred. Four write-offs totaling $1.135 billion were taken between 1985 and 1997. Chronologically, they were:

---

17. These premiums would be well justified by expansions and some synergies with other operations. Enron sold half of Florida Gas Transmission to Sonat in 1986 at its purchase price to break even, as discussed in chapter 3, pp. 150–51, 162.

18. InterNorth agreed to this premium after HNG concocted new profit projections of 15 percent annual earnings growth. See chapter 2, pp. 119–20.

19. See chapter 3, pp. 169–72.

20. Rich Kinder, who replaced Mick Seidl as president and COO in 1989, had been breathing down Seidl's neck as executive vice president and chief of staff. Kinder left Enron before the 1997 write-offs, but both Teesside II and MTBE had been entirely subject to his purview.

1. Peruvian nationalization (1985): Right after the merger of HNG and InterNorth, Belco Petroleum was forced to write down $218 million in assets, owing to expropriation by the government of Peru, with no income-tax benefit.[21]

2. Valhalla (1987): An oil-trading scandal at Enron Oil Corporation in Valhalla, New York, required Enron to restate earnings for 1985 and 1986, write off $142 million ($85 million after-tax) in fourth-quarter 1987, and shutter the unit. Adroit work by an emergency team from Houston reduced the exposure from a high of $300 million, an amount that could have been still higher had the market discovered that Enron was short and out-of-the-money on approximately 85 million barrels.[22] The reduced amount at close gave Enron and Ken Lay a second chance.[23]

3. MTBE (1997): Enron's "clean fuels" bet with reformulated gasoline resulted in a $100 million ($74 million after-tax) charge to earnings, which would have come sooner and been greater except for mark-to-market finagling. The "top dollar" $632 million acquisition of methyl tertiary butyl ether and methanol facilities in 1991 was never profitable, and the unit was eventually sold, only to be scrapped by its new owners.[24]

4. Teesside II (1997): In the Teesside I project, Enron had successfully built and operated the world's largest gas-fired cogeneration plant in England. In 1993, Enron's Teesside II project went long with a 300 MMcf/d fixed-price contract for gas supply. Enron's bet to corner the next phase of UK gas (and power) development was stymied by new gas discoveries lowering prices below those at which Enron could profitably sell the gas it was obligated to buy. The J-Block gas contract write-off was $675 million ($463 million after-tax).[25]

How much of this can be blamed on Ken Lay and his executives? The first of these write-offs was a legacy of the InterNorth side, but it had been identified as a special risk by HNG prior to the merger. (Government insurance and restitution from Peru would reverse most of the write-off years later.) The second write-off also came from InterNorth, but much of the transgression occurred on Lay's watch (as well as Seidl's and Kinder's). Certainly, basic business judgment,

---

21. See chapter 2, pp. 126–28.

22. "If the market moved up three more dollars Enron would have gone belly up," remembered clean-up man Mike Muckleroy. "Lay and Seidl never understood that."

23. See chapter 4, pp. 199–200. The sale of half of Enron Cogeneration Company cleaned up Enron's financials in the wake of Valhalla but reduced an earnings engine.

24. See chapter 6, pp. 295–300; chapter 11, pp. 466–67.

25. See chapter 12, pp. 494–98.

right-and-wrong squarely in the bourgeois capitalist tradition, was suspended in favor of finagling, hope, and prayer.

The third charge resulted from a political-environmental wager that went wholly wrong. The final and largest write-off came from very imprudent contracts—a take-or-pay liability no less, something Enron had spent years cleaning up on its US interstate pipelines.

Nothing ventured, nothing lost, it is said. Write-offs are a part of business life amid capitalism's creative destruction. One expects extraordinary gains to be offset, to some degree, by bets gone bad in a world where economic verdicts are always uncertain. Still, the circumstances and size of Enron's failures put in question its adherence to those long-standing best-business practices that arose spontaneously within commercial capitalism. Corporate autopsies must ask what could have been reasonably avoided by relying on basic prudence—if not play-by-the-rules morality, including transparent and realistic accounting.

As it was, the two write-offs in 1997 (MBTE and Teesside II) would leave the company's Enron 2000 growth narrative in tatters.[26] Momentum-driven ENE, not to mention the strong credit rating essential for Jeff Skilling's trading operation, were put at risk. Enron probably would have taken its later write-offs earlier, and taken other charges to earnings, except for a belief that its troubled assets could be finagled into solvency. That is how 1997 became the pronounced "tipping point" of Enron's slide into spiraling deceit and philosophic fraud, whereby Ken Lay's desired story of Enron came to replace the real one.

"I think one of the unfortunate characteristics of Enron is we tend to financially engineer things to death rather than just take our medicine in a one-off hit and get beyond it," Tom White, an Enron senior executive, complained just months before Enron's death spiral set in. "We expend enormous intellectual capital in trying to engineer around it—less so, I think, in the Skilling days than in the Kinder days—and this caused us some great pain over the years." While White revealingly implicated Kinder, he obviously did not know about what Jeff Skilling and Andy Fastow had under the rug.

Postponing Write-Offs

The aforementioned write-offs were almost joined by others. Construction ceased at the multibillion-dollar Enron-led Dabhol, India, power plant in 1994 and again in 1996, owing to political turmoil and the buyer's limited desire and ability to pay. As it turned out, modest revenue would ever be collected from

---

26. Enron 2000 promised Wall Street an average of 15 percent earnings growth between 1996 and 2000, doubling the size and profitability of the company compared to base-year 1995. Double-digit growth in 1996 was followed by an 80 percent profit plunge in 1997, eviscerating talk of Enron 2000.

the state of Maharashtra to offset $650 million in costs incurred during Enron's solvent life.[27] (Dabhol was written off after Enron's bankruptcy.)

Other write-offs were avoided via the dubious "snowball" treatment of international project expenses that could not be offset by associated project revenues. Snowballing involved rolling the costs of failed ventures into still-to-be-negotiated ones in the same geographical area in order to prop up current-period profit. There were many no-go projects among the 75 or so that Enron Development's Rebecca Mark would work on.

In fact, 5 out of 10 projects listed as in "final development" in Enron's *1996 Annual Report* would be terminated. The International division's snowball reached Kinder's $90 million ceiling and then more than doubled. Yet write-offs were not chosen "because doing so would bring Enron's earnings below expectations," as Enron's top accountant at the time explained to management. Philosophic fraud, not candor and prudence, was the response to unpleasant fact.

———

A high-risk-to-imprudent culture resulted in other close calls in Enron's rocket ride to prominence. One concerned the aforementioned 1,825 MW, $1.3 billion Teesside cogeneration project (1989–93). Enron had a weak balance sheet for self-financing such a large project. Project financing by outside capital required that contracts for gas supply and power sales be finalized simultaneously. Not wanting to wait, Enron employee-turned-consultant John Wing preordered the GE turbines. Enron self-financed construction for $300 million over six months while contract negotiations advanced. The gas sellers and power buyers set a strict deadline for completion—or they could walk.

In the end, the back-to-back contracts beat the deadline on the final day—and not before Enron had agreed to strict construction deadlines backed by financial penalties of £385,000 ($575,000) per day. Completion in 1993 came with just days to spare, dodging another bullet. Larry Izzo, Enron's on-site star with the project, had been hired out of the military for just this emergency by Tom White, who himself joined Enron from the US Army, where he had been a brigadier general.[28]

"We were all very intense," remembered White. "It was a crusade for us … a religious thing" to meet the deadline. The 24/7 heroics and close-call victory erased the cold-sweat memories of a potential disaster. "Few outside Enron knew how much risk the company had taken to build Teesside, and afterward, few cared," stated one account. This ends-justified-the-means episode was a management practice that would not always triumph.

———

27. See chapter 12, pp. 498–502.

28. See chapter 6, pp. 269–71.

In retrospect, Ken Lay's bet-the-company strategy was celebrated as a leap to the international market and global recognition. But Teesside's success led to a naked bet for a second phase that went badly wrong. Facing huge losses, Teesside II would result in the largest write-off in Enron's history, as well as another incurred liability (the CATS transportation contract) that went unreported amid Enron's bigger problems in 2001.

———

Its near-failure forgotten, Teesside I's success led to global adventurism. In developing countries, prospective profit margins, as high as 30 percent, were said to be far greater than in capitalist environs. Consequently, Enron built a string of power plants with the help of taxpayer-aided loans, a clear and recognized deviation from Enron's free-market talk.

This government involvement, pegged at 21 official agencies, reflected a country-by-country environment inhospitable to private-party lending. Enron's closings in more than two-dozen nations depended on getting enough government aid to placate private parties. But judging from the final results, the lure of those extraordinary profits that Enron sought via nonmarket assistance resulted in very normal rates of return (3 or 12 percent per annum for the entire portfolio, according to competing internal calculations).

Apples in noncapitalist gardens looked ripe, with up-front profit recognition and bonuses paid to the project originators. But costs were high, and actual operations proved problematic in many cases. Furthermore, these countries moved from negotiated to bid projects to reduce expected margins. The whole international unit, Enron Development, ceased originations in 1999.[29]

Imprudent Marketing
Pronounced risk also occurred with major contracts by Enron's nonregulated gas-merchant business, which formed the basis of the new Enron. The progenitor was a 15-year sales contract in 1985 between Citrus Trading Corporation (half owned by Enron, with this contract 100 percent guaranteed by Enron) and Florida Power & Light.

The delivered gas price was tied to the delivered price of residual fuel oil (FP&L's plants could burn oil or gas). But the gas supply was not locked in at the wellhead at a netback price to ensure a profitable margin for seller Citrus/Enron. Enron was long oil, short gas—a "big gamble," one Enron executive stated. "We felt that the survival of the company depended upon continuing to make very large gas sales in Florida," remembered Enron economist Bruce Stram.

———

29. See chapter 12, p. 515. Enron's later attempt to apply the same model to underdeveloped Houston-area neighborhoods, Enron Investment Partners, failed miserably.

With unanticipated gas/oil differentials, Enron's position was under water when deliveries began in 1988. With liabilities accruing at several million dollars per month, a $450 million worst-case deficit was calculated over the contract's life. A renegotiation in 1992 resulted in an Enron payment of $50 million to FP&L, with new contract terms that positioned Enron for future profits.[30] This time, an unparalleled risk taker escaped relatively unscathed.

In 1987, the 10-year Brooklyn Union Gas was praised as the "breakout moment" of Enron Gas Marketing (EGM); in 1992, the 20-year Sithe Energy contract was hailed as the "bell-cow transaction" of Enron Gas Services (EGS). But in both cases, Enron had not secured the pledged gas. It wagered that many years down the road it would be able buy and deliver the gas profitably.

The 60 MMcf/d sales agreement with Brooklyn Union Gas had been enabled by FERC Order No. 436, which allowed Enron to demote traditional seller Transco Energy to transportation only. The deal was highly profitable right out of the blocks, with locked-in prices well above the going spot (short-term) price for gas. But Enron did not secure fixed-price, long-term gas in order to lock in a margin for the out months of the 230 Bcf deal. Similar nonhedged bets were made by EGM with Elizabethtown (NJ) Gas Company (10 years) and Northern States Power Company (5 years).

The 195 MMcf/d natural gas contract to fuel a planned 1,000 MW cogeneration plant built by Sithe Energies Group in New York was backed up by 5-year price-hedged gas and 15 years of unhedged supply thereafter. With delivery commencing on the first day of 1995, the unhedged gas was out-of-the-money come the first day of 2000. Worse, Enron had booked profits up front on this gas via mark-to-market accounting, exacerbating the deficit. The problem would balloon to several hundred million dollars, potentially exceeding the value of the plant (Enron's collateral), before more normal market conditions removed the liability.[31]

Little wonder, then, how it would end. "The Gambler Who Blew It All," read one postmortem on Enron in early 2002. "Lay thought he was Horatio Alger, but he may be closer to another archetype: the high roller who believed his own hype." A beau ideal of capitalist theory, Enron's founder was not.

Subquality Income

Investors prefer predictable, repeatable profits instead of fortuitous, nonrecurring earnings. Sustainability—the idea that the present should not borrow from the future but enhance it—applies to business, not only to the environment. Ken Lay himself promoted a long-term orientation among Enron employees after

---

30. See chapter 6, pp. 263–64.

31. See chapter 9, pp. 387–89.

the Irwin Jacobs buyout, saying: *"This agreement removes a major, disruptive uncertainty about Enron's future created by short-term oriented speculators."*

But Enron was going to make its promised earnings, year by year, even quarter by quarter, whatever it took. Ken Lay said so, and Rich Kinder enforced the edict, sometimes by browbeating executives acting prudently. In Enron's parlance, "a sense of urgency" meant *we need earnings.*

Maximizing, and then some, current-period income had two purposes. One was to reduce debt to help future income, a gain typically offset by the fact that future income was given up in the initial move. The second purpose was to make ENE a momentum stock.

Here-and-now supraprofits were gained by selling assets and/or accelerating future income via accounting discretion. Quick fixes violating net present valuation (NPV) were part of this. Enron also relied on fortuitous income to make its short-term goals. In all, *Enron's sell-down/take-now proclivity turned a (normal) physical-asset company with predictable income streams into an image/ momentum play betting on the next big thing.* Ken Lay was, indeed, creating a new type of energy company.

In the early-to-mid 1990s, when analysts rated ENE a Buy, two journalists broke from the pack. Mark-to-market accounting accelerated profits in a way that could not be sustained, Toni Mack wrote in a 1993 *Forbes* piece. Enron's "live-for-today philosophy" should caution ordinary investors, Harry Hurt III concluded in his 1996 *Fortune* article. Only years later would such analysis be appreciated as ahead of its time.

Promises versus Premises. In 1995, Enron boasted eight consecutive years of 15 percent growth in earnings per share—on paper. This record was behind Lay's and Kinder's Enron 2000, a plan to achieve the same growth pace averaged over five years, doubling the company's profitability by year-2000 as part of its quest to become the world's leading energy company.

But on close inspection, the 1988–95 earnings streak was not only about superior performance in Enron's major divisions, although that was present. It was also about core asset sales and artificial income acceleration to reach its aggressive targets.

Nine of the 12 years under review in this book (1985–1996) were marked by major income acceleration. The exceptions were loss-years 1985 and 1987, as well as profitable 1988 when net income of $109 million was a mere one-fourth of what HNG and InterNorth had made just prior to the merger.

Starting with postmerger 1986, 8 of the 11 years (1986–1996) were marked by special-asset sales, the exceptions being 1987 (a loss year), 1990, and 1991.

In sum, five of the eight years between 1988 and 1995 were marked by both income acceleration and special-asset sales; the other three, by one or the other. No year in this period achieved 15 percent earnings growth without special help.

The lack of earnings quality at Enron can be appreciated by looking at 1989, the second year of the streak. Profit of $226 million, high by Enron standards, was modest for a $9 billion-asset company—and well below HNG and Inter-North's premerger net income. Yet asset sales accounted for half of earnings, Mobil stock sales for one-third, and an antitrust settlement for 5 percent. Given the debt service that the operating units had to cover to make Enron profitable, incremental earnings also came from a long-term gas-sales contract between Houston Pipe Line (HPL) and Entex, rejiggered to sacrifice greater future income (as measured by net present value) to increase immediate earnings. Yet Enron investors had been told, in the annual report, no less, that "the number one priority in 1989 will be to build the foundation for substantial earnings growth, both for the short- and the long-term."

The earnings streak was a species of deceit, of philosophic fraud.

_____

The overall earnings story can be retold chronologically. When postmerger problems eviscerated profitability for HNG/InterNorth in 1985, the heat was on. A financially rough 1986 was rescued, in part, by John Wing's refinancing of a Texas City cogeneration project, which sacrificed millions of future dollars to take (smaller) earnings by year end. That same year, one-half of Florida Gas Transmission was sold to reduce debt after the Belco nationalization, no more than a break-even transaction from HNG's (full) acquisition a year before.

After the Valhalla write-off in 1987, Enron sold half of Enron Cogeneration Company (ECC) to Dominion Resources for $90 million to help rescue 1988. In 1989, as mentioned, the hastily redone gas deal between HNG and Entex repeated 1986's violation of NPV to make earnings. This was just a foretaste of the income acceleration to come with Enron's use of mark-to-market account-ing, which began in 1992, was retroactively applied to engineer 1991 earnings, and was abused in later applications.[32]

In the early 1990s, Enron began taking earnings from Teesside two years before the first power was generated—more than $100 million worth—via work payments to the hastily created Enron Construction Company. Teesside would later provide instant income when Enron sold down its half-interest to 28 per-cent, generating $83 million between 1994 and 1996.[33]

Spin-offs in 1992 (Enron Liquids Pipeline) and in 1993 (Northern Border Pipeline) resulted in net income of $225 million and $217 million, respectively. In 1994, the partial sale of Enron Global Power & Pipelines LLC (EPP) brought in $225 million and left ENE with a positive valuation for its remaining

_____

32. See chapter 8, pp. 378–83.

33. See chapter 12, pp. 489, 515.

52 percent share. (Before EPP's third anniversary, however, Enron bought back the outstanding interest to end the have-your-cake-and-eat-it-too foray.) Another public offering, the spin-off of 60 percent of EOTT Energy Partners in 1994, was done at a small profit but with conditions that would create great toil, described in chapter 10.

The biggest cash-out concerned Enron Oil & Gas, yielding the parent $679 million from stock sales in 1989, 1992, and 1995.[34] A final sale in 1999 completely divested EOG. What was arguably the best of Enron would end up outside Enron.

Quarterly earnings goals, not only yearly targets, were part of the momentum. ("This is the thirteenth consecutive quarter in which reported earnings ...," a typical press release read.) One quarter was rescued by a sale and leaseback of the Enron Building, which produced immediate gains in return for higher future costs (the lease payments). Complicated tax strategies, in which high-priced advice saved a greater amount of money in the heat of earnings season, was pursued to unusual ends; the Corporate Tax department would come to consider itself a profit center rather than a cost center by the late 1990s.

In all, core asset sales of $1.4 billion—approaching the combined asset sales of Lay-period HNG ($632 million) and HNG-InterNorth ($1 billion)—were part of the legacy of rich purchasing and business problems. All reduced future income, requiring something *new* to maintain and to increase profits.

———

Fortuitous income is welcome and inevitable in a large corporation, where the opposite can occur for the unluckiest of reasons. Still, relying on such nonrecurring income to meet guidance to the Street represented another form of image making for Enron.

One cookie jar of income was an antitrust-suit windfall from InterNorth's 1983 investment of $5 million in an abandoned coal slurry pipeline project that had encountered right-of-way obstruction from coal-carrying railroads. The Energy Transportation System Inc. (ETSI) project won settlements and received a large court award that provided Enron's 29.5 percent interest with $100 million, which helped Enron regain profitability between 1987 and 1990.

A second cookie jar was Mobil Oil Corporation stock that InterNorth held from the sale of its exploration and production company to Mobil in 1964.

———

34. They were (pretax) $202 million in 1989, $110 million in 1992, and $367 million in 1995, leaving Enron with 61 percent ownership. Enron would further reduce its ownership in 1998 and fully divest EOG the next year.

Between 1988 and 1992, Enron recorded pretax income of $250 million from such stock sales to help begin its 15 percent earnings-growth streak.[35]

Marking to Market? Enron Gas Services' wholesale adoption of mark-to-market accounting for long-term energy contracts was ripe for abuse. It began with a retroactive adjustment in order to juice 1991 earnings as the books closed. By simply tweaking assumptions—what critics called mark-to-*model*—Jeff Skilling's group could produce a variety of profits, or even avoid loss, as desired. EGS, later Enron Capital & Trade Resources (ECT), would liberally compute profits as the decade went on—and reap outsized compensation for false profit.

Mark-to-market was abused in a new way when a liquid market was contrived from two long-term MTBE contracts, part of the ill-fated acquisition of MTBE and methanol facilities from Tenneco in 1991. This financial illusion produced present-year profits in 1993–94 but removed future income, exacerbating future losses. A $100 million write-down of these assets in 1997 was just the beginning; the facilities would be scrapped several years later.

Mark-to-market and mark-to-model accounting became even more abused as Enron found itself in more and larger holes. One was the aforementioned artificiality whereby assets were revalued at "fair value" (mark-to-model) to meet promised earnings during 1996.

Jeff Skilling was the executive in charge. But the financial shortcuts were on Rich Kinder's watch with Ken Lay's support. In fact, COO Kinder was in the meetings that produced the fair-value deceit. External auditor Arthur Andersen, pliable to its lucrative client, went along with the scheme, another canary-in-the-coal-mine moment in Enron's history.

Perceptionism. For ENE to remain a Buy (rather than a Hold), Enron had to meet or exceed its (bullish) earnings projections. And Enron knew that its credit ratings had to be maintained to support the huge trading side of the business, particularly under mark-to-market accounting.

Earnings management was crucial to keep the story going. One strategy was to smooth earnings by shifting profits forward if current-period goals were reached. At the close of 1995, a $70 million transfer to 1996 was executed by ECT for just this purpose.

Shifting income, accelerating income, and monetizing assets to make earnings—quarter over quarter, not only year over year—gave new meaning to the term *financial engineering*. Originally applied to the esoteric field of

---

35. For ETSI and Mobil stock income, see Internet appendix 2.2, "HNG/InterNorth: Joint Ventures, Miscellaneous Assets, and Sales," at www.politicalcapitalism.org/Book3/Chapter2/Appendix2.html.

quantitative modeling (the domain of Enron's top quant, Vince Kaminski), the term came to mean *gaming the accounting rulebook to meet corporate goals*, especially to placate investors and/or trigger internal compensation awards. Such gaming also applied to hiding debt off the balance sheet, a practice critically noted by the financial community in the pre-1997 era. Rich Kinder played his part in this too.

"The Enron debacle represents an extreme example of the selective financial misrepresentation mentality," a review in the *Journal of Accounting and Public Policy* would find. In contra-capitalist terms, philosophic fraud was enabled by a rules-based (instead of principles-based) accounting system. By establishing a system in which intent could be masked by legalese, regulation and regulators had invited gaming by a business underclass and spawned a generation of investors unwilling to better look out for themselves.

Enron's hope was that by reporting a desired reality instead of the true one, painful midcourse corrections could be avoided and outside investors placated. It was an instance of *Just Because You Can Doesn't Mean You Should*, as Enron executive Mike McConnell titled his memoirs. Such short-run deceit became habitual, with one expediency morphing into another. The philosophic fraud of warring against reality instead of understanding and conforming to it would prove unsustainable. "It happened at many levels, from matters with the Board to our contention that 'gray' financial structures were within the rules," McConnell remembered.

The mentality behind financial engineering is antithetical to best-practice capitalism. Good profit is economic profit approximated by cash flow, not contrived accounting or paper profit. It is also comprehending the market (and political) forces behind earnings. But as ECT executive John Esslinger remembered: "People at Enron didn't ask how you made your money but only why you didn't make your money."

Corporate Masks

Enron's communication strategy went beyond the standard business practice of presenting key data in reference to general market conditions with a dollop of optimism. That was for vanilla annual reports and minimally staffed public relations departments. Big-picture Ken Lay—tying business strategies to public policy, launching new profit centers, keeping ENE hot, and, later, looking to retail energy as a national brand—had many constituents to impress and different masks to wear.

Enron's annual reports were businesslike prior to 1988 but bolder and theme-oriented thereafter. Enron's 1992 offering was unusually spirited, even whimsical, playing on the green theme of natural gas. The next report added an international focus, complete with a hologram in the middle of the cover, as shown in Figure I.2.

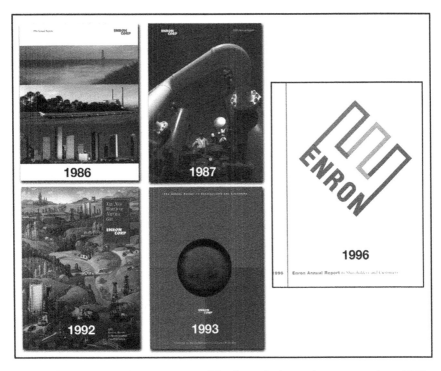

Figure I.2 Enron's annual reports were all business in the early years, such as 1986 and 1987. Themed reports in 1992 and 1993 fashioned Enron as a natural gas company with global reach. Enron's 1996 report highlighted the new logo with the company's plan to retail gas and electricity to homes and businesses.

Inconsistencies, however, marked Enron's self-imaging with regard to so-called green energy and competition, not to mention its supposed allegiance to free-market capitalism. Misdirection and even deceit were present when certain information was highlighted and other equally relevant information was not—and when called-for explanations were absent or falsified. Inconsistent imaging and misdirection characterized the 1985–1996 period; deceit became more prevalent in 1997 forward.

A "Green" Company?

Natural gas was the cleanest burning of the three major fossil fuels.[36] The self-described "leading integrated natural gas company in North America"

---

36. "Natural gas plants emit about 80 percent less nitrogen oxides; 60 percent less carbon dioxide [than a coal plant]; and no sulfur dioxide," read Enron's 1992 annual report. Also, compared to a similarly sized coal plant, gas plants avoided sludge and ash and required half the water.

naturally sought a valuation premium from this differentiation in an era of political environmentalism. But tensions would emerge when Enron's green image clashed with Enron's bottom-line considerations.

"Isn't it wonderful natural gas is invisible so the rest of nature never will be?" asked Enron's national advertising campaign in late 1989. In early 1990, Enron unveiled its new vision, *"to become the world's first natural gas major, the most innovative and reliable provider of clean energy worldwide for a better environment."*[37] Two years later, Ken Lay presented his *Natural Gas Standard* in order to cajole electric utilities and their regulators to choose natural gas in place of coal for new capacity.[38]

Fair enough: Enron tied itself to a fuel that had been artificially held back by government policy and that had both cost and political-environmental advantages, helped by rapidly improving combined-cycle turbine technology to generate electricity. Lay was smartly playing a political angle to promote an advantageous fuel that had been politically victimized by a lesser one.

Green Enron also warred against oil, not only coal. Fuel oil was a competitor to natural gas in Enron pipeline markets from Florida to California. Periodic fuel switching from gas to oil in dual-fuel plants was either occurring or threatening to do so in the mid-to-late 1980s, and after. As a consequence, Ken Lay even came to favor tariffs on imported petroleum to reduce international competition to (domestic) natural gas.[39]

Yet oil, not natural gas, was the energy choice most desired in many underdeveloped countries for the power plants Enron wanted to build. Typically, natural gas was not indigenous, and liquefied natural gas (LNG) cost more than oil. Accordingly, Enron Development touted its "market-led approach" of "finding solutions to a country's energy needs rather than selling a specific fuel [natural gas] or pushing a specific project."

For example, Batangas (105 MW) and half-owned Subic Bay (116 MW) in the Philippines were oil fired, as was an Enron leased-and-operated 28 MW facility at Subic Bay. The 110 MW Puerto Quetzal, a two-barge power plant in Guatemala, half owned by Enron, was oil fired. (These projects were very profitable for Enron, given a government-lending boost.) Oil was also the fuel of choice for the 696 MW Dabhol, India, power plant (Phase I), although it was to be joined by LNG for Phase II once the contracts were in place.

---

37. See chapter 14, pp. 563–65.

38. Rate-base incentives under public-utility regulation favored coal over gas for new capacity, something that was not necessarily good for consumers, much less the environment. See chapter 7, pp. 324–27. New oil-fired capacity was not at issue, since the same power-generation technology can use either fuel oil or natural gas.

39. See chapter 7, pp. 316–19.

At home, Enron's natural gas image also had to square with Enron Liquid Fuels, described in Enron's 1989 annual report as "a fully integrated crude oil entity in North America." Enron's midstream oil assets (what was previously called Enron Oil Transportation & Trading) were assembled and taken public (in March 1994) as EOTT Energy Partners. EOTT's activities in 17 states and Canada encompassed "purchasing, gathering, transporting, processing, trading, storage and resale of crude oil and refined petroleum products and related activities." EOG, on the other hand, although it had oil reserves and drilled for oil, was close to a pure natural gas play.

———

Enron was as anticoal as a company could be, having no coal assets; urging utilities to choose natural gas over coal in power generation; and lobbying for public policies disadvantaging coal emissions and usage. But Enron quietly got into the (profitable) coal business.

In October 2001, in what would prove to be his last conference call with security analysts, Ken Lay revealed a previously undisclosed profit center. Enron, he promised, would transition out of its noncore businesses and stay in trading and pipelines—and in coal.

Coal? Who knew that since 1997, Enron had been building this business, first in trading and then in financing coal companies and taking payment in physical coal (volumetric production payments). Enron's "integrated approach" was explained by one executive: "While we aren't interested in purchasing a coal company outright, we can use ECT's capital in a variety of ways to gain access to production which strengthens our physical position."

To be sure, Enron had already declared itself the world's first natural gas major and had moved on to a vision of becoming *the world's leading energy company.* But Ken Lay's enterprise was still pushing global warming and green energies. When confronted on the discrepancy by one of his coal executives, Jeff Skilling put the matter to rest with the words: "Mike, we are a green energy company, but the green stands for money."

Gone were the jokes at Enron headquarters about coal as "flammable dirt."

The CEO of many masks—procoal at Florida Gas Company and again at Transco—had been against coal upon his arrival at Houston Natural Gas. He continued to be that fuel's number-one private-sector foe until Enron got into the business, even acquiring coal reserves. But the physical side of Enron's coal play was not emphasized; logistics were. "Enron provides a single, comprehensive solution to manage all logistics and risk, whether the coal is sourced domestically or abroad," the last (2000) annual report stated. "In some cases, we have reduced the customer's cost of coal by as much as 10 percent."

YOUR NATURAL RESOURCE

Now there's an all-encompassing coal merchant resource to help you access markets, manage risks and control the bottom line - Enron Capital & Trade Resources (ECT).

FOR **coal** SERVICES

ECT is a business unit of Enron Corp., one of the world's largest integrated energy companies, with approximately $30 billion in assets. ECT's capabilities include market-making in physical energy commodities, creative risk management and financial services.

Recognizing the convergence of energy resources, we've added coal to our portfolio to help us continue our role as a leading global energy solutions firm. Our extensive resources and innovative approach to the coal business can help you further your success.

COAL STILL BURNS BRIGHT

Enron Capital & Trade Resources Corp.

ENRON

Figure I.3 Enron quietly but decisively entered the coal business in 1997, first in trading and then in asset acquisition to enhance trading. The coal unit was a welcome new profit center on the wholesale side of ECT.

Enron's 35-employee coal unit earned $35 million in 1999, a true profit center with $300 million invested in coal reserves to back ECT's physical trading. "Our position as a 'green' company is getting thin," stated Enron's head of European affairs, Mark Schroeder. "We will find it increasingly difficult to even maintain the John Browne imitation, having sold solar (to BP), and sometime next year becoming the largest trader of coal in the world."

Procompetition?

Enron was not an ivory tower, despite its raft of PhD economists (and near PhDs). Ken Lay was a businessman, not an academic or an ideologue. He was a pragmatist first and a visionary second. In the name of profit maximization, Lay was for many things before he was against them, and vice-versa. The iconic institutions of *markets* and *competition* were embraced here but not there, even in contradictory public stances. This was the mixed economy in which Enron operated, and a Ken Lay could reach the top.

Early on, Lay was of two minds about the spot-gas revolution and associated transportation versus the old ways of doing business. "About the time people get all the flexibility and transportation they want," he said in 1985, "they'll find they don't want all of that." Why? Higher prices and profits were needed for his upstream and midstream operations. This from the ex-president of Transco Energy, who had spearheaded the formation of the US Natural Gas Clearinghouse in 1983, not to mention Transco's special marketing programs in 1982–83.

Low spot prices weighed heavily on Lay. Selling gas "below cost," he complained, could compromise the service obligation of pipelines to deliver gas and eventually result in a "severe landing" of price spikes later on.

Was Mr. Natural Gas saying that natural gas was anything but abundant and dependable? To electric utilities, Enron's answer was no ... but maybe yes. In order to get electricity generators to forgo coal for their new plants, Enron said gas was a sure thing. They had to; buyers remembered the mid-1970s when gas deliveries were curtailed. And had not the *Enron Outlook* quantified the robust North American resource base in light of improving technology?[40]

On the other hand, long-term contracts had higher margins than heavily traded, transparent month-to-month spot gas. So, Enron hinted, and a bit more, that gas might not be *quite* so abundant, reliable, and affordable—and electricity generators should execute long-term, price-premium, fixed contracts for some, even much, of their requirements. And by the way, Enron was the preeminent supplier of that long-term gas.

Ken Lay was a bearish bull. In 1985, he complained that "our industry saying big shortages and big price spirals are just around the corner" was not "a very effective way to sell people on making long term commitments to our fuel." Yet three years later, Lay warned that gas produced at less than replacement cost was setting up "a real shock and very severe dislocations throughout the industry."

There was a fence to be straddled. The idea was for utilities to build new gas-fired capacity and to commit to higher-margin long-term supply. Enron would assure them of gas availability just forcefully enough to build, yet it would concern them just enough to sign long-term fixed-priced contracts. In fact, during customer meetings, Enron would present McKinsey's pessimistic view of natural gas supply, follow with the in-house optimistic view, and then pitch the long-term gas option for locking in the (premium) price.

To encourage long-term contracting, Enron also warned state utility regulators about volatile spot prices and possible supply problems.[41] This was done not only for electric utilities but also for gas utilities supplying

---

40. See pp. 52n57, 57–58.

41. See chapter 9, pp. 419–21.

residential and commercial customers—for anyone buying gas at wholesale from Enron.

Make no mistake: Ken Lay knew where Enron's bread was buttered. He saw, early on, how money could be made as a marketer, not just as a transporter, of natural gas. And that long-term contracts were far more profitable than transacting on the spot market.

———

Asset collectivism represented a far more fundamental contradiction for the allegedly free-market Ken Lay. Early on, however, he saw that more money could be made if Enron was an independent marketer of natural gas as well as a transporter. Separating sales and transportation would create two profit centers where before there had been only bundled pipeline sales (no margin) and transport. The same principle—separating sales and transportation—could also be applied to the much larger electricity industry.

Separating sales and transportation required Enron to accept FERC's program of mandatory open access (MOA), whereby interstate natural gas pipelines (and, later, electric utilities) agreed to let all comers use their transportation capability at nondiscriminatory prices and other terms of service. At first, this would apply at the wholesale level (pipelines, transmission wires) but later was also to apply at the retail level.

Using other companies' assets via "infrastructure socialism" allowed Enron to create a unit devoted solely to marketing natural gas and electricity, a very good thing for an asset-light company trying to grow quickly and have a high credit rating at the same time. MOA was procompetition, exhorted Enron, and competition was good, even when it took place on a regulation-communalized playing field.

To Lay, MOA was a means to an end: making money. He was not concerned about *real* deregulation: namely, repealing decades-old public-utility protection to remove franchise protection and to remove rate caps. That was not in political play.

Enron championed MOA, first at the federal (interstate wholesale) level, which allowed Enron to form EGS/EGM/ECT as a new innovative profit center. MOA was now advocated by Enron for retail (the distribution level) as Enron's next big thing, as discussed in both chapter 15 and the Epilogue.

———

Expediency in place of principles created unusual situations for Ken Lay. One tension emerged when potential state-level MOA threatened the profitability of supply sales from two intrastate pipelines. In Texas, a long-term sales contract to Entex by Houston Pipe Line was at risk. What if the Texas Railroad Commission did what FERC had done: issue an open-access order abrogating the very profitable contract in favor of (lower-margin) spot gas?

"There is a need to coordinate our policies, statements, and positions with one another to avoid diverse positioning at Enron," an ECT Legal memorandum stated in 1997. The issue also was alive next door concerning gas sales off of Enron's Louisiana Resources pipeline.

It was all-hands-on-deck to "assist in resolving contrasting interests in order to formulate ECT positions to support the needs of ECT Retail with the least damaging consequences to our intrastate pipelines and wholesale business units." As it turned out, a crisis was dodged (in-state MOA was avoided), and Enron's two-faced policy did not become public at a most inopportune time.

In South America, the same tension emerged. Enron preferred a closed, integrated, bundled approach upon building or buying natural gas infrastructure. Producers would sell gas to Enron, which would then transport and burn the gas in its power plants, capturing profits across stages where little outside competition existed. Open-access pipelining, on the contrary, increasing competition and adding price transparency, would lower returns.

"Can you e-mail folks to set up a meeting ... to discuss infrastructure integration?" an internal memorandum read. "We really need to resolve the two [positions] to give Ken [Lay] some guidance, and right now I'm pretty lost," wrote Enron's director of public policy analysis (the present author).

––––

Other competition-here-but-not-there examples can be cited. By assigning Enron's travel business to his sister's travel agency, an allegedly procompetition CEO was anything but. By accusing major oil companies of predatory pricing with wellhead gas sales in the early 1990s, Ken Lay was really complaining about too much competition (led by his own affiliate, EOG), not too little.

Lay and Enron actively lobbied for the passage of the North American Free Trade Agreement (NAFTA), which on the first day of 1994 prohibited tariffs and other restrictions on oil or natural gas imported from, or exported to, Canada or Mexico. Yet foreign oil was too cheap (competitive) for Lay, who sought a tariff in 1993 to lessen oil's competition to natural gas.[42] Lay also lobbied for a Btu tax to favor natural gas relative to oil and coal—until Clinton's draft proposal had the unintended consequence of gumming up ECT's long-term gas deals then in negotiation.

Natural gas was the natural winner over coal and oil in power generation, Enron claimed from at least 1987 on. EPA's political regulation favored gas because of its emission profile, and 1970s-era regulation favoring coal was repealed, or nearly so. Still, Ken Lay wanted any advantage he could get against his two rival fuels. A tax differential against oil and coal to benefit natural gas was an example of less competition and anticonsumerism for the sake of Enron's

––––

42. See chapter 7, pp. 316–19.

bottom line, given that existing fuel-specific environmental regulation was in place by the early 1990s to equalize the playing field.

Government Opportunity and Dependence

Market competition—or special government favor? Privately controlled assets—or mandatory open access? Oil and coal—or (subjectively defined) green energy? Tensions naturally developed where public policy positions were based on the bottom line rather than on intellectual argument and coherence. The same inconsistency was present in the image of Ken Lay as "the philosopher-king of energy deregulation."

At Transco in 1983, Lay lobbied Congress to terminate negotiated, inflexible producer contracts, a position opposed in the same hearing by better-situated InterNorth. In 1985, with InterNorth and HNG merged, Lay favored private renegotiation.[43] (The combined company, with 14 percent of the national gas market, had only 5 percent of the industry's take-or-pay liability.) Transco's Lay had sought a legislative fix to the take-or-pay problem; Enron's Lay favored self-help in a free market.

The modish idea that Ken Lay and Rebecca Mark's Enron Development were "spreading the gospel of privatization and free markets to developing countries" was a half-truth, or less. With crucial government loan aid, and working with authoritarian governments as counterparties, Enron was practicing crony capitalism—and not without risk. Despite the hoopla surrounding many project beginnings, there would be modest benefits to offset costs.

Ken Lay was shaky on market reliance when Enron's profitability was threatened. As outlined in Book 1 (*Capitalism at Work*), and more fully documented in this volume, Ken Lay was often the "bootlegger" (the business-side participant) in the "bootlegger and Baptist" rent-seeking framework (business interests working with public-interest groups). In fact, Enron was a political company with a first-mover predilection for opportunities created by existing government intervention or opportunities that might come from new regulation, taxation, or subsidization.

A striking example of the calculus of pragmatism, not free-market principles, concerned a rent-seeking play to advance a new energy tax in the context of the global-warming issue. In fact, in 1997, Enron was part of a Clinton-Gore task force recommending just that as public policy.

By the mid-1990s, Enron fiercely advocated MOA for retail electricity, a huge new market for ECT, in the name of *lowering* prices for consumers. "Cheaper

---

43. See chapter 2, p. 106n3.

electricity means economic growth and job creation," Lay intoned in 1992. Two years later, Jeff Skilling pegged California's savings alone at $8.9 billion, "enough money to pay down current debt, to double and triple the number of police officers and teachers in the state's largest cities, and still leave about $1 billion for discretionary purposes."

In a typical Enron speech, Rich Kinder pegged the savings at between 30 percent and 40 percent, or $60 to $80 billion per year, by comparing the average retail rate near $0.07 per kWh to the marginal costs of providing that power at between $0.04 and $0.05 per kWh.[44] If Enron could retail to capture part of this differential, it would become with electricity what Exxon was with petroleum: *an energy major.*

But what if the powerful electric utility lobby, led by the Edison Electric Institute, found out that Enron was trying to *increase* electricity rates via CO_2 rationing, while at the same time urging retail access in order to lower rates? Even if the two policies cancelled each other out, Enron would be a *triple* winner as power marketer, natural gas major, and renewables giant. And quadruple winner if cap-and-trade created a CO_2 emissions market.

Enron's have-it-both-ways position was quietly deemphasized by Lay in the face of a potential exposé that could have compromised Enron's consumerist argument for electricity restructuring.[45] Enron 2000's cornerstone, a new $200 billion market for ECT, was too important to get tangled, at least frontally, with global-warming policy.

Political Capitalism

Chapters 7 and 13 focus exclusively on political opportunity and rent-seeking at Enron, supplementing the chapter-by-chapter discussion of government in particular business situations. This macro/micro treatment underscores the unique dependency of Enron on the political process, quite outside a simple private-property free market.

Political Lay and political Enron were virtually inseparable. The politician-CEO was front and center in all things governmental. Business historians will be hard pressed to find another business leader with more Washington opportunity, drive, and results. Part of this was the nature of the energy business, long regulated at the state and federal levels, as summarized in the Epilogue of Book 2 (*Edison to Enron*). Part of it was Ken Lay's gravitating to regulated

---

44. Enron's estimates assumed that the utilities would not get ratepayer recovery for uneconomic generation that could no longer get rate-base treatment under public-utility regulation. Such "stranded costs," if passed through, would theoretically negate most of the cost savings, at least in the short run.

45. See chapter 15, pp. 557–58.

businesses and championing new interventionist policies.[46] "Ken Lay plays offense, not defense," as one company lobbyist remembered.

Virtually all Enron profit centers benefitted from and/or sought major government intervention: mandated access to interstate (wholesale) transmission for gas marketing; special incentives for independent (nonutility) electric generation; mandated access to interstate (wholesale) transmission for power marketing; special tax treatment of resource extraction (tight-sands gas); regulation of criteria pollutants (and, perhaps in the future, carbon dioxide)[47]; special tax treatment of solar power and wind power production (and, later, state quotas for qualifying renewable output); and loan assistance for foreign projects. These laws and administrative regulations, some originating in the 1930s, were in play in Enron's era, some with crucial Enron drafting and lobbying.

Still, laws could hurt rather than help Enron. The Public Utility Holding Company Act of 1935 was a burden for a nonutility, such as Enron, that built power plants and traded electricity in various states. Exemptions would be required until this law was formally amended in 1992.

Another thorn in Enron's side was environmental regulation, which encumbered pipeline operation and delayed pipeline expansions, although Enron (Transwestern and Florida Gas, in particular) innovatively minimized this inefficiency. With rate base treatment of environmental capital costs, Enron (and competing projects) could live with this hassle factor.

Enron's interstates were more disadvantaged than helped by FERC public-utility regulation of rates and service. A capacity surplus in interstate (wholesale) markets beginning in the early-to-mid 1980s, creating pipe-on-pipe competition, made traditional cost-plus ratemaking unnecessary and counterproductive to the goal of market-responsive pricing. Maximum regulated rates might be above market, requiring a discount lest the rate become zero from lost business.

Such laws could hurt Enron's competitors to lessen the pain, at least relatively. What Ken Lay sought was *government intervention that helped Enron despite its negative effects on competitors, not to mention rate payers or taxpayers.* In so doing, Enron became addicted to special government opportunity—whether a favorable regulation, tax advantage, or check written on the US Treasury.

---

46. Both Lay and John Henry Kirby, who founded Houston Natural Gas in 1930, were private-sector politicians; their parallels are discussed in Bradley, *Edison to Enron*, pp. x, 8–10, 388–400.

47. These are particulate matter (PM), ground-level ozone, carbon monoxide (CO), sulfur dioxide (SO_2), nitrogen oxides (NO_x), and lead (Pb). Of these six, three (PM, SO_2, and NO_x) were part of the natural-gas-versus-coal debate. CO_2, notably, was not considered a criteria pollutant.

But Enron's core competency certainly did not begin with Ken Lay. Rent-seeking alarmed Adam Smith in the 18th century, and leading US political economists explained its nefarious presence in the 19th century.[48] *Natural Gas Week* editor John Jennrich described it succinctly during Enron's day: "This is, after all, not a philosophical discussion," he noted about various industry positions taken about a regulatory matter. "This is about M-O-N-E-Y." Such pragmatism was old hat in the US energy business, where the long tradition of business morality and bourgeois virtue, from Adam Smith and Samuel Smiles onward, was often ignored.

Mixed-Economy Competition

Legislation and administrative regulation enabled politically attuned, politically correct Enron to make hundreds of millions of dollars between 1984 and 1996. Regulation of a different kind (accounting, finance) enabled Enron to self-interpret its results in order to appear to be more profitable and sustainable than it really was. But in some cases, Enron found itself engaged in political lobbying that promoted competition and wealth creation.

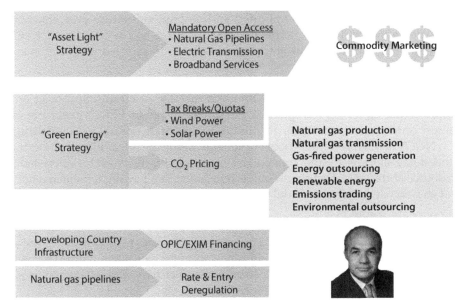

Figure I.4 Enron's asset-light and green-energy strategies, as well as virtually all its profit centers, were dependent on special government favor. A politically connected, politically correct Ken Lay was the common denominator of Enron's public-sector activism.

---

48. See Bradley, *Edison to Enron*, pp. 7–9, 11–13, 33–35, 130–34.

Ken Lay's opening move to acquire two interstate pipelines brought federal regulation to HNG's core. This was about market-side profit-seeking under regulatory constraints, not rent-seeking. Interstate gas transmission was a consumer-driven business that its energy rivals—manufactured (coal) gas and fuel oil—routinely obstructed through the political process. In fact, the entry of Northern Natural Gas Pipeline in 1931 was delayed, and entry of Florida Gas Transmission in 1959 nearly derailed, by interfuel rent-seeking by coal and oil interests.

In a competitive market with FERC leaning toward competition, Enron's regulatory initiatives were procompetition—liberalizing service so that consumers increasingly had choices between gas providers and between fuels.[49] The exception to this was Ken Lay's push for oil tariffs to protect gas pipeline volumes against foreign oil.

Inherited Intervention Opportunities

The Natural Gas Policy Act (NGPA), part of the five-law National Energy Policy Act of 1978 (NEPA), was foundational to what would be Enron's core business. Two lawyers described the phaseout of price controls, as well as the act's other provisions, as "the most complicated and ambiguous statute ever enacted." Total deregulation (to create a true free market) it was not; nevertheless, deregulatory momentum was secured that would lead to more freedom of action and competition.

Section 311 of the NGPA began the process of unbundling the gas commodity from interstate transportation. Spot-gas carriage programs, approved on a case-by-case basis, were supplanted and universalized by FERC's generic open-access orders, which created a new industry: interstate natural gas marketing.

NGPA accelerated the process of federal wellhead price liberalization that ended gas shortages—and created an institutional framework for open-ended resource abundance. Supply problems overcome, Ken Lay implemented a natural gas–focused business model that was sustainable and profitable.[50]

PURPA Opportunity. Another part of NEPA, the Public Utility Regulatory Policies Act of 1978 (PURPA), was a precursor for Enron's new business of power plants. The law was intended to aid renewable energies when natural gas was considered to be a fading resource to generate electricity. Still, efficient new gas technologies qualified for the law's preferences.

---

49. For these money-making initiatives, see chapter 6, pp. 257, 264–65.

50. Lay's much-described free-market advocacy centered on market (scarcity) pricing in place of federal price controls as interpreted under the just-and-reasonable standard of the Natural Gas Act of 1938. But he disputed market prices as too low, once with natural gas (Lay's predatory pricing charge in 1991) and once with oil (his tariff and tax proposals).

Lo and behold, natural gas became plentiful, and natural gas combined-cycle technology rapidly improved in the 1980s, generating increasing amounts of electricity per unit of gas. PURPA predated Enron, but Ken Lay, having seen good results with independent power generation at Transco, his former stop, was an early mover at HNG.

PURPA opened a new market for independent gas-fired cogeneration plants by requiring utilities to buy power at a lucrative, regulatory-assigned "avoided cost" as if the utility had built the capacity itself.[51] Enron Cogeneration Company—a much-needed new profit center and, in fact, Enron's highest rate-of-return business—built or acquired six plants between 1985 and 1988 that contributed tens of millions of dollars to the bottom line. Lay wanted this business right off the bat and found his leader in John Wing, formerly at GE.

Multiple Enron divisions benefitted from Wing's PURPA-enabled deals. The sizeable gap between (low) gas costs and (high) avoided-cost power prices allowed the Texas City project not only to lock in high margins but also to buy 75 MMcf/d from Enron Oil & Gas "at prices substantially above spot market levels."

Texas City's avoided cost was based on the estimated cost of a new coal plant outfitted with expensive pollution-control equipment (scrubbers) pursuant to the Clean Air Act of 1990. The difference between Wing's $300 per kilowatt high-efficiency cogen plant and the regulatory-approved $1,100 per kilowatt of installed coal capacity allowed (regulatory) windfall profits for EOG and transporter HPL.[52]

This power-sales contract was so high that natural gas could be profitably purchased from EOG at $3.25/MMBtu (with a 6 percent escalation factor) at a time when spot gas was averaging less than $2.00/MMBtu. Credit Enron for fully capitalizing on regulatory opportunity, one of many instances that defined a politically alert company operating in a politically shaped industry.

Under a more reasonable interpretation of avoided cost, the power contract would have been based on the utility's constructing its own gas-fired cogen plant (what Enron's John Wing was doing). The gas-purchase price would then have had to be closer to spot. But Texas Utilities as a franchised monopolist was indifferent so long as it could sell the (PURPA) purchased power.

Captive electric ratepayers, in other words, lost what Enron gained in the 1984–89 heyday of PURPA. An energy-crisis law had quite different results in an energy-surplus era, an unintended consequence of government intervention from changed markets.

---

51. This law is described in Internet appendix 1.5, "Public Utility Regulatory Policies Act of 1978 (PURPA)," at www.politicalcapitalism.org/Book3/Chapter1/Appendix5.html.

52. See chapter 3, pp. 165–66; chapter 4, p. 204; chapter 5, pp. 218–19.

Export Aid. Enron's infrastructure projects in the least-developed areas of the world were enabled by long-standing laws that created the Export-Import Bank (Ex-Im) in 1934 and the Overseas Private Investment Corporation (OPIC) in 1971. Rebecca Mark's mandate was to "plant the flag for Enron in as many developing nations as she could."

Why go to the poorest, riskiest markets? Because other energy companies were ensconced in the better markets, and Enron wanted the higher profits that came from greater risk. Government financing and/or government risk insurance, combined with Enron's favorable reputation post-Teesside, were enough to attract other private financing to get projects done.

Ex-Im was reauthorized three times in Enron's solvent life: 1986, 1992, and 1997. When OPIC's reauthorization was blocked by a House vote in 1996, Enron's lobbying went into high gear. "As we move toward projects in Croatia, Mozambique, Bolivia, Poland, and a number of other emerging democracies," Ken Lay wrote in the *Journal of Commerce*, "OPIC will again be a key agency enabling Enron to contribute to private investments to these struggling countries."

Ex-Im and OPIC were joined by other taxpayer involvement with Enron's overseas ventures. According to one study, "at least 21 agencies, representing the U.S. government, multilateral development banks, and other national governments," approved $7.2 billion for 38 Enron-related projects in 29 countries.

No other company before or after could point to the breadth of such assistance. The irony was evident. "There were times when Lay's lobbying seemed at odds with his oft-stated belief in free-market solutions," noted Bethany McLean and Peter Elkind. "A classic example was Enron's dependence on such government agencies as [OPIC and Ex-Im]."

Shaped Intervention

Enron shaped, but did not originate, important legislation and administrative regulation between 1984 and 1996. Two major areas were (1) MOA for interstate natural gas transmission and (2) emissions regulation under the Clean Air Act as amended in 1990.

FERC Open Access: Wholesale Gas. FERC's aforementioned implementation of mandatory open access began with a May 1985 Notice of Proposed Rulemaking that became administrative law later that year.

Regulation of Natural Gas Pipelines after Partial Wellhead Decontrol (FERC Order No. 436) birthed a national interstate gas commodity market. The new regime for pipelines was supported, even championed, by HNG/InterNorth and personally lobbied for by Ken Lay.[53] The rules for MOA were finalized in

---

53. See chapter 2, pp. 138–40; and chapter 7, p. 309. Also see Internet appendix 1.2, "Mandatory Open Access for Interstate Gas Pipelines," at www.politicalcapitalism.org/Book3 /Chapter1/Appendix2.html.

the Pipeline Service Obligations and Revisions to Regulations Governing Self-Implementing Transportation Under Part 284 of the Commission's Regulations. FERC Order No. 636 of 1992 was Enron-stamped: "Many of the proposals advocated by HNG/InterNorth in our written comments are incorporated into the Final Rule," an internal Enron memorandum stated.

Enron's interstates were entirely open access by 1993. No longer did Transwestern, Florida Gas, Northern Natural, or Northern Border buy or sell gas; they only transported gas owned by others (including arm's-length Enron affiliates). From Enron's viewpoint, the transition had gone well. "Order No. 636 will have a positive impact on Enron and the natural gas industry as a whole," read the company's *1993 Form 10-K*. Echoed the annual report: "Full implementation of the Federal Energy Regulatory Commission's (FERC) Order 636 and the successful settlement of all significant regulatory issues on our interstate pipelines during 1993 should provide a constant and reliable stream of cash flow over the next several years from our largest single earnings contributor" (meaning the now-unbundled pipelines).

MOA to all 28 major interstate pipelines, not only to Enron's several, allowed Enron Gas Marketing (1986–90), Enron Gas Services (1990–94), and Enron Capital & Trade Resources thereafter to profitably buy and sell natural gas nationwide. "We're going through a 'once in a hundred years' transition in this industry," Jeff Skilling told employees in 1994. He was speaking about natural gas, but the same "infrastructure socialism" with electricity was ahead, first at wholesale and then, if Enron's massive lobbying bet succeeded, at retail.

Clean Air Act Emissions Control. What became the Clean Air Act of 1990 (aka the acid-rain bill) was of vital importance to the gas industry, partly because Enron made it so. Ken Lay testified on behalf of both the Interstate Natural Gas Association of America and the American Gas Association (the industry's midstream and downstream trade groups, respectively) before the Subcommittee on Energy and Power (House Committee on Energy and Commerce) in September 1989.

Emphasizing how natural gas had "virtually no sulfur dioxide emissions and one-third the nitrogen oxide emissions of coal," Lay argued for a "freedom of choice" approach to allow electric utilities to reduce emissions via SO_2 and NO_x trading. "Legislation should not mandate the installation of scrubbers by utilities," Lay implored. Nor should so-called clean-coal technologies be subsidized beyond the feasibility stage for commercialization.

Emission-reduction requirements should be allocated systemwide, regionally, or statewide, not quantified by individual plant. Lay and the gas industry also supported emissions trading and a tax on other fossil fuels (*not* natural gas) "to help fund the [emission reduction] program."

Enron stood to benefit in existing and potential ways. Higher gas demand benefitted Enron's exploration and production, transmission, and marketing businesses. Prospectively, emissions trading in SO_2 and NO_X could be done by a well-positioned gas company, such as Enron. And methane-intensive oxygenates could be important on the transportation side, a frontier for natural gas. Within several years, in fact, Enron would become a major player in both emissions trading and reformulated gasoline.

The Clean Air Act of 1990 moved the marker for Ken Lay. Before, his lobbying had been about getting back to even with coal, legislatively and administratively. Now, it was about getting ahead. In speeches and in print, Lay cajoled electric utilities to go "beyond Clean Act compliance" with "natural gas co-firing, gas conversion, or new gas-fired capacity [that] would hedge the risk facing ratepayers resulting from potential CO_2 emissions limits or taxes in the future." Carbon dioxide regulation? That was another gas-for-coal and gas-for-oil play that Lay and the Enron-pushed natural gas industry sought.

Championed Intervention
Enron was also instrumental in enacting major legislative provisions. One home run was a clause in the Energy Policy Act of 1992 requiring electric utilities to provide transmission services to outside parties for sale-for-resale transactions. As told in chapter 11, this provision birthed wholesale power marketing, of which Enron became the market leader, and set the stage for retail MOA, the subject of chapter 15.

Another Enron-driven provision was in the Omnibus Budget Reconciliation Act of 1990, which provided a tax credit of $0.52/Mcf for natural gas sales from qualifying tight-sands gas wells drilled in 1991–92. The pretax benefit of $0.80/Mcf for Enron Oil & Gas equated to a *50 percent* increase in the then price of wellhead gas.

Although already producing such gas, EOG "did a 180-degree shift" to became the nation's leading tight-sands company. Enron's 1991 annual report stated the good news: "The supportive role Enron Oil & Gas played in the passage of tight sands legislation … could be worth more than $100 million to Enron on a net present value basis." The cumulative effect, in fact, would be double this.

Far from coincidental, Enron and EOG "diligently" worked to give an expired credit new life. "We spent a lot of time working that issue and actually got an extension of the Section 29 credits, which had, frankly, expired," remembered Joe Hillings, head of Enron's Washington office. "Enron essentially was the biggest winner in that legislation."

EOG tried and failed to extend the start date for qualifying wells past 1992, but drilled wells had a 10-year credit window, which resulted in a nine-figure tax savings as wells drilled in 1991–92 gave their bounty.

———

Enron's Washington office often responded to company emergencies with legislative fixes. One was the aforementioned pushback against funding cuts for

OPIC and Ex-Im. That was defense. On offense, one emergency concerned two Enron pipeline expansions that faced a shortage of pipe and construction delays from a tariff on imported steel. So, in 1989, "Enron succeeded in inserting language into the law that created a short-supply relief mechanism." In this instance, Enron's benefits were shared by consumers.

Joe Hillings, Cynthia Sandherr, and the rest of Enron's staff in the nation's capital were always busy with the day-to-day minutiae of national and international Enron. Setting up visits between Enron developers and foreign dignitaries or trading favors with the US Department of Energy or the US Department of Commerce were the daily fare of a fast-track company in a political world.

Desired Intervention

There was legislation and administrative regulation that eager Enron could not land. One area concerned an oil-import tariff promoted by Ken Lay to reduce oil-to-gas competition. A more ongoing effort was to regulate carbon dioxide by pricing CO_2 emissions either by cap-and-trade or by an emissions levy. Ken Lay preferred emissions trading (in which Enron could be a market maker), but he was amenable to a carbon tax.

A third effort, the biggest of the three, was the lobbying effort to get MOA for retail electricity (and natural gas) either from individual states or via federal legislation that would pre-empt the states. That broad, costly effort would be slow, mixed, and ultimately unsuccessful in Enron's life.

Oil Tariff. Oil was a thorn in the side of the natural gas industry beginning in the mid-to-late 1980s. Fuel switching in dual-fuel power plants was an issue in markets served by Florida Gas Transmission and by Transwestern Pipeline. Cheap gasoline was a barrier to commercializing natural gas vehicles as well.

In the 1980s, Lay flirted with endorsing an oil-import fee, a policy he had championed with Jack Bowen back at Transco. Lay stopped just short of protectionism in the wake of the 1986 oil price collapse. But in mid-1991, after the Gulf War, he endorsed an oil tariff in a speech before the Aspen Institute Energy Policy Forum, a sort of trial balloon.[54]

Lay went all in with a four-page Enron press release in early 1993: "Enron Corp. Chairman Kenneth Lay Cites Means by Which to Rebuild U.S. Energy Infrastructure, Create New Jobs and U.S. Investment." In the *Petroleum Economist*, Lay proposed a $5 per barrel, $75 billion tariff to drive greater domestic oil and gas production, as well as to underwrite crude-oil purchases for the Strategic Petroleum Reserve. Little thought was given to the politics and mechanics of the policy, such as an inability to tax oil from Canada on one side and Mexico on the other, following the passage of NAFTA (which he strongly supported).

---

54. See chapter 7, pp. 317–18.

CO₂ Limits. "I think we need to do something," Ken Lay told a conference of academics and industry leaders in 1996. "Perhaps the first thing will be some kind of an emissions trading system where we will put some limitation on CO_2 emissions.... I do not think we will see a big carbon tax for some time." In fact, pricing CO_2 had been a goal of Enron's CEO since the global-warming issue emerged in 1988. It became part of the Enron-led "corporate green movement" that split the fossil fuel industry into two parts, if not into three.

Lay led the charge, even when he was outnumbered in the gas industry and perceived as ceding to the Democrats and anti-industrial Left. "Maybe we ought to be very careful about leading the fight to kill the carbon tax," he diplomatically suggested to *Natural Gas Week* in 1990. Two years later, Lay endorsed Clinton's Btu tax so long as it had a "heavier tax on dirtier fuels."

Pricing CO_2 was an intervention that promised profit opportunities in divisions across the company. Four were gas production, transmission, and marketing, as well as gas-fired power plant construction. Enron's entry into solar (1995) and wind power (1997) were two more. Outsourcing for electric utilities via Enron Environmental Services brought the count to seven.

Emissions trading rounded out the list. Enron entered this last-named market in early 1993 with the acquisition of the air-emission consultancy AER*X, which traded SO_2 allowances in Los Angeles pursuant to regional regulation. The founder and president of AER*X, John Palmisano, would join Enron and get busy as Enron's chief climate lobbyist to pursue CO_2 trading.[55] Before it was all over, as an ex-Greenpeace official observed, Enron would be "the company most responsible for sparking off the greenhouse civil war in the hydrocarbon business."

MOA: Retail Electricity. The most coveted government intervention, the linchpin of Enron 2000 (the promise to double the size and profitability of Enron in five years), was state-level retail access for natural gas and electricity. Utilities would not voluntarily grant marketers such as Enron access to their customers, whether it was off the last increment of pipe for gas or of wire for electricity. State regulatory authorities would have to compel MOA.

MOA was achieved for wholesale gas via FERC regulations between 1985 and 1992. The same was achieved with wholesale electricity via the Energy Policy Act of 1992, implemented by FERC in the next years. This left retail, which was a state-by-state battleground, short of a federal law to preempt state authority and get it all done in one step. Enron pursued both with vigor, an

---

55. See chapter 9, pp. 405–7. Emissions trading, a proposal championed by the Environmental Defense Fund, led Lay to remark: "In shifting more to market-oriented solutions, environmental leaders are speaking the businessman's language."

effort that began in 1995 and reached its apogee with the California electricity crisis in 2000, a subject of the final book in this tetralogy.

Achievements (in Political Space)

Enron operated in a politicized industry within the US mixed economy. Public-utility regulation governed both natural gas and electricity at the interstate-transmission level and the distribution level. A politicized tax code impacted natural gas exploration and production and particularly qualifying renewable energies. Various laws left over from the 1970s energy crisis offered Enron opportunities and constraints, too.

Enron began and grew amid such regulation. That was simply a given for any company entering into natural gas and electricity. By itself, that framework did not require significant violations of best-business practices or bourgeois morality, although operating successfully within that framework doubtless required some skills and attitudes that were alien to truly free-market entrepreneurship.

Enron's operation within a mixed economy was not by itself what made Ken Lay's enterprise contra-capitalistic. In interstate gas transmission, for example, Enron maximized profits under regulatory constraints by becoming more efficient and user friendly. Amid competition, Enron's pipelines were market based and consumer judged. Government did not enable but constrained this business, and entrepreneurial profits were won by superior performance, not philosophic fraud or political capitalism, much less crony capitalism.

To a lesser extent, the same was true with the natural gas marketing that Enron pioneered in the era of mandatory open-access transmission. The infrastructure socialism that underlay gas marketing was a regulatory inheritance that Enron worked to shape—and lead in marketplace exchanges. In electricity, on the other hand, Enron did not inherit but led, federally at wholesale and state-by-state at retail, as described in chapter 15.

MOA was key to Jeff Skilling's *asset-light* strategy, whereby interstate pipelines did not have to be owned to be used. Without MOA and other government intervention in natural gas, marketing would have been done by pipeline owners in a physically integrated industry from the wellhead to retail, not unlike the oil majors' business-integration model. (Enron itself followed a bundled model on Houston Pipe Line.)

The grand function that Jeff Skilling pioneered, in other words, was a decentralized reinvention of what would have been done in different market form, and one that was aided immeasurably by franchised utilities and their regulators accepting long-term, fixed-priced contracting in place of monthly spot-gas purchases.

MOA has typically been equated to deregulation, since the commodity—methane or electrons—was deregulated for the first time in interstate commerce. But interstate transmission for both remained rate- and service-regulated

and, with the advent of MOA, hyperregulated. So less than "a child of deregulation," as one chronicler concluded, Enron was *a child of mandatory open access*,
not to mention government-created profit centers elsewhere.

The following chronology of Enron's accomplishments—whether concerning the parent overall or the individual units—must be placed in political context and judged in degrees of contra-capitalism. What was profit-seeking under
regulatory constraints that produced win-win outcomes? What was rent-
seeking, whereby others lost what Enron gained? What was lobbying for deregulatory advantage under new frameworks, and what was (crony) lobbying for
special government favor?

Which activities and results were fairly portrayed to the public, and which
were misrepresented by philosophic fraud? When were prudence and humility
exercised, and when were best practices abandoned?

What strategies and acts, in other words, were virtuous or the lesser of available evils within the morality of bourgeois capitalism? Which were neither?

Shades of gray will accompany some or most of the following apparent and
real successes concerning a half-dozen separate business units between 1984
and 1996. Overall patterns, however, foreshadowed what was to come for Enron.
These processes constitute the why-behind-the-why of one of the most consequential episodes in the history of commercial capitalism.

Surging ENE

In its first decade, Enron was relatively successful in a period of industry turmoil, giving the appearance of superior vision and execution by Ken Lay, his
top management, and a motivated, talented workforce. A company valued at
less than $2 billion in the mid-1980s doubled its market capitalization to $3.5
billion in 1991, doubled it again by 1994, and reached a market value of $11 bil-
lion by 1996. A stock valued at $5 per share (split-adjusted) in 1986–88 doubled
by 1992 and doubled again by 1996, soundly outperforming the competition
and overall market.

To be sure, net income was modest compared to the premerger days of
Houston Natural Gas and InterNorth. But ENE was premium priced because of
Ken Lay's narrative about an integrated natural gas play in a new energy era,
one propelled by a fourth industry segment, interstate marketing. "The natural
gas industry lives, and it looks a lot like Enron," one Wall Street analyst opined
in 1992. "Those companies that live beyond the commodity price alone will do
well."

ENE's price/earnings (P/E) ratio tells the story of increasing confidence. The
company's aggregate stock value divided by annual income increased from 14
in 1988–1991 to 20 in 1992–96. If earnings were driving valuation, this meant
that investors gave every dollar of income more market worth in the mid-1990s
than before, much of the optimism being tied to the surge in reported income
from gas marketing.

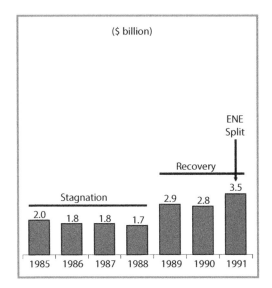
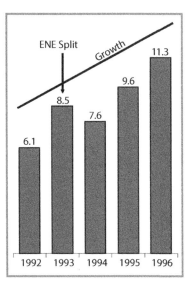

Figure I.5 Enron doubled its original market valuation by the early 1990s (shown in billions of dollars), and doubled it again in the mid-1990s. Increasing earnings, accelerated by mark-to-market accounting, as well as Ken Lay's stature and messaging, made ENE a momentum stock with a high price/earnings ratio.

Was the premium justified? Analyst John Olson, unlike almost all his colleagues, was wary. Oil-trading companies' lower ratio reflected its high risk, and gas-side comparables were scant. Peer companies, mostly with pipeline assets, traded at a half to two-thirds of Enron's P/E ratio. The 20 P/E ratio at which InterNorth valued HNG before the merger proved to be too high also, creating a goodwill account in excess of $1 billion for the new company.

Olson, in fact, had resisted the Enron narrative since 1990, causing Lay to complain to Olson's superiors at the investment firms that did business with Enron. "Ken Lay tried to get me fired three different times," the maverick remembered.

Vindicated in the end, Olson described a company obsessed with money and power. He characterized Enron's "game plan" to "get rich quick" as follows: "buy influence, issue big stock options, play Wall Street, goose the stock." Analysts, auditors, lawyers, and investment banks were paid well to perch ENE as a momentum stock, Olson noted. Enron's board of directors, explicitly supporting and otherwise apprised of Lay's strategy, was culpable, in Olson's telling. So was president and COO Rich Kinder until his departure.

Enron *was* buying political influence across the political spectrum, issuing outsized stock options for the smartest executives in the room, strong-arming the Street to share the narrative, and paying top legal and accounting talent to game the rules. The largesse of Ken Lay and Enron would increasingly compromise external constituencies—not to mention the company's own executives, employees, and board—to bring capitalism (but really contra-capitalism) into disrepute.

Profitable Core

Double-digit earnings growth per share for nine straight years (1988–96), a rarity in energy and practically everywhere else, was done by financial engineering (gaming). Still, Enron had five solidly profitable divisions. They were, in order of importance:

- The "cash cow" interstate gas pipelines, Enron's major asset base and the largest overall net cash contributor in the period under review;

- Enron Oil & Gas, which became Enron's top performer with annual cash-flow growth averaging 19 percent between 1989 and 1996—and with a debt ratio between 20 and 30 percent;

- Gas marketing, which became a notable profit center by 1989 and, with discretionary accounting help, became Enron's largest profit contributor by 1993;[56]

- Power generation (cogeneration), which became a major profit maker between 1986 and 1993 with US projects and Teesside UK;

- Gas liquids, a dependable contributor that offered contracyclical benefits when natural gas prices were low.

International, ensconced in developing countries, was profitable too. But its biggest project, Dabhol, cast a cloud on the whole unit's performance.

EOG was the truest growth story in Enron's stable, even accounting for its significant government-related favor. Unlike its parent, EOG was a low-cost, no-frills operator. Hoglund's rejection of artificial earnings acceleration ("We're not playing the easy type of game") ensured stability. Enron would monetize EOG thrice to keep the parent's earnings story hot before completely selling the company to public investors in 1999.

The interstate pipelines did well, increasing annual earnings by around 5 percent, more when expansion projects came on line. Cost reductions via automation and fully subscribed expansions overcame FERC's regulated rate of return embedded in maximum rates. In the competitive liquids business, finally, annual earnings growth in the mid–single digits was good—and achieved.

Cogeneration and gas marketing were high-return businesses in a market shaped by PURPA regulation and infrastructure socialism, respectively. But

---

56. Enron Gas Marketing earned $29 million in 1990; the renamed Enron Gas Services, under mark-to-market accounting, made $122 million in 1992 to become the second-largest income generator for Enron after the interstate pipelines.

competition was at work in the regulated space, normalizing returns over time. Regulators, too, pulled back their generous interpretation of avoided cost. In John Wing's case, the lucrative US market dried up by 1990, necessitating the move abroad (to a market newly created by privatization). For Jeff Skilling, profit spreads narrowed by the early-to-mid 1990s, bad news since earnings had already been recorded for the out years of the previously done long-term deals.

————

Management talent drove the profitable core. Ken Lay's philosophy to "try to get a game breaker in every key position" paid dividends and might well have been the difference between survival and failure in the dicey early years at Enron. Remuneration and payouts for superior performance, even in excess of that offered by other firms, were his means. Multiyear contracts for John Wing, Forrest Hoglund, and others were quite different from the philosophy back at Lay's Transco, where Jack Bowen believed that top executives were paid by the day. (Hoglund did receive a five-year contract to leave Exxon and join USX back in 1977.)

Lay's incentive approach, comparing stock values against a peer group and general market, proved to be imperfect, as short-term results could and would be overemphasized and overrewarded and as the competition rose to Enron's pay scale. Still, Lay's divisional heads, a few inherited but mostly new, were superior in Enron's first decade.

Landing Forrest Hoglund in 1987 to awaken and grow Enron Oil & Gas was pure gold. Hiring Jeff Skilling, first as a consultant and then as an executive, accelerated product development in wholesale gas marketing. Interstate-pipeline head Jim Rogers was a Lay-alike who had fun shaking up FERC just as FERC was shaking up Enron and the whole industry.

John Wing in cogeneration was a value creator in PURPA-regulated space, albeit a very trying one. Only Ken Lay could keep Wing in the stable as long as was possible, a good thing judged by the projects that got done on time and within budget—and very profitably so.

Mike Muckleroy gave Enron good value, beginning with his first job as director of special projects, selling stray assets after the merger of InterNorth and HNG. Muckleroy successfully merged two liquids units into one and became Enron's savior in the Valhalla crisis. Muckleroy was also a voice of conscience at Enron, questioning mark-to-market accounting as well as International's overreach into unstable, anticapitalistic countries.

————

Two risk-mitigation strategies were instrumental in Enron's superior performance during an industry recession. One allowed the interstate pipelines to remain cash cows; the other helped EOG prosper in a period of low wellhead prices. Both reflected instances of entrepreneurial insight and prudence that gave Enron and Ken Lay a (more-than-deserved) aura of superiority in the industry and to Wall Street.

Lay's charge to the interstate pipelines to expeditiously settle take-or-pay claims proved sound. Producers needed cash, and Enron, unlike other interstates, did not bank on higher wellhead prices to remove its liability.[57] Wall Street liked resolution in place of uncertainty, boosting ENE as Enron's take-or-pay liabilities fell from $1.2 billion in 1987 to "not material" by 1992.[58] This played a role in making the return to Enron's shareholders double that of its peer group between 1987 and 1992.[59]

Risk-minimization strategies helped EOG in low-price periods. "We try to hedge the prices of most of our natural gas, our more modest oil production, and the interest rates we pay," noted Ken Lay in 1995.[60] Another corporate synergy was long-term gas sales sourced from EOG, which produced incremental gains of $131 million for Hoglund in 1990–91 alone.

But what about Enron's naked risk taking elsewhere? Teesside II's open-ended supply contract, for example, ignored the history of take-or-pay problems in the United States for interstate pipelines, including those of Enron. Rushing to anticapitalistic countries, and especially India, was high risk, even with government loan aid. As it was, Enron's advertised prudence masked its *im*prudent strategies elsewhere, part of the false confidence Enron engendered for most of its solvent life.

––––

Other contributions and positives of Enron's rise to prominence should be mentioned. Financing techniques, such as credit-sensitive notes, inaugurated by Enron in 1989, were recognized as innovative in the business world. Derivatives trading with natural gas and electricity was pioneered by Enron. Securitization vehicles, although abused over time, had sound applications, such as Enron Finance Corporation's volumetric production payments in the early 1990s.

The Enron experience was certainly positive for the large majority of employees in the period under review. By the late 1980s, Ken Lay was a nation-

––––

57. Enron disagreed with the analysis of consultant Henry Groppe, a Transco Energy director and Lay confidant, who predicted that the gas bubble would burst with falling production and higher prices. Enron Corp.'s *Outlook for Natural Gas*, first released in 1989, was bullish on production and bearish on prices.

58. Transco Energy nearly collapsed after it reversed its take-or-pay strategy when Lay left to join HNG. See Bradley, *Edison to Enron*, pp. 331, 334, 338, 347–48, 352–54, 359.

59. As defined for incentive pay, Enron's peer group was 11 companies with major interstate gas pipeline assets, including Burlington Northern, Coastal, Columbia Gas, Sonat, Tenneco, Transco Energy, and Williams Companies.

60. Hedging against low gas prices helped make EOG's years in 1992, 1994, and 1995. Hedging backfired for EOG in 1993 and 1996, when locked-in prices were below market prices.

ally known corporate leader and a major figure in energy. In hometown Houston, Enron was considered one of the best companies to work for. Enron was new school, while Exxon (soon to be Exxon Mobil) remained the old-school standard of excellence. Employees were well compensated and then some with two-for-one ENE stock splits in 1991 and again in 1993. A boom was happening inside Enron, not only outside it.

Overall, Enron *did* find a unique niche in the cyclical energy business to outdistance and even separate from its peers. But the first-mover advantage was also becoming contra-capitalist, violating best-business practices, the morality of the market, and the political constraints of the free market itself.

Competitive Pipelining

Enron's 1986 annual report justifiably stated that the company's interstates "led the industry in the creation of innovative ways to serve widely different markets." A year later, the company reported: "Enron supports the move toward deregulation as evidenced by the fact that three of its affiliated interstate pipelines officially opened their systems to nondiscriminatory transportation during the year."

Deregulation in this sense was not FERC deregulation of rate and terms of service for interstate transmission. It referred to competition within the framework of mandated open access, whereby (unregulated) spot gas sent a price signal from the wellhead all the way to the city gate (the gas utility) or the end user (electric generator). California, served by Enron's Transwestern, achieved real-time scarcity pricing when a cold spell in early 1987 increased prices overnight by 15 percent. "We didn't require one regulator from Washington or any other state to allocate anything," one participant marveled.

Enron's intrastate system (Houston Pipe Line, later joined by Louisiana Resources Company); interstate systems (Transwestern Pipeline, Florida Gas Transmission, Northern Natural Pipeline); and four joint-venture lines (Northern Border, Trailblazer Pipeline, Texoma Pipeline, Oasis Pipeline) increased their market share in trying times. In 1985, Enron's 37,000-mile network delivered 13 percent of the US total. Five years later, the 38,000-mile network had an 18 percent national share, where it would remain in the next years.

The interstates for many years led Enron in revenue and earnings, the work of such leaders as James E. (Jim) Rogers (1985–88), Clark C. Smith (1985–88), Oliver (Rick) Richard (1987–91), and Stan Horton (1985–2002). Each devised new means to loosen the regulatory shackles and allow entrepreneurship to generate good profits.[61]

Enron's interstates busied FERC with innovative proposals to liberalize their rates and terms of service. Early on, Enron forced FERC to confront the

---

61. Enron worked to lessen regulatory constraints rather than impose them, creating value for consumers. Had Enron lobbied FERC to block entry or rate and service liberalization by rivals, that would have been rent-seeking for bad profits instead of good.

long-standing public service obligation of interstates (including Enron's) to obtain and deliver supply now that federal policy voided pipeline sales in the open-access era. "Like a velvet hammer, executives of the 37,000-mile pipeline are prepared to break new legal ground in forcing FERC to decide this issue," *Natural Gas Week* reported in 1987.

Transwestern, a relatively simple rifle-shot pipeline to California, received a whole new management team when it was acquired in early 1985. It became Enron's "laboratory" in pushing market and regulatory change. Transwestern, as well as the company's other jurisdictional pipelines, blended market and regulatory activism by several means:

- Supporting and refining FERC's open-access transportation policy, while suggesting how pipeline gas could be competitive with spot gas to avoid wellhead take-or-pay liabilities.[62] "We were, consequently, leaders in the natural gas restructuring process," remembered Stan Horton. "We tried to be first in everything that we did."

- Pricing transportation services at market rather than cost-based regulatory maximums. Beginning in 1985, Enron's rate proposals contained such adjectives as *negotiated, flexible, seasonal, incentive, fair-value,* and *market-based*—all intended to better reflect shifting demand and changing cost.[63] Between legalized flexibility and market competition, the Natural Gas Act of 1938 was becoming anachronistic. "Despite the fact that interstate pipelines still are regulated and the FERC will set minimum and maximum rates for each of our unbundled services," Horton remarked in 1993, "we're finding that competition is determining what we can actually charge."

- Entering new markets to increase competition and pushing FERC to expedite certification for much-needed new natural gas capacity. Regarding the former, Enron-led Mojave Pipeline, first proposed in 1985, challenged a long-standing California monopoly divided between the state's two major gas utilities. Regarding the latter, Transwestern pushed FERC and set "a modern-day record" of 18 months from application to completion (September 1990–February 1992) to end natural gas shortages in the Golden State.[64]

A highlight of Enron's FERC-leading initiatives was a pioneering rate-case settlement by Transwestern (effective November 1996) that effectively

---

62. See Internet appendix 1.2, "Mandatory Open Access for Interstate Gas Pipelines," at www.politicalcapitalism.org/Book3/Chapter1/Appendix2.html.

63. For Enron's liberalization initiatives at FERC, see chapter 2, pp. 140–43; chapter 3, pp. 157–58; chapter 5, pp. 225–32; chapter 6, pp. 256–66; and chapter 7, pp. 308–9; and chapter 10, pp. 441–45.

64. See chapter 6, pp. 262–63. In 1986, Transwestern also became the first out-of-state supplier to sell gas to California's industrial and electricity users (chapter 3, 159–61).

deregulated the pipeline for a decade. The negotiated agreement with some 25 customers, prompted by an immediate revenue shortfall for Transwestern from a large expiring contract, shared risks and rewards, and left the pipeline with *contractual* responsibilities instead of *regulatory* ones, as had been the case. Rates were indexed to inflation, leaving Transwestern with the opportunity to take improved efficiencies to the bottom line for a decade (rather than every three years in the traditional rate case). With this and other entrepreneurial decisions, a nominally FERC-regulated pipeline put itself in position to be "a growth story for Enron."[65]

Transwestern's settlement "shows that tough situations can be handled through the self-regulation of long-term contracts," offering the upside of "eliminated regulatory costs, increasing business certainty, and increasing entrepreneurial opportunity," an internal Enron memorandum by this author noted.

––––––

Enron's pipelines developed new information technology and protocols to compete in the new open-access world. As the largest and most flexible operator, Enron found itself acting as a bank whereby its rivals could borrow (short) gas during tight supply periods for repayment later (profit was not allowed for gas buying and selling by regulated interstates). This led Ken Lay to confront other pipeline CEOs at a 1990 board meeting of the pipeline trade group, Interstate Natural Gas Association of America (INGAA). "Ken Lay's quite forceful language behind closed doors was arguably the beginning of the protocols *operational flow orders* and *operational balance agreements* that became the industry norm by 1992," remembered one participant.[66]

Enron's investment in information technology under MOA transformed a balkanized latticework of pipe into a "single networked system." It began with electronic bulletin boards in 1994 and culminated several years later with the FERC-directed Gas Industry Standards Board (GISB), which codified more than 100 best-practice standards for nominations, allocations, title transfers, and invoicing. All told, Enron led the industry in best practices by which independent marketers (non-ECT, ECT) competed fairly and cleanly.

––––––

Enron had a Teesside-worthy success with the acquisition, revitalization, and growth of the southern side of Argentina's natural gas–transmission system. In 1992, an Enron-led consortium purchased the 1.3 Bcf/d, 3,800-mile Transportadora de Gas del Sur (TGS) for $550 million. Importing its North American expertise, Enron turned an aging, 85-percent-utilized system into a fully utilized modern pipeline and expanded the line by 25 percent the next year. Performance

––––––––––

65. Also see chapter 10, pp. 434–36.

66. See chapter 6, pp. 259–61.

incentives were met to earn extra profit—what FERC could never finalize as incentive ratemaking at home.

Led by such notables as Mike Tucker and George Wasaff, this best-of-Enron venture contributed to what became recognized, at least for its too-brief time, as *the third Latin American miracle.*[67] True, politics was heavily involved with the government as seller and close regulator, and Enron received political-risk insurance from OPIC. But as a case study in the private-sector reform of a hitherto ailing, underachieving government asset, TGS in the 1993–99 era was very successful.

Commoditizing Natural Gas

From the beginning, Enron was the leading gas marketer in the United States. It was in the DNA of both Houston Natural Gas Corporation and InterNorth Inc., the precursors of Enron. Houston Pipe Line was an experienced gas seller in the very competitive, virtually unregulated Texas market; Northern Natural Gas Pipeline's salesmanship culture was necessitated by its "spaghetti lines" serving small Midwest locals.

Interstate gas marketing became a fourth industry segment (joining the traditional production, transmission, and distribution segments) under the mandatory federal rules of infrastructure socialism. At Enron, it began with the Transportation & Exchange division of Northern Natural, which grew into a nonregulated affiliate, Northern Gas Marketing. NGM became the guts of HNG/InterNorth Gas Marketing, renamed Enron Gas Marketing (EGM) in 1986, headed by a new hire from Transco, John Esslinger.[68] EGM became EGS in 1991 and ECT in 1994.

EGM became a notable profit center by 1989, supplementing its short-term sales with high-margin long-term contracts. Gas Bank, described in chapter 5, was the beginning of a portfolio approach offering to gas utilities, electric utilities, municipalities, or independent power generators a variety of products differing in price (variable, fixed, or both); term (multimonth, multiyear, or both); and service (firm, interruptible, or both). What had been chocolate and vanilla (firm or interruptible for the long term) was now 31 flavors.

The second takeoff began in 1990 when Jeff Skilling's Enron Finance Corporation developed new ways to lock up gas supply to satisfy a waiting long-term sales market.[69] The same year inaugurated natural gas futures trading, which gave the gas market a national pricing point from which basis differentials across the country could be tied.

---

67. See chapter 6, pp. 273–76.

68. See chapter 3, pp. 153, 180.

69. See chapter 8, pp. 366, 371–73.

With firm gas supply in hand (no easy task, as described in chapters 8 and 9), EGS ramped up gas marketing to electric generators: first the independents and then the utilities. Business strategist and historian Malcolm Salter recognized a "complete virtuous circle" of buying, selling, and, often, transporting the same gas. Ken Lay's Natural Gas Standard, stressing the economic and environmental benefits of methane relative to coal and oil, was brought to fruition by Jeff Skilling in what was, arguably, Enron's greatest contribution to the gas industry—and business generally.

Enlarging the market from physical to financial products, as well as standardizing complex contracts, thus reducing negotiations from months to weeks, was part of the EGM/EGS/ECT contribution. Calls, puts, options, forwards, hedges, swaps, hybrids, and other "exotic options" were pioneered by Enron for gas and adopted by the industry in the early-to-mid 1990s. Small wonder that Enron was tops of several hundred gas-marketing companies in terms of volume and overall reputation from the late 1980s forward.

―――

Enron made natural gas the "fuel of choice" for electrical generation—intellectually, operationally, and in public policy. Enron's chairman explained time and again (as did virtually all energy economists) that federal price controls on natural gas had resulted in physical shortages and, ironically, artificially high prices in the end. Deregulated prices would coordinate supply and demand, Dr. Lay knew, as well as improve confidence in natural gas for long-lived projects, and none more than for power generation.

Led by economist Bruce Stram, Enron challenged the pessimistic "hard landing" studies of private consultants predicting that then low gas prices would result in declining natural gas production, higher prices, even physical shortages. The first *Enron Outlook for Natural Gas* (1989) forecast year-2000 demand of 18.5 trillion cubic feet at a time when Groppe, Long & Littell (1987) and McKinsey (1988) predicted a much smaller market. (The actual figure of 19.2 Tcf made Enron a tad low but quite accurate.) Enron's 1991 *Outlook for Natural Gas* increased its estimate to 22 Tcf for 2005, which proved exactly on the mark.[70]

Enron's bottom-up forecast correctly captured the growth in gas demand for power generation and strong supply from drilling improvements despite prices that were lower than predicted. EOG proved Enron right regarding the latter, and EOG Resources would continue to lead the upstream gas market (and, post-Enron, eventually become the nation's leading onshore lower-48 oil producer).

―――

70. Enron's *1993 Outlook*, its third, overshot gas demand for 2005 and 2010 by 7 percent and 4 percent, respectively. The *1995 Enron Outlook* broadened its scope to international gas markets, and *1997 Enron Outlook* (its last) added electricity and renewable energy to its analysis.

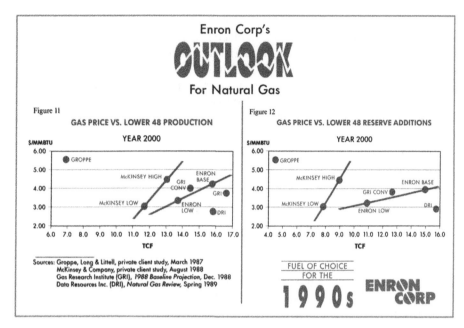

Figure I.6 *Enron Outlook for Natural Gas*, first published in 1989, and updated periodically, portrayed the resource base as prolific and open-ended. More than rebutting supply pessimism from other studies, the *Outlook* challenged electric utilities to build gas plants in place of new coal capacity.

As detailed in chapter 7, Ken Lay and Enron worked tirelessly to level the playing field for natural gas. This meant repealing the Fuel Use Act of 1978 and the incremental-pricing provision of the Natural Gas Policy Act of 1978, both of which artificially advantaged coal in the all-important electric-generation market. Getting utilities and their regulators to think as if they were subject to market forces (rather than maximizing the regulatory rate base) before building a new coal plant (rather than a gas plant) yielded a more efficient outcome, though still a government-influenced one.

———

Enron did more than commoditize natural gas to challenge, and beat, coal in head-to-head competition at home. Teesside's "privatization showcase" sparked England's "dash for gas" in place of government-protected coal-fired generation. British Gas (later BG), which hitherto called the shots in the region, had geographical competition for the first time—from US-based Enron, no less. In the UK and other European markets, ECT commoditized natural gas in the mid-to-late 1990s within what had been a monopolistic, balkanized market.

Contra-Capitalist Enron

Enron's divisions, strategies, and results can be evaluated in light of business insights long enumerated by classical-liberal thinkers and entrepreneurs. Anti-bourgeoise values, philosophic fraud, rent-seeking—these categories have been identified and warned against almost as if classical liberals had Enron and Ken Lay in mind.

Contra-capitalism violates the *means* and *method* of the market, which is: Perceive reality as the given. Transform inputs into more valuable outputs. Exchange goods and services for mutual advantage, without force or fraud and with civility. Repeat to build reputational value.

As a normative ideal, capitalist conformance focuses on *means* before financial results. The simple business verdict—*profits are good, losses are bad*—is secondary; on occasion and for a time, good business practices can result in losses, and bad practices can generate profits.

The future state of the market is unknown. Entrepreneurship is and will always be imperfect, necessitating trial and error in the search for market viability. Enron certainly suffered from entrepreneurial error—and yet it had many successes along the way. Ken Lay's enterprise had solid profit centers that inaugurated and institutionalized best practices. But bad practices and bad divisions drove the final outcome—and systemically so, inspiring the theoretical framework underlying this book.

———

Enron's contra-capitalism begins and ends with Ken Lay, whose prodigious business drive was chancy, hubristic, and ultimately fatal. Eschewing conventional best practices, Lay sought to outpace competitors via a *situational ethics* that compromised the prudential virtues. These deviations began before Enron was born by name, and by 1997, as Book 4 will further document, a uniquely contra-capitalist enterprise was present.

Enron's rebellion was not a form of creative destruction, or innovation within capitalism, as many employees believed. Rather, loosening capitalism's commercial precepts was a slippery slope to decay. But it was a slope, not a cliff. Enroners did not become imprudent, dishonest, prodigal, or arrogant overnight. Indeed, their downward course was concurrent with many solid achievements, impressing outsiders and blinding the company to the need for midcourse corrections to allow *sustainable* growth.

Contra-capitalist Enron can be described typologically or chronologically. The typological approach ties together the philosophic and psychological relationships among flagrant anticapitalist behavior (such as lobbying for special government privilege); violations of fundamental market rules (for example, misleading external parties about financial results); and departures from long-standing free-market precepts (for example, acting imprudently by overvaluing the present). This introduction has presented the typological approach.

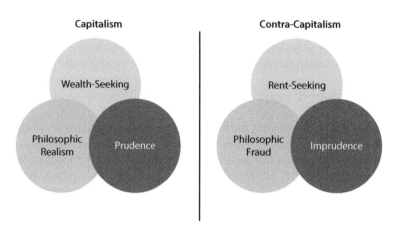

Figure I.7 Enron's practice of contra-capitalism involved not only government intervention but also habits of mind that classical-liberal thinkers long criticized and warned against.

The forthcoming chronological narrative demonstrates how Enron's contra-capitalist practices evolved interactively—with small, reversible deviations turning into large, hardly reversible ones (creating the slippery slope, also called path dependency).

Book 1 in this series documented classical liberals' analysis of personal and business success—and its opposite. Their wisdom is the framework by which this book judges Enron's destructive strategies: the imprudence and unreliability that began with Ken Lay's run-up of company debt on the basis of trumped-up earnings targets; the absence of prudence and even civility by Enron's smartest guys in the room; the scorn toward traditional, mature businesses within Enron; the abuse of finance and accounting norms; and other such behaviors.

Bourgeois Vice

This category of contra-capitalism is the most internal and personal: violations of the "capitalist spirit" that comprise "the bourgeois virtues." One interpreter of Adam Smith listed those virtues as "prudence, restraint, industry, frugality, sobriety, honesty, civility, and reliability."

A century after Smith, Samuel Smiles exalted respect, reverence, honesty, thrift, politeness, courtesy, generosity, forethought, and economy, and, most of all, a focus on the longer term via perseverance. The *anti*bourgeois vices, according to Smiles, included avarice, greed, miserliness, fraud, injustice, thoughtlessness, extravagance, selfishness, and improvidence.

Charles Koch has recently codified the important virtues driving business success. In order to "optimize resources," it is necessary to "adjust value for

risk," proceed by "experimental discovery" (trial-and-error), "challenge hypoth-
eses," and "admit mistakes" and "take responsibility." But Koch goes deeper by
also emphasizing how each employee must have "respect" and "empathy" for
others; act with "integrity"; have "passion" and "pride" in work—yet maintain
"humility" in the face of limitations and ignorance.

————

Enron stressed values in its corporate culture to go along with its aggressive
visions (which circa 1996 was *to become the world's leading energy company*). In its
final and highest form, "Our Values" were *respect, integrity, communication,* and
excellence (RICE, for short).

Three of the four values—respect, communication, and excellence—were
internal, telling employees, in effect, to get along, work well, and get results. But
Enron's other value—integrity—was both internal and external: "We will work
with customers and prospects openly, honestly and sincerely." Then the second
part: "When we say we will do something, we will do it; when we say we cannot or will not do something, then we won't do it."

But was the "something" being done ethically?

Contra-capitalism was not halted by any of Enron's values except integrity.
Moreover, missing from RICE (as interpreted by Ken Lay and Enron) were the
capitalistic virtues of humility, honesty, transparency, and respect for consumer-driven, taxpayer-neutral markets.

Enron's enunciated values were, at best, a safe harbor, a check-the-box exercise, a *mask*, rather than a firm check against employee and company misbehav-
ior. Values were not fixed but adopted pragmatically. The ends (avoiding failure,
declaring success) justified the means; the means were not held to be inviolate
regardless of ends.[71]

Philosophic Fraud

Even when it does not violate the law, philosophic fraud violates the market's
spirit and frustrates its efficient working. The ability of dispersed knowledge to
morph into a rational, undesigned whole is hampered; mutually beneficial
exchange thwarted; and reputational trust (a hallmark of commerce)
diminished.

Market signaling via prices and profits can be compromised to the point
that the guilty firm misleads itself. (Enron's clever finance and accounting executives certainly fooled the rank-and-file.) Worse, the dishonest company must
continue its dishonesty in order to cover up its past. Two disciples of Ayn Rand
described the mental process of the dishonest CEO: "He is shifting his primary

---

71. Earlier Enron values—Your Personal Best Makes Enron Best; Communicate: Facts are
Friendly; Better, Faster, Simpler; Excellence in Everything We Do—were also about internal
efficiency and less about bourgeois virtue, which was evidently thought to be out of date.

focus away from the facts relevant to the conduct of his business and toward the deception of others."

This is the context in which historians of Enron must characterize Rich Kinder's insistence on making the numbers, Jeff Skilling's mark-to-model accounting, Rebecca Mark's snowball, and Andy Fastow's special-purpose vehicles. In Enron's next and final phase, such philosophic fraud would spread and grow, leading to corporate collapse.

––––––

"Contracts, or promises obtained by fraud, violence, or under fear, entitle the injured party to full restitution," wrote natural-rights philosopher Hugo Grotius in 1631. "For perfect freedom from fraud or compulsion in all our dealings is a right which we derive from natural law and liberty." In short, Enron's illegalities cannot be pinned to free enterprise or its rules, traditions, or ethics.

As detailed in Book 1, opportunistic deceit has long been denounced by classical liberals, from Adam Smith to Samuel Smiles to Ayn Rand to Charles Koch. In Enron's case, a variety of contra-capitalism, *philosophic fraud*, was employed to reach Ken Lay's heady goals.[72] Most infamously, Enron gamed the US accounting code in order to portray the company as more profitable than it really was.[73]

When seeking permission to use mark-to-market accounting (not an inherently fallacious method), Enron assured the Securities & Exchange Commission that its calculations of revenue and profits would be based on "known spreads and balanced positions" rather than be "significantly dependent on subjective elements." In fact, as explained in chapter 8, upon receiving SEC permission in January 1992, Enron Gas Services retroactively applied the methodology to 1991 earnings, telling the SEC that the action was "not material."

Yet the switchover gained $25 million, or 10 percent of the unit's total earnings, allowing Lay, along with COO Rich Kinder, to gush about the unit's "exceptional" performance in the 1991 annual report. For Enron as a whole, that increment helped turn single-digit earnings growth into a 20 percent growth story, boosting ENE's year-end price.

––––––

Books and articles have portrayed Enron's financial practices as fraudulent and illegal. (Enron also pioneered financial practices that notably benefitted energy producers and energy consumers in the early 1990s.) But less than criminal were Enron's "exquisitely fine judgement calls" exploiting "the shadowy space of legal ambiguity," as Harvard Business School's Malcolm Salter noted.

––––––

72. This term was coined in Book 1, *Capitalism at Work*, pp. ix, 11, 64, and 321.

73. See chapter 8, pp. 378–83; chapter 9, pp. 413–14; and chapter 11, pp. 462, 465.

"Many of Enron's complex transactions, questionable accounting choices, vague disclosures, and corporate reorganizations" occurred in "the penumbra between the clear light of wrongdoing and the clear light of rightdoing," Salter found. "While an alarming portion of Enron's financial maneuvers had an aroma of deception, lacked respect for the spirit of the law, and thus reflected ethical delinquency, much of this behavior was not clearly unlawful."

Enron's problem was not complex financial deals per se—or the government's tight regulatory controls (which in fact lulled watchdogs into complacency). It was that Enron's "culture of gamesmanship" (aka philosophic fraud), violated classical-liberal entrepreneurship. Enron was contra-capitalistic, not only ethically challenged.

Political Capitalism (Rent-Seeking)

A sociopolitical category of political capitalism joins the moral (bourgeois vice) and the epistemological (philosophic fraud). As developed by the late socialist historian Gabriel Kolko, *political capitalism* refers to the acquisition of political means to achieve economic success. Although Kolko believed it was an inevitable aspect of capitalism, its practice has been denounced by capitalist thinkers as unfair and (socially) uneconomic, from at least the time of Adam Smith.

This book refers to businesses' pursuit of special government advantage as *rent-seeking*. Sociologically, the prevalent practice of firm or trade association rent-seeking is called *political capitalism*.[74] When the advantages are granted to a donor or a friend, political capitalism becomes crony capitalism.

Typologically, the most flagrant forms of contra-capitalism—rent-seeking achieved by political capitalism, even crony capitalism—have been denounced over the centuries by classical liberals. "I expect all the bad consequences from the chambers of Commerce and manufacturers establishing in different parts of this country, which your Grace seems to foresee," Adam Smith wrote in 1785. "The regulations of Commerce are commonly dictated by those who are most interested to deceive and impose upon the Public."

Some 150 years later, Ayn Rand wrote: "I glorify the real kind of productive, free-enterprise businessman in a way he has never been glorified before," but "make mincemeat out of the kind of businessman who calls himself a 'middle-of-the-roader' and talks about a 'mixed economy'—the kind that runs to government for assistance, subsidies, legislation and regulation."

In our day, classical-liberal entrepreneur Charles Koch has denounced "corporate welfare" as bad business. "The role of business is to respect and satisfy

---

74. Political capitalism overlaps with, but is not synonymous with, the mixed economy. The latter usually brings companies unearned benefits, or rents, but simultaneously imposes on them extra-market costs. The term *political capitalism* refers to those acts of government economic interventionism that have been specifically enacted at the behest of businesses for enhanced profitability (Bradley, *Capitalism at Work*, p. 3).

what customers value (even if it's other forms of merchandizing) rather than lobbying the government to mandate what can or cannot be offered," he explains. "Such activities are the ultimate form of disrespect for customers."

———

Enter Enron, whose profit centers time and again benefitted from special government favor, some inherited and much expressly sought in state capitals and in Washington, DC. More than just a strategy, rent-seeking became a core competency at this corporation—and, in the frantic end, a life-preserver out of reach.

Mandatory open access for energy trading; loan assistance for international projects; tax credits for domestic tight-sands production; solar and wind production tax preferences. No less than seven Enron profit centers were tied to Ken Lay's cause célèbre: (government) priced carbon dioxide emissions. Little wonder that Enron had an unmatched donor profile at the local, state, and federal levels—crony capitalism in action.

True, political interference with markets has long marked the American economy. True, identifiable business interests have self-interestedly shaped much of that intervention. But in size and scope, Enron benefitted from government subsidies and regulations as no other leading US company ever had.

Lessons for History

Enron is no more. But its legacy continues, its lessons live. Business strategy and public policy stand to learn the *true* lessons of Enron as opposed to the misleading ones emanating from superficial analyses and flawed worldviews.

Profit growth of 5 percent, adjusted for inflation, was quite commendable for most energy companies in Enron's era. But this was not enough for Ken Lay, whose 15 percent annual earnings figure went from an aspiration to an expectation to a promise and requirement. To realize that vision, Enron went contra-capitalist, violating the ethical, economic, and political canons of a free society.

How ironic, then, that Enron's fall inspired an outpouring of accusations and complaints against free markets, deregulation, privatization, and profit-seeking. The Marxists went further, charging international Enron with corporate imperialism.

Various strands of the capitalist tradition—from Adam Smith's "invisible hand" of self-interest to Milton Friedman's Chicago School of free-market economics to Ayn Rand's Objectivist philosophy of rational self-interest—were linked to Enron's ethical culture and business behavior. In mainstream (Progressive) analysis, Enron became the apotheosis of liberalization and libertarianism gone wrong. "The story about Enron reminds us of a serious fact of economic life—that markets fail," concluded one economics textbook.

Such analyses must be fundamentally reinterpreted—and revised—on several grounds.

First, the mainstream view overlooks the fact that myriad classical-liberal intellectuals *denounced* the business practices and ethical culture that came to define Ken Lay's company, from Adam Smith's self-deceit to Ayn Rand's warning for the guilty executive: "He is free to evade reality, he is free to unfocus his mind and stumble blindly down any road he pleases, but not free to avoid the abyss he refuses to see."

Second, it was the market and its collateral institutions—represented by a few short-sellers, financial analysts, and business journalists—that uncovered and publicized Enron's bad practices, well before federal regulators did. A general loss of investor confidence then overwhelmed Enron's pitiful attempts to stem its death spiral, just as market theory predicts.

"Enron Proves Capitalism Works," wrote Joe Bast, the leader of a free-market think tank, following the company's demise. And in a sense, he was right: Enron's fall proved that capitalism tends to weed out failures, as judged by consumers and investors. But Enron's rise and flourishing illustrated something different: Contra-capitalism can fool in the short run but does not work longer term in (mostly) free economies.

Third, Enron was born, lived, and thrived in the mixed economy where political entrepreneurship or so-called rent-seeking was normal practice. The large majority of Enron's activities were regulated, and most of Enron's profit centers were closely tied to special government preference.[75] Enron also manipulated the mixed economy's regulatory structures, from tax codes to accounting rules to energy trading. Some of these opportunities were sponsored and even created by Enron. But many were opportunities created by so-called public-interest interventions.[76]

Gaming complex rules was fair play in the Progressivist economy—and nobody took it to the extremes that Enron did. When Houston Natural Gas merged with InterNorth to become Enron, for example, the tax department was halved to 40 to eliminate redundancy. By 1996, the staff was past the premerger number, and by 2000 the count would be 253. More than a cost center, corporate tax was a *profit center*, where resources were dedicated to numbingly intricate deals. Although it was legal and maximized profit, this opportunity and practice were far outside a free market's simple tax regimen.

Enron-as-capitalism is the most enduring misconception of post-Enron thought. That verdict deserves a thorough reexamination, as this new draft of history documents.

---

75. Derivatives were not regulated, which was beneficial to ECT. But such an unregulated environment was not the cause of Enron's collapse.

76. The role of government intervention in inciting opportunistic, superfluous private-sector responses is joined by another irony: The Enron-like behavior of public-sector officials, a theme that will be explored in Book 4.

Part I

From HNG to Enron: 1984–1987

Introduction

1984 was hardly Orwellian. Ronald Reagan's America was turning toward free markets and regulatory restructuring after the failed statism of Jimmy Carter. Margaret Thatcher was bringing fresh perspectives and policy reversals to socialistic Britain. Marx was out, Keynes demoted, John Kenneth Galbraith passé. New thinking favored the economics of Ludwig von Mises and F. A. Hayek, the very intellectuals who had been swept aside in the 1930s by the fashion of government planning. Milton Friedman, too, was ascendant and educating a vast popular audience about the merits of capitalism and freedom.

In the realm of energy, economic liberalization was bringing entrepreneurial opportunities that would soon call forth a company named Enron. Partial deregulation from the Natural Gas Policy Act of 1978 set into motion changes that were championed and accelerated by the industry's rising star, Kenneth L. Lay. Aggressive, tireless, smart, and affable, plus a bona fide PhD economist, Lay was determined to be a change maker in his field.

His vehicle for change would be Enron, which he hammered together from his own Houston Natural Gas Corporation (founded in 1925) and InterNorth Incorporated (founded in 1930). The companies' 1985 merger was a strategic response to the regulatory and economic tumult in the natural gas market, both nationally and in Texas, where much of the nation's gas was sourced. Prices and profits were falling. Federal regulators, seeking consumer benefits from the upstream and midstream price reductions, changed the rules, some of which had been in place for 50 years. The harsh new environment resulted in a wave of mergers in an effort to find synergies and reduce costs. For Lay, the new world also demanded a turn away from conglomerates and a return to basics.

"We're going to stay with our knitting and do what we do best," read the cover of Ken Lay's first annual report at Houston Natural Gas (HNG). In Year 1 (1984), Lay extended that knitting from the relatively unregulated intrastate Texas gas market to the highly regulated interstate natural gas market. The new and expanded HNG (chapter 1) sold noncore assets to finance its expansion at the core.

After the InterNorth merger during the following year (chapter 2), the greatly enlarged company was positioned as the largest midstream-upstream operator in the industry. HNG's traditional Texas hub now connected to the Midwest and Canada in the north, Florida in the east, and California in the west. No other gas-transmission company had such reach—much less to three of the fastest-growing states in the nation.

Big things were expected from HNG/InterNorth, which in a postmerger euphoria touted itself as *America's Premier Energy Company*. But markets were not cooperating. The bold moves had come with higher debt amid weakening markets. The oil-price collapse of 1986 affected Enron's natural gas assets, which competed against fuel oil in both industrial and power plant markets. A good story line (America's "coast-to-coast, border-to-border" pipeline system) only went so far.

Things seemed settled by early 1987 (chapter 3). Major cost reductions, asset sales, and a price recovery—not to mention consolidating operations in the energy capital of Houston, Texas—helped the bottom line. "With these adjustments," CEO Ken Lay and COO Mick Seidl wrote shareholders, "we believe all costs associated with the merger and the sharp drop in energy prices are behind us." The major divisions had good leadership, and a new star, Forrest Hoglund, was brought in to revive the sizeable but sleepy exploration and production division. Everything was in place for Lay to begin realizing the promise of his new company—or so it seemed.

1

The New Houston Natural Gas

In 1984, Kenneth L. Lay left the presidency of Transco Energy Company to head Houston Natural Gas Corporation (HNG), a promotion with challenges. Sporting $2.8 billion in assets (about $5 billion in 2017 dollars), Houston-based, Texas-centric HNG, the predecessor of Enron, was cash rich and conservatively financed. But markets were going south, and HNG's revenue and profit were receding.[1] Worse, the storied company did not seem to have a plan to reverse the decline and return to glory. That is why HNG's board dismissed its old-school chairman, M. D. "Bill" Matthews, and brought in the youthful, affable, industry-experienced PhD economist.[2]

The transition away from the roaring-energy 1970s was continuing in 1984. Crude-oil prices were down 25 percent from peak-year 1981. OPEC dropped its benchmark price for the first time in history and began cutting member quotas. Meanwhile, the Crude Oil Windfall Profits Tax of 1980, collecting no revenue at current prices, was headed toward repeal.

Shale oil and coal-liquefaction projects—once thought to be the energy future at Transco, HNG, and elsewhere—were being shelved. Oil and gas in their natural state needed no help from higher-cost substitutes (*sub*marginal

---

1. Part of HNG's prior boom came from federal regulation. With a gas surplus in (unregulated) intrastate markets, HNG was "print[ing] money" by selling its low-priced gas (some under legacy contracts) into the gas-short (regulated) interstate market. This two-tier market equalized by the early 1980s.

2. The history of HNG and of Ken Lay's leaving Transco Energy are described in Bradley, *Edison to Enron: Energy Markets and Political Strategies* (Book 2 in this series), chapter 13.

supply). Although President Reagan had breathed new life into the Carter-era Synthetic Fuels Corporation with major grants in 1981, he now was ready to abolish the agency.

Recessions in the mid-1970s and in the early 1980s, in the face of rising natural gas prices, dampened boiler demand for gas. Periodic winter-time gas curtailments in the early-to-mid 1970s not only reduced current gas usage but also steered new power plants to coal. All told, US gas usage fell from 21 trillion cubic feet (Tcf) in 1970 to 17.3 Tcf in 1985 (17 percent).

First evident in the late 1970s, the natural gas surplus ("gas bubble")—an excess of wellhead deliverability over demand under long-term, must-take, fixed-price contracts—was not going away. The Federal Energy Regulatory Commission (FERC) was more interested in helping gas consumers than producers, although (now) overpriced wellhead contracts were of its doing. The US Department of Energy, meanwhile, was routinely granting exemptions from the Powerplant and Industrial Fuel Use Act of 1978, which prohibited the use of natural gas in new industrial and electricity facilities.[3]

The reversal of the commodity cycle—even for minerals once thought to be fixed, depleting, and increasingly scarce—was reality. Except for Julian Simon and some other technological optimists, few had predicted resource plenty amid the energy shortages of a decade before.[4]

Transitioning in an inhospitable environment was the backdrop for the company that, through acquisition and merger, would become Enron. Needed were new approaches to energy profit making, which a unique new chief executive officer would soon provide.

A New Company

When Ken Lay took over from Bill Matthews in June 1984, HNG was put on a faster track than anybody knew. A company accustomed to success, yet now insecure, had another shot at the top. But the diversification model that had worked under CEO Robert Herring in HNG's heyday was no longer viable. HNG needed to shed assets and acquire new ones to establish a well-defined, vibrant core.

HNG was well capitalized and profitable for the 42-year-old Lay, but financial indicators were negative and the outlook muddled. After a great run between 1969 and 1981, the stock price had faltered, although it experienced

---

3. The Carter-era Fuel Use Act benefitted coal at the expense of gas, an ironic consequence given the push for air quality regulations—and given the global-warming debate that was about to become central to energy policy.

4. See Bradley, *Capitalism at Work: Business, Government, and Energy* (Book 1 in this series), chapter 11.

a speculative rise when Oscar Wyatt and Coastal Corporation launched a hostile takeover bid in early 1984. After the bid was thwarted, however, HNG's share price fell sharply. Speculators were disappointed—and one took action. Prudential-Bache Securities filed suit against HNG and its board of directors for not acting in the best interests of shareholders. Lay, never comfortable with conflict, longed to get rid of his tormenters by giving them the stock price they wanted, either by remaking HNG itself and creating shareholder value or by succumbing to another company's takeover. Ken Lay acknowledged this by ending his first letter to the stockholders: "But most of all, we want to express our appreciation to our shareholders, to whom we commit every possible effort toward increasing their long-term value in the Company."

Still, this was hardly a story of distress. HNG announced a 10 percent dividend increase in 1984, its thirteenth consecutive year of payout growth. A low debt-to-capital ratio gave the company acquisition power. The legacy of Herring and caretaker Matthews was a company with a foundation. And natural gas was a business with untapped potential.

Despite replacing Matthews with an executive described by industry analysts as "exceptionally talented" and "highly respected," the changeover increased HNG's stock price less than 3 percent—to $53.75 per share. An asset makeover and improved operating results, not cosmetics, would be necessary to reach the speculative peak ($63.25 per share) experienced earlier that year from the Coastal offer.

———

With 1,400 employees and $1.1 billion in market value, HNG described itself as "a diversified energy company involved primarily in the transmission, processing, and sale of natural gas and in the exploration, development and production of oil and natural gas," with a goal to "expand its primary operations through internal development and acquisition." Its crown jewel was Houston Pipe Line Company (HPL), purchased in 1956. A 5,100-mile intrastate system, HPL sold more natural gas to industrial users than any other pipeline in the country. HPL also wholesaled gas to Texas Gulf Coast distribution companies, including its former subsidiary Entex.[5]

HPL's total sales and transportation accounted for between 4 and 5 percent of national consumption, rivaling the deliveries of the large interstate gas pipelines serving the Northeast, Midwest, and California. HPL's Bammel gas storage field, positioned just north of Houston, represented 40 percent of total natural gas storage capacity in a state that produced one-third and consumed one-seventh of the nation's natural gas. More than any other company, HPL was at the center of America's natural gas hub.

———

5. See Bradley, *Edison to Enron*, chapter 13.

But the good news stopped there. A recession and intense interfuel competition, not to mention company reluctance to discount gas prices, had eroded gas sales, such as a one-fourth drop to industrial customers between 1980 and 1984. As the new CEO would find out, things were also getting worse with gas demand for electric generation.

Thursday, June 7, was Ken Lay's first day at 1200 Travis Street in downtown Houston. His five-year employment contract began Friday, but he had cleared out of Transco and was eager to get started. Coming with Lay from Transco was his prized assistant, Nancy McNeil. But that was it; Lay had promised Jack Bowen not to raid his former company for executive talent.

Jim Walzel, newly promoted from president of HPL to president and chief operating officer of HNG, introduced Ken around the office. Walzel knew his new boss from trade association meetings, and everyone knew Ken Lay by reputation. An all-employee meeting came next. "I'm here to have fun," Lay began. "Every career decision I've made was where I could have the most fun." Lay used the forum to describe HNG's strong asset base, the status of the restructuring program, and the challenges and opportunities ahead. Lay's accent was down home; his tone reassuring. The crowd sensed that Ken was one of them, writ large. He introduced Nancy McNeil and his wife, Linda, who had come so far since being Ken's secretary at Florida Gas just four years earlier.

More than the audience knew, Linda was also a partner in the company. She had been fully supportive of Ken making the change from number two at Transco to number one at HNG, and she was very enthusiastic about it. "It's fun to be the king," she told a friend.[6] Lucrative, too, fortunately: The Lays' blended family of seven—three children from Linda's side and two from Ken's—meant lots of future bills to pay.

The new boss laid out his goals and management philosophy in the *HNG Annual Report for Employees*. The company was going from a conglomerate to a natural gas enterprise of pipelines and exploration and production. Lay expressed hope that 1984, the second straight year of declining results, would mark a turning point. "I hope in fiscal 1985 that we'll be back on that strong growth curve that the company experienced in the 1970s," Lay said. "Our financial goals for 1985 will be to operate a company which will realize one of the highest growth rates in earnings per share and one of the highest returns on equity of any company like ours in the industry." He added: "We want HNG to be one of the top companies in terms of profitability, growth in earnings and return on investment."

Then the new CEO turned to personal goals:

---

6. See also Internet appendix 1.1, "Linda Herrold Lay," at www.politicalcapitalism.org /Book3/Chapter1/Appendix1.html.

> I'm a strong believer in establishing personal goals, and I would like to encourage each of you to … make plans for yourself. Set some goals. Think hard about your job. How can you do it better? … I want each of you to be as productive, efficient, and professional as you possibly can, whatever your job may be.

In turn, Ken promised to provide transparency, a major theme of his at all his corporate stops.

> I want to keep employees informed about the company's goals and plans. I think people are more productive and enjoy their work more, if they feel like they know what is going on, what the corporation is trying to accomplish, and what its goals and problems are.

One of the first things Ken noticed at his new company was the closed doors. Bill Matthews had often kept his shut. People complained that Matthews was hard to find sometimes. The buzz was that he spent a lot of time reading in a place where all you could see were his two feet.

Communication was disjointed. "Don't tell the board this" was a refrain from no-bad-news Bill. Matthews recoiled at inconvenient information, which made some afraid to share data and others only too willing to accommodate his self-censorship. Lay, briefed on all this, set a new tone by asking the right questions and complimenting those who communicated the whole story. It was a fresh start, and Lay, clear-eyed, wanted to get to the underlying essence of things. There was no purpose in hiding anything or pretending.

Board chairman John Duncan had put everything on the table and expected no less from his new hire. No matter what was found, and no matter how bad it could be, the board expected him to discover, report, and address it.[7] The good news was that the problems at the conservatively managed, old-line company were digestible. This, indeed, was a harmonious, productive period for a fresh CEO whose huge ambitions would soon test the primordial virtue of prudence.

———

Job One was to revisit strategy—and execute. Lay was given free rein from the board to reverse course and halt the ongoing divestment of noncore assets that Matthews had committed to. (He would not reverse it.) But the new CEO had a more immediate problem. Gas sales by Houston Pipe Line were, in his words, "dropping like a rock." HPL's marketers were pricing above the competition on the pitch that their gas was "high quality." Everyone else's supply was considered to be "junk gas." HPL was backed by Bammel storage, after all, and no customer had ever been curtailed in company history.

---

7. This early-period rationality would erode over time as both Lay and Duncan came to deceive themselves about Enron's greatness and invincibility.

"About the third day there," Lay recalled, "I told a bunch of them, 'All the rest of that stuff you tell me is great, and all that plus the cheapest price will sell the gas.'" He added: "So, my real challenge the first few weeks over there is just going around meeting with all the customers, trying to get them to buy our product again."

Lay was no fan of discounted short-term *spot* gas sales. But that was the reality until the gas surplus went away, predicted by Lay to be in the "not too distant future." Given the surplus, coming changes in federal regulation would make sure that cheap commodity gas got to markets on the other side of the interstate pipelines.[8]

Lay, indeed, had committed Transco to become the first pipeline member of the pioneer gas broker, U.S. Natural Gas Clearinghouse (NGC), and in short order he committed HNG to be its fifth member with the same 10 percent ownership interest.[9] In September 1984, the first transaction of the company later known as Dynegy was executed when HPL gas was delivered to Transco for redelivery to four Northeast gas utilities. Ken Lay's footprints were all over that deal, although it was more symbolic than a moneymaker. Because they were merely on loan from members, NGC's pipeline executives naturally wanted to make the same deals for their home companies rather than making a (socialized) $0.10/MMBtu fee for NGC. Few transactions followed.

Lay felt, perhaps more strongly than was prudent, that he needed to address the stock price, which had not recovered from its speculative high after Coastal's takeover attempt was repulsed. The sale of Liquid Carbonic was close to completion, and discussions were under way to offload the marine and coal assets. Looking toward a major acquisition, Lay asked the finance department for cash-flow projections and debt-repayment schedules. Ken had taken few accounting and finance courses in school, but he had learned what he needed to know running Continental Resources as CEO and Transco as COO.

The man on the spot was Michael Pieri, the chief financial officer whom Matthews had picked as his replacement after being promoted from that position by Herring some years before. Lay got numbers—and then new numbers and more new numbers. There had been a lot of turnover in the department, and the manually calculated figures were not reconciling. Ken was not prone to firing people, but Pieri had to go.

---

8. This FERC-directed change in public-utility regulation for interstate pipelines, which created the new world of natural gas transportation and marketing that drove Enron, is described in Internet appendix 1.2, "Mandatory Open Access for Interstate Gas Pipelines," at www.politicalcapitalism.org/Book3/Chapter1/Appendix2.html.

9. For Lay's spadework with NGC while president of Transco, see Bradley, *Edison to Enron*, pp. 346–47.

Others had been around for a long time and were coasting; early-retirement packages were served up to them. The job-for-life culture that had developed at HNG had to change, now that markets were no longer forgiving.[10] Clifford Campbell, Richard Nevill, and H. J. Hass were old hands who left within months of Lay's hiring. James Harrison and John Heap stayed longer but would leave by mid-1985.

In some cases, early retirement was best for both sides. But in other cases, incumbents were being replaced by fresher, better talent, and feelings were hurt. "I didn't have the academic qualifications," said Heap, a 30-year veteran of Houston Pipe Line. "Academic criteria were used as the basis for retention and/or promotion," another former officer complained, adding: "Experience didn't count." Lay did what he could to make sure the severance packages were quite reasonable, if not generous.[11] A culture was born that would morph into the *smartest guys in the room*.

Back to Gas

Two months into Lay's tenure, the books were closed on HNG's fiscal year ending July 31. "We're going to stay with our knitting and do what we do best," announced the front cover of HNG's [FY] *1984 Annual Report.*

That was right out of *In Search of Excellence* (1982), the business bestseller by Tom Peters and Robert Waterman Jr. Principle six (of eight) in this McKinsey & Company study of America's best companies was "remaining with the business the company knows best." Conglomeration was out; back-to-basics in. "Case after case demonstrates the difficulty of absorbing the unusual," the book explained. "Virtually all the growth in the excellent companies has been internally generated and home-grown." When the successful companies did acquire noncore assets, the authors found, it was done incrementally and with a clear exit strategy if needed.

Robert Herring had bought Liquid Carbonic (in 1969), Zeigler Coal (1974), and Pott Industries (1977) at just the right time. HNG's diversification strategy looked brilliant. But Joe Foy, HNG's top gas man, had left the company in 1978 in disagreement with Herring's integrated coal-marine strategy (he remained a board director). And sure enough, Foy's concerns were proved right. The

---

10. Jim Walzel remembered: "You could call it a good-old-boy network. The company basically never fired anybody. I am not saying that was the right policy, but that was the policy. Even when people would turn out to be semi-incompetent, they would be put in positions where you could live with that. It was very benevolent—probably more so than it should have been, looking back on it."

11. See also Internet appendix 1.3, "Ken Lay's New Team," at www.politicalcapitalism. org/Book3/Chapter1/Appendix3.html.

Figure 1.1 Ken Lay's first annual report as CEO of Houston Natural Gas announced a return to the company's core. The strategy, adopted from *In Search of Excellence*, was about incremental improvement, not revolutionary change.

synergies proved scarce, with bundled services not competing well against separate, independent offerings.

By 1983, HNG's still-strong gas side was propping up most of the other businesses. Liquid Carbonic was holding up, but marine and coal were just breaking even. Investors did not know how to value HNG's different businesses, and HNG did not know how to centralize its management. Ken Lay had seen this before when he was at Continental Group, the unwieldy conglomerate that acquired Florida Gas Company.[12]

But HNG's bugle call for natural gas was more than just back-to-the-basics. It reflected Lay's vision that methane was ideally situated for the next energy era. Natural gas had had a troubled decade, but the problem was caused by federal regulations that violated the economic law of supply and demand. There was a surplus of regulation, not a shortage of gas, as Lay liked to say. Lay had flirted with coal at Florida Gas Company and again at Transco, but clean-air

---

12. See Bradley, *Edison to Enron*, pp. 306–12.

issues and labor union strife soured its prospects. The fuel of choice for new electricity-generating plants was—or should be—natural gas.

The gas surplus indicated a much more robust resource base than previously thought, Lay surmised. Demand would catch up to supply given the economic and environmental advantages of natural gas relative to coal and fuel oil—if the ghosts of gas curtailments past could be put to rest. Nuclear power had taken market share away from natural gas, but nuclear-plant construction ceased with the Three Mile Island accident in 1979 and Jane Fonda's coincident movie about a nuclear-plant accident, *The China Syndrome*.[13]

Natural gas demand had one burgeoning market, and HNG was in it. Cogeneration—burning gas to produce both electricity and steam—had Lay's attention at Transco, and his first annual report at HNG, released four months into the job, described six gas deals with cogen plants in Texas.

In mid-1984, HNG signed a "preliminary" 300 MMcf/d, 10-year contract with General Electric for the latter's future cogen projects in the state—with an option to buy an equity interest in the same. "Cogeneration is the single largest new gas market in the state and probably nationwide," Lay wrote. "Our relationship with General Electric should permit us to be a dominant gas supplier to this market."

But Lay wanted to be more than a gas supplier and passive owner; he wanted to *build* or *buy* cogeneration plants. That would soon come with a young rebel hired away from GE.

———

Jim Walzel, responsible for all of HNG's gas operations, was pleasantly surprised when Lay gave him an employment contract guaranteeing four years of salary in case a change in corporate control reduced his job responsibilities. HNG had never had employment contracts; nor had Transco. Mighty Exxon and other oil majors did not have them either. You just worked each day for your dollar until you retired or otherwise left the company. Ken Lay changed that. He also increased compensation for the board of directors.

Clearly, the message was: *I am better than my industry counterparts, and so are you as part of my team. We should be paid accordingly. Everything will be first class, because good people working in top conditions more than pay for themselves.* Aggressive compensation to attract superior employees and reward performance— something that Jack Bowen would not let him do at Transco—would be a defining part of Lay's business strategy from the beginning. It was flattering, of course, and highly enjoyable, but this incremental challenge to strict and even ascetic frugality would become part of an economically and spiritually damaging trend.

———

13. No new nuclear plants began construction in the United States after 1974, although completions in the 1980s continued to take demand away from gas-fired power plants.

Ken Lay, the golden boy of the gas industry, was on a honeymoon during his first months at HNG. Everything was polite—Lay's style. But a lot of work had to be done, and quickly, to reposition the storied company. There were basically no complaints about the new boss from the real doers, just renewed enthusiasm and hope post-Matthews. But Lay came with a bit of baggage, although none dared call it that. It concerned a sister.

Like her brother, Sharon Lay was smart, articulate, likeable, and a bundle of energy. She owned and operated an upscale travel agency that had built up a clientele from businesses that worked for Transco, including the law firm Andrews & Kurth. Transco itself did not designate a preferred travel agency—Jack Bowen was not interested in that. Still, clients of Transco happily sent their business her way; they knew that Ken would know and be pleased. Sharon would tell him, and Ken was big on things like that.

Now, Ken Lay had his own show, and before long the word was out that HNG's travel arrangements should go Sharon's way. Jim Walzel thought it "terrible" to mix the two businesses together, particularly knowing about Ken's financial interest in Sharon's business and after hearing that one employee's international airfare was $1,500 above his prior arrangement. But who could really complain, with frugality deemphasized anyway?[14]

New Talent

The midstream and downstream natural gas business was an industry for engineers and accountants, plus a few lawyers and lobbyists. Good managers were needed on top, but natural gas was not considered a hotbed of entrepreneurship. The business was changing, however. Market challenges and regulatory nuances required smart guys, at least for a company that wanted to help shape the future rather than just respond to it.

In September 1985, the founding editor of *Natural Gas Week* began one of his weekly columns: "WANTED: Lots of competitive executives not mired in regulated rut, for jobs as natural gas executives charged with leading the industry into the modern world." John Jennrich's piece was about a former natural gas regulator who had joined an executive search firm to find "competitive" executives.

Ken Lay could not have agreed more. HNG needed new talent to create the company that he had in mind. Lay had brought in some top talent in his previous stops, and now he had free rein to create *his* management team.

Lay had Jim Walzel to handle everything on the gas side and gained a right-hand man in John A. "Mick" Seidl for restructuring work. Seidl actually was not Lay's hire; Matthews and Walzel had recruited him. But Lay and Seidl were

---

14. This early example of Lay's nepotism and of feathering his family's nest, part of the principal/agent problem recognized by Adam Smith (see Bradley, *Capitalism at Work*, pp. 30–31), created a bad example that would only fester and spread. See chapter 14, pp. 582–86.

friends, intellectually akin, and neighbors in the Piney Point subdivision of Houston. They had first gotten to know each other at the Department of Interior during the Nixon administration when Lay was Deputy Undersecretary of Energy and Seidl was Deputy Assistant Secretary for Programs, Development, and Budgets. Then they went their separate ways, with Seidl first joining the faculty at Stanford Business School and then San Francisco–based Natomas Company, an oil and gas producer with interests in coal mining and geothermal, among other businesses. In 1981, promoted from vice president of corporate development to president, Natomas North America, Seidl relocated to Houston.

After Diamond Shamrock bought Natomas in mid-1983, Seidl was in the job market. Lay tried to hire him at Transco, but Mick did not see a fit. Ken then pointed his friend toward HNG, which needed help with its new restructuring program. Bill Matthews and Jim Walzel liked him. He was friendly and had nearly a decade of hands-on experience in energy. (HNG was not then in the habit of hiring even quasi-academics.) The two men sold Seidl on HNG's need to move away from being a conglomerate, and now, with Lay in place of Matthews, everything was that much better.[15]

Lay needed a senior vice president of corporate affairs immediately, but Seidl was committed to a long-planned family vacation abroad. Upon Seidl's return, Lay walked over to his neighbor's house with a stack of papers and said, "Here is everything I know about the company."

Seidl's job was to evaluate potential acquisitions. He had a happy hunting ground to search, with many energy assets for sale, given the 1980s' reversal of a long commodity price boom. Lay was in the market for natural gas pipelines to complement HPL in order to compete in what was envisioned as an increasingly integrated national transmission grid.

Seidl, who arrived at HNG in July 1984, one month after Lay, promptly hired PhD economist Bruce Stram, a colleague at Natomas, as director of corporate strategy.[16] Stram found his own lieutenant in Mark Frevert, who had worked at Natomas after being plucked from the doctoral economics program at Rice University.[17] Never before had a collection of economists graced the top

-----

15. See also Internet appendix 1.4, "John M. 'Mick' Seidl," at www.politicalcapitalism.org /Book3/Chapter1/Appendix4.html.

16. Enron's PhD parade indirectly involved Dr. Darius Gaskins, who was a classmate of Seidl at West Point and later chaired the Interstate Commerce Commission, where Stram worked. Gaskins was hired by Seidl at Natomas, and Stram followed Gaskins and became acquainted with Seidl.

17. Stram and Frevert would remain with Enron to the end, with Frevert becoming number three as vice chairman in the company's final months. Stram also hired Lou Pai, who would become COO of Enron Capital & Trade Resources and then CEO of Enron Energy Services, and Cliff Baxter, who would head Corporate Development.

management of an energy company. No longer was this industry just for engineers and lawyers—at least not in Ken Lay's company.

**NATURAL GAS PROCESSING
AND HYDROCARBON SALES**
HNG Petrochemicals, Inc.
Houston, Texas

**OIL AND GAS EXPLORATION
AND PRODUCTION**
HNG Oil Company
HNG Fossil Fuels Company
Midland, Texas

SYNTHETIC FUELS
HNG SynFuels Company
Houston, Texas

NATURAL GAS TRANSMISSION
Houston Pipe Line Company
Intratex Gas Company
Oasis Pipe Line Company
Valley Pipe Lines, Inc.
HT Gathering Company
Panhandle Gas Company
HNG Offshore Company
Industrial Natural Gas Company
Black Marlin Pipeline Company
Houston, Texas

Llano, Inc.
Hobbs, New Mexico

Figure 1.2 Ken Lay's first management team at Houston Natural Gas (bottom, left to right) was led by James Walzel (President and COO) and Mick Seidl (SVP, corporate development). The two major divisions were run by Melvin Sweatman (President, HNG Intrastate) and Ted Collins (President, HNG Oil Company).

Another early hire by Ken Lay was J. Michael Muckleroy, whom Selby Sullivan, the tough taskmaster described in *Edison to Enron*, had hired at Florida Gas Company.[18] As HNG's Director of Special Projects, Muckleroy was in charge of noncore asset divestment. An effective, affable negotiator with management experience in petroleum retailing, commodity trading, and gas liquids, Muckleroy had a wide skill set that would come into play in many ways for his new company.

Ken Lay was busy on another front. The HNG board of directors was not weak, sporting such leaders as John Duncan, Joe Foy, and Ed Smith. But in the

---

18. Bradley, *Edison to Enron*, pp. 300–309.

past 15 years, Lay had accumulated important business associations that could enhance this group. Three Lay appointees in 1984 expanded the board to 18. One was Robert Jaedicke, dean and professor of accounting of Stanford University's Graduate School of Business, a former colleague of Professor Mick Seidl. The second was Herbert "Pug" Winokur Jr., senior vice president and director of the post-bankruptcy Penn Central Corporation in Greenwich, Connecticut. The third was Charls Walker, brother of Lay's mentor Pinkney Walker and head of a Washington consulting and lobbying firm, Charls E. Walker Associates. Jaedicke and Walker held PhDs; Winokur, a friend of Lay's from the Pentagon days, was a hard-nosed businessman who had forged a national reputation for turning around a company, Buckeye Pipeline, and also for winding down post-bankruptcy Penn Central. All three provided diverse expertise and new geography to the board. By just about any measure, they had heft.

Ken Lay was attracting the brightest at the top, but it was the job of the human resources department to hire superior talent deeper in the company. Lay wanted more MBAs, only to be told by his hiring director: "Natural gas companies are not able to attract that type person." This gentleman was soon replaced.

Acquisitions

HNG had strong cash flow and a cash hoard when Ken Lay arrived. An aggressive stock-repurchase program was under way to improve earnings per share and lift the share price. Some 8.5 million of an authorized 10 million shares had been purchased by HNG for $400 million on the eve of what would be a major asset-acquisition program. HNG had that kind of liquidity.

HNG's debt-to-capital ratio of 26 percent was quite lean compared to that of most other natural gas pipeline companies (including Transco's 50 percent). A major acquisition adding debt was the best strategy to stay independent. Bill Matthews had passed on a merger with El Paso Natural Gas; Ken Lay saw the future in this type consolidation.

HPL had recently spent several hundred million dollars to interconnect with new pipelines and tap into new gas basins. The company with the best access to gas, Lay believed, would be able to offer the cheapest supply and increase market share. There was first-mover opportunity in all this. But the hub needed spokes to reach high-growth gas markets across the United States.[19]

Ken Lay's vision would become the nation's first coast-to-coast natural gas transmission system. Actually, this description had been used for Texas Eastern Corporation when it purchased Transwestern Pipeline back in 1967. But that was long forgotten compared to what was just ahead.

---

19. The hub-and-spoke concept was well known from the deregulated airline industry, and natural gas was considered to be analogous by Enron's corporate planners.

Transwestern Pipeline Company

Effective November 30, 1984, HNG bought Transwestern Pipeline Company from Texas Eastern Corporation for $390 million.[20] This pricey, gutsy acquisition just five months into Lay's tenure would pay off handsomely in the years ahead.

Transwestern was a medium-sized interstate, delivering natural gas to the Arizona-California border from West Texas and the Texas Panhandle. At this terminus, there was only one take-away pipeline, the one owned by gas buyer Southern California Gas Company (SoCalGas), a division of Pacific Lighting Corp., the nation's largest natural gas distributor.

SoCalGas was a billion-dollar-a-year client for Transwestern by virtue of its exclusive franchise to serve southern California. Customers of SoCalGas, such as Southern California Edison Company and San Diego Gas and Electric Company, did not connect to interstate gas suppliers at the California border; nor could they buy their own gas as a transportation customer of SoCalGas. They were captive to their one utility under state regulations prescribed by the California Public Utilities Commission (CPUC). Transwestern was captive, in turn, to SoCalGas, creating a monopsony situation at the border.

Sized at 350 MMcf/d upon completion in 1960, Transwestern had expanded three times to reach 750 MMcf/d at the time of HNG's purchase.[21] Still, it was less than half the size of El Paso Natural Gas, its rival to Southern California. No stranger to its buyer, Transwestern interconnected to HPL in both West Texas and the Texas Panhandle. And HNG Oil was the interstate's third-largest gas supplier.

Transwestern's SoCalGas agreement had a provision requiring the buyer to pay for no less than 91 percent of its contracted volume, whether or not it took the gas. A complement to the pipeline's take-or-pay contract with gas producers, this clause provided the financial surety that investors required to build an asset that had few or no alternative uses once in the ground.

Like all other interstates, Transwestern received a monthly demand charge just for standing ready to deliver the contractual volume, a fee that covered almost all of the pipeline's fixed costs (capital plant, salaries, etc.). Then, under its minimum-bill

20. Texas Eastern Transmission Corporation was formed with the purchase of the Big Inch pipeline following World War II. Texas Eastern diversified its Northeast gas-transmission business by purchasing Transwestern for $95 million. In 1989, Texas Eastern itself was purchased by Panhandle Eastern Corporation, and the renamed PanEnergy Corporation was bought by Duke Energy Corporation in 1997.

21. A second leg of Transwestern had been built in 1965 from the Texas Panhandle to Oklahoma. A 250 MMcf/d contract with Cities Service Company (later Williams Company) would be reduced and eventually terminated in 1989 because of cheaper supply delivered from the north, the Hugoton field in southwest Kansas, the largest gas formation in North America.

provision, Transwestern received a payment for at least 91 percent of 750 MMcf/d, which covered its remaining fixed cost and all variable costs for the volume taken (or even not taken). So long as the gas was physically deliverable, Transwestern was home free—and under a contract that had no expiration date.

Transwestern thus did not have a marketing department, just supply and engineering departments to make sure the gas arrived every day after its 1,300-mile journey. El Paso Natural Gas, the original supplier to SoCalGas, operated under an identical minimum-bill contract.[22] This is how the Golden State got the capital-intensive interstate pipelines built, backed by long-term supply contracts in the gas fields.

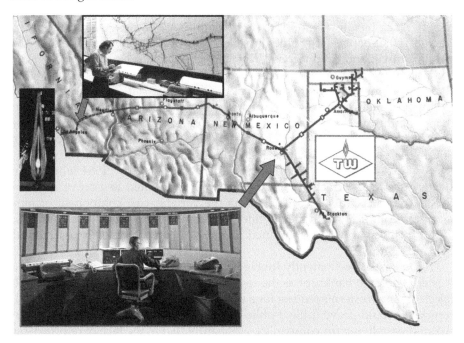

Figure 1.3 Transwestern Pipeline Company, built in 1959 to connect gas supplies in New Mexico and Texas to southern California, was acquired by HNG in 1984. The system's 4,434-mile mainline and 18 mainline compressor stations, moving 750 MMcf/d to California and 250 MMcf/d to Oklahoma, would prove very profitable for its new parent in the years ahead.

The open-ended Transwestern-SoCalGas contract had been approved by the Federal Power Commission (FPC) in 1959 when California needed all the gas

---

22. El Paso's initial entry into California is described in Bradley, *Edison to Enron*, pp. 240–42.

that Transwestern (and El Paso) could deliver. But not even that was enough, as evidenced by periodic gas shortages ("curtailments") in the state from 1974 through 1981. Transwestern's parent, Texas Eastern, had been so desperate for gas (given federal price controls discouraging wellhead supply) that it formed Transwestern Coal Gasification Company (TCGC) in 1971.[23] Texas Eastern also joined a consortium of pipelines interested in building the world's largest pipeline to bring gas from Prudhoe Bay to the lower-48 states (the Alaska Natural Gas Transportation System, or ANGTS). Both projects were abandoned and write-offs of several million dollars taken in the early 1980s when the gas-supply picture improved.

Amid a gas surplus, cheaper spot gas became available to compete against the interstate pipeline's more expensive dedicated ("system") supply. But contractual issues between the pipeline seller and utility buyer on one side, and the pipeline buyer and producer seller on the other, had to be addressed before a switchover to spot gas could occur.

In the falling price environment, gas buyers of interstate-pipeline-system gas, led by the utilities, were eager to shed their bundled commodity and transportation commitments. They wanted to buy cheaper spot gas and contract for unbundled transportation at the regulated rate. Further, FERC, which had replaced the FPC in 1977, pragmatically changed the rules to give them the ability to do so.

For Texas Eastern, the bloom came off the rose in May 1984 when Transwestern's sales contract with SoCalGas was invalidated as part of a generic FERC decision, Order No. 380, ending the variable-cost component of minimum-bill contracts for interstate lines, including that of El Paso to California. (The pipelines, however, continued to receive their aforementioned monthly demand charge.)

Texas Eastern vehemently lobbied against the ruling, warning that Transwestern could go bankrupt as the result of contract nullification. In July, FERC rejected Transwestern's request for a waiver, and subsequent court action by the company would prove futile. Public-utility regulation, once thought to be low risk and easy living for companies, was hardly that in the face of reformer-regulator opportunism.

No longer could Transwestern's gas sell itself. Fluctuating demand, previously the buyer's problem, was now the seller's problem. Texas Eastern feared the change and needed to retire the debt associated with its recent billion-dollar purchase of California-based Petrolane, a retailer of liquid

---

23. TCGC formed a joint venture to build a coal-to-gas plant with Pacific Coal Gasification Company, a subsidiary of Pacific Lighting Corporation (parent of SoCalGas). The Western Gasification Company received its certificate from the FPC in 1975, but regulatory uncertainty and changing economics precluded construction.

petroleum gas (propane and butane). Transwestern consequently was put up for sale.[24]

Transwestern was dwarfed by the parent's two larger pipelines anyway (Texas Eastern Transmission Corporation and Panhandle Eastern Pipe Line Company). But recognizing growth opportunities in one of America's largest gas markets and confident about HNG's managerial capabilities, Ken Lay was more than willing to match wits with the CPUC, FERC, El Paso, and SoCalGas.

———

HNG's winning bid of $390 million was $60 million (or nearly 20 percent) above Transwestern's book value, the original depreciated cost upon which a regulated return was allowed. This premium was partly derived from anticipated pipeline expansions, on which the FERC-authorized rate of return, less borrowing costs, promised pure profit. The rest of the bid premium came from anticipated margins associated with buying and selling gas connected to and transported on Transwestern.[25] This was not yet legal (gas costs were a dollar-for-dollar passthrough as part of a bundled price), but a major policy change was in the air. Deregulating the commodity would become, in fact, FERC policy in 1985, giving the company's marketing side first shot at the contiguous gas.

This was a major change. Traditionally, an interstate could not profit on the gas it bought and sold. This left no upside, only a potential downside should federal regulators find that its gas purchases were not "reasonable" or "prudent" (in regulatory terms). Pipelines rudely encountered this asymmetry in the 1980s with their take-or-pay liabilities.

By *unbundling* transportation from the gas commodity and deregulating the latter, however, *two profit centers would be potentially created where there had been one.* HNG imputed value to Transwestern because of this, whereas other bidders were focused on the loss of the minimum-bill contract and likely take-or-pay claims from voided producer contracts behind it. The two-for-one profit transformation was the difference in HNG's winning bid—and it would be

———

24. Oscar Wyatt's Coastal Corporation, which held 1.2 percent of Texas Eastern stock, filed suit to block the Petrolane purchase. After failing to get a court injunction, Coastal sold its holding at a modest profit.

25. For the bid, HNG based its gas-margin forecast for gas delivered by Transwestern on the estimated difference between gas costs and delivered prices at the California border. The delivered price was the estimated residual fuel oil price available to fuel-switchable power plants served in Los Angeles and San Diego. Although this pricing scenario did not play out, the imputation of value for Transwestern from the commodity side of the business would prove sound.

justified in practice, even as it created confidence (perhaps too much) in the ability of entrepreneurial genius to redeem management's excessive risk.

Florida Gas Transmission Company

In mid-1984, several years after Lay's departure from Continental Resources Company (CRC), Continental Group agreed to merge with Kiewit-Murdock Investment Corporation, an entity owned by Peter Kiewit Sons and Murdock Investments. Sir James Goldsmith had put Continental Group into play with a $2.1 billion offer (soon increased to $2.4 billion), and Kiewit-Murdock, a more likable suitor to CRC, surfaced at the 11th hour. Stockholders approved the $2.7 billion buyout, and a new company, KMI Continental Group, emerged on November 1.

Needing to pay down debt, the new company announced the sale of CRC, whose major asset was Florida Gas Transmission (FGT), the Texas-to-Florida pipeline that Jack Bowen had fathered a quarter century before. (Bowen had hired Lay at Florida Gas Company and again at Transco Energy, as described in *Edison to Enron*.[26]) The 725 MMcf/d pipeline was about the same size as it was in 1970, when the last expansion had been made prior to (regulatory-induced) gas-supply problems setting in.[27]

In addition to the interstate, CRC had onshore and offshore oil and gas production, a gas-processing facility, and a seven-story office building in Winter Park, Florida. CRC's senior management had relocated to Houston's Greenway Plaza, just a few miles from HNG, leaving the operating division's executives back in Winter Park.

HNG's acquisition team, already busy with Transwestern, set a floor value for FGT at $575 million, the net book value of the facilities and the rate base upon which FERC applied an allowed rate of return. A value was also assigned to the nonpipeline assets, primarily oil and gas production and leased acreage, most of which was planned for sale.

Effective December 31, 1984, just two months after acquiring Transwestern, HNG announced its purchase of Continental Resources Company and related affiliates for $800 million. The winning bid easily outdistanced a joint offer from American Natural Resources Company and InterNorth (the parents of, respectively, ANR Pipeline Company and Northern Natural Pipeline Company), as well as third-place Tenneco (the parent of Tennessee Gas Transmission Company). "We were completely blown out of the water," recalled InterNorth's Lou Potempa, whose "aggressive" bid for CRC turned out to be 25 percent too low.

As with Transwestern, HNG's bid for FGT reflected the prospect of unbundling sales from transportation, where two margins could be made instead of one. There was also a perceived synergy between HPL's system (Bammel storage in particular) and the Florida market.

---

26. Bradley, *Edison to Enron*, pp. 295–98, 310–12.

27. See Bradley, *Edison to Enron*, pp. 281–82, 285–87.

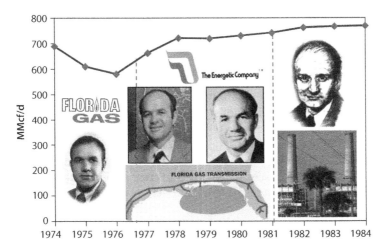

Figure 1.4 Florida Gas Transmission, completed in 1959, was part of Ken Lay's first corporate stop after leaving the Department of Interior in 1973. Succeeding Lay as head of FGT was William Morgan (far right), who would join HNG after the merger. Not expanded since 1970, FGT would triple in capacity with four expansions during Enron's solvent life.

The other premium was FGT's potential for low-cost expansions, which Continental Group had not pursued. The company, in fact, proposed to convert part of the natural gas line to petroleum products. Conceived during the gas-shortage era, the Transgulf Pipeline Project had just been approved by FERC. Also, the Fuel Use Act of 1978, inhibiting gas service to new industrial and power plant boilers, was still on the books, although exemptions could be won for economic or environmental reasons.

A technical analysis of Florida's market by HNG's Bruce Stram and Mark Frevert found that the electric utilities were overspending on new transmission lines to import power from southeast coal plants (coal-by-wire). Building new gas-fired plants was cheaper if the utilities could think that way. The economics indicated a bright future for natural gas so long as innovative contracting could assuage the concerns of utilities that remembered the shortage days.

The winning bid, which Ken Lay set after polling his team, reflected another value: a talent infusion to help Lay run the whole corporation, not just the pipeline. From the beginning, FGT had been a transportation-for-others pipeline, not only a bundled merchant. The open-access era, in which transportation was mandated by new FERC policy, was just ahead. Omnipresent interfuel competition was good training, and good people worked in the Winter Park paradise.

Three CRC veterans would reward Lay's high bid. Richard Kinder would soon become general counsel, replacing HNG veteran Richard Alsup. Ron Knorpp, who had almost been chosen over Lay to run CRC in 1979 by the departing CEO Selby Sullivan, was elected chief information officer of the parent. William ("Bill") Morgan became president of FGT—the pipeline he had been running for CRC. He took the same title with Transwestern, reporting to Mick Seidl, chairman of the new HNG Interstate Pipeline Company.[28]

FGT earned $40 million in 1984 for its previous owner, a nice rebound from prior years. The pipeline was running full at 725 MMcf/d, and margins were up because of contractual provisions with direct-sale customers and a FERC-approved rate case settlement with sales-for-resale customers. Oil prices, though slipping, were not low enough to cause power plants, such as those of Florida Power & Light Company, FGT's largest customer, to switch from gas to residual fuel oil. But to make the acquisition pay off given its new debt, HNG needed to keep the pipeline full—and find new ways to profit.

New Management

Ken Lay flew to Winter Park the day after New Year's with offers for 12 executives of Florida Gas Transmission to join HNG. Kinder and Morgan were in the bag, but middle management was needed. All would receive bigger jobs and salary increases and be officers of HNG Interstate. "I need you guys in Houston," Lay explained. "I bought another company, and Texas Eastern is still running it for me under a service agreement. I need to get out of that agreement. I need to put a team in place who knows the interstate marketplace." Indeed, only field personnel had come with the Transwestern purchase.

Stan Horton, accepting an offer to move to Houston as vice president of rates, was thrown into the fire with the California pipeline. "It was as challenging as you can imagine," he remembered. "Transwestern was going through tremendous regulatory restructuring, tremendous take-or-pay issues, and unfinished rate cases, so we were just trying to get our hands around some basic things."

Horton's first move was to hire Transwestern's rate expert back at Texas Eastern, Rob Kilmer. Already, Rich Kinder had hired Cheryl Foley from Texas Eastern as Transwestern's general counsel, and she was soon joined by the brand new senior vice president of HNG Interstate, James E. "Jim" Rogers. Rogers and Foley began a long business relationship that would extend from Enron to Public Service Company of Indiana, then PSI Resources, later Cinergy.

Rogers, who had earned his spurs at FERC after receiving his law degree from the University of Kentucky, had just the skill set that Lay was looking for. Rogers had been with the Washington office of Akin, Gump, Strauss, Hauer &

---

28. Bill Morgan and Ken Lay had been fraternity brothers at the University of Missouri (UM), and Morgan and Kinder had been in law school together there. All three dated and later married sorority roommates from UM. Lay had hired Morgan at Florida Gas Company in 1975; five years later, Morgan and Lay had hired Kinder at Continental Resources Company, the renamed Florida Gas Company.

Feld, providing counsel to the U.S. Natural Gas Clearinghouse, the start-up gas brokerage in Houston that was co-owned by his firm. It was there that Rogers got to know Transco's president—and now HNG's CEO.

Rogers knew FERC inside and out. He knew that the regulated interstates needed unprecedented flexibility under hitherto inflexible regulation pursuant to the just-and-reasonable standard of the Natural Gas Act of 1938. In April 1985, Rogers and HNG tested FERC for the first of many times with a proposal to replace the current policy of fixed-maximum cost-based rates for interruptible transportation with rates set within a "zone of reasonableness." The "experimental" rate would be negotiated, flexible. It would be cost-based, on average, with below-cost rates offsetting above-cost rates for other volumes. In the current surplus environment, indeed, *discounting* below fully allocated cost, the rate ceiling, was a fact of life, although it was generally a rarity under public-utility regulation.

Rogers moved to Houston as HNG Interstate's senior vice president for rates, regulatory affairs, budgets, and strategic planning, reporting to Bill Morgan. Soon, Rogers would have one of the biggest jobs in Ken Lay's company— heading two and then three major interstate pipelines at a time of great regulatory and market tumult.

There was entrepreneurial opportunity beyond the maelstrom that Horton found at Transwestern. The HNG-Interstate team, which started with the FGT transfers, would get up to speed and run both pipelines expertly. The synergy portion that factored into HNG's winning bids for Transwestern and FGT emerged. The adrenalin of the new team, incentivized and inspired by Lay, supported the 12-hour days and Saturday work. "We all realized that we were in on the beginning of something that had the potential to be pretty great," remembered Horton. "I'm not sure anyone envisioned what it could become, but we all knew that we were in an organization that thought differently about the industry than any other pipeline company in America at that point in time."

The philosophy permeating the HNG building was to embrace change for competitive advantage. "A change is sweeping through the gas industry with the force of a tidal wave that is going to turn it upside down," Rogers would explain to employees.

> There are two approaches to dealing with it: you can either ride the wave, mold the chaos into opportunity, or you can swim against it. It is clearly our mission to mold and shape the changes that are occurring in a way that we can benefit from [change] as a corporation and as individuals, both in terms of growth and development of opportunity.[29]

---

29. In 1989, Rogers (chapter 5, p. 229) would leave Enron to join a coal-heavy electric utility where he supported mandatory open access for power transmission and regulatory limits on carbon dioxide (CO_2) emissions. Rogers and Lay, working from the same contra-capitalist playbook, championed the same causes from different industries.

Tearing another page from the big boss's playbook, Rogers would add: "We should try some new things, and have some fun doing it."

Divestitures

Liquid Carbonic Company, which had been a solid acquisition for HNG for 15 years, was sold in August 1984 to CBI Industries of Chicago for $407 million, plus the assumption of liabilities. The sale necessitated a $7 million write-off, but it was a clean exit that retired debt. Although it culminated on Ken Lay's watch, the sale was really Bill Matthews's last hurrah as CEO of HNG. It was part of HNG's April 1984 (pre-Lay) restructuring plan, which was in response to the sharp drop in stock price that occurred after Coastal Corporation was forced to withdraw its tender offer, and the speculators went back to their dens.[30] But it was get-back-to-the-basics too.

Markets were much weaker for marine and coal assets than for industrial gases. More time and different strategies were required for their sale, as Mike Muckleroy found out when he took over HNG's divestiture effort.

In November, HNG merged its 159-vessel Gulf Fleet Marine Corporation with the fleets of Zapata Corporation and Halliburton Company to form the world's largest offshore marine service. HNG received $130 million in cash and 36 percent ownership in the new company, Zapata Gulf Marine Company. HNG's other marine investment, Federal Barge Company, was sold the next month to Eastern Gas & Fuel Associates for $40 million. Then in January 1985, Zeigler Coal Company was sold in a leveraged buyout to the subsidiary's senior management for $55 million.

After the sale of approximately 80 percent of CRC's onshore oil and gas properties to Apache Corporation for $82 million, HNG's divestment revenue topped $700 million. That was less than what HNG had estimated, but there was still good value left in Zapata Gulf Marine and other stray assets—undeveloped coal properties in five states, two coal transfer terminals, two shipyards, two crude oil recovery projects in West Texas, and a gold mine in Colorado. Mike Muckleroy sold all these by mid-1985.

In December 1985, Alamo Barge was sold for $18.5 million to Hollywood Marine. HNG board director Ed Smith came in second with an offer of $18.25 million, which would have given him the company he had sold to HNG less than five years before—at one-third the price. (It was this transaction that had made Smith HNG's largest stockholder and a member of the board's executive committee.) Depressed energy prices in 1986 made for a tough first year, but Alamo Barge would prove to be a good purchase for Hollywood Marine.

---

30. Coastal's takeover attempt and failings at HNG are described in Bradley, *Edison to Enron*, pp. 470–78.

Momentum—and Debt

It had been almost six months since Ken Lay left Transco to revamp HNG. Instead of 1,400 employees, there were now 3,100. Senior management and the board of directors had been revamped. HNG's collection of gas-processing plants was complemented by the $10 million purchase of a half interest in Petro Source Corporation, a marketer of liquefied petroleum products. HNG's oil and gas production was enhanced by the CRC properties that were not sold to Apache. But most of all, HNG was a focused midstream natural gas company with a Texas hub and a coast-to-coast gas-transmission system ("an intra- and interstate pipeline network") reaching Florida and California—14,300 miles of pipeline in all. It was these three states that had the highest anticipated growth rates in the nation for natural gas and just about everything else.

HNG was now "a fully integrated natural gas company, capable of producing natural gas from the ground, transporting it through its pipelines and distributing it to customers." Lay also described his company as "the undisputed leader in the natural gas industry."

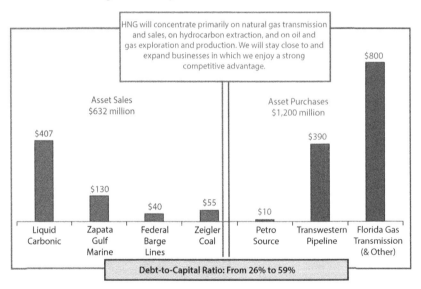

Figure 1.5 Houston Natural Gas returned to its core by divesting its industrial gas, coal, and marine assets and purchasing two interstate pipelines and one small intrastate. The makeover more than doubled the debt-to-capital ratio in Ken Lay's first eight months at the company with purchases outdistancing sales by almost two-to-one.

Ken Lay vacationed between Christmas and New Year's with his family. Much had been done in little time. It was heartwarming to open the business section of the *New York Times* on December 30 to read a boxed article, complete

with his photo, titled "The Maverick Who Transformed an Industry." It vindicated all the decades of hard work that he had put in and was a powerful anti-
dote for the financial setbacks endured by father Omer, as well as for Ken's own
personal challenges—and Linda's too.

"If any one person can be considered responsible for the recent transformation of the natural gas industry," the piece read, "it is Kenneth L. Lay, the hard-
charging 42-year-old former economics professor, who, until last June, was
president of Transco Energy Company." The business practices that Lay pioneered, the article explained, had overcome both regulation and industry rigidi-
ties to create a national spot market for gas. Prices could now balance supply
and demand, in and across regions.

"Now Mr. Lay is bringing his penchant for turning around bad situations to
bear on one company in particular: the Houston Natural Gas Corporation," the
piece continued. "In just six months as that company's head, he already has
taken what had been a poorly managed takeover target operating entirely
within Texas and turned it into an interstate powerhouse—the first in the industry to stretch from coast to coast." Lay's strategy was quoted by the *Times*:
"'We're going to have access to virtually all the Lower 48 gas producing areas,'"
allowing HNG to "'pick and choose'" the lowest-cost gas for customers.

The New York Times

THE MAVERICK WHO **TRANSFORMED AN INDUSTRY**

HOUSTON

If any one person can be
considered responsible for the recent
transformation of the natural gas
industry, it is Kenneth L. Lay, the
hard-charging 42-year-old former
economics professor, who, until
last June, was president of Transco
Energy Company. It was he, more
than any other industry executive,
who was responsible for devising
the first spot market for natural gas.

Kenneth L. Lay

By bringing free-market pricing
to an interstate industry that had
never before been subject to the rigors of competition, he helped
the interstate gas pipelines survive the crippling squeeze brought
on by partial deregulation at a time of recession.

"We tried to build incentives for producers to respond to
the marketplace, even though contracts and regulations did not,"
Mr. Lay said. "The spot market is growing by leaps and bounds,"
he noted with satisfaction. "There are virtually no barriers to
where you can sell gas today."

Now Mr. Lay is bringing his penchant for turning around bad
situations to bear on one company in particular: the Houston
Natural Gas Corporation. In just six months as that company's
head, he already has taken what has been a poorly managed take-

over target operating entirely within Texas and turned it into an
interstate powerhouse--the first in the industry to stretch from
coast to coast.

Mr. Lay has negotiated two giant acquisitions that will about
double, to 14,000 miles, the Houston Natural system, making it
tops in the industry in terms of pipelines mileage.

First, he spent $380 million to acquire the Florida Gas
Transmission Company, the only supplier to the Florida peninsula.
Then, just after Thanksgiving, even before the Transwestern deal
was formally completed, H.N.G. announced that it would spend
$800 million to acquire the Florida Gas Transmission Company,
the only supplier to the Florida peninsula.

"We're going to have access to virtually all the Lower 48 gas
producing areas," said Mr. Lay, noting that H.N.G. will now be
able to "pick and choose" the cheapest supplies for the various
parts of its new transcontinental market, instead of being tied to its
traditional Gulf Coast sources.

**HOUSTON
NATURAL
GAS**

Figure 1.6 Ken Lay's profile in the *New York Times* added to his reputation as an industry visionary. As a former economics professor (as mentioned in the article), *Dr.* Lay had
gravitas beyond the usual business CEO.

But these were *moral* victories. The market was not that impressed by all the commotion that doubled the size of Lay's company. HNG's stock price barely registered the Transwestern and FGT purchases. The share price was mired in the low $40s, about what it had been prior to the speculation surrounding the Coastal offer—and some 20 percent *below* the price on the day that Ken Lay joined the company.

The reasons were not hard to fathom. Lay had bid very aggressively for his new assets, and the takeover speculation was now out of HNG's stock. Standard & Poor's placed the new HNG on its CreditWatch list because the company "would be aggressively leveraged, carry a substantial short-term debt burden, face increased fixed charges and have its access to capital markets restricted."

But the CEO was undeterred. "It takes a little time," Lay allowed. "I'm convinced the company is fundamentally sounder today and has greater growth prospects than it has over the last six months." The eternal optimist would later joke about how "the Board gave me unlimited authority, and I exceeded it."

Acquisitions of $1.24 billion, minus sales of $714 million, had more than doubled the debt-to-capital ratio to 59 percent, the highest anyone could remember. The Robert Herring/Bill Matthews company was reshaped. Concerns over corporate independence became secondary as a confident Lay expected to either acquire or set the terms to be acquired.

Surely, this was a collection of assets with staying power. But the bet was on the come: HNG had to generate new, incremental, *unexpected* earnings to grow its way out of its debt problem and impress Wall Street.

Into 1985

Ken Lay may have been the talk of his industry, but there was no cakewalk ahead. Volumes and margins were squeezed at the core. Earnings in 1984 from HPL's vast Texas operations were off 14 percent from two years before. Yet in contrast to 1981, HPL had maintained its throughput, no small feat in a gas market (Texas) that had shrunk by nearly one-third. HPL's 15 percent market share, up from 11 percent, reflected the system's superior logistics (Bammel storage included), aggressive marketing, and reinvestment. Bill Matthews, Jim Walzel, and HNG's board had done the right thing by keeping the capital flowing to the core.

With its substantial production of oil, gas, and gas liquids, HNG needed—but could hardly expect—help from prices. In a far cry from the Herring era of tight supply and rising energy prices, Lay could only complain about "being in the sixth year of what many estimated was an 18-month to two-year natural gas bubble."[31]

---

31. Normally, free-market price adjustments eliminate surpluses, as they do shortages. But long-term, fixed-price contracts between producers and pipelines—encouraged and backed by government policy—created take-or-pay liabilities and other problems that forced the parties to laboriously negotiate a way out of the problem. FERC created the mismatch by voiding end-use

A stand-alone gas-marketing division—what Ken Lay's company would become famous for—was not yet a reality. For the time being, HNG's interstate lines needed to sell the gas they had under contract with producers—and substitute spot gas and transportation service only as needed to retain price-sensitive load. Marginal income was better than none at all.

Lay the pragmatist, not only the visionary, was of two minds about the changing world of natural gas. "About the time people get all the flexibility and transportation they want," he chided, "they'll find they don't want all of that." On the intrastate side, however, HPL had a marketing arm—a "shadow pipe-line" as the Texas Railroad Commission (TRC) put it—that was changing the way sales were being made to end users. With prices falling, a third or more of the gas consumed in Texas had shifted from multimonth *term* gas to month-to-month *30-day* spot gas. Producers were hurting as much as end users were benefitting, and the producer-friendly TRC wanted to know more about it.

Looking ahead, Lay set two goals for HNG: a return on investment in the high teens or low twenties and a reduction of the debt ratio to 50 percent within 18 months. With the restructuring almost complete, his two priorities were "operating expense containment" and "innovative entrepreneurship." In a vote of confidence, and to support the lethargic stock price, Lay and the board announced a 6 percent increase in the stock dividend for 1985. This increase would not be repeated for some years.

————

HNG had one new business that promised good earnings right off the bat. In late 1984, HNG purchased a 34 percent interest in the Bayou Cogeneration Plant, a $100 million joint venture with GE and Big Three Industries. The project was originated by GE's John Wing and Robert Kelly, both of whom had been hired into the energy business by Ken Lay before he left Continental Resources Company in 1981. By March 1985, Bayou Cogeneration was turning natural gas, mostly purchased from Houston Pipe Line, into 300 megawatts of electricity for Houston Lighting & Power and 1.4 million pounds per hour of steam for Big Three Industries and other industrials.

Best of all, the plant was churning out profits. Not only that, but Wing and Kelly were back with Ken Lay, tasked with creating an independent power business as the downstream leg of HNG's integrated natural gas strategy.

Cogeneration used recent advances in technology to produce a given quantity of electricity and steam (hence, *cogeneration*), while using a third to a fourth less natural gas or oil. The process produced steam at a substantial savings

————

sales contracts but not wellhead purchase contracts, until forced to do so by a court's review of FERC Order No. 436. It then issued FERC Order No. 500, which allowed pipelines to pass along part of the cost of buying out their take-or-pay contracts with producers.

compared to what industrials would pay to produce it themselves—the opening gambit to build such plants.

What made the business viable for newcomers like HNG was a federal law called PURPA (the Public Utility Regulatory Policies Act of 1978), which required utilities to purchase cogenerated power at the utility's *avoided cost* as determined in state regulatory hearings.[32] That, in turn, allowed the upstart nonutility generators to capture at least some of the power that electric utilities hitherto self-generated or bought from another utility or municipality. A new business was created within the bowels of the highly regulated electricity industry, and Ken Lay loved new business opportunity.

———

HNG paid more than top dollar for its interstates, a reason why the stock market did not reward the company. Expansions of both Transwestern and Florida Gas were required to enliven the stock price. The good news was that each system served one of the fastest-growing markets in the country.

In early 1985, Lay and Seidl spearheaded Mojave Pipeline Company with William Wise of El Paso and Lee Harrington of Pacific Lighting Corporation (Pac Lighting, the parent of SoCalGas) to reach the largest untapped gas market in North America: central California.

Jointly owned and operated by the three firms, Mojave would transport natural gas from the termini of Transwestern and El Paso to the heavy-oil fields of Kern County. There, Mojave's gas would produce steam to lift heavy crude to the surface, an enhanced oil recovery (EOR) process. Estimates said that in five years (by 1990), 750 MMcf/d of new gas demand would fuel EOR-related cogeneration plants (themselves aided by PURPA incentives). This was a pipeline full of gas—a *new* pipeline full.

But in California, EOR was being held back because Berry Petroleum, Chevron USA, Mobil Oil, Shell California Production, Texaco, and other operators of Kern County could not secure the long-term, firm (noninterruptible) gas contracts from California utilities. The operators needed contractual assurance that affordable gas would be available on a day-in, day-out basis in order to make new steam-flood investments.

Natural gas was cheaper and less burdensome to burn than oil, and the cost of switching back and forth between the two was prohibitive. But EOR service had a low priority classification under the CPUC-sanctioned service schedules of the state's gas utilities, which put residential and commercial gas customers at the head of the line. Gas for electricity generation was also put ahead of gas

———

32. For discussion of PURPA's provisions and politics, see Internet appendix 1.5, "Public Utility Regulatory Policies Act of 1978 (PURPA)," at www.politicalcapitalism.org/Book3 /Chapter1/Appendix5.html.

for steam flooding. Under the status quo, therefore, EOR operations would get curtailed in any gas-short situation.

But by starting the Mojave project in Arizona and ending in Kern County, California, Mojave would be an interstate pipeline under FERC's jurisdiction, under which a contract was a contract between buyer and seller and beyond the reach of intrastate priority schedules. The CPUC would be bypassed despite the fact that gas service was being provided in-state. Moreover, as an EOR-dedicated line, the oil producers would have firm contracts that, if violated, could be litigated in federal court.

But Pac Lighting and Pacific Gas & Electric, with franchises to serve Southern and Northern California, respectively, wanted the EOR business for themselves. The former joined the out-of-state crowd to get the gas needed to serve the incremental market. PG&E, serving most of the existing EOR gas load, did not join the consortium but chose to fight it.

Pac Lighting saw Mojave as a way to compete with PG&E for a new market, but Harrington and other company executives underestimated the ferocity of the CPUC, which regulated practically everything a utility did. Under pressure, Pac Lighting soon dropped out of Mojave. Thereafter, Pac Lighting, PG&E, and the CPUC presented a united front against the interlopers, arguing that the status quo allowed the utilities' fixed costs to be spread over more sales to reduce gas rates for all its customers.

The efficiency argument of the utilities against Mojave was really a wealth-transfer argument that assumed that gas capacity to California was sufficient to prevent curtailments. But old- versus new-customer welfare aside, capacity was *short*; that was why the EOR operators were adamant about securing their own capacity and the gas to fill it. It would turn out to be a multiyear fight between regulatory jurisdictions and between rival projects to serve the same market, but HNG had forced the issue.[33] Ken Lay was stirring the California pot with his investment in Mojave.

Mojave's president was Ross Workman, an attorney Ken Lay had hired at three places: Florida Gas Company, Transco, and now HNG. Workman's job was to obtain all regulatory approvals and have EOR producers enter into long-term contracts to permit project financing. On April 15, Mojave applied to FERC for certification to build a $300 million, 388-mile line delivering 400 MMcf/d.

---

33. Mojave's formal application with FERC, submitted April 15, 1985, would be joined a month later by a rival EOR certification request from Kern River, a joint project of Tenneco Inc. and Williams Cos. Hearings would begin in 1987, and final certification was granted in 1989 for 400 MMcf/d Mojave, and in 1990 for 700 MMcf/d Kern River. Mojave and Kern would enter service in early 1992, with the final leg in California being a combined 1.1 Bcf/d project.

The gas would come from the southwest on Transwestern and El Paso, either filling up their existing capacity or anchoring an expansion. Transwestern had not been expanded since 1969.

———

On the Florida side, FGT still had plans to convert part of its capacity from natural gas to petroleum products. HNG set a deadline of year-end 1986 to sign enough contracts to build the $400 million, 350,000 bbl/d Transgulf Pipeline.

To stimulate negotiations, FGT placed a $12 million pipe order to build the first 78 miles of the line. It was advertised as the first of several major contracts to build Transgulf, but the order was also good for expanding the line for natural gas. Indeed, HNG was actively pursuing an alternative that would overtake Transgulf: commitments from Florida's electric utilities to expand their gas-fired generation capacity. These contracts would require the first FGT expansion in 15 years. This would be very good news, providing double-digit returns on a rate base that otherwise would see its earnings fall from depreciation under federal cost-of-service regulation.[34]

Intrastate, capital flowed to HPL to gain access to new gas supplies. Matthews and Walzel had purchased Black Marlin Pipeline Company for $17 million from Union Carbide Corporation, giving HNG access to gas supplies off southeast Texas in federal waters.[35] In partnership, HNG purchased an oil line that it would to convert to gas in order to access price-competitive Oklahoma supply. This 650 MMcf/d Texoma Pipeline would enter service in 1985.

In the same year, HPL completed a $100 million, 193-mile link between Oasis Pipeline in West Texas and gas reserves in South Texas, including offshore reserves. The 550 MMcf/d project would provide gas for Transwestern to move to California, or HPL to move to Houston and on to Florida. This hub-and-spoke synergy was central to Ken Lay's business model.

———

By first-quarter 1985, HNG had assembled what Ken Lay called "one of the most innovative and experienced teams in the natural gas industry." Nine new faces were blended with five HNG veterans. The holdovers were:

• Jim Walzel, president and COO of HNG

• Richard Connerly, vice chairman, Marine and Coal

• Richard Alsup, senior vice president of HNG and general counsel of HPL

———

34. See chapter 3, pp. 161–64, for Mark Frevert and Enron's efforts to make natural gas the fuel of choice in electrical generation.

35. Given FERC jurisdiction, the 54-mile Black Marlin became part of HNG Interstate, the division housing Transwestern and Florida Gas Transmission.

- Mel Sweatman, senior vice president of HNG and president of HPL
- Elbert Watson, senior vice president of HNG

They could not help but feel a bit estranged from an organization that was changing more by the day. But Ken Lay was a diplomat amid the change, the type of leader that HNG was used to—in contrast to scary Oscar Wyatt of Coastal.

Three new corporate senior vice presidents had come over from CRC—Richard Kinder, Ron Knorpp, and Bill Morgan. Also new was Keith Kern, who joined HNG in early 1985 as senior vice president and chief financial officer. Kern, taking the position previously held by the ousted Michael Pieri, had been in charge of Shell Oil Company's refining, chemical manufacturing, and marketing finances, including auditing.

Kern had big-league experience, but Houston Natural Gas was no integrated oil major. Ken Lay's company lived closer to the edge. Keith Kern would last less than three years in corporate before joining (and soon leaving) a subsidiary, Enron Oil & Gas Company.

––––––

Upon his arrival in January 1985, 38-year-old John Wing became the youngest officer of HNG as senior vice president and chief planning officer. Wing had received an engineering degree from West Point and then fought in Vietnam, where he received a Bronze Star. He went on to receive an MBA from Harvard University, graduating in the top 5 percent of his class in 1980 as a Baker Scholar. Another Baker Scholar, a year ahead of Wing (although the two did not know each other), was Jeff Skilling, who would soon become part of the Ken Lay and Enron story as well.

In 1980, Wing joined Continental Resources Company as director of corporate development, the very position for which Jack Bowen had hired Ken Lay seven years before. Wing recruited his West Point roommate and Vietnam compatriot, Robert Kelly, to join him in Winter Park. Kelly, who had received a PhD in economics from Harvard, was teaching at West Point when he left for the corporate world.

In 1982, about a year after Lay left for Transco, Wing migrated to General Electric, followed the next year by Kelly. At GE, Wing caught the eye of CEO Jack Welch and became head of GE's new power plant development group, Cogeneration Applications Department (CAD), which became a lightning rod both inside and outside the company. Superconfident, superaggressive Wing was telling the world how GE would become the nation's top independent power plant developer—sooner rather than later. He was not necessarily wrong, but his in-your-face message did not sit well with some of GE's biggest turbine and equipment customers—the investor-owned utilities (IOUs), which wanted to build the plants themselves. The head of Houston Lighting & Power even lobbied Welch to fire Wing. Other big GE clients, such as Southern Company and Florida Power & Light, were nonplussed as well.

For IOUs, building their own plants meant increased profitability. Given the way money was made under public-utility regulation, new rate base meant earnings growth instead of stagnation. But a provision in PURPA required the integrated utilities to negotiate to buy independently generated power. Such intervention was fiercely opposed by most IOUs, leading to lawsuits and years of delay before the 1978 law had its intended effect of politically forcing competition into power development.

Wing's department also ruffled feathers by placing equipment orders within GE whenever project negotiations got hot. That was part of Wing's first-mover strategy, but the old guard complained loudly when some of Wing's orders were not followed by a final purchase.

Still, Wing had a friend in a high place. Jack Welch made Wing the youngest general manager at GE and let his protégé shine before GE's board of directors, senior management, and New York securities analysts. Welch also did not mind Wing shaking things up inside the company. It was a great situation for a Young Turk.

John Wing was not looking to leave GE when Ken Lay called him about a senior management position with Houston Natural Gas. HNG wanted to make cogeneration projects a growth vehicle of the company—a complement to the pipelines that generated more cash than reinvestment opportunities. But there was something else more immediate: mergers and acquisitions. Lay needed a good financial mind and tough negotiator to make sure that HNG did well in the industry's buy-or-be-bought environment.

Wing agreed after negotiating a nice raise for himself and his right-hand man, Robert Kelly, whose new title in the deal was vice president of strategic planning. It was an exciting opportunity on multiple fronts, and the two were soon on their way to Houston from Schenectady, New York, the very headquarters that Thomas Edison had opened and Samuel Insull run nearly a century before, a story told in *Edison to Enron*.

Before leaving, Wing visited with Welch to tell him how much he appreciated his education at GE, one that was even more valuable than that received at Harvard Business School. Welch returned the compliment by retrieving his secret list of top managers, the ones he saw as the future of the company. Wing was on that list. But Wing was not there to renegotiate. In the meeting, Welch predicted that Wing would return. But Wing would stick with cogeneration development, unlike GE. Still, Wing would never forget the GE days—"the lifelong friendships, the advice, and how I was enabled by Jack [Welch]."

John Wing was soon working for HNG and living in a suite at the Four Seasons Hotel in downtown Houston. (Lay, extravagant in small expenditures as in large ones, put people at this luxury spot for interim housing.) Then, out of the blue, Allied Signal offered Wing a superior package to come run its new cogeneration unit. Wing visited Lay, explaining his regret, and offering to reimburse HNG for all moving expenses. But Ken Lay was not going to be outbid. Wing soon had a five-year contract with HNG with a raise and equity kicker for future projects. Regulation-enabled cogen was about the hottest area of the energy business, and Lay's philosophy was that superior talent was worth paying for.

Mercurial and demanding, John Wing would have an eventful, peculiar relationship in the next decade with Ken Lay and the company that would soon become Enron. Part of it was Wing, who would later confess: "I'm basically unemployable and a pain in the ass inside the corporate culture." Wing presented some of the same challenges to Lay as Selby Sullivan had in a different context a decade before, a story recounted in chapter 8 of *Edison to Enron*.[36] But part of the problem would be Enron's own volatility—and Ken Lay's balancing act between many things and people, which sometimes would come at the expense of his iconoclastic doer and closer.

———

HNG Gas Liquids (formerly HNG Petrochemicals), with interests in 19 processing plants, and newly acquired liquid marketer Petro Source were placed under the leadership of Mike Muckleroy, who was now all but done with asset sales. Muckleroy, a former Navy Seal and a protégé of Clint Murchison (see *Edison to Enron*), replaced HNG veteran H. J. Hass and would run the liquids group for the next decade.

Another new officer was E. Joseph Hillings, HNG's senior vice president of government relations. Hillings had run the Washington office of United Airlines, then headquartered in Miami. His work with the Florida delegation led Ken Lay to hire him as vice president of public affairs at CRC. After Lay left for Transco, Hillings left Winter Park to run the Washington office of Fluor Corporation, where Lay found him when HNG needed a chief for its Washington office. Joe Hillings would be involved in more issues than he could possibly imagine until his retirement just prior to Enron's collapse in 2001.

A Final Piece?

"HNG is actively shaping the natural gas market of the future," Ken Lay reported. But the company needed to do more to jolt the post-speculation stock price and end the Coastal hangover. Would it be a new spoke to the company's pipeline system or an entirely new business? Could it be a merger of equals by which new value was created? It would not be long before Wing and Kelly would find out.

In early 1985, Oscar Wyatt and Coastal Corporation began an unsolicited tender offer to purchase American Natural Resources Company (ANR), the Detroit-based parent of an interstate pipeline serving the Midwest and Great Lakes with gas from Texas, Oklahoma, and Louisiana. In response to Coastal's all-cash offer (terms that Wyatt believed would have made his earlier tender

———

36. Bradley, *Edison to Enron*, pp. 302–3.

offer for HNG successful), ANR CEO Arthur Seder asked Ken Lay to be a white
knight. It would be a merger of equals, but HNG shareholders could come out
on top with a full-value offer. ANR Interstate would geographically complement HNG's three major lines too.

Discussions and due diligence moved quickly until a deal killer suddenly
came to light: HNG was still operating under a standstill agreement with
Coastal from the prior year's settlement. Wyatt, a notorious litigant, would
have grounds to sue for "tortious interference." HNG took itself out of the running, and ANR went on to merge on friendly terms after gaining some concessions from Coastal. The stock price of Coastal and ANR both rose when the deal
was announced, and layoffs and disruptions were minimal. It would not be so
easy for the parties of the next megapipeline merger, the subject of chapter 2.

Still, other major gas systems could gain synergies from becoming part of
HPL's hub. In the Midwest, there was InterNorth's Northern Natural Gas Pipeline; in the Northeast, the largest market of all, there were three: Texas Eastern
Transmission (Texas Eastern Corporation), Tennessee Gas Transmission (Tenneco), and Transcontinental Gas Pipe Line (Transco Energy Company).

In February 1985, Lay initiated discussions with the company he knew best.
Transco's 10,000-mile system delivered 6 percent of the gas consumed in the
United States, compared to HNG's three-system 14,000 miles delivering around
10 percent. Transco had emerged as a white knight for HNG during the Coastal
tender offer of early 1984. Perhaps HNG/Transco would have been born at that
time had not Jim Mattox, Texas attorney general, intervened to send Coastal
away, as described in chapter 13 of *Edison to Enron*.[37]

Negotiations began between John Wing and Ken Lay of HNG and Jim Wise,
George Slocum, and Jack Bowen of Transco. HNG was interested in receiving
$65 per share, a one-third premium over its going stock price, but that was too
rich for Transco. The companies then talked about a straight stock swap, but a
rumor-driven increase in HNG's price cooled Transco's interest. There were
also egos involved that would complicate any division of management slots in
the combined company. Negotiations were called off in early April, and HNG's
stock retreated to the mid-40s.

———

Ken Lay and the HNG board were disappointed, but surely there would be
other opportunities. One company in the wings was InterNorth, the Omaha-
based parent of Northern Natural Gas Company. Sam Segnar, InterNorth's
CEO, had visited Ken Lay the previous fall. Their discussion about industry
matters, over coffee, turned out to be far longer than planned. The two had
similar business ideas and prognostications of the industry's future. They also
had like egos, one generation apart.

37. Bradley, *Edison to Enron*, pp. 474–75.

Neither Segnar nor Lay believed that the gas surplus was going away in the near term. Regulatory reform would make interstate pipelines open-access transporters, creating a national market for purchases and sales of the gas commodity. The transmission systems with the best access to gas basins and markets would come out on top. Federal regulation of interstate pipelines needed to be more light-handed. (Northern, in fact, was advocating repeal of FERC certification to expedite entry and exit in the new environment.[38]) The winners would be companies that had the largest, nimblest pipelines with the lowest unit costs.

The two also agreed that their companies were a good fit, although a merger was not brought up. Segnar had to be careful because of a standstill agreement executed between InterNorth and HNG during their Coastal-related white-knight discussions. Any deal had to be friendly, and this meeting was certainly that.

Lay was pleased to be in sync with his guest. InterNorth was a big customer, purchasing 1 Bcf/d of offshore Texas gas and using HPL and others to move the gas up to Northern Natural Gas Pipeline. Lay learned that InterNorth had once offered Matthews a cool billion dollars to purchase HPL.[39] The offer had been turned down, but the companies had negotiated cordially, just as they had during their white-knight discussions.

The hub-and-spoke romance of HNG for InterNorth was there. Segnar left with a very good feeling about Ken Lay and the new HNG. Segnar, more than Lay knew, was on a mission. InterNorth's 1984 annual report, projecting capital spending between $500 and $700 million for 1985, spoke of small- to medium-size acquisitions but added: "An exception would be an opportunity to acquire a large company with the ability to make a major contribution to earnings combined with better-than-average prospects for long-term growth." There were also other reasons that InterNorth needed to merge. This company would be heard from again—soon.

---

38. See Internet appendix 1.6, "InterNorth and Interstate Pipeline Deregulation," at www .politicalcapitalism.org/Book3/Chapter1/Appendix6.html.

39. InterNorth was not interested in buying the whole company, because HNG's nonenergy businesses (industrial gases, marine transportation) were incongruent with InterNorth's energy-focused diversification program.

2

HNG/InterNorth

Omaha-based InterNorth was eager to merge in the spring of 1985. Sam Segnar, the company's 57-year-old chairman, saw consolidation and streamlining as the future. His company was looking for new gas markets with higher growth rates than those in the Midwest. He and a group of his top executives were edging toward retirement. But most of all, InterNorth was in play on someone else's terms.

Irwin "Irv The Liquidator" Jacobs was accumulating InterNorth stock with the intent to gain control. In all likelihood, Jacobs would sell the company in five parts: natural gas transmission, natural gas distribution, exploration and production, gas liquids, and petrochemicals. A merger, though, might make InterNorth too big to swallow, and already mergers were hot among the 20 or so major interstate gas pipelines, the most recent being Coastal Corporation's $2.5 billion takeover of American Natural Resources Company (ANR). "In natural gas," a *Business Week* headline announced, "it's buy or be bought," and Segnar's company was a good candidate.

InterNorth's 1984 annual report had been titled *A Banner Year*. A record $297 million was earned on $7.5 billion in revenue. All divisions were profitable, thanks in part to a prior housecleaning that resulted in the sale of underperforming assets, discontinued operations, and write-offs.[1] Cash flow in 1984 of $652 million left the company's debt-to-capital ratio at a healthy 38 percent,

---

1. A $64 million charge against 1982 earnings wrote down the value of the company's Colorado coal properties, two liquid petroleum gas vessels, and the soon-to-be-cancelled Alaska Natural Gas Transportation System. "Challenges faced … in 1982 were as difficult as any faced in the 52-year history of our Corporation," InterNorth stated.

even after making the largest acquisition in company history the year before: the $768 million purchase of Belco Petroleum Corporation, an exploration and production company headquartered in New York City.

Northern Natural Gas Company, the interstate pipeline division, accounted for 40 percent of InterNorth's earnings in 1984. Its flagship Northern Natural Gas Pipeline (NNGP) was the nation's longest, after adding up all the mainline between southern Texas and upper Michigan—23,000 miles in nine states.[2]

NNGP enjoyed relatively low gas-acquisition costs. Its modest take-or-pay exposure in its producer contracts was quite the opposite of Transco Energy, where Ken Lay had struggled with the problem. In 1983, in fact, in his role as president of Transco, Lay asked Congress for contract abrogation, a "quick fix" that NNGP president Dan Dienstbier argued against in the same hearing.[3]

InterNorth, one of the strongest companies in its industry, would buy Houston Natural Gas in 1985 to form HNG/InterNorth. The next year, HNG/InterNorth would become Enron.

Northern Natural Gas Company

In 1931, Northern Natural Gas Company built the first megapipeline in the United States. It would have been sooner, but years were needed to overcome the political maneuvering of coal-mining companies, coal labor unions, and coal-hauling railroads—all seeking to preserve their manufactured (coal) gas business.[4]

NNGP's 1,150-mile system, twice as long as any other gas line then in service, had an initial capacity of 200 MMcf/d. Only later would thousand-mile lines become commonplace, beginning with Tennessee Gas Transmission in 1944 and continuing with, among others, El Paso Natural Gas Company (1947), Transcontinental Gas Pipe Line Company (1951), Pacific Northwest Pipe Line Corporation (1956), and Florida Gas Company (1959).

NNGP, as well as Northern's gas-distribution arm, Peoples Natural Gas Company (Peoples Gas), was born during the Great Depression and endured

---

2. Transcontinental Gas Pipe Line (Transco) was the longest straight-line system, stretching from South Texas to New York City, about 1,500 miles.

3. Said Dienstbier: "Precipitous action in the form of a quick fix [to inflexible producer contracts] would certainly impair the ability of the industry to deal with these problems and to meet the needs of consumers and the nation in the longer term." Lay, citing "the inherent difficulty of contract renegotiations" with the company's 1,050 contracts and 1,400 producers, argued for "a legislative mandatory 'market out' applicable to all existing gas purchase contracts."

4. See also Internet appendix 2.1, "Regulatory Delay under the Natural Gas Act," at www .politicalcapitalism.org/Book3/Chapter2/Appendix1.html.

the Midwest's lean World War II years. But the postwar economic boom changed everything. Demand caught up to the capacity of the pipeline, necessitating expansions. NNGP would reach 1.1 Bcf/d by its 25th anniversary, five times its original size. By 1955, the parent had added an exploration and production division, creating one of the nation's most integrated gas companies.[5] Northern Natural Producing Company would explore for oil and gas near the mainline and in Alberta, Canada.

Regulation was a major part of the company's business. Peoples Gas was regulated as a public utility in its four states: Iowa, Minnesota, Nebraska, and Kansas. NNGP's rates were capped by the Federal Power Commission (FPC). Even the production unit, by selling gas to the pipeline, came under FPC price ceilings, precipitating its sale in 1964 to Mobil Oil Corporation for Mobil stock. It was a nice divestiture. "Hell," remembered Willis "Bill" Strauss, president of Northern at the time, "the dividends were income we hadn't been seeing!"[6]

Following a strategic plan unveiled in 1958, Northern diversified into unregulated areas near its core. In the early 1960s, Northern Gas Products Company built the largest hydrocarbon extraction plant in the Free World. The Bushton, Kansas, facility produced butane, propane, helium, and natural gasoline from 900 MMcf/d of NNGP's Btu-rich gas.

In the same period, Northern Propane Gas Company purchased more than 100 small firms selling bottled gas to rural communities. Later that decade, a $200 million petrochemical processing plant put Northern Petrochemical Company in competition with such giants as Union Carbide, Dow Chemical, and DuPont. By 1970, Northern was a diversified energy company with distinct regulated and nonregulated sides.

Inadequate gas supplies under federal wellhead price ceilings made the 1970s a troubled decade for interstates. Natural gas reserves attached to NNGP's system, which stood at 15 Tcf in 1966, were 11.5 Tcf by 1973 and falling. Pipeline expansions ceased, and NNGP urgently sought to avoid customer curtailments in wintertime. Tough times led to an austerity program at Northern in 1972, which included the first early-retirement program in company history.

A financial turnaround began in 1973 as energy prices began their sharp ascent. As federal price ceilings gave way—and because such regulation had

---

5. Motivated by the fall of Samuel Insull's empire, the Public Utility Holding Company Act of 1935 (PUHCA) enforced a one-state, contiguous-system rule, which required many divestments by companies that had integrated interstate transmission with local distribution (Bradley, *Edison to Enron*, pp. 219, 406, 433, 513). But as "a single integrated public utility system," Peoples Gas was exempted, which allowed Northern to stay intact.

6. Two decades later, the value of Mobil shares would be $180 million, which provided cookie-jar income for HNG/InterNorth and then Enron, whenever the decision was made to sell the stock with its very low-cost basis. See chapter 5, p. 247.

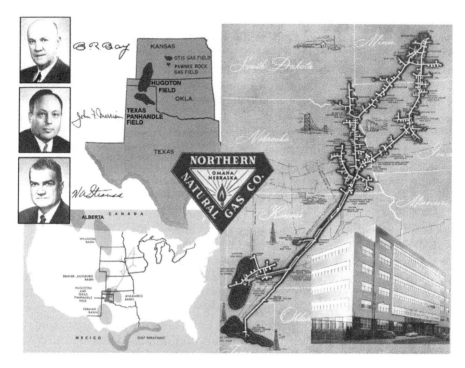

Figure 2.1 Northern Natural Gas Company began as a gas pipeline and distribution company and later diversified into exploration and production, gas liquids, and petro-chemicals. In 1951, the company consolidated its operations at 2223 Dodge Street in Omaha. The company's longest-serving presidents (top to bottom) were Burt Bay (1939–50), John Merriam (1950–60), and Bill Strauss (1960–76).

reduced supply—gas liquids, natural gas, and oil increased in value time and again.[7] Riding the energy commodity price boom, Northern Natural split its stock two-for-one in 1975 and again five years later.

Canadian gas, a focus for Northern in the 1950s, became a major priority.[8] In 1978, Northern Border Pipeline Company (Northern Border) was formed to bring Canadian gas down to the Midwest. InterNorth was managing partner

---

7. Disputes about Northern Liquid Fuels Company products under federal price controls led to litigation and a final settlement of $48 million with the US Department of Energy in 1988.

8. Northern Natural's determined effort to access Canadian gas under CEO John Merriam is discussed in Bradley, *Edison to Enron*, pp. 254–55.

and 22.75 percent owner of the six-company, $1.3 billion consortium.[9] This north-side supply strategy was joined by a south-side initiative beginning in 1976: purchases of offshore Gulf Coast gas for delivery to NNGP. It wasn't cheap, but every cubic foot was needed. Indeed, in winter 1976/77, NNGP curtailed its customers by 126 Bcf, about 15 percent of its annual system deliveries. But by the time Northern Border's 975 MMcf/d system entered service in 1982, the gas picture had changed.

Coal gasification, intensely studied as a third strategy, was rejected. Under the aggressive leadership of Sam Segnar, Northern purchased coal operations in Colorado and Wyoming. Conservation initiatives also became a priority to stretch available gas supplies.

As energy prices peaked in the early 1980s, InterNorth executives eyed new investments in coal, renewable energies, and synthetic fuels. Gasohol (grain alcohol used as a transportation fuel) was also studied. But the company was joined at the hip to natural gas. In 1982, Northern Border's 823-mile system began delivering Canadian gas from the international border to regions deep in Northern's territory. The project was supposed to have an eastern leg fed by the Alaska Natural Gas Transportation System (ANGTS), but this $15 billion (or more) project was cancelled in 1983. The natural gas picture had drastically reversed itself in only a few short years.

The 50th anniversary of Northern Natural Gas Company (1930–80) was a time of celebration and change. In addition to a stock split, supply was back in sync with demand on the flagship asset, which now had a capacity of more than 2 Bcf/d. To better reflect its disparate operations—gas pipelines, gas distribution, oil and gas exploration and production, gas liquids, petrochemicals, and bottled gas—Northern was renamed InterNorth Inc. Northern Natural Gas Company, hitherto the whole company's name, was the new name for wholesale natural gas operations.

Also in 1980, Bill Strauss transferred the CEO title to his president, Sam Segnar, while remaining chairman. Four years later, Strauss reached InterNorth's mandatory retirement age of 62, ending a 36-year career as the most effective and beloved chief executive in the company's history. Sam Segnar was now InterNorth's one and two man.

Segnar, an engineer by education, had worked at a refinery in Lake Charles, Louisiana, before joining Cities Service Gas Company. In 1960, his boss at Cities Service, Rocco "Rocky" LoChiano, assigned him to a consulting job at a start-up unit of Northern: Northern Gas Products Company. The consultant became an employee of the client a year later. Segnar progressed on the liquid fuels side

---

9. For more detail on Northern Border and other joint ventures, as well as miscellaneous assets and sales, see Internet appendix 2.2, "HNG/InterNorth: Joint Ventures, Miscellaneous Assets, and Sales," at www.politicalcapitalism.org/Book3/Chapter2/Appendix2.html.

before becoming president of Northern in 1976; president and CEO of Inter-North in 1980; and president, CEO, and chairman of InterNorth in 1984.

Though in some ways introverted, Segnar's sizable ego and aristocratic style resulted in unprecedented pizzazz for the company. InterNorth's 1981 annual report showed the flags of 39 countries where the company now did business. An InterNorth advertising campaign pictured Segnar by a globe with the tag line, *We work for America*.

As part of the patriotic theme, Segnar invoked the wisdom of Thomas Jefferson and Thomas Paine to pay tribute to "our free market system [that] is constantly under attack by some who choose to march to a different drummer." Of course, InterNorth itself was tapping taxpayers for a synthetic-fuel study, and NNGP had used both eminent domain and a gas-conservation law against flaring to build its line and then secure the gas to fill it.[10] But that was small potatoes. The real problems for Segnar (and other industry executives) were remaining natural gas price controls and the crude oil windfall-profit tax.

A Marketing Pipeline

NNGP was the premier gas-marketing pipeline in the country. With its sister Peoples Gas, a local distribution company, NNGP also marketed appliances to increase gas demand. NNGP was mostly a system of "spaghetti lines"—small-diameter trunk lines branching out from the mainline to delivery points all around the upper Midwest. NNGP was just the opposite of rifle-shot Transwestern Pipeline (a future sister pipeline at Enron), which delivered almost all its gas to a single terminus at the Arizona-California border. Because the central United States was thinly populated compared to other gas markets, such as California, Florida, the Texas Gulf Coast, and the Northeast, NNGP's personnel had to knock on many doors and make many phone calls.

The result was a salesmanship culture. "Some interstate transmission companies have almost no marketing staff, but we sort of grew up with our customers and shared our expertise with them," one executive recalled. "[By] the mid-1960s, businessmen from the Netherlands, Germany, France, and Great Britain came all the way to Omaha to learn more about Northern's marketing techniques and strategy."

The goal was to sell more gas to expand the pipeline, thus enlarging the rate base upon which regulated earnings were made. Otherwise, earnings

---

10. NNGP used state-level eminent domain law to secure right-of-way during construction at a time when most interstate gas lines relied solely on voluntary contracts. In another example of political capitalism, NNGP successfully lobbied the Texas legislature to outlaw open-air discharges of gas at the wellhead, as well as the use of gas for so-called inferior uses, both of which required the gas to be sold to gas pipelines (including NNGP).

would fall with the pipeline's net book value (cumulative original cost, less depreciation).

————

In 1978, NNGP inaugurated a Transportation and Exchange group (T&E) in response to Section 311 of the Natural Gas Policy Act, which allowed self-implementing transportation agreements in place of a Section 7(c) certification by FERC. In simple terms, under Section 311, an interstate could now transport gas on short notice and file the paperwork afterward, rather than go through a regulatory process and await permission from Washington.

Before, NNGP had been mostly an island unto itself, buying gas in Texas, Oklahoma, and Kansas to sell in Iowa, Minnesota, Wisconsin, and Michigan. Now, the interstate could trade gas with another pipeline or have another line move gas to take advantage of momentary opportunities.[11]

Being in the upper Midwest, NNGP's system gas could go in three directions: east, west, and south. Other pipelines were more boxed in and did not want to engage in off-system deals, preferring a closed world in which they did not enter other markets, and other pipelines did not enter theirs.

By allowing companies to reclassify gas from *sales* to *transportation*, Section 311 deals opened up a new world of possibilities. The initial opportunity was transportation agreements between gas-short interstates, such as NNGP, and gas-rich intrastates, such as Houston Pipe Line (HPL), the major subsidiary of Houston Natural Gas Corporation. Even after supply and demand came into better balance beginning in 1979, there were deals to exploit system efficiencies. NNGP's T&E department, the industry's largest, was helped by the complexity of its system, as well as the flexibility provided by a bidirectional leg between West Texas and southern Oklahoma (the K-B line, which could receive and deliver gas either way).

Coming or going, on system or off, meeting system requirements and minimizing costs was the name of the game. Physical transportation could be avoided with gas exchanged at different points—or if the contractual flow was opposite from the physical flow (a *backhaul*). Given that every dollar spent in T&E was recoverable as a (regulated) pipeline cost of service, gas-sale revenue in excess of cost was returned to ratepayers pursuant to NNGP's FERC rate case. Still, at least nominally, T&E-driven cost efficiencies were motivated by FERC prudency reviews, under which penalties could be levied for inaction.

————

11. Gas exchanges between pipelines were not new but long-standing arrangements premised on Section 7(c) certification. In 1952, for example, NNGP entered into an agreement whereby El Paso Natural Gas delivered Permian Basin gas to NNGP, and NNGP delivered a like amount of Texas Panhandle gas to El Paso, avoiding cross-hauling and, in NNGP's case, the construction of a West Texas leg to the mainline.

In addition, agreements with producers for take-or-pay relief required Northern Natural to find new markets for its gas that was surplus to NNGP's native load (on-system demand). That was incentive aplenty to market the gas off system, given that the pipeline did not know whether unresolved take-or-pay liabilities, absent the agreement, would be recoupable in future rates.

Julie Gomez became NNGP's first T&E accountant in January 1980. She arrived to find boxes of unorganized paperwork describing a variety of deals under which the gas, in her words, "wasn't purchased, it wasn't saled, it really did not fit in any one person's job." Such transactions represented the beginning of what would become a coordinated natural gas grid, a logistical *network*. Like linear programmers, the T&E specialists were getting their hands around the cost-minimization and revenue-maximization possibilities of a system with hundreds of receipt and delivery points.

This was new territory, and a cultural divide developed at InterNorth between the new group and NNGP's traditional account executives. Remembered Gomez:

> We were a group of 10, 15 people, and the rest of the organization hated us! We were the upstarts. We were the ones stealing their markets. We were screwing up their relationships with the producers.... We were punching holes into the pipe in places it shouldn't be punched. It was massive change, and Northern Natural Gas had not gone through change.

As the supply and demand for spot gas grew, the sharp minds in T&E increasingly encountered price differentials that invited profit making. But NNGP was held back by federal regulation, at least FERC's interpretation of it. ("We were, believe it or not, a not-for-profit organization," Gomez recalled.) The rebels needed to make profits for their own account, not just reduce costs for NNGP, to get noticed and grow.

———

Effective January 1, 1983, NNGP's new rate case built in incentives with the new gas-marketing function in mind. The interstate was assigned a level of transportation revenue past which earnings would accrue to the company and not to ratepayers. In response, Northern formed Northern Gas Marketing (NGM), a bona fide profit center separate from Gas Sales on the one side and T&E on the other.

The timing could not have been better. NNGP found itself with a surplus of gas under contract beginning in mid-1982; by spring 1983, the surplus reached 50 percent of the contractual total.

Part of the problem was lost sales at the far end of the system, where delivered-gas prices were the highest, owing to transportation costs. In upstate Minnesota, gas used for taconite reduction was being displaced by bottom-of-the-barrel petroleum produced by an oil refinery near Minneapolis owned by Koch Industries. The consultancy McKinsey & Company was hired by InterNorth to devise a counter strategy. The project went to Jeffrey Skilling, a rising star in McKinsey's Houston office.

Skilling saw nontraditional marketing as the only solution. NNGP's on-system gas needed to be released (via producer permission and a federal filing), relabeled as (cheaper) spot gas, and marketed off system. Producer-contract reformation was necessary to minimize take-or-pay liabilities. In the longer term, pure profits from such innovation would be even better.

———

The rate case that opened up nonjurisdictional (unregulated) profit making was a bellwether moment for InterNorth. The director of rates who designed the incentive and who lobbied regulators to allow profits from off-system sales was Ronald J. Burns.

Everyone knew that Ron Burns was going places as soon as he arrived at Northern in the summer of 1974 as a 22-year-old accounting trainee, fresh out of the University of Nebraska at Omaha. A hulking, athletic man at six feet four inches, gregarious and smart, and a scratch golfer to boot, Burns inspired warmth and commanded respect. The All-American boy and Superman look-alike would find his niche in the regulatory affairs department, where he grasped the interplay between business opportunity and the Natural Gas Act. Burns soon became General Manager of the Transportation & Exchange Department and would go on to be a key figure in unregulated gas marketing at Inter-North, HNG/InterNorth, and Enron.

While T&E focused on off-system pipeline logistics to mitigate NNGP's take-or-pay liabilities, as well as keep FERC placated for minimizing system costs, NGM marketed gas to at-risk industrial customers who were threatening to switch fuels or even suspend operations. Both groups were nontraditional and complementary. So in May 1983, just several months after NGM was founded, T&E separated from Operations to join NNG to "provide a more integrated company sales effort by placing gas sales and transportation sales activities in one division." Ron Burns, T&E general manager, reported to Bill Kellstrom, the newly named vice president of Northern Gas Marketing.

NGM's job was to buy and sell spot gas (which was selling at a large discount to pipeline system supply) and arrange for its transportation.[12] Spot-gas sales could range from one month to six months at fixed prices or for longer terms at variable prices. The sales pitch was size; NNGP was the nation's longest, with 23,000 miles of transmission through 14 states and interconnected

———

12. InterNorth's 1983 annual report described NGM's role as "arrang[ing] for direct gas purchases from producers and pipeline transportation for potential large volume consumers not presently using natural gas." Under its Agency Gas Program, NGM would not take title to the gas but would arrange for the purchase of gas at the wellhead (and transportation) for end-users, avoiding a sale-for-resale that would require a marketing certificate from FERC.

with 26 other major lines. "Northern's unique geographic position not only offers you competitive sources for natural gas but a dependable gas supply—wherever you are located," the marketing brochure explained.

In early 1985, just months before InterNorth would acquire HNG, T&E and gas sales merged within NGM. Joining newly promoted vice president Burns in the T&E/Gas Sales Services Unit were Bill Kellstrom, executive vice president of marketing, and Bill Houston, general manager of gas sales. Julie Gomez was named director of operations, responsible for volume allocation and interfacing with Gas Control. In NGM's trenches were talented young marketers, including Ken Rice and Steve Bergstrom, both of whom would go on to be leaders in the new natural gas industry.

———

Northern Natural's off-system marketing group was the first and best in the industry. Thus it was not surprising that InterNorth's Burns and Dan Dienstbier, after attending a meeting hosted by Transco Energy and Ken Lay in spring 1984, declined to have Northern become an equity member of U.S. Natural Gas Clearinghouse (NGC). Six other pipelines joined, including Ken Lay's old company, Transco, and his new company, Houston Natural Gas. Northern Natural had its own show.

T&E had Ron Burns as its dynamic leader. He also had the crucial support of Dienstbier, a man who welcomed change as president of Northern Natural Gas, the largest division of the company.

In his early 40s, Dienstbier recognized the benefits accruing from both T&E and for-profit marketing. He noticed the impressive talent migrating to both areas. Market conditions and regulatory trends pointed toward much more growth on this side of the business. "Marketability" was the buzzword.

The upstarts were making a splash. "The Natural Gas Group successfully responded to intensified competition from alternate fuels," wrote Sam Segnar in the 1984 annual report. "It also increased significantly its transportation services for other companies and sharply reduced operating expenses." Dienstbier added:

> The transportation of gas for other companies and opportunities in brokering and trading on a national basis have developed into major business activities. The two programs accounted for a significant increase in transportation revenues in 1984.

Looking to 1985, $35 million was budgeted to "pursue revenue opportunities through gas brokerage, direct sales, and transportation and exchange activities … to increase its share of the national natural gas transportation and exchange markets." Ron Burns, vice president of the Transportation and Exchange Department, was at the epicenter. Of particular interest was constructing unregulated small-diameter *gathering* lines to move gas from the wellhead to the mainline. "It is 'good business sense' to make short-term investments for long-term returns, instead of paying other pipeline companies or natural gas producers to gather for us," Burns explained.

Prelude to a Merger

"At his fiercest," *Forbes* reminisced, "corporate raider Irwin L. Jacobs … terrorized chief executives, forcing them to either fix their problems or sell them off to him, if possible." Jacobs purchased stakes in Borg-Warner, Pabst Brewing, Kaiser Steel, and Walt Disney, among others, "financing his predations with his own cash, then selling for a quick profit."

Sam Segnar was among the scared. In 1984, Jacobs quietly accumulated a significant stock interest in InterNorth, a company he believed was more valuable in its parts than as a whole. First were the pipeline systems—not only NNGP but also Northern Border and some smaller lines that cumulatively accounted for nearly one-half of InterNorth's earnings. Belco Petroleum Corporation, the oil and gas unit, was marketable in whole or in part. Northern Petrochemical Company, recently bolstered by the acquisition of Chemplex Company from Texaco, was profitable and salable. There was value in Northern Liquid Fuels Company, which housed InterNorth's gas-liquid facilities and marketing groups and accounted for 5 percent of corporate earnings. The retail natural gas distribution division, Peoples Gas, contributed small (3 percent) but steady rate-base earnings under public-utility regulation. The newest of the major divisions, International, included an oil-trading operation located in Valhalla, New York, which was very profitable by all appearances.

What did the notorious Minneapolis financier have in mind? Sam Segnar met with his stalker, but Jacobs said little other than that he liked the company. Segnar knew that this could mean the end of a storied enterprise—no, a Midwest institution—that had finally achieved its desired balance between its regulated and nonregulated divisions. InterNorth's merger and acquisitions team, formed in 1979, got busy looking for a synergistic deal that would make InterNorth too big or expensive for Jacobs or any other corporate raider.

InterNorth had another problem that pointed toward a fundamental restructuring. Although worth billions in replacement cost, NNGP had a rate base south of $1 billion. Even with plenty of low-priced gas, expansions were modest in a market with slow population growth. "We had connected the last outhouse in the area," joked InterNorth executives. But it was not very funny when it translated into stagnant earnings on a vanishing (depreciating) rate base under federal public-utility regulation.

———

On March 15, 1985, InterNorth's stock jumped 13 percent in heavy trading. Takeover speculation that had already pulled the stock out of the 30s was now a fever as the price reached $53 per share. Sam Segnar, sometimes accompanied by McKinsey's two top energy specialists—John Sawhill and his protégé, Jeff

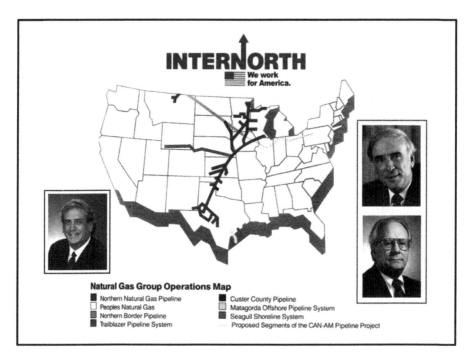

Figure 2.2 InterNorth was a rock-solid, mid-America company centered on natural gas transmission. In 1984–85, CEO Sam Segnar (upper right) instructed Rocky LoChiano (lower right) to find a merger partner before Irwin Jacobs (left) could gain control and break up the company.

Skilling—were talking to potential suitors, including American Natural Resources Company (ANR, which would end up being acquired by Coastal Corporation), Burlington Northern Inc. (the new owner of El Paso Natural Gas Company), Southern Natural Gas Company, Natural Gas Pipeline of America (Samuel Insull's creation, still headquartered in Chicago), and Texas Eastern Transmission Corporation.

The arbitrageurs thought that Burlington Northern would bid for Inter-North, but its El Paso Natural Gas was just discussing a joint venture with Northern Natural. Rumors of a bid quieted, and InterNorth's stock fell back to the mid-40s.

The company atop InterNorth's wish list was Houston Natural Gas. The two firms had opened their books and cordially negotiated not once but twice. Six months before, InterNorth lost out to HNG in its joint bid (with ANR) for Continental Resources Company, the owner of Florida Gas Transmission. It was a blow given that, on the southern end of its system, NNGP had excess gas needing a home now that Northern Border Pipeline was filling the line from the north.[13] That led to Plan B: a major pipeline-marketing push within Texas to get InterNorth's surplus gas to market.

In February 1985, two agreements were reached with San Antonio–based Valero Energy Corp. The first was buying a half interest in Valero's 450-mile West Texas pipeline for $80.5 million. The second was a new joint venture, Nor-Val Gas Company, to sell gas off of the pipeline to Texas customers. The main competitor of InterNorth (and Valero) in the midstream-downstream market was Houston Pipe Line, the major subsidiary of Houston Natural Gas.

Still, InterNorth's new Texas strategy could be upended for a greater good. HNG's coast-to-coast pipeline network was centered beneath Northern's Midwest market. Texas, Florida, and California were growth states. Segnar liked Ken Lay, and the InterNorth board was interested in the affable young man with a stellar past who by all accounts was leading his company toward the industry's future. With Segnar nearing his 25-year anniversary with the company—and with the other top brass at InterNorth approaching InterNorth's mandatory retirement age of 62—Ken Lay and his young team were considered as valuable as the iron in the ground.

In first-quarter 1985, InterNorth's earnings and revenue were three times that of HNG. InterNorth had twice the number of employees and had earned twice the profits of HNG in 1984. But the companies were closer in market value. Still, even if Wall Street saw more potential in HNG than in InterNorth, there could be no question about who was the big dog. For 1984, InterNorth earned $297 million versus HNG's $123 million; total assets were $6.1 billion versus $3.7 billion for HNG; stockholder equity was $1.8 billion for InterNorth versus HNG's $1 billion.

Parts of InterNorth were already in Texas, which was the hub for much of the interstate gas industry, including the Midwest gas industry. InterNorth's half-interest in the Seagull Shoreline pipeline system at Matagorda Island joined HNG's 25 percent. InterNorth, based in Omaha, had numerous Gulf Coast transportation agreements with HPL and more than a thousand employees in Texas, almost half of them in Houston, the site of InterNorth's 1984 stockholders meeting.

HPL and NNGP were the marketing dynamos of the intrastate and interstate market, respectively. The future belonged to spot gas and transportation, not traditional pipeline sales. No other company would be able to rival a combined HNG and InterNorth, at least out of the blocks. Scale economies and cost savings were likely from merging their respective exploration and production, liquids, and petrochemical operations. Lastly, the stray assets of each could be sold to reduce the debt associated with the purchase.

---

13. InterNorth did not pursue Transwestern Pipeline Company (as it did CRC), despite the fact that California was a coveted market, and InterNorth had once owned 16 percent of Transwestern before its sale in 1967 to Texas Eastern Transmission Company.

On the other hand, Omaha and Houston were very different places. Inter-North's corporate culture was more traditional and hierarchical than the corporate culture at Ken Lay's remade HNG. But this was no time for convenience or nostalgia; InterNorth had to pick the best partner for the rough road ahead. Not surprisingly, the search led to Houston.

———

On Saturday, April 20, 1985, Segnar contacted Ken Lay about a merger. "We would buy you, or if you want to pursue it, you can buy us," Segnar proffered. Lay, drawing on positive impressions of Segnar and InterNorth from their meeting six months before, and cognizant of the need to increase his stock price to heal the Coastal-offer wounds, put John Wing, HNG's chief planning officer, right on it. Segnar tapped Rocky LoChiano, InterNorth's chief technical and developmental officer, who put his deputy, Lou Potempa, in the room with Wing. HNG retained Lazard Frères & Company and InterNorth Goldman Sachs for advice.

For both companies, it was mainly updating the numbers they already had. For Wing, it was laying out the conditions that HNG had to have to make the deal work. One condition was the price; the second was who would be in charge of the combined company. Lay had little doubt about both with such a game suitor. The stock-buyout price would have to be no less, and preferably a little more, than that reached at the height of the Coastal take-over attempt ($63.25). He, Ken Lay, would have to be on top—sooner or later. Wing, who had crossed paths with InterNorth on the cogeneration front two years before, fast-forwarded the negotiations with both conditions in mind.

Briefed by Wing, Lay visited Omaha a week later. Segnar explained his merger hunt and his concerns about Jacobs. Lay explained the need for more value in HNG's stock price and how HNG's discussions with ANR and Transco had fallen short—but maybe for the best. The two described their major assets and company positions. Both saw a good fit—better than any other merger they could think of.

Lay, sensing Segnar's urgency, and knowing that any deal had to be on HNG's terms from the standstill agreement that InterNorth was operating under, reiterated the conditions that Wing had already set forth.

InterNorth, the bigger company, would be the acquiring party. The stock buyout would need to be in the range of the rejected tender offer from Coastal, maybe higher. (HNG stock was then selling at around $45 per share versus its Coastal-driven high of 14 months before.) Over half of HNG's stock was held by institutional investors, Lay explained, who were antsy to pocket the several hundred million dollars they had once had on paper. This way the shareholder suits hanging over HNG would go away.

As the acquirer, Segnar would be chairman and CEO, with Lay as president and COO, and InterNorth would have a majority of seats on the board of directors. But Lay and Segnar each knew of the other's ambitions. Come January 1, 1987, about 18 months hence, Lay would become CEO and Segnar senior chairman. This would become Lay's company—unless the board reversed.

On the sensitive question of corporate headquarters, the answer was Omaha unless the board declared otherwise. NNGP would certainly stay in Omaha, but Houston was attractive for almost every other division. Some preliminary ideas were exchanged on the postmerger organization chart melding the executives from both companies.

Goldman Sachs valued HNG for InterNorth at $45 per share—about where the current stock price was—and a good negotiating point for its client. Lazard valued HNG for Lay and Wing at a rich $77 per share. Splitting the difference would be a price in the low 60s. In fact, upon hearing the rumors, natural gas specialists John Olson of Drexel Burnham Lambert and Curt Launer of L. F. Rothschild, Unterberg, Towbin valued HNG at $60 per share, tops. LoChiano, who had done due diligence on HNG when it was run by Matthews and then Lay, saw $65 as his ceiling.

But with InterNorth committed to a merger and not negotiating elsewhere, HNG decided to strike quickly. Wing rejected LoChiano's $65 and offered take-it-or-leave-it $70 per share. "I think I get this," LoChiano replied to Wing. "We're the rich old ugly guy with all the money, and you're the good-looking blonde."

But LoChiano was firm. He would not go to Segnar, and Segnar would not go to the board, with that price. HNG's own projections of postmerger income could not justify it. Goldman Sachs had done the math too. The debt service was just too high, he explained.

Wing informed Lay that $70 per share needed help. Lay convinced himself that he needed $70 price, even though $65 was above the speculative peak reached during the Coastal fight. (That HNG's self-tender offer was $69 during the heat of the Coastal battle helped Lay persuade himself.) Once again, Lay pushed an imprudent gutsy-pricey bid confident that his smartest guys could make it work.

HNG upped its projected earnings to sway its suitor. The estimate showed that HNG would make $136 million in 1985, increasing to $227 million by 1989, a compound growth rate near 15 percent. With this came Lay's "personal assurances" that HNG would make those numbers after the merger.

InterNorth quickly lined up a $2.5 billion credit line led by Citibank of New York "for general purposes," and its board was called into special session.

Lay *was* feeling confident. HNG was off to a strong start in 1985 with first-quarter earnings up one-third from the year before, and its debt-to-capitalization ratio falling toward 50 percent from year-end's 59 percent, a goal Lay had not expected to meet for another 6 to 12 months. HNG's board could not be more pleased with their golden boy.

Goldman Sachs signed on in light of HNG's new projections, while recognizing $70 per share as a stretch. LoChiano went to Segnar, who hedged by saying he was 49 percent in favor of the merger at this price, which was almost 20 times HNG's 1984 earnings.

It had been a long road, and HNG seemed serious in both its final offer and holding up its end of the profitability goal after the merger. Segnar envisioned a grand exit for himself and a grand entrance for Lay. So Segnar agreed and had LoChiano, the deal's chief booster and a man greatly respected by InterNorth's board, present to the directors. They unanimously accepted the terms of the merger on May 2, 1985, as did the obviously delighted HNG board.

Just 10 days had passed from the moment when Sam Segnar phoned Ken Lay about a merger. Two long-standing companies—Houston Natural Gas Corporation (established 1925) and InterNorth (established 1930)—were now to be HNG/InterNorth.

This was all very good news for the Lay household as well. Ken Lay's 150,000 HNG stock options with a grant price of $50 per share now meant $3 million. His personal expenses were very high, with his divorce settlement of two years before, his household of seven (his two children and Linda's three), and his role as the family banker. But he would need this and more, a lot more, with the lifestyle that he and Linda were embarking upon.

HNG/InterNorth

InterNorth's offer to HNG stockholders totaled $2.4 billion. With the assumption of debt, the purchase price was $3.8 billion. HNG's stock price jumped by more than one-third; InterNorth's fell 10 percent. However, much of this occurred the day *before* the announcement. Indeed, the *Wall Street Journal* reported that a "blatant" leak had provided "reasonably good details" of the transaction. Using insider information as it turned out, takeover specialist Ivan Boesky purchased several hundred thousand HNG shares that he would sell two weeks later for a $4 million profit.[14] HNG and InterNorth executives, flying from Houston to New York City to present the deal to their boards, were flummoxed when they were greeted by reporters at the airport. HNG's stock price had jumped 25 percent during the plane ride, and the press wanted an explanation.

Segnar and Lay gave a very positive picture of the merger on their analyst call. Lay stressed the geographical reach and integrated nature of the combination, particularly the new 37,000-mile, four-pipeline cross-country *network* that had access to all of the country's major gas basins in the United States, Canada,

---

14. The leak, as documented by the Securities & Exchange Commission, originated from Robert Wilkis of Lazard Frères, the company that was HNG's merger advisor and would receive $7 million in fees. Wilkis tipped off Dennis Levine of Drexel Burnham Lambert, who in turn told Ivan Boesky. All three were sentenced to jail for violating laws prohibiting insider trading.

and even Mexico. Segnar waxed eloquent about now having "the competitive, operational, marketing, financial and managerial strengths which will, simply put, enable us to truly fulfill our mandate consistent with the restructuring of the country's energy industry." On the analyst side, Curt Launer, who just days before valued HNG at $60 per share tops, praised the $70 purchase as "a good deal" for creating "the premier pipeline in the country." Launer would be on the new company's bandwagon for a long time to come.

The market's immediate verdict indicated a wealth transfer from InterNorth to HNG stockholders, at least equivalent to the $5 per share that InterNorth had originally resisted (and prudence dictated). Wing himself saw $65 as his ceiling if he had been negotiating on the other side. But Lay's desire for pain-avoidance demanded that he end the shareholder litigation left over from the Coastal fight. And what about the future of the combined company, given the too high price? Ken Lay was very confident that his smartest could make his gamble work.

Segnar remained chairman and CEO of InterNorth, and Lay chairman and CEO of HNG—now two divisions of the merged company. Lay was also president and COO of InterNorth—number two to Segnar. But in 18 months, contractually, Ken Lay would be the unequivocal number one.

Still, this was InterNorth's company with 12 of 20 board seats. All 12 of the acquirer's directors continued, while the HNG side had to pare down from 18 to 8 directors.[15] Among the survivors were Lay's recent appointees, as well as HNG veterans John Duncan and Joe Foy. The merger agreement specified that two additional board directors would be jointly recommended by Segnar and Lay the next year, bringing the total to 22.

A kicker to discourage third-party encroachment was the right given to InterNorth to buy a two-thirds interest in Houston Pipe Line for $867 million, giving HNG's "crown jewel" a paper value of $1.3 billion. It was this asset that InterNorth had offered to buy two years before for $1 billion.

———

The mood was upbeat in Houston. The local papers bellowed the good news for HNG. Stockholders, who included most every HNG employee, had received a full price. Ken Lay himself reaped the biggest payday of his life by far, and it was comforting that the 43-year-old had positioned himself to be on top, an outcome that was not surprising given his reputation.

Lay's enthusiasm at an all-employee meeting put any doubts about the merger to rest. HNG's assets were what InterNorth coveted to complement its core, he explained. This was the final piece, at least for the foreseeable future, to

---

15. The eight surviving HNG board members were Lay, Duncan, Foy, John Harbert III, Robert Jaedicke, Charles LeMaistre, Charls Walker, and Herbert Winokur. Among the displaced were Ed Smith, James Walzel, and Bryan Wimberly.

HNG's divestiture and acquisition plans. It would be mostly status quo on the HNG side. A bigger company would mean more opportunity for all.

But the 1,500 employees gathered at Omaha's Orpheum Theatre the Monday after Thursday's announcement were apprehensive at best. Some were not hiding their displeasure. Most employees were second-, third-, or fourth-generation Nebraskans who went to college in the state and married into another midwestern family. InterNorth was the acquiring company, yet Houston was energy central, and Ken Lay was destined to call the shots.

InterNorth was more diversified and gangly than what it was buying, and asset sales were likely to reduce the debt load of the pricey acquisition. Yes, InterNorth directors controlled a majority of the new board, but they had approved what was already being described as a reverse merger. A few swing votes could make anything happen—including moving headquarters to Houston.

Segnar opened the meeting. "As we go through deregulation and face highly competitive marketplace situations, we will not have the same life that we've had in the past." He continued:

> I concluded some time back that our best interest is served by being aggressive rather than defensive.... The two systems fit. A Houston business writer used the phrase, "border to border and coast-to-coast." As we pursue efficient transportation and a lot of options in the marketplace, border-to-border and coast-to-coast certainly becomes a unique circumstance in the pipeline industry.

HNG, Segnar added, served gas markets with a summer demand peak, reflecting gas demand for electric generation, which complemented NNGP's winter-peak residential market. HNG's pipelines were embedded in the nation's three growth states—Texas, Florida, and California—that "we have been making an intense effort to enter." He concluded: "This is what we've been trying to do for three years.... I think the fallout will be good for everybody."

Rocky LoChiano, whose acquiescence to HNG's hell-or-high-water price was decisive, described the purchase price as "somewhere in the middle" of what the two companies wanted, which was not quite philosophic fraud but close to it. Other options had been considered, he explained to the solemn audience. After rumors caused InterNorth's stock price to jump nearly 15 percent in mid-March, management decided that decisive action was required. The company first considered a leveraged buyout whereby employees would control the company through an Employee Stock Option Plan (ESOP). But the resulting debt ratio of 90 percent would have required a massive cut in capital spending, jeopardizing future earnings. Management then visited one of their two top choices for a merger partner, Burlington Northern, the parent of El Paso Natural Gas Company, only to be turned down. Other conversations with Texas Eastern Corporation and Natural Gas Pipeline of America had not even gotten that far.

So InterNorth turned to its first choice, HNG, which had rejected its offer for HPL back in 1983, as discussed in chapter 1. Ken Lay, fresh off the Transco rejection of a HNG combination, was open to a merger. The new debt ratio of 70 percent (about $5.4 billion of debt versus a $7.7 billion capitalization, approximately $5 billion of which was from InterNorth and $2.7 from HNG), while substantially higher than the company's prior 38 percent ratio, was digestible compared to the ESOP leveraged buyout.

"Ken Lay is a very decent, straight-forward person," Segnar assured his employees. Segnar described his role as making sure that Ken and Omaha got to know each other. It would be an equitable transition over the next 18 months, he promised.

The HNG side was well protected in the deal. Lay did not foresee layoffs, and the agreement obligated InterNorth to honor all of HNG's employee benefit plans, including vacation and severance, for a period of not less than two years. Ken Lay had not forgotten the little guy. After all, in just about every way, he once had been the little guy.

Buyer's Remorse

Omaha soon developed a bad case of buyer's remorse. Sure, Irwin Jacobs, owning 5 percent of InterNorth's common stock, had opposed the deal from the start. "I don't like it, and I'm not going to sit here and take it," he said. The market spoke loudly when the deal sent InterNorth's stock down $5.25 a share and HNG's up $20.25 per share. "It looks like a great business combination until you get to the terms," quipped one financial expert. Said industry analyst John Olson upon looking at the fine print: "It makes you wonder who is taking over whom."

That InterNorth overpaid was one thing. But adding insult to injury for Omaha were well-placed rumors that the new company's headquarters was Houston-bound. The impression was that the InterNorth side—the acquirer, the bigger company—was playing soft. *Houston Chronicle* reporter Barbara Shook, a former HNG employee, saw the natural gas capital as logical and documented Segnar's ties to the city. Like Ken Lay, Segnar was a director of Houston's largest bank, First City Bank Corp., and had recently married a Houstonian, rented an apartment in town, and was looking to buy a house in The Woodlands north of Houston.

But Segnar and Lay denied that Houston had been chosen. It hadn't. Still, it did not take a genius to know where Lay wanted the company to be. All this was happening just as InterNorth's new $108 million headquarters building—dubbed Segnar's "pink palace"—neared completion.

On July 16, the merger became final with all stockholder and regulatory approvals. June 1 was chosen as the official merger date. Several divestments of the two companies' combined Texas intrastate pipeline interests were necessary to satisfy the Federal Trade Commission on antitrust grounds. HNG sold its interests in Oasis Pipe Line Company, Red River Pipeline, and Llano Inc.; Inter-North divested its just-bought half-share of Valero Energy's West Texas pipeline and dissolved its interest in the Nor-Val Gas Company Partnership.[16] An interim name was announced: HNG/InterNorth. HNG came first, Lay explained, "because it came off the tongue better."

The inaugural HNG/InterNorth newsletter described the company's 37,000-mile network, serving five million customers from all the major gas basins in the United States and Canada. For each division, it was business as usual, the publication commented. Segnar and Lay were all smiles in an accompanying photograph.

Figure 2.3 The dual corporate communications and public affairs departments went into high gear to meld two corporate cultures and improve morale. The tag line *America's Premier Energy Company* would soon be forgotten with what was to come for the balance of 1985 and in 1986.

---

16. Prior to the asset divestitures, the merger was considered negative for producers in the Permian Basin—an area accounting for one-fifth of national gas production—because of the buying strength of a combined HNG and InterNorth. The scale economies originally envisioned by Lay and Segnar were disallowed by regulators, so that antitrust law, in this instance, was arguably pro-producer rather than pro-consumer.

The public relations department replaced *We work for America* with *America's Premier Energy Company*. "Strategically, few mergers have made more sense," a glossy company brochure explained, adding:

> InterNorth's low-cost gas supplies and extensive pipeline system along with HNG's growing markets offer greater operating and marketing efficiencies. The nationwide system provides unparalleled flexibility and competitive opportunities.

The novel idea of a synergistic coast-to-coast, border-to-border gas-pipeline system created opportunity if management could be properly aligned and if regulatory flexibility could be gained.

A new reality set in just weeks after the merger announcement. In June, the major rating agencies reduced the senior debt of the to-be-merged company by several notches, including Standard & Poor's reduction from A to BBB. That was still investment grade but not by much. That is what brought Ken Lay to Michael Milken. His company, Drexel Burnham Lambert, made a $614 million "junk bond" placement for HNG/InterNorth in October 1985,[17] the first of eight deals in the next three years, totaling just under $3 billion. This was the beginning of a long friendship between Milken and Lay, one that would bring the formerly jailed financier to speak at Enron's last management meeting in late 2000.

HNG/InterNorth's 70 percent debt ratio—and downgraded debt at that—left interest expenses eating up more than half of operating earnings. Segnar and Lay set a goal to reduce the debt ratio to 60 percent, or less, from cash flow (estimated to be in excess of $1 billion per year), capital expenditure reductions, and asset sales.

At least out of the gate, economic value was destroyed by the (imprudent) terms on which the two companies had combined, but that was value pocketed by HNG stockholders (including Ken Lay) at the expense of InterNorth stock-holders.[18] With pre-merger HNG valued at $1 billion versus InterNorth's $2.4 billion payment, the goodwill account was approximately $1.4 billion, a figure that would have to be handled via future earnings or a write-off.

On June 27, the first consolidated organization chart was released. Lay and LoChiano, head of acquisitions and sales, reported to Segnar. Just about all the

---

17. "HNG/InterNorth was one of the first big leveraged buy-out deals with junk debt—very expensive debt," Jeff Skilling remembered. "We had a very strained balance sheet."

18. The debt ratios of HNG and InterNorth were 59 percent and 38 percent, respectively, at year-end 1984, creating a weighted average of 46 percent. A year later, HNG/InterNorth's debt ratio peaked at 70 percent from increased debt and less stockholder equity. (This was later restated to be 73 percent.) Investors viewed the new company as higher risk, and of lower value, than the two companies standing alone.

other senior executives reported to Lay.[19] At employee meetings (held in Omaha, Houston, and points between), it was announced that some layoffs would be required.

A company-wide severance or early-retirement plan was released two weeks later, specifying two weeks' pay for every year of employment, plus a week again for every $10,000 of salary. For veteran employees, this summed to a year or more of pay. "I hope you can feel that the provisions will go a long way toward eliminating financial hardship," Sam Segnar wrote. "That is certainly the intent."

But Omaha could not help wondering why this was even occurring. Some in Houston remembered what Ken Lay had breezily told the press the day after the merger was announced, "I don't think there's any redundancy in Houston." It would not be the last time that Lay would prove to be over-optimistic in the face of imprudence. Before the year was out, the employee count would shrink by 900, and a nonrecurring charge of $55 million would be taken to cover early-retirement, severance, and relocation costs. But the severity of the transition reflected unanticipated factors as well.

A Postmerger Stumble

As the merger approached completion, Ken Lay flew to Washington to meet with his new head of government affairs. Joseph Hillings had been around the international block. His work with National Airlines and with Fluor Corporation had educated him in the politics of dozens of countries. When things were rough, he hired former CIA heads and ambassadors for real-time intelligence and advice.

"Joe, you will love this job because you have worked for years on international issues, and InterNorth has a number of international projects, including one in Peru," Lay said.

"Ken, you don't mean Peru!" Hillings responded. "At Fluor, we had an army protect our mines because of the terrorist group Shining Path." Hillings realized right there that his CEO was inexperienced when it came to doing business in international hot spots.

The assets in question were offshore oil-production facilities owned by Belco Petroleum, one of InterNorth's major divisions. Arthur Belfer, the company

---

19. Reporting to Lay were Bill Morgan (SVP and assistant to the chairman and president); Tommy Thompson (EVP and CFO) and Keith Kern (SVP and deputy CFO); Mick Seidl (EVP and chief of staff); Dan Gardner (EVP, gas operations); and Gordon Severa (EVP, petrochemicals, liquids, and exploration-production). Reporting to Gardner was Dan Dienstbier, who as head of natural gas operations arguably had the most important job in the company next to Lay.

founder, had operated in Peru since 1959. His company pioneered offshore drilling techniques that reduced the number of needed platforms. He and his son Robert, who now ran the company, wisely sold Belco to Sam Segnar in August 1983 to remove a "structural imbalance," namely, "too much of our income … coming from one foreign country." Both men knew that this country had nationalized the operations of Exxon Corp. in 1967 and Gulf Oil Corp. in 1975.

Peru was a democracy at the time, operating under a constitution adopted on July 28 (Independence Day) 1980. President Fernando Belaúnde was a friend of Belco Petroleum Corporation of Peru (BPCP), but there was political unrest. The Belfers sought US government insurance from the Overseas Private Investor Corporation (OPIC), but Peruvian law did not allow disputes to be tried in a third-party nation, a requirement for such protection. The Belfers worked with their senator, Jacob Javits (R-NY), to change the law, but to no avail.

InterNorth required Belco to buy political-risk insurance as a condition of the purchase. A $200 million policy was secured from AIG—about half the book value of the properties. That was enough for Sam Segnar and the board, given InterNorth's strong cash flow and interest in diversification.

Peru's statist economy was weak. Inflation was running high. The Maoist Shining Path was terrorizing rural areas. In April 1985, Alan García, the candidate of the left-wing American Popular Revolutionary Alliance (APRA), won the presidential election. Private companies operating under government contract, energy and otherwise, domestic or international, were on notice.

On August 29, García promulgated a restructuring of BPCP's 50/50 production agreement with Petroleos del Peru—the alternative was expropriation.[20] Renegotiations had occurred as oil prices soared in the 1970s, but now oil prices were falling. Robert Belfer had even broached more lenient contract terms with the previous government. The company refused García's demand that it repay $50 million in old tax credits and agree to new conditions going forward. A 90-day negotiation period was followed by a one-month extension—all fruitless.

On December 27, 1985, the Peruvian army surrounded BPCP's office in Lima and occupied Belco's operations in the coastal town of Talara. The company's 111 offshore platforms, producing about 24,000 barrels per day, were now under the supervision of the Peruvian government. The action sent HNG/InterNorth's stock down 4 percent.

---

20. Peruvian authorities accused BPCP of misusing tax exemptions granted under the prior regime and asserted, "This is not a measure against foreign capital [or] … an anti-American position." García, in fact, was having his cake and eating it too, inasmuch as the US government had given Peru $600 million since 1980.

All the rosy projections for the combined company were squashed. Net of expected recoveries, lost properties with a book value of $393 million resulted in an extraordinary charge of $218 million in fourth-quarter 1985, wiping out most of the year's operating profit. (The charge did not incur any tax benefit.) Postponing a planned debt issue, HNG/InterNorth exhaled when both Standard & Poor's and Moody's reaffirmed HNG/InterNorth's (already lowered) ratings.[21]

Every dollar was needed to reduce debt, which was $5 billion after some asset sales and repayment from cash flow. The nationalized assets had provided annual cash flow of around $20 million, approximately 3 percent of the corporate total. Ken Lay got his first taste of the vagaries of international business. Given that the merger was very much his baby, it represented a rare if entirely foreseeable business setback for him.[22]

Getting Together

HNG/InterNorth established five divisions: Gas Pipeline Operations, Exploration and Production, Liquid Fuels, Petrochemicals, and International. Inter-North executives Dan Gardner (EVP, Gas Operations) and Gordon Severa (EVP, Petroleum and Chemicals) were atop it all. But there was much HNG-side talent just beneath the surface of this $9 billion entity, variously self-described as "an international energy company," "America's Premier Energy Company," a "premier energy network," and as having "the makings of the very best diversified energy company in the country."

Headquarters aside, each division had to choose a home. Before long, the major units were heading south.

InterNorth's most valuable managerial talent resided in Northern Natural Gas Company, key members of which were among the first to move to Houston, even ahead of their families. President Dan Dienstbier relocated, as did Ron Burns, vice president of NGM. They liked the natural gas business, and Houston was the place to be.

In mid-July, the natural gas divisions of HNG/InterNorth held a three-day integration session at InterNorth's ranch near Granby, Colorado. There was time for socializing and recreation (horseback riding, fishing, hiking, bowling, trap shooting, and more—Sam Segnar went first class). But it was time for all to get their hands around the vast grid that had been created. Each pipeline gave

---

21. See Internet appendix 2.3, "The Nationalization of Belco Peru: A Personal Recollection," at www.politicalcapitalism.org/Book3/Chapter2/Appendix3.html.

22. Lay left Transco Energy Company right before its $92 million after-tax write-off of a 20 percent interest in the Great Plains Coal Gasification Project, a pet project of Transco chairman Jack Bowen.

a presentation, and task forces made presentations recommending who did what. All were looking for synergies and ways to maximize company-wide profits.

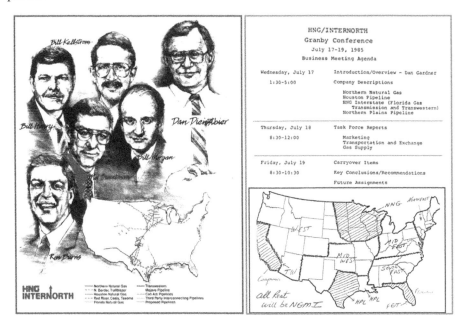

Figure 2.4 A mid-1985 meeting of top gas executives from HNG and InterNorth formed an opening strategy for the new company's intrastate and interstate grid, including the formation of a national marketing company.

Dan Gardner was nominally in charge, but Ron Burns was presiding. Ken Lay planned to attend but had to cancel, and Sam Segnar was who knows where. But just about everyone else of import, newly titled, was there. Corporate was represented by Mick Seidl, EVP and chief of staff; Bill Morgan, Lay's special assistant who had been with Florida Gas; and Jim Walzel, whose reduced responsibilities in the restructuring triggered his buy-out clause and who would soon be gone. A dozen folks from Northern Natural, in addition to Dienstbier and Burns, were present, including Bill Kellstrom, EVP of marketing; Don Hepperman, manager of strategic support; Fred Hollinger, VP of gas acquisitions; and Bill Houston, VP of gas sales.

Leading the HNG Interstate contingent were John Wing, the newly named president (who would soon leave the company); Jim Rogers, EVP of marketing, T&E, and supply; Claude Mullendore, SVP, marketing; E. J. Bergin, EVP, operations; and Harry Stout, SVP, gas supply. HNG Intrastate was represented by Mel Sweatman, president of Houston Pipe Line; Gerald Bennett, EVP, supply and administration; Bob Kelly, SVP, development; and others.

The big five who would emerge as leaders for HNG/InterNorth and, later, Enron were Dienstbier, Burns, Bennett, Mullendore, and Rogers. New talent, among the industry's finest, would soon be joining them.

To nobody's surprise, NNGP was given responsibility for the upper Midwest; Houston Pipe Line for the Texas Gulf Coast and Dallas areas; Florida Gas Transmission for Florida; and Transwestern for California. Each of the four pipelines had marketing responsibility on its system for released gas (that is, contracted system supply released as price-flexible spot gas).

Northern Gas Marketing's wide reach made it the logical choice to be the *systemwide* gas marketer. This company, soon to be renamed HNG/InterNorth Gas Marketing Inc. (HIGMI), had two years' experience, a full staff, and working information systems. It was moving as much as 800 MMcf/d, more than Natural Gas Clearinghouse or any other marketer.

Confident and cocky, InterNorth's T&E group described itself at the meeting as the "#1 ass-kicker in the national, natural gas industry" and a "fully integrated, team-oriented, aggressive machine." Playing off of its coast-to-coast, border-to-border base, T&E envisioned itself as a "service center" and "nerve center" providing "total grid management." All this would be needed; by mid-1986, some 70 known marketers and brokers—and many more entrants with little more than "a phone and a folding table"—were populating the gas-logistics field in the US open-access interstate (wholesale) transmission markets.

———

Gas processing and liquids was another major HNG/InterNorth division requiring consolidation and streamlining. InterNorth's Northern Liquid Fuels Company (NLF) had to be merged with HNG Gas Liquids, run by Mike Muckleroy. NLF, headed by Roland Beasley, was several times larger than that its HNG counterpart—but not as well managed. Muckleroy, who had evaluated each Northern plant prior to the merger, explained to Lay his ideas for improvement. McKinsey & Company was engaged for advice. The decision was to make Muckleroy COO of the combined group, effective September 1985, while making Beasley EVP for liquids and petrochemicals at Northern Petrochemical Company (Norchem).

Muckleroy quickly announced Houston as headquarters and told the InterNorth side that the faster they relocated, the better their choice of jobs and houses. Relocation allowances were generous, giving each family a chance to start with extra equity. Muckleroy received some boos at the Omaha Christmas party, but most NLF staffers would come Houston's way. Those electing to stay were placed in jobs, some outside the company. Best of all, significant operational improvements in the months and years ahead would make for a happy ending.

Norchem—with world-class olefin and polyolefin production facilities in Illinois and Iowa, and smaller plants in Ohio, Illinois, and Massachusetts—had no counterpart at HNG, so it was business as usual after the merger. Norchem, in fact, was busy with its own merger, which was the job of James Schorr, who had run Chemplex Company for Texaco before it was purchased by InterNorth in late 1984. There would be no need for Norchem (briefly Enron Chemical Co.) to move to Houston, given that the division was an early candidate for sale to reduce corporate debt. Roland Beasley, who had stayed in Omaha, turned into expensive overhead when the petrochemical division was sold in November, and he left the company early in the next year.

In October 1985, HNG Oil Company and BelNorth Petroleum, both located in Houston, consolidated as HNG/InterNorth Exploration Company, responsible for all domestic drilling and production. Ted Collins, formerly head of HNG Oil, was placed in charge of what was the fourth-largest independent oil and gas operation in the country.

Collins reported to Robert Belfer, chairman of Belco Petroleum Corp., which held Belco's international properties, including the rights to the nationalized Peruvian assets. A month later, with Belco's move from New York City to Houston imminent, Belfer resigned but remained on the board of directors as one of HNG/InterNorth's largest stockholders.[23]

InterNorth International, responsible for all nondomestic ventures outside of exploration and production, did not have an HNG counterpart either. The conglomeration of energy businesses, mostly assembled under Sam Segnar, continued as a stand-alone entity under its prior head, John Harding, in Omaha.

———

Market vagaries ruled every division. Falling oil and gas prices hurt all except for petrochemicals. The pipelines were steady but faced a depreciating rate base and, given the upheaval in federal regulation, some nonrecoupable transition costs to the open-access environment. Open access promised profits for the most efficient commodity market makers, but that was still a bird in the bush.

Cogen projects were here and now. Done right, lucrative and even extraordinary rates of return could be locked in with long-term energy contracts, thanks to the political capitalism aimed at creating independent electricity producers to contest generation from vertically integrated electric utilities. Regulation and regulatory change were particularly appealing to Ken Lay, whose energy game was about seizing profit opportunities from the government-enabled side.

———

23. Belfer recollected: "It became apparent to me that either I should move to Houston and get a divorce, which is expensive, or sever my employee relations with [HNG/InterNorth], stay in New York, but continue with the company as a board director. I clearly chose the latter alternative."

Enron's vision of a roaring independent power division faced a choice between two captains. One was General Electric's cogeneration star John Wing, age 39, whom Lay had hired 18 months earlier. Wing had completed HNG's lucrative merger with InterNorth and now, pursuant to his contract, was to run the cogeneration division. But HNG was now HNG/InterNorth, and the combined entity was heavy with HNG-side appointments. Furthermore, Lay's guy was not going to get points for having been the negotiator of the deal that the still-powerful InterNorth side had grown to like less and less.

Most important, Segnar and his board majority had their own man—a good one—in Howard Hawks, age 50, president of Northern Natural Resources Company (Northern Resources). Hawks had joined Northern Natural in 1966 and had been elected vice president of finance and administration five years later. In 1977, he was promoted to president of the division constructing Northern Border Pipeline. In 1982, he did well after taking over a major division, Northern Liquid Fuels Company. So in 1984, Hawks was tapped to run Northern Resources, which was tasked with finding good investment opportunities for InterNorth's sizeable cash flow. Cogeneration projects topped that list.

The former head of Northern Resources, Robert Raasch, knew Wing prior to the merger, as did Sam Segnar. In 1983, Northern Resources turned to GE after failing to ink a cogen alliance with equipment manufacturer Crouse-Hinds Company (today Cooper Crouse Hinds) and equipment supplier Bucyrus-Erie Company (Caterpillar). To close a deal, executives from GE's Cogeneration Applications Development Group were invited to InterNorth's Granby ranch to negotiate.

There was some reason for the two competitors—employees of which were negotiating projects against each other on phone calls even at the retreat—to join hands. But hopes were squashed at the end of an otherwise festive opening-night dinner when Wing rose to toast his hosts. GE's rep said nothing about a North America alliance. His vision was about joint ventures in InterNorth's territory, the ones that could benefit from the gas and transportation services of Northern Natural Gas Company.

InterNorth didn't need a partner for that, even mighty GE. Flummoxed, Raasch said little in his reply toast. After some perfunctory recreation the next day, the meeting broke up.

Still, by the time InterNorth bought HNG, Northern Resources, now run by Hawks, sported letters of intent to develop and equity-finance three cogeneration projects: two in California (enhanced oil-recovery projects, all courted by HNG's Mojave Pipeline) and one in Texas City, Texas.[24] InterNorth had $300

---

24. The Texas City cogeneration project would become one of the most successful in Enron's history. See chapter 4, pp. 203–4.

million earmarked for these projects, with plenty more for subsequent deals. Northern Natural Gas Pipeline generated large free-cash flow, far in excess of reinvestment needs. Cogeneration was just the investment home that Inter-North needed to be a growth company. Consequently, Ken Lay acquiesced to Segnar and assigned HNG/InterNorth's cogeneration activities to Howard Hawks's Northern Resources, a division well ensconced in Omaha.

What to do with John Wing? Lay tried to assuage his star by giving him the interstate pipelines, nominally one of the biggest jobs at the company. But Wing would have none of it. "I divide the world in two parts: creators of wealth and custodians of assets, and pipeline people are custodians to the nth degree," Wing recalled. Calling Lay on the terms of his contract, Wing negotiated an exit agreement under which he would consult with HNG/InterNorth but also pursue cogeneration projects on his own.[25] This five-year agreement was extraordinary, for it meant that Wing could negotiate on both sides of a deal involving Enron, setting a precedent for future waivers when (contra-capitalist) conflicts of interest arose. In fact, Enron got a clause in the contract giving the company a right of first refusal on any of Wing's deals.

The Hawks-for-Wing drama was just the beginning of the fits and starts experienced by Ken Lay's cogeneration business. Hawks would soon be out and Wing back in, as explained in the next chapter.[26] But it hardly stopped there, as Wing would again exit and return as Enron's top power plant developer.

Ken Lay Takes Charge

Amid all the internal and external winds buffeting HNG/InterNorth, the one constant was Ken Lay. Sam Segnar, on the other hand, whose 18-month interim position was designed to ensure a smooth transition from two companies to one, would not last that long.

Segnar was the antithesis of Bill Strauss, yet Strauss picked him as his successor. Strauss's solid entrepreneurial instincts were complemented by his honest, value-driven, tell-it-like-it-is persona. His knowledge and sincerity inspired trust. But Segnar, particularly after he reached the top, acted genteel and was aloof—not endearing traits in a public company embodying midwestern American values.

It was Segnar who bought InterNorth's first corporate jet and liked to fly in it by himself. It was Segnar who restricted the 15th-floor executive dining room

---

25. As part of the buyout of his five-year agreement, which was but several months old, Wing agreed to a two-year consulting agreement for $265,000 a year (a raise), while keeping his perks and equity interest in new projects.

26. See chapter 3, pp. 168–69.

to members of his *office of the president*, each served by white-gloved waiters. It was Segnar who bought a dude ranch in Colorado for the corporation and aggressively entered into ventures far away from Omaha, including a stand-alone position-taking (speculative) oil-trading enterprise in Valhalla, New York. And now, in a reverse merger, Segnar had executed a grand exit strategy for himself.

In a commissioned history commemorating InterNorth's 50th anniversary in 1980, Segnar was described as "both a humble and a proud man who is nostalgic about his simple beginnings but openly fond of the finer things of life." He was variously described as "intense," "highly intelligent," and "not afraid to take chances." A fellow executive was quoted, "Segnar may not always be right, but he will give it a try."

Such descriptions may have been more than was wanted by Segnar and the company—and ditto for the university professor's colorful characterizations of the prior presidents of Northern, warts and all. The 300-page manuscript was not published as Segnar and Strauss had planned. The would-be book was locked away in a bank vault in Omaha and a sanitized 25-page illustrated booklet published instead.[27]

––––

In September, just two months after stockholders gave approval to the merger, Ken Lay invited the InterNorth-side directors to Houston to meet with the city's top business, civic, and political leaders. The reception did not go as planned. These directors were not interested in hobnobbing where they did not want their headquarters to be. While Lay, Segnar, and the HNG-side directors greeted the guests, the recalcitrant directors convened their own meeting to air complaints that Lay and Segnar were privately cutting deals, including one that would move the headquarters to Houston.

Given this discord, the full board engaged McKinsey & Company for a recommendation. The hot potato fell to Jeff Skilling, who had distinguished himself as the consulting firm's go-to energy analyst.

Meanwhile, things were not going well for Sam Segnar. The HNG-side directors had never warmed to the man who was heading for the door on day one of the merger. But Segnar was also losing support from his own board. His business judgment did not look as sharp as it did in "banner year" 1984. Coal was a bust, and the insurance that underlay InterNorth's purchase of Belco in 1983 was exposed as inadequate relative to the nationalized segment's book value. Segnar had also become increasingly distant in his interim role. He decided to have Lay report to LoChiano, not himself as originally set up by the board of directors.

––––

27. See Internet appendix 2.4, "The Suppressed History of InterNorth," at www
.politicalcapitalism.org/Book3/Chapter2/Appendix4.html.

Bill Strauss, still a board member, saw the estrangement and asked his fading protégé to meet one-on-one with the directors to clear things up. Segnar was not interested. Worse, he was getting defiant. When a key director called him to complain, Segnar erupted: "Well, God damn it, if you don't like it, buy me out!"

McKinsey's John Sawhill and Jeff Skilling flew to Omaha for HNG/Inter-North's November 1985 board meeting to recommend a headquarters. Just prior to their presentation, however, the board terminated Segnar, giving him a $2 million severance and stripping him of his titles and board position. A press release announced Segnar's resignation as chairman, CEO, and board director effective November 12, 1985, more than a year ahead of schedule. The fireworks continued when McKinsey made a case for replacing Omaha with Houston, which the board emotionally debated and voted down.

InterNorth-side directors were hopping mad about nearly everything.

Segnar should not have been surprised at his fate, but he was—or pretended to be. Just days earlier, he told New York security analysts, "A successful melding of two good companies into one great one is well under way." He also had reconfirmed HNG/InterNorth's intent to reduce the debt ratio to 55 percent from 63 percent by year-end 1986.

Ken Lay was promoted to CEO in addition to keeping his president's title. But Segnar's chairman title went to Bill Strauss, age 63, who reluctantly came out of retirement to serve out Segnar's term. Morale in Omaha was terrible; it was Strauss's job to field complaints and work with Lay for the duration of the transition. In fact, upon hearing about the board's decision to can Segnar, Lay urged Strauss to "pull the teams together" and "give me air cover in Omaha."

"Ken Lay is a most talented and capable chief executive for HNG/Inter-North," Strauss told the press. "While he'll be in charge of managing the company, I'll be on hand to provide advice, consultation, and guidance." Lay added how he was "delighted that Bill Strauss is aboard as chairman."

Strauss warned the board that stepping back in "was the last thing I wanted to do." Sure enough, he soon found himself in a no-win position. All Strauss heard were complaints about Houston and Ken Lay. Cooperation and teamwork, old InterNorth trademarks, were in short supply. Strauss felt concern when the board overruled Lay by choosing InterNorth's longtime auditor, Arthur Andersen, over HNG's Deloitte Haskins & Sells. The decision was driven by civic nepotism: Andersen would close its large Omaha office if not retained, and the InterNorth-side directors, led by Charles Harper, CEO of Omaha-based ConAgra, were civic minded and in little mood for compromise.

An important reason for using Deloitte for auditing and Andersen for consulting, as had been recommended to the board by CFO Keith Kern, was avoiding the conflict of interest involved in one firm's doing both. An auditor needed to judge a consultant's strategy at arm's length, a best-practice that would be sorely missed at Enron in the next decade. Robert Jaedicke, chairman of the audit committee, had made this very point, seconded by Georgiana Sheldon, at the January 1986 board meeting. Obviously, Ken Lay was not the only company leader ready to forsake such prudence.

Two-headed HNG/InterNorth was making compromises that would have long-lived consequences.

———

One Saturday morning, three senior Omaha-side executives visited Strauss at his house with disturbing allegations of illegal activity down in Houston. Leaving on vacation, Strauss asked his general counsel, Dean Wallace, to investigate and have a report on his desk upon his return.

Two weeks later, Strauss returned to find nothing. Strauss called Wallace. "Damn it, I asked you ...." But before he could finish, Wallace answered, "Bill, I can't find any illegalities!"

Realizing that he was being used to further the dissension between Omaha and Houston divisions, not lessen it, Strauss changed course. After meeting with every director to size up the situation, he met with Lay. After Ken reviewed all the problems he was having in both Omaha and Houston, Strauss asked about Ken's multimillion-dollar golden parachute that could be opened with just two words, *I resign*.

"I would disavow that contract," Strauss told Lay. "I don't know how to better get through to people." Open to the idea, Ken said he would talk to his wife and confidante, Linda. The next week, Ken Lay embraced the bourgeois virtue of perseverance, voided the provision, and announced to employees, "I am here for the long term."

With that, Strauss went to the February 1986 board meeting at the Florida Gas Building in Winter Park with a plan. Presiding as HNG/InterNorth's chairman, Strauss opened the meeting by asking the insiders (company executives who were not on the board) to leave the room before he began speaking. "There is a hell of a problem here, and I don't want the problem to get hold of things," he began.

> We've got deregulation ... [and] debt running out of our ears. I am worried about the survival of this company. And yet, I think we've got a lot of good people, and I am convinced that the only way to move forward is with one guy. And therefore, here is my letter of resignation.

Before the surprised directors even noticed, Bill Strauss was gone. Despite seven limousines at the building and seven private jets parked on the runway, no one even saw him leave. As it turned out, the man who minutes before had all the trappings as chairman of a Fortune 500 company had taken a cab to the airport and flown commercial back to Omaha, retired for good.

Reconvening, the board immediately and unanimously elected Ken Lay chairman, CEO, and president, effective February 11, 1986. When finally tracked down, the former chairman said, "My retirement is designed to strengthen Ken Lay's role as the chief executive officer of the company."

"I am a student of Bill Strauss," board member John Duncan would later recall. "He is my hero ... my total hero." But Strauss was not after applause. He just knew that a company could not serve two masters.[28]

Ken Lay's riveting ascent in the postmerger period needed support from more than just the HNG-side directors. The balance of power came from Arthur and Robert Belfer, InterNorth's largest stockholders. They liked Lay and were compassionate about how their former company's Peruvian nationalization had made his job harder. "We were immediately cognizant that Ken Lay was a dynamo, a very effective leader, and somebody who thought outside the box," Robert Belfer recalled. (Belfer remained loyal to the end and reportedly lost the largest sum of anyone in Enron's collapse: $2 billion.)

Lay also gained power from his and Segnar's choice for the two open board seats, made in accordance with the merger agreement. Each pick, however, was a step back from Lay's HNG appointments back in 1984. Both appointees were in their sixties and on the downside of their careers. Recently retired from government, Georgiana Sheldon had been a former FERC commissioner (1977–85). To critics, she was just a diversity choice who had a natural gas background. P. Scott Linder was a Florida industrialist sometimes mentioned for governor; his daughter was married to the brother of Ken's second wife, the former Linda Phillips Herrold. Linder, in fact, had arranged for Linda to come to Florida Gas Company, not long after Ken joined the company, where she would become Lay's secretary—and more. Sheldon and Linder together owned 212 shares of company stock, worth less than $10 thousand.[29] A bit of cronyism was evident, but this was now Ken Lay's show, even to the existing board.

Competitive Pipelining

Ken Lay's jab against spot-gas transportation service in the April 1, 1985, issue of *Natural Gas Week*, ironic given Enron's market leadership to come, was no joke. Gas prices were falling, which meant lower margins for HPL and less profit for HNG Oil Company. On the interstate side, lower spot prices were disrupting the market for traditional long-term service and leaving HNG's new pipelines with take-or-pay liabilities, a problem that Lay knew all too well from his Transco days. Higher prices and longer-term commitments from new buyers, multimonth to multiyear, were sought by HNG's chairman.

---

28. The worst species of this problem is one business plan governing two different companies (rather than one plan per company), as occurred with Houston Oil Company, the enterprise that founded HNG in 1925. See Bradley, *Edison to Enron*, pp. 378–85, 425.

29. Linder served for less than two years before becoming honorary director in 1987. He died in 1990. Sheldon did not stand for reelection in 1993 after two terms, at which time Wendy Gramm, the former head of the federal Commodity Futures Exchange Commission and wife of then Sen. Phil Gramm (R-TX), joined Enron's board.

Ken Lay knew that the future was direct marketing and unbundled transportation services, which had captured a third of the market in 1984 (two-thirds still being integrated wholesale service, whereby interstate pipelines bought, delivered, and sold gas at one bundled rate). It was Ken Lay the president of Transco who had helped create the Natural Gas Clearinghouse (NGC), a gas-brokerage firm that opened its doors in summer 1984. And now, Lay was cheerleading HNG/InterNorth's entry into gas marketing on a national scale.[30]

End users were clamoring to access cheaper spot gas, and federal regulators were eager to give it to them. FERC's proposal for open-access transportation in May 1985 put the new world on a fast track. Independent marketers would soon spring up, not only companies such as Hadson Gas Systems (founded by Vinod Dar) but also some nonprofits. One was Community Gas Acquisition, run by industry gadfly Edwin Rothschild, energy director for Citizens/Labor Energy Coalition. Another was Citizens Energy, founded in 1979 by Joseph Kennedy, which added natural gas to its oil offerings in response to open-access transportation.

Mandatory open access (MOA) was a well-developed theory for network industries (e.g., long-distance telephony). Lower-priced spot gas that just needed transportation to beat the price of bundled pipeline supply made the changeover economically attractive.[31] Regulators were driven by the idea despite encountering much more opposition than support from major segments within the natural gas industry (producers, pipelines, or distributors).

The Reagan administration's Department of Energy also advocated MOA for interstate gas transmission as procompetition and a step toward the free market.[32] Total deregulation, even the abolition of FERC (as proposed by the *Wall Street Journal* editorial board), was not in play either in Congress or in the executive branch.[33]

---

30. HNG joined NGC as an equity partner under Lay but sold its interest back to the company for a nominal fee the next year when NGC reorganized from a gas brokerage (working on commissions) to a gas marketer (taking title to the gas and profiting on price spreads). Lay's HNG, in other words, was a competitor of the new NGC.

31. The US Energy Information Administration predicted a natural gas price decline of $0.30 per MMBtu, about 15 percent. In fact, gas prices averaging $2.28/MMBtu in 1985 fell to $1.76/MMBtu a year later (23 percent)—and still more in 1987 as lower spot gas substituted for higher-priced pipeline-system supply.

32. Reformers drove MOA more than business interests, at least initially (see Internet appendix 1.2), which was a notable exception to most so-called reforms under political capitalism, as explained in Bradley, *Capitalism at Work*, chapters 5 and 6.

33. "Given the total success of oil deregulation, it's hard to believe that anyone today denies the wisdom of getting the government completely out of the energy business," the editorial read. "FERC should be decommissioned and a monument erected to remind everyone of the follies committed in the name of the 'energy crisis' in the 1970s."

In the same month that HNG and InterNorth merged, FERC proposed to transform interstate pipelines away from their merchant (bundled) role, leaving others to buy and sell the physical commodity for profit. The "Magna Carta of the natural gas industry," issued in October 1985 as FERC Order No. 436, set forth the rules and conditions for nondiscriminatory, open-access transportation. The voluntary order allowed a pipeline to elect to enter into the program.

Figure 2.5 Ideas have consequences. The advent of MOA for interstate natural gas pipelines was championed by a young FERC Commissioner, Oliver "Rick" Richard, who credits the 1984 book shown above for his inspiration and direction. Richard would go on to become CEO of Enron's Northern Natural Gas in 1988.

By terminating the FERC-approved special marketing programs and congruent Section 311 transportation on November 1, leaving the pipelines without a way to move spot gas, the 650-page mimeographed order carried a big stick.[34] "The Commission continues to take the position that the Final Rule is voluntary," an internal Enron memo concluded. "If, however, pipelines are to continue to have any flexibility in offering exchange and backhaul service, they must accept a blanket transportation certificate."

---

34. Section 311 transportation, part of the Natural Gas Policy Act of 1978, was the first and only way interstate pipelines could transport spot gas prior to open-access election. See Internet appendix 1.2, "Mandatory Open Access for Interstate Pipelines," at www .politicalcapitalism.org/Book3/Chapter1/Appendix2.html.

Business necessities and prior FERC policy had already pointed HNG/InterNorth's interstates toward transportation. Before FERC's order, Transwestern and FGT were carrying 40 percent and 20 percent transportation gas, respectively. NNGP was in this range as well. All three were negotiating with producers to release gas from unmarketable long-term contracts for carriage as cheaper, marketable spot gas, giving producers cash flow and pipelines take-or-pay relief. And HNG/InterNorth Gas Marketing (HIGMI, the renamed Northern Gas Marketing) was buying and selling gas, including for off-system delivery to New York, Massachusetts, and Pennsylvania.[35] Accordingly, HNG/InterNorth, both before and after the merger, supported FERC Order No. 436.

"We're looking at all our systems to see which ones [Order No. 436] makes sense for," reported Jim Rogers, executive vice president of HNG Interstate Company (Transwestern Pipeline and Florida Gas Transmission). It was a tough but practical choice. "There's no turning back," Rogers explained. As it turned out, Transwestern in 1986 was one of the very first interstates to open. Northern Natural followed the next year. FGT would not open until 1990, owing to unique competitive circumstances.[36]

The new regulatory politics went upstream too. The Independent Petroleum Association of America (IPAA), representing independent oil and gas producers, added legal staff to intervene in FERC proceedings and in pipeline rate cases. "Behind open transportation is the clear intent to drive prices down," Washington attorney Gordon Gooch told attendees at IPAA's mid-1986 meeting. In fact, the buyers' market for gas was the impetus for FERC to change the rules of the game to get (cheaper) spot gas to end users. "Open transportation is a two-edged sword," Gooch explained. "Order 436 will help some of you, but Order 436 will hurt some of you bad."

The other upstream producer group, Natural Gas Supply Association (NGSA), founded in 1965 during the price-control era and representing integrated oil companies with sizeable gas reserves, was also lawyering to make open access producer friendly (relative to marketers and pipelines). NGSA would be heard from again when renewable-energy mandates emerged to back out gas in the next decade.

———

Southern California jumped the gun on the new world of spot gas and transportation, which put Transwestern in the middle of the commotion. For a quarter

———

35. "The key role of [HIGMI]," Dan Dienstbier explained to employees, "is to complement, not compete with, the individual operating pipeline companies. It's obvious that if we do not clearly define the responsibilities between the three operating companies and the new marketing company we've set up, we run the risk of less than optimum results."

36. See chapter 6, pp. 257–59.

century, Transwestern's gas sold itself under its 91 percent minimum-bill contract with Southern California Gas Company (SoCalGas), the local distribution company serving Los Angeles and surrounds and, indirectly, San Diego. Then came FERC Order No. 380 (May 1984), which prohibited pipelines from receiving revenue for gas not delivered and sold—a rebuke of Transwestern's minimum-bill. In the face of such uncertainty, Texas Eastern Corporation bailed out, selling Transwestern to high-bidder HNG.[37]

FERC Opinion No. 238 on July 1, 1985, made it official: Transwestern no longer could operate under the prior arrangement. Instead of 91 percent, SoCalGas under state-level (California Public Utilities Commission) instruction could choose to nominate as little as 60 percent of Transwestern's contract quantity (450 of 750 MMcf/d). Needing gas just as before, SoCalGas could turn to cheaper spot gas transported on Transwestern.

With El Paso's sales contract already cut back to 60 percent, SoCalGas purchased 650 MMcf/d of auction gas for July delivery. Overnight, Southern California became the nation's epicenter for spot gas and related interstate transportation.

Transwestern's newly formed spot-gas affiliate, Pacific Atlantic Marketing Inc. (PAMI), successfully submitted a bid into SoCalGas's new program, which allowed Transwestern to deliver as much volume as before.[38] But the difference was price: SoCalGas bought spot gas at $2.73/MMBtu, 15 percent below the rate for Transwestern's system supply.

This was complicated, risky business. To compete against other gas-supply options available to SoCalGas, and in particular against gas packages delivered off of El Paso, which also served Southern California, Transwestern:

1. Sent *force majeure* notices to system producers, requiring them to reduce prices or be shut in by a zero nomination at the wellhead;

2. Arranged releases whereby system producers could assign their gas to PAMI for spot-gas pricing;

3. Bid PAMI gas, as well as other spot-gas packages from HNG/InterNorth affiliates and outside marketers, to flow on the pipeline each month;

4. Set transportation rates so that the delivered price of spot gas was competitive enough to be accepted in SoCalGas's bid process.

---

37. See chapter 1, pp. 86–88.

38. Each interstate pipeline company began with its own marketing arm. Before consolidating as Enron Gas Marketing in 1986, the HNG/InterNorth-related affiliates were Panhandle (Houston Pipe Line), PAMI (Transwestern), and Northern Gas Marketing (Northern Natural Gas). Effective June 30, 1986, with the sale of half of Florida Gas Transmission to Sonat Inc., marketing off FGT would shift to Citrus, an independent marketer.

If this were done right, Transwestern-qua-transporter could make as much money as it did before under FERC ratemaking. Further, if Transwestern could design its rate case creatively—assigning its fixed costs for automatic recovery and setting maximum interruptible rates that rewarded higher volumes than forecast—it could make *more* than before. (It would, in spades.) But the downside was the producer-contract reformation to get to the new world. Transwestern represented the majority of HNG/InterNorth's take-or-pay costs, estimated at $125 million at year-end 1985, a figure that would soon balloon.

In just months, SoCalGas was managing a 1 Bcf/d spot market, equivalent to 2 percent of all the gas consumed in the United States. Dozens of companies were bidding into their program, creating intense gas-on-gas competition between and within El Paso and Transwestern. Nothing like this had ever been seen since at least the passage of the Natural Gas Act of 1938.

In Washington, DC, SoCalGas representatives explained their program to both House and Senate energy committees. Compared to higher-priced system supply before FERC Opinion No. 238, spot gas was saving SoCalGas and its customers $10 million a month. Price-discounted (pipeline) system supply created more savings, given the pressure that spot-gas prices put on pipeline tariffs.

Transwestern in 1985 was running full and playing the new game better than its rival El Paso. But nothing was automatic about this. A hand-picked, premium management team had been assembled, given that the handoff of Transwestern from Texas Eastern to HNG had come with 500 field personnel—but no senior management or midlevel analytic capability. Transwestern simply had not needed strategic thinking in the cushy minimum-bill era.[39] (As mentioned in chapter 1, prime talent for Transwestern came from the Winter Park office of Florida Gas Transmission, one of the few pipelines in the country to have grown up around transportation gas.)

Stan Horton was one of the first to grapple with Transwestern, an experience he described as being "as challenging as you can imagine." While he dealt with fires from below, help atop came from new hires Jim Rogers and Cheryl Foley, as mentioned in chapter 1.

Marketing was next. Rogers hired Clark Smith, El Paso's loaned executive to Natural Gas Clearinghouse. Smith had just returned to the El Paso headquarters to work on the July 1985 inaugural spot-gas bids to SoCalGas. Only weeks later, he was in Houston helping arrange the August spot-gas bids for Transwestern. Quick thinking and a doer, Smith, age 31, proved to be the right man at the right time as Transwestern began to morph from a merchant pipeline company to a spot-gas transporter.

---

39. For further discussion about Transwestern as a major success stories of the Order No. 436 era, see Internet appendix 2.5, "Transwestern Pipeline: 'Enron's Laboratory' amid Regulatory Change," at www.politicalcapitalism.org/Book3/Chapter2/Appendix5.html.

For Transwestern analytics, Lay and Rogers landed Cathy Abbott, the head of research for the interstate pipeline trade group, Interstate Natural Gas Association of America (INGAA). With a master's degree from Harvard University's Kennedy School of Government, Abbott hired similarly credentialed Steve Harvey, whom she had groomed at INGAA. Both Abbott and Harvey would have long careers in the gas industry, with and after Enron.

All this was quite a change for a pipeline that a year before did not have analytic capacity. It was one of the biggest analytical buildups in the history of the formerly staid, regulated industry, if not the most.[40]

Positioning for the Future

The Peruvian nationalization was not the only problem plaguing the merger. Prices for natural gas and gas liquids were falling. The pipelines faced take-or-pay liabilities, given that they were transporting cheaper spot gas in place of (producer-obligated) system supply in order to retain fuel-switchable industrial and power plant customers.

In September 1985, Lay imposed a hiring freeze. Two months later, a company-wide reorganization resulted in several hundred layoffs. This was not what Segnar or Lay had forecast just months before. Nonessential assets—such as Segnar's Granby Ranch playground—had to be sold. Gutsy-pricey imprudence was taking its toll.

HNG/InterNorth closed the books on 1985 with a net loss of $79 million—very disappointing for a corporation sporting $10 billion in assets and more than 11,000 employees. The damage was done by fourth quarter's $197 million loss. The Peruvian write-off was the big item, but there were other charges, led by $55 million to cover early-retirement, severance, and relocation costs, and $10 million to complete the InterNorth side's 1982 exit from the coal business. On the positive side, Peoples Natural Gas, InterNorth's old retail gas-distribution arm, was sold for $250 million, registering a $42 million profit.

As 1985 drew to a close, Ken Lay wrote his annual year-end memo to employees. But before getting to his holiday wishes, the letter called for pulling together to create a stronger company. An "unusually challenging" year lay ahead, given the uncertain price environment and the regulatory transformation of the interstate gas pipeline industry, Lay explained. Open jobs would be decided by merit, as promised, not by which side of the merger the candidate came from. "We all have the opportunity to create the most successful enterprise of our type in the country, but this will only happen if we all commit to work together as a single team to realize our enormous potential," he concluded.

---

40. The author joined Abbott and Harvey at HNG Interstate in September 1985, remaining at Enron until December 3, 2001. Another Abbott hire at INGAA was R. Skip Horvath, who would go on to head NGSA in Washington, DC.

To the Shareholder:

The year 1985 brought dramatic change to our Corporation.

Most significant was the merger in June of Houston Natural Gas Corporation and InterNorth, Inc. which created one of the largest and most strategically located natural gas pipeline systems in the nation. In essence, we joined two successful corporations, which had been pursuing similar strategies, and created an even stronger corporation better positioned to deal with an increasingly competitive business environment.

Respectfully submitted,

Kenneth L. Lay
Chairman,
President and
Chief Executive Officer

HNG
INTERNORTH
1985 Annual Report   *Managing change*

Figure 2.6 In just under 10 months, HNG/InterNorth president and COO Ken Lay became chairman, president, and CEO. "The present business climate provides no margin for error," Lay sternly stated on the opening page of the *1985 Annual Report*, but his penchant for overspending and going first class belied his prudent words.

Pulling Together in '86, the subtitle of a company brochure released in the first quarter of the new year, reviewed the current situation and what had to be done to get the new company on track. "There have been setbacks," Lay explained. "To say that we're facing a tough year is an understatement." He continued:

> My number one priority in 1986 is to get our organization settled and get everybody concentrating virtually 100 percent on their jobs. I want to put the discussion, conflict, uncertainty and rumors behind us. We must all devote our full energies to what we are paid for, and that is making money for our shareholders.... My second priority in 1986 is to pay down a significant amount of our debt.... In our current situation, we have no room for error. We have to be the best—in our own jobs and in the industry.

Annual cash flow that had been expected to be $1 billion in 1985 would come in near $600 million. But Ken Lay had good people in place to run what he described as "the making of the very best diversified energy company in the country." A rebound in energy prices would do wonders for normalcy and growth. Further, there was great potential in natural gas marketing with what was decided at the Granby conference.

Nervousness surrounded HNG/InterNorth. But Ken Lay was confident, even hubristic. The 1985 annual report audaciously set out a vision to "substantially enhance shareholder value by becoming America's most successful energy company."

The physical assets were there, certainly, although tagged by a high debt load. But Lay saw the company's *intellectual* capital—aka its smarts—as its trump card. "The Corporation is fortunate in having a management team that ranks as one of the most talented and creative in the energy industry," Lay posited. "Given the current business environment, we believe this is one of the Corporation's greatest assets."

A New Name

HNG/InterNorth was a two-company moniker. A wholly new name was needed to leave the past and unify. That job went to Lippincott & Margulies in New York City, considered the best in the business, having invented the most familiar word in energy marketing—Exxon. Ken Lay wanted something like that and paid millions of dollars for what Lippincott called a "crash program" with "about 400 serious [name] candidates."

Several months later, the answer came in three syllables—*Enteron. En* stood for energy and the environment, *ter* connoted international (but also interstate), and *on* was the trailer that worked so well instead of *co* for oil majors Exxon and Chevron. Its industrial definition was "a pipeline system transmitting nourishment." A lot of marketing could grow up around it.

The new name was announced the week after Ken Lay was named CEO in Orlando. Seizing the PR moment, Lay heralded it as a new beginning: "The merger joined two great energy companies into one, and a new name to illustrate a new beginning could not come at a more appropriate time." The InterNorth side was upset that HNG had received first billing in the prior name, and some thought that the new name rang toward InterNorth, not HNG.

But this was cosmetics, and the cosmetics got bad instantly when an embarrassment came to light. The trade press discovered something that mighty Lippincott & Margulies had apparently missed: "Enteron" was a dictionary term for the alimentary canal—right down to the anus. Ken Lay's company was all about natural gas. There were hearty laughs all across the industry.

The Houston brass did not find it funny. Sentiment developed to keep the name and ride out the storm. Besides, with the printers busy with the new name, it would be a six-figure hit to stop the presses. But Ken Lay had the ultimate vote. Virtually alone, he ordered Lippincott & Margulies to come up with a new name or HNG/InterNorth would remain.

A week later, a simple and obvious solution was found. Dropping the "ter," left short-and-sweet *Enron*. Ken Lay liked it. It was major league, akin to the moniker of mighty Exxon, the company Ken had worked for and had the audacity to believe he could eventually rival and even surpass. Also, it would be good not to confront the meaning of Enteron come every bad turn. Lay knew marketing and had made the right move.

HNG/InterNorth was replaced by Enron Corporation, complete with the common stock symbol ENE, by vote at the annual shareholders meeting held April 10, 1986. But this was gloss. The dividend was frozen, and things were tight all around. The debt-laden company had to create new earnings to work its way out of its postmerger hole.[41]

41. The new logo was ENRON CORP, with a congruent slash in each "O" to signify the joining of two pipeline companies.

3

Foundations

Effective February 11, 1986, Ken Lay was elected chairman of HNG/Inter-North, joining his titles of president and CEO. The Fortune 100 company was solidly his, although corporate raider Irwin Jacobs was still in the picture. In April, stockholders approved a new name, Enron Corporation (Enron Corp, with no period, for marketing purposes); a month later, Houston was declared company headquarters.

Six months before, McKinsey's Jeff Skilling had laid out the reasons to replace Omaha with Houston. The InterNorth-dominated board unanimously rejected the move, but with the handwriting on the wall, some of InterNorth's operating divisions were migrating south. Still, Omaha was home for cogeneration developer Northern Natural Resources Company, wholly owned Northern Natural Gas Pipeline (NNGP), and the joint ventures Northern Border Pipeline and Trailblazer Pipeline.[1]

In May 1986, J. M. "Mick" Seidl was promoted to president and chief operating officer, giving Enron a formal one and two executive. Lay, who put a premium on credentials and brainpower, was pleased with the Harvard PhD and former Stanford professor. The affable Seidl was a close personal friend as well—and always would be.

---

1. Enron's joint ventures and miscellaneous assets are reviewed in Internet appendix 2.2, "HNG/InterNorth: Joint Ventures, Miscellaneous Assets, and Sales," at www .politicalcapitalism.org/Book3/Chapter2/Appendix2.html. The decision to make Houston headquarters is discussed in Internet appendix 3.1, "Houston Headquarters," at www .politicalcapitalism.org/Book3/Chapter3/Appendix1.html.

A New Home

Some much-needed celebration came in July when employees moved from the aging 28-story Houston Natural Gas Building on Travis Street, the company home since 1967, to the shiny new 50-floor Enron Building on 1400 Smith Street. The several-block move in downtown Houston made a world of difference. The new home was not a monument, like the art deco Transco Tower. But Enron's mirrored, racetrack-shaped structure was modernistic, fully outfitted, and reconfigured to house a company cafeteria (*Energizer*), an underground health facility (*Body Shop*), and executive dining rooms. The multilevel 50th floor housed executive suites, a cavernous boardroom, and meeting rooms. Everything was stately, the best that Gensler, one of the world's top interior architectural firms, could design.

Reducing costs was a priority, but Ken Lay's pride would not let him moderate Enron's first-class image. His business model demanded the *best* for his *brightest*. Only Tenneco and Transco in energy-mecca Houston offered the full range of headquarter amenities that Enron employees would now enjoy. Enron's field workers could only wonder about—and question—company priorities when hearing about the Body Shop's stationary bikes with television screens.

The Enron Building was advertised as the region's most secure facility next to NASA. Magnetic cards were required to gain entrance on each floor. Everything was user friendly—almost. The salt and pepper shakers were missing when the Energizer opened, replaced by a seasoning mix atop each table. That quirk had come straight from the top. Ultra-health-conscious Ken Lay, the picture of health, was following a strict diet, part of a daily regimen that included jogging or some other strenuous activity. (Lay, unbeknownst to his employees, had a heart condition.[2]) But the salt and pepper would soon reappear. There were too many complaints, and Ken Lay was dining elsewhere.

———

Pomp aside, Enron was in a tight financial position. Much had changed since May 1985, when Sam Segnar and Lay confidently predicted an annual cash flow of a billion dollars or more to expeditiously retire debt. A year after the merger, indebtedness was still above $4 billion, leaving Enron's debt-to-capital ratio above 70 percent—versus 46 percent prior to the combination. Bankers did not like ratios above 50 percent and preferred below 40 percent. Bill Matthews had HNG's ratio near 25 percent when he was fired in 1984 for his passivity.

Deteriorating industry conditions in first-quarter 1986 prompted a stern-faced Lay to declare in the *1985 Annual Report*: "The present business climate provides no margin for error." Energy markets were soft, particularly in Texas,

———

2. Lay's heart problems would not become public until his death from heart failure at age 64, just weeks after his fateful trial concluded in mid-2006.

where Houston Pipe Line's margins were a fraction of those enjoyed in the Herring/Matthews heyday. Also, a regulatory restructuring of the interstate gas industry by FERC left Transwestern Pipeline, and to a lesser extent Florida Gas Transmission and Northern Natural, with growing take-or-pay claims from producers. Whereas Lay had earlier predicted the dissipation of the gas surplus, he now saw a multiyear gas bubble. "The most thoughtful forecasts we look at show an annual surplus continuing out for the next five years," he told a Houston audience in early 1986. "Changes in OPEC philosophy threaten significant downward pressure on oil prices as well."

Ken Lay had to be the consummate leader. The operating units had to have superior management. Everyone had to perform. (*Having the most fun* was now deemphasized.) The bankers were nervous; investors, impatient. The merger had done nothing to get rid of a block of dissidents, led by Jacobs, who were increasing their stake with the intent, if history were any guide, of gaining board seats and restructuring the company.

A *Business Week* profile on HNG/InterNorth in February 1986—Jo Ellen Davis's "A Mega-Pipeline with a Massive Identity Crisis"—was less than flattering. Playing off the fact that the company's stock was down nearly one-third from its (speculation-induced) 52-week high, the article included negative comments about the merger, complete with a photo of a goonish-looking Lay with his fist in the air. The insinuation was that the aggressive CEO had bitten off more than he could chew.

Ken Lay resented that article. Challenges abounded, but he had never failed. Good ideas, hard work, positive thinking, and blessings from above had always spelled success, from his preteen jobs in rural Missouri to leadership positions in college to successful tenures in business and government after college—and then at top executive positions with Continental Resources Company, Transco Energy Company, and now the company soon to be Enron.[3] HNG had had a strong first quarter prior to the InterNorth merger, vindicating his early moves at the company.

Business failure only brought back memories of the events that had overwhelmed his father, Omer Lay. Ken swore to prove the naysayers wrong—and to improve his look. From now on he would wear contact lenses, not glasses. Instead of emotional displays, the photo ops would portray a quiet, confident man, one perceived to have superior vision and business acumen. Image was much.

---

3. On Lay's early life and career, see Bradley, *Edison to Enron*, pp. 20, 291–95, 310–12. See "Kenneth L. Lay: A Chronology," pp. 677–88.

Figure 3.1 The Enron Building (upper right) was a big step up from the HNG Building and a world apart from Ken Lay's childhood in Rush Hill, Missouri. The challenges of 1986 brought out some criticism of Ken Lay, including an article in *Business Week* (upper left).

Ken Lay was not about to scale back his expectations. "We intend to outperform our industry in bad times and good times," he responded to a complaint at the annual shareholders meeting that Enron was a "beached whale." "Our goal," he wrote to shareholders in spring 1986, "is to substantially enhance shareholder value by becoming America's most successful energy company."

Still, this marked a retreat from the braggadocio of nine months earlier, when Segnar and Lay had tagged their creation *America's Premier Energy Company*. Since then, strongman Alan García of Peru had nationalized the heart of Belco Petroleum, energy prices had collapsed, and the costs of consolidating two feuding companies had mounted. What had been a claim was now a goal. And even this vision would be forgotten amid a tough 1986, which included the debt-reducing sale of half of Florida Gas Transmission to Sonat, an Alabama-based interstate natural gas pipeline company.[4] Such a move was not

---

4. The partial sale of Florida Gas left operational control with Enron, preserving this part of the hub-and-spoke synergies of its multi-pipeline system, as well as generating income from operational fees.

what Ken Lay had planned when he had bought Florida Gas less than two years before.

In spring 1987, Ken Lay unveiled what officially became the first of his four visions for Enron: *to become the premier integrated natural gas company in North America*. This goal had more focus, applicability, and staying power than *America's premier energy company*. The new goal better reflected the company's congruent businesses in natural gas pipelines, exploration and production (primarily gas), liquid fuels, and gas-fired cogeneration. With a 14 percent market share of US gas consumption (as measured by volumes handled), this vision was a fitting moniker.

Yet just months later, Lay's "singular mission"—not to mention the company itself—was nearly derailed by oil-trading losses at Enron Oil Corporation, a stand-alone unit headquartered in Valhalla, New York. As described in the next chapter, deft work by an emergency team from Enron Liquid Fuels would save the day. But the chilling crisis—one that should never have reached its tipping point, given prior documented activity in the unit—was sanitized and tossed down the memory hole. Ken Lay had always been successful—even when it wasn't quite true.

The Valhalla scandal was "unforeseen," Enron's *1987 Annual Report* reported. And with that fresh start, Enron would finally get its footing and begin to excel in a difficult industry environment. Thus began a period, the subject of chapters 5 and 6, that would (with Valhalla forgotten) make Dr. Kenneth L. Lay *the* leading man of his industry.

The New Team

The merger was less than a year old, but many InterNorth veterans were gone. Chairman Sam Segnar had been terminated by the board less than 6 months into his planned 18-month tenure. Bill Strauss, InterNorth's storied CEO, kindly came out of retirement and gracefully exited—all within 3 months. W. G. Thompson, who began as chief financial officer overseeing Deputy CFO Keith Kern, was replaced by the HNG-side Kern. Gordon Severa, originally overseeing petrochemicals, liquids, and exploration and production, briefly became chief of staff before leaving. Mick Seidl was now in charge of all that.

Roland Beasley, who had taken over liquids and petrochemicals from Severa, was now gone. Rocky LoChiano—EVP, asset redeployment—stayed a year before his function was assumed by his longtime deputy, Lou Potempa, who had painfully negotiated the one-sided merger with John Wing just a year before.

Dan Gardner, another InterNorth mainstay, survived 1985 but left the next year. Howard Hawks, who was chosen over John Wing to run cogeneration, was gone a year later. One of the few InterNorth survivors to last past 1986 was John Harding, the head of Enron International, an apparently high-flying subsidiary that turned out to be anything but.

Sam Segnar was right: InterNorth was buying not only businesses but also Ken Lay and his team. But what Lay got from InterNorth management was Dan Dienstbier, who was immediately appointed head of natural gas operations, the heart and soul of the company, and who brought with him the youthful Ron Burns and the makings of the best natural gas marketing team in America. Ken Lay had been instrumental in forming Natural Gas Clearinghouse back at Transco and had HNG become its fifth partner in 1984. But Lay's real entrance into gas marketing, which was destined to be Enron's defining division, began with InterNorth.

There was shakeout on the HNG side too. The initial HNG/InterNorth organization chart in June 1985 found some veterans a rung or two down the ladder. Jim Walzel, the COO of HNG, soon resigned, as did Richard Alsup, who had been HNG's general counsel before Richard Kinder came aboard. Jim Harrison, another mainstay, promoted to chief administrative office by Lay back in September 1984, left seven months later. Mel Sweatman, who took over for Walzel as head of Houston Pipe Line, left in January 1986, ceding the reins to Gerald Bennett, a rising talent hired by Walzel and Lay prior to the merger.

All this was a second remaking for HNG. Only a few from the Bill Matthews era were left. Gary Orloff was moving ahead in legal. C. O. "Ted" Collins, a Matthews hire, headed the newly consolidated Enron Oil & Gas Company. Another survivor was Don Gullquist, vice president and treasurer, who in 1987 would find himself party to a corporate imbroglio (the Valhalla trading scandal) that could scarcely have been imagined in the Herring/Matthews era at HNG.

The big three behind Ken Lay were Mick Seidl, President and COO; Dan Dienstbier, EVP and President, Gas Pipeline Group; and Richard Kinder, EVP, Law and Administration. Keith Kern continued as EVP and CFO.[5] So did, among others, Ron Knorpp (SVP, Chief Information Officer) and Joe Hillings (SVP, Federal Government Affairs). Two corporate vice presidents who would buck the changeover and have long Enron careers were Robert Hermann running the tax department and Jim Barnhart directing administration. It was Barnhart whom Selby Sullivan had trained the hard way back at Florida Gas Company a decade before.[6]

---

5. As shown in Figure 3.2, senior management (upper right, clockwise) comprised John M. "Mick" Seidl, Kenneth L. Lay, Dan L. Dienstbier, Keith D. Kern, and Richard D. Kinder. The board of directors (top row, left to right) were James J. Renier, John H, Duncan, Herbert S. Winokur Jr., William F. Dinsmore, Charles A. LeMaistre, Ronald W. Roskens, Charls E. Walker, Dienstbier, and John M. Harbert III; (bottom row, left to right) Robert A. Belfer, Seidl, Arthur Belfer, Lay, Georgiana H. Sheldon, Joe H. Foy. Not pictured: Robert K. Jaedicke and P. Scott Linder. (Four honorary directors, all from the InterNorth side, were Edward J. Brock, Russell E. Dougherty, David L. Grove, and Thomas S. Nurnberger.)

6. For a discussion of Enron employees previously hired at Florida Gas Company, including Barnhart, see Bradley, *Edison to Enron*, pp. 290, 302–4, 309.

Figure 3.2 The *Houston Chronicle* documented the management changes at HNG/
InterNorth compared to the year before. Only 1 of 5 senior executives and 6 of 17 board
directors had come from InterNorth. Meanwhile, HNG's senior management prior to Ken
Lay's arrival had all but departed.

Three key divisional executives were Gerald Bennett, intrastate gas pipelines; Jim Rogers, interstate gas pipelines; and Mike Muckleroy, liquids. They
would be joined in 1987 by a new strong leader for Enron Oil & Gas Company,
Forrest Hoglund. With burgeoning talent in the nonregulated gas-marketing
division—beginning with Ron Burns and continuing with two veteran hires
from Transco, Claude Mullendore and John Esslinger—Ken Lay could say that
he had the best management team in the natural gas industry. What Enron was
creating was unprecedented in a sector that had long been subject to sleepy
management, owing in part to inhibiting state and federal regulation.

The rank-and-file was changing too. By first-quarter 1986, 500 employees
had retired early or been severed, and 400 had left for other reasons. An additional 750 jobs were slated for elimination by the first anniversary of the merger.
Still, quality new hires were coming in. From top to bottom, Enron's aggressiveness, coupled with Ken Lay's reputation, were attracting a new level of expertise and brainpower to the cause. By first-quarter 1987, Enron's head count of
7,200 was 18 percent below that of late 1985.

Enduring 1986

The big loss taken in fourth-quarter 1985 was intended to clear the decks for a strong new year. Although replicating the half-billion dollars that HNG and InterNorth earned in 1984 was a pipe dream, several hundred million dollars were in sight for 1986.

HNG/InterNorth earned $80 million in first-quarter 1986. Although 25 percent below the prior-year quarter because of lost Peruvian income and lower energy prices, cash flow was supporting the dividend and retiring some debt. But this would be the last profitable quarter from continuing operations for the year. The culprit was a precipitous fall in oil prices that would bring down values of both natural gas and gas liquids.

In late 1985, Saudi Arabia announced that it would no longer cut back its crude production to support prices but instead would sustain its market share. This meant a price war; oil prices had to fall until demand met supply—or output was pared by some combination of well abandonments and shut-ins.

The new reality hit in March 1986, when the spot (immediate delivery, short-term) price of West Texas Intermediate crude oil, which had been $28 per barrel several months before, fell below $10 per barrel. Prices for natural gas and related liquids, competing against oil products in many US markets, fell sharply. Averaged over the year, composite US fossil-fuel prices would be one-third below that of 1985, bad news for Enron as for virtually every upstream and midstream energy company.

Image-driven Ken Lay would not show his sweat, much less panic. "I'm having a lot of fun with this," he would say as 1986 wound down. The eternal optimist, it seemed, could do what few others could—walk through thunderstorms and not appear wet. Behind the scenes, though, Lay froze salaries for the 60 highest-paid employees, and tough-guy Rich Kinder formed a company-wide cost-reduction committee.

But more was needed, given that Moody Investors Service was about to lower Enron's credit rating from low investment grade to high speculative grade (junk bonds). Noting that "debt leverage has not improved," Moody's predicted that "neither cash flow nor capital structure will show substantial improvement in the near term." In contrast to later years, the credit agencies were not beholden to Enron or Ken Lay, and his pricey-gutsy purchases were taking their toll.

Operating Results

Enron's three divisions—natural gas transportation, exploration and production, and gas liquids—sagged in the new price environment.[7] The Gas Pipeline

---

7. These divisions at year-end 1986 accounted for 98.5 percent of Enron's assets, the residual being joint interests in cogeneration projects and small foreign energy ventures. At year-end 1985, with petrochemicals still in the mix, the three divisions had accounted for more than 90 percent of total assets.

Group (GPG) lost volume to residual fuel oil and had to discount transportation rates from the FERC-set maximum to be competitive. At the same time, take-or-pay liabilities increased for Enron's three interstates, given fewer takes of system supply and lower prices paid at the wellhead. Year-end 1985 claims of $125 million, which had been expected to rise to $395 million in 1986, would end the year at $750 million. Still, after establishing a financial reserve for expected losses, well-managed GPG earned $191 million in 1986, only 9 percent below the previous year.

Enron Oil & Gas (EOG), advertised as the second-largest domestic independent oil and gas producer in the United States, reported a slight loss in 1986, although cash flow was strongly positive.[8] A nearly 50 percent increase in gas production—the result of an active, successful drilling program—negated most of the 40 percent drop in gas prices. EOG pruned its workforce by one-fourth. Operations were consolidated, and headquarters was moved from Midland to Houston. All awaited a price rebound.

Enron Liquid Fuels reported a yearly loss with lower revenues from ethane, propane, butane, and natural gasoline sales, as well as lower margins for gathering and transporting crude oil and petroleum products. Mike Muckleroy was aggressively consolidating the operations of two companies, but there was just too much supply relative to demand for profitability.

Overall, Enron recorded a net operating loss in 1986 of $81 million. But asset sales ("earnings from discontinued operations") produced a $139 million gain, which allowed Enron to report net profits of $78 million in a depression year for upstream-to-midstream oil companies. Transco lost $23 million in 1986, and its problems were just beginning. Still, *Enron's net income was a mere 15 percent of what HNG and InterNorth had reported separately just two years before*.[9] Under federal public-utility regulation, GPG's rate base was entitled to several hundred million dollars alone.[10]

What rescued Enron's year was the $600 million sale of Enron Chemical Company to National Distillers and Chemical Corporation, netting $121 million after taxes. Falling energy prices substantially helped the company previously known as Norchem, which had been earning about $25 million per year (before capital costs). Sharply lower fuel expense increased margins for polyolefin

---

8. EOG's loss turned into a positive cash flow by adding back depreciation and depletion expenses, which were sizeable for exploration and production by independents under US tax law.

9. Two years later, earnings for 1986 would be restated at $557 million (versus $78 million), reflecting a reduction in deferred income taxes from a tax-law change in 1986.

10. A 10 percent return on $4 billion—the approximate depreciated original cost (book value) of Northern Natural Pipeline, Florida Gas Transmission, and Transwestern Pipeline—would be $400 million.

resins and other chemicals used primarily for making plastics. But going forward, a cash generator was lost, and Ken Lay no longer had this countercyclical division. Enron was now betting on higher energy prices to benefit all divisions excepting Liquids.

The income statement showed no effect from Enron's other major asset sale in 1986: 50 percent of Florida Gas Transmission Company sold to Sonat Inc., for $360 million. Ken Lay had paid a pretty penny for the pipeline 15 months before, and the general market for energy assets had weakened. But on the strength of Florida Gas's expansion plans, Enron was able to recoup half of its investment. The break-even deal removed debt from the balance sheet, reducing interest expense and making almost everyone a tad less nervous. (A contemplated half-sale of Transwestern was not consummated.)

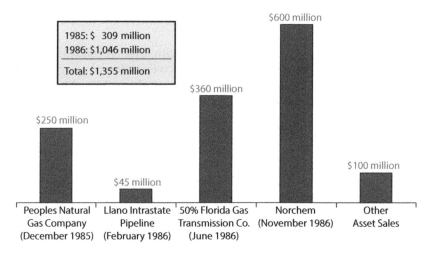

Figure 3.3 More than $1.3 billion in asset sales in 18 months after the HNG and Inter-North merger left Enron's debt-to-capital ratio little changed, given other developments. Not until 1992 did this ratio fall below 50 percent, still above where the two companies were on a consolidated basis at year-end 1984.

The appreciated presale value of Enron Chemical in 1986 was a rare bright spot in a tough year. Another positive—or so it seemed—was Enron Oil Corporation (EOC), the oil-trading division of Enron International; EOC recorded earnings of $27 million in 1986. What could be better than a profitable subsidiary requiring virtually no capital investment? Enron's *1986 Annual Report* pictured EOC president Lou Borget and explained: "The volatile oil prices experienced during 1986 benefitted earnings of this group as profits are generated on margins and on the skill of the trader, not on the absolute price of the product." Was this Enron's answer to price volatility in either direction? Or was it too good to be true? Ken Lay and Enron would soon find out.

Innovative Pipelining

"During 1986," Enron's annual report trumpeted, "[our natural gas] pipelines led the industry in the creation of innovative ways to serve widely different markets." Necessity inspiring innovation, Enron's four major systems (Houston Pipe Line, Transwestern Pipeline, Florida Gas Transmission, Northern Natural Pipeline) and four joint-venture lines (Northern Border, Trailblazer Pipeline, Texoma Pipeline, Oasis Pipeline) collectively increased their market share in a year when natural gas usage fell 6 percent across the United States. Enron's 37,000-mile network delivered 14 percent of the US total, up from 13 percent the year before. Still, this relatively good performance could not mask a bleak fact: Gas demand had not been this low since the 1960s when Robert Herring received HNG's baton from Bus Wimberly.

HNG's previously segregated interstate and intrastate units were consolidated in late 1986 (the second consolidation that year) to create the Gas Pipeline Group, headed by James E. ("Jim") Rogers. Gerald Bennett, still over HPL and Bammel storage, now reported to Rogers, as did the three interstate pipeline heads and Ron Burns, now executive vice president, gas transportation.

In early 1987, the interstates integrated as Enron Gas Pipeline Operating Company. The "single networked system," as described in Enron's *Annual Report*, was an industry first. Centralized supply procurement was introduced with Enron Gas Supply Company, headed by Transco-ex Claude Mullendore. To deal with FERC, a Regulatory & Competitive Analysis group was formed.

"This consolidated management and business philosophy allows Enron's separate natural gas businesses to use their combined strengths to greater advantage," the annual report stressed. Still, as compared to hub-and-spoke organization, which itself might have been "more theory than fact," integration and centralization were hype and hope. The pipelines were not built as a system, and federal open-access banned intracompany preference.

The challenge for each pipeline was to stay fully utilized between sales and transportation, maximizing revenue and minimizing take-or-pay liabilities. But with national gas demand down 20 percent from 1979, owing in large part to federal policies favoring coal in electrical generation, the natural gas transmission grid was overbuilt just about everywhere. The result was intense gas-on-gas *and* pipe-on-pipe competition, not to mention interfuel rivalry (oil-to-gas, purchased power-to-gas, and so forth).

It was showdown at the pipeline corral. FERC Order No. 436, effective November 1, 1985, ended the special marketing programs (SMPs) that many interstates had used to substitute (spot-gas) transportation for their (noncompetitive) system sales.[11] Electing open-access transportation under

---

11. See chapter 2, p. 139; and Bradley, *Edison to Enron*, pp. 339, 344, 347, 348.

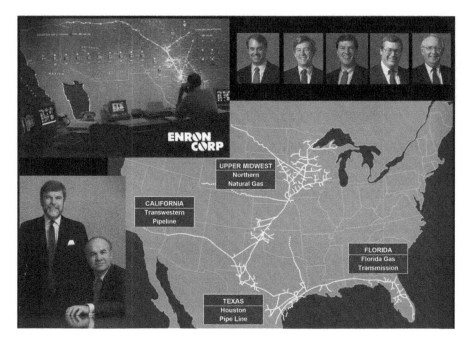

Figure 3.4 Attempts by Mick Seidl and Ken Lay (lower left) to integrate Enron's four pipelines into one synergistic system were limited by federal regulation. Enron's senior natural gas management included (top right, left to right) Jim Rogers (interstate pipelines); Gerald Bennett (intrastate operations); and Ron Burns, John Esslinger, and Claude Mullendore (national marketing).

the restructuring rule was a tough call given that take-or-pay liabilities would mount when customers bought lower-priced spot gas and paid transportation fees. But few pipelines could continue in the old world of bundled deliveries if a rival elected to go open access because markets had surplus carriage capacity.

In April 1986, Transwestern became the first interstate to accept the provisions of FERC Order No. 436 and open access. Northern Natural Gas Pipeline soon followed. Florida Gas, situated as the lone pipeline serving peninsula Florida (although Coastal Corp. was making noises about building an interstate to there), would not open for several more years.

The fact that Transwestern and Florida Gas bracketed the industry's transformation was all about the bottom line. Ken Lay was not a philosopher; nor was Enron an ivory tower. Lay and Enron were pragmatic profit seekers operating in a mixed economy. "Markets" and "competition" could be embraced here but not there—and sometimes in contradiction to company rhetoric and even stated company policy.[12]

Transwestern's move to nondiscriminatory transportation was part of a negotiated settlement of its three-year (FERC) rate case, which conveniently coincided with the implementation of Order No. 436. The key sign-off came from Transwestern's predominant customer, Southern California Gas Company (SoCalGas), the local distribution company for most of Southern California, with approval from FERC and the California Public Utilities Commission (CPUC). The wide-ranging agreement included an obligation by SoCalGas to buy a reduced quantity of system supply and otherwise choose from a menu of transportation rates offered on Transwestern. Abolished was the minimum-bill provision of the sales contract, which had been already been cut to 40 percent from 91 percent pursuant to FERC instructions and was also in legal jeopardy.

Transwestern had substituted transportation for sales to deliver at capacity to California in 1985. But gas demand fell in first-quarter 1986 when mild weather lowered heating demand, and electric power plants behind SoCalGas burned cheaper low-sulfur residual fuel oil. Transwestern's throughput fell to 60 percent of capacity, the lowest in company history.

Reduced gas demand for space heating could not be helped. But if a complex of private-sector agreements could be combined with regulatory change, the loss of sales to oil was reversible. Jim Rogers, the head of Enron Interstate, sent Transwestern marketing vice president Clark Smith to California to begin the process.

Job One was negotiating a delivered spot-gas price with San Diego Gas & Electric (SDG&E) that would return its power plants to gas. Working backward, SoCalGas first agreed to discount its intrastate transportation rate, as Transwestern would do interstate. For both transporters, some revenue was better than none. Producers selling to Pacific Atlantic Marketing Inc. (PAMI, Transwestern's gas-marketing affiliate) were also accepting a lower price at the wellhead as a shut-in alternative, so all the permissions were in place to back out oil with competitive gas. With regulatory approval from the CPUC—the incentive being cleaner air by burning gas rather than resid—the first direct sale by an out-of-state gas supplier to an end user in California's history commenced. It had been a whirlwind two weeks for Smith and all parties.

This *bypass*—Transwestern–PAMI contracting directly with a customer of SoCalGas—inaugurated a new era of gas competition in the state. Transwestern–PAMI would open a California office to market transportation and released

---

12. Enron supported the *goal* of FERC Order No. 436 ("the latest in a number of sweeping deregulatory moves by the government to increase competition in the natural gas industry") more than the rule itself, which did not grant pipelines full recovery of their transition (take-or-pay) costs in the open-access environment.

gas directly to end users, coupling its deliveries to the border with in-state carriage by SoCalGas in the latter's new transportation program. Reporting to Clark Smith was a young talent hired away from rival El Paso Natural Gas, George Wasaff, who would have a long career at Enron in different capacities.

In the first year alone, Transwestern added 15 accounts, where before there had been only 1—SoCalGas. Two of the new accounts were electricity heavyweights: Southern California Edison Company and the Los Angeles Department of Water & Power. The marketing effort even reached Northern California, where Transwestern's released gas, transported on the Northern California leg of El Paso Natural Gas, was sold to Pacific Gas and Electric Company.[13]

Figure 3.5 HNG Interstate, composed of Transwestern Pipeline and Florida Gas Transmission, expertly navigated a changing regulatory landscape. Stan Horton and Rod Hayslett came with the Florida Gas purchase; the other five joined HNG after Ken Lay took over in mid-1984.

---

13. George Wasaff was simultaneously selling Transwestern's system supply to SoCalGas and released spot gas to customers served by SoCalGas. "Imagine my predicament walking into a utility selling regulated gas and the next day walking into another door at the same company with a handful of transportation contracts to bypass them," he remembered. See also Internet appendix 2.5, "Transwestern Pipeline: 'Enron's Laboratory' amid Regulatory Change," at www.politicalcapitalism.org/Book3/Chapter2/Appendix5.html.

Ken Lay and the top Enron brass, particularly Jim Rogers, were all smiles at Clark Smith's presentation, "How the West Was Won." The interstate gas industry, regulated since 1938, had few entrepreneurial episodes as good as this one. Multiple Enron profit centers, not just Transwestern–PAMI, were involved in California's huge spot-gas market. Other Enron affiliates selling gas to California and transporting on either Transwestern or rival El Paso were Enron Gas Marketing (the company's national gas seller, run by John Esslinger) and Panhandle Gas Company (the released gas arm of Houston Pipe Line, whose supply was escaping from Texas's gas surplus).

Transwestern synergies were not only paying off for other Enron units; the interstate's own revenue was exceeding its FERC-authorized margin on invested capital (depreciated original cost). Transwestern was bringing home between $60 and $65 million annually beginning in 1987, versus an authorized return of approximately $42 million. This feat was achieved not only by keeping the pipeline at maximum throughput day after day but also by a rate design whereby pipeline space could be sold twice: once to firm customers paying a demand charge, and again to interruptible customers paying a volumetric rate to use the pipeline space not used by firm customers. (Capacity-release programs, under which firm customers could sell their unwanted firm rights, would come later.[14]) Unsung heroes in Transwestern's rate department had designed three-year rate cases that offered incentives for such extra performance.

————

Florida Gas Transmission had its own oil problem in 1986. Facing lost sales in Florida Power & Light's (FPL) dual-fuel-capable plants, Florida Gas renegotiated its delivered gas price to a percentage of the Btu-equivalent price of low-sulfur residual fuel oil. A locked-in discount was a sure way to keep oil out—so long as gas producers would accept their netback price (the price received at the wellhead after subtracting the costs to reach end users) rather than the shut-in price, which was zero but had a take-or-pay claim.

The renegotiation worked as planned. FGT throughput stayed at capacity, despite some pain. In one month, July 1986, the formula tying gas to 65 percent of the price of resid resulted in a wellhead netback of $0.93/MMBtu, less than half that received the summer before.

This was defense. Florida Gas needed to play offense to justify the premium price paid by HNG to Continental Resources for the system less than two years before. Pipeline expansions would do this, but that required firm, long-term

————

14. In 1999, FERC Order No. 637 allowed customers holding but not needing firm capacity to release their capacity and cease demand-charge payments. But for now, a regulated pipeline could overcollect revenue by using its (spare) capacity in this way.

shipper agreements in addition to the contracted gas already being delivered. The goal was to ensure that FPL use FGT to build new gas-fired plants.

FGT had both tailwinds and headwinds. More electricity was needed in the state. Natural gas firing was environmentally preferred. Rapidly improving combined-cycle gas plants added to this advantage over burning oil in existing facilities and committing to coal in new facilities. But FLP had to demonstrate to the Florida Public Service Commission that electricity generated from gas was competitive with or cheaper than other alternatives, including imported power.

Could Enron guarantee on a multiyear basis what Florida Gas was already doing on a short-term basis: delivering gas at a discount to resid?

FGT's capacity to ship gas to the state had not increased in a quarter century. FPL had a life-of-field warranty contract from Amoco, for 200 MMcf/d of gas delivered on FGT, but the field was depleting and the contract faced expiration. The state's largest electric was contractually committed to transportation charges for gas that might not be there.

With gas shortages in the 1970s, the electrics had idled some of their gas-fired plants. Meanwhile, FPL built intertie transmission capacity to import surplus electricity generated by Southern Company's coal plants just north of the state.

This situation created opportunity for both buyer and seller of transportation capacity. Enron's Bruce Stram and Mark Frevert determined that new gas-fired generation was more economical and reliable than power imports. Replacing coal-by-wire with gas-fired capacity would also provide Florida's electrics with more capital investment (rate base) for profit making.

Putting Enron's money on the table, Frevert in May 1985 executed a letter of intent to supply an average 343 MMcf/d over 15 years to FPL (more in the summer; less in the winter). The gas was priced at a discount to resid, guaranteeing savings for the buyer. A contractual price ceiling kept coal-by-wire at bay.

FPL signed the contract, committing to the first expansion project on FGT since 1970, for 100 MMcf/d. The Phase I expansion would enter service in July 1987, and a similarly sized (Phase II) expansion was planned for two years later.

Enron's Jim Rogers called the supply deal "a big gamble," since the producer contracts were not yet in place. FPL was not obligated to pay for transmission on volume that Enron could not deliver under the contract, but the electric wanted full deliveries to meet its generation goals.

With the contract's gas-delivery date commencing in mid-1988, Frevert had dual tasks. First, he had to get final approval for the transportation contract from the directors of FGT's new parent (Citrus Corp., as of June 30, 1986), which held the half-interests of Enron and Sonat. Second, he had to secure 1.9 Tcf of flexibly priced gas. Citrus had, in effect, sold short, imprudently taking a naked risk on the equivalent of about 10 percent of annual US gas consumption.

As part of the deal, Citrus cancelled the Transgulf project, which would have converted part of Florida Gas to petroleum transportation, instead applying to

FERC for a (second) 100 MMcf/d, $28.5 million expansion. FPL had helped anchor the original Florida Gas project in the late 1950s; new contracts were anchoring the first expansions since the Jack Bowen era.[15]

The supply risk turned out to be all Enron's. Sonat CEO Ron Kuehn adamantly opposed increasing his company's exposure beyond that already being taken with his company's new investment.

With the contract hanging in the balance, Ken Lay put his company's corporate guarantee behind the deal to get Citrus's board to unanimously concur. Enron's warranty assumed the risk of what otherwise would have been split equally with Sonat. So if FGT did not receive transportation revenue on supply that was contractually committed but not delivered to FPL, Enron would be liable to Citrus.

This done, Frevert and FGT executive Stan Horton executed a resid/gas price differential hedge with the global commodities conglomerate Louis Dreyfus as they worked to line up long-term supply to meet the contract.[16] The bet was that gas could be found to meet and beat resid prices. After all, oil prices could not get much lower than in 1986, and Florida Gas still had been able to attract gas from producers. For his part, Frevert intuited that "markets would create [their] own supply," a reversal of Say's law of markets, namely, that supply creates its own demand.

Frevert's hunt began at Enron Gas Supply (EGS), the newly formed procurement arm serving all of Enron's pipelines. But EGS demurred, stating: "We don't have it, nor can we buy gas like that!" So Frevert formed a team and went outside the company, where they found two megasuppliers: wellhead gas from Amoco, the nation's largest holder of gas reserves; and liquefied natural gas (LNG) from Panhandle Eastern Corporation. The agreement for 120 MMcf/d, signed in April 1987, allowed Panhandle to reopen its Lake Charles facility to import Algerian (Sonatrach) supply.[17]

Importantly, and fortunately for Enron's sake, both Amoco and Sonatrach were comfortable with a netback price tied to the market price of resid. This gave Citrus about 90 percent of the gas needed for the 15-year contract. The rest would come from spot-market purchases, which seemed to be a manageable risk.

---

15. For the history of Florida Gas Transmission during and after the Bowen era, see chapter 8, Bradley, *Edison to Enron*, pp. 271–312.

16. Stan Horton remembered such hedging as "probably one of the first derivative contracts ever done in the gas business."

17. Sonatrach and Panhandle Eastern's stormy history began with a 1972 LNG agreement and ended in 1986 with a $530 million payment by Panhandle to void the contract. The Citrus LNG contract was a new beginning for this underutilized multibillion-dollar LNG infrastructure.

FGT's complicated spot-gas contract, priced off going residual fuel oil prices, with a variety of provisions to try to keep the deal affordable for both parties, began favorably for Enron. FGT was making its full margin on existing capacity, and Phase I capacity (as of July 1987), and Phase II capacity (as of September 1989). Profits were being made on the gas-supply contracts for Enron Gas Services.

But things reversed beginning in late 1990 and early 1991. Large monthly losses (to Enron, not Citrus) were being incurred with no relief in sight. The resolution of this contract, estimated to be $450 million in net present value and requiring an up-front payment to FPL, is described in chapter 6.

––––

Northern Natural Gas Pipeline, the granddaddy of Enron's interstates, faced stiff competition from other Midwest pipelines, some of which were bringing in cheap Canadian gas (as well as resid) to many of Northern Natural's industrial markets in 1986. Using a new regulatory mechanism whereby rates could be changed on a day's notice (as opposed to laborious filings with FERC or as periodically scheduled), Northern Natural was able to reduce tariffs, stay competitive, and retain throughput. It had been Transwestern, in fact, that first asked FERC for a flexible purchased-gas adjustment clause ("flex PGA").

Northern did well in the transition away from old methods of doing business, for several reasons. In addition to flex PGAs to change rates, Northern benefitted from on-system and off-system marketing. Northern's producer contracts were also more market responsive (price flexible) than most such interstate pipeline contracts. Compared to the competition, including Natural Gas Pipeline of America, one of the last great projects of Samuel Insull,[18] Northern Natural did well with take-or-pay costs.

––––

Proactively unbundling sales from transportation created two profit centers instead of one for Enron. Fending off oil with innovative contracts kept Enron's throughput high in states two thousand miles apart. Designing and performing under rate cases won extra profit. Capacity was expanded not only to stay ahead of the market but also to *create* an incremental market that would otherwise go to a rival energy. This was what Lay's new breed could do in the changed world of FERC pipelining.

It took much more smarts than ever before to keep the pipelines as cash cows. By getting ahead of transition (take-or-pay) costs and offering innovative products, Enron was earning what other interstate pipelines, such as Transco, were not. Many interstate pipelines, in fact, were not making their authorized rate of return in the late 1980s, given overcapacity. At the same time, pipelines

––––

18. See Bradley, *Edison to Enron*, pp. 187, 257, 413, 503.

were replacing their old "20-year, firm, fixed, and forgotten" supply contracts with two-to-five-year agreements that had price flexibility and market-outs.

Reorganizing Cogeneration

Cogeneration was a new technology that used 20–35 percent less oil or natural gas than prior technology producing the same amount of steam and electricity. Cogen became a business for independents when a provision in a federal law required utilities to buy the cogenerated power at a price determined to be the "avoided cost," so long as certain conditions were met.[19] John Wing and Bob Kelly got HNG into this business just months after Lay arrived from Transco Energy Company.

After negotiating the merger between HNG and InterNorth, Wing was set to develop a thriving cogeneration business pursuant to his employment contract. But InterNorth, the top dog in the merger, had its own cogeneration activity in Northern Natural Resources Company, ably run by Howard Hawks.

Northern Resources was off to a fast start with two excellent projects. Thus Hawks's Omaha-based division assumed responsibilities for power development for the combined company. Wing left HNG/InterNorth under a five-year consulting agreement that gave him room to develop cogen projects independently, while giving Enron a right to invest.

Into 1986, Hawks's mission, unchanged from the InterNorth days, was "to create new grass-roots businesses which are attractive in their own right and complement the Corporation's various operations." That was the case with the Central Basin Pipeline, a $70 million, 143-mile CO_2 pipeline project running from New Mexico to West Texas, that began operations in late 1985 and produced high up-front earnings. At about the same time, aligned contracts allowed construction to begin on a $152 million, 440 MW cogeneration facility adjacent to Union Carbide's petrochemical complex in Texas City.

Both projects were equity financed by InterNorth but not off the balance sheet, which would involve other parties putting up the capital and taking the risk. Not that such financing was a bad business practice; cash-rich InterNorth did not need it, and Hawks's company liked simplicity and transparency. What you saw is what you got with this Midwest-culture company.

The Texas City project, originally named Northern Cogeneration One, had come together nicely. The contract specified that the sales price of steam and of power flexed up or down with natural-gas input prices, creating an arbitrage spread. (Fixed-priced multiyear gas was not yet available.) The 140 MMcf/d needed to produce the steam and power utilized existing InterNorth agreements for offshore gas and for transportation on Houston Pipe Line. Dan Dienstbier's

---

19. See the discussion of PURPA in Internet appendix 1.5, "Public Utility Regulatory Policies Act of 1978 (PURPA)," at www.politicalcapitalism.org/Book3/Chapter1/Appendix5 .html.

Northern Natural Gas Company made the arrangements, but it took some prodding from Hawks—he threatened to go outside the company for gas—to finally get things done.

Union Carbide agreed to buy all the steam and 30 percent of the power from the proposed plant. That left 70 percent of the plant's cogenerated electricity for sale. Houston Lighting & Power Company (HL&P), a franchised utility, was building coal and nuclear capacity and did not need the power—at least not at a high-enough "avoided cost" price to make the project viable. But there was a potential solution. Dallas-based Texas Utilities Electric Company needed power and could pay an attractive avoided cost—if the power could be delivered to North Texas.

The bottleneck was broken by some (more) political capitalism when the Texas Public Utility Commission intervened to force HL&P to deliver ("wheel") the power up to Texas Utilities. (Actually, a power exchange between the two utilities would eliminate the need for physical transportation altogether.) The 12-year contract was for 393 MW, the largest power contract ever executed between a cogenerator and a utility. The deal, completed just when InterNorth announced its acquisition of HNG, was a triumph for Northern Resources. Construction began later that year, and, on paper at least, the arbitrage returns between locked-in input and output prices were substantial.

But circumstances had reversed. After energy prices collapsed in March 1986, Northern Resources found itself stuck in neutral—and worse. Given its imprudent debt, Enron needed cash coming in, not going out to construction payments. The word from Houston was to wind down outstanding negotiations and sell Central Basin Pipeline. That left Texas City, just several months in construction, facing the prospect of being financed by Enron's treasury (but indirectly debt-financed for the most part, given Enron's indebtedness).

Enter Michael Milken and Drexel Burnham Lambert, whose high-yield junk bonds were used with 50 percent ownership going to Drexel. For $10 million, Enron owned half and operated the 450 MW plant. The facility would become operational in early 1987. But Enron had sacrificed much in the process of getting money in the door by year end—and demoting Hawks in the process, explained in the next chapter.

Another cogen project that Enron wanted to do—even with its own scarce capital—did not originate from Northern Resources. It was a project that Howard Hawks told Mick Seidl he would not authorize without renegotiating its terms, creating a rift between Houston and Omaha. The project concerned a proposed $120 million, 165 MW plant in Bayonne, New Jersey, sponsored by Cogen Technologies Inc. (CTI), a company founded by Robert C. "Bob" McNair.

McNair was new to the business. He had precious little equity, coming off a setback in which one of his trucking companies declared bankruptcy amid the industry-wide retrenchment that followed deregulation.[20] But McNair was smart, diligent, likable, and an able negotiator. He would eventually repay his creditors, exit trucking, and enter a field that would turn out to be phenomenally successful. He would also eventually sell his company to Enron and go on to bigger things.[21]

McNair originally presented a 22 MW cogeneration project to Mick Seidl, who sent him to John Wing. The two met, but McNair's 50/50 profit-sharing proposal was a nonstarter given that HNG would be putting up the equity. Talks were suspended when Wing was pulled away to consummate the merger between HNG and InterNorth.

Postmerger, Wing was out and Hawks in. But McNair was not going to fly to Omaha to negotiate with Hawks. Wing was the key to getting a deal done, something he agreed to do for a 1 percent personal-interest carry, given that things were falling into place with a gas provider, steam buyer, power purchaser, and project constructor (GE). Better yet, the project was growing well beyond its original size, and McNair was proving adept at resolving the politics of siting and permit issues.

It was a strange situation—Wing as McNair's consultant, negotiating with Enron, where he also consulted. Enron's board had to approve this arrangement given the conflict of interest. But far from fooling anyone, Wing's contract required that he give Enron the right of first refusal to invest in any of his new projects. This became moot given Enron's capital constraints, but it showed to what extent Wing had Lay's ear.

While negotiating on behalf of HNG, Wing had wanted 85 percent of the free-cash flow to go to the company, not 50 percent as McNair proposed. That was still a good starting point. Now, wearing three hats—his own, McNair's, and Enron's—Wing saw a compromise to flip from 85/15 to 50/50 should the project's return on investment (ROI) reach 23 percent.

This was doable and good for all sides. But given how well the project was coming together, McNair, in return for the 85 percent concession on the front end, wanted a second flip in his favor should the project reach a still higher profit threshold. Maybe it was because few really thought that a 30 percent

---

20. The federal Motor Carrier Act of 1980 eased entry restrictions and liberalized rates for interstate trucking companies. "By 1984, hundreds of firms, including some of the biggest names in the industry, entered bankruptcy proceedings." McNair's truck-leasing company was also felled by a recession that hit in 1982.

21. McNair sold Cogen Technologies to Enron in 1998 for $1.1 billion, which enabled him to start a new NFL franchise, the Houston Texans, to replace the departed Houston Oilers. McNair's effort was enabled by a taxpayer-supported stadium that resulted from a come-from-behind effort led by Enron and Ken Lay personally to get voter approval for such public monies. (See chapter 15, p. 617.)

ROI was possible. Maybe it was McNair's likability and effective one-on-one negotiations with Lay and Seidl at a Young Presidents' Organization retreat. Maybe it was Wing's strong support of the deal and Lay and Seidl's respect— or fear—of Wing. But whatever the reasons, McNair got the Houston brass to agree. If Bayonne's ROI reached 30 percent, Cogen Technologies would receive 85 percent of the free cash, leaving Enron with 15 percent for the life of the project.

It was this three-tiered proposal that Howard Hawks wanted to renegotiate—not approve as Mick Seidl, Enron's president, wanted him to do. Thus the Bayonne project was in stalemate in the spring of 1986.

Given the order from Houston for Northern Resources to retrench, as well as the impasse with Bayonne, Hawks began eyeing life after Enron. Ken Lay too knew that major changes were necessary, so he turned to Wing for help. Could Wing refinance Texas City to free up Enron's $152 million in committed project costs, even if it meant selling part of the project? Lay also wanted to pursue cogeneration projects off–balance sheet, something that Wing, a superdeveloper-promoter-closer, could do.

Wing agreed and renegotiated his consulting contract with Enron for a third time, upping his monthly stipend and establishing a special payout, assuming that Texas City could be profitably refinanced. As part of the deal, Enron Cogeneration Company (ECC) would be created, with Robert Kelly running the division from Houston, where he was already reporting to Hawks. At the same time (June 1, 1986), Northern Resources became Enron Development Company (EDC), with Hawks as president, charged with selling the CO_2 pipeline and, if capital became available again, investing in new projects.

But Hawks had had enough. With permission from Lay, Hawks set out to buy Central Basin Pipeline from Enron as part of his exit strategy. A few calls to the right energy companies resulted in an $87 million offer, but Lay decided to sell Central Basin externally.

Hawks negotiated a severance payment and began networking around Omaha, where resided a number of severed InterNorth employees who were capable and interested in work. In a matter of months, Hawks found a stalled cogeneration project that he and a few others got back on track. April 1, 1987, was the first payday for a company that christened itself Tenaska, a sort of reborn Northern Natural Resources Company.

Today, Tenaska is one of the top-20 privately held companies in the United States, with assets of $3.3 billion, annual revenue of $8 billion, and an enterprise value of $1.5 billion. With 10 percent of the nation's natural gas either sold or managed and more than 24,500 MW of electricity under management,

Howard Hawks's company is what Ken Lay's (contra-capitalist) enterprise ultimately failed to be.[22]

_____

With Wing on the outside and Hawks gone, Robert Kelly was now in charge. He hired former Omaha talent, such as Jay Berriman, and new talent, including Rebecca Mark, who had been in the treasury department of Continental Resources Company when it was acquired by HNG in late 1984. Kelly also had straight access to now-Enron consultant John Wing.

Kelly's ECC began to revise the Texas City contracts to allow refinancing, which Wing did pronto. The 165 MW Bayonne deal was executed with Enron agreeing to invest $14 million for a 42 percent interest. Other partners that Wing brought in with Bayonne were GE (the builder), Jersey Central Power & Light (the power buyer), and Transco (the gas supplier). The extraordinary profitability of the project that launched Bob McNair's Cogen Technologies is discussed in chapter 5.

Buying Independence

Takeover specialist Irwin Jacobs took a blow from the merger of InterNorth and HNG. InterNorth stock, which had been selling in the low $50s per share from takeover rumors, fell to $47 after HNG was acquired. But rather than sell out, Jacobs increased his stake. By third-quarter 1986, Jacobs and associates owned 5.1 million shares of common. In July, New York–based Leucadia National Corporation disclosed an ENE accumulation of 2.3 million shares.[23] Together, the arbitrageurs (*arbs*) had accumulated 16.4 percent of Enron's common stock, which was mired in the low-to-mid $40s.

What to do? Lay's first plan was to take Enron private, with senior executives taking ownership positions. Lay, Rich Kinder, Jim Rogers, and Gerald Bennett flew to New York to work with leveraged-buyout specialist Kohlberg Kravis Roberts & Co. Lazard Frères was busy assisting Enron on the deal as well.

The trick was finding a price that stockholders would accept—say, $55 per share—while not assuming so much debt as to endanger ongoing profitability. But to get to a marketable buyout price, projected earnings had to be sweetened

_____

22. For an interpretation of Tenaska as a *contra-Enron* company (like Kinder-Morgan and Koch Industries Inc.), see Internet appendix 3.2, "Tenaska: Escape from Enron," at www.politicalcapitalism.org/Book3/Chapter3/Appendix2.html.

23. Leucadia was controlled by Ian M. Cummings and Joseph S. Steinberg, both from the Class of 1970 at Harvard Business School. Once, after hearing himself described as a takeover coyote, Cummings embraced the comparison by saying, "Coyotes eat carrion."

from what the Enron divisions originally projected. Thus they were pressed to up their volume and margin forecasts—not unlike what HNG had done to get its $70 per share price from InterNorth. But energy markets were much worse now than then, and Lay was joined by more prudent colleagues.

The concerns came out during the last night, dinner consumed and drinks flowing. "I have been pushed way beyond my level of comfort," Bennett confessed to Lay in reference to his intrastate gas assets. Rogers, speaking for the interstates, chimed in: "I am probably the best regulatory man in the country, but I am not this good." Lay responded: "Well, if you guys don't think we can make it work, then we'll drop it, get back to Houston, put our heads down, and try to make it work."

Enron then asked Lazard Frères and Drexel Burnham Lambert to explore other options for remaining independent. Lay visited some deep pockets in search of equity. But nothing clicked, so negotiations ensued with Jacobs and Leucadia to purchase their shares.

On Monday, October 20, 1986, Enron announced a buyback of the 7.4 million shares for $47 per share, a 6 percent premium to the prior day's close. A special charge to earnings of $20 million would be taken for this difference.

But the real hit was a $180 million devaluation of Enron from a $4 per share fall in ENE upon the announcement. One million shares were dumped, mostly by disappointed speculators. The takeover premium was now completely out of the stock. Wall Street arbs, taken by surprise, exacted their revenge.

Lay and the board had hoped to avoid this by simultaneously authorizing a potential stock buyback of up to 10 million shares, depending on market conditions and business considerations. Enron also estimated a $45 million increase in annual cash flow from the tax benefits of the transaction. The market was little impressed.

Clear-the-decks, get-this-behind-us would be Ken Lay's pain-avoidance strategy—now and all the way up to the final months of Enron's solvency. Each time, Lay was nothing but positive. *"This agreement removes a major, disruptive uncertainty about Enron's future created by short-term oriented speculators,"* he wrote in an all-employee memo. "Our directors, our employees and our shareholders are now in command of the company's destiny." The decision, Lay added, *"brings to a close the long period of restructuring, realignment and reorganization* that began with the merger of InterNorth and Houston Natural Gas." Still, he admitted, "this freedom has a cost."

The deal disadvantaged general stockholders and worsened the company's debt ratio at a vulnerable time. And unfortunately for Ken Lay, who treasured good public relations, a fellow industry leader, T. Boone Pickens, was crusading for shareholder rights at the time.

"Greenmail is a symptom of weak management, and Enron's executives folded in a big way," complained the chairman of the newly formed United

Shareholders Association (USA). Digging hard, Pickens called the event "Black Monday" and characterized the buyout as "an 'ongoing job security program' for Enron executives."

Ken Lay had been a big Boone Pickens fan. After all, this was the man who had shaken the cage of the stodgy oil majors with his attempt to buy Gulf Oil Company, something Ken enjoyed watching. But Boone had gone too far—way too far—by ridiculing Enron in a press release for the national media.

Lay fired off a three-page rebuttal to his critic. The missive mentioned how Pickens's Mesa Limited Partnership had recently paid Irwin Jacobs a "slight" premium in its takeover of Pioneer Corporation. Lay argued that Enron's value decline would be eventually regained from the benefits of the buyout, including a better-motivated workforce. It was "careless" for Pickens to denounce Enron's senior management as "weak" and "entrenched." Lay added:

> I have been chief executive officer of Enron Corp. less than one year, which hardly seems long enough to be too entrenched. More importantly ... many people in our industry ... believe Enron Corp. has one of the strongest and deepest senior management teams of any company in the natural gas industry.... Many of the innovations within the industry in attempting to adapt to the rapidly changing market and regulatory environment have been initiated by this team.

"My respect for Boone has certainly diminished substantially because of this matter," Lay scribbled in a note to his old boss and friend Jack Bowen at Transco, attaching a copy of his letter.[24] But otherwise the communication remained private. As much as Pickens violated his ego, Lay thought it best not to feud in public over the matter. This was a hard time, and a war of words with an industry icon would scarcely help. Only a more profitable Enron would vindicate the stock buyout and enhance his (Lay's) image.

Enron's special friends in the investment banking community spoke up. "It is a black mark on the investment business that arbitrageurs are able to wreak havoc on a well-run operation due to their concern only with short-term gain," commented Joseph Culp of First Manhattan Company. Still, he and virtually everyone else had to agree: This was another clear-the-decks action for Enron's balance sheet. Even after profitable asset sales of over $1 billion, Enron's debt ratio would end 1986 at 69 percent, a slight improvement from the year before but a far cry from Lay's goal, announced just 11 months earlier, to end the year at 55 percent.

Even if the buyout failed to impress externally, the major selling point internally was the creation of a new employee stock option plan (ESOP) from the stock purchase, financed by a tax-free $230 million transfer from an overfunded

---

24. For further discussion, see Internet appendix 3.3, "Letter from Ken Lay to T. Boone Pickens," at www.politicalcapitalism.org/Book3/Chapter3/Appendix3.html.

retirement plan that had been earmarked to retire company debt, as well as $105 million of new bank debt.[25]

Coupled with the stock already distributed to employees from prior programs, one-third of Enron's outstanding common stock would be employee owned. To Ken Lay, this put the incentives in the right place.[26] But short-term stock performance might become overemphasized within the company, particularly one run by hurried, über-confident Ken Lay.

The ESOP would prove to be an employee bonanza in the coming years. And it created a thirst for continual stock appreciation by virtually every Enroner—and pressure to get it. Removing "investors who we believe sought short-term profits at the expense of higher long-term returns" would itself over time create a hyper-short-term bias.

High-risk debt securities (*junk bonds*) issued by Drexel Burnham Lambert financed part of the deal with Jacobs, which continued the relationship between Lay and Drexel star Michael Milken. (Between 1985 and 1988, Drexel financed eight Enron transactions, totaling nearly $3 billion.) Milken would always be a favorite to Enron's chairman, even after the financier's (controversial) criminal conviction on finance and tax charges and Drexel's bankruptcy in 1990.

Public Policy Overtures

Government intervention in energy markets had long been driven by competitively harried executives, not only by outside reformers invoking the common good or consumer groups seeking a free lunch. The political capitalists, aka *rent-seekers*, could come from small or large companies. The common denominator was effective organization and follow-through to obtain the requisite services of the right politicians or bureaucrats at the right time.[27]

Not surprisingly, the collapse of energy prices in 1986 inspired acts of political capitalism. Transco Energy CEO Jack Bowen used his annual report to call for an oil tariff sufficient to guarantee a domestic floor price of $25 per barrel (about double the current price). Oscar Wyatt championed oil protectionism at

---

25. The move increased pension risk for retirees, given that a prior consolidation of the HNG and InterNorth retirement programs had left a 10 percent cushion above the asset valuation required by the Internal Revenue Service and Pension Benefit Guaranty Corp. But the move was done partly in response to a new tax incentive.

26. "Perhaps more important [than cost savings] for the long-term future of this company," Ken Lay and Mick Seidl wrote in the *1986 Annual Report*, "all our employees—from the lowest paid to the highest paid—will be shareholders and will have a strong, additional incentive to make the company as efficient and productive as possible."

27. The theory of political capitalism and the long history of US government economic intervention are surveyed in chapters 5 and 6, respectively, of Bradley, *Capitalism at Work*. For a review of major electricity and natural gas regulation, see Bradley, *Edison to Enron*, pp. 495–521.

Coastal Corporation. Richard O'Shields, CEO of Panhandle Eastern Corporation, called for the federal government to prorate (limit) gas supply to gas
demand and to stabilize (*increase*) prices. "The odd thing about free enterprisers
is that they can't stand free enterprise," observed John Jennrich, a University of
North Carolina political science major and now editor of *Natural Gas Week*.
"They want certainty."

Enron's fortunes were tied to oil and gas prices. Announcing a 38 percent cut
in planned capital spending in 1987 from the prior year, CFO Keith Kern calculated a $15 million hit to Enron's annual cash flow for every drop of $1 per barrel of oil or $0.10 per Mcf of gas at the wellhead. Thus Enron was keenly
interested in promoting public policies to increase energy prices—natural gas
(and gas-liquid) prices for their own sake and oil prices to help natural gas and
liquid prices. (Enron had no coal investments at the time.)

Dr. Lay and Dr. Seidl—PhD economist and PhD political economist, respectively—ominously noted the "sharp swing toward dependency on foreign oil"
in Enron's *1986 Annual Report*. But they stopped short of advocating an oil tariff.
They were not averse to such a policy but viewed it as politically undoable.
They also believed that they had cleared the decks one last time, meaning "all
costs associated with the merger and the sharp drop in energy prices are now
behind us" and foresaw a price rebound from "fundamental economic and
political forces." But such optimism and patience would be tested in the future,
and Ken Lay would be partial to quick-fix political solutions in lieu of (slower)
market adjustment, as discussed in chapter 7.

———

On another front, Ken Lay donned a free-market cape to help his industry
and Enron. Part of natural gas's problem was a federal law passed after the
severe gas curtailments of the winter of 1976/77, which restricted the use of
oil and gas in existing and new industrial facilities and power plants. "The
choices now for electric utilities are basically coal and nuclear power," the
Carter administration's National Energy Plan concluded at the time. The idea
was to ensure that the supposedly dwindling resource of natural gas would
not go to "low priority" boilers at the expense of "high priority" residential and commercial markets. Natural gas was "too good to burn," a refrain
went.

Despite a gas surplus that began almost on the day that Carter signed the
Powerplant and Industrial Fuel Use Act of 1978 (Fuel Use Act), the law remained
on the books. Exemptions were being granted, particularly for new gas-fired
cogeneration projects that its sister federal law PURPA encouraged.

Still, the Fuel Use Act sent a chilling signal that long-term commitments to
natural gas were a political risk. By 1986, the American Gas Association
(AGA) made repeal a legislative priority, and in March of the next year, Ken
Lay testified before the House of Representatives in Washington to that end.
Enron's pipeline expansions required long-term commitments from these big

gas users, and every bit of incremental gas demand was needed to help raise prices.[28]

"Everyone agrees the 'gas bubble' will soon disappear," Senator Howard Metzenbaum of coal-rich Ohio said in his opening statement, to which Lay replied that the "18-month/2-year gas bubble has been about to burst for eight or nine years." It was a sad story for the upstream industry. Gas deliverability was increasing, while gas demand had fallen almost 15 percent in five years. What the gas industry needed—and deserved with new technology turning gas into electricity more efficiently and cheaply than ever before—was a level playing field, a policy of "let the market be the test."

Lay issued a challenge at the hearing. "We say to our friends in the coal industry: 'You build a coal unit: We will build a combined cycle,' and then we'll go head-to-head to see who will sell electricity to our friends in the electric business."

Ken Lay was on a crusade. But as much as he enjoyed external matters, particularly those in his old haunt of Washington, DC, his attention would soon have to be back inside Enron's walls in Houston. His creation was not yet on track two years after the merger, and a big festering problem was just ahead.

Brightening 1987

The bust in oil and gas prices in 1986 meant pain and retrenchment for most of the upstream and midstream oil and gas business. The precipitous fall in oil prices worsened feeble natural gas prices as fuel oil displaced gas in power plants. Transwestern Pipeline, arguably the most entrepreneurial interstate in the industry, regained markets but could not recoup lost throughput.

Still, foundations were set in Enron's core businesses and would blossom in 1988–89 and continue in the 1990s. One was the management changeover in Enron Oil & Gas; the other was the takeoff of Enron Gas Marketing to become the top wholesaler in the open-access environment.

A Star for Enron Oil & Gas
After integrating InterNorth's properties, Enron Oil & Gas Company ranked as the second-largest US independent oil and gas producer in terms of reserves. Concentrated in South Texas and New Mexico, with some Canadian operations

---

28. Lay's testimony was also aimed at repealing the incremental pricing provision of the Natural Gas Policy Act of 1978, which disproportionately loaded gas costs on industrials and power plants to advantage residential and commercial gas users. But large gas users could switch fuels, and oil-for-gas left the intended beneficiaries with higher rates—and the gas industry with lower demand. For more detail, see Internet appendix 3.4, "Fuel Use Act, Incremental Pricing, and Gas Demand," at www.politicalcapitalism.org/Book3/Chapter3/Appendix4.html.

and a number of Gulf of Mexico blocks, daily production in 1986 averaged 350 million cubic feet of gas and 10,720 barrels of crude oil and liquids. Gas production increased nearly by half from the year before, and low selling prices were partially offset by lower drilling costs.

EOG's fortunes rose and fell with prices. The price depression in 1986 resulted in a one-fifth staff reduction, closed regional offices, and consolidation in Houston "to position the company for the future."

EOG's lineage went back to 1951, when HNG formed Houston Natural Gas Production Company. Two decades later, Robert Herring bought Roden Oil Company as part of a West Texas gas play, renaming the division HNG Oil Company. When W. F. Roden retired in 1982, Ted Collins Jr. became head of HNG Oil, which was still operating in Midland. By 1986, Collins presided over a much bigger enterprise, post-InterNorth.

There was room for improvement. Seidl had his strategic planner, Bruce Stram, compare HNG Oil's return on capital to its cost of capital. The answer was sobering. McKinsey consultant Glen Sweetnam reconfirmed that what HNG Oil thought to be strength—profitably finding oil and gas relative to other operators—was instead a weakness.

EOG's 1986 cash flow of $205 million was respectable, given a 50 percent fall in received natural gas prices and one-third drop in oil and condensate prices from a year before. But the subsidiary was bulky. Properties needed to be sold and others developed. The tumult left the unit disorganized at its new home in Houston. Collins, tiring of corporate meetings at his new headquarters, was ready to cash out. A makeover of EOG under a new entrepreneurial eye made sense.

Ken Lay wanted the best in the business and had something valuable to offer: an equity stake in EOG, a unit that Prudential-Bache Securities valued at $1.7 billion if taken public. EOG had strong upside under the right management, a McKinsey & Company study for Enron concluded.

Lay first approached the head of Anadarko Petroleum Corporation, Robert Allison, who was interested and took the offer to his board, which informed him that a new compensation package was in the works. The sweetened deal kept him home.

Next on Lay's list was the architect behind the stellar growth of Texas Oil & Gas (TXO). Forrest Hoglund was courtable. His company had recently been purchased for $3 billion by United States Steel Corporation (USX), adding a layer of management above him. Hoglund had signed a long-term agreement with his new bosses and was rumored to be in the running for the top USX job, but his contract had an out clause. What Ken Lay offered was the chance to participate in the appreciation of a valuable set of assets that were akin to what he had mastered at TXO.

Hoglund was presented with a five-year contract agreement that was competitive in base salary but superior in incentives. The kicker was a grant of

1 percent of the valuation of EOG when it was taken public.[29] EOG was worth at least a billion dollars, so that was $10 million and counting. This was not something that the Pittsburg-based company wanted to match, so Hoglund accepted Enron's offer.

Figure 3.6 Enron Oil & Gas received new leadership in 1987 with Forrest Hoglund, Ken Lay's most rewarding hire. Hoglund is shown in 1977 upon joining Texas Oil & Gas and in 1989 with the top Enron brass at the New York Stock Exchange when EOG went public.

---

29. Hoglund's five-year employment agreement stipulated a floor for base pay of $550,000 annually and options on 100,000 shares of ENE, in addition to 1 percent of EOG stock payout, vested at 20 percent per year of employment.

Forrest Hoglund was a veteran of the upstream industry. After graduating from the University of Kansas in 1956 with a degree in mechanical engineering, he began his career as an engineering trainee at Humble Oil & Refining Company. At Exxon, Hoglund rose to vice president, worldwide natural gas, before he was hired away by TXO as its new president in 1977. Hoglund became COO of Texas Oil & Gas two years later and CEO in 1982. His company roared with one of the highest and most profitable growth rates in the industry. One of TXO's prime assets was Delhi Gas Pipeline Corporation, the owner of the South Texas gas lines that Jack Bowen had built in the 1950s.

Effective September 1, 1987, Hoglund became chairman and CEO of Enron Oil & Gas Company, advertised as the third-largest US independent, with a reserve equivalent of 1.7 Tcf. Similar to TXO, 85 percent of EOG's reserves was natural gas and 94 percent domestic. Another similarity: the reserve positions were geographically concentrated and capable of benefitting from affiliated transportation and marketing services. Enron's synergies and Hoglund's entrepreneurship would make for a happy story starting in 1988.

Enron Gas Marketing

PURPA-driven independent power generation was not the only regulatory opportunity for Enron in the mid-1980s. The law of the land for interstate pipelines (under FERC Order No. 436, later taking final form as FERC Order No. 636) was mandatory open access that opened a profit door for buying and selling gas in interstate commerce. Natural Gas Clearinghouse (NGC) was the first out of the gate on a national scale, but, as Jeff Skilling would later explain, "they had the wrong concept." NGC was a gas broker, not marketer, and its incentive and ability to secure interstate pipeline space for delivery was limited.[30] Northern Gas Marketing (NGM) had the right plan. But to be national, it needed transportation access on pipelines other than its affiliate Northern Natural.

The merger between HNG and InterNorth was just months old when open-access transmission became FERC policy.[31] InterNorth's NGM became the guts

---

30. In NGC's first 15 months (1984–85), the entity did not take title to gas but acted as a *broker*, receiving a commission for putting together parties that did pass title in the transaction. NGC employees, loaned from member pipelines, returned home to form their own marketing affiliates after parochialism stymied deals. Under the new leadership of Chuck Watson, NGC reorganized in the last half of 1985 as a stand-alone gas marketer to become the major rival to Enron.

31. FERC's policy shift from closed pipeline carriage to mandatory open access is described in Internet appendix 1.2, "Mandatory Open Access for Interstate Gas Pipelines," at www .politicalcapitalism.org/Book3/Chapter1/Appendix2.html. The (regulatory) rise of gas marketing as the fourth segment of the industry is described in Internet appendix 3.5, "Rise of Gas Marketing" at www.politicalcapitalism.org/Book3/Chapter3/Appendix5.html.

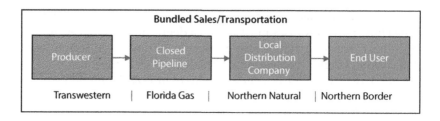

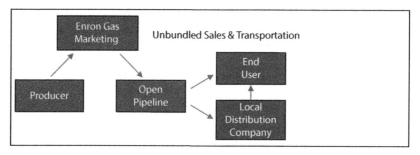

Figure 3.7 FERC's open-access regulation led interstate pipelines, including Enron's, to leave the bundled sales and transportation function. Independent marketers assumed the buy/sell commodity function, leaving the interstates as pure transporters. This created two profit centers for Enron where there had been only one before.

of HNG/InterNorth Gas Marketing, soon to be Enron Gas Marketing (EGM). The opportunity was there, but many customers for long-term contracts were haunted by the gas problems of the 1970s. Curtailments and moratoria had sent electric generators to coal, and even to nuclear, for their new capacity. Fuel oil also gained from federal price controls on wellhead natural gas.[32]

The coal rush did not mean problem-free solid fuel. There were periodic labor union problems in the mines, and pollutants from coal plants were greater than from natural gas facilities for generated power. Still, coal was a known, abundant commodity. As prolific producers and as net exporters (in contrast to oil or gas), US coal companies offered power companies a secure input that was one-third to one-half cheaper than gas in terms of heating value. But coal plants were more expensive to build than gas plants, so much so that low gas prices flipped the economics.

But memories were long. Curtailments in interstate markets in the 1970s led to a federal law intended to phase out gas from industrial boilers and power

---

32. Interstate gas shortages (and intrastate surpluses) in the 1970s led to the federal mandatory open-access era. See Bradley, *Edison to Enron*, pp. 505–9.

generation. Price spikes, too, were an issue for gas versus coal. And even if gas supply was secure and cheaper, utilities were biased toward new coal capacity, given public-utility regulation. Capital-intensive coal plants created more rate base to be multiplied by the allowed rate of return. To utilities, coal was profit maximizing whether or not its generated power was more economic than from a gas-fired plant for their captive customers.

The statistics told the story. Between 1973 and 1988, the use of natural gas for electric generation fell 28 percent nationally, while the consumption of coal in its three flavors—anthracite, bituminous, and lignite—almost doubled. In Texas, gas usage fell 26 percent, while coal for power generation, starting practically from zero, increased tenfold. Robert Herring's coal-for-gas vision in the early 1980s for Houston Natural Gas seemed prescient.[33]

But North America's gas resource base was not running down, judged economically, as Herring and many others in and out of the industry had assumed. Record prices in the 1970s and expanding technology in the 1980s did what few thought possible: create a surplus of supply relative to demand. The overhang of gas supply sent wellhead prices south—from approximately $2.25/MMBtu in 1985 to $1.75/MMBtu in 1986 and about $1.50/MMBtu thereafter. Given the lower capital costs of gas plants when compared to coal plants, this price reduction made the *overall* production costs of gas-fired electricity less than its major rival over the life of a prospective plant.[34]

Low gas prices led to warnings of expensive gas to come—a so-called hard landing between supply and demand. McKinsey & Company's John Sawhill, a former energy regulator, pumped this scenario. So did Groppe, Long & Littell's Henry Groppe, a Transco Energy Company board director whom Ken Lay knew, liked, and retained as a consultant at Enron. The National Coal Association's Richard Lawson self-interestedly spread this message as well, as told in chapter 7.

Thus Enron and Ken Lay faced a major challenge—and an opportunity. Utility commitments to build new gas plants required supply and price certainty to lock in the present advantage of gas relative to coal. (Nuclear power was stymied after the Three Mile Island accident in 1979.) Ken Lay understood this very well, as did McKinsey energy specialist (and Sawhill protégé) Jeff Skilling. Their response would define Enron's first boom, as discussed in later chapters.

———

In early 1987, Enron's largest subsidiary, Gas Pipeline Group, reorganized. The biggest change was separating the nonregulated merchant function from the pipelines. Enron Gas Services was created, housing Enron Gas Marketing

———

33. See Bradley, *Edison to Enron*, pp. 456–57, 465.

34. See also the discussion in chapter 7, pp. 323–24. Gas costs that were 50 percent higher than coal on a Btu basis in 1985 shrank to one-third higher by 1990.

(EGM) on one side and Enron Gas Supply (EGS) on the other. Reporting to Enron Gas Services head Gerald Bennett were EGM's John Esslinger and EGS's Claude Mullendore, both formerly with Lay at Transco. Bennett, who continued to head Enron's intrastate properties at Houston Pipe Line and Oasis, reported to Dan Dienstbier, as did Jim Rogers from the interstate pipeline side.

Bennett's job was to rebuild nonregulated markets, which meant securing gas supply to make long-term sales commitments. Enron Gas Supply was now charged with procuring supply for EGM, which prominently included released gas off Enron pipelines. Take-or-pay resolutions were part of this effort.

EGS/EGM was focused on markets outside the areas served by Enron pipelines, leaving the majority of on-system sales coming from the pipelines, from either their FERC-blessed jurisdictional supply or their released-gas spot affiliate. But some EGS/EGM gas was sold in Enron's pipeline markets along with spot-gas packages from non-Enron marketers. All was at arm's length; Enron's transportation and gas marketing were "classy" compared to other interstates where the pipeline and its marketing affiliate could preferentially team up at the expense of independent marketers.[35]

———

The highlight of EGM's 1987—its "breakout moment" as remembered by head marketer John Esslinger—was a 10-year agreement to sell up to 60 MMcf/d to Brooklyn Union Gas Company, the fifth-largest gas-distribution company in America. Transco had provided this gas to Brooklyn Union ever since its line entered service in the early 1950s; now Ken Lay's old company would provide transportation for EGM pursuant to FERC Order No. 436. The transaction, accounting for approximately 25 percent of the requirements for the New York City–based company, or enough gas for as many as 125,000 homes, began in November 1987.

Brooklyn Union president Elwin Larson stated: "[We are] convinced that Enron's extensive supply and pipeline network will make a substantial contribution to our supply portfolio and will provide customers with a reliable and competitive source of natural gas well into the future." Dienstbier spoke of "the opportunities available in a free-market environment for both buyers and sellers to benefit from market-responsible pricing mechanisms." But mandatory open access, which enabled such third-party marketing, was part deregulation (of the commodity) and part reregulation (of interstate pipelines). It was a new FERC interpretation of just-and-reasonable pricing under the Natural Gas Act of 1938.

———

35. This controversy would lead to FERC Order No. 497, the Marketing Affiliate Rule (1988), which functionally divorced marketing from (interstate) transmission within a company. See Internet appendix 5.2, "Marketing Affiliate Rule (FERC Order No. 497)," at www .politicalcapitalism.org/Book3/Chapter5/Appendix2.html.

The terms of the agreement were not disclosed, but secrets were hard to keep in the industry. The long-term, guaranteed gas was fixed at a "hefty premium" to the then spot price, higher than any other contract but a portfolio hedge for Brooklyn Union should prices trend up. However, the contract contained "price bumpers" to trigger renegotiation should severe price swings occur.

The contract generated immediate high profits for EGM. But Enron did not have fixed-price, long-term gas to lock in a margin on the out months of the 230 Bcf deal. EOG production and reserves, not to mention Bammel storage, could come into play in a pinch. But Enron's corporate credit backed EGM to perform—even to buy gas at a loss to honor the contract.

Brooklyn Union was a landmark deal. No commodity contract of this size had ever been made to a gas-distribution company in the history of the (regulated) interstate market. It represented "the first long-term nonjurisdictional contract that had been done on a 10-year basis," remembered Esslinger, and it was just the beginning. Making bets that the buyers' market in gas would continue, EGM consummated similar deals with Elizabethtown (NJ) Gas Company (10 years) and Northern States Power Company (5 years).

———

Multimonth, noninterruptible (firm) contracts commanded a price premium to spot.[36] Buyers were willing to pay more for first-in-line gas, if it was backed (at least implicitly) by a corporate guarantee. Those were the deals that Enron wanted as a producer and a marketer. Generally, the longer the term, the better the margin, at least compared to the current spot price.

Profits were not separated out by Enron, reflecting the embryonic and sensitive nature of margin making in this early period. What customer would want to read about how much profit Enron was making on the deal? Volume information was provided for the first time, and it was strong: 700 MMcf/d.

Ken Lay was pleased. He didn't mind taking chances—big ones—in order to lead the market. Florida Gas and Citrus, after all, had done it on a grand scale in signing its 1.9 Tcf, 15-year deal with Florida Power & Light. The press noticed too as headlines told the business world how innovative Enron was. A story within the story was that Ken Lay's new company was beating his old one with

---

36. Daily spot gas prices at dozens of points were reported in trade publications, each of which gathered information from buyers and sellers. Longer-term contracts—with durations of a few months to a season to a year or more—were often priced off a reported spot price for a particular location. For example, a November–March winter contract might reference a spot price reported in *Natural Gas Week* in October and then be adjusted by the agreement of the parties, plus or minus several cents per MMBtu. These price indexes were the gospel until it became public that traders were increasingly reporting false prices and volumes to drive the index in self-serving ways, a practice that began in the late 1990s.

ex-Transco executives Claude Mullendore on the procurement side and John Esslinger on the sales side leading the way.

Conclusion

With his fourth anniversary as a Fortune 500 CEO just ahead, Ken Lay had transformed the old Houston Natural Gas into a Fortune 100 company and an industry leader—though not in the mold of the integrated oil majors. There was good block-and-tackle with the pipelines and with liquid fuels and an exciting new beginning with oil and gas exploration and production.

Best of all were the new (regulatory-driven) profit centers in which Enron was out front. Cogeneration was highly profitable with limited balance-sheet liabilities. Natural gas marketing, not only using company pipelines but also off-system nationally, was a new way to make money without buying hard assets, although the required investment in information technology was neither cheap nor foolproof.[37] Regulatory change, market conforming or not, was Ken Lay's playground.[38]

Despite perilous industry conditions, Lay was confident, perhaps hubristically so. ("Instead of reacting with fear and paralysis to the problems that plagued us," Ken Lay would later reminisce, "Enron Corp saw an opportunity to establish ourselves early in the game, as a leader of our industry.") Lay considered each of his divisional heads superior to the competition. Many risks had been taken, and most had been won, albeit at a very high long-term price considering what behavioral patterns were set.

Ken Lay had never failed in business, only overachieved, in his and so many other minds. This track record, however, would change dramatically with a scandal at Enron Oil Corporation, described in the next chapter. The scandal almost ruined Enron, and it dimmed, at least for a time, the halo of Ken Lay.

---

37. After much trial, error, and in-house expense, Enron outsourced its information technology (IT) function to Electronic Data Systems (EDS) in 1988 under a long-term contract. See chapter 6, pp. 260–66.

38. See Internet appendix 3.6, "'Market Conforming' Intervention: Free Market or Not?" at www.politicalcapitalism.org/Book3/Chapter3/Appendix6.html.

Part II

Peril and Progress: 1987–1989

Introduction

Normalcy and steady growth had eluded Enron since the merger. The Peruvian nationalization ruined 1985. The collapse in wellhead prices—nearly one-half for crude oil and one-fourth for natural gas—dampened 1986. Buying out Irwin Jacobs was expensive. What else could go wrong?

Now, surely, it was Enron's time to shine. The core assets in the gas divisions were in place. Top leadership had Jim Rogers over the interstate pipelines, Gerald Bennett over (Texas) intrastate pipelines, John Esslinger over wholesale marketing, Michael Muckleroy over liquids, John Wing (either as an employee or a consultant) over cogenerated power, and Forrest Hoglund running exploration and production. Richard Kinder, executive vice president and chief of staff, was increasingly complementing the Big Six, a good thing given the mediocre presidency of Mick Seidl and the external proclivities of Ken Lay.

Yet something suspicious was going at the high-flying Enron Oil Corporation in Valhalla, New York. The stand-alone, speculative oil-trading unit was reporting large, consistent profits—and bragging about them at management get-togethers. Experienced traders in Houston did not think that such profits were possible, quarter after quarter. And Mike Muckleroy was raising a stink about it.

What was too good to be true became just that in 1987, when Enron was hit by a major scandal—the story of chapter 4. In their annual report for the year, Lay and Seidl could claim only "progress" toward becoming "the premier natural gas company in North America," owing to "a number of unexpected events which hindered but failed to diminish achievement of that goal."

A second try at normalcy and progress was necessary—and accomplished to some degree in 1988–89. Still, as described in chapter 5, heavily indebted Enron was relying on nonrecurring earnings to report profitability. Young Enron was living on the edge, reflecting the ambition and nonstop drive of its founder and CEO, and thus foreshadowing the fate of a company that would die far too young.

4

Crisis at Enron Oil Corporation: 1987

Ken Lay was a good story. *Natural Gas Week* described the man "who hopped from Transco to HNG, and then had InterNorth for breakfast, even fooling some people into thinking that he was picking up the tab." But this momentum was gone. The $70 per share buyout of HNG stockholders made for a happy ending, but the same transaction made for a precarious beginning.

At Lay's insistence, InterNorth had overpaid for HNG by $5 per share, probably more. If everything had gone right, the premium could have been worked down. But the Peruvian nationalization of 1985, followed by the industry's price collapse the next year—both of which had warning signs—made the acquisition's high debt load lingering and constraining. Nonrecurring earnings were propping things up, not recurring, *quality* earnings.

In their first 19 months together, HNG and InterNorth recorded losses north of $100 million. Debt remained at over 70 percent of capitalization, which also meant higher interest rates than a better capitalized company would have paid. Speculative-grade "junk" bonds from Michael Milken's Drexel became Enron's debt instrument of necessity.

Still, Lay set a tone of high expectations. He announced the restructuring complete with the stock buyback and ESOP programs; his management team was mostly in place; and moral victories abounded. After all, wasn't Enron the industry's most innovative natural gas company? It was high time to have a big 1987 to support the (frozen) dividend, reduce debt, and achieve a credit upgrade, thereby creating a virtuous circle of lower interest costs and increased profitability.

The first quarter of 1987, the high season for natural gas, produced $67 million in earnings. The second quarter barely broke even, however, indicative of tough industry conditions and the company's debt burden. Then came a ray of good news: a proposed recapitalization plan to reduce the debt ratio from 73 percent to 60 percent by year's end.[1] Enron's stock, which had ended 1986 at $39.50, was trading at $51.00 nine months later in a down market. A ratings increase was under consideration by Moody's Investor Service.

———

One profit generator being counted on for 1987 was Enron Oil Corporation (EOC), a 28-person oil-trading operation headquartered in Valhalla, New York, with offices in London and Singapore. The "flashy part" of Sam Segnar's Inter-North, and now Lay's Enron, was a company unto itself. EOC did not market for Enron Oil & Gas Company. Nor did it make trades related to physical infrastructure, as did Enron Oil Transportation & Trading (EOTT), a division of Enron Liquid Fuels run by Mike Muckleroy. EOC traded paper barrels of crude oil and just about any petroleum product; EOTT traded mostly physical barrels that were moved from one place to another. EOC's arbitrage and speculation was profit for its own sake; EOTT was about logistics. And 1,400 miles—three hours by Enron jet—separated Smith Street in Houston from EOC's headquarters just north of New York City.

EOC had reported profits ever since Segnar hired Lou Borget from Gulf States Oil & Refining Company in early 1984 to set up a trading shop for Inter-North. Earnings of $10 million in 1985 were followed by $27 million in 1986, the latter accounting for a third of Enron's total profit for that year. And that was *after* paying bonuses to EOC of $3.2 million in 1985 and $9.4 million in 1986, as aggressive as any on Wall Street, and *after* absorbing such costs as company cars and limousine service, not to mention the fine caviar and champagne that were always on tap at the office. After all, there were many more good days than bad—seemingly.

John Harding, the head of Enron International, the parent of EOC, described Lou Borget to Enron's board as the best in the business. Borget had an edge on price movements because of his special relationship with some leading OPEC officials, his boss explained. For his part, Borget wrote in a board report: "As done by professionals in the industry today, using the sophisticated tools

———

1. Enron offered to exchange 2.2 shares of common stock for 1 share of preferred, lowering interest expense, and sell 18 percent of wholly owned Enron Oil & Gas to raise an estimated $275 million.

available, [oil trading] can generate substantial earnings with virtually no fixed investment and relatively low risk." And as explained in Enron's *1986 Annual Report*: "The volatile oil prices experienced during 1986 benefited earnings of [Enron Oil Corp.] as profits are generated on margins and on the skill of the trader, not on the absolute price of the product."

Like virtually all trading houses, EOC operated under in-house guidelines limiting *open* or *naked* positions (*long* or *short* obligations not offset in the other direction). In this case, the maximum nonhedged position was eight million barrels, and any position had to be liquidated if its paper loss reached $4 million (equating to a $0.50 per barrel loss-limit on the maximum volume).

Rules limiting unhedged risk also limited the home run, making profitable trading a game of small ball and perseverance. An outfit like EOC might be expected to earn $3 million in a decent year or as much as $7 million in a banner one. But if it was not skilled and careful, a trading house could lose money too.

Ken Lay liked Louis J. Borget—just as Segnar did. Borget, a New York native, had overcome an abusive father and put himself through night school at New York University while working full time at Texaco. Borget was intelligent, articulate, and debonair. He strode well in social settings. Mick Seidl respected him too.

Plus, Borget was tough and persuasive under the gun. His traders were devoted to him. But best of all, in Houston's eyes, he was a moneymaker. To Lay, Borget was just another smart performer like his other operating heads: Gerald Bennett (intrastate gas operations), Mike Muckleroy (liquids), Jim Rogers (interstate pipelines), and, soon, Forrest Hoglund (exploration and production).

Sirens and Denial (Valhalla 1)

Borget had a few skeptics. Early on, Howard Hawks of Northern Liquid Fuels warned his InterNorth superiors that Lou Borget might be rolling his losses forward. Speculative trading invariably had dry spells, and Borget never seemed to lose.

At Enron, Borget had one mighty skeptic: J. Michael Muckleroy. The two first met at a company management conference in 1986. EOC was reporting big earnings, yet Borget was strangely evasive when Mike quizzed him about it. Muckleroy had once been an active commodity trader for his own account and knew that it was a tough game. Trading orange juice futures in the early 1960s, he had made $1.2 million in two weeks, only to lose most of it over the next months. What seemed so easy—he had played a citrus freeze just right—turned excruciating.

Muckleroy gained respect for how price-driving factors could change unpredictably. He knew the pain of margin calls that forced him to liquidate open positions that just needed *a little more time*. Muckleroy finally quit his sideline when his wife threatened to leave him. He did not believe that anyone could be a trading Midas, much less Lou Borget.

How did EOC's earnings stay so strong and for so long? This was not the regulatory arbitrage of the 1970s, when price-controlled oil could be traded up to its market level. Back then, almost all traders had been winners.[2] But with oil decontrol in early 1981, hundreds of trading outfits had folded. Only the real pros remained, mainly those trading around their company's assets, such as oil production and refining.

EOC was working in a volatile price environment, which created opportunities for big gains—and losses. But even the best traders have bad runs, Muckleroy knew. There just are too many acts of man and of God for moneymakers not to be moneybreakers on occasion.

But most of all, Muckleroy knew that self-imposed company trading limits scarcely allowed the type of profits that EOG was reporting. To achieve earnings that high, Borget's traders would have to be consistently winning in marathon trading. Yet Borget described EOC's niche as low risk, combining arbitrage gains (simultaneous buy and sell orders locking in a price differential) and sure-bet tips about where prices were headed. Seasoned traders had reason to doubt both stories: Arbitrage is small, hard money because sure things are difficult to come by.

Muckleroy's Houston operation was actually larger and more global than that of EOC. EOTT's oil traders had the pulse of the industry, and the whisper was that EOC was making aggressive bets. Muckleroy warned his boss, Mick Seidl, who as Enron's president and COO presided over both Enron Liquid Fuels (EOTT's parent) and Enron International (EOC's parent).

Mick had been in the oil business from his days at Natomas. But, curiously, he was not responsive to the red flags that Muckleroy found alarming. The same was true of Ken Lay. Richard Kinder, now Enron's general counsel, did not give Muckleroy a beachhead either. With Lay setting the tone, top management was content with what came through official channels: the audited and recorded profit, the result of Lou Borget's consummately turning superior knowledge into superior returns.

Enron was lucky to have Borget, people thought. Any fuss about him was just one more case of company infighting—and at a target whose 1986 bonus was 50 times that of the complainant (Muckleroy). Plus, Muckleroy went too far when he brought his concern to New Yorker Robert Belfer, Enron's largest stockholder and a board director, who until recently had run Belco. Muckleroy had broken the chain of command. He was not being a team player.

———

2. Regulatory arbitrage with price-controlled oil ("daisy-chaining") is described in Bradley, *Capitalism at Work*, pp. 260–62.

On Friday, January 23, 1987, alarm bells went off for David Woytek, Enron's vice president of auditing and one of the corporation's 21 officers. A New York bank alerted him about large wire transfers to secret international destinations for the personal account of EOC treasurer Tom Mastroeni, Borget's right-hand man. Woytek alerted Rich Kinder, who alerted Borget's boss, John Harding, the head of Enron International. The first Valhalla scandal had begun.

Investigation by Woytek found trouble. A member of Woytek's team, John Beard, scribbled notes such as: "Misstatements of records, deliberate manipulation of records, impact on financials for the year ending 12/31/86."

A meeting in Houston was quickly convened with Borget and Mastroeni in the hot seat. Seidl was traveling, so Lay presided.[3] The CEO was in a tight spot. Lay simply could not do what he might have done in more prosperous times—and should have done, period. Enron's (low) earnings were in danger of violating its loan covenants, and a confidence crisis could lead to a ratings downgrade, if not worse.[4] This was a baby that had to be split, Lay decided.

Harding, to his relief, got a viable explanation from the two. The funny stuff was just a means to smooth earnings between quarters and even years—just as Enron executives had instructed him (Borget) to do. Bankers preferred steady, recurring earnings, and EOC had little trouble finding another trading house to perform a *net-out* transaction to shift costs and revenue as desired. In this instance, the intent was to get a solid jump on 1987 earnings, something that 1986's success happily allowed.

Ken Lay nodded sternly but appreciatively when he heard this explanation. But Woytek and his auditing team were ready to drop the hammer. Several million dollars were missing, and internal audit had turned up what appeared to be criminal behavior. Worse, right before the meeting, they had discovered that a key document brought in by Borget and Mastroeni had been forged. The incriminating fund flows on the original copy obtained from the bank had been suspiciously removed. The two had to be fired, maybe prosecuted. The whole Valhalla operation had to be reaudited and closed or at least merged into EOTT.

Mastroeni gave a plausible explanation of the peculiarities, but there was just too much smoke not to signal fire. A recess was called. Beard and Woytek walked over to Rich Kinder, Enron's top lawyer. "They just lied to you," Beard

---

3. This account follows Eichenwald, *Conspiracy of Fools*, pp. 15–19. McLean and Elkind say that John Harding maintained Lay was not present. But if Harding was right, it merely suggests that Lay's conflict-avoidance syndrome was more crippling still to the company.

4. Just weeks before this meeting, Moody's Investors Service downgraded the company's long-term credit rating to "junk" (below investment grade).

complained. Kinder allegedly responded: "Well, if it was up to me, I'd fire them all right now."

But then the meeting turned in favor of the visitors. Borget and Mastroeni got moral support from Harding and Steve Sulentic, both of Enron International in Houston. (EOC's performance had meant bigger bonuses for them that might have to be returned.) Borget and Mastroeni argued for EOC and promised to do things differently going forward.

This was Lay's call, and the CEO did split the baby. This should not have happened, Lay said. There needed to be income restatements between quarters and years to achieve compliance. The money in question had to be retrieved. Privately, Lay instructed Woytek to get an auditing team up to Valhalla to review everything. New controls and a new treasurer had to be put in place. This could not happen again, Lay told Borget and Mastroeni point blank.

Still, Woytek and Beard left the meeting feeling defeated. Muckleroy, upon hearing it all, was perturbed. Borget and Mastroeni could not be trusted. For his part, Lay shared his decision with key board members and moved on. This was the last thing that he wanted to deal with, but EOC had to be watched very carefully. Henceforth, EOC vigilance was Mick Seidl's number-one priority with daily examination of positions. Finally, to examine things more closely, an Enron board meeting was scheduled for that summer at EOC's offices at the Mount Pleasant Corporate Center in Valhalla, New York.

———

Valhalla 1 was far from over. Woytek's on-location audit work was troubled from the start. Borget kept a tight leash on his unwanted guests, and his books came without documentation. Still, the auditors pressed, and just when Borget seemed cornered, Woytek got a call from Houston to disengage. The new plan, explained Seidl, was for Arthur Andersen to take over. As it turned out, Borget had called Mick, complaining that the audit was disrupting trading. There was a danger of not making plan, Borget said. Enron could not afford that, Seidl knew.

The Lay-ordered investigation found a variety of irregularities. Borget had sold a company car for his own account. There were secret payments to a fictitious M. Yass (code for "my ass"?) that in all probability went to Borget and Mastroeni. Some of the companies involved in the countertrades did not seem to exist. Mastroeni had once been sued by his bankers for fraud. Internal audit took the report to CFO Keith Kern, who did not seem to want to get involved. Despite Lay's order, this was not something that people at the top of Enron wanted to confront—at least not yet.

Now engaged in Valhalla, Arthur Andersen also encountered roadblocks. Borget was not providing information, such as daily trading reports that could be checked against Enron's trading limits. In fact, Borget and Mastroeni admitted that they had routinely destroyed the dailies. This was a damning story, but the Valhalla cowboys had Houston on their side, as indicated by one note from nice-guy Mick Seidl to Borget after a conference call between the parties:

> Thank you for your perseverance. You understand your business better than anyone alive. Your answers to Arthur Andersen were clear, straightforward, and rock solid—superb. I have complete confidence in your business judgment and ability and in your personal integrity. Please keep making us millions.[5]

In April, Arthur Andersen presented its findings to the Audit Committee of the Enron board of directors, chaired by Robert Jaedicke, a Stanford business professor who would continue in this capacity through Enron's solvent life. Andersen's conclusions were hardly reassuring. EOC had "demonstrated the ability" to engage in unrecorded commitments. Although more improprieties had not been found, there could be no assurance that more did not exist.

Some board directors were uneasy, including Ron Roskens, one of the few InterNorth holdovers, who expressed his concerns. But ending the operation was not on the table, only Mastroeni's part in it. Borget had evidently felt confident enough about his own standing to call Lay just before the meeting and personally plead for Mastroeni, saying that the operation could not work without him. When Lay saw that the discussion was going against Mastroeni, he stepped in. According to the minutes of the meeting, "Management [Lay, clearly] recommended the person involved be kept on the payroll but relieved of financial responsibility." One source claims that Lay said: "I have decided not to terminate these people. I need their earnings," as though all of EOC was under the gun, but there is no confirmed source for that impression or for that quotation.

According to Muckleroy, there also existed a letter composed by John Beard, Carolyn Kee (of Arthur Andersen), and David Woytek, with input from Muckleroy, that detailed findings of criminality and wanton disregard of company policy by Borget and Mastroeni. If that is true, the Enron board's dereliction in not terminating EOC root and branch would itself seem to border on negligence. But the allegation may not be true as described.

In any case, Muckleroy said, these four were apparently content to feel that, should EOC implode, their exposé would serve to exonerate them as having made their best efforts at diligence. It was the whistle blow, the smoking gun, which any external investigation would surely uncover.

As it turned out, EOC *would* go into crisis, but the damage would be contained and the investigation internalized. Not until many years later, with Enron and Lay under the microscope, would the full story of Valhalla come out.

———

5. Ron Burns remembers Seidl as "a good guy" who "never really knew the business" versus "the really strong operating types who really started to take control [such as] [Dan] Dienstbier, [Mike] Muckleroy, [Rich] Kinder."

Dodging a bullet at the April meeting, and perhaps knowing that this was their best or last chance, Borget and Mastroeni and a few of their traders who were on the take put their clandestine operation into high gear. They were in a hole and had to get out of it—*again.*

Big bets outside of their trading limits had been made back in 1986, but a fortuitous jump in oil prices at year end helped paper over the problems. Now more rabbits had to be pulled out of the hat to keep reporting profits in the dailies that Mick Seidl reviewed every workday morning at eight o'clock. Things were not going well, and rumors were flying. Don Gullquist, Enron's treasurer, was getting calls from his New York bankers about how EOC was "lighting up every trade on the screen." Enron seemed to be on one side or the other of an inordinate amount of cargos.

The caviar and champagne remained on ice. The bets were scarcely winning. Long positions made at an average $21 per barrel had lost as oil prices fell, and short positions made at an average $19 per barrel went out of the money as prices rose.

To provide some cover for their growing limit violations, Borget went to Seidl with a request to increase their trading limits. Seidl put it on the agenda for Enron's August board meeting in Valhalla. At that meeting, Borget made his case, comparing his risk profile to that of holding Treasury bills. Despite skepticism by a number of people in the room (attendee Robert Kelly described the presentation to his boss, John Wing, as "alchemy, selling fool's gold"), the board voted to increase the open-position limit from 8 to 12 million barrels.

The verdict was decided before, not during, the meeting. Gullquist remembered how he and others on the plane ride up tried to move Ken Lay against Borget's request. Lay ended this discussion by stating Enron's need for earnings. As Lay went, so would the board.

Meanwhile, EOTT was hearing new rumors that EOC was on the wrong side of the market. More warnings by Muckleroy to the Big Three—Seidl, Kinder, and Lay—went unheeded, although Lay did phone Borget about the whispers to make sure they were not true. (Borget said absolutely not.) Muckleroy was "paranoid," it was said in the chairman's office.[6]

EOC was up some $12 million for the first half of 1987, the books showed. Thus it was not out of particular concern that Seidl on a New York swing set up a lunch with his star trader at the Pierre Hotel in New York City. It was Friday,

---

6. "We had reached a total impasse," remembered Muckleroy, referring to himself and members of Enron's internal audit team. "Ken, Mick, and Rich told me to 'butt out,' that the Valhalla operations were 'none of my business,' that I was simply jealous of the success of that unit and the bonuses that Lou was receiving, and to cease my harassment."

October 9, 1987, about a year from when Muckleroy first complained about EOC and about nine months after Valhalla 1.[7]

Crisis and Cleanup (Valhalla 2)

At lunch, Seidl got shocking news. "I've got a big problem," Borget stated, alluding to trading imbalances that were under water. "How big is it?" Seidl shot back. "I think it may be as much as $50 million before tax," answered Lou. Borget confessed to busting through his newly increased trading limits but expressed optimism about winnowing his way out of the predicament with some time and support from corporate.

Mick was crestfallen. EOC was his responsibility. Lay had made it his number-one priority. John Duncan, who had dealt with sugar traders back at Gulf & Western, had warned him to be vigilant. ("Seidl, pay really careful attention. These people have a different mentality than everybody else.") Mick had visited the large trading houses in New York and London to understand their systems and controls to get things right at EOC. He had worked hard at a professional and personal friendship with Lou Borget. This unit had never lost a penny. Its presentations were crisp and persuasive. The daily reports indicated another big year for Enron.

The deficit that Borget alluded to was enough to ruin Enron's year—and cancel most, if not all, the profit that the EOC had made for Enron from its inception. *And what if the hole was even deeper?* Given the "screwy" things that had gone on at EOC, Seidl feared a worst-case scenario. Enron was just turning the corner—and now this.

After suggesting Borget do what he could to unwind the bad deals, Seidl jumped on his plane to intersect with Ken Lay, who was coming home from Europe. Lay and Seidl would return to Valhalla to meet with Borget, and Lay's plane would return with its other occupants to Houston.

Lay had been touring Europe with Forrest Hoglund, the new chief of Enron Oil & Gas Company, in anticipation of taking EOG public. Lay had lured Hoglund, an industry star, away from Texas Oil & Gas Company. If Valhalla had blown up six weeks sooner, Hoglund might have stayed put.[8]

In Houston, Rich Kinder tracked down Muckleroy with the news. Kinder was no fan of Borget or EOC but had followed the leader on this one. He now

---

7. Muckleroy's account is at odds with that of Seidl and of Borget, who agree that the shockingly bad news came out at lunch. Muckleroy says that at 11:45 a.m. on Monday, October 5, he learned that Enron International had recent margin calls of $100 million. By Muckleroy's account, he told Seidl, who then flew to New York to see Borget.

8. Hoglund's decision to join Enron is discussed in chapter 3, pp. 174–77.

had that cold feeling of financial doom—one he remembered from when some bad personal investments bankrupted him back in Missouri.

Muckleroy, previously the skunk at the lawn party, was now the company's hope. He had experience. Get right to Valhalla with a team to unwind EOC's positions, Kinder bellowed.

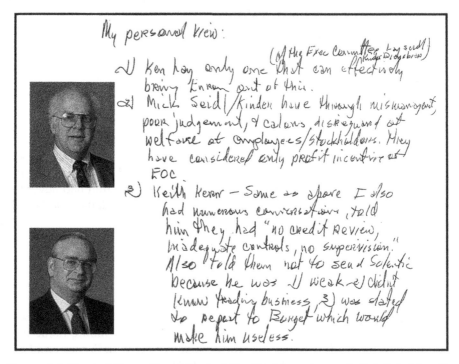

Figure 4.1 Head of Enron Liquid Fuels, Mike Muckleroy (upper left) futilely blew the whistle on Enron Oil Company's Lou Borget (lower left). Muckleroy cleaned up Borget's mess, a fiasco that was not fully appreciated until after Enron's bankruptcy in late 2001.

Muckleroy was prepared. Having anticipated this crisis, he had a team on notice. The red alert was to pack for three weeks, wheels up in two hours. Joining Muckleroy were John Fetzer, EOTT's most experienced trader, and Roger Leworthy, EOTT's treasurer and credit manager. Internal audit and support staff would follow early the next week.

Muckleroy, in fact, had gotten Clint Murchison (the father of Florida Gas Transmission, among other pipelines[9]) out of a tight spot in the early 1950s, when an underwater pipeline owned by Delhi Oil broke near Corpus Christi,

9. See Bradley, *Edison to Enron*, pp. 230–45.

interrupting wintertime gas deliveries. The repair job by the former scholarship swimmer and Navy Seal earned special kudos from Murchison himself. Now, using every interpersonal and business skill in the book, Muckleroy had to save Enron by carefully unwinding a slew of out-of-the-money contracts without tipping off the market.

Muckleroy arrived at EOC's offices in the early evening to find the employees in a daze. Friday trading was over. Many were in the dark about what was going on. Little had been done after Borget returned from lunch with Seidl. Borget had informed the floor of problems and had everyone in their chair pending Houston's arrival.

Muckleroy first dismissed Borget, telling him to tell the floor and those who had to know that he was going on a two-week vacation, with EOTT running the office until his return. Other than that, he was to say nothing.[10]

Everyone else was likewise told to say nothing, not even to share trading positions with each other, or they would be fired on the spot. All communication would be centralized and come from the top—from Muckleroy. But there was a carrot. If everyone did as asked and performed well, each would receive a bonus and a letter of recommendation. It was a foregone conclusion that EOC would no longer be a going concern after the crisis passed.

After Borget, Muckleroy met with Mastroeni. His voice shaking, Muckleroy said:

> Tom, I do not believe that you are the originator of what has happened, but you are certainly the facilitator. Borget is going to prison, but I'm giving you a choice. If you bring us the *real* books and help clean up this mess, I will do everything I can to keep you out of jail. If you flee, however, I will go to the ends of the earth to find you. And I want you to know that I have killed people in my [military] past and slept like a baby…. I'll see you first thing tomorrow morning.

Mastroeni arrived at eight o'clock sharp on Saturday morning with two crates containing the off-the-books records. The salvage operation, what Mike Muckleroy would later call "the biggest poker game ever played in Crude Oil Trading," was on.

The weekend was spent figuring out where EOC stood. The ugly truth was an out-of-the-money short position of *84 million barrels*, not the feared worst-case scenario of 50 million barrels. Some 76 sham transactions had been made from as far back as November 1985 to hide the problems. No oil-trading house

---

10. According to Eichenwald's account, Lay called Muckleroy from Newfoundland and ordered him to Valhalla, then summoned Borget to his hotel on Saturday morning. Borget arrived, believing he would be unwinding the company's difficulties and was stunned when Lay fired him (*Conspiracy of Fools*, p. 38). Borget said that Lay did not fire him at the hotel and that his notice of termination came by telex, more evidence of Lay's confrontation avoidance, if true.

had been short this much, ever. As Enron would state in court documents, this short position was the equivalent of three months' oil production from Britain's North Sea fields.

The market could not be permitted to find out how badly Enron was in the hole. Credit cutoffs and margin calls would test Enron's liquidity at the worst possible time, given that the bankers were in the middle of Enron's recapitalization plan. All indications had to be business as usual—except that the ENE price was falling. Something was up, but no one at Enron would comment on why.

Monday began cautiously with Fetzer purchasing a few cargos and Leworthy working with Mastroeni to figure out EOC's short position. The market saw that Enron was covering but little else. Still, losses of between $10 and $15 million were incurred in about five million barrels of unwinding.

With a few more million barrels purchased on the European market, Enron had covered some 10 percent of its open position. But early Tuesday morning, the bleary-eyed crew got a news flash: Iraq had attacked a supertanker carrying Iranian crude oil in the Strait of Hormuz. Oil in Europe was up over $1 a barrel, increasing Enron's contract exposure another $100 million, or about $300 million overall.[11]

Then came Muckleroy's finest moment. Tuesday morning, a half hour before the New York open, EOC offered one of the largest traders in the New York harbor market one million barrels at $1.25 over Monday's close. This was a bold play. Enron needed to cover its obligated barrels, not sell new barrels, and any sale at this price would mean a large loss. Muckleroy had EOC make the same offer to other large houses before the bell.

The market got the message: *Enron was not as short as believed*. No one bought Enron's cargo, thankfully, and the market opened less than a dime higher, which was even better. The bluff worked. Enron quickly bought two million barrels, followed later by some European cargo buys. One purchase was made from Shell International, which did not know that Shell USA had cut off credit to Enron on the rumors.

Enron had now covered 20 percent of its position at a manageable loss. It was hectic work, but the first laugh in days came when a trader asked Muckleroy what he would have done if Enron had had to sell cargos at the Monday close plus $1.25. "I would have just had to kill myself," came his reply.

Credit was a worry. If Exxon cut off Enron as had Shell USA, the whole market would find out quickly, and Houston would be drawing down its lines. The bankers would find out everything, and oil sellers could name their price. Enron

---

11. This was Enron's maximum exposure, contrary to estimates made in some accounts that put the figure at $1 billion. That inflated figure was a what-if—if the price of crude oil had gone up another $5 to $10 per barrel, partly as a result of the market's finding out about Enron's desperate short position.

might even enter into a liquidity crisis. Ken Lay's old employer held a sword over him, even if both he and the venerable oil major did not know it.

But Muckleroy had a high card to play. Enron Liquid Fuels had done a lot of business with Paribas ever since the merger. Philippe Blavier of Paribas particularly liked Mike Muckleroy, as did just about everyone. Mike asked Philippe for a $300 million line of credit, explaining that he was unwinding some bad positions and needed backup.

"What size position are you dealing with," Blavier asked, only to add, "I don't want to know, just tell me later."

"Philippe," Muckleroy replied, "I will explain it to you in 30 days over the best meal and finest bottle of Chateau Lafitte at the Four Seasons in New York City."

Enron would owe Paribas that and a lot more, although the line would not have to be used. It made a world of difference for EOC just to be able to tell its trading partners to call Paribas if they needed a letter of credit in addition to the usual corporate guarantee.

The oil market calmed by midweek. Prices were within striking distance of most of the remaining open positions. It was now just a matter of buying cargos—but not too quickly. The loss was looking like $175 million—about $2 a barrel averaged over the entire short position. But there would be some offsets to the trading loss: $6 million of Borget bonuses that were in a deferred income account at Enron and a $15 million court-ordered award that would come from a Japanese trading company that participated in Borget's ruse.

———

After 11 days, it was time for Muckleroy to return home. The scotch was flowing, and one of the Enron pilots kindly called Mrs. Muckleroy to come pick up her husband, although, yes, his car was at the airport. The EOTT team, with help from various Enron divisions, had lassoed the losses. EOC was now on a glide path to extinction.

Mike Muckleroy had just enough of an ego to look forward to getting back to the office. Would the Big Three look him in the eye? In particular, what would Ken Lay say? Lay had not once talked to Muckleroy during the ordeal, leaving that to Seidl. Seidl and Lay had stayed away from Valhalla; any sighting of these two would have charged the rumor mill.

The damage could have been worse. What if Mastroeni had not appeared with the real books on the morning of October 10, complicating efforts to unwind the positions and likely leading to the market's learning about Enron's huge naked positions? What if Exxon had cut off credit or Paribas had not extended a large credit line? What if oil prices had moved up several dollars per barrel? Maybe such a combination would not have sunk Enron—the company's hard assets had a net market value north of a billion dollars before Valhalla. Unquestionably, though, recovery would have been much more difficult. And just maybe Ken Lay would have had to go.

Sanitization

The announcement came October 22: Unauthorized transactions in the oil-trading unit would result in Enron's taking a charge of $142 million—$85 million after taxes—against third-quarter 1987 earnings. Net income for the company would be restated all the way back to 1984, the year that InterNorth hired Borget to set up EOC.[12] The ENE share price, already down on rumors, fell on the official news for a total EOC-related loss of 30 percent.

This was bitter medicine.

But what could be worse was a *full* explanation of the debacle. Public disclosure of Enron's year-long civil war would stain Ken Lay in particular. ENE had always enjoyed a management premium centering on Lay's aura of special talent. Should he be exposed as a pain-averse Big Thinker, his PhD credential would go from halo to Hamlet, and Enron's board of directors would seem compliant with a fact-evading CEO.[13]

The press release, employee meeting, and follow-up interviews were exercises in half-truth. Enron had to tell a story but not fully. Corporations did this all the time, and certainly Enron had done this before, albeit on a much smaller scale. Press releases concerning the parting of a fired or demoted executive, for example, were typically half-truths (strategic deceit, aka philosophic fraud). And so it would be in 1991 when Transco fired CEO George Slocum (who back in 1984 took the place of departing Ken Lay as COO) but described it as *his* decision to leave—and only after great contemplation.[14]

The sanitized version of Valhalla went as follows. Oil trading is a secretive business depending on the integrity and highly specialized skill of the trader. The scandal was a classic case of unforeseen criminality where all signs pointed the other way. Lou Borget and Enron Oil Company were highly successful before the shocking turn of events, earning $50 million in two and a half years. There had been rumors, but every precaution had been taken. There were meetings, audits, and reaudits—and even an Enron board meeting held at EOC's offices where everything was scrutinized.

---

12. InterNorth auditors were suspicious about Valhalla from the beginning but could not uncover anything. It was also discovered that Borget had left Texaco abruptly and had lost money while trading at Gulf States Oil and Refining. Sam Segnar had not done the proper due diligence.

13. A worse financial outcome out of Valhalla could have triggered a full airing of Ken Lay's culpability, which could have roiled the financial community and forced the board to ask for Lay's resignation. If so, Lay would have received benefits under two employment agreements worth several million dollars. This almost unimaginable end for the industry wunderkind would have been far gentler than what transpired in 2001–2002 and after.

14. See Bradley, *Edison to Enron*, pp. 359–61.

During a period of unusual volatility in oil markets, the narrative continued, EOC got on the wrong side of a bet and tried to recoup the losses quickly,
all the while violating company policy on both volume and margins. They
went long and lost—and went short and lost again. To hide the deficits and
violations of company policy, secret books were kept by EOC's two most
senior executives. But when the hole got too deep for the renegades, Enron
was notified.

Enron found out on October 9—three days before the next scheduled
audit—and acted quickly and prudently. Borget was fired, and the open positions were unwound in a matter of days. Enron's full board, meanwhile, called
into emergency session in New York City, shut down the unit as a going
concern.

Enron was fooled but had been otherwise prudent. It was an "expensive
embarrassment," Lay told the *New York Times*. The business press, including a
feature in *Texas Business*, portrayed Lay as shocked, dismayed, and helpless,
given that, as the magazine described, "safeguards had been in place."

Compliant analysts buttressed Enron's whitewash. "How do you protect
yourself?" asked David Fleischer of Prudential-Bache, an Enron investment
bank that had recently sued HNG's board over its payment of greenmail. "You'd
have to hire an accountant and a marshal with a gun and have them peering
over the shoulder of traders all day long." But on closer inspection, a string of
obvious management failures was behind the ruse of Borget et al.

———

"I promise you," Lay told employees packed in the Hyatt Regency ballroom,
"we will never again risk Enron's credibility in business ventures without first
making sure we thoroughly understand the risks." At the meeting, Lay
expressed his regret that several crooked employees could cancel out the profitable effort of thousands. As in golf, Lay analogized, Enron now had to scramble
after a bad shot to make par.[15]

But wasn't this the man who the year before told all that the business climate
provided no margin for error? The man who just weeks before Valhalla 2
exploded told *Forbes* how much fun he was having with the disorderly market?
Words aside, Ken Lay was an inveterate optimist—and a riverboat gambler.

Muckleroy left the employee meeting upset. He had expected a more forthright explanation and even contrition from the CEO. Instead, Lay professed
total innocence. At one point, Muckleroy thought of standing up from his front-
row seat and asking for the real story. But he was not going to embarrass the

———

15. By memo, Lay bluntly expressed himself as "damn mad" and told employees: "If there
is any lesson to be learned from the recent trading losses, it is that everyone—and I do mean
everyone—must abide by the company's policies, procedures and controls."

chairman, although two colleagues sitting on either side of him were ready to lean over to keep the peace.

Mike did get the real story out to the lawyers, which he supplemented with pages of hand-scribbled notes for the record. If heads were going to roll, he thought, it sure did not need to be his. He had been warned by a Vinson & Elkins attorney investigating the fiasco for Enron's board: "Mike, never underestimate their ability for damage control."

Others in the know were scared too. David Woytek duplicated all his papers for home storage. It could get ugly if Lay or another high-up needed to manufacture distance from the fiasco.

———

Muckleroy would never receive any one-on-one, heartfelt thanks from Lay, Seidl, Kinder, or Kern. But a layer down, Ron Burns, Forrest Hoglund, and others were congratulatory. Otherwise, the subject was over and done with—and verboten. In Lay's mind, he had hired Mike, and Mike had come through—just another vindication of the smartest-guys strategy. It would not always have to be this way. Once Enron got its footing, such chances would not need to be taken again, Lay thought.

But a *mea culpa*, at least behind closed doors, was what was needed and entirely appropriate. "I was desperate for earnings," Lay might have confessed to his inner circle and Muckleroy in particular. "Next time, I'm going to put Kinder on this and sooner—he is better with the hammer than me." And finally, "Thank you Mike for your deft cleanup, and I apologize for downplaying your warnings."

With the passage of time, Lay might have even revisited the issue for all employees. "I did not walk the talk about Enron's core values when it mattered the most," he could have admitted. "It is easy to look the other way or rationalize amid the pressure of earnings." The lesson going forward: "Forbid shortcuts, and courageously solve problems before they get bigger and unmanageable."[16]

As it was, Valhalla would soon be forgotten. It would be an afterthought when in March 1990 Enron filed suit against 21 plaintiffs, beginning with not only Borget and Mastroeni individually but also a raft of companies involved in the sham transactions and illegal transfers of money. Borget pleaded guilty to three felonies and was sentenced to a year in jail and five years of probation. Mastroeni pleaded guilty to two felonies but got only two years of probation after Muckleroy, as promised, pleaded for leniency.

———

16. Years later, with setbacks accumulating around him, Lay added a new slide to his standard presentation about confronting and learning from problems, the most prominent example being Valhalla.

Federal investigations did not find Enron liable, although the criminal defense lawyers, seeking to broaden blame, argued: "Any honest competent management, confronted with the conduct of Borget and Mastroeni, as revealed to Enron's senior management in January 1987, would have fired these gentlemen without delay."[17]

Costs and Consequences

Valhalla's loss ruined Enron's 1987. Paltry earnings of $6 million would be restated the following year as a $29 million loss. ENE's fourth-quarter share price sagged from a high of $50.50 to a low of $31.00, before a year-end rebound to $39.125. Lay's goal to end 1987 with a debt-to-capital ratio near 60 percent was eviscerated, although Enron's recapitalization plan (which was completed only because the bankers were not alerted to Valhalla) resulted in a 70 percent ratio, slightly higher than the year before but still down from 1985's 73 percent.

"Enron Is Upbeat Despite Poor 1987," read a news item in *Natural Gas Week*. Valhalla aside, cash flow was significantly above 1986, the industry's depression year. And take-or-pay liabilities were cut by more than half, from $1.1 billion to less than $500 million.

————

With the balance sheet wounded, it was necessary to sell a core asset, continuing the habit of monetizing good assets to pay for bad habits.[18] Enter Enron Cogeneration Company (ECC), whose sale in part or in whole would help the income statement and balance sheet, at least in the short run. Cogeneration was a new technology and great new business for independents, thanks to political capitalism. With power-demand growth and the nuclear option closed after the Three Mile Island accident in 1979, many electric utilities needed new generation capacity. It all came together to create Enron's highest rate-of-return business—and most marketable asset.

After ECC was reorganized, the inside-outside team of Robert Kelly and John Wing was able to redo the necessary contracts with Texas Utilities to get Texas City's financing off the balance sheet. Fixed-priced, long-term gas was purchased from Enron Oil & Gas, a key modification that made the project bankable.

————

17. For further discussion of Valhalla issues, see Internet appendix 4.1, "Valhalla Redux," at www.politicalcapitalism.org/Book3/Chapter4/Appendix1.html.

18. As discussed in chapter 3, the prior instance was the sale of half of Florida Gas Transmission in March 1986 when HNG's pricey-gutsy bid for FGT was followed by the Peruvian nationalization and higher-than-expected merger costs. *Business Week* reported that Enron was considering a half sale of Northern Natural Gas Pipeline for "nearly $750 million" post-Valhalla.

Project finance from a bank consortium was not the path chosen by Wing. Enron needed money fast, with 1986 drawing to a close. While negotiations with Texas Utilities were being completed to secure the contracts requisite for financing, Wing pushed forward with Drexel Burnham Lambert, already an Enron mainstay. Michael Milken's company agreed to finance 90 percent of the project's cost with high-yield junk bonds in return for a 50 percent equity kicker. The deal was done to help rescue Enron's year after 1985's net loss.

Wing cut several months off the usual process of bank financing and equity solicitation. But it was very expensive in terms of both the interest rate paid and the surrendered equity. More than this, though, the opportunity cost for Enron was having Harold Hawks in charge rather than consultant Wing. Hawks had put together the project initially. Hawks respected net present value economics. Enron, as it was, neutered not millions of dollars but *tens* of millions in its hurry.[19]

Texas City began full operations in May 1987. Wing collected a $1.5 million bonus, based on assured payouts, as well as a cut of the plant's future profits. The plant was technically sound and highly profitable. Three years after start-up, Ken Lay and Rich Kinder would tell shareholders in Enron's annual report: "Our state-of-the-art facility in Texas City has established Enron as a key player in this new market."

Indeed, Texas City was a *triple* win for Enron. HPL carried 75 MMcf/d of gas to the plant. And EOG, supplying two-thirds of the gas to the operation, got a company-building contract far above the going spot price for gas, which the quirks of avoided-cost regulation under a federal law afforded at the expense of captive utility customers.

The genesis of EOG's sweetheart contract came when Wing, after failing to interest Ted Collins at EOG, contacted Boone Pickens, who had recruited him to join Mesa Limited Partnership (formerly Mesa Petroleum Company) after he left Enron as an employee to consult. Mesa was interested in providing long-term gas at a premium to spot for Texas City. But when Lay found out that Pickens (his nemesis since the Jacobs-Leucadia buyout) was about to get a piece of his own deal, Collins and EOG agreed to a multiyear fixed-priced contract for two-thirds of the plant's requirements. That deal, paying $3.25/MMBtu plus a 6 percent annual escalation factor—compared to spot gas just above $1.00/MMBtu—would prove invaluable for EOG and thus for Enron as gas prices remained low through the next decade.[20]

---

19. In fact, Hawks was not a good fit at Enron and left in 1987 to form his own company. Tenaska, prudent and profitable from the start, would prove to be the multifaceted natural gas company that Enron set out to be. See chapter 3, pp. 168–69.

20. The regulatory (PURPA-related) reason behind this gas price is discussed in chapter 5, pp. 218–19. See the PURPA discussion in Internet appendix 1.5, "Public Utility Regulatory Policies Act of 1978 (PURPA)," at www.politicalcapitalism.org/Book3/Chapter1/Appendix5.html.

Enron needed more projects like this. But despite talk about new large projects (as many as six were in discussion), nothing had reached the construction
stage. So in August 1987, in keeping with Lay's way of doing things, Enron
signed Wing to a new five-year contract, complete with a 5 percent equity interest in ECC. But Wing remained a consultant, not an Enron employee, although
he could no longer work on non-Enron projects. It was a peculiar arrangement,
but Wing was fiercely independent—and Enron's own twists and turns were at
work.

Figure 4.2 The PURPA-driven cogeneration work of John Wing (center) was a much-
needed profit generator for Enron in the in the mid-to-late 1980s. Enron's other two top
cogen developers were Wing lieutenant Robert Kelly (upper right) and, from the Inter-
North side, Howard Hawks (upper left), who would leave Enron in 1987 to found his own
company, Tenaska.

The company Wing inherited had interests of around 400 MW in three
cogeneration plants with a capacity of 915 MW, a portfolio soon supplemented
by a 50 percent purchase of an operating 377 MW plant in Clear Lake.[21] Arthur

---

21. The projects in Enron's portfolio were a 34 percent interest in the 300 MW Bayou Cogeneration Plant; a 50 percent interest in the 450 MW Texas City Plant; a 42 percent interest in the
165 MW Bayonne Plant in New Jersey (1987); and a pending 50 percent interest in the 377 MW
Clear Lake Cogeneration Plant. Enron would soon have 100 percent interest in Clear Lake
when Mission Energy sold its half-interest at cost to Enron in return for having an exclusive
offer to buy half of ECC, which it declined to buy.

Andersen valued ECC for Enron at $30 million, giving Wing a $1.5 million stake at the get-go. But this valuation did not account for future projects, and discussions were under way concerning an additional 900 MW.

But come Valhalla, Wing's new instruction was to sell part of his unit to improve the balance sheet and to create earnings.[22] Lay blamed it on the oil-trading losses and more specifically, to the surprise of Wing, on the oversight failures of Mick Seidl and Keith Kern regarding Valhalla. In any case, Enron's and Lay's relationship with Wing was ruptured, and the future income from one of Enron's top profit centers was halved.[23] This cost from the oil-trading debacle would last for the rest of Enron's life.

Lesson Unlearned

With his interpretation of Valhalla, Ken Lay fooled not only his employees, Enron's investors, and general public. He fooled himself. The two-act scandal was chock-full of lessons. But by not volunteering the whole truth, by parsing it instead—a narrative that struck those closest to Valhalla as blatant lying—much instruction in bourgeois morality went undone. Scarcely realized at the time, the episode was "the canary in the coal mine" for what would ultimately bankrupt Enron and destroy Ken Lay professionally and personally.

Ken Lay—and Enron's public relations team—committed *philosophic fraud* by engaging in *half-truths*, which philosopher Ayn Rand characterized as "a very vicious form of lying." Not telling "the whole truth," she explained, "is more misleading than simply lying, which is bad enough." She continued:

> It's especially evil to claim honesty when you are deceiving somebody. This is why the oath you're asked to take in court is so wise: You're supposed to tell the truth, *the whole truth*, and nothing but the truth.

By condoning the well-documented indiscretions of Borget and Mastroeni, Lay also violated Adam Smith's "sacred regard to general rules" and Samuel Smiles's "path of common sense." Classical liberalism's wisdom of the ages applied to misjudgment at Enron.[24]

---

22. This goal would be accomplished by mid-1988, as discussed in chapter 5, pp. 210–11.

23. Wing's complicated relationship with Enron is also described in chapter 1, pp. 100–102; chapter 2, 132–33; and chapter 5, p. 211.

24. The wisdom of Smith, Smiles, and Rand for best-business practices constitutes Part I of Bradley, *Capitalism at Work*, pp. 17–89.

For more than a decade, Enron's philosopher-king would not refer to Valhalla in his many presentations about Enron's history.[25] Had Lay forthrightly admitted how earnings-over-rules, ends-justify-the-means pragmatism had caused Enron's "expensive embarrassment," one that could have turned out far worse, humility might have been institutionalized for the good of himself and the company.

Instead, Lay began (or perhaps continued) talking the talk but not walking the walk. He would create safe harbors (such as a company vision-and-values statement) as if words trumped deeds.[26]

"Facts are friendly," was one of Lay's oft-repeated values. But the reality at Ken Lay's Enron, even back in the 1980s, was *"friendly* facts are friendly."

Almost 20 years later, commenting on Ken Lay's conviction by a Houston jury and what was likely to have been life in jail, Enron whistleblower Sherron Watkins said: "Much of Ken Lay's mistake was really continuing to let ethically challenged employees stay at the company if they were providing results." That is what had happened, in bright lights, back in 1987.

---

25. In a 1990 address to the Newcomen Society on the history of Enron and its two predecessors, Lay described the merger as a "tough, chaotic time" but said nothing about Valhalla 1 or 2. Lay mentioned the oil-trading scandal in a January 2000 presentation at Harvard Business School in passing. But come another crisis situation, Lay attempted to rally the troops in October 2001 by mentioning how Enron overcame Valhalla, which "could have taken the company down." Two months later, Enron went down.

26. Enron's value statement of *respect, integrity, communication,* and *excellence* was featured in the *1997 Annual Report,* released in March 1998.

5

Recovery: 1988–1989

Ken Lay had made big bets in precarious markets. At HNG, he had richly bid to win Transwestern Pipeline and then Florida Gas Transmission, over-paying somewhere between $100 million and $200 million (10–20 percent of the purchase price). Lay then had InterNorth overpay for HNG by at least $5 per share, or about $150 million. Although pushing that imprudence was arguably his fiduciary duty as the seller in the transaction, it was also driven by his desire to remove a pending shareholder suit. In a further act of pain avoidance, he then bought out Irwin Jacobs and Leucadia at a shareholder cost of $200 million.

Roughly $500 million—or about one-eighth of Enron's total debt of $4 bil-lion entering into 1988—was attributable to Lay's aggressiveness, even hubris. And then came Valhalla's $142 million oil-trading loss ($85 million, after-tax), which could have been far worse. If not for some deft cleanup, Ken Lay's career might have taken a new turn in 1987 and changed business history.

As 1988 dawned, capital spending was down to a maintenance level of $185 million, about two-thirds of 1985's actual. ENE's dividend was frozen, as were the salaries for Enron's top 60 corporate officers. A hiring freeze was in effect for major parts of the corporation. But greater efficiency was the good news amid the bad. From the time of the merger, pipeline cost per unit of gas delivered was down one-fourth, which included a reduction in field personnel of 23 percent.

Half sales of Florida Gas Transmission (in 1986) and Enron Cogeneration (in 1987) redeemed Lay's weak balance sheet but left Enron's earnings engine smaller. A minority sale of Enron Oil & Gas Company, scheduled for late 1987, was postponed owing to negative market conditions. Wall Street was uncom-fortable with Enron's 70 percent debt-to-capital ratio, as evidenced in rating downgrades by Moody's and Duff & Phelps in 1987. Prior to Valhalla, Lay had promised 60 percent by year's end.

Still, the dividend had been maintained, and expectations were high. The pipelines were beating the parent's reserve for their transition (take-or-pay) costs, and growth was ahead from innovative rate-case designs and expansions. Gas marketing was a whole new profit center, with Enron the national leader. Regulation-enabled cogeneration remained lucrative even with Enron's domestic pullback. And new expert leadership at Enron Oil & Gas created a significant upside.

Restructuring complete, Enron had a synergistic natural gas core, along with the perennial hope "to believe that the worst is over for the energy industry." Consumer choice and national energy policy were trending toward gas and away from oil and coal for economic and environmental reasons, Lay and Seidl also noted in their 1987 annual report.

Ken Lay exuded optimism. His down-home, caring style made him likeable and believable to the Enron nation. "You can imagine," Lay lieutenant James E. "Jim" Rogers, told *Forbes*, "how excited young people four or five levels down in the organization get when the chairman of the board calls to tell them, 'You're doing great.'" Upbeat, witty, confident, visionary—Enron had a *leader*. Who was to question a PhD economist with a storybook past and a seemingly unblemished business track record? (Valhalla just snuck up on him, remember.) This was the industry's mover and shaker, according to the local, industry, and national media.

Enron was a well-regarded, first-class place to work. Despite the pressures, opportunities abounded for many in Enron's workforce of 7,000. The buzz was that the smartest guys worked for Ken Lay and that there was always room for brainy people and top performers.

Enron had strong interlocking assets and superior divisional management. What was needed was normalcy, *no surprises*, to let the units work down the parent's debt load. It was time to dust off and get to work on the mission Ken Lay had set the previous year: *to become the premier integrated natural gas company in North America.*

———

The year began with Enron's letter of intent selling 50 percent of Enron Cogeneration Company (ECC) to Dominion Resources for $90 million. This was the price that had to be paid for Valhalla. But the good news was that by the time John Wing completed the sale five months later, the price had reached $104 million, thanks to some promising new projects in negotiation. All proceeds went to reduce debt, and a $40 million profit was taken for 1988 earnings.[1]

---

1. As part of the sale, the 50 percent interest of the 450 MW Texas City plant held by Drexel Burnham Lambert was purchased to make the facility wholly owned by the new partnership.

Figure 5.1 Financing with high-yield bonds (*junk bonds*) proved crucial for Ken Lay from the time of the HNG/InterNorth merger in 1985 through project financings in 1989, when Michael Milken was indicted for securities violations. Drexel Burnham Lambert filed for bankruptcy protection in 1990.

Wing would not run the renamed Enron/Dominion Cogeneration Corporation, however. Despite his new contract to run the independent power business for Enron, Dominion wanted one of its own in charge of the partnership. Lay really needed that deal, and so once again Wing was the odd man out, despite a redone contract that had four years to run. Wing negotiated yet another lucrative contract (each of the four better, with two coming and two going).

Some of this was about John Wing, a hot personality in a febrile business. Some of it was about working for a debt-laden, mistake-prone company and a chairman who had to please a whole lot of people.

Managerial Depth and Change

Through his personal dynamism and industry-leading compensation packages, Ken Lay had assembled a top management team heading into 1988. Each of Enron's three major divisions (absent cogeneration) had strong, innovative leadership, starting with the Gas Pipeline Group (GPG) in its three dimensions: intrastate, interstate, and national marketing.[2]

Intrastate, Gerald Bennett was doing as well as could be expected in the overbuilt, low-margin Texas market. Houston Pipe Line was Enron's weak sister, although the synergies provided by Bammel storage redounded to the benefit of the rest of GPG. In this respect, Ken Lay's restructuring moves looked smart compared to Bill Matthews's cocoon strategy for the old Houston Natural Gas.

Interstate, all three pipelines were evolving from gas merchants to transporters, while getting their take-or-pay costs under control. Jim Rogers and team were playing the FERC liberalization game expertly, offering new products with customer support and reaching rate-case settlements with upside profit potential. Transwestern was setting an industry standard by entrepreneurially working within regulatory constraints. Florida Gas was making natural gas the fuel of choice at Florida electrics for the first time since 1970. And Northern Natural Gas Pipeline was its usual solid self, just needing some winter cold snaps to keep its volumes high.

On GPG's nonregulated side, Enron Gas Marketing was emerging as a bona fide profit center, pointing the industry into a new era of gas commoditization.[3] Ron Burns was EGM's leader, aided by Transco-exes Claude Mullendore (supply) and John Esslinger (sales). Armed with a blanket certificate from FERC, EGM was buying and selling gas nationally under short-term and long-term contracts. Enron was building up unique capabilities with a first-mover advantage.

Enron Liquid Fuels (ELF), under Valhalla hero Mike Muckleroy, had been reshaped amid tough industry conditions and was back to profitability. ELF's asset base of $750 million was housed in five divisions: liquids processing,

---

2. Enron Gas Marketing would remain as part of Enron's Gas Pipeline Group until January 1991, when it was renamed Enron Gas Services and placed in a new division, Natural Gas.

3. EGM's major rival was U.S. Natural Gas Clearinghouse (NGC), the company that Ken Lay had helped start in 1984 as president of Transco Energy. Lay's Houston Natural Gas became NGC's sixth industry member (and 10 percent owner) but sold its interest after the InterNorth merger. All told, more than 300 independent firms were marketing gas by 1988–89.

213

liquids retailing, liquids pipeline, oil transportation and trading, and international.[4] And Forrest Hoglund was hard at work reconfiguring the valuable assets of Enron Oil & Gas Company.

Ken Lay's talent was not lost on Enron's rivals—and the energy industry more generally. At a time when companies were restructuring and looking for change agents, Enron executives were at the top of many headhunter lists. By first-quarter 1989, four Enron notables had left to take top jobs elsewhere. "While we will miss their ideas and leadership talents," Ken Lay remarked, "their departure gave us the opportunity not only to promote equally aggressive and innovative mangers but also to streamline further our management organization and thus further reduce overhead costs." Losing experience seemed not terribly important at the time, but some of Enron's emergency brake for Lay's hyper-speed would no longer be in place.

Enron's competition was being upgraded. Clark Smith left Transwestern Pipeline to become CEO of Coastal Gas Marketing Company, a start-up within Oscar Wyatt's Coastal Corporation, which would go head-to-head against EGM. Jim Rogers jumped industries, becoming CEO of Public Service Company of Indiana (PSI Holdings Inc.; later Cinergy Corp.; then Duke Energy). His blend of political capitalism and market entrepreneurship made him in demand at the troubled Midwest electric utility, one that needed a fresh start with state and federal regulators, as well as a new strategic direction.

Dan Dienstbier, Rogers's boss as head of GPG, left to lead a smaller gas company, escaping a corporate culture in which he was never really comfortable.[5] With Dienstbier's departure, the old InterNorth imprint was with a new generation: Ron Burns and, behind him, Ken Rice and Julie Gomez, both of whom would excel within EGM and its progeny.

Another Omaha talent who would eventually assume responsibility for all of EGM's back-office operations (accounting, contracts, etc.) was Cindy Olson. She would later head community affairs for Enron, among other responsibilities,

---

4. The divisions were *Enron Gas Processing Company*, a major producer of ethane, propane, butanes, and natural gasoline; *Enron Gas Liquids Company*, a major seller of ethane, propane, butanes, and natural gasoline; *Enron Liquids Pipeline Company*, the owner-operator of a 1,537-mile pipeline and other gas-liquid loading facilities; *Enron Oil Trading & Transportation Company*, a petroleum-gathering, transportation, and marketing company; and *Enron Liquid Fuels International*, the holder of various gas-related foreign operations.

5. "The culture at Enron was totally foreign to me," Dienstbier later recalled. "It was much less team-oriented and much more individual-oriented than I was used to or comfortable with."

becoming a top lieutenant to Ken Lay as his outside ambitions got bigger and bigger.[6]

———

A change at the top of Enron occurred in early 1989. Mick Seidl had been Ken Lay's fix-it man almost from inception, with mixed results. Valhalla, in particular, blew up on his watch. Richard Kinder, even before becoming chief of staff in August 1987, had been asserting himself as Lay's fix-it man—with good results.

Over time, Seidl became redundant between nice-cop Lay and tough-cop Kinder, although there was always plenty for Mick to do. So it worked out well when Maxxam's Charles Hurwitz offered Seidl the presidency of Kaisertech Ltd. (Kaiser Aluminum and Chemical Company). Upon Seidl's departure, Lay retook the president's title but left the COO position open. Rich Kinder had been promoted to vice-chairman and elected to Enron's board of directors in December 1988, as well as becoming head of the Gas Pipeline Group, replacing the recently departed Jim Rogers.

As EVP and chief of staff, Kinder had been involved in practically every urgent matter. Just about every department reported to the hands-on Kinder: accounting, administration, corporate development, finance, human resources, information systems, law. With a photographic memory and an intuition for numbers, he knew what needed to be known about the myriad businesses beneath him. Ken Lay was also gifted but more interested in issues and events outside the window.

Kinder lived between Enron's walls, and though he was tough, he was approachable. "He was with you and on you, every week," remembered one pipeline head. For those who worked hard, stayed focused, and spoke straight, Rich Kinder was cordial; for everyone, this taskmaster was a good custodian of assets.

Kinder made his mark at a momentous meeting to resolve the conflict between the pipelines and marketers over the future of the gas merchant function. In Enron lore, it would become known as the Come to Jesus meeting.

The pipelines wanted to remain in their familiar role as buyers and sellers of gas. After all, they had gathering systems, contracts with producers, and time-honed procedures that ensured reliable supply. Only acts of God, such as well freeze-offs and hurricanes, could keep them from their appointed rounds. But marketing affiliates could make a margin on the purchase and sale of gas in interstate commerce under the new rules from Washington. The gas historically

———

6. See chapter 15, pp. 609–10, 615. Olson's memoir was published in 2008: *The Whole Truth: So Help Me God* (Mustang, OK: Tate Publishing). It covers her early career, followed by her 23 years at InterNorth and then Enron, including her appointment as head of global human resources and a member of the executive committee; and the turbulent post-Enron years.

controlled by the interstates needed to be relinquished for Enron Gas Marketing to buy, sell, and arrange transportation.

The pipelines were uncomfortable with this shake-up. With the culture conflict between Houston and Omaha largely overcome, the future of the gas-merchant function was *the* major issue at Enron.[7]

Lay supported EGM as the future of the gas business. It was simple: Two profit centers were better than one, even with the transition costs (take-or-pay liability) of pipelines exiting the merchant function. A new generation of information technology, Lay and others believed, would ensure reliability in the new world where marketers, not the pipelines, coordinated gas supply.

Lay opened the meeting of Enron's top corporate officers and division heads with polite reasoning to this effect. The merchant function *should* transition to EGM for the overall good of Enron. Kinder took over from there. His voice rising, he presented example after example of the warring factions' politicking, back stabbing, and power plays. "There are alligators in the swamp," Kinder yelled. "We're going to get in that f------ swamp, and we're going to kick out all the f------ alligators, one by one, and we're going to kill them, one by one."

The room got the point. Lay liked how Rich got things done. This was a defining moment for Enron and Kinder personally. It cleared the crossing, allowing EGM to speed ahead and become the largest and most profitable gas marketer in the United States.

The weekly corporate staff meetings changed too when Kinder took over from Seidl. No longer was the go-around a beauty pageant for each divisional head to describe good things happening in the unit. It was now bad-news-first and getting hard decisions made. It was about bottom lines and accountability.

Ron Burns remembered a "huge cultural change" at the Monday confabs, which began with lunch and could last into the evening. "Kinder took charge to really make sure that all the issues were on the table, that all the alligators were on the table, and we slayed as many as we possibly could." And Kinder never forgot what was said or promised to him.

Monday afternoons were tough. But for the performers, airing the issues and getting consensus behind tough courses of action were prized. "As long as you had your act together and made your pitch, you could get a decision that day," Burns remembers. "That is when we went from playing defense to playing offense."

Rich Kinder was the clear number-two executive at Enron by late 1988. After a strong close to 1989 (discussed later in this chapter), Lay and the board would

---

7. "The pipeline guys were absolutely, adamantly dead set against" the transfer, remembered Jeff Skilling, then a McKinsey consultant. "Their belief was that the purpose of a merchant business was to support the pipes. They had a temporary problem [take-or-pay], so they wanted to … fix their temporary problem. Then we would go back to business-as-usual."

name him Enron's new president and COO, with Lay remaining chairman and CEO. The Lay-Kinder era would continue through 1996.

Repositioning EOG

Forrest Hoglund and Ken Lay were courting potential investors in Europe about taking Enron Oil & Gas Company public. The two were on the plane when Lay got the phone call from Mick Seidl about Valhalla. Had the trading fiasco erupted a month earlier, Hoglund might not have been in Enron uniform. He already had a good job, and just about everyone wanted Forrest Hoglund for their exploration and production company.

Lay's winning courtship was the talk of the industry. "Hiring Hoglund shows Enron is serious about putting more emphasis on this end of the company," remarked one securities analyst in the *Wall Street Journal*. "It gives them instant credibility." True to form, EOG's new leader would create a thriving, valuable enterprise—and prove to be one of Ken Lay's best moves.

Hoglund relished the idea of building up the company and making himself and his colleagues wealthy in the process. But EOG could not be like Enron. The company-within-a-company had to have its own rules and culture to be able to go public. And then there were expenses. When Ken Lay offered the use of an Enron plane to commute between Dallas and Houston (the Hoglunds maintained dual residences), Forrest demurred. "It costs $2,000 to take the plane off, and I can ride Southwest Airlines for $100," he responded. "Why would we do that?"

Looking back, Hoglund contrasted his "much different outlook on costs" to Lay's. Industry conditions precluded such luxuries, and the CEO set the example. As a minority shareholder of the company that was going public, Hoglund was thinking of himself too.

EOG needed reshaping to become, in Hoglund's words, a "low-cost, basic, get-it-done kind of company." Its properties needed to be grouped into core for development and noncore for disposal. Intellectual capital needed to be reshaped from an incumbency that seemed to have "cornered mediocrity." In his introductory meetings, Hoglund told his managers that half of them would not get it and leave, and the other half would become millionaires. "I undershot on both cases," he would later say. About 80 percent of the managers would be changed out, and most of the new team would become wealthy.

EOG needed to restructure its South Texas joint-venture ("farm-out") contracts that were too skewed toward the partner, devise a plan to develop and market its large gas reserves at Big Piney in Wyoming, and enter into marketing arrangements to extract more margin. But rather than consolidate EOG in Houston, as had been done in the past year, decision making needed to be near the action. Separate offices and profit centers were set up in Corpus Christi, Denver, Midland, Oklahoma City, and Tyler—creating companies within Hoglund's company.

Drilling required cash, but EOG's cash flow was needed by Enron. That was why Lay and Hoglund were touring Europe in search of investors when Valhalla 2 hit. An initial public offering (IPO) was set for pricing on October 19, 1987. But that turned out to be "Black Tuesday," the day that the Dow Jones Industrial Average (DJIA) fell 22 percent, almost double the percentage fall of the Great Depression's "Black Monday" in October 1929. EOG would have to be a wholly owned subsidiary of Enron a while longer, which gave Hoglund an opportunity to strengthen and streamline the company and create a better story for analysts and would-be buyers.

In April 1988, with the stock market fully recovered, Enron decided to put Enron Oil & Gas up for sale. Enron and its bankers floated a value for EOG at as much as $2 billion, and both expressed some hope that EOG's proved reserves of 1.4 trillion cubic feet of gas and 42.3 million barrels of oil would fetch a $1.50/ MMBtu equivalent, valuing the company at $2.5 billion.

But oil and gas prices were in the doldrums, and Tenneco and other large companies were also selling large reserves. Analysts were valuing EOG between $1.25 and $1.75 billion, every dollar of which was needed by Enron to pay down its $3.6 billion debt in order to lower interest costs and raise net income.

Nearly a dozen formal bids came by the July deadline. Internally, Enron was looking for $1.8 billion, but the high bid was $1.3 billion, about 15 percent below EOG's book value—and a straight discounted valuation for EOG's proved reserves. There was no premium for undeveloped properties or management.

Hoglund, Lay, and Enron's board were of one mind: It would be disadvantageous for Enron stockholders to sell. All the bids were rejected; EOG would again stay wholly within Enron for the time being.

Still, Lay expressed his hope that wintertime would bring increased demand for long-term, higher-priced gas contracts, thus increasing the value of reserves in the ground. "Reducing our debt is still a real high priority for us," Diane Bazelides of Enron's media relations added, "and we'll continue looking to all avenues until we've reduced that debt." Wall Street, however, reacted sternly to the news, sending ENE down 7 percent to 38⅞.

With debt of $3.9 billion at the end of third-quarter 1988 and a loss that quarter of $14 million from continuing operations, Enron still needed to monetize its value in EOG. Plan B was for EOG to sell between $200 million and $300 million in nonstrategic properties. In fact, $253 million would be sold in the fourth quarter, representing most of EOG sales that year of $282 million. Better yet, reserves were reduced by only 13 percent. EOG was left with the assets it wanted to take public.

Meanwhile, things were getting cleaned up at the core. Hoglund's first full year produced income before interest and taxes (IBIT) of $13 million, a rebound from a loss of $41 million in 1987. In retrospect, this was EOG's turnaround year.

Enron's *1988 Annual Report* described a good year for EOG's "decentralized, profit-conscious management team." EOG's 84 percent drilling-success rate was a company best. A major gas find near Matagorda Island in the Gulf of Mexico added to proved reserves. Overall reserve additions costing $0.60 per Mcf joined sales made at $1.56 per Mcf. EOG's aforementioned property sales reduced Enron's debt, contributing to a credit-rating upgrade for the parent. EOG was unlocking value that was only partially reflected in ENE.

But something else kicked in that would be a real moneymaker. Thanks to regulatory opportunity exploited by John Wing, a 48 MMcf/d contract between EOG and Enron/Dominion's cogeneration plant in Texas City was executed "at prices substantially above spot market levels." In fact, it was almost *double* the going price for gas, a premium that alone increased EOG's revenue by $44 million in 1988, the first full year of the contract.

More than purely free-market forces were at work with this sweetheart deal. Specifically, the Public Utility Regulatory Policies Act of 1978 (PURPA) set forth a methodology that tied the power-sales agreement to the purchasing utility's *avoided cost*, or the cost of power that it would otherwise generate or buy.

For Texas Utilities Electric Company, the ultimate buyer (via a wheeling arrangement with Houston Lighting & Power, which did not need the power), the avoided cost was based on constructing a new coal plant. Coal plants, which now had to be outfitted with scrubbers and other pollution-control equipment, were more capital intensive than gas plants, particularly a state-of-the-art high-efficiency cogen plant.

So, in this case, the avoided cost was determined in state regulatory hearings to be $1,100 per kilowatt of installed capacity—versus Enron/Dominion's $300 per kilowatt cost. The power-sales contract was so high that natural gas could be profitably purchased (from EOG, providing a windfall) at $3.25/MMBtu (with a 6 percent escalation factor) at a time when spot gas was averaging under $2.00/MMBtu.

This was a home run compared to what regulators could have required: basing the power contract on an avoided cost tied to the cost of constructing an efficient cogen plant. The gas-purchase price would then have had to be done closer to spot. But Texas Utilities did not care, because its profit under public-utility regulation was based on rate base, with gas costs a ratepayer passthrough. Unlike a free-market company, this franchised monopolist had no incentive to maximize the spread between costs and revenue.

Federal power law was very kind to Enron at a time of great need for Ken Lay.[8] State regulators were very generous too, blessing high avoided costs and thus, indirectly, premium pricing for long-term contracts. It was good eating at the trough of public-utility-regulated companies, at least during the 1984–89 heyday of PURPA.

---

8. PURPA is described in Internet appendix 1.5, "Public Utility Regulatory Policies Act of 1978," at www.politicalcapitalism.org/Book3/Chapter1/Appendix5.html.

In October 1989, Enron floated an IPO for 16 percent of EOG, priced at $18.75 per share. The offering's 11.5 million units were placed, trading on the Big Board under the symbol EOG. Enron netted $202 million, and its remaining interest, coupled with debt owed by EOG to the parent, gave Enron an asset on its balance sheet worth $1.6 billion.

Forrest Hoglund, with help from the extraordinary Texas City contract, had created a lot of enterprise value to help Ken Lay and Enron turn the corner. And it would get better. The offering price appreciated by one-third by year end, giving Enron a $2 billion asset. This equated to about $40 per share of ENE, leaving $17 for the rest of Enron: the pipelines, the gas-liquid assets, the cogen interests, and the emerging marketing division. But far from irrational, the drag was the debt burden associated with these valuable assets. Still, optimism abounded. "It is obvious," stated Ken Lay and Rich Kinder, "that potential remains for continued growth in shareholder value."

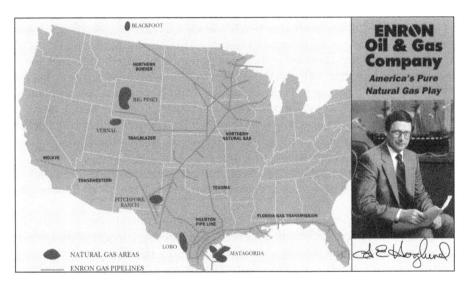

Figure 5.2 Enron Oil & Gas, advertised as "America's Pure Natural Gas Play," launched an October 1989 public offering that valued the company at $1.6 billion. Forrest Hoglund, chairman and chief executive officer, was off to a very fast start in a low-price environment.

EOG's public offering was accomplished despite uncooperative natural gas prices—at least in the spot market. Long-term deals that could be priced at a premium to spot were sought, and Ken Lay would become a spokesman against "irrationally low" gas prices in the years ahead.[9]

---

9. See chapter 7, pp. 312–15.

Recommitting to Cogeneration

Cogeneration was an exciting new business driven by technological advance, low natural gas prices, and a federal law requiring electric utilities to favorably contract with qualifying independent developers. Ken Lay had pushed cogeneration back at Transco; as CEO of Houston Natural Gas, he got into the game by hiring John Wing and Robert Kelly away from Jack Welch at GE.

Enron was well situated near the industrial belt of the Texas Gulf Coast, a top market for cogenerated steam and power. As a gas-transmission company, Enron was pursuing another prime market for cogen: steamflood-enhanced oil recovery in central California. This was the planned destination of the upstart Mojave Pipeline Company, a joint project of Enron and El Paso Natural Gas Company.[10]

Enron had done well with its investment in the Bayou Cogeneration Plant. Ken Lay wanted a stable of such projects, but Lay crossed Wing in the wake of the InterNorth merger by giving the combined companies' cogen responsibilities to Howard Hawks's Northern Natural Resources Company (NNR).

After a brief heyday, during which the Texas City project ("Northern Cogeneration One") was agreed to and entered construction, things changed radically at NNR. The Omaha division found itself going from growth to retrenchment, then Hawks departed. Lay got Wing back to refinance Texas City off–balance sheet, with Enron taking full ownership (up from 50 percent), to complete the 377 MW Clear Lake Project, and to wind up a cogen project in New Jersey.

John Wing may have been a bucking bronco, but he was immensely talented and someone Enron needed in-house, or at least under a contractual collar. Not just anyone could execute a fast-track moneymaking cogen project, particularly when a multitude of contracts had to be buttoned down to allow the project to be self-financed (the type of project that Enron had to have, given its weak balance sheet).

Building and operating steam and power plants utilizing the very latest in technology required technical expertise and precise, urgent management. Cogeneration could be the highest return-on-equity (ROE) opportunity for an energy company, offering estimated pretax returns of 18–20 percent, but only if the projects were done right. And the competition was getting intense, as utilities and regulators tightened up the rules.

It was far better to have John Wing on your side. InterNorth found that out the hard way in the 1985 merger negotiations with HNG. Enron found it out a year later by leaving big money on the table regarding its 42 percent investment in a $120 million, 165 MW plant in Bayonne, New Jersey. Wing, negotiating for the developer and receiving a 1 percent override for his trouble, cut the deal of

---

10. The Mojave project, connecting gas from Transwestern and El Paso to Kern County's heavy oil fields in central California, would become part of a competing project and enter service in 1992 as the 1.1 Bcf/d Kern-Mojave Pipeline.

all deals. It wasn't that the investment for Enron was not good—it was very good. But it could and should have been better.

Newly formed Enron Cogeneration Company (ECC) signed the deal with Cogen Technologies Inc. (CTI), an upstart private company majority owned by Robert McNair. The agreement began with 85 percent of profits going to Enron, the major equity investor. But then profit sharing flipped: a 50/50 split if and when the project's ROE reached 23 percent and then another readjustment, to a 15/85 split (in favor of CTI), should the project reach a 30 percent return.

Figure 5.3 Bayonne Cogeneration Plant in New Jersey was the inaugural project of Robert McNair's Cogen Technologies. A decade later, Bayonne and two neighboring CTI plants would be sold to Enron for $1.1 billion and debt assumption, enabling McNair to found an NFL franchise, the Houston Texans.

Entering service in September 1988, Bayonne quickly reached and exceeded these thresholds, making tens of millions of dollars for McNair and CTI. But how did something so extraordinary happen?

Working closely with GE—the prime contractor and the turbine supplier—McNair and Wing brought the plant into service ahead of schedule and below budget. But this was just the start of something extraordinary. A federal investment tax credit was enacted just as the project was being completed, adding 10 percent to the rate of return. Accelerated depreciation in the same law further sheltered profits from income taxes. Thank you, political capitalism.

A fourth factor concerning risk versus reward came out all roses for McNair and his other private investors (including Wing). Anticipating rising gas prices, the major electricity purchaser, Jersey Central Power & Light, required CTI to enter into a power-sales contract based on a spread reflecting fixed gas prices as of 1985.

Without forward markets for natural gas to lock in prices, McNair could not effectively hedge his exposure under his sales contract. Jersey Central, meanwhile, was impervious to (falling) price risk because its power-purchase contract was approved by its state regulators. A floating power price, alternatively, which McNair's CTI preferred, would have locked in a spread with a market-price purchase contract. As it was, a big bet on the future price of gas was made at the power buyer's insistence.

Jersey Central guessed wrong—badly. Instead of escalating, gas prices plunged in 1986 and stayed low. Bayonne's profit margins increased by one-third after the project came on stream, with spot gas purchased at well below 1985 levels.[11] Continuing low prices well into the 1990s would add to the win for McNair—and the loss for customers of a monopolist utility that, as the customers' agent, bet wrong.

All said, Bayonne achieved its 23 percent rate of return in two years and 30 percent return in three, leaving CTI with 85 percent of the profit for the life of the plant. So, with McNair putting up the sweat equity and several million dollars in development costs versus Enron's $14 million, McNair found himself making more money from the project each month than Ken Lay made in a year as Enron's CEO.

"You're making so much money!" Ken complained to Bob. But Enron had received a handsome return from the project, and a deal was a deal, even if Wing and McNair bested Lay and Seidl—and the man caught in the middle, Robert Kelly, who was now heading Enron Cogeneration Company.

Cogen Technologies would go on to become one of the very top independent power developers in the nation. The sale of CTI's major asset to Enron in

---

11. "We were scared to death," recalled McNair, "so we ran the numbers out to see how high the price of natural gas would have to go in 1986 before it wiped our profit out.... So, they really tried to take advantage of us. Well, as it turned out, the delivered gas was about $4.20 per Mcf in 1985 and dropped to $3.00. So our profit margin increased about 30 to 35 percent."

1999 (McNair took cash, not stock) would make McNair one of Houston's wealthiest men and provided the means to buy an NFL football team for his hometown, a deal that was also made possible by a new taxpayer-supported stadium, in no small part the result of an intense lobbying effort by Ken Lay and Enron several years before.[12]

———

Robert Kelly had followed Wing out the door in early 1988 when the top job of Enron/Dominion Cogeneration Company went to David Heavenridge from Dominion. (The half sale was necessitated by Valhalla's oil-trading loss.) Kelly and Wing formed Wing Group in The Woodlands north of Houston and advised Enron and other clients.

Heavenridge's Houston-run operation was not getting deals done. There were no ground breakings, just managing Enron's 1,000 MW interest in four plants.[13] Other companies were more active and announcing projects—CTI, Mission Energy (Southern California Edison Company), even Enron-ex Howard Hawks's Tenaska, based in Omaha.

With Heavenridge's heavy-handed management causing dissent, Ken Lay summoned Wing, necessitating a *fifth* long-term (five-year) contract (all occurring within four years of each other). Wing would agree to the contract but would remain a consultant, not an employee.

In early 1989, Enron Power Corporation (EPC) was formed as a second cogeneration division, separate from Enron's half-stake in Enron Dominion Cogeneration Company, now a passive investment. Wholly owned EPC was about the future; EDCC was the past. With John Wing as chairman and Robert Kelly as president, EPC was run out of The Woodlands. (Wing's new contract required that his office be within 25 miles of his primary—Woodlands—residence, and the Enron Building was 30 miles away.) The Wing Group, meanwhile, continued in non-Enron spheres.

But cogeneration activity had slowed down considerably in the United States. The domestic projects that were on the drawing board of ECC/EDCC were stuck in negotiations. The new opportunity was *international*. England, in particular, was ripe for a new technology that could underprice the coal-fired power that the country had grown up on.

———

———

12. Enron's role in a referendum authorizing public funding of sports stadiums is discussed in chapter 15, pp. 612–18.

13. Enron's cogen assets were a 34 percent ownership in the 300 MW Bayou Cogeneration Plant, a 100 percent interest in the 450 MW Texas City Plant, a 42 percent interest in the 165 MW Bayonne Plant in New Jersey (1987), and a 100 percent interest in the 377 MW Clear Lake Cogeneration Plant.

Margaret Thatcher was privatizing and otherwise liberalizing the electricity sector in the United Kingdom, and new gas finds were coming from the North Sea. The prospects looked very interesting for an interloper such as Enron to shake things up. But compared to the status quo, this required back-to-back contracts allowing everyone—gas sellers, steam and power buyers, and project developers—to win.

Enron Power Corporation was reorganized to do just that. Wing was chairman, and under him as president and CEO was Rebecca Mark, now with a Harvard MBA. Robert Kelly was named chairman, Enron Power UK.

In late 1988, what would become the world's largest gas-fired, combined-cycle electric-generation plant was born when Wing and Kelly met at London's Heathrow Airport with two executives of Imperial Chemical Industries (ICI), a major consumer of steam and power. EPC's spreadsheets showed a substantial cost savings for ICI from a new state-of-the-art combined-cycle plant under a variety of price scenarios with gas from the North Sea. But Enron could not buy that gas. ICI had the legal means to break into British Gas's stranglehold—and the incentive to do so, given the prospect of buying cheaper steam and power.

The proposed project was big—larger than any such project built in the United States. Financing a new North Sea platform was very expensive, and the cost of gas had to be driven down to offer the savings that the purchase contracts required. Customers other than ICI were needed to make the project viable. Within the United Kingdom's restructured power market, the old regime of several generators selling to a dozen distributors was giving way to new independent contracting.

The new project that Wing and Kelly had in mind played right into the public policy changes that allowed self-interested buyers and sellers to intersect. A five-utility consortium signed on to more than double the purchases that ICI alone committed to.

Gas supply was now the trigger point. Kelly initiated simultaneous discussions with Amoco (Everest-Lomond Field), Statoil (Sleipner Field), Marathon-BP (Bray Field), and Phillips (J-Block Field). With discussions advancing, Enron signed a letter of intent in February 1989 to build a 1,750 MW gas-fired cogeneration plant near the town of Teesside in England. The project, the world's largest, priced north of $1 billion, compared to the net worth of Enron itself ($1.6 billion). Ken Lay's temerity again prompted him to throw the dice, betting on the smarts and fortitude of the mercurial John Wing.

———

At decade's end, PURPA-driven independent power market was responsible for 30 percent of new US electrical generation capacity versus 5 percent in 1984. Enron was right there. The *1989 Annual Report* described EPC as "one of the nation's largest independent producers of electric power via natural gas-fired combined cycle and cogeneration technology."

Now, "Enron's total package concept offering a wide range of coordinated services" was going abroad. The future, Lay proselytized, belonged to natural gas—a cheaper, cleaner alternative to coal and fuel oil and certainly a cheaper alternative to nuclear power.

Pipeline Entrepreneurship

Enron was spreading its wings, but natural gas transmission still represented two-thirds of the company's assets and income. Generating several hundred million dollars a year in cash flow was no small feat. Interstate pipelines as a whole saw their return on equity fall in half during the 1980s—from around 15 percent to 7 percent. Not Enron, whose collection, including its interest in Northern Border, remained consistently in the double digits.

Jim Rogers declared in 1986 that interstate transmission "is no longer a rate base business." How true. To make its FERC-authorized rate of return, an interstate needed to do more than just keep its compressors running and shiny. This was not the 1950s and 1960s, when such investment was akin to holding a bond, or the gas-short 1970s, when financial undercollection in one period could be recouped in the next.

Now, pipeline earnings were at risk. The minimum-bill contracts guaranteeing income whether or not the customers took the gas were gone. Rate-design changes allowed the customer to avoid some fixed charges if the gas was not physically taken. Pipeline payments to reform its take-or-pay contracts with producer contracts were not automatically passed through to customers in rates, legally or even economically. The pipeline itself would have to absorb some of its take-or-pay costs—a compelling reason to minimize those expenses.

All said, the pipeline had to earn every dollar it could, whether by increasing revenue or decreasing expenses. Customers had to be courted with a menu of sale and transportation options to maximize a pipeline's throughput. Pipelines needed to be competitive to deliver gas below the cost of fuel oil to dual-fuel-capable customers—and in some cases to keep a customer in business.

————

Enron was well positioned. Its four-pipeline hub-and-spoke system offered logistical opportunities that smaller or less congruent systems could not. Gas could be purchased from more regions, and Bammel storage ensured flexibility at the center. Geographical overlaps between Enron's pipelines (HPL and FGT to the east; HPL and Transwestern to the west; Transwestern and Northern Natural to the north) allowed consolidation of field operations.

At headquarters, the traditional gas-transmission functions—accounting, administration, finance, marketing, rates, regulatory affairs, and supply—did not need to be done by each pipeline. Some functions (buying gas, dispatching) went corporate-wide beginning in 1987. Even before then, Transwestern and Florida Gas shared managerial talent. ("We found out that we could manage two pipelines at about the same cost that you could manage one," Stan Horton remembered.) Northern Natural, however, located in Omaha to be near its customers, operated more autonomously.

In March 1988, Enron's interstate pipelines under Jim Rogers dispensed with its presidents and centralized administration, finance, marketing and supply, and rates and regulatory affairs. Horton, previously president of Florida Gas, was named vice president of marketing and production for Enron Interstate Pipelines. William "Bill" Cordes, previously vice president of regulatory affairs for Northern Natural, was now director of rates for Florida Gas, Northern Natural, and Transwestern.

This centralization involved 90 layoffs and relocating 140 employees from Omaha's Northern Natural to Houston. Each pipeline, though without a president, had an executive vice president: Don Parsons, Florida Gas; Clark Smith, Transwestern; and at Northern Natural, the former FERC boy wonder Rick Richard, who had pushed through open-access restructuring, jumped to industry, and soon landed a job at Enron.

Still, this integration had its limits. FERC regulation was based on a separate rate base and cost allocation for every interstate. Each pipeline had its own customer base. Within a year, the president titles were back with the pipelines. Nevertheless, functional integration occurred with costs savings.

———

Enron did not wait around for gas prices to rise before renegotiating its uneconomic producer contracts. Ken Lay rejected that strategy as more heart than head. The interstates were instructed to settle their take deficiencies quickly in the belief that protracted negotiation and litigation would backfire and that money could be saved by offering cash-strapped producers instant liquidity. Wall Street did not like uncertainty and did like resolution.

The strategy exceeded expectations. Enron's take-or-pay liabilities, which peaked near $1.2 billion in mid-1987, ended 1988 at $570 million and fell to $160 million a year later.[14] Compared to its 14 percent share of the national gas market, Enron's total exposure was never over 5 percent of the interstate industry's bill. Transco Energy, meanwhile, was stymied by take-or-pay. Payouts of $688 million through 1987 would surpass $1.1 billion by the time an embattled

———

14. Take-or-pay was subsequently estimated to be $100–$150 million, partly from new claims after Florida Gas became an open-access transporter in August 1990. By 1992, however, take-or-pay exposure was reported as "not material." Actual payments, by year or in total, were not disclosed in the annual reports.

George Slocum resigned in 1991, and hundreds of millions in claims still lingered.[15]

Whereas Transco's Ken Lay had sought a legislative fix to a big take-or-pay problem, Enron's Ken Lay favored self-help to resolve a smaller problem. It was all about competitive position, not free-market philosophy.

———

The man in charge of Enron's interstate pipelines was described by *Natural Gas Week* as "the visionary missionary of natural gas marketing and Wunderkind executive of Enron Corp." Jim Rogers—who declared back in 1986 that "we're all getting comfortable with chaos"—had to run fast in a chancy environment. It was tough to maintain earnings, let alone increase them, given a depreciating rate base upon which regulated returns were calculated—even assuming that a pipeline could *make* its authorized rate of return. Many did not.

Rogers knew the regulatory game from the other side, having previously worked at FERC as deputy general counsel for litigation and enforcement. His entrepreneurial side was devising strategies to probe, even stretch, the regulatory boundaries for efficiency and financial gain.

The Kentucky native also had a gift for oratory, giving more than 30 speeches between 1985 and 1988 on the political economy of the midstream gas sector. In one, Rogers asked why the mighty dinosaur went extinct and the lowly cockroach thrived. Enron-the-roach was practicing "resilience and ability to change direction"—and surviving in the natural gas industry. No wonder he was a Lay favorite, a protégé. And little wonder that when Rogers spoke, the gas industry and its regulators listened.

Back in mid-1986, with Transwestern fighting the California natural gas wars, Rogers proposed a new rate design to reward producers who stood ready to supply gas whether or not the customer took it. Californians and their regulators were having their cake and eating it too by buying cheaper interruptible 30-day supply yet expecting long-term, guaranteed gas to still be there. "Spot gas is very seductive," Rogers analogized, producing "a narcotic effect on those who start taking it."[16] Supply security, he argued, required the customer to pay a *demand charge*, a fixed monthly fee separate from the variable costs of taken gas, for producers standing ready to provide firm gas. Such revenue for producers would alleviate take-or-pay payments that pipelines would otherwise have to make.

———

15. See Bradley, *Edison to Enron*, pp. 331, 334, 338, 347–48, 352–54, 359.

16. "California consumers have been living a lie," Rogers added, referring to the rate-design policy of the California Public Utilities Commission (CPUC), which forced the state's power-plant and industrial-gas buyers to subsidize residential and commercial customers. In fact, such cross-subsidization had the unintended consequence of reducing gas demand to the noncore, thus leaving higher costs for core customers to pay.

The next year, FERC Order No. 500 included a provision authorizing a gas-inventory charge (GIC), more or less what Rogers had in mind. Transwestern Pipeline would be the first to implement a GIC, an idea-to-action plan that characterized Rogers's pipelines, although customers avoided it by electing not to buy pipeline gas in favor of (cheaper) spot supply.

Enron's interstates were market and regulatory leaders, not unlike Transco Energy under Ken Lay. Transwestern in 1989 became the first transportation-only interstate in FERC's open-access world. The multidecade service obligation was removed, with marketers selling gas and pipelines transporting it. The GIC and the flexible purchased-gas adjustment (PGA) clause, described in chapter 3, were Enron ideas. Northern Natural was the first interstate to get blanket authority to sell its gas off-system and, like Transwestern, had been one of the early pipelines to go open access back in 1986.

Other innovative proposals teed up at FERC were less successful. Rick Richard and Jim Rogers proposed that Northern Natural set rate maximums with seasonal (monthly) pricing within the (averaged) cost-of-service constraint, replacing one set maximum price. "Pipeliner Rick Richard is building a better mousetrap," opined John Jennrich in *Natural Gas Week*. "What he hopes to catch is more certainty in gas supply planning and pricing."

Mick Seidl, at the time Enron's number two behind Lay, joined Jim Rogers's push for less FERC and more market forces. Market and regulatory change was remaking the industry, but "cradle-to-grave" Natural Gas Act regulation was inhibiting and unfair to pipelines.

"We at Enron support the move toward deregulation and simplification of the natural gas industry," Seidl remarked at the annual Cambridge Energy Research Associates (CERA) conference in Houston.[17] "We are firmly convinced that over time the *invisible hand* of Adam Smith can more effectively and efficiently protect the interests of natural gas consumers than can the most thoughtful and well-meaning efforts of federal regulators."

As it was, the industry was immersed in regulatory-related matters from routine filings to formal rate cases. "The btu value of the paperwork now exceeds the btu value of the gas," one wag complained about FERC Order No. 500. Pipeline expansions were in slow motion, part of FERC's backlog of pending certification requests totaling $14 billion in costs and 18 billion cubic feet per day of capacity, a multiple of that of Enron.

Still, Enron was not pushing for a true deregulated market. "Regulation is in the public interest because it tends to protect gas pipelines from risks to which they would be exposed in a competitive environment, and hence promotes stability and thereby reduces costs of capital and benefits consumers," reported

---

17. Industry consultancy CERA was founded by Daniel Yergin and James Rosenfield in 1983. CERA's flagship conference in Houston was crucially supported by Ken Lay.

the Council on Economic Regulation, an ad hoc group that included Enron's Richard, previously a FERC commissioner who had helped author Order No. 436. "If deregulated, economies of scale in transportation would result in competitive entries into the market, exercise of market power, and probable predatory pricing and eventual consolidation."

This was the case for regulating a so-called natural monopoly, little changed from that espoused by Chicago Edison's Samuel Insull to the electric industry a century before. But several years later, Ken Lay would reject this case for public-utility regulation in a speech before the Cato Institute in Washington, DC.[18]

For now, however, regulatory balance was sought. Peter Wilt, head of Enron Interstate's regulatory and competitive analysis, complained at industry conferences about FERC's "dual approach to supply availability"—regulation here and free-market forces there. Wilt and Enron favored deregulation so long as pipelines received fair value for its public-utility service. The policy chief of the Interstate Natural Gas Association of America (INGAA), the pipeline trade group, similarly urged "a market-responsive commission." As it was, FERC was taking a guilty-until-proven-innocent approach to proposals from a market-responsive industry.

In a stubborn buyers' market, pipelines were stuck with take-or-pay liabilities and public-service obligations just as their customers were unilaterally freed by administrative fiat to buy cheaper nontraditional supplies. The "uneven mix" of edict and markets needed more of the latter, Seidl complained. The escape from a regulatory balkanized past, including wellhead decontrol for the first time in several decades, deserved a bilateral, lightened approach.

In the fourth quarter of 1988, Rogers (just 41) was hired away from Enron by a struggling Midwest electric utility, Public Service Company of Indiana (PSI), whose coal-dominated generation assets needed modernization. PSI had suspended its dividend because of a failed nuclear project and was stuck in neutral. The folksy Rogers was just the leader to bring new thinking and urgency to state and federal regulators, customers, and investors. Tumult in the gas industry was good training to this end, PSI's board determined.

Rogers would turn things around at his new job in the next years, although a financial home run was precluded, given the strict rate-base regulation governing his assets. In the process, Rogers would actualize the political capitalism model that Ken Lay was employing at Enron by embracing—ahead of his electric utility peers—the global-warming issue and mandatory open access for electricity.[19]

---

18. For the beginnings of electricity and gas regulation, see Bradley, *Edison to Enron*, pp. 500–515. On Lay's reversal, see chapter 10, p. 442.

19. Rogers's post-Enron career is discussed in chapter 7, p. 322.

Ron Burns, 36, took Rogers's place running the interstate pipeline group. There was only one Jim Rogers, but Burns had cut his teeth in rates and regulatory affairs and sported hands-on experience in transportation and marketing. Burns's contagious can-do spirit made him a superior leader, helped by his all-American build and looks. With Seidl, Dienstbier, and now Rogers gone, Burns reported to Rich Kinder, who was both president of the gas pipeline group and vice-chairman of the parent.

Reporting to Burns from the nonregulated gas side was Gerald Bennett, by now an Enron veteran, who oversaw both Houston Pipe Line and Enron Gas Marketing. The pipeline presidents under Burns were Stan Horton (Florida Gas), Rick Richard (Northern Natural), and Terry Thorn (Transwestern).[20]

Horton, in particular, was a rising star who was on his way to becoming Enron's top pipeline executive. He had been on the regulatory side of Florida Gas when Ken Lay and HNG called in late 1984, had helped Transwestern on the fly, and now had his own pipeline to run, something he could have scarcely imagined just four short years before.

Oliver "Rick" Richard was a talented, colorful character who had gone from being the youngest commissioner in the history of FERC (1982–85), where he led the regulatory restructuring of the interstate gas industry, to general counsel for Tenneco's gas-marketing arm, Tenngasco. He joined Enron in early 1987 as vice president of regulatory and competitive analysis. A Rogers hire, Richard would run Northern Natural until 1991 before becoming CEO of New Jersey Resources and then Columbia Gas System (later Columbia Gas Group).

An HNG lobbyist in Washington, Terry Thorn's business acumen allowed him to take over Enron Mojave from Ross Workman in 1987. Thorn's plans for a PhD and academic career had stopped at the dissertation stage. An intellectual, partisan Democrat and an effective and likable boss, Thorn offered Enron a versatility that Ken Lay would utilize expertly in the years ahead.

In August 1988, Thorn became president of Transwestern Pipeline Company. About a year later, Transwestern became the nation's first transportation-only interstate when SoCalGas nominated zero under its long-standing gas-purchase contract, choosing to buy cheaper gas than that offered by the pipeline. Gas sold by marketing companies to SoCalGas and other California customers on a monthly basis, aided by as-needed transportation-rate discounts, kept Transwestern full. The days of Transwestern as gas buyer and

---

20. Thorn replaced Clark Smith, who was hired away by Coastal Gas Marketing, the counterpart of Enron Gas Marketing at Coastal Corporation. For background on Oscar Wyatt's multifaceted energy company, see Bradley, *Edison to Enron*, pp. 470–75.

seller were over, but revenue was just fine, given favorably designed rate cases and growing gas demand in the Golden State.[21]

___

All of Enron's interstates were in an expansion mode. Florida Gas's Phase I expansion (its first in a quarter century) came on stream in 1987, and a second 100 MMcf/d expansion was planned (it would come on stream in 1991).[22] After a depressed 1986, Transwestern's throughput to California rebounded, and discounts off the maximum transportation rate lessened. In November 1989, Transwestern announced a $153 million, 320 MMcf/d mainline expansion to California, the pipeline's first capacity increase in more than 20 years. Northern Natural, meanwhile, judiciously expanded; the Midwest was not like Florida or California, a reason why InterNorth bought HNG back in 1985.

Mojave Pipeline, a proposed interstate intended to move gas from Transwestern and El Paso to central California's enhanced oil-recovery plants, was navigating its way through two regulatory jurisdictions: the friendly FERC and the obstinate CPUC. Southern California Gas Company, the nation's largest gas distributor, facing bypass in its service territory for the first time in its history, was also vehemently opposed to new entry. When it came to open access, SoCalGas wanted to receive but not to give.

"SoCalGas Turns Environmentalist to Fight Rival Pipeline Companies" stated an *Energy Daily* headline. The article reported: "In a somewhat novel twist, [SoCalGas] has now taken up the cudgels in favor of the endangered desert tortoise and the San Joaquin kit fox," joining such groups as Sierra Club and Friends of the Earth. Such environmental opportunism by profit-seekers would go from novel to commonplace in the years ahead, with California utilities rent-seeking via state and federal *green* energy programs.[23]

As it turned out, Mojave would merge with another expansion project and be completed in 1992, after seven years of effort and much regulatory delay, to serve central California. Enron would sell its half-interest to El Paso Natural Gas the next year.[24]

___

21. Transwestern's market-conforming innovation to escape the profit ceilings under FERC's cost-of-service regulation is described in Internet appendix 5.1, "Transwestern vs. FERC Cost-based Regulation," at www.politicalcapitalism.org/Book3/Chapter5/Appendix1.html.

22. For a history of Florida Gas Transmission, see Bradley, *Edison to Enron*, chapter 8. For subsequent developments through 1996, see chapter 6, pp. 263–64; and chapter 10, p. 437.

23. See chapter 15, pp. 598–99.

24. See chapter 6, p. 263n13.

Together, Enron's pipelines delivered almost three trillion cubic feet of natural gas in 1989, 17.5 percent of the national total. This compared to just above two Tcf in the industry's depression year of 1986, a 14 percent market share. A lot of innovation and hustle went into this improvement. Among other things, GPG's operating expenses fell by one-third (from $0.36/MMBtu in 1986 to $0.24/MMBtu in 1989), helping Enron win gas markets against oil-generated electricity and from purchased power.

Enron's pipelines were negotiating their way out of their producer contracts, but that did not mean that they did not need sourced supply. Even if bought and sold by others, gas needed to be physically connected to the pipeline via gathering lines from the wellhead—or throughput would be short no matter how high end-user demand.

In 1987, Enron Gas Supply Company (EGS) was formed within the interstate group for company-wide gas procurement—an industry first. EGS's 1988 goal to connect 400 MMcf/d to Enron pipes ended the year with that and 50 percent more. Claude Mullendore was president of the unit, reporting to Gerald Bennett, head of the newly created Enron Gas Services, a holding company that was also over Enron Gas Marketing.[25]

Thanks to advancing technology, low prices were not impeding gas supply. Better finding rates, improved drilling and completion techniques, and management efficiencies were allowing consumers to pay less and get more. "America has a large natural gas resource base that is recoverable at reasonable prices that are competitive with alternate fuels in generating electricity," Enron's *1989 Annual Report* concluded. In fact, as documented in its periodic Outlooks, bullish Enron was right on the mark with its resource optimism—and for the right reasons.[26]

Capturing Gas Marketing

Federal open-access rules were transforming a key part of the wholesale natural gas business. Before, interstate pipelines could not make a margin on their wellhead gas purchases. Now, with the merchant function removed from the (regulated) pipelines, independent marketers could buy and sell gas for profit. Thus, a whole new entrepreneurial element emerged, as described in chapters 2 and 3.

It had been an eventful, productive several years since John Esslinger joined Enron Gas Marketing from Transco in August 1986. "It was starting basically from scratch," Esslinger remembered. "I thought there was a great deal of opportunity to do marketing in a different way than it had been done

---

25. Enron Gas Supply in 1988 would negotiate LNG agreements with two Norwegian gas companies, but the needed capital investments would not materialize.

26. See Introduction, pp. 52n57, 57n70.

traditionally," including moving the market away from the "foolish" idea of pure spot (30-day) reliance.

EGM's core activity was making buy-and-sell margins from its advantages of "logistics, scale, scope" and "[having] as much market knowledge as anybody," Esslinger stated. The huge Bammel storage field (part of Houston Pipe Line) gave EGM flexibility. Strategic transportation buys by EGM provided leverage for higher margins. ECT's reputation of fair dealing—being truly arm's length from Enron's pipelines even before FERC regulation required it— was important to all parties: producers, end users, and regulators.[27]

Bid Week was the big event each month. For three-to-five business days near the end of each month, it was all hands on the phone, buying gas here and selling it there for net margin. It began in each person's office, but it was soon decided to create a trading pit of about 16 desks in a large conference room, making communication much easier. For the rest of the month, that space stood empty.

What were profits per MMBtu? At the time, no one knew except for a very chosen few inside the walls of Enron. Volumes, not margins, were broken out for analysts and investors having a need to know. But now it can be told. In comparison to eventual "grocery store type margins" (around 2–3 percent), earlier EGM margins could be 20 or 30 percent ($0.50–0.75 per MMBtu on $2.00–$3.00 gas).

Strict trading guidelines limited position-taking (versus back-to-back arbitrage transactions). The in-house rules were an outgrowth of the oil-trading debacle at Valhalla (chapter 4). But there was also humility. "There is just no way you can figure out the market," Esslinger knew. With limited hedging, particularly with larger deals, going short (selling gas not yet possessed or contracted for) or long (buying gas not yet sold) was scary for the trader. Trading limits, skill, and some humility (Valhalla was still a fresh event), and maybe some good fortune too, prevented a major trading loss during EGM's era of physical trading.

Enter Ken Lay and the art of the big deal. When new gas capacity for power generation hung in the balance (competing with coal), Enron went short on gas with its corporate credit on the line. Enron had some flexibility that competitors did not (Bammel storage for short-term deliveries and Forrest Hoglund's EOG for longer-term supply), but the risk was buying expensive gas for its

---

27. Expecting to compete well on Enron pipes, EGM's real effort was "getting markets on pipelines that we don't own—Transco, Texas Eastern, Panhandle [and] all the other pipelines."

fixed-price sales commitments. Helped by wellhead prices that stayed low, Enron profitably met its long-term sales contracts.[28]

——

"Natural gas now is an industry more of marketers than it is of lawyers," noted John Jennrich in 1988. "That's not to say that a battalion of legal beagles isn't needed to track down the nuances of rules from the Federal Energy Regulatory Commission, the National Energy Board [Canada], and key state and provincial agencies," he wrote in *Natural Gas Week*. "But natural gas is now a commodity—it has a price that fluctuates according to rumor, whim, cold weather, real or perceived shortages, and competing fuels."

In 1988, EGM's sales rose 10 percent, the slowest annual increase since inception. Yet this was almost double the volume averaged just three years before, and the bigger news was a shift toward higher-priced/higher-margin agreements with contracts running from 4 to 15 years, totaling 164 MMcf/d. "We were creating a forward market in 1988," Jeff Skilling would remark many years later about the subsidiary he masterminded as a consultant and then ran as an Enron executive.

The year's jewel was a 100 MMcf/d, 10-year deal with Pacific Gas & Electric (PG&E), California's largest gas and electric utility. The gas would be transported on the El Paso Natural Gas Pipeline (Transwestern did not connect to PG&E). That was the beauty of open access for Ken Lay. The government mandated that pipelines not owned by Enron were on call to EGM at nondiscriminatory rates and other terms of service.[29] The new FERC-driven regime negated part of Ken Lay's coast-to-coast, border-to-border strategy, but unregulated (intrastate) HPL and Bammel storage (now within EGM) were at the core. Government-driven open access was the enabler of EGM.

In July 1988, a regulatory change consolidated Enron's spot-gas marketing programs into EGM. FERC's Marketing Affiliate Rule (Order No. 497) required that interstate pipelines divest themselves of their released-gas (spot-gas) programs. Functional divorcement between transmission and commodity sales was intended to get pipelines out of the merchant function, where conflicts of interest or just preferential treatment disadvantaged independent marketers. FERC Order No. 497, in other words, was a regulatory progression from Order No. 436 and Order No. 500, illustrating the cumulative process of interventionism

——

28. See Introduction, pp. 22–23; and chapter 3, pp. 162–64. Beginning in 1990, new strategies by Enron Gas Services filled the long-term supply gap. See chapter 8, pp. 364–67.

29. FERC open-access rules prohibited a pipeline from giving better terms to one marketer than to another, even the carrier's own affiliated marketer. For example, Enron pipelines could not discriminate against NGC to favor EGM, although Enron would have benefitted by doing so. On the other hand, other interstate pipelines with marketing affiliates (such as Coastal Corporation) could not discriminate against EGM.

whereby new regulation addresses the shortcomings, *the gaps*, created by earlier regulation.[30]

With this order, PAMI (Transwestern), Northern Gas Marketing (Northern Natural), and Panhandle Gas (HPL) merged into EGM. No employee could work for both the regulated ("jurisdictional") pipeline and the unregulated ("nonjurisdictional") marketer. No preferential information could be communicated between the two, under penalty of law. Open access for interstates was not a free-market program but one mandated by FERC to transform the former application of public-utility regulation. It was not deregulation despite Ken Lay's shorthand. It was half-slave, half-free: transportation regulated, gas sales unregulated, and interaction between the two once-merged functions also regulated.[31]

———

By the late 1980s EGM was a bona fide profit center, offsetting take-or-pay costs absorbed by Enron's three interstate pipelines as they moved out of the merchant (buy and sell) function. The future looked bright with new FERC initiatives to increase the competitive arena of independent marketers, including a 1988 proposal to allow purchases of excess transportation capacity from interstate pipelines, called *capacity brokering*.

While EGM's business swelled with FERC Order No. 436 declarations by interstate pipelines, as well as end users executing long-term, price-guaranteed contracts, a major constraint surfaced. *Producers were not stepping up with long-term supply*. A market disconnect was forcing EGM to assume nonhedged risk (really *Knightian uncertainty*, as defined in chapter 4 of Bradley, *Capitalism at Work*), by buying short-term spot gas to meet its long-term, fixed-price deals. Prices had cooperated so far by staying flat, even falling. EOG provided a backstop that other marketers scarcely enjoyed. Still, EGM could not keep playing this game. Given what happened at Valhalla, investors would sooner or later notice and penalize Enron for its growing unhedged positions.

How might EGM create a hedged long-term forward market? Gas producers were not eager to commit their future production in the wake of the take-or-pay debacle with pipelines—especially with a price keyed off (historically low) current prices. These risk-taking optimists always thought that a price rebound would be just a year or two or three away. Consequently, EGM could not simply buy long-term, fixed-price gas to mirror its sales.

———

30. See Bradley, *Edison to Enron*, pp. 493–98.

31. The politics and substance of FERC Order No. 497 are further described in Internet appendix 5.2, "Marketing Affiliate Rule," at www.politicalcapitalism.org/Book3/Chapter5/Appendix2.html.

Somehow, Enron had to restructure the supply side to create a vibrant, profitable market between producers and end users. This innovation would be part of Enron's remaking the national gas market, described in chapter 8.

———

EGM broke out in 1989. The open-access world was maturing, gas sales by interstate pipelines were shrinking, and a national transportation grid was mostly open for business. Total EGM volumes doubled from a year earlier to 1.14 Bcf/d, reaching a peak day of 1.9 Bcf.

Spot sales increased more than 20 percent from the year before as more markets opened up and new ways of doing things, including a gas swap, were discovered.[32] But the real story was "significant margin improvements … through innovative programs and other long-term sales contracts." Long-term sales tripled to nearly 300 MMcf/d in 1989 from the prior year. Fifteen customers executed deals totaling more than 114 Bcf of annual gas sales, the largest being a 200 MMcf/d contract with SoCalGas. What Transwestern and other interstates lost in commodity purchases (on which they could not make a margin, only incur take-or-pay liabilities), EGM won with real profits.

Ken Lay's Enron was actually profiting amid a painful transition for interstate pipelines. And once take-or-pay settlements were done, there was no reason not to make more, much more, from two profit centers in place of the previous one.

The last two months of 1989 were EGM's best, enabled by a new program, *Gas Bank*. Its genesis was gas-supply dedications in the unregulated Texas market by Texas Oil & Gas (the parent of Delhi Gas Pipeline Company, where Forrest Hoglund had once presided). Its supply was partitioned into discrete what-when-where units to meet the terms of heterogeneous end-use contracts. Because these contracts were long term, calculating the related gas *reserves* and future deliverability was crucial. Gerald Bennett had been involved in this prior to coming to Houston Natural Gas in 1984, and it was the progenitor of a whole new concept that would later be credited to Jeff Skilling and Enron Gas Services.

McKinsey's Skilling was tasked with creating a supply portfolio that would reduce the risk of EGM's long-term deals to something more scalable and tailored than previously. Size and differentiation would allow EGM to cut both its price and its supply risk, locking in margins and consummating more sales.

———

32. A swap replaced a physical sale and delivery of gas with a (derivative) financial contract under which a price was guaranteed (by Enron), with the gas delivered by a third party. Jeff Skilling, credited with this innovation to meet the needs of a Louisiana aluminum producer, executed the deal in 1989, which followed the first known swap with oil made three years before.

Skilling's innovation, with input from Bennett,[33] was "nothing less than the first serious effort to diminish the level of risk for everybody involved in natural-gas transactions." Large gas packages had to be procured and divvied into sales packages in order to meet a variety of end-user time profiles. Somewhat akin to bank deposits that could be lent for investment, these *supply buckets* were validated by Enron's own reservoir engineers and then sold to end users. That was the theory of the Gas Bank, something that Skilling described much later as "pure intellectually" and as "ma[king] all the sense in the world."

As logical and successful as the program turned out to be, the idea behind the Gas Bank was not initially embraced by Enron's old guard. About a year before the Gas Bank hit the market, Rich Kinder called a meeting to hear out Skilling's concept. A contingent from the interstate pipelines, led by Jim Rogers, came to the McKinsey presentation. Kinder's Come to Jesus meeting just months before had been a victory for EGM. But questions lingered about how far and fast EGM could assume these pipelines' well-oiled interface between the wellhead and the city gate or burner tip.

Skilling's presentation was unexpectedly brief—one slide and less than a half-hour. The room went silent. Then Rogers spoke: "I've got to say, that's the dumbest idea I've ever heard in my life." Other critics chimed in, pointing out how EGM could not and should not be responsible for ensuring reliable supply. Some alligators were crawling back into the swamp that Kinder thought was drained.

After the vetting, a humbled Skilling headed back to Kinder's office. But the boss was hardly disappointed. "As soon as I heard Rogers say it was the dumbest idea he's ever heard, I knew it's exactly what we need to do," Kinder told Skilling. But really, Kinder had grasped the concept both from this meeting and from prior discussions with Skilling. McKinsey's new marching order was to pony up EGM's resources and make it work.

———

Supply in hand, Kinder and Skilling visited major gas customers interested in diversifying with some known supply-and-price quantity in addition to their shorter-term commitments. Many customers jumped at the idea of supply and price security backed by an Enron corporate guaranty. In the last two months of 1989, EGM placed 366 Bcf of 10-year, fixed-priced gas—generating income for Enron of as much as $200 million in net present value. Such profit required gas streams backed by good reservoir engineering and the requisite long-term transportation to the delivery point, something that mandatory open access enabled.

---

33. For Gerald Bennett's role, see Internet appendix 5.3, "On the Formation of Gas Bank," at www.politicalcapitalism.org/Book3/Chapter5/Appendix3.html.

But the success came with concerns. First, the long-term gas was not hedged. Only if prices stayed down (they would) would the margins be large. The other problem was a depleted Gas Bank. Low wellhead prices and scarce bank financing in the wake of the energy-price collapse of several years were limiting the product that end users wanted. A new generation of supply-side product was needed. And that required an innovative leader to engineer new approaches to the business—and to construct the institutional architecture that would turn ideas into action.

As 1989 drew to a close, Rich Kinder and Ken Lay asked Jeff Skilling to join Enron. But the 36-year-old had just been elected partner at McKinsey with a salary that Enron could not match. Enron was a bird in the bush, not the hand. Skilling was not quite ready to stop being a schemer, the outside set-up man for the most innovative gas company anywhere. Moreover, consulting fees paid to McKinsey by a continually reorganizing, reanalyzing Enron were huge.

Liquid Fuels: Profitable Incrementalism

Enron Liquid Fuels (ELF) had the lowest profile of Enron's major divisions. It was not sexy like exploration and production, where each new prospect brought suspense and potential riches. Unlike the interstate pipelines, ELF did not operate in a regulatory maze where industry news was made with FERC filings and Rogers speeches.

ELF wasn't an upstart like EGM, blazing new territory and making history along the way. No, it was relatively quiet business to turn natural gas into ethane, propane, butane, and gasoline; pipe these liquids around the Midwest and Southwest; and trade liquids or petroleum. For Ken Lay, this midstream was not too exciting but integral to Enron's natural gas model.

ELF's Mike Muckleroy had gotten rid of most of the top managers he inherited from InterNorth, including all five division presidents. Their replacements all had been found internally. InterNorth was like that; middle managers could often be as good as or better than their tenured superiors.[34]

---

34. Principals in ELF's revamping and turnaround in 1985-89 (listed with Muckleroy's comments) were general counsel Mike Moran ("we never had one major legal problem in any of our companies"); human resources head Mary Ellen Coombe ("she was in on every major change-in-management decision I made"); Enron Gas Liquids' Dave Rousell ("he ran all of our liquid plant operations and participated in acquisition decisions"); Enron Oil Trading & Transportation's Chuck Emel ("he guided growth from handling 200,000 daily barrels to over one million barrels a day in the U.S. and Canada"); and Enron Liquid Pipelines' Jim Spencer ("he reorganized EOTT and then successfully ran the pipeline operations"). Two other key team members were Dave Woytek in accounting and audit ("he detected the accounting/marketing fraud at Enron Oil Company") and Ron Jones of information technology ("he made the IT systems work behind the huge growth volumes in every one of our companies").

Best of all, ELF went from net losses in 1986 and in 1987 to income before interest and taxes (IBIT) of $58 million in 1988 and $89 million in 1989, the last figures being between 10 and 15 percent of Enron's total. Reorganizations and a major reduction-in-force in late 1988 were part of the turnaround.

Strong margins in liquids had formerly depended on high selling prices. But in a low-price environment, profitability was about controlling cost, value-adding services, and marketing. That is where the affable Muckleroy earned his keep. He liked to find out where the problems were and get out in front of them. He led by example, regularly walking the floors to talk to people and inspire them to do a little more—and be rewarded for it. He was considered close to ideal by his thousands of employees.

_____

When Ken Lay reset Enron's sights as a global natural gas company, ELF provided a platform as the world's sixth-largest nongovernmental marketer of liquid products. With major offices in the United Kingdom, France, and the Netherlands, international opportunities were expanding, in part from the growing US position as a net importer of petroleum and gas liquids. "Demand for natural gas liquids continues to grow worldwide while supply is abating domestically," Enron's 1989 annual report stated.

With a growing linkage between foreign and domestic markets and a forecast that ELF's foreign side would be a net product provider to the United States, Muckleroy merged Enron Liquid Fuels International into Enron Gas Liquids in 1989. Five divisions were now four—Enron Gas Liquids; Enron Oil Trading & Transportation Company; Enron Gas Processing Company; and Enron Liquids Pipeline Company.[35]

Muckleroy found out how hard it was to operate in noncapitalistic parts of the world or where a joint venture was lacking parental attention or where the operation was distant and obscure. For example, Enron and GE jointly owned a Venezuelan manufacturer of GE appliances—Madosa—which turned into a money drain, in part from a bad economy and also from government controls. Small investments in Puerto Rico and the Dominican Republic were or would be problematic as well.

Some success came from just being able to say *no*. A case in point was when Muckleroy inaugurated a meeting between Ken Lay and the Russian Minister of Energy, which resulted in a highly publicized letter of intent in December 1989 for Enron to develop a full range of natural gas projects there. But Muckleroy knew better than to make investments in unstable, unpredictable jurisdictions. What ELF did do was enter into a marketing agreement for refined

---

35. Each of the four divisions was several years old, with only Enron Gas Liquids experiencing a name change (shortened from Enron Gas Liquids Marketing).

products whereby Russian deliveries were paid for only when they reached Baltic ports. It was profitable, and Ken Lay had gotten his photo op.

Muckleroy also stopped short of making capital-intensive investments in LNG infrastructure. Prior to its merger with Houston Natural Gas, InterNorth had taken a big hit when it had to cancel an LNG tanker order. ELF left the big infrastructure projects to those companies with time-honed expertise. Muckleroy was sufficiently risk averse to stick to his knitting, and there was plenty to do, given ELF's economies of scale and scope. Such prudence would be missed at Enron a decade later when Muckleroy and other experienced executives like him were gone.

In 1989, ELF acquired CSX, Louisiana's largest gas-liquids processor. In the same year, contracts were executed to build a 100-mile, 30,000 bbl/day ethane pipeline from Mont Belvieu, Texas, to Lake Charles, Louisiana. Although its $55 million capital budget for 1990 was down from 1988's $89 million, ELF was one of Enron's Big Five divisions heading into the new decade.

———

With ELF and EGM, Enron offered customers an entire portfolio of energies at a variety of prices for periods from one month to multiple years. No other company could do this, Ken Lay proudly pointed out. Even on the petroleum side—which Lay would not emphasize—ELF described itself as "a fully integrated crude oil entity in North America."

Trading was part of ELF, but it was not speculative like at the old Enron Oil Corporation. Betting on future price movements was quite secondary to trading around the company's hard assets. Traders who violated ELF's strict limits "fired themselves," as Muckleroy put it. One who did, ironically, had come down from Valhalla where, unlike some of his colleagues there, he had played by the rules.

Mike Muckleroy, Valhalla hero and company builder, was rewarded in 1989 with total compensation near $1 million. He was Enron's third-highest-paid executive after the chairman and the vice chairman. In December 1989, Muckleroy entered into a new five-year contract with an increase in minimum base pay. To the board and Lay and Kinder, he was a man to keep.

Getting Political

Enron's profit centers in the 1980s were particularly, even uniquely, tied to federal energy policies. FERC regulated the interstate pipelines with complicated rate cases affecting the difference between authorized and actual rates of return. PURPA drove independent cogeneration to create a competitive arena for nonutility providers. Mandatory open access enabled gas marketing on interstate pipelines. And Forest Hoglund's EOG was lobbying to get a tax break that would contribute to a roaring 1990s.

But there was another political card to play for natural gas–oriented Enron. Coal gained the upper hand on natural gas as an unintended consequence of federal policy in the 1970s. Price controls on natural gas, specifically, created shortages that turned electric utilities to abundant, non-price-controlled coal. On the belief that natural gas was geologically constrained rather than governmentally discouraged ("we had a surplus of regulation, not a shortage of gas," Lay would say), federal law instructed industries and utilities to substitute coal for gas in new facilities.[36]

Even in the face of gas surpluses, coal interests continued to disparage natural gas as unreliable—something that caught in Ken Lay's craw. There was public relations work to do—such as rebutting the anti-gas rhetoric of Richard Lawson, president of the National Coal Association. More important, there was Enron's *marketplace* rejoinder with the Gas Bank and other innovations that reduced price and supply risk to clinch the economics of gas plants relative to coal plants.

Natural gas had another card to play against coal: *less pollution* per kilowatt hour of electricity produced. A table in Enron's 1988 annual report showed these reductions for a gas-fired power plant relative to a coal facility: 99 percent for sulfur dioxide (SO_2); 43 percent for nitrogen oxide (NO_x); 53 percent for hydrocarbons; and 96 percent for particulates (PM_{10}). These were traditional, *criteria pollutants* as defined by the Clean Air Act of 1970 and subsequent legislation. In addition, the table identified a 48 percent reduction for natural gas relative to coal in electric generation for the major manmade greenhouse gas, carbon dioxide (CO_2). CO_2 was not a pollutant in the classic sense but a heat-trapping gas that contributed to global warming (aka climate change), other things being equal. This became a national issue in the hot, dry summer of 1988 when NASA scientist James Hansen testified before a Senate subcommittee chaired by Al Gore (D-TN). "Global warming is now sufficiently large that we can ascribe with a high degree of confidence a cause and effect relationship to the greenhouse effect," Hansen testified.

Fellow climatologists were less sure. "What really bothers them is not that they believe Hansen is demonstrably wrong, but that he fails to hedge his conclusions with the appropriate qualifiers that reflect the imprecise science of climate modeling," reported Richard Kerr in *Science*. But media reaction to Hansen was swift and supportive—anthropogenic (manmade) global warming was here *and* problematic (the United States was experiencing heat waves and drought at the time). The 1970s concern about global cooling or even a new ice age (global average temperatures had been falling since 1945) was forgotten.

---

36. See Bradley, *Edison to Enron*, pp. 454, 508–9. After Department of Energy program administrators routinely granted exemptions, the Fuel Use Act would be partially repealed in 1987 and 1989 and then totally repealed in 1992.

The Popular Vision, or what climate scientist and critic Patrick Michaels called *apocalyptic environmentalism*, was born—and not to abate in Enron's lifetime.[37]

In Enron's 1988 annual report, Ken Lay brought in the (enhanced) greenhouse effect as part of natural gas's comparative advantage against oil and coal:

> Renewed interest in clean air could mandate anti-pollution measures that will favor the use of natural gas, the cleanest fossil fuel. Natural gas contributes the least of all fossil fuels to emissions thought to contribute to the greenhouse effect, acid rain, and reduction of the ozone layer in the upper atmosphere.... Because of these developments, the company fully expects the 1990s to be the decade for natural gas.

Enron's 1989 annual report referenced "the discussion concerning the dangers of a global warming trend" with natural gas being "a key component of the solution."

The natural gas industry got right on board the global-warming bandwagon. The American Gas Association (AGA) met with environmental groups on a strategy of substituting gas as a "bridge fuel." "Our effectiveness depends on how the industry reacts," explained the Sierra Club about the new alliance. The World Resources Institute stated: "We believe that discouraging new uses of natural gas is bad energy policy, economically unsound, and environmentally damaging." The National Coal Association, meanwhile, labeled such thinking "shortsighted," while the nuclear group US Council for Energy Awareness complained about being left out of the discussion.

The *Exxon Valdez* oil spill in Alaska in spring 1989 stained petroleum, not only Prince William Sound. Commenting on the development, Lay pointed to global warming as the bigger driver of future gas demand and thus price. The "operating and environmental benefits of gas" should (and would) be "reflected in gas prices," Lay opined. Compared to about $1.60/MMBtu at the wellhead, Lay estimated a full-value gas price at between $3 and $4 per MMBtu. To get gas prices up, given gas-on-gas competition at the wellhead (including from EOG, advantaged by a tax credit), other fuels needed to be made more expensive. An oil tariff was too problematic to Lay, but he was all for a "heavier tax on dirtier fuels," aka an environmental surcharge.

Enron's involvement with the global-warming or climate-change issue would only grow in the years ahead. Existing profit centers were well aligned to benefit from mandatory carbon dioxide reductions, and new such profit centers would be created in the 1990s. Enron, superaggressive politically, would

---

37. See also chapter 7, p. 328. The global-warming issue, involving the enhanced greenhouse effect, primarily from fossil-fuel burning, is discussed in Internet appendix 5.4, "Global Warming and Greenhouse Gases," at www.politicalcapitalism.org/Book3/Chapter5/Appendix4.html.

work behind the scenes for national and international government policies to ration (price) emissions of hitherto unregulated CO_2.[38]

_____

In late 1989, Enron rolled out an environmentally themed advertising campaign, its first nationally. "We've been quietly but consistently making a name for ourselves in the natural gas industry, and our chairman, Ken Lay, has become its undisputed spokesman," the company magazine *Enron People* explained to employees.

Ads in *Forbes*, *Barron's*, *Roll Call*, and the *Economist*, as well as in Audubon Society magazines, brought attention to Enron's role in reducing the emissions associated with acid rain and global warming. "Isn't it wonderful natural gas is invisible so the rest of nature never will be?" the message under flying golden eagles read.

The target audience was policymakers. "This is a particularly active period in Congress in terms of topics that affect us," explained Ed Segner, vice president over public and investor relations. "When clean air issues, reform of the Public Utility Holding Company Act, and other energy policies are being discussed by our legislators, we want them to consider natural gas as a vital part of their strategy."

"Working natural wonders in the energy world." "Natural gas. A fuel to stop growing foreign oil dependence in its tracks." "Our smartest instincts for the future run to natural gas." Enron was branding itself with investors, policymakers, and environmental groups. Coal interests were nonplussed, and oil interests were conflicted.

Imaging Enron as a superior, socially conscious company, however, would not confine Enron's bottom line. Oil, not natural gas, typically would be the fuel of choice with Enron International's power plants in the developing world.[39] And coal was just a few years away from (quietly) being a moneymaker for Enron.[40] What would eventually confine Enron's bottom line—to zero—was its growing disposition to consider imaging as a substitute for reality.

Vision Accomplished

Results from 1988 were a welcome change from the previous three years. Yet industry conditions remained depressed, and natural gas marketing was just evolving into the sort of profit center that could impact Enron's overall earnings. Cost cutting was still necessary at the core, as it was for most other energy companies.

In the fourth quarter of 1988, GPG merged its operations with that of corporate staff, reducing redundancies. Lay and Kinder, nominally at least, were pipeliners as well as overseers. Layoffs of 250 resulted in annualized savings

_____

38. See chapter 7, pp. 327–30, 332–40; and chapter 13, 529–30, 552–59.

39. See Introduction, p. 30; and chapter 7, pp. 319.

40. See Introduction, pp. 31–32.

estimated at $15 million. "We continue to be affected adversely by declining oil prices, gas-on-gas competition resulting in lower gas prices, and depressed margins in our liquids businesses," Ken Lay explained in an all-employee memo. "To respond to these market conditions, Enron must position itself as one of the least-cost providers of natural gas in the country." Lay apologized: "Staff reductions are never anything the management committee nor I consider lightly, and I sincerely wish that market conditions did not force us to make these types of decisions."

Back to basics (which included Lay and Kinder dealing directly with the pipelines) was defense. Lay liked to play offense. "Cost cutting does not lead to prosperity," he would say. But this would be the last all-employee cost-containment memorandum from Ken Lay until the dark clouds of 2001. Enron's architect and chairman believed that first movers, the best and brightest, should chase dollars rather than pinch pennies.

Still, things were looking up as 1988's final results were tallied. The first quarter of 1989 was coming in well. Enron *was* the industry leader in many of its businesses. So Ken Lay announced victory on the mission he had set for his company back in 1986.

Enron—the 1988 annual report declared—was *the premier integrated natural gas pipeline company in North America*. At the same time, with all divisions in a growth mode and a major new UK project in Teesside in the planning stage, Ken Lay set a grander, more creative vision for Enron: *to become the world's first natural gas major*.

———

The year 1989 was a big step up. Net income of $226 million was almost double the previous four years combined. The debt overhang was being erased by cash flow. All divisions were profitable. Best of all, ENE's price had appreciated by more than half, a sign that Wall Street was buying into Enron's natural gas story. "The successful accomplishment of virtually all our 1989 priorities has given Enron the proper building blocks for future growth in an exciting but challenging era for natural gas," Rich Kinder and Ken Lay exuded in the annual report.

Ken Lay's halo was in full glow. After all, his unique strategy had—finally—turned around the company in an unforgiving environment. In energy-capital Houston, Enron was emerging as an energy star—and a different, more exciting company from the local icons: Exxon, Shell, Tenneco, and certainly Transco.

Enron *was* a breed apart, Lay explained. "Enron employees are not afraid to take risks, and they are not content to do things the way they have always been done," the 1989 annual report explained. "They constantly are looking for a better, faster, simpler way to get the job done with quality." Every employee was an Enron shareholder pursuant to the 1986 ESOP program, and they were told that the key to corporate success would be an attitude of "do it right/do it now/do it better." Going beyond words, Lay issued a special thank you. When ENE first traded in the $50s in late 1989, Lay surprised every salaried employee with a crisp new $50 bill.

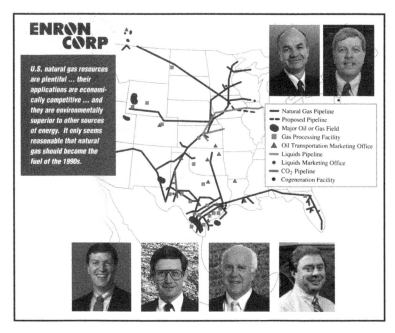

Figure 5.4 After much turmoil, Ken Lay had a top team in place by 1989 to manage Enron's North American gas assets. Under himself and Rich Kinder (the new vice chairman and soon president) were (lower, left to right) Ron Burns, who oversaw interstate pipelines and marketing; Forrest Hoglund, for exploration and production; Mike Muckleroy, running liquids; and John Wing, handling cogeneration.

But beneath the gloss was a company with a lot of work to do. In fact, some 11th-hour financial shenanigans made turnaround-1989 less than it was heralded to be. Valhalla had been a canary in the coal mine; what happened in late 1989 was a foretaste of Ken Lay's modus operandi as well.

As the fourth quarter dawned, Enron was in danger of not making its projected earnings—bad news for a debt-heavy company that had presented itself to Wall Street as a momentum stock. The search was on for earnings to meet plan. Exceeding plan and any other good news would send the stock price up—something that Enron's ESOP-laden workforce was eager for—not to mention Enron's top management, whose compensation packages were tied to meeting earnings targets, ENE's appreciation, and the price of ENE relative to a peer group of 11 chosen companies.

It was at this time that Gerald Bennett, head of Houston Pipe Line, was in final negotiations with gas-distributor Entex over a long-term contract renewing a range of wholesale services. It had been laborious, figuring out the costs of different components (such as Bammel's storage functions) and the value this represented versus Entex's next-best opportunity.

In the process, Bennett discovered something: The contract's lifetime earnings could be accelerated to the present in the context of removing a $40 million take-or-pay liability that had been assigned to HPL at the time of HNG's merger with InterNorth. The problem was that this number had to be increased, and Enron faced a loss unless an offset was found.

With some new provisions and accounting help, the HPL-Entex contract could accelerate future income into fourth-quarter earnings. Bennett informed Rich Kinder about the possibility as a *you should know about this*, not *let's do it*. Kinder talked to Lay, and both agreed that they had to have the earnings, the future notwithstanding.

Job one was for Kinder to get Enron's new CFO and Keith Kern's replacement, Jack Tompkins, to get his former colleagues at Arthur Andersen (where he had managed the Enron account), to sign off on the earnings acceleration and take-or-pay reversal. Despite grumblings that the acceleration was outside of generally accepted accounting principles (GAAP)—the income should have reduced the *goodwill* account that was created at the time of the merger—Andersen consented.[41]

Kinder then interjected himself in the negotiation, working with Entex's Jimmy Terrell to rework the contract for getting the contract just right for accounting discretion. Present income aside, there was a price for Enron to pay; Entex, playing off of Enron's urgency, cut a better deal—taking away as much as a third of HPL's profit margin, a loss in the many millions of dollars.

So not only was HPL's future earnings neutered in an accounting sense, the deal's net present value for Enron was lessened compared to what would have occurred without the legerdemain. "The name of the game," Bennett recalls, "was to make this year's earnings, come hell or high water; so the decision was made to go forward."

Jeff Skilling, working closely with both Bennett and Kinder as a consultant, took note of the earnings acceleration. In fact, this birth of mark-to-market accounting at Enron would later become Skilling's forte at Enron Gas Services, later to become Enron Capital & Trade Resources. A slippery slope created in 1989 would become an addiction at Enron in the 1990s.

———

Meeting projected earnings was a necessary but not sufficient condition to raise the stock price. Something else was necessary to cause a jump in ENE by year end. Gerald Bennett found himself in the middle of this too.

Enron Gas Marketing was successfully placing its Gas Bank inventory with end users desiring locked-in prices for some of their purchases. But Bennett was

---

41. David Woytek, Enron's internal auditor at the time, would call the reversal "wrong" because "it went against every accounting rule there is." The goodwill account, which housed the overpayment for HNG by InterNorth, originally $1.2 billion, was being amortized against net income over 40 years, as dictated by GAAP.

blindsided at his 7 a.m. staff meeting on Monday, November 27, by a page 1 *Wall Street Journal* article: "Enron Is Selling Gas on Long-Term, Fixed-Price Basis." The piece explained how Enron was "locking in premium prices for now and allowing customers a hedge against the rising tide of future gas prices," an industry first. Gas Bank volumes of 200 MMcf/d were flowing, and cumulative multiyear deals with 11 customers had reached 430 Bcf, the paragraphs read.

There was little holding back in the piece. Ken Lay estimated that EGM's profit margin—the difference between average purchases and sales—at 7 cents per MMBtu in 1989, up from 5 cents in 1988. Next year's average margin looked like 11 cents, he added. On a net present value basis, earnings were calculated at $60 million for just the first four years of the contracts.

Ed Segner, formerly of Drexel Burnham Lambert, and now Enron's vice president of public relations, confirmed Enron Gas Marketing as a major profit center going forward. EOG, he added in the piece, was also benefitting as a supplier for EGM's premium-price sales.

Bennett was nonplussed, even incensed. Many deals he was negotiating had not been completed. No one had cleared the story with him; worse, it appeared to have been done *around* him to goose the stock. Gas Bank *was* going well, but this was not the time to tell the world about it. Such a premature announcement skated a fine line for a public company. But the top of Enron felt that, with the holiday season just unfolding, this was the time to break the big news.

The story did its work, propelling ENE to an all-time high of $61 per share before ending the year at 57 5/8. The dividend remained frozen at $0.62 per share. Enron was now a growth stock, not a yield stock.

Enron's 1989 income of $226 million, while high by postmerger standards, was modest for a company sporting $9 billion in assets. Earnings were still below what HNG alone had made back in 1984, even before adjusting for inflation. More troubling, at least in retrospect, was earnings *quality* given that non-recurring items accounted for the majority of net income.[42] Asset sales accounted for most of the after-tax income: $107 million from the partial sale of EOG; $73 million from the sale of Mobil stock; and $6 million from the sale of Enron's investment in Zapata Gulf Marine Corporation (ending an unfruitful diversification made by Robert Herring back in the mid-1970s). Another $12 million came from an antitrust settlement.[43] All this left divisional earnings below $50

42. Jeff Skilling commented on this period at Enron: "There were some reasonable profit numbers showing, but if you look at the quality of those profits, they were just awful." He went on to add, in his characteristic black-and-white tones: "There was a period of time there where it was dicey whether the company would survive. It was that bad."

43. The ETSI settlements, concerning an ill-fated coal slurry pipeline proposal, which resulted in nearly $100 million of income to Enron in the 1987–90 period, is summarized in Internet appendix 2.2, "HNG/InterNorth: Joint Ventures, Miscellaneous Assets, and Sales," at www.politicalcapitalism.org/Book3/Chapter2/Appendix2.html.

million. Income before interest and taxes was almost $700 million, but servicing Enron's $3.2 billion debt took a toll.

Meeting earnings expectation and generating optimism improved business too. A higher stock price improved Enron's capital value, lowering the debt-to-capital ratio to bolster ENE's credit standing. With a better credit rating, now or later, borrowing costs would fall, generating millions for the bottom line.

There was something else. Enron's senior executives, whose compensation was tied to ENE's price, scored big. For the first time, a number of Enron's top brass could exhale for their years of risk taking alongside Lay.

Still, the higher net worth of the company—$1.8 billion—was one-third below the two companies' premerger value. The debt ratio of 63 percent, while down from 75 percent during 1986, was burdensome. "Management is very comfortable with the current debt level and continues to target debt to total capital ratio of 60 percent or less," the 1989 annual report stated. But EOG's Forrest Hoglund sure liked his ratio of 41 percent a lot better.

———

Enron was living on the edge—still. But with take-or-pay liabilities under control, the Gas Pipeline Group (the largest in North America) was performing at the very top of its peer group. Enron Gas Marketing was the industry's largest and most profitable gas merchant—and unregulated. "America's Pure Natural Gas Play," Enron Oil & Gas, was making top money in a low-price environment. Enron Liquid Fuels was judiciously expanding and solidly in the black. And with John Wing doggedly pursuing a bold new opportunity in England, Enron Power had home-run potential.

But was Enron really the leading integrated natural gas company in North America? *Leading* is a relative, not absolute, standard, and there were no purely integrated natural gas companies, defined as upstream-midstream-downstream and more than regional. Enron was not in downstream, having sold its Inter-North-side gas-distribution business, Peoples Natural Gas Company, right after the merger.

Enron was a strong upstream-to-midstream company performing atop its peer group (e.g., El Paso Natural Gas, Tenneco, Texas Eastern, Transco Energy, Sonat, among others). And should commodity prices recover—say, to levels anywhere close to 1985—Enron would be more of a money machine. But, alas, Enron would have to prosper without much help from commodity prices well into the 1990s.

Part III

Natural Gas, Natural Politics: 1990–1993

Introduction

"Enron enters the 1990s with a focused business strategy, a strong set of values, and a vision to become the premier integrated natural gas company in the world," Ken Lay and Richard Kinder reported to investors, customers, and employees. The well-focused company had four major divisions: exploration and production, pipelines, liquids, and cogeneration—all profitable enough to overcome the parent's extraordinary debt load (chapter 6). Another area would soon break out as Enron's fifth major division—gas marketing, the subject of Part IV.

Significant progress had been made in a tough business environment. Enron led the nation with 18 percent of the gas market. Take-or-pay liabilities in pipeline contracts, as high as $1.2 billion in mid-1987, were under control, leaving each interstate with double-digit profitability, quite unlike troubled peers Transcontinental Pipe Line and Columbia Gas Transmission. Enron's debt-to-capitalization ratio, at a precarious 73 percent after the 1985 merger, was in the low 60s and falling. Enron, by all counts, was ready to capitalize on what its annual report described as "the decade for natural gas."

A wave of legislative and regulatory change was propelling the company. Inhibiting 1970s regulation on natural gas was being removed in the surplus era. Political capitalism was also providing a major boost: Federal regulation of sulfur dioxide (SO_2) emissions, associated with acid rain—as well as newfound concern about carbon dioxide (CO_2), the major manmade greenhouse gas emission—advantaged natural gas relative to coal and petroleum.

Federal energy policy inspired two profit centers. A provision in the Public Utility Regulatory Policies Act of 1978 (PURPA) prompted the emergence of a non-utility (independent) power-generation sector, of which Enron Power Corp was a market leader. Technological advances in gas-fired cogeneration—the simultaneous production of electricity and heat—played right into this government-sponsored opportunity.

Revamped rules by the Federal Energy Regulatory Commission (FERC) enabled the burgeoning Enron Gas Marketing—soon renamed Enron Gas Services—to offer national sales services in the wholesale market (retail was the franchise of gas utilities). While pipelines made their profits as before, gas sales in interstate commerce could make margins for the first time since the 1938 passage of the Natural Gas Act. Desktop computers were just in time, too, as hundreds of EGM/EGS employees mastered the open-access pipeline grid.

Internationally, the "greatest sale in the history of the world" was on. Cash-strapped socialist countries were turning to private parties to build and operate energy assets for deficit reduction and improved economic performance. Enron

Development, constructing new power plants and other energy infrastructure, rushed into high-risk/high-return underdeveloped countries. But these unfree economies would produce more risk than return for Enron in the final counting.

America's political capitalism offered Enron unique opportunity, such as mandatory open access (MOA) for interstate pipelines. And Enron was winning special government favors elsewhere, too, including a tax credit for tight-sands gas production; MOA for electricity in wholesale markets; and loan guarantees for foreign projects. Not coincidentally, a Washington-wise CEO was shaking the money trees in a very political economy.

Ken Lay knew and liked the nation's capital, where he had worked for six years in different governmental capacities, the subject of chapter 7. There were always rumors that Lay would take a high-level political appointment. But Enron provided a seat of power for Lay across federal agencies. Besides, there were too many bills to pay with a blended family of seven to take a government job.

———

Enron circa 1990 was the product of temerity, problem solving, get-this-behind-us, and real progress. The years 1988–89 were about overcoming and repositioning; 1990–93 Enron was fast-forwarding into the future with divisional progress and breakout profit centers.

But the company's 15 percent annual earnings growth, well beyond that of almost all major energy companies, was placing ambition ahead of bourgeois virtue. Mark-to-market accounting at EGS, Enron's fastest-growing unit, inflated current earnings. Nonhedged commodity-price contracts were accruing liabilities. Rash bets overseas (and none greater than in Dabhol, India) would leave a huge bill for exciting beginnings. And off-balance-sheet financing was beginning a bad habit of selective reporting to investors in the company.

Enron was embarking on imprudent, slippery tracks. Aggressive visions and bullish talk made ENE a momentum stock. Everyone was in, including an Enron workforce that owned more than 20 percent of the company's common stock. Honest talk, tempered expectations, and prudent adjustments were needed for future sustainability. But those would prove increasingly rare as the 1990s went on.

6

Natural Gas Majoring

T he four years 1990–93 witnessed great change and growth at Enron. Total assets increased 26 percent to $10 billion. Net income rose almost by half to $332 million. Shareholder equity grew to $2.6 billion, up 47 percent.[1] Financial engineering was behind some of the profit, however, and big bets were being made that would trap capital and require future write-offs. Far from unique, this continued a future-is-now philosophy that dismissed steady, solid, and good as not enough.

Enron joined the *Forbes*, *Fortune*, and *BusinessWeek* lists of largest US companies in the early 1990s. In the nation's energy capital, only Marathon Group and soon-to-be-dismantled Tenneco topped Enron. (Exxon and Shell, Houston based for their domestic operations, were headquartered elsewhere.) In terms of local employment, Enron was sixth behind Continental Airlines (now United), Houston Industries (now CenterPoint Energy), Compaq Computers (now HP), Baker Hughes, and Cooper Industries (now part of Eaton).

Chapter 6 details five (of six) Enron divisions: natural gas pipelines, still the largest part of the company; international, a very aggressive division that would record notable profits but create major problems going forward; liquids, which went from highly profitable to a problem area with an ill-fated acquisition for

---

1. The financial comparisons are between year-end 1989 and year-end 1993, except for income, which compares 1989 and 1993. Total revenue rose by 72 percent between 1989 and 1993 (to $8 billion). Pipeline revenues fell by approximately one-fourth, while EGS picked up this revenue (and much more) as gas merchant.

producing methyl tertiary-butyl ether (MTBE); power, which quieted as the US independent cogeneration boom played out; and exploration and production, the prized subsidiary led by Forrest Hoglund.

Natural gas marketing, a multitudinous story of entrepreneurial development, is reserved for Part IV.

A New Vision

In first-quarter 1990, Ken Lay declared victory on his vision set less than three years before. Enron was "the premier integrated natural gas company in North America." But this commanding height was no resting point. It was a beach-head for sustained first-mover advantage given the company's unique business niche and attractive corporate culture.

With international aspirations, and sensing major growth in all its (gas-oriented) divisions, Lay assigned Enron its second vision: "to become the world's first natural gas major; the most innovative and reliable provider of clean energy worldwide for a better environment." Dr. Lay awed his top lieutenants at an off-site meeting on this one. *Natural gas major* was really what Enron was all about—and a new way to think about the energy business.

What would the new vision require? "Since there are no natural gas majors today," Lay explained, "we must make our own model." The analogy was the oil majors: those "integrated companies that are able technically and financially to do virtually any and all aspects of the oil business anywhere in the world." It was about total integration "from the production platform through the electric power plant" on a global scale—and sooner rather than later, Lay explained.[2]

True, there were no natural gas majors, in terms of large-scale integrated, international specialization. But there should have been. The oil majors were gas-ready with their large domestic production and strong international upstream and midstream operations. But federal energy policy intervened. The Public Utility Holding Company Act of 1935 required divestiture for almost all integrated gas-transmission and -distribution companies. For example, Jersey Standard—later to acquire Humble Oil & Refining (Ken Lay's old company) to become Enco, then Esso, and then Exxon—for one, divested its gas holdings to stockholders as five separate companies.

Second, the Natural Gas Act of 1938 placed interstate transmission under cost-based rate regulation. The core competency of integrated oil majors was not in public-utility-regulated businesses. And when the same law imposed wellhead price controls on the production of integrated gas companies in the 1940s, upstream divestment followed.

---

2. For further discussion, see Internet appendix 6.1, "Natural Gas Visions at Enron," at www.politicalcapitalism.org/Book3/Chapter6/Appendix1.html. There were four Enron visions in all, three by 1996. Later missions are discussed in chapter 14, on pp. 565–70.

Downstream, at the local distribution company (LDC) level, state utility commissions regulated rates and service under traditional cost-based principles. The incentive for firms was to maximize capital investment, to maintain and add to the rate base, and to earn the authorized rate of return. So long as the regulated margin was greater than borrowing costs, pure profits were won by such investment in a market where consumers were captive to their utility.[3]

The result of state and federal regulation was a nonintegrated gas industry with firms specializing in production, transmission, or distribution. There were no natural gas majors, no integrated behemoths.

———

Going into the new decade, Enron had five major divisions (with International to come). Natural Gas housed three: Pipelines, Gas Services, and Power. Gas-centric Liquid Fuels, along with Exploration and Production, were the other two divisions.

- *Pipelines*, the 38,000-mile, five-pipeline system of interstates Northern Natural, Transwestern, and Florida Gas Transmission; intrastate Houston Pipe Line; and the interstate joint-venture Northern Border

- *Enron Gas Services*, the nonregulated gas finance and marketing subsidiary at the forefront of the spot- and term-gas commoditization in interstate markets

- *Power*, a leading independent developer of domestic and international electricity generation (gas-fired cogeneration)

- *Liquid Fuels*, the nation's fifth-largest natural gas processor, as well as a large marketer and transporter of gas liquids and a midsize gatherer of crude oil

- *Exploration and Production*, one of the nation's largest independent, nonintegrated oil and gas companies, with 90 percent of its energy reserves in natural gas and 90 percent domestic

Enron was not a wholly integrated gas firm, since it did not own an LDC. InterNorth's Peoples Gas was sold in 1985, and that was about it except for small retail gas meters scattered off the pipelines. But Enron was getting very large in the new unregulated gas-merchant business, as discussed in chapter 8. Enron Gas Services (EGS) wholesaled gas at the city gate, where LDCs, exclusively serving geographical areas under a franchise monopoly, bought gas for resale to commercial, industrial, and residential customers. As discussed in chapter 9, EGS would expand its marketing reach to customers behind the LDC

———

3. The evolution of public-utility regulation for both manufactured and natural gas and for electricity is described in Bradley, *Edison to Enron*, pp. 500–515.

as part of Enron's quest to become the leading gas merchant in North America.[4]

Enron was a virtually pure, multifaceted natural gas play. Oil accounted for about one-tenth of Enron Oil & Gas. Enron Oil Trading & Transportation (within Liquid Fuels) was an island unto itself. Coal was not even traded, much less produced, transported, or burned in Enron power plants.[5]

The term *natural gas major* was unique and heady, if not sexy. But that only went so far. Business comes down to earnings and cash flow, now and in the future. The word from the Street was *no more surprises*. The Peruvian nationalization in August 1985 and the oil-trading loss in 1987 came amid high debt load and trying industry conditions. A rebound from those skittish years was due mainly to nonrecurring earnings in 1988–89. Ken Lay's shine had to be joined by quality, recurrent profitability that could retire debt and master new competitive arenas. Managerial expertise and new profit opportunities were required, given that first-class Enron was not a low-cost provider.[6]

In their last year as separate companies, HNG and InterNorth earned a combined $500 million, generating cash flow of nearly $1 billion. A $10 billion combined company needed to move toward this kind of profitability, which was about double that recorded by Enron in 1989. Lay as the inspirational leader and Mr. Outside provided the framework. But it was up to Lay's hard-nosed chief operating officer, Richard Kinder, to identify and fix problems and keep the divisions hard-wired for actualizing promised earnings.

Growing the Interstates

Ken Lay's Enron journey began by transforming the largest gas pipeline company in Texas into the largest and most diverse gas-transmission system in the nation. Beginning with Houston Pipe Line as his hub, Lay added three multistate spokes in 1984–85: Transwestern Pipeline (Texas to California), Florida

---

4. Enron Gas Marketing (1986) was joined by Enron Finance Corporation and Jeff Skilling in 1990. The two divisions merged as Enron Gas Services (EGS) the next year.

5. Enron did receive income from an antitrust-related legal settlement regarding a coal-slurry pipeline project, ETSI, of which InterNorth had purchased an interest prior to its acquisition of HNG. See Internet appendix 2.2, "HNG/InterNorth: Joint Ventures, Miscellaneous Assets, and Sales," at www.politicalcapitalism.org/Book3/Chapter2/Appendix2.html.

6. By the late 1980s, generic cost cutting was completed at Enron. "You cannot cut costs to prosperity," Ken Lay used to say. There would be no all-employee cost-cutting directives from corporate between 1987 and 2001, a fact reflective of Lay's preoccupation with the revenue side of Enron's equation and his overoptimism in the face of accounting (but not economic) profit.

Gas Transmission (Texas to Florida), and Northern Natural Gas Pipeline (Texas to the Midwest).

Six years in, natural gas transmission remained Enron's core. Houston Pipe Line was mired in Texas's overbuilt market, but each interstate was running at full capacity with plans to expand. With take-or-pay costs under control, each was recording double-digit profits and rates of return. The story was quite different at Ken Lay's old haunt, Transcontinental Pipeline, not to mention Columbia Gas Transmission Corporation, a major interstate that humbled the industry by declaring bankruptcy in mid-1991.[7] This was not your father's gas-pipeline business.

The FERC-authorized rate of return was set in excess of borrowing costs, a good start for those who carefully navigated the regulations. But Enron's interstates were cash-flow engines exceeding their assigned profitability, known in the trade as *beating the rate case*.

Maximum tariffs set in three-year FERC rate cases assumed a certain level of throughput and cost. Extra revenue could be won if gas volumes were above forecast (an old-fashioned efficiency incentive) or if a nuanced rate design allowed a pipe to over-recover its costs. Enron, and Stan Horton in particular, were very good at that.

Extra profits could also come from actual costs being below the assigned level. And so automation and other efficiencies made layoffs regular news at Enron gas operations. Modernization, multitasking, and consolidation flattened the organization to reduce expense and increase productivity. This substitution of capital for labor had another benefit: more rate base for future earnings.

All this was hard work—and a difficult starting point for the next (three-year) rate case. The more a pipeline accomplished, the higher the performance hurdle in the next go-around. Such penalization was not only an irony of public-utility regulation but also a reason being advanced by Enron and the industry for lightened regulation at FERC.

Going Open Access

In the mandatory open-access era (1985–), Transwestern and Northern Natural led the transition from gas merchants (buyers and sellers) to fee-based transporters of supply owned by others. Incurred take-or-pay costs from exiting the merchant function were mitigated by legal terminations (force majeure clauses), early settlements, and partial recoupment from customers in regulated rates. But the remaining write-off was well spent in Enron's case because *two profit centers replaced one.* Enron's interstate pipelines made margins on transportation,

---

7. In 1995, Columbia Gas would turn to Enron-ex Rick Richard, who in turn hired Cathy Abbott and Steve Harvey from Enron Gas Services, to bring the company out of bankruptcy with a new business focus.

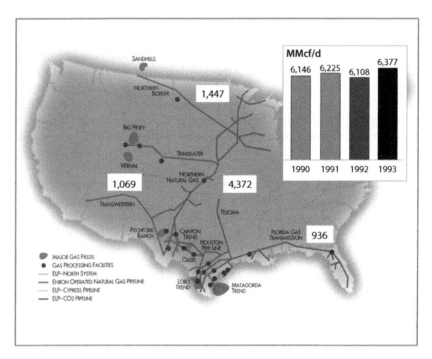

Figure 6.1 Enron's 41,000-mile, 7.8 Bcf/d gas-pipeline systems were (as of 1996) limited synergistically under federal open-access regulation. Northern Natural's capacity exceeded the combined size of Enron's (wholly owned) Transwestern Pipeline, (half-owned) Florida Gas Transmission, and (35 percent owned) Northern Border Pipeline.

and Enron Gas Marketing (under its evolving names) made money buying and selling gas and offering ancillary services.

Florida Gas Transmission (operated and 50 percent owned by Enron) and Northern Border (operated and 35 percent owned by Enron) were among the last interstates to accept open access under the provisions of FERC Order No. 436. As with the early adopters, the reason was pecuniary, not philosophic.

Running at full capacity as the sole provider to Florida and with customer contracts that needed to reach their full term, FGT entered the new world in August 1990. Northern Border, a cost-of-service pipeline fully subscribed by producer shippers, continued to operate as before.

"At the end of fiscal year 1990," reported FERC, "all 23 of the major pipelines held blanket certificates and provided non-discriminatory access to the gas transportation market." But this was under FERC Order No. 436 and did not include Northern Border. The final restructuring rule, FERC Order No. 636 (1992) required new comparability rules and new rate designs to complete the transition to open access.

"The challenge is to take the broad framework and flexibility FERC has given us in Order 636 and adapt the system to fit the needs of customers," Ron Burns explained to the *Oil & Gas Journal*. "[A] cookie cutter approach will not work." Transwestern, operationally the simplest interstate of Enron's four, was approved by FERC in 1992. The next year, Northern Natural and FGT also converted to final open access. Northern Border Pipeline, which went public in 1993 as a master limited partnership (MLP), received final approval under Order No. 636 last, in October 1993.

"Full implementation of the Federal Energy Regulatory Commission's (FERC) Order 636 and the successful settlement of all significant regulatory issues on our interstate pipelines during 1993 should provide a constant and reliable stream of cash flow over the next several years from our largest single earnings contributor," Enron told investors.[8] Automation and modernization, too, substituting profitable rate base for passthrough labor costs, put "Enron's interstate pipelines … in optimum shape from both an operational and regulatory perspective."

Operational Order

The role of interstate pipelines as transporter, not merchant, came to a head at a trade association meeting in early 1990. The instigator of change was Ken Lay; the result was new protocol and industry standards regarding *operational flow orders* and *operational balance agreements* that became standard by 1992. Therein lies a story.

Few knew that Ken Lay had a temper. Patience and pleasantry were his public persona. But when he lost his cool, it was something to behold. For Lay had a bigger monkey on his back than most realized or understood. His psyche carried memories of his dirt-poor past—including the business failures of his father, Omer. The smart, energetic, and über-productive Lay had gone through life accommodating less talented, more moneyed colleagues. Lay had always worked his rear off to have a jingle in his pocket. He was well coordinated but physically short, too, which held him back in sports competition against some of his more statured opponents.

It was not easy being in such a hurry yet having to deal with just about everyone else's slower pace. But Ken worked (and prayed) hard at patience and got good at leading others to perform so he could succeed that much more.

---

8. By 1993 all gas that was moving interstate was on open-access pipelines, meaning that pipelines transported spot gas of others for a fee. The previous *merchant* practice involved selling a bundled product at the terminus of the pipe to distribution utilities for resale to end users. The FERC orders behind this transition are summarized in Internet appendix 6.2, "Mandatory Open-Access Orders: 1985–92," at www.politicalcapitalism.org/Book3/Chapter6/Appendix2.html, and Internet appendix 6.3, "Other Federal Natural Gas Regulation," at www.politicalcapitalism .org/Book3/Chapter6/Appendix3.html.

When his inner ego was violated, as when his business was being hurt unjustly, the invectives could fly. Lay had mixed it up with Selby Sullivan during the 1970s back at Florida Gas Company, a story told in chapter 8 of Bradley, *Edison to Enron*. John Wing could really get his goat, too. But if someone was nice and innocent, Ken found patience. After all, he—Ken Lay—was the underdog too, in a different sort of way, and he empathized.

But it was an unforgettable moment when a furious Ken Lay walked into a January 1990 board meeting of the Interstate Natural Gas Association of America (INGAA), the interstate pipeline trade association. Staring down his fellow CEOs one by one, he yelled: "You f---ing stole my gas." "You owe me gas." Around the table of pipeline heads Lay went.

A severe cold snap had badly tested the interstate gas system just weeks before. The interstates were borrowing, and even shorting, gas to each other in the frantic search to meet peak demand. Enron, which had upgraded its gas operations for the open-access world and had the widest reach of any one company, found itself on the short end of many transactions. Formal operational controls were not yet in place. It was relationships and handshakes where Enron unwittingly became the bank.

"Ken Lay's quite forceful language behind closed doors was arguably the beginning of the protocols *operational flow orders* and *operational balance agreements* that became the industry norm by 1992," remembers Skip Horvath, INGAA's vice president of analysis. The fire lit that day would be a catalyst for new best practices and better performance in the winter of 1991–92 and beyond.

————

The computerization of gas logistics in a nonintegrated industry made information technology (IT) a top expense at Enron, as at other companies. For pipelines, unbundled transportation was more complicated than it was before, when they acted as bundled gas merchants; for national marketing companies such as Enron Gas Marketing, the complexity was beyond what could have been coordinated in the days of manually handled information.

Expensive mistakes with IT resulted in a master contract with Ross Perot's EDS in 1988. Enron's IT expense of $70 million in 1987 was followed by a 10-year outsourcing contract that began at $16 million and was set to escalate to $140 million in year 10.

As the Enron-EDS alliance matured, a number of disputes arose that required a rethink from Enron's side to improve IT service at a more manageable cost. In mid-1991, an Information Services Team was formed with all the units represented to develop new guidelines, improve coordination, and centralize dispute resolution.

Four years into the agreement, a major restructuring of the contract was announced to "improve the flexibility of both organizations to deal with new and evolving technology." Three years were added to the contract (through

2001), and Enron subsidiaries were assigned a part of the cost and instructed to manage and improve their IT function. Some services were unbundled to allow more tailored provision per unit. Performance bonuses and penalties were built into the contract too.

In a separate transaction, EDS acquired 3.5 million new shares of ENE to reduce Enron's debt-to-capital ratio by two percentage points. The transaction was expected to be nondilutive to earnings with better efficiencies and aligned incentives.

The new contract was the work of Rich Kinder from Enron's side, given that the EDS-Enron alliance was a key variable on the cost side of the business equation. IT was that important in the new natural gas—and later, electricity—world.

Back to Decentralization

In late 1992, Enron Pipeline and Gas Liquids Group was formed to house the regulated pipelines, as well as Producer Field Services (the newly deregulated feeder pipes from the field to the large-diameter interstates); Clean Fuels (MTBE and methanol plants purchased from Tenneco); and Enron Liquids Pipeline. Ron Burns was chairman; Stan Horton was named president of the pipeline division in addition to his position of president, Northern Natural Gas.

Reporting to Horton were Terry Thorn, president of Transwestern; Bill Allison, president of Citrus and FGT; and Larry DeRoin, president of Northern Plains. The heads of the still-centralized accounting, finance, and legal functions reported to Horton as well.[9] Intrastate Houston Pipe Line remained in Enron Gas Services as part of the unregulated merchant-gas side, as would Louisiana Resources Company (LRC), an intrastate purchased in early 1993.

Commercial-side decentralization was the major thrust of the reorganization. One size did not fit all when it came to meeting specific customer needs. Each president had a lot of customer touch to do that was lost in the previous organizational structure, not only at the terminus of the pipeline but also at the source. Producers were customers; without gas, there would be no sales at the other end.

Regulation also limited economies of scale for Enron's hub-and-spoke system. The network synergies that Lay envisioned for his adjoining coast-to-coast, border-to-border pipelines were neutralized by FERC pipeline-specific regulation, not to mention nondiscriminatory open access. This could have been anticipated. Still, some functions were centralized, and best practices and standardization were achieved by rotating employees between pipelines.

---

9. Horton would assume additional responsibilities the next year as president of the newly formed Enron Operations Corporation, reporting to chairman Tom White.

Transwestern: Expedited Certification

With Enron's interstates in expansion mode, timely FERC authorization was crucial for the parent to retire debt and increase profits. Yet getting Section 7(c) authority under the Natural Gas Act to enter a market or expand an existing pipeline was a time-honored forum for delay by rival projects and fuels. Back in the 1950s, Florida Gas Transmission narrowly overcame fuel-oil interests to receive a certificate to build to the Sunshine State.[10] Northern Natural Gas Pipeline beat coal interests for its federal certificate a quarter-century before. Receiving its certificate in 1959 after only 15 months, Transwestern had an easier time in gas-needy California.

In June 1990, Transwestern applied to FERC for a 340 MMcf/d, $160 million mainline expansion to (once again) gas-short California, coupled with a 520 MMcf/d, $90 million lateral expansion to receive surging supplies of (tax credit–aided) coal-seam gas from New Mexico's San Juan Basin.[11] With Transwestern's 18-month construction schedule and a full customer subscription, Enron wanted the project's double-digit incremental profits as soon as possible.

When Iraq invaded Kuwait two months later, making oil geopolitics a national security issue, Ken Lay went into overdrive with a gas-for-oil substitution argument to speed Transwestern's approval. FERC and the US Department of Energy, indeed, were already on record favoring expedited pipeline certification to increase gas-on-gas competition and support the cleanest fossil fuel.

Transwestern's expansion stood to displace as much as 55,000 daily barrels of oil imports. (California power plants, under periodic gas curtailments, were reluctantly burning fuel oil.) Industry-wide, Enron put the gas-for-oil substitution opportunity between 250,000 and 500,000 barrels of imported oil per day.[12]

In September 1990, Transwestern reapplied to FERC for an expedited certificate. "Providing this nation with stable supplies of domestically produced, environmentally safe fuel has never … been more critical," Transwestern's filing stated. Terry Thorn quipped to the trade press: "We can save the country

10. See Bradley, *Edison to Enron*, pp. 272–76.

11. The $0.87/Mcf Section 29 (of the IRS Code) tax credit for coal-seam gas applied to wells completed before January 1, 1991. October 1990 legislation would extend the date through 1992 and add the tight-sands-gas credit, a boon to Enron Oil & Gas, discussed in this chapter.

12. Compared to Enron's reasonable (but debatable) estimate, the American Gas Association's "longer term" oil-displacement figure of one million barrels per day assumed that natural gas from new capacity replaced oil on a Btu-equivalent basis and also included natural-gas vehicular demand. "But the industry shouldn't be fooled by its own advertising campaign," *Gas Daily* commented. "The fact remains that the gas industry continues to compete mostly with itself for new load. Coal is far more likely to be displaced by gas."

from Iraq and El Paso [Natural Gas] with just one filing." Transwestern's president was like that: a bit irreverent to go along with his business and professorial sides.

The new plan resulted in a preliminary certificate whereby Transwestern could embark on preconstruction business matters, while hiring its own environmental firm to remediate the right-of-way for artifacts pursuant to the Historic Preservation Act. With this head start, the full certificate resulted in "a modern-day record" of 18 months between federal application and gas delivery (September 1990–February 1992).

Chopping months off the process for a project with an IBIT of $40 million per year added millions of dollars to Enron's 1992 bottom line. Transwestern, the little pipeline that could, was the last to apply for FERC certification and the first to provide new capacity to gas-short California.[13]

Besting Oil in Florida

Enron's grand plan to ride economic growth in California and Florida encountered an unexpected problem when oil prices precipitously fell in 1986. Discounting was necessary to regain or retain markets for gas in dual-fuel power plants. But in the case of Florida, where Florida Power & Light (FPL) was the world's largest residual fuel oil buyer for electrical generation, a complicated 15-year gas contract by Enron priced to resid turned problematic. Throughput on Florida Gas Transmission hung in the balance.

In fact, Citrus/Enron was losing several million dollars per month on buying and reselling under the terms of Mark Frevert's 1985 deal. The tracking account—designed to carry losses forward in low-resid-price months and erase them in months when higher prices for resid prevailed—was not working as planned. Falling demand for resid, for environmental and other reasons, resulted in perennially low prices and delivered-gas price losses for Citrus. And all of it was Enron's problem, not Sonat's.

The historic gas-to-resid price ratio had blown up. Monthly losses between $3 million and $7 million had no relief in sight. Consecutive losses that were supposed to trigger contract termination did not quite work as planned either. Enron calculated a $450 million net present liability, requiring a new contract, as

---

13. Just weeks and months later, the 700 MMcf/d Kern River Gas Transmission Company (Wyoming to Southern California) and the 400 MMcf/d El Paso Natural Gas expansion entered service after years of regulatory delay. Both fed the 1.1 Bcf/d Kern-Mojave Pipeline inside California to directly supply end users. El Paso would purchase Enron's 50 percent interest to become the sole owner of Mojave in mid-1993.

well as payments and concessions to FPL. It was a problem one-third that of Enron's infamous J-Block contract in the United Kingdom to come.[14]

The problem contract became one for Enron Gas Services to solve. That job went to Geoff Roberts, formerly of FPL, who had negotiated the deal on the other side of the table from Enron's Frevert. Roberts assigned Mike McConnell to lead the renegotiation.

As McConnell would later explain in his memoirs, Enron's number-one corporate goal for 1992 was settled with upside. The large liability was resolved with a $50 million check to the buyer, and the restructured contract actually put Enron in the money as resid prices strengthened. Enron's brightest, including Vince Kaminski, had done a good job. Roberts's former colleagues wanted to amend a deal that seemed to go more and more Enron's way with pricing relationships. The contract also created a mark-to-market profit of $60 million, which got McConnell a nice bonus and promotion to vice president.

Full Utilization

It had been nearly a decade since Ken Lay restructured the old Houston Natural Gas by entering the federally regulated midstream gas market. By 1993, each Enron interstate was transportation only, with arm's-length affiliate Enron Gas Marketing or nonaffiliated independent marketers buying and selling the (transported) gas. Once-feared operational problems in the transition from purchased supply to received supply proved immaterial. Rich Kinder's Come to Jesus meeting in 1988 had set the stage for the old-guard pipeliners and new-guard marketers to divide (unbundle) and conquer.

Capacity in 1993 on Enron's four interstates (including joint-venture Northern Border) was almost 8 Bcf/d, 10 percent greater than in 1990 and just ahead of national market growth. Utilization was at or close to capacity year-round except on Northern Natural, which was built to meet high winter demand (the peak versus the shoulder months). Northern Border's 25 percent expansion to 1.7 Bcf/d to meet the 1992/93 winter heating season was running at full tilt. Houston Pipe Line, on the other hand, was relatively margin-poor in the over-supplied Texas gas market.[15]

On many days, excess capacity on Enron pipelines necessitated discounting below FERC-authorized maximum rates, which were based on depreciated original cost, not replacement costs. Pipeline-to-pipeline rivalry characterized

---

14. Compared to FGT's $50 million payment (not charge), Enron's write-off from the J-Block contract reformation, taken in 1997 (chapter 12), was $675 million.

15. The commercial side of unregulated HPL (and later, Louisiana Resources Company) was run by Enron Gas Services. Physical management of the intrastates, the interstates, Transportadora de Gas del Sur (Argentina), and the liquid plants was in Enron Operations, part of Ron Burns's Enron Pipeline and Gas Liquids Group.

every market except that of Florida Gas Transmission, which was the sole supplier to the state. But Enron's former head of pipeline operations, E. J. Burgin, was knocking on doors to get contracts to build a second pipeline to the Sunshine State, a proposed 800 MMcf/d, $1.4 billion project cosponsored by United Pipeline and Coastal Gas Transmission.

"Despite the fact that interstate pipelines still are regulated and the FERC will set minimum and maximum rates for each of our unbundled services," Stan Horton explained, "we're finding that competition is determining what we can actually charge." Being the low-cost provider was essential, the head of Enron's interstates explained. "We want to ensure that our customers are not going to leave us to receive service from Natural Gas Pipeline of America, ANR, El Paso, or Sunshine or whomever the competition is." But being low cost at Enron would not be easy with Ken Lay's first-class tendencies (a corporate charge to the interstates); Horton could not quite do what Forrest Hoglund could do at Enron Oil & Gas.[16]

––––

One of Enron's goals in the 1991 annual report read: "Abandon strict rate-base mentality and expand pipelines only when economically justified." Enron's real world was different from the textbook natural-monopoly model, bringing into question the public interest rationale of the Natural Gas Act of 1938 for public-utility regulation. And so Ken Lay and Enron stumped for lightened regulation with rates, as with entry.

In 1990, Lay floated the idea of a new maximum rate based on "fair value" (such as replacement cost instead of original depreciated cost) to "respond to market forces." This was how interstate oil pipelines were regulated at FERC, and cost as redefined could meet the cost-based, just-and-reasonable criteria under the Natural Gas Act. This was also the position of INGAA.

The next year, Lay reiterated his plea that pipelines needed extra incentive to go the extra mile via an expanded risk-and-reward frontier.[17] As part of their rate cases, both Northern Natural and FGT filed rate cases proposing incentive rates in 1991. But FERC head Martin Allday (1989–93) put a heavy burden of proof on applicants. Lay could only complain: "It is time FERC stopped talking about incentive rates and started granting them."

––––––

16. One strategy to lower costs was *variable pay*, which Enron implemented in 1993 to better reward results rather than effort. Encouraging individual risk taking and ownership instead of group (bureaucratic) resolution to resolve issues faster (improve customer service) was also emphasized.

17. Lay based his case on a new FERC-required rate design, *straight fixed variable*, which reduced at-risk cost recovery, thus dulling pipeline incentive for maximizing throughput. For more discussion, see Internet appendix 6.4, "Incentive Regulation and Enron: 1989–92," at www.politicalcapitalism.org/Book3/Chapter6/Appendix4.html.

Allday's predecessor as head of FERC, Martha Hesse (1986–89), had put incentive rate making on the agenda to allow pipelines to keep a greater share of their productivity (efficiency) gains. Invoking a dynamic (versus a static) view of competition, she explained: "I don't think that there's any doubt that the extensive regulation of gas from the gathering line to the burner tip is at least partially responsible for the gas industry's sluggish performance over the last 20 years." The lure of pure profits (profits higher than FERC-assigned "reasonable" profits) was necessary for Schumpeterian innovation, Hesse explained, describing incentive rates as an "attempt to emulate the life cycle of entrepreneurship."[18] The industry had transitioned, she said. FERC "has to transition too."

Hesse gave specific examples of inefficiency. Risky projects might not be built without higher profit potential. Cost-reducing projects beyond the three-year rate-case period might not be done. Rate discounts (below fully allocated cost, the rate maximum) to increase volume would accrue against the pipeline in the next rate case when assigning volumes. Still, the static view of competition, versus the dynamic entrepreneurial view, would be too hard to overcome despite Hesse's proposal, not to mention Ken Lay's and Enron's best efforts, as well as that of the entire interstate pipeline industry.[19]

Going International

When Ken Lay turned a Texas gas-transmission system into a national hub-and-spoke assemblage, international aspirations were secondary. Indeed, Houston Natural Gas Corporation sold Liquid Carbonic, the world's leading supplier of carbon dioxide, to help fund the domestic gas expansion. And two InterNorth international ventures were discontinued after ruining Enron's years in 1985 and 1987: Belco Petroleum's Peruvian operation (nationalization) and Enron Oil Company (trading scandal), respectively.[20]

Canada was about the extent of Enron's non-US operations. Joint-venture Northern Border Pipeline Company carried Canadian gas from the Saskatchewan

---

18. Invoking Joseph Schumpeter (1883–1950), Hesse explained: "An entrepreneur or innovator is, for a time, a monopolist. If successful, greater-than-normal profits are enjoyed. But success invites imitators and competition. [So] ... early profit ... gradually erodes over time." Schumpeter's economics is described in Bradley, *Capitalism at Work*, pp. 97–103.

19. For greater discussion of two theories of competition, one guiding FERC and another driving reform, see Internet appendix 6.5, "Mandatory Open Access Reconsidered," at www.politicalcapitalism.org/Book3/Chapter6/Appendix5.html.

20. A third InterNorth-side international subsidiary, Protane Corporation, part of Enron Americas, would bite Enron in 1996 when a propane leak from San Juan Gas Company exploded, killing 33 and injuring 69 in Puerto Rico. See chapter 12, pp. 502–4.

border to the US Midwest. Nine percent of Enron Oil & Gas's reserves were in western Canada, where Enron Gas Services would get going with its merchant activities.

Neighboring Mexico, with its closed, socialistic energy sector, was not part of Enron's operations.[21] But there was always hope. The North American Free Trade Agreement, which became law on January 1, 1994, was strongly supported by the gas industry—and Enron particularly. Lay's testimony on behalf of the Greater Houston Partnership before the House Ways and Means Committee in 1993 signified as much.

Enron was a proven builder and operator of pipelines and power plants. Natural Gas Major was a *global* vision. "We also want to continue our expansion into the international marketplace with the intent of establishing worldwide markets for all our integrated operations," Lay remarked in 1990. But established international energy companies were also scouring for deals in business-friendly nations. How could Enron break out?

————

In early 1990, Ken Lay fielded a request from his friend in the White House. President George H. W. Bush had chosen hometown Houston for the 16th Economic Summit of Industrialized Nations, scheduled for July.[22] Planning had fallen behind. Could he (Lay) help?

This was a perfect opportunity. Over three days, the leaders of Canada, the United Kingdom, France, Germany, Japan, and the European Commission—and their many delegates and an international press—could be introduced to Enron and to energy, natural gas style. Appointed cochairman along with Houston philanthropist George Strake Jr., Lay put his able assistant Nancy McNeil in charge with the company's many resources.[23] This was for America and the City of Houston—and Enron.

The informal working sessions of the Group of 7 would produce little. But there was plenty of Texas-style entertainment and merriment, and Lay got quality time with not only Bush but also Margaret Thatcher, whose country was about to sport Enron's ambitious gas-fired cogeneration power plant.

———

21. Mexico declared ownership of its subsoil minerals in 1917, and the country nationalized its oil and gas industry in 1938. Petróleos Mexicanos (PEMEX) was founded in that year. Enron negotiations with PEMEX in the 1990s would not result in any executed agreements.

22. "The fact that [Secretary of State] Jim Baker is from Houston, and I'm from Houston, and [Secretary of Commerce] Bob Mosbacher's from Texas should have nothing to do with where the next Summit's going to be," quipped Bush in 1989.

23. McNeil, promoted to vice president of corporate affairs in 1994, would become Mrs. Richard Kinder and leave the company early in 1997.

Visiting delegates toured Enron's handsome building and the modernistic gas-control room on Floor 42. The international press was courted. The message: Enron is big, proven, and the future. Enron can finance, build, and operate. Enron is the energy major you might not have heard about. Cochairman Strake, without an Enron agenda, was amazed—and perturbed—about how his colleague sought to take over the event.

Figure 6.2 Ken Lay put Enron at the forefront of the 16th Economic Summit of Industrialized Nations, held in Houston, Texas, in mid-1990.

Houston's prodigious effort with the summit, which included a $20 million beautification effort involving thousands of volunteers, went well. Tens of thousands of Houstonians turned out to salute the dignitaries. One small hitch was a bomb scare with a car carrying a mysterious cylinder in the trunk. It was Enron's retrofitted natural gas vehicle, just a small piece of Ken Lay's natural gas theme.

———

Enron's two major international forays in the early 1990s would come from its core. One was the construction of the world's largest gas-fired combined-cycle power plant in the northeast England industrial community of Teesside. The other was the acquisition and modernization of a large gas-transmission line in southern Argentina. Amid regular reorganizations, a revamped Enron Power would launch an ambitious sequel to Teesside in Dahbol, India, with Rebecca Mark in place of John Wing.

From Teesside to Enron Europe

By 1990, "Iron Lady" Margaret Thatcher had liberalized the United Kingdom's socialistic electricity sector, which supported the heavily unionized coal sector with an exclusive long-term contract. Market competition was needed to bring down power prices and remove cronyism, as well as demote labor strife. British Gas, a monopoly, also needed competition.

About the same time, discoveries of natural gas in the North Sea created potential competition to coal. Coupled with advances in gas-turbine technology, a new competitive arena was created for private firms, particularly for newcomer Enron with its cogeneration expertise and sense of urgency.

John Wing, under a consulting contract with Enron, got right on it. Ken Lay did too, visiting Thatcher's energy minister, John Wakeham, to lobby for fast-track approval.

Wakeham found Lay to be "very sensible" and "very determined"—a man who "understood his subject better than perhaps the competition did." The Energy Secretary (1989–92) welcomed the "nitty-gritty" discussions that "helped to prove that my system of electricity privatization, complete with a competitive market, was moving very substantially in the right direction."

Permissions would be expedited for the 23-acre, modernistic project. Wakeham himself would have celebrity honors when the Teesside Power Station opened in March 1993. Prince Charles reputedly turned down the opportunity—but not from a lack of Enron effort, including donations to the Prince's Trust. Ken Lay was that way.

The project began when John Wing and his top lieutenant at the Wing Group, Robert Kelly, ventured to London in 1988 to line up contracts for the world-class project. The project needed commitments for power and steam, gas supply to generate both, and a pipeline to get the offshore gas to the plant.

By year end, a long-term sales agreement was reached with Ralph Hodge of Imperial Chemical Industries (ICI) for all the steam and 700 MW of power. Teesside was home to ICI's major facility, and ICI joined the project as 10 percent owner. A group of utilities led by Midlands Electricity increased the power commitment to 1,750 MW, with the remaining 125 MW (to 1,875 MW capacity) being discretionary peak output for spot sales.

Gas supply was a major challenge. For the economics to work, a pipeline had to be built at a scale beyond Teesside's required 150 MMcf/d. The problem was partially solved with the addition of a 7,500 bbl/day gas liquids plant

Figure 6.3 It was all smiles with the completion of the world's largest cogeneration plant in Teesside, on April 1, 1993. Ken Lay and Tom White (center) join together with other principals of the UK project.

requiring 90 MMcf/d, which resulted in a 15-year, 240 MMcf/d gas contract with a 70 percent take-or-pay clause. Enron committed to a 300 MMcf/d transportation contract with the Central Area Transmission System (CATS) pipeline, a consortium led by the major North Sea producer Amoco (later BP) to move the gas 140 miles to Teesside.

To win his customers, Wing not only offered cheaper power and more power and steam. He also entered into strict completion-date contracts with bonuses and penalties. Enron had upped its ante to finalize the contracts necessary to build the plant.

Before project financing could be secured, Enron self-financed construction—as if it were already the energy major that the project was to help it become. For "six nerve wracking months," Enron poured $300 million of its precious capital into the project. Wing hired some of the US Army's top infrastructure managers to speed construction. Thomas White, Larry Izzo, and Lincoln Jones would be part of the Enron story to come.[24]

---

24. "Tom White and Larry Izzo did a spectacular job of overcoming lots of obstacles," remembered Robert Kelly. "At one point, we were turned down for the permit! Tom got that overturned, mainly through his charisma with the local people."

Round-the-clock activity, daily 7 a.m. staff meetings, and ferocious Wing management proved barely enough.[25] The gas contracts were finalized with just minutes to spare. Plant completion was two days ahead of its April 1, 1993, deadline—a 29-month record for a project of this scope.

Goldman Sachs provided $1.3 billion to take out half of Enron's interim cost, leaving Houston with a $150 million investment for 50 percent of the $1.2 billion asset. Already, $100 million in-construction profits—earned by Enron Power as builder and operator—had been recorded in 1991 and 1992 to bolster earnings.

"Few outside Enron knew how much risk the company had taken to build Teesside, and afterward, few cared." The bet-the-company strategy worked; later such moves would not end this way.

———

The Teesside project was recognized in Enron's 1990 annual report as the first of "numerous" opportunities for "Enron's total package concept offering a wide range of coordinated services." To meet this goal, Enron Europe was formed in mid-1990 to manage all gas activities throughout the continent, whether pipelines, liquids, power plants, and even exploration and production.

"Enron Europe, Ltd., is an integral part of the company's vision to become the first natural gas major worldwide and will allow Enron to expand all of its core businesses in the international arena," the 1990 annual report stated. The operations around Teesside were seen as just the beginning for the London-based subsidiary, which was featured on the cover of Enron's 1991 annual report.

In mid-1992, an agreement in principle was announced with Eastern Generation for a $300 million, 380 MW gas-fired power plant, with construction in 1993. Phase II of Teesside's liquids plant was planned for 1994. Enron also foresaw a need for gas marketing, all part of an ambitious "mini-Enron" UK plan.[26]

The United Kingdom's "dash for gas" in place of dirty coal seemed to be all going Ken Lay's way. So in March 1993, Enron Europe (now part of Enron International) contracted for 300 MMcf/d of J-Block North Sea gas for 15 years, commencing in 1996. Enron's purchase commitment was necessary for Conoco/

———

25. The "volcanic" Wing would manipulate his own staff with a self-described "combination of 'cheerleading and ass kicking'." Said one direct report: "We were all fired at least ten times." One top staffer was Rebecca Mark, whose stormy, intimate relationship with Wing was legendary.

26. The 1992 annual report said it all: "Enron will market the additional 300 MMcf/d to new gas-fired power projects and other natural gas customers in the U.K…. The [liquids] output will be more than doubled when the J-Block volumes come on line. The liquids also will be marketed in the U.K. and throughput Europe." The 1993 annual report reiterated this optimism: "Phase II [liquids plant] construction is expected to begin soon…. J-Block gas … will support Enron's future marketing programs."

Phillips, British Gas, and Agip to develop the Judy and Joann fields in central North Sea—a billion-dollar proposition. A 300 MMcf/d send-or-pay transmission contract with the Central Area Transmission System (CATS) supported coastal delivery. The enlarged 1.4 Bcf/d system, led by British Gas, Enron's entrenched rival, needed such shipper certainty to build the line.

But there was a major difference between Enron's gas-supply commitments of September 1990 and those of March 1993. Neither Eastern Generation nor a second-phase Teesside gas-processing facility was a done deal; both the supply and transmission contracts were *speculative*. As he had done before (and would do again), Ken Lay made a naked bet that locking up gas supply on the front end would ensure Enron's preeminence for a grand European strategy.

Riskier still, J-Block gas was purchased at fixed, escalating prices without a market-out clause to protect against falling prices—as if the 1980s US experience could not happen in the UK gas market. This 300 MMcf/d had a 100 percent take-or-pay financial requirement and a minimum physical take of 260 MMcf/d to all but ensure that 95,000 barrels of oil per day (the gas was associated) could be produced. More than a trillion cubic feet of gas was estimated to reside in the Judy and Joann fields in the central North Sea—and Enron wanted all of it.

Enron's obligations were "firm, extremely firm," noted Mike McConnell, the Enron employee who later was tasked with fixing the contracts. "It seemed that almost every possible item was against Enron," he recalled. "Phillips and the original negotiator took such advantage of Enron's need that they 'almost punished' them in negotiations." He could only conclude: "I was frustrated with the agreements."

Robert Kelly, head of Enron Europe, who was responsible for J-Block, cited the goal to "become a major competitive supplier of gas in the United Kingdom to electric power stations as well as other customers." (He also was convinced that gas would become less, not more, plentiful.) Teesside's 4 percent share of the UK power market left plenty of growth for gas, Ken Lay (and Rich Kinder) believed back home.[27] And Enron's board was not going to buck its golden boy.[28]

The Eastern Generation deal faded, and a liquids expansion at Teesside was short of customer commitments. Worse, a lot of new North Sea supply that Enron did not anticipate spelled trouble for prices. Neither was this good for

---

27. "Enron was convinced it could replicate [the Teesside] structure and began its power development growth strategy," McConnell remembered. The new gas-demand projects were "almost ready to go" and at "impending closure." But firm, executed demand-side contracts would not result.

28. John Wing seconded Kelly on J-Block, and Claude Mullendore (allegedly spending too much time in an English pub with his counterparty) negotiated a deal that got worse and worse for Enron with every draft. Jeff Skilling was the most critical of the deal.

Enron Oil & Gas's purchase of a quarter-interest in four undeveloped North Sea blocks, initially celebrated as "further integrating [our] European activities."

Enron was dangerously long on gas supply and transportation. J-Block and CATS II would turn into a billion-dollar problem. Only desperate, nimble negotiation and a much stronger Enron could weather this very expensive mistake.[29]

Transportadora de Gas del Sur (Argentina)

An all-employee memo from Rich Kinder in late 1992 shared the good news: An Enron-led consortium successfully bid for 70 percent ownership of a major natural gas pipeline system and adjacent liquids facility in southern Argentina under a 35-year concession, with an option for 10 more years. As operator and 17.5 percent owner of the plant under a fee agreement, Enron was exporting its capabilities in a second key region after Teesside. As in the United Kingdom, Argentina was newly privatizing, and Enron was first,[30] aided by generous government loan guarantees.

In addition to the prospect of providing "immediate earnings" for 1993, Kinder lauded Transportadora de Gas del Sur (TGS) as "consistent with Enron's vision of becoming the first natural gas major and the most innovative and reliable provider of clean energy worldwide for a better environment." Natural gas had a 40 percent market share in Argentina, and two-thirds of it was in TGS's territory.

The approximately $550 million winning bid for 70 percent of the system was $100 million above the sole other offer submitted by Tenneco and below the bottom of the range authorized by Enron management. Kinder and Lay were concerned, even upset, that the offer might fail. But Mike Tucker's team had researched the opportunity to identify real value but not overvalue. Enron's 25 percent equity investment, $25 million, would create an equity return near or above 20 percent in its first years, as much or more than Enron's domestic pipelines.

———

Argentina was a Third World, populist country disdainful of the ideals and rigor of market capitalism. Anti-American sentiment was prevalent. The

———

29. Enron's J-Block imbroglio would be settled in 1997 for $675 million ($463 million after taxes), equating to $1.82 per share. See chapter 12, pp. 494–98.

30. Argentina sold the smaller northern gas system to a consortium led by Nova Corp (Canada) for $210 million, also representing 70 percent of ownership. Enron outbid Nova, but the rule was that the same company could not win control of both systems. Five gas LDCs were also sold by Argentina, making the privatization as a whole second only to that of the United Kingdom. For greater detail, see Internet appendix 6.6, "TGS (Argentina's Privatization)," at www.politicalcapitalism.org/Book3/Chapter6/Appendix6.html.

country had been "a capitalist wonder during 1860–1914, enjoying phenomenal growth rates and rising prosperity." But spiraling intervention set in, particularly during the Juan Peron era (1946–55). Government corruption, rent-seeking, hyperinflation, punitive taxation, price controls, nationalism, and nationalization predictably created crises and coups. Foreign debt of $65 billion held by Argentina had enabled much crony socialism.

Crisis can bring fundamental reform. In the early1990s, Carlos Menem, Argentina's president, embarked on a new policy of privatization and market reliance. Part of this was privatizing state enterprises to reduce annual budget deficits, which were 15 percent of Argentina's GDP in 1989.

Privatization was advantageous on the merits, but Enron had to be very careful not to spook ENE investors. The Belco nationalization by Peru, discussed in chapter 2, was not quite settled after seven years of effort. To align incentives and minimize expropriation risk, Enron put together a unique, diversified consortium: Perez Companc, a local industrial powerhouse; Citicorp Equity Investments, the largest bank in the country; and Argentine Private Development Trust Company Limited, composed of 21 international banks. Outside of the consortium, 30 percent of TGS was owned by the government and company employees. Finally, $53.6 million in risk insurance was secured from the Overseas Private Investment Corporation (OPIC), which put US taxpayers into the game.[31]

Enron had not parachuted in to win the bid. Enron had previously tried to launch a gas-liquids business in Argentina, and Enron Development was looking for power plants there. EOG's joint-venture negotiations in the country had broken down, in fact, because of a lack of transmission capacity for new discoveries in the south. Little surprise that Enron heard about Argentina's privatization plan early and was all-in when the official announcement came. And little surprise that Argentine officials visited 1400 Smith Street en masse to secure a bid. (A false but widely believed story says that Argentina was forced to accept Enron's bid by George W. Bush, at a time when his father was the US president.)

The 1.3 Bcf/d, 3,800-mile system had averaged 85 percent utilization from four major gas-distribution customers under long-term firm contracts that fully subscribed the line. But TGS was in disrepair. Expertise and capital were badly needed, and the Enron-led consortium promised a minimum of $75 million on the front end.

"Enron expects to realize significant profits over time from this transportation-only pipeline via improved operating efficiencies." Goals for 1993 were

---

31. The project's OPIC insurance was increased to $62.6 million the next year before falling in 1994 and thereafter.

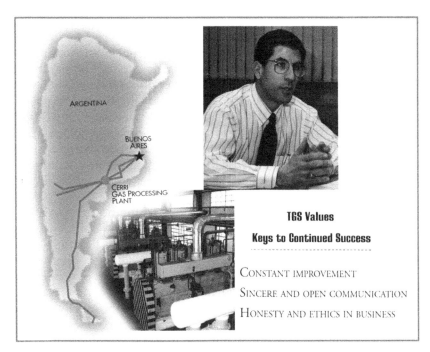

Figure 6.4 Transportadora de Gas del Sur (TGS) was a second major international step toward Ken Lay's vision of Enron's becoming the world's first natural gas major. George Wasaff, in particular, brought best practices from Enron's US interstates to Argentina between 1993 and 1998.

higher throughput from better marketing, new capacity from better use of existing compression, and a 30 percent workforce reduction—all preapproved by the government. Such restructuring allowed Enron contractually and profitably to lower transportation rates, which were pegged to the US dollar to manage currency risk. The five-year rate agreement, in effect, offered incentive rates for the project.

On December 29, 1992, just weeks after winning the concession, 40 Enron executives arrived to oversee the remaking of a large pipeline system. One hundred additional hires would be made from the operator side. The incumbents, each government-approved, were interviewed in competition for positions. Several hundred would be laid off with severance.

TGS was a mini-Enron, beginning with "a vision, core values, and key corporate objectives that covered every aspect of the business." State-of-the-art gas-measurement controls were installed, as were new systems for accounting and finance, information technology, and human resources. Compensation and a new corporate culture strove to create a meritocracy where seniority and crony-ism had previously ruled. It was, compared to Argentine standards, *progressive*.

The new, improved TGS increased its historic throughput under Enron man-agement. But large industrial customers were being curtailed during the winter peak, when households and small businesses got priority. An open season was held to see whether users would underwrite an expansion to get firm instead of inter-ruptible service. Expecting 90 MMcf/d, subscriptions came in for 210 MMcf/d.

At a cost of $86 million, TGS capacity would be increased 25 percent (240 MMcf/d) in mid-1994. An Enron-led construction bid was chosen by Energas, the Argentine authority. This increased Enron's net investment within its $75–$115 million forecast and was the first part of the consortium's $153 million, five-year requirement.

TGS "positions Enron for future growth opportunities in Argentina and South America," Enron told investors in the *1992 Annual Report*. Transmission and liquids marketing today, electricity generation and gas trading tomorrow; TGS was seen as a "springboard," even a "'once-in-a-lifetime' opportunity," for Enron. Ken Lay now had a beachhead in South America, not only in Europe.

Enron could take some credit for what, during a period of time, was *the third Latin American miracle*. The best of Enron translated into the best for natural gas for southern Argentina. In addition to broader economic reforms that tamed inflation and generated prosperity, revenue from privatizations such as TGS produced "unheard of" budget surpluses in 1992 and in 1993. "By doing away with debt-ridden state-owned enterprises," President Menem announced in August 1993, "we have eliminated very important pockets of corruption."[32]

Reorganizations, Multiplicity

Reorganizations were commonplace as autonomous Enron units built and man-aged projects outside North America. Reshuffling was also necessary to accom-modate strong personalities, and none more than superdeveloper John Wing, who rotated between employee and consultant as circumstances changed.

In May 1991 came the first of the five major restructurings of 1991–93. A hold-ing company, Enron Power Corp., was created to house (the renamed) Enron Power–U.S. and Enron Europe Ltd., with Wing as chairman of the holding com-pany and its two units. Tom White was number two at the holding company as president and CEO, as well as president and CEO of Enron Power–U.S. Bob Kelly, still head of Enron Europe, was named vice chairman of the holding company.

Rising executive Rebecca Mark, vice chair of both subsidiaries, was named chief development officer to "coordinate all development activities." This pro-motion put Mark in position to "plant the flag for Enron in as many developing nations as she could."

---

32. After some good years, Argentinian politics would overtake TGS. See chapter 12, pp. 490, 511n16, 515.

Two months later, Wing resigned his positions to again become a highly paid Enron consultant. Wing could cash out his equity stake now that Teesside's contracts and financing were done. His new arrangement also contained a big bonus to complete Teesside by deadline, his major responsibility. The Wing Group also was free to pursue its own power projects, while giving Enron a right of first refusal as investor.

With Wing nominally departed, Tom White replaced the man who had originally hired him and became the new chairman of Enron Power. Robert Kelly as head of Enron Europe reported to White. At the same time, Jack Urquhart, a member of Enron's board of directors and a retired 41-year veteran of GE's power side, joined Enron's office of the chairman to advise Enron Power and "be responsible for coordinating our international strategies among our various business segments." All this was to replace John Wing as much as possible— and provide stability. But strong personalities and fiefdoms within Enron's far-flung international operations remained.

———

In early 1993, a major reorganization was implemented. Consolidating offices in Houston, Enron International (EI) was created with Robert Kelly in charge. EI's main division was Enron Europe, which had jurisdiction for integrated gas-project development in the United Kingdom, the rest of Europe, the Middle East, and the former Soviet Union. EI was also given international liquids marketing (including Enron Americas) and the newly created Enron LNG.

"We believe this new organizational structure will allow Enron to manage its growing presence in the international natural gas marketplace," Ken Lay and Rich Kinder wrote employees, "and enhance our position as the world's first natural gas major."

Kelly went over his big plans in a feature in *Enron Business* magazine. EI's "first priority" was a 700 MW gas-fired combined-cycle plant, at Humberside, 150 miles south of Teesside. With construction permits secured and gas supply and transportation under contract, Enron and partner IVO, a Finnish company, awaited power-sales contracts to build. (This contract mismatch would not be rectified; the project was not built.)

Three power plants in Turkey were in negotiation with the Turkish government, the most likely for year-end completion being a 400 MW gas plant in Marmara. A joint agreement was near completion with Russia's Gazprom to upgrade a major gas pipeline in the Volgograd region, the major conduit to supply southern Europe. (Bigger projects, such as one in the Russian republic of Kalmykia, would not materialize.)

A proposal to refurbish a 300 MW power plant in Kuwait was envisioned as the start of a Middle Eastern presence. An international strategy to market gas liquids and petrochemicals (including MTBE and methanol) was under way. A 30-year "non-binding joint venture agreement" with the Chinese city of

Shenzhen by Enron Liquids International for liquid petroleum gases (LPG) was executed six months later.

Kelly saw economies of scope as Enron's niche. "Synergy may not have a lot of meaning in other companies," he intoned, "but at Enron International, it's one of the secrets to our growth and continued success." Project-financed LNG projects were also envisioned in the Middle East and in the Americas.

———

Three separate Enron divisions were active internationally as Kelly consolidated EI. One was Enron Development Corporation (called EDC or just ED), which was headed by Rebecca Mark. ED housed Enron Power, the unit that had jurisdiction over integrated gas projects in Latin Americas, India, and the Far East (including the Pacific Rim)—all the areas not within Enron International's Enron Europe. Enron Power also held all the US cogeneration projects that John Wing and Rebecca Mark had previously developed, but new US projects were not being begun.

ED's "market-led approach," defined as "finding solutions to a country's energy needs rather than selling a specific fuel or pushing a specific project," resulted in several completions. Two Philippine projects—Batangas (105 MW) and half-owned Subic Bay (116 MW)—came online in April 1993 and February 1994, respectively. Enron leased and operated a 28 MW facility at Subic Bay as well.

Another start-up was the 110 MW Puerto Quetzal plant in Guatemala, half owned by Enron.[33] The two-barge facility, the first in Central America to be privately owned, as well as project financed, supplied one-fifth of the country's electricity.

Oil was the fuel choice for those projects despite Enron's public relations image, which began and ended with natural gas. (This discrepancy between talk and walk would also be the case later in the decade when coal quietly became part of Enron's portfolio.) Most of the same projects were remote and risky, requiring taxpayer aid, and not all would live up to the profitability expected from them.

The other two international divisions were subsidiaries of major domestic operations. Enron Pipelines and Liquids Group was the parent of Transportadora de Gas del Sur (Argentina), the earnings of which were reported in Enron International. A subsidiary of Enron Oil & Gas, Enron Exploration Company, was responsible for upstream activities outside North America.

———

---

33. Enron was buying too, purchasing a half-interest in the 125 MW Bitterfeld gas-fired plant in Germany. Negotiations were also active in Columbia, the Dominican Republic, Greece, Indonesia, Italy, and Yemen.

Negotiations and soft agreements, trumpeted with press releases and photo opportunities, were commonplace at Enron. Outside of Teesside, TGS, and small oil-fired power plants, however, legal contracts to build and operate were elusive.[34] With Enron negotiating with sovereign governments at every turn, political help was needed.

In February 1993, Enron hired as consultants James A. Baker III and Robert Mosbacher, two Bush Cabinet members who were back in Houston with the reelection defeat of George H. W. Bush. Lay lauded the two's "wealth of international experience" to help Enron "in the development of natural gas projects around the world."

Baker, who as secretary of state got to know many foreign leaders intimately, pushed projects in Kuwait, Turkey, Qatar, and Turkmenistan. Mosbacher, the former secretary of commerce (and, briefly, Enron board member), knew energy by trade. In addition to lucrative up-front fees, the two would receive an interest in any project they helped to secure. None, however, would result.

Figure 6.5 A 1993 issue of *Enron Business* was full of photo-ops on Enron's early agreements with Russian and Chinese officials, but little activity would follow these heady beginnings.

A third consultant, Thomas Kelly, who had joined Enron's board after winning fame as a Gulf War commander, was hunting down international business

---

34. For greater detail, see Internet appendix 6.7, "International Starts, Not Finishes," at www.politicalcapitalism.org/Book3/Chapter6/Appendix7.html.

too, both for Enron and for John Wing's Wing-Merrill Group. To help in China, if not elsewhere, Henry Kissinger also joined Enron's stable of highly paid consultants. Ken Lay left no stone unturned.[35]

In June, a second major reorganization was announced. To "speak with one voice" internationally, Enron International Group (EIG) was formed with two divisions: International Development (Rebecca Mark) and Enron International (Ray Kaskel). Regional vice presidents would be assigned within each group.

With John Wing carrying his own torch and Robert Kelly taking a new job as chief strategy officer reporting to Ken Lay in Houston,[36] Rod Gray was named head of EIG. Gray's tenure would be short-lived, as discussed in chapter 12, all part of the trial-and-error of a still-young international company.

Separate from EIG, Enron Operations Corporation (EOC) was formed to take over international building and operating activities previously assigned to Pipeline and Liquids Group. Tom White was in charge, fresh off his triumph at Teesside. Earnings from TGS and other internationally operated projects were recorded within EIG—not EOC, which operated on a fee basis. Enron Oil & Gas, meanwhile, being a publicly traded company 80 percent owned by Enron Corporation, continued to operate independently.

Dabhol (India) Project

A Rebecca Mark power project in India was envisioned as a Teesside-like opportunity for Enron Development. To Ken Lay, this was the beginning of a $20 billion Enron program to modernize the country's electricity sector via a two-phased power project that represented the largest foreign investment in the history of the Republic of India.

India's central planners were desperate. Their Eighth Plan (1992–97) forecast an 8 percent power shortage on average, 19 percent at the peak. Electricity was mispriced between user classes, and much of it simply disappeared. It was *planned chaos*, the term free-market economist Ludwig von Mises coined for economies run by politicians.

The options were few. The quality of India's indigenous coal was going down and its price up. New domestic supplies of natural gas were limited. Government funds were scarce. India's weak currency and volatile politics inspired little confidence.[37] Recent energy ventures there had burned the World Bank and other international parties. India's downgraded credit ratings reflected the real chance of an international debt default.

---

35. See also chapter 7, p. 341.

36. Kelly would bring Enron into renewable energy, discussed in chapter 13, pp. 526–28.

37. The Indian Electricity Act of 1948 left generation and distribution to local state electricity boards (SEBs), which dealt with national (central) corporations: one for hydro, another for fossil fuels, and another for the grid. Enron dealt with the State of Maharashtra.

Enron was all ears when Indian officials came prospecting in Houston in early 1992. Never mind that the traditional energy majors had little interest in a country hostile toward foreign capital. Contrarian Enron was hot to be the first—and exclusive—partner to rectify India's power shortages. Lay bragged about going where the strategic planners said not to, and he had a flamboyant executive whose deals "positioned Enron not as the low-cost option but as the solver of the unsolvable problem."[38]

In late 1993, a $2.8 billion, 2,014 MW combined-cycle power project was inked with India's Maharashtra State Electricity Board (MSEB). The all-in price of $0.073 kWh—denominated in US dollars given India's double-digit inflation—was a jolt compared to the country's current subsidized price that was estimated to be one-half of the long-run marginal cost of power.

The chosen site was near Dabhol, about 100 miles south of Bombay. The state of Maharashtra was the industrial region of the country, although it was desolate and impoverished.

The $930 million, 696 MW fuel-oil-fired first phase—"which we expect to have financed and under construction in 1994"—would be followed the next year with the LNG phase once contracts were in place.

Phase I's 20-year, $26 billion power-sales agreement was the work of Rebecca Mark. Out of the shadow of John Wing, her decision making at Enron in different international capacities would make her one of the most consequential figures in Enron's history—and a model for entrepreneurial shortcoming.[39]

Enron got its tough terms in the purchased-power agreement (PPA). The project was technologically doable. But *was it affordable*—or even *politically salable* for a government du jour? Moody's had just downgraded the country's credit, and the World Bank rejected aid to a project it saw as too much, too soon. Phase II's LNG was far more expensive than indigenous coal, not to mention oil. And who could ignore that about one-third of the region's power was stolen or just not metered, which left MSEB chronically poor?

The lure of 30 percent returns—triple that earned in home markets—was a powerful one if Enron could lay off risk. Equipment supplier GE and contractor Bechtel each took 10 percent, leaving Enron with 80 percent. The plan was for Enron to sell down 30 percent of Phase I to become half-owner for an equity

---

38. Rebecca Mark notoriously went over her superiors to work directly with Ken Lay, who had a soft spot for her in terms of shared history (they both grew up in rural Missouri) and similar ambition. Lay welcomed her presence for (female) diversity and smiled at her press and sex appeal.

39. According to author Robert Bryce, "[T]he enormous losses Enron took on Mark's projects accelerated the company's downfall.... Mark's high-living globe-trotting style was a constant drain on Enron's cash coffers."

Dabhol Power Project at a glance

The 2,015 megawatt (MW) natural gas-fired, combined-cycle power station is being developed in two phases:

Phase I   895 MW
Fuel supply – distillate fuel oil
Construction begins 1994

Phase II   1,320 MW expansion
Liquefied natural gas (LNG) as primary fuel
Construction begins 1995; contingent upon LNG supply

Dabhol Power Company (DPC) joint venture partners:
Enron – owner, developer and operator
Bechtel – owner and turnkey contractor
General Electric – owner and turnkey contractor

Power Purchase Agreement:
Between DPC and the Maharashtra State Electricity Board
Provides for power sales from the plant
Guaranteed 90 percent availability by DPC
20-year term

Figure 6.6 The Dabhol, India, project of Rebecca Mark was a bold attempt to replicate Teesside in an undeveloped country. Contracts were completed and construction commenced in 1993, but political problems would soon engulf the project to leave Enron and its partners with a nonperforming, in-construction project.

investment of $135 million, comparable to that of Teesside. But because India was a developing country, government financing was also sought (as it was not with Teesside), to better Enron's chances for project financing.

Enron's contract, the result of one-on-one negotiations rather than a bid process, built in not only high returns but also protections. Under a 90 percent take-or-pay clause, payments were denominated in the US dollar, not the Indian rupee, to limit currency risk. The buyer (MSEB) was liable for cost escalations associated with fuel costs or plant operations (including transmission service). Government guarantees were secured at the regional and central levels.

Mark got her terms across the board. But the Dabhol contract was J-Block in reverse; the sell was executed but with a poor, unstable sovereign. The paper-strong project was trouble waiting to happen, despite the flood of good press and goodwill that both parties bestowed upon each other.

Export-Import Financing

Enron Development's goal was "to reduce Enron's risk on the international market to those similar with normal commercial operating risk that one might have in this business in the United States." But how was this doable outside of Canada and the United Kingdom, particularly in capitalist-unfriendly undeveloped (or *developing* in euphemistic terms) countries?

In fact, Enron was taking risks that others would not. But such daring was aided by taxpayers, the major agencies being the Overseas Private Investment Corporation (OPIC) and the Export-Import Bank (Ex-Im). "In most cases, in other countries we insist on OPIC insurance, expropriation insurance," Ken Lay told *Natural Gas Week* in 1991. "We certainly look for higher rates of return in these projects than we would in the U.S., and even then we want to make sure to tie together the cost of the project, the marketing arrangement on the product and so forth."

OPIC insurance help for Enron in 1992–93 included TGS-Argentina ($53.6 million in 1992; $62.6 million in 1993), Puerto Quetzal-Guatemala ($73.8 million in 1992), and Batangas ($50 million in 1993). A gas-liquids project in Venezuela (Accrogas LNG III) received an Ex-Im loan of $65 million, as well as public financing from France ($90 million) and Italy ($40 million). Enron Production Company, the foreign arm of EOG, also got into the act, receiving $100 million in OPIC insurance approval for its 1993 Trinidad play.

Then came the granddaddy. The Dabhol, India, plant was teed up with tax-payer assistance: a $302 million loan by Ex-Im and $300 million in insurance from OPIC.

That was just the beginning of taxpayer involvement with Enron's overseas ventures. Before it was all over, "at least 21 agencies, representing the U.S. government, multilateral development banks, and other national governments," approved $7.2 billion for 38 Enron-related projects in 29 countries. Many of the projects would not have gone forward without the guarantees or actual investment.[40]

But the half-truth evolved that Ken Lay and Rebecca Mark's Enron Development was "spreading the gospel of privatization and free markets to developing nations." In fact, Enron was applying crony capitalism to inhospitable areas and press-spinning its global aspirations to swell its stock price. The result was more politicking at home and loosened business norms that would create problems for Enron later in the decade.

Breakout—and Peril

Enron's breakout year for international was 1993. Teesside was in full operation. TGS was off to a very profitable start. Smaller power projects were getting done. Negotiations in a variety of countries, many remote, promised an earnings future.

Momentum was in the air with fancy press releases. But too many agreements to negotiate did not result in agreements to build. A toehold in Russia (pipeline repair) did not turn into projects. The Middle East did not provide even a toehold, much less a beachhead. Shenzhen did not turn into Enron's "China Connection."

This left large bets with the J-Block/CATS deal for expansion in the United Kingdom and the European Union, as well as with Dabhol in India. Neither would come to replicate Teesside. Worse, each would become an albatross

---

40. See also chapter 12, pp. 491–92, 498–99.

around Enron's neck. Ken Lay's fast-forward ambitions to become an international energy major would leave him with a heavy price to pay.

Enron Power

"Enron remains committed to the development of independent power and cogeneration projects both in the United States and around the world," stated the *1990 Annual Report*. The gold rush by independent power producers in the United States pursuant to 1978 federal legislation had peaked, and John Wing and Enron were hunting abroad.[41]

Domestically, Enron was idling at 1,282 MW in four gas-fired cogen projects: 440 MW Texas City (50 percent); 377 MW Clear Lake (50 percent); 300 MW Bayou (17 percent); and 165 MW Bayonne (22.5 percent). Although no new projects came on stream in 1990, profits were strong, with Texas City and Clear Lake operating at 95 percent availability, reconfirming the technology as world class, even world best. This success led to the 1,725 MW Teesside UK project and to the formation of Enron Europe, leaving Enron Power Corporation for US projects, outside of build-operate contracts abroad.

One new domestic project was taking shape: a $136 million, 150 MW gas cogen plant in Milford, Massachusetts, just south of Boston. The Enron-operated project, half owned by Enron, entered service in 1993. Meanwhile, prospecting in Texas, Florida, and New England failed to add a sixth plant for Enron Power.

In the saturated market, the game plan turned to acquisitions where improved operations could win incremental profits. This job went to two newly titled Enron Power executives: President and COO Lincoln Jones and senior vice president of project management Larry Izzo. In mid-1992, these two had their first purchase to operate: a half-interest in a 250 MW plant in Richmond, Virginia, that sold cogenerated electricity to Virginia Power under a 20-year contract. Just four months after start-up, Enron made capital improvements, restructured fuel contracts, and refinanced the plant for gain.

"Five years ago our efforts were focused on building power plants within 50 miles of our office," Tom White, head of Enron Power told employees at the close of 1992. "Now we have operations thousands of miles away." The shift from domestic to worldwide spawned a long list of countries in Europe, Asia, the Middle East, and elsewhere.

At the four-year mark, Enron Power (housed under Enron Development) was more of an operating and investing company than a project originator. Enron Europe and the rest of Enron Development were doing the originations

---

41. John Wing (and Robert Kelly) had left Enron but were working on Enron's Teesside project through Wing's consultancy, Wing-Merrill Group Ltd. In their absence, as mentioned, Enron named John Urquhart vice chairman to nominally oversee Enron Power and Enron Europe.

abroad. Domestically, Jeff Skilling's fast-paced Enron Gas Services was taking over electricity with its subsidiaries Enron Power Services and Enron Power Marketing, the subjects of chapter 8 and chapter 9, respectively.

Enron Oil & Gas Company

Ken Lay found a star to revitalize Enron Oil & Gas in Forrest Hoglund, the builder of Texas Oil & Gas. "America's Pure Natural Gas Play" had been under-performing in a challenging environment. Gas prices that fell by half between 1985 and 1987 nearly did the same to EOG's cash flow. Net income was turning negative. EOG was also having trouble reorganizing for the new reality of $1.50 gas (about double this amount in 2017 dollars).[42]

Fortunately, Hoglund was on board when the Valhalla oil-trading scandal became public in 1987. Had the news broken a month or two earlier, Lay might not have landed him. As it was, the new CEO righted the ship well enough to take EOG public in 1989 to net Enron $202 million in profit for its 16 percent sale—and record an asset value of $1.8 billion for its 84 percent remaining share.[43] A second sale of 4 percent of EOG by Enron in 1992 would yield $110 million, showing the value appreciation in the period under review (1990–93).

A turning point for EOG occurred in 1990. Net income went positive, and cash flow rebounded to $269 million. Low gas prices were ameliorated by low finding costs; production surged one-third; and reserve replacement was strongly positive.

Far bigger things would evolve with 1993's net income nearly triple and cash flow nearly double that of 1990, while proved reserve additions continued to outpace production. EOG's bright story in the low-price environment reflected a tax credit, very large and expertly played; profit-rich synergies with Enron; and an emerging technology boom. Forest Hoglund's touch was also attracting, retaining, and directing talent within the organization.

Tight-Sands Gas: The Tax-Credit Boom

"A significant event occurred for EOG in late 1990 when federal legislation was passed providing tax credit incentives for developing natural gas production in tight sands areas," reported Hoglund in EOG's 1991 annual report. Such reservoirs, he explained, otherwise would require "production enhancements limiting their economic viability for drilling and development at today's prices."

---

42. "America's Pure Natural Gas Play," describing an asset base of 90 percent natural gas (versus oil), adorned the cover of EOG's annual reports from 1989 (the year it became a public company) through 1993.

43. For the history of EOG before and after Hoglund arrived in September 1987, see chapter 3, pp. 174–77.

The Omnibus Budget Reconciliation Act of 1990 provided a tax credit of $0.52/Mcf for natural gas sales from qualifying tight-sands gas wells drilled in 1991–92. The pretax benefit of $0.80/Mcf equated to a *50 percent* increase in the then wellhead price.[44] "If one were to describe a tight sands company," Hoglund told shareholders, "EOG would probably fit the description better than any other company in the industry." Far from coincidental, Enron and EOG "diligently" worked to give an expired credit new life. "We spent a lot of time working that issue and actually got an extension of the Section 29 credits, which had, frankly, expired," remembered Joe Hillings, head of Enron's Washington office. "Enron essentially was the biggest winner in that legislation."

With the changed economics, EOG "did a 180-degree shift" to develop, or acquire to develop, qualifying properties. The result? EOG tight-sands gas reserves were about double that of the US-company average of 25 percent. Parent Enron rejoiced. "The supportive role Enron Oil & Gas played in the passage of tight sands legislation … could be worth more than $100 million to Enron on a net present value basis." Texas, too, aided tight-sands gas, and thus EOG, with a 10-year severance-tax exemption for sales from wells spudded between May 1989 and August 1996.[45]

The newly tax-incentivized reservoirs were already in play. In 1989, two trillion cubic feet of unconventional gas was produced with the trend sharply upward. Tax incentives and federal grants between 1980 and 1990, $2.4 billion and $250 million, respectively, were having their effect. Still, with the Gulf War creating an anti-oil environment, natural gas reaped new political hay.

The huge tax-side revenue enhancer was yet another example of industry-driven—and Enron-driven—*rent-seeking*. As part of the National Energy Strategy project of the US Department of Energy under Bush-appointee James Watkins, important segments of the oil and gas industry concentrated their efforts on tax breaks to improve the after-tax economics of domestic drilling. The Independent Petroleum Association of American (IPAA) and the Natural Gas Supply Association were joined by gas associations of the midstream (Interstate Natural Gas Association of America) and downstream (American Gas Association). The battle cry was gas-for-oil in the name of energy security and national security. The energy majors got into the act, complaining about the relatively higher tax burdens at home than abroad.

----

44. For a technical discussion of this tax credit, as well as parent Enron's gaming to utilize the credits for the consolidated balanace sheet, see Internet appendix 6.8, "The Tight-Sands Gas Tax Credit of 1990," at www.politicalcapitalism.org/Book3/Chapter6/Appendix8.html.

45. In 1998, EOG reported cumulative federal tax savings of $211 million with another $27–$30 million expected before the end of the program in 2002. Parent Enron used the tax credits that were more than its subsidiary could use.

Some free-market voices dissented. Noting the historically low price of natural gas, equating to $7 per barrel of oil (1991), and the failure of government energy subsidies, economist and industry consultant Arlon Tussing argued for government neutrality. "I simply don't see why," he testified before Congress, "it is necessary for government to subsidize [natural gas] ... to penalize the production or consumption of conventional fuels." Public policy should simply be "opening up the access to natural gas supplies throughout the economy" and "removing the barriers to the cheap and efficient delivery of this commodity throughout the country."

The 1990 political coup for gas created some buyer's remorse the next year when prices collapsed. Summer (off-peak) prices of a meager $0.50/Mcf, if not less, were reported in the Rocky Mountain region. Oil's price woes in 1986 were now joined by natural gas in 1991. Both the IPAA and NGSA reversed course to oppose extending the benefit for wells drilled after 1992. But the math was complicated, given that one-third of all active rigs were in Section 29 formations. IPAA went back to favoring an extension just months after opposing it; other groups were too conflicted to take a position.

It could be state versus state. Oklahoma producers complained that New Mexico, rich in tight-sands gas, was taking away the California market. "It's another energy subsidy, and it distorts the whole damn system," complained one Sooner State producer.

EOG, however, stayed the course as the top beneficiary. "If properly focused," Hoglund told a congressional subcommittee in early 1992, "the section 29 credit is the best vehicle to stimulate domestic natural-gas production and reserves." His argument: "The producer is required to assume all the drilling risk, and the U.S. contributes to the investment only if the venture is successful and gas reserves are increased and the gas is produced."

A scorecard of what a company produced in what proportions of conventional versus nonconventional gas drove the debate. "This is, after all, not a philosophical discussion," as John Jennrich noted in another context, in *Natural Gas Week*. "This is about M-O-N-E-Y."

———

Tax policy would steer EOG in the next years. Hoglund announced tight-sands gas drilling as "the most important emphasis for 1991." A budgeted $100 million for 150–200 new wells was expected to create $10–$15 million in incremental income.

In 1991, wellhead gas prices fell almost 10 percent to $1.37/Mcf—more than 50 percent below the average EOG received in 1985. Still, a good year was recorded with tight-sands gas production leading. Not only did the company beat its forecast by earning $17 million from the credit alone, but also the benefit accrued to the parent. "Tight gas sand income tax credits resulted in a significant contribution to Enron's after-tax net income," Lay and Kinder reported.

EOG's tax play peaked in a "tremendously successful" 1992, with "optimization of tight sands tax credits" resulting in 500 wells producing $42.5 million in tax-credit income. Seen another way, 95 percent of EOG's natural gas reserve additions in 1992 was in "tight sand qualified areas," which contributed to a record gas versus oil production tilt of 94 percent to 6 percent. (Oil never had a similar credit.)

EOG's profitability would have been less in a more neutral tax environment. But production from its conventional properties would have been higher, onshore and off. And wellhead prices would have been higher, a factor that led companies lacking in tight-sands gas to oppose the credit, such as Anadarko's Robert Allison, the very executive Lay tried to recruit before pursuing Hoglund.

EOG could not get an extension of qualifying wells past 1992, although it tried.[46] But spudded wells had a 10-year credit window. In 1993, EOG's tax gain would fall by half and decline thereafter. Still, more than $100 million in legacy tax savings would accrue in the next decade as wells drilled in 1991–92 gave their bounty.

In first-quarter 1993, the total active US rig count sagged from the end of the tax credit for new wells. Still, EOG was optimistic as a "low cost producer" with "a large inventory of non-tight-sands gas prospects that have been developed and/or on hold." There was another reason, although left unstated: Gas prices could be helped only by less drilling and less production in tight-sands gas.

A curious sidelight of EOG's involvement with tight-sands gas was the role of prepayments from Chase Manhattan bank. Said a congressional staff report in 2003: "Enron would not have been able to utilize its Section 29 tax credits in 1992 and 1993 without the taxable income generated by prepayment transactions." The same prepayment scheme was then continued by Enron to produce the cash flow that wasn't coming in under mark-to-market accounting. Bankruptcy examiner Neal Batson argued in 2003 that the prepayments had amounted to "unsecured loans" from the bank, but British Justice Jeremy Cooke ruled that Enron had a plausible justification under US accounting principles for giving them non-debt status.

Technology "Mini-Renaissance"
Unlike Ken Lay across the street, Hoglund emphasized cost cutting and personally set the example.[47] "We run a lean, decentralized organization at EOG," he

---

46. "We ... are working very diligently for the passage of legislation to extend tight gas sand incentives beyond 1992," Hoglund wrote shareholders in March 1992.

47. Hoglund, for instance, took the *company plane*, as Southwest Airlines advertised itself, rather than *the* company plane, which EOG did not have.

emphasized, invoking his company's industry-wide reputation as such. A company profile in early 1993 announced, "EOG is well on its way to becoming the Walmart or the Southwest Airlines in the exploration and production (E&P) industry."

Between 1989 and 1992, EOG reported a one-fourth decline in operating and interest expense: $0.48/Mcf. New technology, readily adopted and sometimes pioneered by EOG, reduced the time and effort to find and produce energy.

"EOG also has benefitted from what I have described as a 'mini renaissance' within the oil and gas industry," Hoglund explained in the 1991 annual report. "At the same time that gas prices are depressed and drilling rig counts are down, there have been some very significant technological advances which have provided tremendous opportunities for EOG." Viewing underground formations in 2-D and 3-D seismic at "state of the art" geophysical workstations was one improvement; improved well-site equipment and more experienced crews were others. An employee-invented drill bit resulted in six- to seven-figure savings for EOG.

Figure 6.7 New technology was necessary to increase natural-gas production in a low-price environment. Technologies such as 2-D and 3-D seismic and forays into fractionation and horizontal drilling were used at EOG in the early 1990s.

Most interesting was a technology that only decades later would become the talk of the industry. "New reservoir fracturing technology has significantly increased production capacities, making many drilling areas economical that wouldn't have been within the realm of possibility three to five years ago, particularly in tight-sand areas," Hoglund reported to investors in early 1992. This had started earlier; tripled delivery in 1990 from the Frio and Lobo areas of south Texas was attributed to "the company's extensive seismic experience in the area and leading-edge use of modern hydraulic fracturing technology."

Enron Synergies

Approximately half of EOG's gas production was sold to either a pipeline or marketing affiliate of Enron. "The numerous synergies between EOG and other Enron Corp. companies are expected to provide additional benefits in the 1990s as the industry trends toward longer term supply arrangements," Enron's 1989 annual report stated.

Indeed, a long-term contract with Enron Power, priced at a hefty premium to the going spot price (regulatory related, as described in chapter 5), helped EOG in 1988 and 1989.[48] Gas Bank 1 prominently included EOG supply. A series of long-term contracts with Enron Gas Marketing (EGM) in the early 1990s added to EOG's financial category: "other gas marketing revenues." Marketing by Enron Oil Transportation & Trading was synergistic for both parties.

Combined with production hedges executed by EGM at EOG's request, which in 1990 covered 30 percent of EOG sales, Enron synergies produced incremental revenues of $51 million in 1990 and $80 million in 1991. Hedging won revenue for EOG again in 1992 before 1993's price rebound shrank the gains.

Enron's need for EOG's bountiful tax credits was another synergy. A Tax Allocation Agreement required Enron to pay EOG the value of utilized tax credits. Numerous service agreements between parent and affiliate were carefully done, given Hoglund's fiduciary responsibility, and the benefits of sound economic calculation. "Enron Oil & Gas intends that the terms of any future transactions and agreements between Enron Oil & Gas and Enron Corp. will be at least as favorable to Enron Oil & Gas as could be obtained from third parties," EOG told investors.

International (non-Canadian) exploration and production was facilitated by Enron's growing global presence and reputation, particularly from Teesside. The strategy was to invest in areas with low up-front costs potentially yielding large reserves. Acquired tracts in offshore Malaysia, onshore Egypt, the North Sea, eastern Syria, and Indonesia (South Sumatra), however, accounting for 3 percent (1990), 6 percent (1991), and 4 percent (1992) of EOG's capital budget, did not result in significant finds. Deal hunting in Australia, China, France, Kazakhstan, and Russia, some involving coal-bed methane, would come up dry.

---

48. Power contracts priced at a utility's (state) regulatory-determined avoided cost, pursuant to the Public Utility Regulatory Policies Act (PURPA), allowed above-market gas costs. See chapter 1, p. 97; chapter 3, p. 165; and chapter 5, pp. 218–19.

EOG recorded its first major success outside of North America in 1993 with a major find off the southeast coast of Trinidad. The "fast track" project, commercialized in the first year of the concession, would grow into an important profit center in the years and decades to come.

Jawboning and Politics

While EOG reaped large tax profits, Enron complained about low wellhead prices and advocated state-level regulation to reduce supply to increase price (market-demand proration).[49] Therein lay a major public policy irony.

In 1991, Ken Lay roiled the industry with his accusation that the majors were exhibiting "economically irrational behavior" by selling their gas "below replacement cost."[50] While stating that "EOG is not dependent upon rising commodity prices," and roundly benefitting from the tax credit that effectively boosted its wellhead price by half, Forrest Hoglund jawboned for higher prices too.

EOG calculated that every $0.10 shift in wellhead prices was worth $8.5 million at the bottom line. Deeming low prices unacceptable, Hoglund aggressively shut in production with EOG's short-lived wells, which provided between one-fourth and one-third of EOG's total deliverability in the years 1990–92. "With prices at $1.20/Mcf, I think we can make a pretty good case for not selling what we have rather than drilling for new reserves," he explained. This was for non-tight-sands gas; tax-credit gas was really $2.00—and more adding Texas's severance-tax exemption.

At a state-of-the-industry gathering hosted by the Texas Railroad Commission (TRC) in 1991, Hoglund complained about "a truly chaotic market for producers, featuring month-to-month sales on the spot market." EOG was shutting in gas that would otherwise (according to the company) sell below its replacement cost, and instead of following suit, other firms were "dumping" their gas in the market.[51]

"Buyers of natural gas are a whole lot smarter than the sellers," Hoglund chided. "Unfortunately," he added, the inexorable forces of supply and demand would have to make the correction. EOG's chieftain advocated market-demand proration whereby the TRC and like state authorities would set allowables (force shut-ins) to restrict supply to increase prices to the proverbial replacement

---

49. Earlier state-level regulation to increase wellhead gas prices, including proration, is detailed in Bradley, *Oil, Gas, & Government: The U.S. Experience*, pp. 191–200.

50. Lay defined replacement cost as "the finding and development cost to add new reserves and acquisition costs to buy reserves, plus production and operating costs, and a nominal after-tax return on investment." See also chapter 7, pp. 313–314.

51. EOG shut in more than 25 percent of its 600 MMcf/d deliverability in 1991, but this was for tiring wells. Its financial cushion of long-term contracts gave the company an overall selling price of $2.63/MMBtu in 1990, almost double the spot-price average.

costs. This, to proration advocates, reduced "waste," defined by Hoglund as gas lost, owing to uncompleted reserves, scaled-down fracturing of new wells, older wells becoming uneconomic, and unconnected new wells.

Lay supported mandatory proration only as a last resort. While EOG banked on its voluntarily shut-ins to qualify as mandatory proration, leaving the competition with more of the pain, Lay's broader Enron math included two offsets. State proration might reduce the gas needed to maximize pipeline throughput, and higher gas prices would narrow the margins of Enron Gas Liquids.[52]

Meanwhile, other upstream industry parties were bemoaning that unconventional gas—not only from tight-sands gas but also coal-bed methane—was flooding the market and depressing conventional prices. Calculating deliverability of 22 Tcf/d chasing 18 Tcf/d of gas demand, at least at the desired price, and witnessing growing reserve additions, one conventional driller described the credit as "another special-interest, pork-barrel budget boondoggle benefiting only a handful of natural gas producers."[53]

Hoglund's Touch

Hoglund's approach was more than low cost; it was judiciously stocking the cupboard. The balance sheet was "extremely conservative" with low debt and high cash. Reserve replacement was steadily positive with the years 1989–93 recording 165 percent, 128 percent, 146 percent, 135 percent, and 139 percent, respectively. Well-timed hedges and long-term sales that beat spot prices—such as an innovative $326 million, 124 Bcf, 45-month volumetric production sale from EOG's biggest field, the Big Piney in Wyoming—were part of this result.

By 1993, Hoglund was a star performer at a star company—and a hedge of sorts to the living-on-the-edge parent. Average wellhead prices and production in 1993 increased 21 percent and 25 percent, respectively. The wellhead average—$1.92/Mcf—was the highest since 1985's $3.19/Mcf. Net income and cash flow soared to $138 million and $521 million, both records.

Tax-credit production of 295 MMcf/d, 42 percent of the total, generated special revenue of $65 million, 47 percent of the total. Investors were quite pleased too; EOG's stock price at year-end 1993 was 50 percent above 1989's close.

With his five-year employment contract maturing in September 1992, Enron extended Hoglund by three years to 1995. Hoglund's hiring, and this extension, would be among the best decisions made by Lay and Enron's board of directors in their all-too-brief 17 years. The Enron-enacted tight-sands-gas tax credit ("We decided to take advantage of this tax credit by going all out," remembered

---

52. Enron Liquid Fuels's big year in 1990 combined low gas prices with high oil prices, discussed below, on p. 293.

53. The beneficiaries included not only Enron, Transco, and Coastal but also Amoco, Arco, and Exxon.

Hoglund) certainly was behind EOG's success. But sans tax farming, with well-head prices that much higher, Hoglund and EOG would have still done well— as they would in the future.

Liquids

Enron Liquid Fuels (ELF) processed and transported natural gas liquids, considered a *midstream* business along with transmitting and storing natural gas. ELF was one of Enron's five gas divisions, joining exploration and production (EOG), transmission (HPL; interstates), electric generation (Enron Power), and marketing (Enron Gas Marketing, renamed Enron Gas Services in early 1991). (Teesside, within Enron Power, would be split out to become the core of Enron International in 1992.)

In 1990, ELF had five subsidiaries: Enron Gas Processing Company; Enron Gas Liquids Inc.; Enron Liquids Pipeline Company; Enron Oil Trading & Transportation Company (EOTT); and Enron Americas Inc. Although rarely newsworthy, and not as visible as Enron's other divisions, Mike Muckleroy's unit was dependably profitable for a parent lacking in recurrent, quality earnings.[54]

ELF profit centers were also countercyclical to the rest of Enron. Lower natural gas prices reduced the cost of (extracted) ethane, propane, normal butane, isobutane, and natural gasoline. These liquids competed against petroleum products, which were priced by other factors. So other things being the same, lower gas prices improved liquid margins.

———

Liquids profits jumped in August 1990 when the Gulf War caused oil prices to spike. Just months before, Enron had fortuitously purchased CSX Energy, which owned the largest gas-processing facility in Louisiana. The Eunice plant joined ELF's Bushton, Kansas, plant to create a billion-gallon integrated gas liquids company: in Enron braggadocio, the fifth largest in America.

With margins doubling and volume increasing by half, ELF earned $187 million before interest and taxes (IBIT) in 1990, exceeding that of 1988 and 1989 combined. For Muckleroy's unit, this more than made up for the troubles of Enron Americas in statist Venezuela and low returns from EOTT.

In 1991, IBIT of $152 million, while strong, was a return toward normalcy. Weak-sister EOTT achieved "a turnaround year," much needed given a plan for the unit to go public as a separate company. Oil was not core to Enron and would be disadvantaged by many public policies championed by Ken Lay.

Earnings at Enron Liquid Fuels in 1992 dropped by almost half from the year before. Part of this was due to reduced liquid margins, domestically and

---

54. Muckleroy's reorganization and profitable incrementalism are discussed in chapter 5, pp. 238–40.

internationally; part reflected the August spin-off of several gas-liquids plants into a master limited partnership (MLP).[55] EOTT's sale was to take advantage of tax laws (MLPs did not pay corporate tax), raise equity to reduce the parent's debt, and improve focus on core competences.[56]

McKinsey & Company was hired to prepare a specific business plan and place personnel for an independent EOTT. The stand-alone company needed an external auditor, a trust agent, a stock-exchange listing (NASDAQ in both cases), and office space (in Houston). An information statement filed with the Securities & Exchange Commission required pro forma financial statements and a general description of benefit.

A major reorganization in early 1993 heralded the breakup of Liquids as a stand-alone major Enron division—and marked the end of the Mike Muckleroy era. It had been an eventful 10 years for the liquids executive who was one of the most-respected figures at Enron. But despite his accomplishments, he had made enemies up high. Muckleroy had challenged the executive suite, even Kinder, over the whole handling of Valhalla. He was critical of the Dabhol project in impoverished India. He complained early on about mark-to-market accounting by Enron Gas Services, discussed in chapter 8. With all the changes, it was now time for him to depart, several million dollars richer.

The new Enron Pipeline and Liquids Group (EPLG), chaired by Ron Burns, had four units: interstate pipelines; Producer Field Services (gathering lines); Clean Fuels (methanol and MTBE plants); and Enron Liquids Pipeline (a public company operated and 15 percent owned by Enron). Producer Field Services was a new unit created by a FERC policy change whereby newly unregulated small gathering lines were separated from (regulated) large-diameter interstate gas lines.

Enron Gas Liquids was moved to Enron Gas Services along with Enfuels, a modest natural gas vehicle (NGV) joint venture.[57] International marketing of gas liquids, methanol, and MTBE was also separated, with head Bill Horwitz

---

55. Enron Liquids Pipeline LP went public with an offering of 5.65 million shares priced at $23 per share, indicating a market value of $130 million. The main assets were a 1,600-mile gas-liquids pipeline and a petroleum-products line from Kansas to Chicago; a 100-mile liquids line from Texas to Louisiana; a CO_2 pipeline in West Texas; and a 25 percent interest in a liquids fractionation plant at Mont Belvieu, Texas.

56. While announced in fourth-quarter 1992, EOTT's spin-off occurred in March 1994, a year behind schedule. Mike Muckleroy, the transitional chairman and CEO for EOTT, left the company before its independence. EOTT Energy Partners LP, was led by president Philip Hawk and board chairman Edward Gaylord.

57. Enfuels' Houston-based experiment would result in a loss of several million dollars for Enron, as discussed in chapter 9, pp. 400–401.

reporting directly to the Office of the Chairman (Lay and Kinder). EOTT, as before, was headed for corporate independence.

Jim Spencer had a good asset base to work with at Enron Liquids Pipeline and would report a good 1992–93 for unit holders. But Darrel Kinder (no kin to Rich) had his hands more than full with Enron Clean Fuels, which crucially depended on new reformulated gasoline rules from the US Environmental Protection Agency (EPA).

―――

Enron never ventured into oil refining or marketing, for good reason. The midstream-downstream petroleum sector was mature, capital intensive, and increasingly burdened with environmental rules. Enron's CEO liked regulatory change that offered upside, not downside. Unlike its sister fossil fuels, natural gas offered much governmental upside.

How could Enron penetrate the transportation market, where petroleum was king? How could natural gas compete on the nonstationary side, which represented more than one-fourth of total US energy use? Natural gas competed in virtually every other market: residential, commercial, and industrial, and in electrical generation. Lay wanted to penetrate transportation to boost natural gas consumption and buoy prices.

Compressed-gas vehicles, as Enron would find out, was a niche, money-losing market. That left an indirect opportunity if Enron could manufacture a natural gas–based additive to reformulate gasoline. Specifically, the oxygenate MTBE, blended 10–15 percent with oil-based fuel, reduced carbon monoxide (CO) emissions by approximately 15 percent. CO reduction in urban areas was a priority of the EPA and lawmakers from both sides of the aisle.

Ethanol was made from biomass; Enron had no competitive advantage there. But MTBE was made with methanol; methanol, from natural gas. This gave reformulated gasoline a natural gas component, offering room for Enron and a rare transportation-side entry "to be a provider of clean fuels worldwide."

Enron began studying the MTBE market in 1988–89 when proposed legislation pointed to a regulatory, even rent-seeking, opportunity. The Clean Air Act Amendments of 1990, which Enron had pushed for other reasons,[58] instructed 39 metropolitan areas out of compliance with federal air-quality standards to market cleaner-burning gasoline in the 1992/93 winter driving season, beginning November 1 and ending March 31. Representing nearly one-third of

―――

58. Enron's interest centered on the sulfur dioxide (acid rain) reduction program for electric utilities, which promised substitution of natural gas for coal in both existing and new plants. See chapter 7, pp. 324–25.

national demand, these cities could elect to enter into the program in this season and the next; mandatory participation began in 1995–96.[59]

Federal instruction for reformed gasoline had a dual attraction to Enron's Darrell Kinder, head of Enron's gas-processing venture. Normal butane had to be removed and MTBE added to produce the cleaner burn. Displaced butane was an input for MTBE too. Would Enron build or buy to enter into the reformulated-gasoline market? Would it have a methanol plant, MTBE plant, or both?[60]

––––

In 1991, distressed Tenneco announced a major corporate-restructuring program, which included the sale of its chemical units, along with an MTBE plant under construction in La Porte, Texas. Envisioning a shortage of the gasoline additive and calculating synergies with Enron's butane plant at Morgan's Point and methanol facility in Pasadena, Texas, Darrell Kinder sold Rich Kinder and Ken Lay on Enron's taking almost 10 percent of the national MTBE market.

In late 1991, Enron Gas Processing Company acquired Tenneco Natural Gas Liquids Corporation and Tenneco Methanol Company for $632 million: $523 million in cash, $7 million in debt, and $102 million to complete construction.[61] Most of the purchase price was financed off-balance sheet with a bank syndicate led by Citicorp, thanks to 75 percent of the 15,000 bbl/day MTBE output under contract for terms between three and five years.

"Along with our existing natural gas liquids operations, the Tenneco acquisition allowed us to accelerate our MTBE plans by approximately two years," Darrel Kinder told *Enron People.* "Now we're in the marketplace ahead of the competition." He pointed to Enron's reputation and assumption of contracts with three major oil companies (refiners). Another oxygenate, ethyl tert-butyl

––––

59. In early 1994, EPA finalized a two-part, year-round reformulated-gasoline program: Phase I commencing January 1, 1995, and Phase II beginning January 1, 2000. For greater detail, see Internet appendix 6.9, "Reformulated Gasoline and the Clean Air Act of 1990," at www.politicalcapitalism.org/Book3/Chapter6/Appendix9.html.

60. Ethanol was never part of Enron's clean-fuel portfolio. Nor, prior to the Tenneco purchase, did Ken Lay extol methanol or reformulated gasoline as clean fuels.

61. The purchased assets included a 15,300 barrels per day (BPD) MTBE plant being constructed at La Porte on the Houston Ship Channel; a 17,000 BPD isomerization plant at La Porte; a 9,100 BPD methanol plant at Pasadena on the ship channel; 9 million barrels of natural gas liquids (NGL) storage at Mt. Belvieu; the Dean Pipeline, which transports NGLs from South Texas through the Gulf Coast petrochemical region to Mt. Belvieu; the 1,600 BPD Magnolia processing plant near Corpus Christi; a 78 percent interest in the 3,600 BPD Sabine Pass processing plant in southwest Louisiana to be operated by Enron Gas Processing; a 25 percent interest in a 126,000 BPD fractionator located at Mt. Belvieu; and a 19 percent interest in the Blue Water processing plant in south-central Louisiana.

ether (ETBE), was producible with slight modification at Enron's new facilities. "We consider ourselves to be oxygenate producers—not just an MTBE producer," Kinder added. With growing demand on both coasts and Enron Petrochemical Company marketing in 22 countries, all seemed in place.

"This acquisition significantly expands and strengthens our existing natural gas liquids businesses and allows Enron to further vertically integrate our natural gas and natural gas liquids businesses with the additional isomerization capacity and the addition of methanol and MTBE to our product offerings," stated Ken Lay in a press release. That was "consistent with our objective to become the first natural gas major" and integrating "into environmentally preferred fuels and fuel components related to natural gas," Lay added.

Enron's broadened clean-energy vision created a tension, because natural gas vehicles (Enfuels) competed against gasoline—and now reformulated gasoline, as discussed in chapter 9. Lay's speeches emphasized natural gas for transportation to lift the industry; now, Enron was at the forefront of making oil-based transportation more environmentally friendly, diluting a selling point of compressed natural gas.

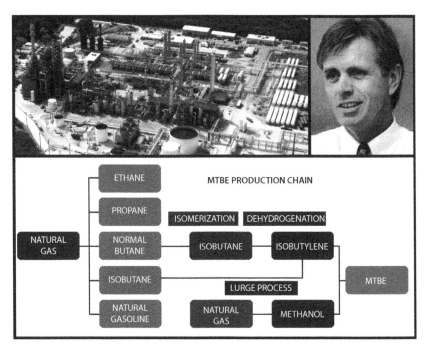

Figure 6.8 Enron's big bet to enter into the reformulated-gasoline market concerned the natural gas–derived oxygenate, MTBE. This foray went south quickly, when the demand expected to emanate from new federal environmental standards pursuant to the Clean Air Act of 1990 failed to materialize.

Enron forecast incremental earnings from its new investment of $40 million for 1993, a nearly 50 percent return on the highly leveraged equity Enron had invested. Investors shrugged off the news, however, sending ENE down a hair. With its premium price, Tenneco's stock rose 6 percent on the day of the announcement.

"[The] MTBE project is on budget and on schedule for operation by early November [1992] and is expected to be a significant incremental earnings contributor for the liquid fuels group in 1993," Enron reported in its second-quarter 1992 report. Expectations were high; Enron now estimated earnings of $60 million before interest and taxes.

Such upsizing at ELF was also intended to "provide Enron with a counter-cyclical balance to its natural gas production, pipeline, and marketing businesses." But what Rich Kinder would later call his biggest mistake at Enron began to unravel within a year of its purchase.

———

The MTBE facility opened as planned on November 1, 1992, producing 13,000 barrels per day for blending at refineries. This was the very day that the EPA's Phase I program commenced for nonattainment CO areas. But demand was weak, reducing volumes and margins. Federal regulators had given local officials leeway, and opt-ins were slow in the face of a 10 percent price premium for this reformulated gasoline. Meanwhile, new capacity was coming on stream; other firms also envisioned what Tenneco and Enron did.

"Today's MTBE prices are significantly weaker than those originally forecast at the time of the acquisition," Enron stated in March 1993, "reflecting the non-uniform implementation of the Clean Air Act provisions that were to be effective last November." Margins down by 20 percent from mid-1992, the new IBIT figure was $10 million, maybe less. This was bad news given Enron's expectations—and purchase price from Tenneco.

Operational problems joined in. A problem with the heat exchangers at the isomerization plant curtailed output by 20 percent and then required a full shut-in during the summer, leading to a suit against and settlement with plant-builder Kellogg. Once the unit came back, problems elsewhere caused the plant to be shut down again in early 1994.

Effective May 1993, the commercial side of Clean Fuels was assigned to Enron Gas Services. (Enron Operations Corporation, a new division, was responsible for the physical side of the methanol and MTBE plants.) Twelve employees were assigned from Enron Liquid Fuels to Ken Rice, who (reluctantly) transferred from Enron Power Services (which was marketing gas for electrical generation) to head the new Enron Clean Fuels Marketing. Jeff Skilling and John Esslinger, skittish about inheriting the unit's contracts in such an unfavorable market, informed employees that "a more integrated marketing and risk management approach for all the EGS commodities" would mean "better opportunities in structuring the MTBE and Methanol businesses."

Ron Burns lamented Morgan Point's "production limitations," as well as the fact that spot-index pricing hurt margins. "We [have] targeted June 1995 to convert these into fixed margin type contracts, over and above the spot index." It would mean going to term contracts to get mark-to-market earnings, a solution papering over the problems, a controversy described in chapter 11.

The second winter driving season, starting November 1, 1993, found conditions little improved. Clean Fuels earnings ended the year little changed from 1992, with increased MTBE volumes offset by weaker margins. The vision, at the time of purchase, of high profitability—$40 million annual IBIT or more—was dashed. Ken Rice's group could improve marketing to bring in some incremental profit, but something bigger was needed. This would lead to mark-to-market earnings shenanigans that would have a longer-term price to pay.[62]

Looking ahead to Phase I of the Clean Air Act's reformulated-gasoline mandate in 1995, when nine major cities would be required to sell reformulated gasoline year-round, MTBE demand was seen as tripling.[63] "MTBE remains the value-added oxygenate of choice among gasoline refiners looking for ways to comply with the Clean Air Act," Enron assured investors.

Enron again miscalculated, not to mention the EPA, which had internal knowledge of a problem waiting to happen. A 1980 CBS *60 Minutes* program reported the problem to a national audience. "Clearly," the *Oil & Gas Journal* was later to comment, "it was only after it was first reported to be a groundwater threat that MTBE was effectively mandated as a gasoline additive."

MTBE, a carcinogen, mixes easily with water and drives through the soil to find it. Should an underground gas-station tank leak or MTBE otherwise escape, the taste and smell of groundwater would be fouled—and powerfully so. (Two or three drops of MTBE in a swimming pool leave an odor.)

Complaints about water contamination first surfaced in Alaska in the first month of the program (November 1992). Flu-like health symptoms were also reported. Other states where MTBE was in use began to add to the problem map.

Ethanol interests stepped up their intervention in EPA rulemakings to get a slice of the reformulated-gasoline pie, differentiating ethanol as renewable and capitalizing on MTBE's falling reputation. EPA in March 1993 granted ethanol a

---

62. In 1997, a $100 million MTBE-related charge to earnings ($74 million after tax) would be made.

63. The ozone nonattainment areas were the metropolitan areas of Baltimore, Chicago, Hartford, Houston, Los Angeles, Milwaukee, New York City, Philadelphia, and San Diego.

30 percent share of the reformulated-gasoline market. Enron's political bet was in political, not only market, trouble.

Corporate Culture

There were many things for employees to like about Enron. From Day 1, Ken Lay had tried to impart realism, smarts, and graciousness to every business situation for a better Enron. In an industry dominated by engineers and lawyers, Lay's infusion of MBAs and PhDs was unique. And every Enron worker was an ENE stockholder under a five-year stock-ownership benefit plan inaugurated in 1986. By the early 1990s, every tenured employee was keenly following the (increasing) stock price and enjoying newfound wealth.

Enron's 1990 annual report introduced the Natural Gas Major vision and addressed the challenges presented by low prices. Subsequent annual reports focused on corporate values in addition to the mission—and boasted about the industry's finest workforce.

"Our goal is to compete on the basis of a unique set of people skills that we believe are unmatched not only in the United States but also worldwide," the 1991 annual report read. "We have the best and most creative employees in the industry," intoned the next year's report, adding: "We will continue to promote from within as well as hire talented individuals from the outside."

Rewarding individual initiative and rooting out bureaucracy would ensure Enron's continued "ability to move faster and more creatively than our competitors." And one of Enron's six goals in the 1993 annual report was: "Attract, hire, retain, and motivate the best people available in any industry."

Value statements were emphasized. Two were: "better, faster, simpler" and "do it right/do it now/do it better." In 1992, two new values appeared. The new charges appeared on the letterhead: "Your Personal Best Makes Enron Best" and "Communicate—Facts Are Friendly."

Compensation was upper end. "We continue to be a [pay] leader for all levels of employees," Ken Lay informed employees in 1990. "Bonuses at Enron generally are distributed through lower levels of employees more than other companies," he added. For those not otherwise eligible for bonuses, a $500,000 Employee Performance Award Program rewarded contributions "above and beyond the call of duty."

There were happy surprises too. When ENE broke $50 per share in February 1993, every employee received a crisp Ulysses Grant. (EOG had its own cash surprise when its stock surged.) With two stock splits, and ENE's value tripling in the last four years, Enron paid off its bank loan ahead of schedule to allow its Employee Stock Ownership Plan (ESOP) to pay ENE dividends directly to employees.

Figure 6.9 Ken Lay liked to celebrate Enron's success, such as awarding each full-time employee a $50 bill and when paying off the ESOP bank loan to allow stock dividends to go straight to employee ENE holders.

While generous, compensation was still legacy driven. An employee's salary had been built up over many years, and there were no base reductions for some to reward high achievers. To become more of a meritocracy, Enron implemented a *pay-for-performance* system in the early 1990s whereby automatic salary increases were slowed to industry norms, and the bonus pool was commensurably enlarged to benefit top performance. Total compensation in the new system remained at or near the top of Enron's peer group.

Jeff Skilling's arrival at Enron to restructure gas marketing and affiliated services, described in chapter 8, created a corporate culture within a corporate culture. Titles were simplified and job descriptions made open ended. Walls gave way to open space, and walls of glass promoted transparency. All this was one decade removed from the time when the CEO of Houston Natural Gas spent his time in a closed office—or in a reading place where all you could see were his two feet.

With so many new employees in Enron's most rapidly growing division, Skilling practically presided over a start-up. His quest was "a perfect meritocracy, where smart, gifted—and richly compensated—people would be pitted against one another in an endless battle for dominance, creating a free flow of ideas that could push the business past its competitors." Lay and Kinder were on board with that.

Still another corporate culture was developing at Enron Development under Rebecca Mark. As head of Enron Development and then Enron International, her approach of we're-the-smartest, don't-say-no proved ever more reckless in the 1990s.

Arguably, there were *multiple* corporate cultures at Enron, beginning with Ken Lay's kind-and-gentle culture, designed for all employees and for public consumption, balanced and complemented by tough-guy Rich Kinder. Beneath corporate, the regulated pipelines were relatively old school but innovative in their competitive arena. Skilling's Enron Gas Services and Mark's Enron Development were new school, the former out to reinvent the gas-merchant business in North America and the latter out to redefine *possible* around the world.

Forrest Hoglund's EOG and Mike Muckleroy's Liquids group were somewhere in the middle of these cultures. Just perhaps, they had the best corporate culture of all.

———

A comfortable, fun work environment was another part of Lay's emphasis on providing the best to Enron's 7,000 employees. The Enron Building was first class, replete with the company cafeteria (The Energizer) and a fancy below-ground workout facility and locker room (The Body Shop).

Enron was among the first major downtown Houston companies to implement a no-smoking policy inside the building. Starting the first day of 1990, pools of employees could be seen smoking outside the building. The same year, casual dress was introduced for summer Fridays. The dress-down policy—no coats and ties, but professional attire when meeting with customers—was extended for summers (1991) and then year-round (1992).

Other workplace issues were at the forefront for Enron: flexible work hours and unpaid leave for dependent care; flexible benefit plans; diversity training and mentoring programs; fostering women in management; addressing procedures for employee complaints against their boss.

Perennial reorganizations and regular downsizing were angst issues that management tried to explain and ameliorate. ("Every effort is being made to place and train employees who are directly affected by these actions," was one common refrain.) Ron Burns, head of the Gas Pipeline Group, the major area of retrenchment, ended one memo: "Believe me, the sole motivator of the moves we are making is to assure that Enron is the 'first natural gas major' and do our part to help that stock price continue to climb!" Making money and creating employee wealth was the best palliative.

Overall, Enron was a fun and rewarding company to work for. Ken Lay was well liked by the rank and file with his charming, down-to-earth demeanor (complete with his Friday blue jeans). And there were company acts of kindness, many private and some public. Terminally ill Neil Oring shared his story in *Enron People* about the outpouring of support he received from people at work and how an Enron jet came to the rescue when he fell sick on family vacation a thousand miles from home in what would be his last trip.

"A collective heart of generosity, caring and love—beyond what anybody could ever expect" made Oring particularly sad about not being able to return to work. "It is not just words any more when I read in our annual report that Enron has achieved its goals largely through the kind of people we employ," he wrote.

"Enron is successful because of its people," Lay wrote back to Oring. "The creativity and hard work of all of our employees has allowed us to differentiate ourselves from other natural gas companies. But as your letter so eloquently states, our people are extraordinarily compassionate and giving."

Ken Lay's ascent from corporate chieftain to Great Man only fueled his belief that he could disproportionately corner the industry's brain market at Enron, now the largest public corporation headquartered in Houston, and with fast-track international aspirations. The "premier New Age man in the natural gas business" had white-noise machines working at 1200 Smith Street. In his personal life, Lay was paying six figures for the latest in self-help and medicine. Lay gobbled down pills with his low-cal food and exercised religiously. Everything was to get ahead, everyone thought. But behind it was something else: a secret heart condition that seemed almost impossible given his regime.

Change and betterment via differentiation were key components to Ken Lay's vision for Enron. The necessary change outside Enron's walls required a new mentality within the company. Instead of don't-fix-what-is-not-broken, the open invitation was to break routines to make them better. "Overcoming barriers may require organizational and institutional change for the gas industry and the electric utility industry," Lay stated in 1992. "Admittedly change is difficult; it is wrenching and painful. But like many things in life, change often makes us a better people and leaves in its wake a better way of doing things, a better system or even a better society." But that philosophy could be taken too far and be proven unsustainable.

Conclusion

"Management's strategy of growth through vertical integration has allowed us to provide five years of solid performance," Ken Lay and Rich Kinder wrote shareholders and customers. "During 1993, we continued to fine-tune our organization to increase the benefits of our integrated natural gas strategy both in the U.S. and worldwide."

"Outstanding" performance in each major division created earnings-per-share growth of 20 percent in 1993 compared to a year earlier. Earnings growth of 15 percent or more was forecast for 1994 and for 1995: a very aggressive target given that the pipeline earnings did well to register 5 percent increases. Strong cash flow allowed Enron to lower its debt-to-capital ratio to 47 percent, a vast improvement from 70 percent six years earlier. Two MLP sales in 1992–93, as well as lower interest rates, were part of the positive results.

Credit analysts agreed, keeping Enron at investment grade, unlike many of its peers, including Arkla, Coastal, Texas Eastern, and Transco (the lowest-rated interstate gas company and Lay's old haunt). This rating gave Enron a lower interest rate on corporate debt, as much as 2 percent below the competition, paramount for Enron Gas Services' rapidly expanding marketing and credit services.

A 2-for-1 stock split in 1993, the second since 1990, reflected ENE's momentum.[64] "Over a five-year period, we have given our shareholders a total return of about 252 percent compared to a total return of 90 percent for the S&P 500 and the industry peer group average for each of the past five years," the 1993 annual report gushed.

Financial analysts rated ENE a BUY. "Judged against the roiled energy markets of the last three years, Enron Corp's success has been remarkable," wrote Lawrence Crowley of Rauscher Pierce Refsnes. "Enron has clearly emerged as the leading company in the natural gas group [with] a focus and management style that is becoming the standard in the industry." No problems were brought up in the 10-page report except with Liquids. There was no mention of EGS's the-future-taken-now accounting method or potential problems abroad.

Enron could have written the analysis itself. Such adulation would increasingly be the case as investment banking firms sought to win the company's underwriting business.

Meanwhile, the Texas intrastate gas market—the province of Ken Lay's original company—remained oversupplied with low pipeline margins. Competitor pipelines to Enron, less well run and without new profit centers, were mired in mediocrity in most cases. Two—United Pipeline and Columbia Gas Transmission—entered Chapter 11 bankruptcy from unrecouped, unresolved take-or-pay costs. In this environment, Ken Lay was the wonder boy of his business—and Mr. Natural Gas, a designation never held before in the industry.

Still, Ken Lay had not yet declared victory on its 1990 vision of becoming the world's first natural gas major. But with a calculated 20 percent share of the domestic market, Enron declared itself "America's leading natural gas company" in various 1992 press releases. And 1993's advertising campaign in such

-----

64. The catch word "momentum" was used six times in Enron's *1991 Annual Report*, once in the opening letter and again for each of the five business units. Enron shuffled talent away from its operating units to Investor Relations (corporate), with Mark Koenig and Rebecca Carter moving from Treasury and Accounting, respectively, in 1992.

publications as the *Wall Street Journal* and London's *Financial Times*, fresh off the Teesside completion, extolled Enron as an international energy company with "World Vision." That complemented the company's environmentally themed US-side advertising that began in 1989.[65]

Success was seen as prologue. "We are striving to maintain this superior financial performance well into the future," Lay and Kinder added in the 1993 annual report. But questions remained. Could the magic of mark-to-market accounting be compounded for such growth? Would the naked price risk of J-Block gas in the United Kingdom be rescued or exposed by the market? Would politics in India, Argentina, and points between stall or haunt Enron investments? EOG's bonanza could only go so far.

Would interstate pipeline expansions in future years be enough to generate mid-single-digit compounded earnings gains? Would the large short position incurred by Citrus Trading to enlarge the Florida gas market turn out well? Could the liquids business be profitable with higher gas prices? Could the troubled MTBE acquisition be turned around?

Don't worry, Enron insisted. The future of natural gas was bright, international opportunities "tremendous." Risk management would "emphasize locked-in spread related businesses versus commodity risk businesses" and "continue to hedge commodity risk, such as our share of EOG's production." The shareholders letter ended: "[W]ith Enron's collective sense of urgency we can achieve these [aggressive] goals with the continued support of our shareholders, including our employees, who have a stake in the company through their approximately 15 percent ownership in Enron."

Political Enron was looking ahead too. In Washington, DC, a provision tucked into the 1992 Energy Policy Act would prove to be an entry into a whole new business: wholesale electricity marketing. Power did not have its FERC Orders No. 436 and No. 636 as did natural gas; Enron was politically seeking to create a market that was far bigger than that of natural gas.

---

65. Enron also advertised itself as No. 3 on the Fortune 500's list of largest diversified companies (behind only AT&T and Cargill), and 45th of the Forbes 500 in terms of revenue.

7

Political Lay

Six years into Lay's Enron career, the *Houston Chronicle* ran an in-depth Sunday feature: "What Makes Kenneth Lay Run? Big Business May Not Be Big Enough for Enron Chairman." Author Kyle Pope interviewed many movers in search of the common denominator behind "Houston's best-known rainmaker."

Pope described the 49-year-old business, civic, and political force as "an anomaly" and "one of the oddest natural gas executives in America." A former employee gave praise, yet called Lay "an enigma." An industry consultant opined: "The rap on him is that his ambitions are in places other than the natural gas business."

Here was a businessman seemingly after something other than business at its highest. (Enron was about to edge out Tenneco as the largest Houston-headquartered company.) A politico who was neither Republican nor Democrat—and certainly not libertarian. A business and civic dynamo who sought alliances in numerous, unusual places. He was, although the term escaped Pope, a *private-sector politician*.

This change maker had doubters and detractors. Lay's two-front civil war within the fossil-fuel industry—between natural gas and coal on one side, and natural gas and petroleum on the other—made enemies. ("All fossil fuels are not created equal," Lay would say.) Many industry toes were being stepped on, although important segments of the gas industry were coming around to Enron's political model.

Kyle Pope found one Lay enthusiast in a sitting member of the Federal Energy Regulatory Commission (FERC). Jerry Langdon described Lay as "the premier New Age man in the natural gas industry." Some leading environmentalists, otherwise foes of all things related to fossil fuels, would similarly characterize Lay as a new voice, a new force, inspiring a rethinking about energy choices.

Pope's subject was highly educated, very smart, and extraordinarily accomplished. Ken Lay was socially gifted, with a diplomat's tact and a soulful persona. He was a master of the written and spoken word. Aided by busy-bee executive assistants, Lay was prolific and tireless.

Behind it all was a gargantuan ambition. Lay was running from a past and hurrying to a self-created future. John D. Rockefeller and Samuel Insull took decades to remake the petroleum industry and the electricity industry, respectively. Lay, emboldened by legislative and regulatory change, some of his own making, wanted to transfigure his industry in years.

Pope's extensive profile missed two things. First, Lay had a secret heart condition that was behind some of the observed personal characteristics. Second, Lay had a proclivity to assume large risks, sometimes because he was rushing but also because his prior actions dictated them.

The market did not seem to know or at least note all of the risk. Enron's whitewash of Valhalla had worked (Enron's near-death brush was not mentioned at all by Pope), and other big bets were either successful and unknown or in the making.[1]

Natural gas was a rising resource. Energy was politicized, with natural gas having upside—and coal and oil downside. Enron provided a growing world stage. For Kenneth Lee Lay, poor Missouri farm boy made good, these were means for *power* and a self-sought legacy of greatness.

———

Just months into his top job, Ken Lay paid a risky price to acquire two major assets regulated as public utilities by FERC. The interstate pipelines served growing markets, and Lay was confident that his new talent could figure out how to profit handsomely from them despite cost-based, regulated-returns. The stakes were high, even higher than when he ran an interstate at Florida Gas Company and then at Transco Energy.[2]

Lay doubled his FERC bet when Northern Natural Gas Pipeline joined the family, at an even riskier price, to create America's largest natural gas transmission network. Beginning in 1985, and more so in 1986, there was much work to do at FERC's 825 North Capitol Street offices in Washington, DC, concerning entry, exit, rates, and other terms of service.

———

1. The two-part Valhalla scandal and its sanitization are described in chapter 4. Gambles concerning the UK J-Block and the India Dabhol projects are described in chapter 6, pp. 271–73 and pp. 280–82.

2. For Lay's previous business life with FERC-regulated interstate natural gas transmission, see Bradley, *Edison to Enron*, pp. 291–312, and 334–51.

Enron's FERC agenda was heavy on relaxed, liberalized regulation. As generic policy, Lay favored a cost-based range for interstate-gas-pipeline rate making, where the ceiling was based on (higher) *replacement* cost, not original cost. Incentive rates, too, were endorsed by Lay, although repeated FERC efforts to set rules were thwarted by industry infighting and regulatory inertia.[3] FERC Order No. 636, the mandatory open-access rule for interstates, was "well balanced" to Lay, but total deregulation of rates and terms of service was not considered as a viable option in the post-636 era.

Transwestern, Florida Gas, and Northern Natural needed explicit approval—*legalization*—to market innovative new products and to expeditiously change rates and increase capacity. Unlike much of what was to come elsewhere, Enron's FERC work was market-conforming, not market-inhibiting (predatory) or market-manipulating. Filings and lobbying by Enron were for new consumer-friendly entrepreneurial arenas, not for restricting competitors as was so common in the history of US political capitalism.[4]

———

Enron had no coal position and few oil assets. Thus, coal and fuel oil, competing against natural gas, competed against Enron—and Ken Lay personally. Interfuel competition was fierce in the marketplace. And in state capitals and Washington, DC, political competition raged between rival energy firms and their trade groups. The political work of newcomer Enron was thus twofold. The first job was reactive, or *defensive:* using politics to remove unfavorable preexisting, rival-sponsored intervention by government. But the second job was proactive, or *offensive:* using politics to create wholly new intervention that would disadvantage rivals.

Nuclear and hydropower competed against natural gas but not at the scale of coal and oil. Once a power plant was built (and the capital cost was sunk), the power generated from nuclear fission and flowing water was cheaper than the power generated from natural gas. Nuclear and hydro thus were first-take—*baseload supply*, in industry vernacular—versus higher-cost *swing supply*.

Energies that were high cost on an operating (or marginal-cost) basis—gas, coal, and oil—competed to generate electricity on a day-to-day, even hourly, basis. So Ken Lay set his political sights on coal and oil, not on nuclear and hydro.

Enron's interfuel politics revved up with a new generation of environmental regulation that resulted in the Clean Air Act Amendments of 1990. (The 1963

———

3. See chapter 2, 140–43; chapter 3, 157–65; chapter 5, 225–32; chapter 6, pp. 256–66; and chapter 10, pp. 441–45, for a review of FERC rate policy in light of Enron positions.

4. The US rent-seeking experience is a major theme of Bradley, *Capitalism at Work*, especially chapter 6.

law had been previously amended in 1970 and 1977.) Reducing pollution from coal was central on the stationary-source side, which gave an advantage to cleaner-burning natural gas. Reformulated gasoline was central on the transportation side, something Enron invested in heavily with the gasoline additive methyl tertiary-butyl ether (MTBE).[5]

The year 1990 was also notable because the Gulf War raised national security concerns about oil imports relative to domestic production and usage. Ken Lay would not let that crisis go to waste.

———

As Enron grew to become companies within a company, in terms of its management, politics became ubiquitous and a core competency: encouragement for independent power development by the Public Utility Regulatory Policies Act (PURPA); sizable tax credits in exploration and production; regulatory relaxation for interstate gas transmission; open-access interstate pipeline requirements to facilitate natural gas marketing; taxpayer subsidies for foreign-investment risks; mandates for reformulated gasoline. Each was important, if not enabling, for a major Enron division.

And there was future opportunity. Should carbon dioxide (CO_2) emissions be priced, whether through a tax or a cap-and-trade ceiling, multiple Enron divisions stood to benefit. An Enron-sponsored legislative tweak in the Energy Policy Act of 1992 would be the opening wedge for an entirely new business: wholesale electricity trading.[6]

Mr. Natural Gas

"In the staid natural gas industry," *Business Week* reported in 1986, "Kenneth L. Lay stands out like a well flaring in the night sky." While at Transco Energy, Lay testified before Congress on energy issues. As chairman of the Interstate Natural Gas Association of America (INGAA), the trade group representing companies piping 90 percent of the nation's gas, Ken Lay brought a new approach. Instead of confrontation, Lay sought collaboration; instead of seeking legal recourse to pipeline transition-cost problems (as he had at Transco), he now saw them as negotiable, solvable business issues that would create difficulties for his competitors.

Skip Horvath, first as policy director at INGAA and later as president of the Natural Gas Supply Association, remembers Lay as "the most highly educated person on our board, and arguably the smartest," a CEO whose "forceful personality and persuasive manner of putting an issue forward helped establish the agenda for the gas industry." Lay "kept pricking imaginations and pushing

---

5. See chapter 6, pp. 295–300; and chapter 9, 413–14.

6. See chapter 9, pp. 418–19; and chapter 11, pp. 461, 469.

the envelope," getting people to think and behave differently. Horvath elaborated:

> By and large, Ken broke the mold. He was an idea man. He liked talking about ideas with people. And if you were someone who could throw a ball back at him as fast as he threw it at you, he would talk to you. He was personable, not condescending, and interested in getting the job done rather than people's station in life, which was quite refreshing for those of us on staff at the time.

The stature of Ken Lay, INGAA's chairman in 1989, would only grow. "He's really become the spokesman for the industry, and a very good one at that," reported a *Wall Street Journal* publication in 1992. In his farewell column at *Natural Gas Week*, John Jennrich put Lay first in his list of best speakers with the comment, "like the voice of God, with a sense of humor." In fact, Lay would achieve a position in his industry unmatched by anyone before or since: *Mr. Natural Gas*. Such a pedigree in the business history of the US energy industry was held by a precious two: petroleum's Rockefeller and electricity's Insull. That was high company, however brief Lay's reign would turn out to be (less than two decades versus twice as long for the other two).[7]

Mr. Natural Gas did not come out of nowhere. Lay was first noticed as the bright young CEO of Continental Resources Company, the parent of Florida Gas Transmission Company. His reputation surged at Transco as he creatively grappled with its gas-oversupply problem. In his first six months as CEO at Houston Natural Gas, he repositioned the company from a regional powerhouse to a national player.

Beginning in 1987, Ken Lay was challenging the coal industry on political, economic, and environmental grounds in a way that no other representative of the fragmented gas industry had ever done.[8] The prize, he knew better than anyone else, was gas-fired power plants capturing not just a majority but the great majority of the new generation capacity to increase demand and strengthen wellhead prices for a stronger industry.

Enron's business model was all about natural gas, reflecting a fertile confluence of events—deregulatory, regulatory, technological, and market—that positioned methane as the fuel of choice in stationary markets. (Natural gas for transportation was a niche market that Lay would push too.[9]) But gas was

---

7. Lay's natural gas reign can be dated from 1983, when he made a name for himself with his work on special gas-marketing programs (SMPs) at Transco, until the mid-to-late 1990s, when Enron's focus shifted to energy services, broadband, water, and renewable energy. Ken Lay's last natural gas speech was given in September 2000.

8. Federal regulation discouraging or prohibiting vertical integration created within the gas industry a "three-headed monster" of production, transmission, and distribution.

9. For Enron's unsuccessful venture into natural gas vehicles and compressed natural gas, see chapter 9, pp. 400–403.

hardly on automatic pilot to achieve this. Much had to be done politically and in the marketplace to get electric utilities to commit to long-lived gas plants.

External issues needed to be championed for his company and his industry. In Lay's mind, wellhead gas prices had to rise for short-term profitability and longer-term supply. Electric utilities had to be weaned away from their rate-base mentality, which put relatively capital-intensive coal plants in front of gas plants on their want list. Utility regulators needed to confront the gas-versus-coal issue to ensure that management would do the right thing for their rate-payers in the monopoly-franchise world.

Another high card to play was the environmental advantage of gas over coal, even if the proposed coal facilities were in compliance with existing regulation. Ken Lay wanted utilities and regulators to think about environmental quality *beyond compliance* and next-generation regulation *now*.

Ken Lay's multifaceted challenge began with sweeping away failed gas-shortage-era regulation. Enron then joined mainstream environmentalists against traditional pollutants where neutral regulation would hurt coal relative to gas. This was soon joined by Enron's full embrace of the nascent global-warming, climate-change movement to bring carbon dioxide (CO_2) into the emission-control mix. There, natural gas beat oil but particularly coal.

Talking Up Prices

Forecasting the end of the "gas bubble" was an exercise in futility. *He who looks into the crystal ball will eat shattered glass*, Enron executives liked to say. Economist and industry wise man Ken Lay proved to be no exception.

In early 1985, Lay predicted market balance in the "not too distant future."[10] But a year later, collapsing oil prices brought gas to rock bottom too. "The most thoughtful forecasts we look at show an annual surplus continuing out for the next five years," Lay now admitted. He frustratingly told the US Senate the next year, "this 18-month/2-year gas bubble has been about to burst for eight or nine years."

Lay's optimism returned in 1988 with a touch of strategic alarm. "We are very, very close to the balance between supply and demand," Lay stated at a *Gas Daily* conference. However, "the industry's security net is being eroded," he added, warning that "a small shortage can cause very large price increases." A year later, Lay reiterated his view that the market was balancing—but cautioned that "some fairly short supply situations … are likely over the next two or three years."

---

10. Market balance, surplus, and shortage, as used by Lay and by the industry, were relative terms used in reference to *higher prices*. From the viewpoint of lower, current prices, there *was* market balance, not shortage or surplus (which normally indicates an inability of markets to clear because of institutional constraints, prominently including regulation). In this case, a contracts problem at the wellhead (a legacy of regulation itself) created overpricing and a surplus.

But not only would Dr. Lay's prognostication prove errant; he was also mixing his messages. Just four months before sounding his *Gas Daily* alarm, Lay complained before the Natural Gas Supply Association that "producers are always forecasting that the next shortage is 18 months to two years away," thus encouraging "utilities and end-users to make commitments to coal and nuclear power." Then, before a different audience, the good doctor warned against "a real shock and very severe dislocations throughout the industry" with "damaging repercussions."

Such two-sidedness was not confined to the microphone. It was part of Enron Gas Marketing's sales pitch behind closed doors to end users to lock in long-term, fixed-priced deals. EGM's presentations would begin with a McKinsey & Company hard-landing (price-spike) forecast, followed by Enron's in-house robust projections about the gas-resource base. The message was: *Lock in now, be at the front of the line, and your gas will be there.* The extra cost—the price premium to the then-going spot price—will be worth it.

As it would turn out, gas deliverability remained high relative to demand. The industry was drilling less but finding more, thanks to new technology and wellhead tax preferences. Gas reserves were increasing, reversing an eight-year decline, in the face of weak wellhead prices.

Having been disappointed for a decade about the gas glut, Ken Lay lost his patience on Wednesday, February 7, 1991, at the annual meeting of Cambridge Energy Research Associates (CERA), hosted by Daniel Yergin in energy-capital Houston. Lay's was "easily the hardest-hitting address at the two-day conference attended by more than 400 people."

Complaining about "economically irrational behavior," Lay accused the major oil companies—the biggest gas producers—of engaging in *predatory pricing*, where wellhead sales at prices below the cost of replacement were distorting the market. *Predatory* had a clear meaning in economic theory and under antitrust law, and Lay's words were clear: The pricing practices of deep-pocketed integrated firms were destroying small rivals to create a less competitive future in which fewer companies and less supply would send prices up.

"Selling below cost is particularly difficult to understand when many of these same companies could scarcely wait 24 hours after the Iraqi invasion of Kuwait to increase gasoline prices so that they were not selling their gasoline inventories below replacement costs," Lay charged.[11] "I strongly doubt that it has been intentional," Lay allowed. "Rather, I expect it is a breakdown in communication between those people in some of the larger companies charged with

---

11. Lay defined replacement costs as "the finding and development cost to add new reserves and acquisition costs to buy reserves, plus production and operating costs, and a nominal after-tax return on investment." The next year, Jeff Skilling estimated replacement costs at $2.30/MMBtu, one-third higher than market.

replacing or expanding natural gas reserves and those people in the same companies charged with aggressively marketing their natural gas production."

As evidence, Lay pointed to the current Gulf Coast spot price of $1.30/MMBtu, the lowest same-month, inflation-adjusted price since 1976, a period of stringent federal price controls. He cited the statistic that 3,000 independents, or almost a fourth of domestic gas producers, had left the industry in the last five years in the face of depressed prices.

Lay came in for some heat, in fact more than he had ever experienced from an address to the industry. "This does not appear to be vintage Lay," an industry compadre told the *Houston Chronicle*, without attribution. A major company representative rebutted Lay with an economics 101 explanation of sunk costs and profit maximization. This was *not* about gas sales where marginal revenue was below marginal costs, after all.

Lay's cannon shot was chalked up to frustration. "You're seeing here what you saw when oil prices went to $10 a barrel a few years ago," commented Mike German of the American Gas Association.

But Lay was not only distorting economic theory with his predatory-pricing charge. He also was the pot calling the kettle black. Open-access competition and EGM logistics were lowering gas prices from the wellhead to burner tip, as Jeff Skilling knew. (Lay would champion this fact five years later, when Enron lobbied for similar open access for electricity.) Enron Oil & Gas Company (EOG), 86 percent owned by Enron, secured a tax break for tight-sands production, which effectively increased the wellhead price by $0.80/MMBtu, a boon for Enron and a driver of excess production (compared to a tax-neutral situation).

EOG, a top independent, *was* shutting in (not producing) some of its deliverability from shorter-lived gas wells in the belief that higher future prices would justify the delayed revenue. Lay was probably upset because of EOG's having to do just that. Nevertheless, EOG was highly profitable in the low-price environment with its negative tax rate, discussed in the previous chapter.

In fact, EOG had just completed a banner year with its average finding cost of $0.82/MMBtu and a combined finding and acquisition cost of $0.95/MMBtu.[12] EOG's Forrest Hoglund was telling shareholders: "This year [1991] is shaping up to be another exciting one with significant opportunities for EOG in spite of early indications that natural gas prices will be lower than desirable." Lay's point about the industry liquidating itself by selling gas below replacement cost was not happening with EOG, which was increasing

---

12. Industry-wide, gas-drilling costs fell substantially. Compared to peak-cost year 1982, when the drilling cost of a gas well per foot averaged $173, this cost fell to $80 in 1987 and remained below $100 well into the 1990s.

reserves even after its record production.[13] Technology was bringing finding (replacement) costs down.

But there was a method to Lay's madness. His accusation—which he sugar-coated as only a "possibility" raised only with "great reservations"—affected the psychology of the industry. *Natural Gas Week* reported ("When Lay Speaks ....") that Louisiana producers were no longer selling their gas below $1.45/MMBtu, their estimated cost of replacement.

Ken Lay had the megaphone of his industry. And he was speaking not only to the market but also to state regulators, who were under pressure from some in the industry to use their authority to reduce production to an alleged market demand. *Market-demand proration*, as it was called, was about increasing well-head prices in the name of reducing "economic chaos," as the head of the Texas Independent Producers and Royalty Owners Association put it. EOG and Hoglund supported the political capitalism of mandatory proration to go along with their own voluntary shut-ins; Lay less so.[14]

But economics was economics. Rapidly improving drilling technology, coupled with very generous new tax credits for tight-sands drilling, were increasing deliverability at a time of stagnant gas demand. The surplus, estimated by EOG's Hoglund at between 5 and 30 percent (depending on the season), could not be jawboned away by Lay or even himself. ("Buyers of natural gas are a whole lot smarter than the sellers," Hoglund complained at an industry gathering hosted by the Texas Railroad Commission.)

Gas prices reached a nadir in the summer of 1991. National wellhead prices fell to a dollar—and some reported spot sales fell below $0.50/MMBtu. This was happening despite voluntary shut-ins by EOG and others—*and* mandatory wellhead proration. State agencies in Texas, Oklahoma, and elsewhere, by limiting production to a calculated market demand, were keen to raise prices for their political patrons.[15]

Ken Lay had a vibrant business model, not to mention a robust ego. He really did not want anyone to feel too sorry for him or his company. So Lay let himself brag a bit in a feature interview with *Natural Gas Week* eight months after his accusatory CERA speech. "Basically, whatever natural gas prices are, we think we can

----

13. EOG would shut in more than 25 percent of its 600 MMcf/d deliverability in first-quarter 1991, but this was for poorer, tiring wells, and EOG had a major financial cushion of long-term contracts that gave it an overall selling price of $2.63/MMBtu in 1990, double the spot-price average.

14. See chapter 6, pp. 291–92.

15. So-called market-demand proration laws for natural gas began in Louisiana (1918), Texas (1935), Oklahoma (1937), and New Mexico (1949), among other states.

do well," he informed his industry. *Natural Gas Week* news reports, meanwhile, had headlines such as "Lay Predicts Solid Growth for Enron for Next 2 Years" and "Enron Sets High Earnings Goal Despite Low Natural Gas Prices."

Still, Enron could use higher gas prices, not only for EOG but also to improve margins for the company's very large transmission and marketing operations. But EOG was going to get a $0.80/MMBtu effective price increase from a special tax provision whether or not wellhead prices rose. Before Lay's CERA bomb, Enron secured passage of a tight-sands tax credit that would reap more than $200 million for the parent in the next seven years. That same provision was helping to create the very supply glut that Lay decried.

Technology, too, was at work. "The headline is basically our ability to add natural gas at fairly low cost is relatively substantial," explained William Fisher of the University of Texas Bureau of Economic Geology. The wellhead bonanza made natural gas its own best friend to beat coal and keep nuclear sidelined. *Enron's Outlook* said as much.

In a speech the next year, Lay retreated from his predatory-pricing insinuation made at Yergin's CERA conference. Independents, not only majors, were selling "below replacement cost—certainly some of the time." He was now "totally convinced" that predation was not at work, since "the [retrenching] majors ... have driven themselves out of the [domestic gas] business." In his address at the annual meeting of the producers' Independent Petroleum Association of America (IPAA), Lay changed the subject from supply to demand in order to address the industry's woes.

The gas-price rebound in 1993 quieted Lay's price crusade, one that he would not revisit when prices again weakened. This reversal ruined EOG's price hedges, which had worked so well in the previous low-price years. Still, Ken Lay, the PhD economist, had some peculiar notions of sunk costs, operating costs, and the oil-major business strategy, which raised questions throughout the industry about his professorial view of markets versus real-world markets.

Fighting Oil

In 1982, Transco Energy president Ken Lay had called for an oil-import fee. Transco Exploration needed higher prices, and Transcontinental Gas Pipe Line was losing business to fuel oil in industrial and power plant markets. Lay's position was that of his boss at Transco, CEO Jack Bowen, who was partial to government quick fixes.

At Enron, Lay continued to make energy-security arguments for reducing oil imports—and reducing oil usage per se. But he stopped short of calling for an import tax, even after the 1986 oil-price plunge hurt EOG and reduced pipeline volumes and margins.[16] Oil tariffs were a hard political sell, and Lay kept

16. See chapter 6, p. 292. Houston Natural Gas Corporation dropped its membership in the American Petroleum Institute the year after Ken Lay became chairman in 1984.

his powder dry. Still, Enron pushed the belief that natural gas as "a reliable, clean domestic fuel ... should sell at a premium price"—and belittled oil on grounds of balance of trade, national security, and domestic jobs.

Ken Lay elevated his gas-for-oil offensive in 1990 and 1991 in response to the Gulf Crisis and subsequent war. Lay had two additional company reasons. One was the need to expedite FERC approval of Transwestern's oil-displacement-themed expansion to California.[17] The other was Enron's entry into the compressed–natural gas refueling market to compete against gasoline and diesel. Lay, who cautiously backed a carbon tax in 1990 ("INGAA Opposes Carbon Tax but Lay 'Not Quite as Negative'," one headline read), began making a case for an oil-import levy.

––––

The *Exxon Valdez* oil spill in Alaska in Spring 1989 stained petroleum, not only Prince William Sound. Commenting on the development, Lay pointed to global warming as an even bigger driver of future gas demand. The "operating and environmental benefits of gas" should—and would—be "reflected in gas prices," stated Lay. Compared to about $1.60/MMBtu at the wellhead, Lay estimated a full-value gas price at between $3 and $4 per MMBtu.

To get gas prices up, given gas-on-gas competition at the wellhead (including from tax-advantaged EOG), other fuels needed to be made more expensive. Even before advocating an oil tariff, Lay supported a "heavier tax on dirtier fuels," aka an environmental surcharge.

At an Aspen Institute Energy Policy Forum, Lay contended that oil policy must go beyond energy security to also confront environmental and domestic supply issues. On all three grounds, Lay recommended a tariff for the first time in his Enron career.[18] "An oil import fee would essentially act as a price premium, captured by the market, to reflect the national security externality," he reasoned in July 1991.

Lay characterized his proposal as "market based" because it changed price signals in one fell swoop, as opposed to the mishmash of oil price and allocation rules enacted by the 1970s' "massive government intervention." But was imported oil really an externality to penalize consumers, and could he as philosopher-king really know the right tax? In any case, Lay's tax proposal did not take into account self-help toward future price uncertainty, such as oil hedging, something Enron pioneered with natural gas internally and externally.

Enron's natural gas vision had been all about power plants, not much else. Now, with oil policy front and center, the vehicular market was targeted too.

––––––––

17. See chapter 6, pp. 262–63.

18. See chapter 3, pp. 172–73 for Lay's earlier views on oil tariffs at Enron.

"Any policy to reduce the potential harmful economic impact of oil shocks must include measures to diversify transportation fuels," Lay opined.

Enter Enfuels, an Enron-led joint venture capitalized at $10 million, to open natural gas refueling stations in Houston. As part of the project, launched in 1992, Enron and partners would convert some of their company vehicles as well.[19]

"Three or four years ago, I was an agnostic at best," Lay told a panel convened by the National Association of Regulatory Utility Commissioners. "Since then, I've become a true believer." Natural gas vehicles (NGVs), Lay added, could account for 1.5 trillion cubic feet per year by 2005, about 5 percent of total demand. Next to electric generation, transportation was seen as the major growth market.[20]

Lay's gas-for-oil ethic was part of his energy-sustainability view. "I would maintain that the end of the oil era has either occurred or soon will occur" he pitched. "Natural gas will increasingly substitute for oil and coal and will be the primary growth fuel used to bridge the ultimate transition to renewable energy, probably sometime in the second half of the next century."

———

In early 1993, Lay went public with a political proposal to levy a $5 per barrel tax on imported oil as an alternative to the Clinton administration's Btu tax to reduce the federal budget deficit and to (politically) redirect energy usage. In an article for the *Petroleum Economist*, Lay calculated that replacing one million barrels per day with natural gas (2 Tcf) would generate 160,000 new US jobs, $37.5 billion in new investment, and a $7.5 billion decline in trade deficit. If this was good energy and economic policy, free-trade economists from Adam Smith to Milton Friedman had been completely mistaken.

Independent producers were about the only industry segment on board with such a proposal, and Lay was looking for political help to stimulate an Enron-estimated $75 billion in annual upstream investment needed to increase gas production by 20 percent (to 22 trillion cubic feet) in the next seven years. More government fiddling, in the form of a payroll-tax rebate, was recommended by Lay to soften the effects of a "short-term negative [price] effect."

Lay's oil-import tax was premised on a perceived social cost (negative externality) of such imports. Yet government intervention to replace internationalism with protectionism would have to consider more than the allegations of

———

19. Enron, half-owner and operator of Enfuels, exited the consortium in 1995 after losing $4 million. See chapter 9, pp. 400–403.

20. The US Energy Information Administration began tracking usage of compressed-natural gas (in NGVs) in 1997, then estimated to be 8 Bcf. Lay's estimate for 2005 would turn out to be about 1½ percent of the actual amount for that year (23 Bcf).

market failure. There were also questions of *analytic failure*, a false prescription (by Lay himself in this case), and of *government failure*, the suboptimal implementation of the desired policy. There were also *unintended consequences*, a defining characteristic of such protectionism. But such arguments would be for another day; this PhD economist was driven by the bottom line, and sooner rather than later.

Lay's antipetroleum philosophy and politics created a tension within Enron. The company's international power plant projects burned fuel oil when the economics of natural gas did not work. The just-signed North American Free Trade Agreement (NAFTA), behind which Lay had put Enron's full muscle, and for which he testified as chairman of INGAA in 1993, made protectionism illegal with Canada and Mexico, the two leading oil suppliers to the United States. Effective the first day of 1994, NAFTA made US oil tariffs economically unworkable, short of a three-country protectionist bloc, something that Lay did not address.

Warring Against Coal

Decades before it became a cause célèbre with Barack Obama, Ken Lay declared political war on coal. Enron's crusade began after Lay left coal-positioned Transco and turned Houston Natural Gas into a pure natural gas play. It continued even after Enron decided to enter into coal trading and then to acquire coal reserves in its last years.

Lay had once been coal-too. "Coal will inevitably be a growth business over the next two decades despite itself, and a well-rounded energy company should attempt to gain a position in it," the director of corporate planning at Florida Gas Company wrote in 1974. "Over time we as a nation, and the world for that matter, will have to increasingly rely on coal as one of our basic energy fuels, along with oil and gas," the Transco Energy president opined eight years later.[21] But at both corporate stops, Lay resented the fact that procoal regulation had unnecessarily and unfairly hurt natural gas.

The first order of business at Enron was to convince lawmakers to repeal coal-biased legislation. The mentality of electric utilities and state regulators also had to change, given the demonstrable economic and environmental superiority of gas. Both fronts, while political, were market oriented, quite different from anticompetitive *rent-seeking* (in the jargon of political capitalism).[22] "From

---

21. Lay stated the next year (with Transco CEO Jack Bowen): "Only with the use of our abundant coal, peat, and oil shale resources can we be assured that we will not have to return to a dangerous reliance on imported energy."

22. Rent-seeking is the practice of politically connected business to obtain special government favor, such as a self-serving regulation, tax carve-out, or check written on the public treasury. See Bradley, *Capitalism at Work*, pp. 122–24; Bradley, *Edison to Enron*, pp. 515–22.

the standpoint of natural gas," in Lay's words, "it's a matter of removing barriers."

The next phase, beginning in the late 1980s, when global warming became an international issue, was to price (regulate) CO_2 emissions politically, to disadvantage coal (and oil) relative to natural gas. Enron's Washington, DC, office pushed the climate issue to Republicans in particular—and no one more than George H. W. Bush. Alliances were formed with environmental groups to promote natural gas at the expense of its fossil-fuel rivals. Unlike before, this *was* proactive rent-seeking, not a quest for fairness.

There had been no love lost between natural gas and coal, and few companies were big enough in both to broker a truce. Coal had started the politicking many decades before when (coal-derived) manufactured gas began to face natural gas delivered by pipelines, first near and then from afar. Facing displacement by a cheaper, cleaner fuel, incumbent coal interests—the mining companies and their unionized workers, as well as the coal-hauling railroads—delayed the entry of natural gas in any governmental forum available.[23]

Coal's major weapon was Section 7(c) of the Natural Gas Act of 1938, which required federal certification of new or expanded pipelines crossing state borders. That gave rival fuels a political forum to delay, if not prevent, gas projects that otherwise linked willing buyers, sellers, and financiers.

In the 1930s, as discussed in chapter 2, coal interests delayed the entry of Northern Natural Gas Company, whose product would displace inferior coal gas. Two decades later, as chronicled in Bradley, *Edison to Enron*, Florida Gas Company had to overcome fuel oil and coal interests in federal hearings to introduce natural gas to the Sunshine State. This was a national story: "With their participation rights secure, alternate-fuel interests intervened regularly in FPC hearings in the 1940s, 1950s, and early 1960s, eager to forestall displacement of coal by cost-competitive, clean-burning gas."

And in the 1970s, with natural gas short and coal abundant, the Powerplant and Industrial Fuel Use Act of 1978 (Fuel Use Act), as well as a provision of the Natural Gas Policy Act of 1978 (NGPA), hurt gas demand in its most price-sensitive market.[24] A political "holy war" predictably ensued between coal and gas in the 1980s; Ken Lay and Enron would be right in the middle of it.

---

23. See also Internet appendix 2.1, "Regulatory Delay under the Natural Gas Act," at www .politicalcapitalism.org/Book3/Chapter2/Appendix1.html.

24. Until its repeal in 1987, the incremental pricing provision of the NGPA (Title II) required that more gas costs be assigned to industrial users to subsidize gas rates for residential and commercial users. Victimized industrials left gas for fuel oil and coal, leaving the intended beneficiaries worse off. See also Internet appendix 3.4, "Fuel Use Act, Incremental Pricing, and Gas Demand," at www.politicalcapitalism.org/Book3/Chapter3/Appendix4.html.

Getting to Even

Although gas markets turned from regulatory shortage to market surplus, the National Coal Association, American Mining Congress, United Mine Workers of America, and allied railroad interests worked to restrict gas under federal law. At first, the coal lobby began to contest applications by gas users seeking exemptions from the Fuel Use Act's prohibition of new gas service. The coal lobby then fought against repeal of the Fuel Use Act, raising fears about a return to shortages and price spikes. Power plants were their market, coal argued, leaving gas for "higher priority" households and businesses.

The debate began when Ken Lay supported repealing the Fuel Use Act and Title II of the NGPA in 1987 testimony before a US Senate subcommittee. Enron's chairman pointed out that gas became abundant, and even surplus, at about the time these laws were passed. Natural gas was a prolific resource that boded well for consumers. Lay ended his remarks with a zinger: "There are some of us in the gas industry who think coal ought to be husbanded for coal gasification in the next century."

The gas industry had the better arguments and the facts. With the backing of the Reagan administration, both procoal federal laws were struck down in 1987. But hurt had been done and memories linger long. Moreover, state and federal favor toward coal remained. In one speech before the IPAA, Lay reviewed how the coal lobbies "were instrumental in:

- Passing the Fuel Use Act, which ... prohibited the use of natural gas for power generation.
- Successfully enticing state regulatory commissions and legislative bodies in eleven states to mandate scrubbers to meet the requirements of the Clean Air Act Amendments of 1990—even if natural gas co-firing or natural gas repowering is cheaper for the consumer.
- Obtaining approximately 30 percent of the DOE R&D budget for years, as compared to 6 percent for natural gas even though both fuels contribute about the same percentage of our nation's total energy needs.
- Obtaining billions of dollars for treatment of black lung disease and reclaiming old strip mining areas because the industry is unwilling to pay for its own problems."

"The natural gas industry is willing and even eager to compete with coal in a truly free market," Lay concluded, "but we have had enough of the preferences, biases, and artificial incentives which greatly benefit coal."[25]

———

25. Under questioning from a coal-state senator, Wendell Ford (D-KY), Lay in 1989 advocated co-firing with natural gas in place of closing coal plants to reduce emissions. "I think we all understand that coal is our largest fossil fuel resource in this country and we have to utilize it," Lay opined.

Natural gas needed to grow out of its problems. Consumption in 1990 was 13 percent below its early 1970s peak. Winters were not cold enough for gas companies to bank on any surge in space-heating demand. The bright spot was electricity demand, which was growing around the country. If new power plants were gas fired, pipelines would grow and wellhead prices rise—things that Enron needed in order to underwrite its global ambitions.[26]

New electrical generation capacity *should* go to gas, Lay believed. Utilities were no longer constructing nuclear plants. California was legislating an end to oil burning in dual-fuel plants when gas was available. Oil in Florida's electric market was all but locked out by Enron's long-term gas contracts. The market was between coal and natural gas for new plants, which meant a 20-year demand stream for the winner.

Regulatory trends were breaking toward gas. After fuel neutrality was significantly advanced in 1987, the Clean Air Act Amendments of 1990 tightened air-emission rules and introduced emissions trading for sulfur dioxide (SO_2), which replaced the *best-available control technology* (scrubber) instruction from the prior (1977) amendments to the same law.

Coal interests opposed trading, which would promote gas firing in place of hitherto installing pollution controls that would increase rate base and thus maximize profits at existing plants. West Virginia regulators, for example, allowed a coal plant to spend $800 million on scrubbers instead of replacing the capacity with a $120 million gas-fired cogeneration facility.

Instead of SO_2 trading, coal interests sought a national fee on all electricity sales (including gas-generated sales) to fund scrubbers. Enron-ex Jim Rogers, now head of the coal-heavy Public Service Company of Indiana (PSI), argued for a "cost sharing mechanism" to help underwrite five scrubbers (each costing in excess of $200 million) that his coal plants needed to comply with what he called the "Bush bill." Without such help, PSI's rates would rise around 20 percent for the anticipated two-thirds-plus reduction in SO_2 emissions.[27]

The gas industry got "90 percent" of what it wanted in the 1990 amendments, according to the American Gas Association. It was Ken Lay, in fact, who represented AGA and INGAA before Congress to argue in favor of emissions trading—and against a power-sales fee that his former protégé Rogers wanted.

---

26. Lay defined Enron in 1989 congressional testimony as "a diversified energy company whose core business is the gathering, sale, and transportation of natural gas to markets throughout the United States."

27. Rogers nominally supported emissions trading but worried about the regulatory risk surrounding the bank of credits that PSI (later Cinergy, then Duke) would accumulate for sale from reduced emissions. Federal regulators could depreciate the value of credits with a rule change, and state regulations could give the value to ratepayers rather than shareholders. Such credits, in other words, were not a property right.

There was other legislative tilt toward gas. The same 1990 law tightened nitrogen oxide standards and allowed emissions trading for power plants, which disadvantaged coal. (Per kWh, gas emitted two-thirds the NO_x that coal did.) Regarding wellhead gas, the tight-sands gas credit was a preferential bonanza, particularly for EOG. And the global-warming issue put coal's carbon-dioxide-rich emissions on the firing line.

New gas turbines made cogeneration and combined cycle increasingly efficient for turning methane into electricity and for utilizing its waste heat. Coal plants were improving but not as much as was the gas side. And low prices made natural gas its own best friend with gas-for-coal substitutions for utilities with spare gas capacity.

Still, long-term commitments to natural gas faced obstacles with the utilities' decision makers. Had not even gas-industry heads preached that the North American gas-resource base had peaked? Robert Herring of Houston Natural Gas had said as much from 1979 until his death two years later. So did Transco's Ken Lay, although no one seemed to remember. Utility heads considered coal, superabundant and domestic, as a hedge against price uncertainty in power generation.[28]

All that was reinforced by the aforementioned perverse incentives under public-utility regulation. Utilities made money by maximizing their rate base upon which the allowed rate of return was multiplied. Coal plants were more capital intensive than were gas plants, and the difference created an extra pot of dollars on which the coal-burning utility could earn a profit during the life of the investment.

Ken Lay saw the disconnect between consumer economics and utility economics; between business-as-usual utility choices and the environment. The electrics had to be cajoled to do the right thing for their customers, not to mention the environment. State-level utility regulators had to be energized in their oversight capacity as well. This battle in a biased regulatory framework had to be very public.

Ken Lay went public almost five years after he first challenged coal to head-to-head competition before the Senate Committee on Energy and Natural Resources. His clinching argument was Enron's long-term, fixed-priced gas contracts that could virtually lock in cost savings for utilities and their customers. This new product came from Enron Gas Marketing and later, Enron Gas Services Group, the subject of the next chapter.

But old habits were hard to break. Don Jordan, CEO of Houston Lighting & Power Company, the nation's second-largest gas user, continued to tout coal over natural gas in public and regulatory forums, to Lay's dismay. Yes, HL&P

-----

28. See Bradley, *Edison to Enron*, pp. 341–45, 452, 454, 459, 490–91, and 518–19.

had been victimized by natural gas shortages in the 1970s, but that was then. Price controls were long gone. And low spot prices were prompting Jordan's power plants to back off coal in favor of gas.

"The Natural Gas Standard"

Enron carefully researched and marketed the key environmental statistics of natural gas relative to coal, per unit of electricity produced. A table in Enron's 1988 annual report showed these reductions for gas: 99 percent for sulfur dioxide (SO_2); 43 percent for nitrogen oxide (NO_x); 53 percent for hydrocarbons; and 96 percent for particulates (PM_{10}).

How could low gas prices, rapid improvements in gas-to-electricity technology, and across-the-board emission reductions win the competition for new power capacity? Education, public relations, and politics were called for.

In March 1992, Ken Lay unveiled *the natural gas standard* for new power plants. Lay's letter, adjoined by an Enron press release, read:

> The advantages of generating power from a gas fired combined cycle plant are overwhelming: It is cleaner, cheaper, and more reliable than the coal and nuclear options. I propose that electric utilities and state [public-utility commissions] adopt the "Natural Gas Standard" for power generation capacity additions. The standard should be applied in the following way—no new coal or nuclear power generating stations should be built unless they:
>
> > produce electricity cleaner than gas combined cycle plants;
> >
> > produce electricity cheaper, per [kilowatt-hour], than gas combined cycle plants;
> >
> > produce electricity more reliably than gas combined cycle plants.
>
> I am obviously confident natural gas combined cycle generation will win when all three of these standards are considered.

Lay's analytics came from Bruce Stram and Mark Frevert at Enron, working with consultant ICF Resources. Using realistic assumptions, the levelized cost of electricity from a state-of-the-art gas plant was about one-third below that from a best-technology coal plant. The gas unit could be sited and built more quickly. There was less financial risk for gas, given fixed-priced contracts by Enron for up to 20 years. Guaranteed supply at floating prices was available for 30 years, about the expected life of a new facility.[29]

Pollution reduction was a big political plus across the board. Updating earlier estimates, a gas unit emitted virtually zero sulfur dioxide (SO_2) and solid waste (ash or scrubber sludge). And when Enron compared gas to coal

---

29. Enron had entered into long-term commitments for four trillion cubic feet of gas, about 20 percent of the annual US gas consumption by comparison. With a probable resource base in the lower 48 of 70 years of present usage, there was room to lock in long-term supply for any new gas plant.

with regard to the emission of nitrogen oxides, it decided to up its carefully researched estimate from 43 percent lower to 80 percent lower, per kilowatt-hour.

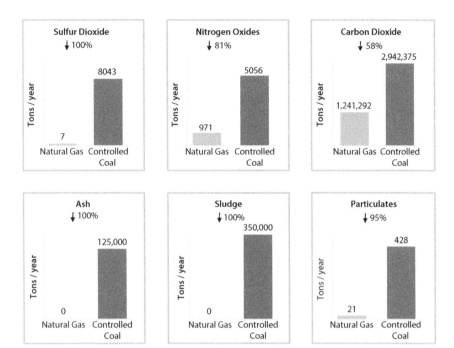

Figure 7.1 Enron continually educated energy constituencies about the environmental advantages of natural gas under current technology. This summary from a company brochure (circa 1995) showed the emission reductions of a similarly sized gas plant versus coal plant in six relevant categories.

Then there was the politics of the greenhouse gas that was in the news: carbon dioxide. Gas-fired generation emitted about half the CO_2 of a coal plant for the same electricity generated.

On the speaking circuit, Lay sold the Gas Standard as a win-win, free-lunch, no-regrets strategy for better economics and a better environment. "In the case of electric power production, cleaner can be cheaper," Lay explained.

> The old paradigm suggests just the opposite: If you want a cleaner environment, you have to pay for it through higher electricity prices. Not true: cleaner air and lower levels of pollution are "free" when a natural gas fired power plant produces electricity, because natural gas power production is generally 30 percent cheaper, per kWh, than coal fired power production. A cleaner environment is a byproduct of choosing the least costly economic alternative.

Meanwhile, Enron's president and COO Richard Kinder urged state regulators in a meeting of the National Association of Regulatory Utility Commissioners to facilitate, and even force, electric utilities to end their coal bias. Kinder insisted that regulators had a responsibility to ensure that utilities fairly weighed all costs, capital and operating, as well as preapprove long-term gas agreements that locked in cost savings up front. Regulators should also resist the practice of favoring indigenous coal in certain coal states, Kinder added.

Coal pushed back. Richard Lawson of the National Coal Association (NCA) wrote a four-page letter, even screed, to the American Gas Association and INGAA (the two gas-industry trade groups of which Enron was a member). Potential pipeline explosions and a "notorious historic record of gas prices to spike on any pretense" were among the "substantial and as-yet unremedied weaknesses" of gas, Lawson warned. A Natural Gas Standard could lead to a "Solar Standard" or a "Wind Standard"—and "more regulation than even Eastern Europe's unemployed central planners dreamed."

Lawson also reminded gas interests that they were fossil fuels too: "Those who would live in the figurative greenhouse shouldn't throw stones from inside to those outside it; they are likely to be thrown back sooner or later."[30]

"We have 300 years of coal and know we can sell it without a lot of price volatility," another NCA official told the press. "Coal is still the cheapest fuel on a Btu basis and with clean coal technology, it can be burned cleanly to meet all the new emission requirements."

This rebuttal ducked the let-the-market-decide call of the Natural Gas Standard. Enron's long-term, fixed-priced offerings allowed coal and gas investments to be economically assayed up front. ("I repeat," Lay would say, "Enron is now prepared to guarantee gas supply and gas prices for fifteen years, even under contracts starting two to three years from now.") Fuel costs might still be cheaper for coal than for natural gas, but the higher up-front costs for a coal plant had to be factored in. Enron had done this math, using realistic assumptions.

The Natural Gas Standard was the start of Enron's move from reactive to proactive messaging and politics. But the standard itself was about removing malincentives in public-utility regulation that worked against free-market consumerism.

Environmentally, the standard was about best-technology to meet existing law and what might legislatively or administratively come next. And that could involve not only tightening standards for criteria pollutants but also expanding the regulated list to include CO_2 emissions, where gas handily beat coal.

---

30. INGAA head Jerald Halvorsen responded: "We'd rather not fight with the coal people, but if they want a fight, they'll get one." He added elsewhere: "You don't see me pointing a finger or opposing a half-billion dollars of Clean Coal Technology money every year."

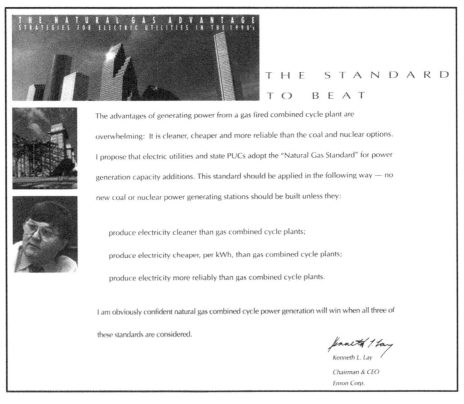

Figure 7.2 With strong arguments developed in part by fellow PhD economist Bruce Stram (pictured), Ken Lay challenged electric generators to choose natural gas instead of coal for new capacity. Less rent-seeking than moral suasion, Enron's Natural Gas Standard was targeting franchised monopolists to do the right thing in the face of a rate-base bias towards coal.

Beyond Even: Global-Warming Activism

Coal had gained the upper hand on natural gas as an unintended consequence of federal energy policy in the 1970s. Price controls on natural gas, specifically, created shortages that resulted in coal-for-gas regulation and new coal-plant construction.[31]

_____

31. See Bradley, *Edison to Enron*, pp. 454 and 508–9. After DOE program administrators routinely granted exemptions, the law would be weakened in 1987 and again in 1989 before being repealed in 1992.

Getting to even was one thing. Getting beyond even, as coal had previously done, was now the opportunity. Opportunity present, Ken Lay jumped on the global-warming bandwagon when it became a national issue during the hot, dry summer of 1988.

In Enron's annual report that year, the enhanced greenhouse effect was added to other environmental metrics:

> Renewed interest in clean air could mandate anti-pollution measures that will favor the use of natural gas, the cleanest fossil fuel. Natural gas contributes the least of all fossil fuels to emissions thought to contribute to the greenhouse effect, acid rain, and reduction of the ozone layer in the upper atmosphere.... Because of these developments, the company fully expects the 1990s to be the decade for natural gas.

The 1989 annual report referenced "the discussion concerning the dangers of a global warming trend" with natural gas being "a key component of the solution."

Yet carbon dioxide was not a contaminant that dirtied the air or was unhealthy to breathe. It was not a criteria air pollutant under Clean Air Act regulation as were sulfur dioxide (SO_2), oxides of nitrogen (NOx), carbon monoxide (CO), particulate matter (PM), lead (Pb), and ground-level ozone.

Quite the opposite, CO_2 was a colorless, odorless, inert, trace gas that is naturally present in the air. Humans exhaled it, and plants absorbed it (via photosynthesis). The so-called gas of life had a variety of industrial uses, including for enhanced oil recovery.

In the atmosphere, on the other hand, CO_2 traps heat (the enhanced greenhouse effect), offsetting SO_2 emissions thought to have the opposite effect. NASA scientist James Hansen made headlines during a 1988 heat wave with such statements as "Global warming has reached a level such that we can ascribe with a high degree [99 percent] of confidence a cause and effect relationship between the greenhouse effect and observed warming." US Senators Al Gore (D-Tenn.) and Tim Wirth (D-Colo.) were behind Hansen's historic political moment.

Concern about global cooling and a new Ice Age from industrial soot from such scientists as Reid Bryson, Paul Ehrlich, John Holdren, and Steven Schneider were quickly forgotten. A new Malthusian scare related to fossil-fuel usage and thus population growth and industrialization was born. "Journalists loved it," remembered Schneider, whose book on global cooling was followed by one on global warming. "Environmentalists were ecstatic." This did not go unnoticed by Ken Lay and another PhD at Enron.[32]

----

32. The global-warming issue, involving the enhanced greenhouse effect, primarily from fossil fuel burning, is described in Internet appendix 5.4, "Global Warming and Greenhouse Gases," at www.politicalcapitalism.org/Book3/Chapter5/Appendix4.html.

With less relative CO_2 emissions than oil and particularly coal, the natural gas industry got right on board. The American Gas Association sold environmental groups on a "bridge fuel" substitution strategy. "Our effectiveness depends on how the industry reacts," explained the Sierra Club about its foray into fossil fuel advocacy. The World Resources Institute upped the ante: "We believe that discouraging new uses of natural gas is bad energy policy, economically unsound, and environmentally damaging."

The National Coal Association labeled such thinking "shortsighted," while the nuclear group US Council for Energy Awareness complained about being left out of the discussion. This was coal versus gas.

With new environmental regulations kicking in under the Clean Air Act of 1990, as well as political interest in tightening existing standards and expanding the list of pollutants, Lay took his no-regrets case a step further in speeches and interviews by exhorting electricity executives to go "beyond Clean Air compliance" with gas-for-coal substitution. This meant some combination of "natural gas co-firing, gas conversion, or new gas-fired capacity [that] would hedge the risk facing ratepayers resulting from potential CO_2 emissions limits or taxes in the future."

John Jennrich in *Natural Gas Week* seconded Enron's ecological argument. "Environmentalism leads to greater use of natural gas," he ended one piece. "And only with increased demand will there be opportunities for higher prices and economic pressure for greater access to supply." It was Jennrich who elsewhere got a lot of chuckles with his term for coal: "flammable dirt."

Ken Lay fashioned an attractive climate message for both sides of the political divide. To Republicans, he stressed the no-regrets strategy of using natural gas to address climate change: "While we complete the research on global warming, we have a significant opportunity to reduce one of the major causes of global warming without paying any economic penalty." To Democrats and to allied environmentalists, Lay went further. "Global climate change is ... potentially ... a horrendous problem," Lay opined in one interview.

"I don't know of any evidence to suggest that larger and larger accumulations of greenhouse gases—and particularly CO_2 emissions—in the atmosphere has any—and I do mean any—beneficial effects for our globe and mankind," Lay iterated elsewhere.

Lay's climate alarmism was opportunistic, self-serving, and intellectually myopic. There were top-drawer arguments against this eco-scare, just as there had been about the population bomb in the 1960s and resource famines in the 1970s.[33] A vast literature existed on the *positive* ecological and economic benefit of higher concentrations of atmospheric CO_2 for plants and woody matter, such

---

33. For a critical review of Malthusian and neo-Malthusian alarms, see Bradley, *Capitalism at Work*, chapters 7–11.

as that document by the (coal-funded) Greening Earth Society. But Ken Lay was not in a mood to think impartially about a new weapon against the energy enemy.

Lay was pliable on many things political and social in his quest for a mighty Enron. In time, he would confess to the opportunism presented by the global-warming meme. "If there is one thing I have been impressed with over the last decades, it is that when the environmental community defines a number one priority, something happens," he remarked in 1997. "Not always something good—but something."

Getting Gas to Green

Enron's two-front civil war within the fossil fuel industry had natural gas warring against coal on the one side and petroleum on the other. But Ken Lay's well-researched, ably orchestrated effort inspired another split, this one within the hitherto anti–fossil fuel, anti–industrial environmental community.

"Natural gas, until recently, tended to be lumped in with the bad guys," wrote natural gas scribe Daniel Macey. "Now the question is whether to let natural gas into the environmental camp." Behind the rethink? "Natural gas executives are trying to turn the blue flame green as they find in environmentalists a new marketing tool for their 'clean-burning fuel'."

The most notable gas-is-green convert was Worldwatch's energy specialist Christopher Flavin. Flavin took a liking to Lay and vice versa. Flavin understood not only that natural gas was environmentally superior but also that industry infighting could break hydrocarbon's grip on government policy. "A major political realignment in the energy world could lead to enormous policy changes and, ultimately, to a new energy system," Flavin strategized. Ken Lay, he knew, was a powerful industry friend, a change maker, for the Environmental Left.

The National Wildlife Federation also looked to gas. "Considering natural gas as a bridge fuel means just that," stated president Jay Hair. "Accelerated work has to go forward on renewables and efficiency so that the bridge gets us where we want to go."

Not so fast, retorted Greenpeace. "Natural gas is paving over these clean renewables and efficiency programs," stated Fred Munson of the organization's global-warming campaign. "Natural gas is not clean and is not any better than oil and coal as far as emissions go," referring to methane leakage in particular, a potent greenhouse gas.[34]

---

34. The 5 percent methane leakage rate claimed by Greenpeace compared to less than 1 percent estimated by others, including the US EPA. Greenpeace, however, recommended new gas plants to retire nuclear plants.

Worldwatch ~~Desk~~
Paper 91

Slowing Global Warming:
A Worldwide Strategy

Christopher Flavin

October 1989

"If there is one thing I have been impressed with over the last decades, it is that when the environmental community defines a number one priority, something happens. Not always something good—but something."

-Dr. Kenneth L. Lay, June 1997

Figure 7.3 Ken Lay, looking for the next big energy thing, was attracted to the global-warming issue and the analysis of Christopher Flavin of the Worldwatch Institute (see "Desk" written at top). Lay at times revealed his pragmatism on this issue, as this quotation attests.

The natural gas–environmentalist alliance was an example of the Bootleggers-and-Baptists lobbying strategy, whereby profit seekers (bootleggers) ally with public interest groups (Baptists), such as, in this case, environmental groups organized as the National Clean Air Coalition, to win a special regulation, a tax provision, or public money.

Compromise and short-sightedness were necessary. Gas interests sold out their fossil fuel brothers to join environmental pressure groups that might later turn on them; environmentalists had to embrace the least-polluting fuel for the time being. This alliance was the result of the planning and salesmanship of Ken Lay.

The alliance reflected something else: the demotion of ad hoc, command-and-control policies by environmental groups in favor of holistic emission fees and tradable permits from which decentralized choice would result. "In shifting more to market-oriented solutions," Lay noted, "environmental leaders are speaking the businessman's language." The Environmental Defense Fund, in particular, would champion setting an overall allowance cap for trading the right to emit carbon dioxide emissions, joining air-permit trading for SO_x and NO_x legislated in the 1990 Clean Air Act.

Enron as a market maker for emissions was more interested in cap-and-trade policy than in a carbon tax. Enron-ex Jim Rogers, who was eager to convert his electricity units from coal to gas to receive CO_2 credits to sell, was even more partial to cap-and-trade. Rogers, like Lay, was waging civil war with his fellow electric utility executives, using Lay's political capitalism model.

Getting gas to green needed a fractious industry to come together for common goals. In late 1991, the major gas trade groups (AGA, INGAA, NGSA, IPAA) united to form the Natural Gas Council. Its $15 million advertising budget was intended to improve methane's image and increase annual demand 13 percent in five years (to 22 Tcf by 1996).[35]

"The gas industry has talked for a long time about burying the hatchet and then burying coal, and this council seems like the right thing to do," an industry analyst opined in the *Wall Street Journal*. A somewhat skeptical John Jennrich reminded his *National Gas Week* readers that this was new territory. "Competition within the gas industry is just as keen as interfuel competition," he remarked. "History has seen members of this new Natural Gas Council at each other's throats in courtrooms, commission hearing rooms, and legislatures all over the land."

But incremental cash flow was a great peacemaker, and the gas industry writ large—facing low prices and squeezed margins on one end and disgruntled customers on the other—would give it a try.

Getting Bush to Rio

President Bush was a moderate Republican, not the second coming of Ronald Reagan. When it came to environmental issues, Bush the elder wanted applause from the green-colored intelligentsia and media. And some of his trusted advisors, such as EPA head William Reilly and White House Counsel C. Boyden Gray, liked the progressive nature of the global-warming issue.

Bush restored federal subsidies to the Carter-era renewable-energy and energy-efficiency programs that had been cut under Reagan. All-Things-to-All-People Bush also signed the Clean Air Act of 1990, which took the acid-rain scare at face value, a signal about his openness towards the global-warming issue to come.

Bush needed a push on climate given the tepid support or outright hostility of his political party. It came from Bush's go-to business executive on energy and related environmental issues, Ken Lay, whom Bush had appointed to advisory committees with the Environmental Protection Agency, the Department of Energy, and the Department of Commerce. Lay was chosen for the President's Commission on Environmental Quality as well.

Lay's embrace of climate-policy activism made him a natural to be chosen as the founding chairman of the Business Council for a Sustainable Energy Future

---

35. The Natural Gas Council was chaired by AGA chairman Richard Farman, head of the Southern California Gas Company. SoCalGas was AGA's largest member, and AGA was the largest Council member.

(1992), later Business Council for Sustainable Energy (BCSE). The group was composed of firms out to benefit from CO_2 regulation. Joining Lay in leadership roles were Arkla CEO Thomas "Mack" McLarty, soon to become White House Chief of Staff in the Clinton administration; Michael Baly, head of the American Gas Association; and Senator Tim Wirth (D-CO). The Business Council's advisory panel was headed by Christopher Flavin, vice president of research at Worldwatch Institute, whose work was central to the sustainability views of Lay.[36]

———

The environmental movement had its business-friend-in-a-high-place with the Bush administration. And Lay did not disappoint when he went all out to persuade a conflicted George H. W. Bush to attend—to *legitimize*—the Earth Summit in Rio de Janeiro in June 1992, which kicked off a global effort to address a global-commons issue of manmade greenhouse gas emissions.

"I am writing to urge you to attend the upcoming United Nations Conference on Environment and Development scheduled for early June in Brazil and to support the concept of establishing a reasonable, non-binding, stabilization level of carbon dioxide and other greenhouse gas emissions," Lay wrote Bush on April 3. "This stabilization level should serve as a useful public policy guide, not a policy mandate," the letter continued. "Moreover, I believe a market-based policy approach is the most cost effective and environmentally beneficial method to achieve greenhouse gas stabilization."

Getting the president to Rio was no small task for a political party that was highly suspicious of the global-warming scare and a UN-led global governance push. Lay's letter sought to stake out the middle ground.

"The demagoguery on both sides of this issue has been extraordinarily fierce." Lay allowed. "Frankly, I do not believe the oceans will boil in a few years if we don't address greenhouse gas emissions, but I also do not believe the U.S. will suffer from economic ruin if prudent steps are taken to reduce CO_2 emissions in order to protect the global environment." Then came his no-regrets pitch:

> In fact, if pursued through market-based policies, a reduction in greenhouse gases should result in a cleaner environment, cheaper electricity, and more American jobs.

———

36. The BCSE evolved out of a joint study published by the American Gas Association, the Alliance to Save Energy, and the Solar Industries Association, titled *An Alternative Energy Future* (April 1992). The legwork for the Council was done by Enron's Bruce Stram. See chapter 13, p. 524.

Among other industries, I am convinced that America's hard-pressed domestic natural gas industry would benefit substantially from a market-based approach to reducing CO_2 emissions. Natural gas is our cleanest fossil fuel and through its increased use in electric power generation could play a major role in reducing CO_2 emissions and delivering lower electricity prices to consumers....

Natural gas electric power generation is not only cleaner, it is cheaper—at least 30 percent less costly than coal-fired electricity generation over the life of the plant using long-term natural gas prices currently offered by Enron and others. Natural gas power plants have also proven to be significantly more reliable than coal or nuclear power.

The letter ended:

I urge you to provide leadership on this important global environmental issue. Not only will many U.S. industries benefit from measures to reduce greenhouse gas emissions, including the natural gas industry, but with the appropriate market-based policies, the measures will result in a cleaner environment, cheaper electricity, more American jobs, and a reduced trade deficit.[37]

Bush went and spoke. Although environmental pressure groups wanted more, the president gave the global-climate negotiations a beachhead. "The United States fully intends to be the world's preeminent leader in protecting the global environment," he stated. "Environmental protection makes growth sustainable [as recognized] ... by leaders from around the world [at] ... this important Rio Conference."

Bush signed the Framework Convention on Climate Change Treaty at the Summit, which the Senate unanimously ratified, given its voluntary—not mandatory—greenhouse-gas GHG reduction goals. The issue was now joined, with tens of thousands of intellectuals, campaigners, and government representatives working on the next steps to override market choices with edicts.

Enron's involvement with the global-warming and climate-change issues would only grow in the years ahead. Existing profit centers were aligned to benefit from mandatory carbon-dioxide reductions, and new profit areas would be added. Superpolitical Enron would work behind the scenes for national and international government policies to ration (price) emissions of this otherwise unregulated nonpollutant.[38] The Lay-led effort would lead one expert to declare Enron "the company most responsible for sparking off the greenhouse civil war in the hydrocarbon business."

---

37. Lay forwarded his letter to DOE deputy secretary Linda Stuntz with a cover note. "I realize ... some limitation on carbon dioxide emissions ... may be contrary to DOE's policy position," Lay stated. "But I think it is both good economics and good politics."

38. See chapter 13, pp. 523–24, 553–59.

From Bush to Clinton-Gore

"Lay said he does not consider himself a Republican," wrote Kyle Pope in his Lay profile in 1991. Indeed, Lay had supported a variety of Democratic candidates and office holders, and some of his most important issues had more Democratic than Republican attraction. Still, Lay remained all-in with his friend in the White House, George H. W. Bush.

Lay had chaired the Bush-Quayle Houston Finance Committee in 1988 and was a member of its National Steering Committee. At Bush's request, Lay was the force behind the Economic Summit of Industrialized Nations, hosted by Houston in 1990. Lay helped plan the Presidential Thank You Celebration in Houston in the same year.

Bush reciprocated, appointing Lay to the President's Council on Environmental Quality, as well as the President's Export Council. Lay was on the advisory board to the Secretary of the Department of Energy, and DOE head James Watkins invited Lay to continue serving on the National Petroleum Council.

What Lay did not do is join the Bush administration, despite an opportunity to succeed Robert Mosbacher as Secretary of Commerce. "I did meet with the president, and I told him that I'm not ready to leave Enron for a variety of personal and professional reasons." With four children in college and many other financial obligations, as well as a growing worldly perch in Houston, few found his decision surprising or difficult to make.

Come reelection time, Lay chaired the host committee for the 1992 Republican National Convention, held in Houston. Enron donated $250,000, and Lay raised much more, just as he had four years earlier. But Bush had real competition on the energy front, and Ken Lay found himself in the middle of it—partly for reasons of his own making. With presidential candidate Bill Clinton and mainstream environmentalism buying into natural gas as a bridge to energy sustainability, and with the upstream industry struggling in a low-price environment, Lay had some shoring up to do for the incumbent. The civil war within the fossil fuel industry was now a civil war between political parties in a presidential election.

Gas executive Robert A. Hefner III called Clinton "the first candidate ever to run for president who really understands that natural gas is different from oil and what natural gas can do for our country." And Clinton's running mate? "Al Gore has been a long-term friend for the natural gas industry and helped pass the Natural Gas Policy Act to get the deregulation of natural gas on the road." But it was more than Hefner. Shell, Texaco, the American Gas Association, Enron, and others were splitting their contributions evenly between the political parties.

Lay answered Hefner in *Natural Gas Week*. "The good news is that both the Clinton-Gore team and the Bush-Quayle team say they are strong supporters of natural gas." But, Lay continued, Bush's first-term victories for gas were decisive. Bush enacted the Clean Air Act Amendments of 1990, which helped gas politically at the expense of coal. Bush's National Energy Strategy, much of which was about to become law as the Energy Policy Act of 1992, streamlined natural gas pipeline permitting; amended the Public Utility Holding Company Act of 1935 to facilitate independent power production (such as by Enron); subsidized compressed natural gas to break into the commercial transportation market; and provided alternative minimum-tax relief to independent drillers. Comparatively, Lay added, it was Democrats who were behind most of the 1970s energy legislation, including the infamous Carter-Mondale Fuel Use Act of 1978.

"Let me conclude by saying that I am also putting my personal support into the re-election ... for what I am confident they will not do," Lay closed. "They will block by veto or otherwise any attempt to reimpose wellhead price or other regulation on our industry as markets continue to tighten up."

This debate attracted other vigorous voices. Warned Vinod Dar, former head of gas-marketing pioneer Hadson Gas Systems: "The gas industry should ponder carefully before rushing to embrace groups who claim that the organizing principle of the world today is the environment." Industry gadfly Edwin Rothschild, the energy policy director of Citizen Action, begged to differ. Noting how the Bush administration had lost opportunities to help natural gas, Rothschild predicted "a natural gas industry revitalized by a Clinton-Gore administration."

As Election Day approached, Hefner took a page out of Ken Lay's playbook to argue in *Natural Gas Week*:

> Clinton and Gore believe that by meeting global carbon dioxide goals we will *not* lose jobs (as the Bush administration insists we will), but will increase domestic employment as well as enhance our economy.... [They] believe all of this is possible *because* of their belief in the American people and their great spirit, ingenuity, and technical ability.

He closed: "Vote for Clinton and Gore—the natural gas industry's Dream Team."

In his final defense before Election Day, Ken Lay called Bush the "energy president" for his 100-proposal National Energy Strategy, "the most comprehensive and balanced energy policy I have seen in over 25 years in the energy industry." Lay concluded: "President Bush not only knows energy policy, he has lived it. George Bush is the 'energy president'."

Although Clinton-Gore won the election, the contest in the gas industry was a virtual tie. *Natural Gas Week*'s Jennrich summarized the tickets on election eve: "In the end, energy appears to be an important part of Clinton's economic plan, and within the energy spectrum, natural gas seems to be Clinton's major fuel of choice." The verdict? "He deserves the natural gas community's vote." Industry elders George Mitchell and Oscar Wyatt also declared for Clinton.

Bipolitical Enron was ready for either outcome, given Lay's concurrence with the Clinton-Gore administration on the global-warming issue. Still, after the election, the Lay-Bush relationship continued. Lay fundraised for the George Bush Presidential Library Foundation, although his choice of the University of Houston (where Lay received his doctorate) was bypassed in favor of Texas A&M University as depository.

Soon, Bush *fils* would become the object of Lay's entreaties. George W. Bush would be elected governor of Texas in 1995, whereupon Lay would be (re)-appointed to the Governor's Business Council. Tellingly, it was Democratic Governor Ann Richards who had first appointed Lay to the council.

———

Enron favorably described to employees the prospects of a Clinton-Gore administration. "President-elect Clinton has said that the cornerstone of his national energy policy will be the increased use of domestic natural gas, both to reduce imported oil as well as to clean up the environment." The November 1992 newsletter added:

> There probably will be a great deal of attention devoted to global warming and a strong push for limitations or reductions of CO_2 emissions. Senator Gore has been an avid proponent of a strong global warming policy and has advocated reducing CO_2 emissions to 1990 levels by the year 2000. This should provide a real opportunity for gas since it emits 1/2 less CO_2 than coal and 1/3 less than oil.

Inside Enron, Terry Thorn was the big winner from the election. The former president of Mojave Pipeline and then Transwestern Pipeline, the quasi-academic with business sense and an affable management style, the core Democrat and Friend of Bill, had a new title: Senior Vice President, Government Affairs and Public Policy. Operating from Houston, Thorn would oversee the busy Washington office led by Joe Hillings and Cynthia Sandherr.

The regime change was hailed by the natural gas industry. "Natural Gas Industry Sees New Ally in Clinton" read the headline in *Natural Gas Intelligence*. "Oklahoma Cheers 'Dream Team,' Sees Gas as Priority Issue" reported *Natural Gas Week*. INGAA and AGA gushed positively, while gas producers were supportive but concerned about drilling policies under Gore.

"New Energy Secretary Good for Gas" read another headline when Clinton tapped Hazel O'Leary as Secretary of the US Department of Energy. Enron's Thorn wasted no time inviting O'Leary to Houston to explain the Clinton administration's energy agenda. "Quite frankly, you are an unknown quantity for many people in the industry and few are aware of the aggressive and innovative initiatives you are pursuing at DOE," he wrote.[39]

———

39. Introducing himself to O'Leary (they had not met), Thorn added: "Before my recent promotion, I was President and CEO of Transwestern Pipeline Company, a strong supporter of Clinton, and active in the campaign."

Meanwhile, Rich Kinder reached out to O'Leary's number two, Deputy Secretary of Energy Bill White, a Houstonian who would now learn energy on the fly as a Friend of Bill. "You are exactly the type of dynamic, hard-charging person we need in federal government today," Kinder wrote. Many more missives would come from Enron's Washington office as Lay's political vision of natural gas atop the environmental and economic agenda took shape.

———

At the 1992 Rio Earth Summit, President Bush signed a 178-nation agreement called Agenda 21 (as in 21st century) calling for the international community to take a "more integrated approach to decision making ... to facilitate the integrated consideration of social, economic and environmental issues" for sustainability. Pursuant to this agreement, and on its first anniversary, President Clinton created the President's Council on Sustainable Development (PCSD) to "develop and recommend to the President a national sustainable development action strategy that will foster economic vitality." The crucial term *sustainability* was defined as "economic growth that will benefit present and future generations without detrimentally affecting the resources or biological systems of the planet."[40]

Ken Lay was appointed to the 25-member group, joining energy CEOs Kenneth Derr of Chevron and Richard Clark of Pacific Gas & Electric. The rest of the group was from the Environmental Left, with administration officials and such pressure-group leaders as Fred Krupp (executive director of the Environmental Defense Fund) and John Adams (executive director of the Natural Resources Defense Council). A few other corporate representatives were mixed in with mostly nonprofit advocacy representatives—but none from the free-market side.[41]

"There has to be an increased dialogue between the private sector, environmentalists, and the government," Lay told the press, "if we are to solve some of these environmental problems ... in ways that are economically efficient." Clinton himself commented on the new task force: "America can set an example by achieving economic growth that can continue through the lifetime of our children and grandchildren because it respects the resources that make that growth possible."

PCSD was Al Gore's pet creation. "We must make the rescue of the environment the central organizing principle for civilization," he had stated several years before in *Earth in the Balance*. "Whether we realize it or not, we are now

———

40. For a description of the (politicized) term *sustainable development*, as well as the author's history with PCSD as Ken Lay's representative for Enron, see Internet appendix 7.1, "PCSD and Sustainable Development," at www.politicalcapitalism.org/Book3/Chapter7/Appendix1 .html.

41. For more detail, see chapter 13, pp. 553–59.

engaged in an epic battle to right the balance of our earth, and the tide of this battle will turn only when the majority of people in the world become sufficiently aroused by a shared sense of urgent danger to join an all-out effort."

Figure 7.4 While nominally a Republican, Ken Lay became a favorite of President Clinton and Vice President Al Gore with Enron's support of their administration's global-warming position. Lay joined other corporate executives, including Kenneth Derr of California-based Chevron, to split the fossil fuel industry on the climate issue.

Ken Lay, privately, was not a big Al Gore fan. But he was happy to let Gore arouse concerns for natural gas to exploit. "In my judgment," Lay lectured to environmentalists, "natural gas will play a dominant role in helping us achieve 'sustainable development'—not only in the U.S., but around the world."

Environmental Enron

"At Enron, we always had a sensible environmental ethic," reminisced Mick Seidl five years after the company's collapse. Lay's former president at Houston Natural Gas and then Enron explained:

> We tried to be as green as possible. We were pushing natural gas as an alternative to diesel fuel and coal, which are heavier polluters.... We always cared and

talked about the environment because we thought it gave us a competitive advantage.

"I'm not an apologist for capitalism, nor am I an apologist for the environmental movement," he concluded. "I'm an apologist for good common sense."

Lay too favored reasonableness in the abstract: "What we really need in this country and others is to prioritize our environmental goals based upon some good cost-benefit analysis" instead of "a fairly emotional and ad hoc basis." Indeed, as a large vertically integrated energy company, Enron had many environmental issues that were more about EPA command-and-control than efficient environmental remediation. Lay mentioned toxic-waste remediation, whereby cheaper cleanup alternatives were foregone. Transwestern Pipeline was at the center of a multimillion-dollar PCB cleanup that was not of Enron's making.[42] Lay heard the stories from the field, where zealotry trumped science and common sense. He wanted *reasonable* regulation, the natural gas advantage aside.

Both before and after Seidl's exit in January 1989, Enron was playing its high cards—and exercising its fiduciary responsibility. But when Lay's lobbying went from reactive to proactive, from removing regulation to imposing it, from promoting market neutrality to rent-seeking, Enron crossed a major public policy line.

Lay's oil-import fee was problematic legally, practically, and intellectually. Enron's all-in climate crusade controversially accepted one interpretation of physical science as decisive and ignored the hard political-economy questions of how to regulate carbon dioxide effectively and economically. When it came to CO_2, it was Enron first, and energy consumers and taxpayers last.

Lay's climate crusade also positioned Enron for what would soon come: investments in solar power, wind power, and energy-efficiency services. "The energy company of the future has to be very much involved in three energy forms: natural gas, renewable energy, and conservation," Lay opined. But none of Enron's forthcoming investments in these areas would prove profitable, quite unlike Enron's coal bet later in the decade.[43] Enron's forays into wind and conservation also took business away from natural gas. On the transportation side, Enron's modest NGV investment would be lost, and the company badly overplayed its hand with its MTBE bet. Still, natural gas had plenty of politics going for it, and green imaging helped ENE as a momentum stock. Lay, in other words, had his reasons.

---

42. Enron inherited the problem with the purchase of Transwestern from Texas Eastern Transmission Company in 1984. Polychlorinated biphenyl was a lubricant manufactured by Monsanto and used in compressor stations moving natural gas over long distances. Transwestern's $10 million tab was shared with Monsanto and passed through to consumers as part of FERC-set maximum rates.

43. See Introduction, pp. 31–32.

Politicking Elsewhere

Enron's multitudinous political interactions kept its founder busy elsewhere, as it did the company's growing government affairs staff. Business-unit executives were not immune. At Lay's urging, and by setting the example, virtually all executives donated to Enron's political action committee (PAC), which in 1992 dispensed $281,000 for federal political races.

Politically powerful consultants were signed up. Gulf War hero Thomas Kelly, who briefly joined Enron's board of directors after retiring from the military in 1991, was hired to push a gas-fired power plant project in Kuwait. In 1993, Lay hired former Secretary of State James A. Baker and former Secretary of Commerce Robert Mosbacher to push negotiations in the Middle East (Mosbacher briefly joined Enron's board). Not much would result from Lay's "Big Shot buying binge," but press releases about early negotiations kept Enron in the news.

A risk-taking, first-in mentality made Enron the leading recipient of tax-payer-backed financing from the Overseas Private Investment Corporation (OPIC) and the Export-Import Bank (Ex-Im), as discussed in chapter 6. When OPIC and Ex-Im funding was threatened by Congress, Lay and Enron's Washington office went on red alert to counter fiscal conservatives and some environmental groups.

PUHCA Reform

Legislative reform of electricity, allowing independent generators and marketers to enter markets previously monopolized by utilities, was a major policy front for Enron. The Public Utility Regulatory Policies Act of 1978 (PURPA), joined by rapidly advancing technology (gas-fired cogeneration), had fortuitously helped Enron create a politically based power-generation profit center, discussed in chapter 5. But another inherited law, the Public Utility Holding Company Act of 1935 (PUHCA), limiting electric utilities to one contiguous system, prevented Enron and other independents from selling power on the open market in more than one area without special exemption.

PUHCA reform got on a fast track in 1991 as part of major legislation teed up by the Bush administration. In speeches, Lay took issue with Houston Power & Light and other utilities lobbying for the status quo. HL&P was content with its franchise-protected market and not interested in acquiring or being acquired by another company. PUHCA reform favored independent generators specializing in gas versus Don Jordan's coal-heavy company.[44] The new world was also welcomed by a few progressive utilities, and none more than PSI Energy Inc., headed by Enron-ex Jim Rogers.

---

44. HL&P opposed reform "designed to promote the increased use of natural gas" for potentially "plac[ing] our nation's electricity supply system in serious jeopardy."

Houston witnessed a tiff between two of its largest energy companies. The stakes were high as Enron envisioned how an expanding market share for nonutility generators would lead to (mandatory) open access for electricity. This "hidden agenda," in the words of one entrenched utility, was Enron's next frontier. Jeff Skilling salivated at a North American trading market that he estimated at six times larger than that of natural gas. (This was later revised to three times larger.)

With Enron taking the lead, most of the gas industry united behind reform. When the American Gas Association did not (it had some gas and electric utility members), Enron withheld part of its AGA dues to cover its own lobbying for PUHCA reform. Victory came with a provision in the Energy Policy Act of 1992 exempting from PUHCA independents generating or selling power at wholesale (as opposed to utilities that sold directly to consumers). So-called exempt wholesale generators (EWG) included a new division of Enron Gas Services: Enron Power Marketing.

Tax Policy

Ken Lay's negative-externality argument against oil and coal relative to natural gas led to his advocacy of differentiated tax policy. An oil-import fee was a border tax, better known as a tariff. Lay also advocated a carbon tax, although he preferred cap-and-trade regulation of CO_2 emissions (a back-door tax) to give Enron another commodity to trade in air emissions.

Natural Gas Week

VOLUME 6, NUMBER 26   JUNE 25, 1990

Inside This Issue . . .
• High court limits antitrust suits . . . . Page 3
• FERC must defend bypass jurisdiction . . Page 7
• Gulf Coast gas prices tumble . . . . Page 20

Late News . . .

INGAA Opposes Carbon Tax But Lay 'Not Quite as Negative'

Natural gas consumers would shoulder the bulk of the estimated $7.2 billion annual cost of the proposed carbon tax being considered as a way to cut the federal deficit, according to an analysis conducted by the Interstate Natural Gas Association of America (INGAA) . . .

VOLUME 9, NUMBER 10   MARCH 8, 1993

Inside This Issue . . .
• Mexico: no gas exports for 20 years . . . . Page 3
• Comments on Btu tax proposal . . . . Page 4
• Canadian, U.S. prices drop . . . . Pages 14, 20

Late News . . .

Enron's Lay Touts Deregulation, Calls Gas 'Winner' With Btu Tax

Saying that "natural gas has been burdened significantly with a difficult regulatory inheritance," Kenneth L. Lay, chairman and CEO of Enron Corp. last week apparently became the first major-pipeline CEO to call for complete interstate pipeline deregulation.

Figure 7.5 Ken Lay looked to tax policy to penalize oil and coal relative to natural gas. This could be done with either a tax on the carbon dioxide content of each fuel or a Btu measure. Only later would Enron quietly get into the coal business.

The Clinton Btu tax proposal in early 1993 was relatively advantageous to natural gas, with a 13 percent price increase ($0.26/MMBtu) compared to oil's 18 percent ($3.47 per barrel) and coal's 26 percent ($5.57 per ton). Renewables, as well as methanol/MTBE and ethanol/ETBE were not covered.

Lay's support, however, evaporated when the Treasury Department decided to tax natural gas at the city gate, not at the wellhead, which severely impaired negotiation of Enron Gas Services's term deals between February and July of that year. EGS, Enron, and the entire gas industry united in opposition.

"BTU Tax Is Dying Death of a Thousand Cuts as Lobbyists Seem Able to Write Own Exemptions," read a midyear headline in the *Wall Street Journal*. The tax proposal died. "Our industry stopped the Btu tax by making our voices heard," crowed Ron Burns, now vice chairman of EGS. But with so many losers and so few winners, the verdict was virtually predestined.

––––

In his role as chairman of the ad hoc lobby group Coalition for Competitive Capital, Ken Lay lobbied for a permanent 10 percent investment tax credit (ITC) in place of a one-year credit as proposed by the Treasury Department. Lay justified his request before Congress as an "economic recovery strategy" and a requirement for "international competitiveness." Equipment used to produce and transport energy, of which Enron had plenty, explained Lay's interest.

Lay warned against increasing the overall corporate tax rate to offset the ITC revenue loss (estimated to reach as much as $17 billion annually). He also recommended reducing the capital-gains tax rate as "another potentially significant spur to our economy." Lay also urged lawmakers to extend the Section 29 tax credit for tight-sands gas, the top public policy priority of Enron Oil & Gas.

An Energy Philosopher?

The private-public dynamo with such titles as Mr. Houston and Mr. Natural Gas was *All Enron, All the Time*. Mighty Lay and Mighty Enron was the gist of Kyle Pope's profile. How else to explain the man who was doing so many things in so many places with so many constituencies?

With his academic credentials, a novel strategy that split the fossil fuel industry in three, and deft lobbying of pragmatic environmentalists, Lay donned the mantle of energy expert and big thinker. Whereas other energy executives thought in terms of quarters and the upcoming year, Lay's messages had a social-good, longer-term quality that *seemed* to set him apart.

The Age of Oil was about to decline, Lay declared. Natural gas would bridge the fossil fuel era to a renewable-energy epoch. "I would guess that, within a century or so, we are going to see a big share of our total energy needs served by renewable energy," Lay stated. A complete transformation to 100 percent renewables was forecast in the range of 200 to 300 years.

But was Enron's architect an energy prophet—or a faux philosopher sanctimoniously promoting his bottom line? Ken Lay certainly read Christopher

Flavin, the most thoughtful of the environmental energy activists. Flavin's books and booklets championing a government-directed transition to renewables were worth study.[45] But the Worldwatch expert *assumed* rather than *justified* his fossil-fuel alarmism. His lawyer-like briefs did not carefully consider opposite views. His footnote-laden work was glorified advocacy, not true scholarship.

Lay did not consider the *fundamental physics behind consumer energy choices.* Conventional energies were cheaper and more reliable than politically correct renewables (wind and solar) because of their density (versus diluteness) and built-in storage (versus intermittency). William Stanley Jevons explained the difference in his 1865 tome *The Coal Question* (described in chapter 7 of *Capitalism at Work*). Vaclav Smil and others explained the why behind market choices in Lay's time, if he had really wanted to know.

Dr. Lay (as he liked to be called in public) was a corporate executive in a big hurry, not an analyst. Rather than work from consumer-driven market reality out, he worked inward from politics and imaging. "To [Lay] knowledge was a means to an end," remembered Terry Thorn. "He lacked what I would call an intellectual curiosity, by which I mean acquiring knowledge outside what you specifically benefit from."

Natural gas was Lay's niche, and he did not despair going from his high cards (gas for electric generation) to the low cards (compressed gas for vehicles). Lay was not satisfied with gas's emission advantage with the politically defined criteria pollutants; he was ready to indict what had hitherto been deemed a nonpollutant, carbon dioxide, to help natural gas at the expense of oil and particularly coal.

Lay was fork-tongued at times. He was all for lower electricity prices when it came to natural gas in power generation ("cheaper electricity means economic growth and job creation"). But he was for higher prices when it came to pricing CO_2 for fossil-fueled electricity generation, not to mention higher gasoline, diesel fuel, and fuel oil prices from oil tariffs.

The PhD economist forgot his education when convenient. Lay's complaints about "irrationally low natural gas prices" and accusations of predatory pricing by integrated major oil companies contradicted the basic economics of variable-cost production and opportunity-cost decision making.

The balance-of-trade argument—which reasons that nations gain greater wealth from money coming into the country (because of exports) than from money going out of the country (because of imports)—had been refuted by

---

45. "Renewable energy has now come of age," Flavin and coauthor Daniel Deudney declared as far back as in 1983. "Increasingly, solar collectors, wind machines, biogas digesters, and many other renewable energy technologies are becoming practical everyday devices used throughout the world." Flavin would spend the next quarter-century writing on energy transformation with the added argument of climate change.

economists since Adam Smith's time. Yet Lay deployed it to urge the use of natural gas instead of oil. "The U.S. balance of trade deteriorates as America's growing dependence on foreign oil increases," he opined, not recognizing that imports pay for exports and that trade per se was good. A negative trade balance for Texas or Houston versus its neighbors, after all, meant nothing. The statistics were not even collected.

Compared to Lay, Samuel Insull (of *Edison to Enron*) was an intellectual and truth-seeker despite the flaws that overtook him late in his career. "Insull was *authentic ... hands on ... realistic*"—a true company builder and leader in his prime. Insull was a Samuel Smiles man; Lay was otherwise, and thus imprudence came to envelop his corporation. That would make for a risky, rough road ahead. So would a political capitalism model of management that contradicted the epithets bestowed on Lay: "the philosopher-king of energy deregulation" and "Enron's free-market visionary."

Part IV

Jeff Skilling

Introduction

Enron's breakout in the early 1990s centered on natural gas commoditization. Enron Gas Marketing (EGM), renamed Enron Gas Services (EGS) in 1991, was the locus for turning the power-generation market from coal to gas as part of Enron's quest to become the *world's first natural gas major*. This bold vision, which had deep public policy implications (via environmentalism), began with gas demand but quickly went to supply in order to allow end users to get their preferred product.

The EGM/EGS heyday marked a high point for the natural gas industry. Other marketers, the most prominent being the U.S. Natural Gas Clearinghouse (later NGC, then Dynegy), also sprang up in response to the business opportunity created from mandatory open-access (MOA) rules promulgated by the Federal Energy Regulatory Commission (FERC).

By the late 1980s, EGM was supplementing its short-term (spot) sales with multimonth and multiyear contracts. (The large capital requirements of the industry—estimated by Enron to be $25 per Mcf per year from exploration and production to marketing and transmission to power generation—required price certainty under long-term contracts.) In the early 1990s, EGS created a macro-market in gas products. The old days, when one company's gas would literally flow point to point, gave way to network economies and financial (derivatives) trading.

Between 1990 and 1993, Enron's burgeoning natural gas merchant function would expend $60 million on proprietary systems "that permitted the organization to function as the trading desk of an investment bank." The buying and selling of gas and related transportation services across North America—varying in time (multimonth, multiyear, hybrids), quality (firm, interruptible, hybrids), and price (variable, fixed, hybrids)—represented a major advance in methane merchandizing. It was also the most enduring contribution of Enron in its brief life.

The Enron of fame and infamy arguably began with the 1990 hiring of Jeff Skilling, formerly of the consultancy McKinsey & Company, and with his assignment to energize the newly created Enron Finance Corporation. The challenge was to create a long-term gas-supply market to meet the demand for long-term contracts that had been proved by Gas Bank (discussed in chapter 5). This foundation, coupled with the successful launch of gas-futures trading (via NYMEX), would lead to financial products (derivatives based on physical products) for hedging and other purposes.

With John Esslinger remaining in place atop EGM's physical trading, a new team would emerge in the Skilling era: Gene Humphrey (long-term gas supply),

Mark Frevert (long-term gas sales), Joe Pokalsky and Kevin Hannon (derivatives), and Andy Fastow (structured finance, also known as *securitization*). Lou Pai would take over for Pokalsky and hire a quantitative specialist, Vince Kaminski, to model EGS's book of business in order to better price products and gauge overall risk for the corporation.

With a new accounting methodology that immediately booked estimated future earnings from long-term contracts, EGS became Enron's second-largest income generator in 1992. Mark-to-market accounting became central to Enron's 15 percent annual-earnings growth story, which propelled ENE as a momentum stock. But this future-now philosophy would have negative consequences as the decade progressed.

———

Enron Finance was just the beginning of three years of innovation, restructuring, and expansion at EGM/EGS. Three new divisions were formed in 1991: Reserve Acquisition, Enron Power Services, and Enron Risk Management Services. The next year, three more were added: Enron Producer Services, Enron Gas Transportation and Trading, and an EGS–Canada unit to reach North American scope.

In 1992, EGS's domain grew when the methanol and MTBE facilities, as well as the commercial side of Houston Pipe Line, were assigned to Skilling. In that same year, EGS bought retail-natural-gas-marketer Access Energy, followed in 1993 by emissions trader AER*X and intrastate pipeline and storage company Louisiana Resources.

Some innovative offerings by Enron would not survive the creative destruction of the marketplace. A group of geographical gas-pricing points (hubs) did not take as an alternative to the central NYMEX point of Henry Hub, Louisiana. EnGas and GasTrust were other offerings that fell short (see chapter 9, p. 387). A game effort to commercialize natural gas vehicles (Enfuels) was discontinued.

EGS became a very large company within a company in the period under review. In becoming the largest buyer and seller of natural gas in the United States, EGS did not record any write-offs, much less scandal. On the contrary, the unit's reputational value in the outside market was very high, important for both counterparty confidence and credit ratings.

At year-end 1993, EGS's thousand employees provided one-fifth of Enron's income, three-fourths of its revenue, and nearly one-half of its assets. Better yet, EGS was *asset-light*, using other companies' transmission systems as easily as it used Enron's own interstates. The secret of EGS, and thus Enron, was its entrepreneurial alertness to a once-in-a-generation regulatory opportunity.

8

Gas Marketing: 1990–1991

Gerald Bennett understood where the interstate market was going. As head of Houston Pipe Line and related operations, he saw how intrastate pipelines were tailoring gas packages for end users. Bennett was at the drawing board in 1988 with a McKinsey & Company consultant tasked by Ken Lay and Richard Kinder to better commoditize interstate gas in order for Enron to increase volume and improve margins.[1]

That collaboration with Jeff Skilling resulted in Gas Bank, described in chapter 5, a way to partition gas supply at known prices for future delivery to help long-lived power plants obtain financing for construction in a PURPA world. With demand outstripping long-term supply, Enron's effort shifted from traditional Enron Gas Marketing (EGM) activity to a new unit, Enron Finance Corp. (EFC), described by a Harvard study as "a developmental laboratory for the financially linked products and services related to [Gas Bank]."

Skilling, the head of McKinsey's energy and chemical practice and soon to become one of Enron's top executives, was unique. Ken Lay was very smart and knew it, but he diplomatically labored to get things done. Tough-guy Rich Kinder was approachable and fair, excepting for those times when he had to *make earnings* in Enron's hothouse. John Wing was a nonpareil prima donna yet talented enough to survive and thrive. Jeff Skilling was the smartest of the

---

1. Gerald Bennett's role is examined in Internet appendix 5.3, "On the Formation of Gas Bank," at www.politicalcapitalism.org/Book3/Chapter5/Appendix3.html.

smartest guys in the room, whose strengths and weaknesses would contribute to Enron's heights—and ultimate demise.[2]

More than *creative destruction*, Enron's gas-merchant business was the story of *creative construction*, the assemblage of new ways of doing business for a new era of customer choice. "The company was intent on finding voids in the gas market and then filling them with new services," one study explained. Adam Smith's invisible hand was at work in that new competitive arena, but the visible hand of government had created the particular forum via mandatory open access (MOA) for interstate natural gas pipelines.[3]

Regulatory Change, New Markets

Prior to the 1980s, the (regulated) interstate pipeline purchased gas at the wellhead in one state for sale to a gas distributor (or municipality) in another state under long-term contracts. Deliveries were either firm or interruptible, and most of the gas was purchased from the pipelines for resale, with the utility or municipality offering the end user a few basic choices. There were no intermediaries to *customize* supply to a particular end user.

Also, pursuant to administrative regulation by the Federal Energy Regulatory Commission (FERC), there was no profit in the buying and selling of the gas commodity in the interstate market. The profit came in the embedded transportation charge, part of what was a single bundled price at the terminus of the interstate line. For example, gas bought at the wellhead for $1.50 per MMBtu with transportation costs of $0.40 was sold at the city gate for $1.90 per MMBtu. The gas commodity was simply a dollar-for-dollar passthrough, bought and sold for $1.50 per unit, subject to FERC reasonableness reviews. The $0.40 per MMBtu summed up to the interstate's nongas costs plus an allowed rate of return on its invested capital (called the *rate base*).

MOA for interstates created a new industry segment: *for-profit gas commodity marketing*. The old world of interstate pipelines—selling a bundled product of gas (at cost) and transportation (for profit)—was over. FERC Orders No. 436, No. 497, No. 500, and No. 636 got the interstates out of the commodity function by the early 1990s, and FERC granted EGM and many other independents certificates of public convenience and necessity to buy and sell gas at negotiated

---

2. The term "smartest guys in the room" comes from the title of an Enron history. Another author described Skilling as a person who "never doubted that he was the smartest person in every room he ever entered."

3. The debate about what is free market or not in a mixed economy is discussed in Internet appendix 3.6, "'Market Conforming' Intervention: Free Market or Not?," at www.politicalcapitalism.org/Book3/Chapter3/Appendix6.html.

EVOLUTION OF THE NATURAL GAS MERCHANT SYSTEM

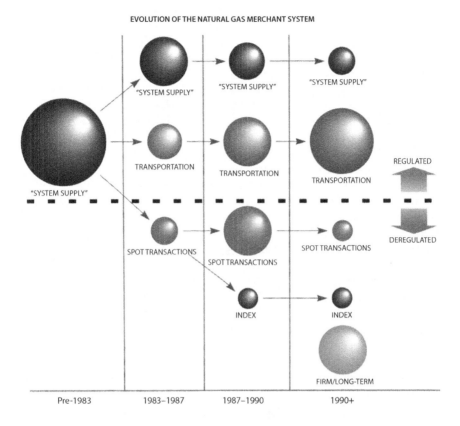

| Pre-1983 | 1983–1987 | 1987–1990 | 1990+ |

Figure 8.1 FERC's regulatory restructuring of the natural gas industry is shown in this illustration from Enron's *1990 Annual Report*. Unbundling sales from transportation gave Enron two profit centers in place of one, a key reason why Ken Lay refocused his company toward interstate gas transmission in 1984–85.

(nonregulated) rates in interstate commerce. EGM was *jurisdictional* to federal regulation but federally unregulated.[4]

Now, independent entities bought and sold the gas and turned to the pipeline for transmission only. To continue the example, instead of $1.90 per MMBtu,

---

4. *Jurisdictional* means that the buying and selling of gas in interstate commerce (involving interstate transmission) was potentially subject to FERC regulation. *Jurisdictional but unregulated* represented a new stanza in the history of just-and-reasonable regulation by the Federal Power Commission, later FERC, under the Natural Gas Act of 1938.

the pipeline received $0.40 per unit to recover its transportation costs and make its authorized return. But the pipeline also did not have to spend $1.50 per MMBtu for the gas. Intermediaries bought and sold that gas and typically bought transportation to make the delivery. EGM thus rebundled the market, making a profit margin on the hypothetical $1.50.

Breaking take-or-pay contracts with producers to exit the merchant function created special costs for interstate pipelines. FERC required all interstates, including those of Enron, to write off some those transition costs rather than pass them through to their customers. The salvation, however, was the opportunity for the same gas companies to profit from nonjurisdictional sales formerly made (at cost) by their interstate lines.

Ken Lay saw the future in two profit centers where one had existed before. Richard Kinder's Come to Jesus meeting (chapter 5) got Enron's interstates to cede their merchant function to EGM (and Citrus Trading in the case of Florida Gas Transmission). This changeover was natural because Enron's two predecessor companies were marketing leaders: Houston Pipe Line in Texas and Inter-North in the Midwest. In fact, Northern Gas Marketing (NGM), founded in 1983, was far enough ahead of the pack to decline the invitation of Ken Lay (while he was at Transco) to join the U.S. Natural Gas Clearinghouse (later named NGC, then Dynegy). NGM became the guts of the postmerger HNG/InterNorth Gas Marketing unit, soon to be EGM.[5]

"Enron has been a proponent of [FERC] Order 636 because it effectively deregulates the merchant function," the 1992 annual report explained. "It also provides customers a wide variety of sales, transportation, and storage options from pipelines, producers, and marketers, such as Enron Gas Services, rather than just a single regulated sales service that had been offered by pipelines until the mid-1980s." Added Ron Burns from Enron's transmission side: "Pipelines will play an important physical role, but aggregators and marketing companies will play much bigger roles." Make no mistake: Enron was a pipeline company *and* a merchant.

Gas-merchant deregulation was tied to new regulation elsewhere. Interstate pipelines, the conduits to move gas for merchants and marketers in order to consummate deals, were federally required to offer nondiscriminatory rates and otherwise provide comparable service to all customers. This ensured that an outside marketer could compete with the pipeline-affiliated marketer that otherwise could (and would, in the early 1980s) limit access to independents to move its own gas. EGM would staff up to intervene in interstate-pipeline rate cases before FERC, even those of Enron pipelines, to ensure such neutrality.[6]

---

5. For Lay's early effort to form a fourth industry segment (marketing) at Transco and nationally, see chapter 1, pp. 76, 90–91; and Bradley, *Edison to Enron*, pp. 339–41, 346–47.

6. See chapter 9, pp. 416–17.

EGM interventions included its sister pipelines Florida Gas, Transwestern, and Northern Natural. The goal was to treat interstate carriers the same, affiliated or not, to ensure that transportation favoritism was not a bottleneck to deal making from the marketing side. Yes, in a nonregulated world, EGM could preferentially deal with Enron's three pipelines to exclude other marketing companies, but then several dozen other interstates could do the same against EGM. In this way, Enron gained access to the *whole* national grid, even where its own pipelines did not traverse. Thus, it could be *asset light,* having *reach* rather than *ownership.* (This would be much more the case with open-access electricity, for which Enron did not have interstate transmission assets.)

——

Enron did not create the new regulatory regime that would portend its greatest hour. The transformation of one profit center into two was well on its way when Houston Natural Gas Corporation purchased Florida Gas Transmission and then Transwestern Pipeline.[7] But the company to be renamed Enron, seeing large profit in MOA's infrastructure socialism, provided early industry support for the DOE-inspired, FERC-led transformation, as did InterNorth's Northern Natural Gas Pipeline, the major interstate that merged with HNG in 1985.[8]

Absent federal price and service rules, the gas industry would have been dominated by vertically integrated majors: megafirms with joined production-transmission-distribution operations, not unlike the oil majors that produced, transported, refined, and marketed oil.[9] Given state and federal regulation, the natural gas industry *de-integrated* between (upstream) exploration and production, (midstream) pipelines and storage, and (downstream) retail distribution. This cleavage led to coordination problems between arm's-length parties, or what integration proponents called the "three-headed monster."[10]

Enron chose not to formally integrate because of regulatory disincentives, none greater than a 1935 federal law limiting outside ownership of local gas

————

7. See chapter 1, pp. 87–88.

8. See Internet appendix 1.2, "Mandatory Open Access for Interstate Natural Gas Pipelines," at www.politicalcapitalism.org/Book3/Chapter1/Appendix2.htm.

9. Public-utility regulation, which came to dominate natural gas, never took hold in the oil industry, because of a lack of interest from either the independents or majors and because (from a reformer perspective) there was workable competition from the wellhead to the service station.

10. US natural gas regulation began downstream at the local distribution level and expanded to the midstream (transmission) and then the upstream (wellhead) in the quest for just-and-reasonable pricing. For the nature of industry integration versus nonintegration, aka the theory of the firm, see Bradley, *Capitalism at Work*, pp. 113–17.

distribution to one contiguous system.[11] Instead, Enron established quasi-independent divisions at or near the top of their respective industry segments.

Enron Oil & Gas was a top natural gas–focused exploration and production independent. Enron's four interstate pipelines had coast-to-coast, border-to-border reach, although open-access regulation limited their synergies as one system. Enron's gas marketing would become the national leader, although under federal open-access rules, it could not preferentially use its affiliated interstates. This was not the case with Enron's intrastate Houston Pipe Line and later-purchased Louisiana Resources Company.

Peoples Natural Gas, InterNorth's distribution company, was sold to reduce debt soon after InterNorth acquired HNG in 1985. But with gas-fired cogeneration plants at home and abroad, Enron could claim to be in the downstream arena, although not as a traditional utility buying gas at the city gate to resell to residential, commercial, and industrial customers.

Enron Gas Marketing: 1990

EGM had an active year in 1990 outside of creating Enron Finance Corp. Sales averaged 1.5 Bcf/d, a one-third increase from 1989, equally divided between West, Midwest, and South/East. Revenues rose commensurably, with earnings between $10 million and $15 million before interest and taxes. This return was on invested intellectual capital, not physical capital that had to be built or purchased from either retained earnings or new debt. Still, this was a small, evolving profit center. The bet was on the future.

EGM finished the year strong with a 23-year, 33 MMcf/d contract with New York Power Authority to fuel a proposed cogeneration plant on Long Island. The first 10 years of the $1.3 billion deal would come from Gas Bank 2. With other executed contracts, Enron proudly reported that EGM's year-end sales mix had risen to one-half long-term, one-half spot.

Gas Bank 2 placed 190 Bcf of multiyear, fixed-priced gas with eight customers. This was half as much as Gas Bank 1 (which drew heavily on EOG for supply), and that lit a fire under Enron and consultant Jeff Skilling to create a new division within EGM to procure long-term gas. Still, with Gas Bank and other commitments, long-term contracts as a percentage of total sales averaged 40 percent in 1990 versus 26 percent the year before.

Forty percent of EGM's volume did not involve use of an Enron pipeline, indicative of how federal regulation made Enron bigger than physical Enron, that is, *asset*

---

11. The federal Public Utility Holding Company Act (PUHCA), described in Bradley, *Edison to Enron* (pp. 219, 236, 309, 433, 513), was a thorn in Enron's side as the company developed independent cogeneration plants that might be in violation of the law. PUHCA was also a barrier to EGS's aspirations to trade electricity, which would require an exemption from FERC.

light. Sixty percent of EGM's volume in 1990 was in the short-term spot market, delivered on interruptible (best-efforts) basis. Forty percent was under firm (guaranteed delivery) contracts, which were longer term, higher margin, and *noninterruptible* (backed by Enron's corporate guarantee). The latter was where EGM wanted to go—and needed to be to beat coal for new capacity for electric generation, whether built by a utility, a municipality, or an independent power producer (IPP).

Enron Gas Marketing
(MMcf/d)

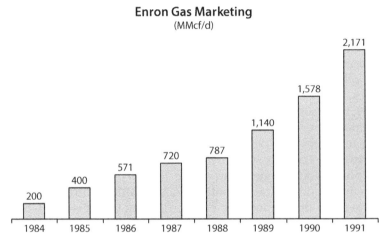

Figure 8.2 Gas marketing, a new business in the mid-1980s, grew significantly beginning with Gas Bank in 1989–90, Enron Finance in 1990, and Enron Gas Services in 1991.

Multiyear deals were higher margin, but spot prices needed to hold steady given Enron's lack of price hedges. (How much Enron was buying short versus selling long was a guarded secret.) Full hedges were not possible given an illiquid, scattered market, and Enron was accustomed to shouldering uncertainty to capture market.

Hedges needed a central pricing and delivery point, in place of regional prices voluntarily reported in *Gas Daily*, *Inside FERC Gas Market Report*, or *Natural Gas Week*—and for later months, not only the upcoming one quoted in the trade rags. A futures market for price discovery and liquidity was well on its way with benefits to Enron, although Enron decided to compete against it with a four-hub proprietary pricing program.

Hub Services vs. NYMEX

A major innovation by EGM in 1990 was *hub pricing*, a program designed to compete with the new gas-futures market offered by the New York Mercantile Exchange (NYMEX). Enron and other gas firms had freely advised NYMEX officials to ensure a successful launch, but Enron wanted to do something bigger by offering futures at centrally accepted locations (hubs) other than NYMEX's Henry Hub in Louisiana.

NYMEX gas futures were conceived after the successful launch of an 18-month crude-oil futures contract in March 1983 at Cushing, Oklahoma.[12] With open-access transportation and spot markets just developing, however, the idea of gas futures was not ripe. Getting pipelines committed to supply a geographical hub—physical delivery to which would serve as the basis for comparable pricing—and obtaining FERC's blessing for open-access carriage, proved slow.

By 1988, the frontrunner for geographical pricing of NYMEX gas was Katy, Texas, where dozens of interstate and intrastate pipelines intersected near a large Exxon gas-processing plant with excess pipeline capacity. Several pipelines consented to a NYMEX short-haul rate at Katy, but Enron's Houston Pipe Line and others held out, looking to see whether they could make a market themselves.

In 1989, interest shifted to a point in Erath, Louisiana, where more intersecting pipelines were interested, and new capacity was being built for a hub. Although not a physical player at Erath's Henry Hub, Enron representatives helped create the contract structure and delivery mechanism, knowing that a NYMEX point would benefit the whole industry. Now with critical mass, NYMEX's application to trade monthly 10,000 MMBtu contracts out 12 months was approved by the Commodity Futures Trading Commission (CFTC, established 1974) for an April 1990 start.

Five months in, the *Wall Street Journal* described Henry Hub as "the most successful commodity trading vehicle launched in seven years." NYMEX gas contracts brought speculators and hedgers together to determine real-time prices—supplanting reported prices to trade magazines in over-the-counter deals. Monthly spot-price swings of 20 percent or more gave plenty of reasons to play futures. Bid week, the monthly exercise of buyer-seller matching and next-month nomination by marketing companies, adjusted its schedule to mesh with that of Henry Hub.

The one-national-price market became a basis from which to price gas in different locations: plus or minus Henry Hub in cents per MMBtu. In first-quarter 1992, with CFTC approval, NYMEX gas futures were extended to 18 months, and options trading, based on futures contracts, was added in October. Early resistance to NYMEX in some parts of the gas patch all but evaporated.

————

EGM's Cathy Abbott was tasked with all things related to gas futures. Beginning in 1988, she and other industry executives—such as Lance Schneier of Access Energy (later bought by Enron)—advised NYMEX's team, led by vice

————

12. For a history of oil-futures trading in the 1970s and prior, see Bradley, *Oil, Gas, and Government*, pp. 1048–55.

president of research Robert Levin. Abbott was part of Enron's so-called Group of Six to devise an alternative to Henry Hub in order to make margins on Enron's selected points.

With NYMEX gas trading imminent, EGM announced a four-location receipt and delivery program, under which Enron would take title and set prices. In addition to buy and sell quotes at Henry Hub for East delivery, the hubs were Wharton, Texas, serving Texas and the South; Waha, Texas, for gas to California; and Kiowa County, Kansas, covering the midcontinent. The Pacific Northwest was out of reach of EGM's program, as were Canada-US flows.

"We will quote prices as far into the future as a balance of buyers and sellers can be reasonably ensured," EGM president John Esslinger told the press. With EGM offering continuous prices and firm transportation for those with hub-pricing master agreements (300 sent in the first wave), customers could hedge, speculate, physically move, and swap between the four locations for any start date, 10 days out. In contrast to the monthly spot market, there would be no bid week. Shorter than NYMEX, EGM quoted forward prices for each of the next six months. If interest and liquidity followed, longer strips (time periods of months beyond six) would be considered.

While calling gas-futures trading at Henry Hub "the right idea," Esslinger predicted that the market would come Enron's way because of regional price differentials and Enron's firm transportation services. But NYMEX as *the* national, liquid price became the benchmark from which basis differentials were added (Henry Hub plus or minus cents per MMBtu) in Enron's three areas, as elsewhere. By year end, EGM had executed only 85 contracts, aggregating 80 Bcf, far below the "very ambitious goals [set] at the start of the project," Esslinger admitted. NYMEX, meanwhile, was executing thousands of contracts by the day.

Other hubs were evolving, such as Carthage, Texas (by Union Pacific), and Blanco, New Mexico (by Gas Company of New Mexico for Pacific Northwest deliveries). Katy, Texas, too, was (finally) coming together. Still, NYMEX was king, with basis differentials joined by firm transportation backup to perfect hedges.

Enron Finance Corp.
In 1987, Enron turned to the consultancy McKinsey & Company for ideas to enhance Enron Gas Marketing, which had Claude Mullendore buying gas for John Esslinger to sell, mostly in 30-day spot markets. Supply was scarcely available for long-term fixed-priced commitments, which promised higher margins than the 4–5 percent average on spot sales.

What was missing was a committed pool of long-term gas from which quantities could be assigned to discrete packages in order to serve a forward market for utilities, independent power producers, industrials, and municipalities. The buyer was interested in hedging supply risks and/or price risks in place of chancing the short-term market. EGM, too, needed to lay off risk when buying short and selling long, which would require derivative (financial) products around physical gas supply.

Enron's Gerald Bennett went to work with consultant Skilling on how to customize gas supply to demand. The result was *Gas Bank*, wherein trusted engineering estimates of reservoir deliverability and longevity backed long-term sales. Pipeline space to get the gas from the field to the customer was doable with MOA contracting by EGM or the customer.

The Gas Bank idea had been coolly received by Enron pipeliners in a late-1988 meeting, but Kinder empowered Skilling to get EGM into high gear. Kinder was right: He and Skilling had little trouble selling out Gas Bank in late 1989. The placement of 366 Bcf of 10-year, fixed-priced gas generated $200 million in net present value, Skilling later calculated.[13]

The concept was proved, but Gas Bank 2's smaller placements the next year indicated that a scale-up and new approaches were needed. A whole new supply approach was required to intersect with ready demand in order to create a forward market in long-term, price-certain natural gas.

Formed in early 1990, Enron Finance needed special leadership. Lay and Kinder approached Jeff Skilling, who was coming off a major promotion at McKinsey. After Skilling passed, the two settled on Don Gullquist, previously Enron's treasurer. But several months and little change later, Gas Bank 2 placements were exhausting the supply bucket. Traditional ways of doing business were not working.

"What Enron needed—and, what the whole natural gas industry needed—was someone who could show them the way" in natural gas commoditization. Lay and Kinder again turned to the consultant, first with InterNorth and now with Enron, who seemed always to find the right answer. This time, he accepted.

Jeff Skilling. Jeffrey Keith Skilling (1953–) was born in Pittsburgh, Pennsylvania, the second of four children of Tom and Betty Skilling. Tom, a Lehigh University graduate in mechanical engineering, made a career selling valves to water plants, power plants, and other heavy industry in the Midwest. His employment moved the family from Pittsburgh to Westfield, New Jersey, and then, when Jeff was 12, to the Chicago suburb of Aurora. Here, Tom rose to vice president of sales for Henry Pratt Company, but his expectation to head the company fell short.

With Tom on the road, Betty Skilling ran the house. The family had to be frugal; still, it was solid middle-class urban living, well above the rural Missouri farm life experienced by Kenneth Lee Lay, 11 years Jeff's senior.

---

13. See chapter 5, pp. 236–38.

Jeff attended public schools in Aurora and graduated as a member of the National Honor Society. He was bright, inquisitive, focused, and a doer; his demeanor was quiet and thoughtful. He was also melancholy, behind his dry sense of humor, but his shyness belied a rebel quality that lay beneath the surface.

Like Lay, his smallish size and average coordination kept him from competitive athletics. But he excelled at just about everything else. He "waltzed" (his mother's term) through school to graduate with distinction and receive scholarship offers from Princeton and Southern Methodist University to study engineering. But a break-out moment occurred when the teenager assumed operational responsibilities at a UHF community-access station in Aurora. He had been doing all the menial tasks when a programming crisis fell to Jeff. He demonstrated technical ability by keeping WLXT-TV on the air, rewarding all for the extra time he had spent with the operators. From then on, Jeff found himself in the control room. The long, paid hours at the station were fulfilling compared to school's "sheer boredom" (his words), at least until the station closed.

Skilling's formative years foreshadowed things to come. He led in boyhood adventures and technical projects with his brothers and friends in tow. Jeff had a propensity to test the odds physically, which resulted in accidents. "Jeff spent half of his life in a cast," remembered brother Tom III, whose fascination with weather patterns would lead to a distinguished career at Chicago superstation WGN-TV. (Tom had also gotten his meteorological start at WLXT-TV.)

College was next for the "scholastic achiever, part techno-geek, and part comer." Settling on SMU in bustling Dallas, the 17-year-old engineering student's major hobby was investing his dutifully saved money. The exhilaration of monetary gains and the agony of losses (he lost big) led him to investigate money management. One influential book (self-described as "the first scientifically proven method for consistent stock market profits") was *Beat the Market*, covering such things as "marking to the market."

With poor grades in engineering, Jeff left the field to study business, which he found creative and stimulating compared to engineering's "mind-numbing" exactitude of numbers and formulae. One assigned paper in business class particularly caught his attention: securitizing commodity contracts.

At SMU, Skilling joined the Beta Theta Pi fraternity, making him, coincidentally, a brother-in-the-bond to Ken Lay, who had been president of the University of Missouri chapter a decade before. But while Omer Lay instilled an optimistic streak in Ken, Jeff's mother was just the opposite, always fearing that Jeff's accomplishments would never be enough. ("Sooner or later," she would say, "they'll get you.")

Skilling's 4.0 grade point average in business mitigated his 2.6 GPA in engineering, good enough to get job offers after graduating in May 1975. After marrying his college sweetheart, Sue Long, Jeff moved to Houston to join the asset and liability group of First City National Bank. At Houston's largest bank, he started in operations before moving to corporate planning, becoming (in two years) the youngest officer at the bank. One highlight was a formula Jeff derived that helped the bank identify check kiting.

———

But Skilling wanted more than a banking career. A master's in business would elevate his prospects, he decided. Night school at the University of Houston would allow him to remain corporate planning officer at the bank. Yet there was another option: going for the top—entry in Harvard University's two-year MBA program.

It so happened that the dean of the program was interviewing in Houston after Jeff decided to apply. The most famous of the pre-Enron Skilling stories occurred during this meeting. At the Hyatt Regency downtown, the site of many Enron all-employee meetings to come, the dean challenged Jeff to distinguish himself—and he did. By the end of the day, an offer from Harvard Business School (HBS) was won. He called his mother in tears. This was big, really big, in Skilling parlance. In August 1977, he resigned from First City to relocate in Cambridge, Massachusetts, with Sue.

Remembered as "razor-sharp" and personable by his Harvard classmates, Jeff was enthralled by the give-and-take classroom dissection of real-world business. He took an interest in business history and energy, particularly in how John D. Rockefeller had rationalized the oil industry in the late-nineteenth century. Jeff was remembered for his cold, calculating approach analyzing the HBS case studies, suggesting an amoralism to come.[14]

Skilling graduated in 1979 as a Baker Scholar, an honor reserved for the top 5 percent in his class. After a year as an associate with the business consultant MJH Nightingale, he joined the more prestigious McKinsey & Company in its Dallas office.[15] Skilling's interest in and focus on energy resulted in a move to Houston six month later. Soon, he was head of McKinsey's North American natural gas practice.

Skilling's mentor at McKinsey was John Sawhill, formerly deputy secretary of energy under Jimmy Carter, and previously head of Richard Nixon's Federal Energy Administration. One client was InterNorth, which Skilling helped to recapture lost gas sales through a strategy of discounting spot gas. Another

———

14. Skilling's amoralism was described as "his harshly libertarian view of business and markets." However, as documented in Part I of Bradley, *Capitalism at Work*, classical liberals since at least Adam Smith have described, defended, and urged a character-centered moral view of business and free markets.

15. McKinsey was founded in 1925 around the talents of James McKinsey, a University of Chicago accounting professor and management expert whose consulting took on a life of its own. His firm became "known as much for its arrogance as for its enormously high—and nonnegotiable—fees."

project involved the headquarters debate after InterNorth and HNG merged. (Skilling recommended Houston, not Omaha.)

Skilling was elected a director at McKinsey in 1984. Five years later, as head of the firm's worldwide energy and North American chemical practice, he was elected partner, an unusually young selection. Skilling's rumored pay, near $1 million annually, reflected his great skills, tireless hours, and a top client list, led by Enron.

It had not been an easy decision for a top McKinsey executive to take a flyer on Enron. Kinder and Lay had first approached Skilling in the triumphant aftermath of Gas Bank's sellout. But Jeff wasn't ready to take a large pay cut and put all his eggs in one basket. He enjoyed the diversity of projects (only half his time was dedicated to Enron), and he was not sure he had the personality to be a corporate manager (he might not have).

Five months later, having found himself in too many managerial meetings as a McKinsey partner, and worried that what he started at Enron would not get finished, he thought differently. Gas Bank was very one-legged. Supply could not meet the pent-up demand for long-term, price-secure gas. New gas-procurement strategies had to be coupled with a way to transfer the long-term purchase and sales contracts to outsiders, given Enron's capital constraints. In short, a whole new business awaited creation. "How often do you get a chance to change the world," Skilling thought to himself.

With a large pay cut from his McKinsey salary, but with a pile of incentives from Enron, Skilling agreed to a multiyear employment contract lasting through 1994. The minimum base salary of $275,000 was joined by 75,000 stock options, letting him participate in ENE appreciation risk free. And as was done for EOG's Hoglund, Skilling received an equity grant in Enron Finance Corp., with appreciation that began at 5 percent of the first $200 million ($10 million) and continued from there, reaching $19 million at $400 million and $31 million if EFC's value reached $1 billion in assessed value. Additionally, a $950,000 corporate loan would be forgiven in the normal course of events so long as he remained at Enron. A noncompete clause ensured that Skilling would not leave to start his own company or join a rival like Natural Gas Clearinghouse.

Compared to other employment contracts atop Enron, Skilling's was behind Lay and Kinder and ahead of Mike Muckleroy (CEO, Enron Liquid Fuels), Ron Burns (CEO, Enron Gas Pipeline Group), and Jack Tomkins (Chief Financial Officer).[16] Based on recent history, Skilling could expect to double his

----

16. Under the terms of their 1989 multiyear employment contracts, the minimum annual salaries were Lay $750,000, Kinder $500,000, Muckleroy $350,000, Burns $245,000, and Tompkins $235,000. Stock options and company loans were similarly ranged, with Lay at 250,000 shares and $2.5 million in loans and Kinder at 150,000 shares and $1.5 million in loans. Compared to their minimum base salaries, actual cash compensation was about double for the five in 1990. Forrest Hoglund, meanwhile, had a separate package at EOG.

base salary in annual cash compensation and earn a lot more in equity appreciation.

Lay also agreed to support a special request from Jeff: an accounting change to recognize the revenue of long-term contracts not as cash received (the *accrual basis*) but on a present-value, *mark-to-market basis*. Skilling had his reasons, professional and personal. Historical, cost-based accounting was imperfect and could even be illogical at times. Mark-to-market was logical—when it could be based on known realities (SEC-designated Input 1 and Input 2 levels of data). But when it was unsupported (using Input 3 models), it amounted to counting one's chickens before they hatched.

Such a changeover would require extra diligence and integrity given its judgmental, even subjective, nature—and its premium on the present at the expense of the future. Strong bourgeois virtue was needed where the accounting rules allowed discretion.

A Running Start. "I am very pleased to announce," wrote Ken Lay to employees in June 1990, "that Jeff Skilling has been named chairman and chief executive officer of Enron Finance Corp. effective August 1, 1990." It would be Enron's most significant hire since Forrest Hoglund joined the company nearly three years before—and a new beginning. Lay explained:

> Jeff is joining us at a critical point in the financial development of the natural gas industry. Enron Finance has the opportunity to provide needed financial resources to producers to fund drilling. Due to the decline in funding available to producers, the opportunities for Enron Finance are significant, and we expect additional staffing as the company grows over the coming year.

Enron Finance sought to rectify a major industry problem: scarce credit for gas production given weak and uncertain prices, as well as from bank regulators all but shutting down production lending in the wake of the energy price crash of 1986.[17] Producers needed financing to mine the gas required for long-term sales, particularly given stagnant prices. For EGM to receive higher margins (versus month-to-month sales), sizeable quantities of known, in-place, *secure* gas were needed to anchor long-term contracts.

While basking in (historically) low prices, gas buyers knew that the spot market could reverse, leaving any new gas-dependent power plant stuck.

---

17. Between November 1985 and March 1986, the spot price for West Texas Intermediate crude oil fell from $28 per barrel to below $10 per barrel. With posted prices in 1986 about half as much as the year before, cash flow and asset values fell proportionally. Employment in the upstream industry fell by approximately one-third; many energy-focused banks and savings and loans had crashed. Fully half of the S&L debacle took place in Texas, and federal banking regulators made traditional energy lending very hard in order to prevent another boom-and-bust cycle.

Enron's opportunity was to reallocate risk to get higher, known prices for producers and known, competitive prices for gas plants.

"Our charter is to develop new mechanisms to lower inherent risk in the business and to lower the cost of capital," EFC's marketing material explained. New financial products offsetting risk for different parties ranged from "traditional loans to gas-denominated financings to complex, long-term fuel price hedges." Specifically,

> For upstream players (producers, gatherers, processors), EFC offers traditional reserve loans, hedged and leveraged reserve loans, non-resource project finance, non-monetary production payments, and acquisition financing. For downstream players (pipelines, cogenerators, gas consuming industries), EFC provides individually designed price hedges, hedged loans, and non-resources project finance.

This was the business that the energy banks once did—and more. In fact, reservoir engineers once employed by banks to calculate collateral (gas reserves) were now working at Enron.

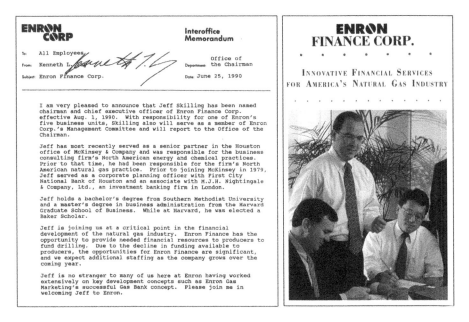

Figure 8.3 The hiring of Jeff Skilling in 1990 would bring highs and lows to the corporation in the next decade. Two key early hires by Skilling (standing) were Gene Humphrey (left) for producer finance and Lou Pai (right) for derivative products.

Without greater supply and price certainty, natural gas would lose to coal in terms of new power-plant capacity to meet electricity growth. Utilities and their regulators did not mind a default to unquestionably abundant coal. Had not

natural gas been curtailed in the 1970s? And did not a coal plant offer more rate
base (on which to calculate a regulated rate of return) compared to a gas plant?

But EFC sought more than just receiving interest payments in return for col-
lateralized risk capital, as would a bank; EFC sought to obtain call rights to the
found gas. Volumetric production payments (VPPs), as devised by Enron, supported term-sales contracts, provided hedging services at the wellhead, and
securitized the contracts to free capital and remove the risk to Enron.

There would be modest activity to report by Enron Finance in 1990, but Skilling
was drafting a team to win in this new competitive arena. The first hire was
Gene Humphrey, a Citibank energy banker in New York City who had interviewed with Kinder for the job that Skilling had just accepted. Humphrey was
well known inside Enron for helping finance the employee stock option plan
(ESOP) that had put up the money to remove Irwin Jacobs from the picture
several years before.

Joining EFC August 29, Humphrey's task was to create a quasi-banking
function to serve gas producers, replacing the lending function all but abandoned by Texas banks and other institutions. His first hire was Monte Gleason,
a reservoir engineer formerly with First City Bank in Houston (where both Jeff
Skilling and Rebecca Mark had worked). Gleason, in turn, would staff up for
the work ahead: estimating the proved reserves and flow rates years out for the
gas that Humphrey would finance.

Two executives were found within Enron. George Posey came from Enron
Gas Services to oversee accounting and finance for EFC. Lou Pai was picked
from Enron Gas Marketing, where he had been vice president of gas supply for
the Gulf Coast and for Gas Bank. Before that, Pai had been in a small unit under
Bruce Stram, Corporate Strategic Planning, which became an incubator for new
talent. (Mark Frevert and Dave Duran were other alumni.) Pai's logistical mind
(his father was an aeronautics professor) would find a good home putting
together key pieces that went into the new gas-merchant business, though his
career at Enron would later flame out.

Long-term gas and a trading operation needed money; long-term sales contracts required working capital. Jeff Skilling wanted to grow—fast. How would
all this be financed? Rich Kinder did not want to borrow the money; his job was
to reduce the debt-to-capital ratio for a higher credit rating, the very rating that
EGS needed. (Already, Enron's ratings were problematic for AAA
counterparties.)

This left *securitization*, whereby long-term executed contracts could be bundled together and sold as securities to outside parties. Doing so both removed
the liabilities from Enron's balance sheet and generated cash to fund the next
deal. The job of securitization went to Andrew Fastow, a whiz-kid securitization
specialist hired from Continental Bank in Chicago by Gene Humphrey. (To
secure the hire, a position was found in Enron Treasury for Andy's wife, the

former Lea Weingarten, an ex-Houstonian who happily returned to family and friends.)

As manager of finance at EFC, Andy Fastow received a starting salary of $75,000, a signing bonus of $20,000, and a minimum bonus of $25,000 for the next year (he joined in December 1990). He also stepped into a corporate culture that he would help define.

Pai and Fastow were "guys with spikes," to use a Skilling term. Unlike the gentlemanly Humphrey and studied Posey, Pai and Fastow were not only talented but also moody and difficult. Outside of the 39th floor, Ken Lay checked such personalities, as did Forrest Hoglund across the street at EOG. Rich Kinder was tough but respectful, although apologies were occasionally in order. The mercurial John Wing from cogeneration was outside Enron's walls.

In the new year, other key executives joined EFC, including Mark Haedicke as head of legal. His job was not only to oversee all commercial contracts of the group but also to devise a way to secure long-term natural gas yet stay out of exploration and production, which was the purview of EOG, not EFC. The final result would be a legal invention for the history books, the aforementioned VPPs.

Partnering was also part of Skilling's initial plan. With gas-futures trading under way on the NYMEX, Skilling approached Bankers Trust in mid-1990 to form a joint venture to develop a derivatives and trading market in natural gas. By year end, a memorandum of understanding was reached: In return for 40 percent of the profits, Bankers Trust assigned a three-member team—two in New York and one in Houston—to work with Lou Pai's group.

The collaboration profitably tapped into a new field. Six months in, Enron paid its partner $3 million, which Bankers Trust considered too low under its arrangement. Enron was concerned about how much value was in play—what it envisioned earning for itself. Negotiations on a final deal broke down in July, whereupon Kevin Hannon, on loan from Bankers Trust, was told by New York to copy the collaborative technology (risk books and pricing models), delete the remaining files, and return home.

Hannon's weekend exit caught Pai and Enron by surprise. Joe Pokalsky, a financial-products trader experienced in basis risk (geographical differentials for the same product), was hired from Chemical Bank in New York to fill the breach. Pokalsky, "the man who was the real star behind the gas trading business, the one Skilling relied on," immediately elevated the financial trading desk, finding the margin on natural gas to be much higher than interest rates. (Pokalsky, a strong personality, left Enron in 1993 after losing a power struggle with Lou Pai.)

Hannon rejoined EGS nine months later. "I initiated the first natural gas book for Bankers Trust after returning to New York," he remembered, "but I realized the core of the business was still in Houston." His new job was to form a transaction-structuring group to review and approve all ECT's natural gas pricing for North America. Six months later, he formulated and managed EGS's index and basis risk books for exchange-for-physical trading. (*Index* referred to pricing based on a published quotation; *basis* referred to pricing at one particular location relative to another.) Hannon's foundational work would be part of an ascension that led him to the presidency of Enron Capital & Trade Resources, North America, and then to CEO of Enron North America.

Bankers Trust would go on to compete against Enron in the natural gas arena, as did Morgan Stanley and AIG Financial. Jeff Skilling would not partner in that way again.

———

Skilling arrived to find different shades of corporate culture at 1400 Smith Street in Houston. Public-utility regulation made for a slow (but prudent) culture at the interstate pipelines, more so at Northern Natural Pipeline and Florida Gas Transmission and less so at start-over Transwestern. Houston Pipe Line was steeped in the good-ol'-boy Texas network, although intense competition was upending things. Then there were Ken Lay's brainy hires—the smartest guys—probing the industry's new competitive contours.

The fast folks at Enron Gas Marketing, the logistics mavens and the deal makers, had been attracting the best from the other three cultures. It was from here that EFC would build.

McKinsey-like, Skilling sought a meritocracy characterized by transparent, open communication; pay for performance; creative destruction; and employee rivalry. The workplace was about upending norms, not just linear improvement. The attitude was *break-it-and-make-it-better*, not *if-it-ain't-broke, don't-fix-it.* Joseph Schumpeter, Peter Drucker, and Gary Hamel were iconic thinkers for the Lay-Skilling model of Enron amid industry tumult.[18]

The 31st floor was reconfigured, with central trading areas replacing long corridors of offices. Remaining offices received glass walls for transparency. Gone were the "formal decor and hushed atmosphere that characterized the activity on other floors of the building." An open staircase between two floors, another Enron first, further connected Skilling's army.

The number of job descriptions was compacted from two dozen to four: associate, manager, director, vice president. Compensation reflected performance (*mark-to-market performance*), not seniority, with peer review replacing hierarchical review. This was all new; Enron Finance, to Skilling, was a breed apart, on a par with Microsoft as one of the major start-ups of its era.

Enron Gas Services Group: 1991

"Over the past several years, Enron has focused on creating a range of new, unregulated natural gas services geared toward providing longer-term price

———

18. See Bradley, *Capitalism at Work*, pp. 83–84, 101–3, 116 17, 126–30, 158.

and volume security," Rich Kinder announced to employees in January 1991. "Through our Gas Bank, firm index contracts, [and] Hub Pricing, Enron Finance has been on the leading edge of what we believe is a major growth area in our industry." In fact, gas buying and selling was emerging as a top Enron money-maker and a business unto itself, "raising a range of issues related to internal management processes, accounting and legal treatment, and supply and marketing execution," Kinder noted.

"As a result, I am pleased to announce the formation of the Enron Gas Services Group [combining] the activities of Enron Gas Marketing and Enron Finance." The support activities of both units would come together "to build the entire range of Enron's nonregulated natural gas merchant services." The one exception was gas bought and sold off of Florida Gas Transmission by Citrus Corp., which was only half-owned by Enron and unaffiliated.

Jeff Skilling was named chairman and CEO of the Enron Gas Services Group (EGS); John Esslinger, president and COO. Of EGS's two subsidiaries, EGM remained focused on long-term marketing and EFC on producer financing and derivative products. Accounting and Finance were consolidated under George Posey; Legal, under Mark Haedicke; and Regulatory Affairs, under Shelly Fust. Fust's job included making sure that the interstates were easily accessible routes for EGS gas under federal open-access regulation.

A third unit, Power Services, was formed to market gas to electricity generators, whether independent, utility, or municipal. Mark Frevert, who had previously done much at Enron to capture power plants for gas, was named head. Joining Frevert's group was Ken Rice, who would soon distinguish himself as a top gas dealmaker and a Skilling confidant—and the soiled soul who would flame out with Enron Broadband Services at decade's end.

Other divisions reporting to the Office of the Chairman (Skilling and Esslinger) were Marketing under Dan Ryser, Structured Finance under Gene Humphrey, Derivative Products under Lou Pai, HUB services under Peter Weidler, Basis Management under Cathy Abbott, and a new Analysis group headed by Mike Walker. Under Marketing (Ryser), the regional divisions were Western, Midwestern, and Eastern, each with a supply and a marketing head. Operations was under Julie Gomez; Operational Planning, under Mary Lou Hamilton.

"With these changes," Kinder's memo concluded, "I am convinced that the new Enron Gas Services Group is positioned to lead the company to great success in 1991 and beyond."

————

The merger of physical and financial, with some shared employees, would be followed two months later with more tweaks. With tepid market interest in HUB Services, Weidler's new assignment was vice president of Reserve Acquisition, to buy and trade gas-reserve pools in order to supply long-term (8- to 15-year) fixed-priced contracts, as well as place tax-advantaged gas (certain gas categories paid less tax) with gas distributors and municipalities.

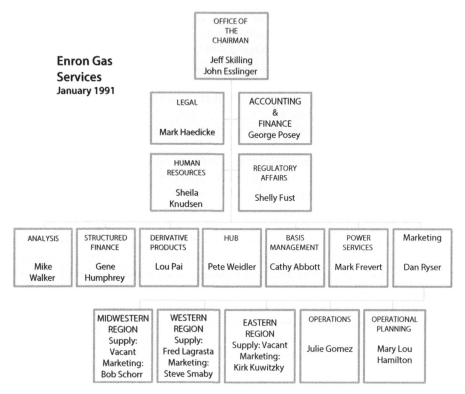

Figure 8.4 The organization chart for Enron Gas Services in first-quarter 1991 showed five support groups, six profit centers, and five marketing sections.

A pricing team was formed under Lou Pai to create and maintain month-by-month multiyear quotations at which EGS would buy and sell gas per location (hub). The so-called bid/ask curve, offering instant pricing for long-term transactions of different durations, was key to both deal profitability and internal compensation. An executive committee was created to review the numbers and set strategy, policy, and personnel issues for EGS. There was much to do to prevent the upstart from getting ahead of itself amid the rush to capture market share.

An off-site meeting several weeks later brought together 16 leaders to define and evaluate the new organization and identify and confront "gray areas" of responsibilities. Skilling set the tone for the organization by imparting his "tight/loose" management philosophy, with risk management, legal, and financial being tight and everything else loose.

Reserve Acquisition Corp.

A division of Enron Finance, Reserve Acquisition Corp. (RAC), was tasked with securing gas in order to mirror EGM's long-term sales. Price-certain supply matched to (higher) price-certain sales meant arbitrage profits, if done right.

But producers, perennial optimists, did not want to lock in what they saw as a depressed base price for multiyear payments. Even worse for EGS, producers were having a hard time getting drilling capital from the hitherto heralded energy banks in Texas and elsewhere. This was the job for Gene Humphrey of Enron Finance.

"In a state reeling from the [1986] energy bust, Enron became the bank of choice—it was the only bank, really, to support the industry." But rather than buying reserves or acreage as Enron Oil & Gas did, EGS devised a contract under which it had first rights to buy the gas flow and in-the-ground supply from a producer. The producer was responsible for operations, but contracts could allow the producer to deliver a like amount of gas to Enron from a third party.

Thus, this volumetric production payment exchanged up-front Enron cash for gas obligations from the producer. Enron's cash-for-gas, unlike a bank's cash-for-cash-with-interest—was for a future gas stream that was legally protected in the event of producer insolvency. (The VPP trumped the royalty owner's rights.[19])

The crucial part for Enron was the engineering knowledge to forecast the gas reservoir's stock of recoverable reserves and achievable flow rate. Such information became an in-house competency at EGS under Monte Gleason, helped by new technology (3-D imaging in particular) that could map reserves and estimate long-lived flow rates.

EFC's first VPP ("the first kind of Special Purpose Entity in which Enron would dabble") was executed in April 1991 by Gene Humphrey. A $45 million prepayment to Forest Oil bought five years of deliverability totaling 32 Bcf (about $0.71/MMBtu). Better yet, netted against sales, this VPP alone generated an estimated $7 million in profit.

The next month, a $24 million VPP by Humphrey funded Zilkha Energy, drilling in the Gulf of Mexico, again for future production. Rather than sell properties or borrow against proved reserves, Zilkha sold a set amount of future production from its offshore properties but retained title to the reservoirs themselves. EFC then eliminated the risk of its "carve out" by hedging prices and

---

19. The overriding royalty, a synthetic debt instrument, created a legal interest apart from the rest of a producer's assets in a bankruptcy proceeding. The VPP, which had precedent in the gold and coal industries of an earlier era, reputedly took Enron 18 months and millions of dollars in legal costs to perfect.

interest rates to create arbitrage profits in the firm price of its end-user contract.

Enron made money coming and going from VPPs. First, producers paid an up-front fee to Enron for the arrangement. Second, between gas costs and gas revenue, there was a locked-in spread that was greater than the cost of capital. Better yet for profit-hungry, image-driven Enron, future profits became immediate earnings through mark-to-market accounting.

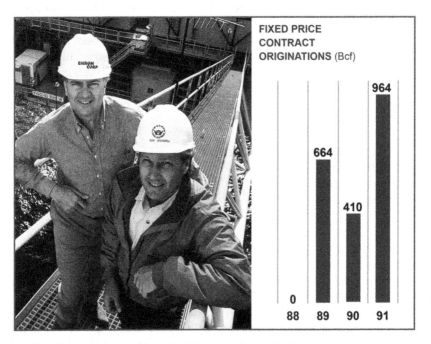

Figure 8.5 VPP was a major Enron legal innovation to fund gas producers and thus supply end-user contracts. Gene Humphrey, vice president of Enron Finance (left), is shown with Rob Boswell of Forest Oil Company (right) after their first VPP in April 1991. VPPs took off to support long-term fixed-priced contract originations.

A *New York Times* stocktaking of Enron's reconstituted merchant function counted 35 producers providing long-term gas to 50 customers as of May 1991. "We're conducting an activity like asset-liability management at a bank," Skilling told the newspaper of record. "To the buyer, it's all coming from Enron in the sense that Enron has a corporate guarantee behind the contract."

Managing risk and lowering capital costs, all the while putting money into the hands of the producers, was a major innovation of EFC's Reserve Acquisition Corporation. "If you offered to buy gas at a fixed price for 20 years, they would throw you out," reminisced Jeff Skilling. "But if you offered to hand the producer $400 million to develop reserves, he saw you as a partner."[20]

Reserve Acquisition Corp. ended 1991 with $121 million in production payments, compared to $4 million the year before. Reserves of 76 Bcf and one million barrels of crude oil were under contract. But most of all, price-competitive gas was finding a home downstream.

Enron Power Services

Enron Power Services (EPS) was formed in February 1991 to market gas to electricity generators. Mark Frevert, who cut his teeth on the Florida power market for Enron, was the vice president in charge of the new unit, which joined EGM and EFC within Enron Gas Services.

The most active market for long-term gas was independent power producers (IPPs), which under federal law sold their generation to electric utilities at the latter's (regulatory-approved) avoided cost.[21] This mandate by the Public Utility Regulatory Policies Act of 1978 (PURPA) was intended to force competition where before only the franchised, monopolistic utility generated power for its needs.

Ken Rice joined Frevert's new unit as head of IPP marketing. With fixed-priced input (gas) contracts to join fixed-priced output (electricity) contracts, such projects were made creditworthy (bankable). Coal could not play the supply-fear card in the new world of Enron.

It was different with electric utilities that preferred to build coal plants for their new capacity. Rate-base regulation meant that coal's higher plant costs (capital investment) resulted in more profits compared to lower-cost gas plants. This perversity played to a fear that gas shortages would return. The price controls responsible for forced curtailments were all but gone, but experts such as McKinsey's John Sawhill, not to mention the coal lobby, preached gloom for gas. State laws encouraged utility regulators to favor coal over gas as well.[22]

EPS was eager to market gas as reliable and affordable for new capacity built by utilities, not only for independent power producers. Reaching that was the mission of Geoff Roberts, hired by Frevert six months after Rice to market gas to utilities. (Roberts had negotiated against Frevert several years before as an

---

20. Another niche for Enron Reserve Acquisition Corp. was "tax-advantaged long-term reserve packages to municipal local distribution companies and municipal power companies," another aspect of EGS's government-enabled niche.

21. For a discussion of IPPs and avoided cost, see Internet appendix 1.5, "Public Utility Regulatory Policies Act of 1978 (PURPA)," at www.politicalcapitalism.org/Book3/Chapter1/Appendix5.html.

22. See chapter 7, pp. 323, 326.

employee at Florida Power and Light.) Even more than Rice, Roberts needed facts, facts, facts to sell his portfolio.

———

Enron needed to educate others about the fact that gas was cheaper than coal on a life-of-plant cost basis. Ken Lay's Natural Gas Standard came from an EPS study coauthored by ICF Resources that estimated gas-fired power to be one-fourth cheaper than coal for highly utilized (baseload) plants—and still cheaper for low-utilized (cycling, peaking) units.[23]

"Contrary to some previous projections," ICF concluded, "natural gas will regain a significant market share of the electric power generation market in the 1990s." The rapidly improved economics of combined-cycle gas generation and "innovative gas supply options available from firms like Enron" drove the analysis, said ICF, adding that coal economics could still win in certain situations, necessitating a case-by-case evaluation.

There was much for gas to regain in the electrical-generation market. What was a 4 Tcf market in the early 1970s had fallen to 2.6 Tcf in 1986 and again in 1988. ICF anticipated 5.8 Tcf by 1995 and 7.7 Tcf by 2000. Growth would be forthcoming, but these projections would prove to be a decade slow in materializing.[24]

On the supply side, Enron updated its internal study of gas resources in 1991 to find that in a market-based, non-price-controlled world, gas resources were abundant and open ended. The "development and rapid diffusion of new technology" "enhanced seismic techniques, such as 3-D seismic, improved evaluation and completion techniques supplemented by refined fracture diagnostics and enhanced drilling technologies, such as horizontal drilling" were the drivers, found an Enron study authored by Bruce Stram. This "new reality" promised "reasonable prices over the long term."

A 22 Tcf market was envisioned by 2005, which was only returning gas to its historic usage in the early 1970s. In 1983 and again in 1986, consumption fell below 17 Tcf, a one-fourth drop from the peak. Enron's 2005 forecast would prove accurate, despite the fact that gas demand for electric-generation growth would be slower than forecast.

Enron uniquely rebuilt the gas market in the 1990s. Gas Bank had done much to get long-term gas into the mix; the Gas Standard elevated the debate to reverse the 1970s (regulatory-driven) coal-for-gas bias. Enron's market breakthrough came in early 1992 when Sithe Energies Group, a large planned

———

23. See chapter 7, pp. 320–27, for Lay's effort to sell the economic and environmental superiority of gas over coal in electricity generation.

24. ICF's estimate for 1995 was reached in 2006; its estimate for 2000 was finally surpassed in 2012.

cogeneration plant in upstate New York, chose gas on the strength of a long-term supply deal with Enron Power Services, discussed in chapter 9.

Enron Risk Management Services

In March 1991, Enron Gas Services Group formed a fourth major division, Enron Risk Management Services (ERMS), which joined Enron Gas Marketing (1986), Enron Finance Corp. (August 1990), and Enron Power Services (January 1991). Calls, puts, options, forwards, swaps, and sister products—how could any combination of these affect Enron on any day, next month, or in a future year given the company's existing portfolio and new deals? With its formation, figuring that out systemically became ERMS's task.

"Risk management services, broadly defined, are becoming a larger and larger proportion of our business," Skilling and Esslinger explained. "For the calendar year 1991, we are estimating that risk management products will directly or indirectly generate close to 60 percent of EGS's gross margin." The portfolio of long-term contracts, and the Gas Bank and Hub Services contracts in particular, were all about bets on the future: some hedged, some not, and some needing to be.

The creation of EGS in early 1991 included Basis Management, a new function to manage the long-term volume and pricing commitments for different locations. Cathy Abbott left Transwestern Pipeline to become vice president of Basis Management, in charge of setting price differentials for dozens of gas hubs countrywide. Rising executive Lou Pai, meanwhile, vice president of Derivative Products, drew heavily on Abbott's numbers.

Now, Pai was vice president of Risk Management Services and chairman of the weekly Pricing Team meetings. With Abbott and other senior executives, including Skilling and Esslinger, Pai and his team worked out long-term bid/ask curves for gas.

"The challenges of [our risk] growth are many," Skilling and Esslinger wrote to employees. "We need to continue to add quality staff, build and improve our processes and systems, and create and develop new service offerings." Indeed, computing risk for illiquid, developing gas markets was highly subjective compared to the financial-product world that Skilling sought to emulate.

With too few deals at various points to establish basis (point-to-point) differentials, Abbott had to model relative transportation rates to estimate future delivered-gas costs. There were also Gas Bank deals that contractually set a maximum delivered price despite floating, unpredictable transportation costs between the field and delivery point. Enron needed to get a handle on its obligated risks and calculate rational risk-return profiles for its next deals. The segregated, ad hoc deal making of before could no longer sustain itself in EGS's growth mode.

ERMS hired Mark Peterson from First City Bancorporation, Skilling's old haunt, as vice president in charge. Reporting to Peterson were Abbott and Pai.

Figure 8.6 The hub of Enron Gas Services Group was gas marketing, which was divided into three regions (lower right). Jeff Skilling's open-office concept is shown by the cubicles and transparent offices.

But Pai, not Peterson, would emerge in the role of the chief forward-price maker, estimating the price at which traders would sell gas in future periods. And new talent coming the next year would bring Enron's risk-management capabilities into higher orbit. Peterson, meanwhile, played auxiliary roles before departing Enron in early 1993 after only 18 months.[25]

Structured Finance/Derivative Products

VPPs created a cash-flow problem for capital-constrained Enron because EFC paid present money to producers for future gas that only then would be sold for revenue. Andy Fastow was hired to do what the company needed: *securitize* the contracts so that Enron could cash out its profits from locked-in contracts and remove future obligations from the balance sheet.

In the second half of 1991, Enron sold its VPPs to a limited-partnership SPE (special-purpose entity) and issued a corporate guarantee that Enron would purchase at set prices the future gas that the SPE would receive from the VPPs. Enron's gas purchases (needed to fulfill its own long-term contracts) thus created a revenue stream for the SPE not unlike that of a bond for investors. Consequently a 15-bank consortium led by Texas Commerce Bank (where Ken Lay

---

25. Peterson, who had been treasurer at First City, returned to treasury-type activities after Enron with several different firms.

was a director) gave the SPE a $340 million loan, which the SPE would repay from Enron's gas purchases. And this loan was joined by a small contribution from General Electric Credit, for which it would also receive payments. The latter contribution was necessary if the SPE and its debt were to be considered independent of Enron.

All this was an extra step from just dealing with producers, but securitized deals gave Enron present cash to repeat the process to enter more buy-now/sell-later gas deals. Enron was quite open about the existence of the SPE, calling it a "$500+ million 'permanent funding facility'."

Cactus Funding Corporation, the new financial legal instrument, had precedent in home-mortgage pools. The SPE for gas VPPs was devised by Enron Finance's Fastow working with accountants at Arthur Andersen, led by Rick Causey, and lawyers from Vinson & Elkins, Enron's most-used outside counsel. But arcane accounting rules, such as a 3 percent minimum-ownership requirement for outside investors, as well as outside control, had to be observed to ensure independence.[26]

Cactus had various iterations (Cactus Investments). One involved an EOG VPP in 1992 for 124 Bcf of its Wyoming gas for $327 million. By 1993, Enron's securitizations totaled $900 million—all off the balance sheet.

SPE securitization closed the circle for what Enron needed to do to create buyer confidence in long-term commitments to natural gas. Multiyear sales of price-certain supply to end users were packaged and sold to outside investors, allowing EGS to fund its next iteration. "It was the Gas Bank in its final form; outsiders provided cash, producers received financing, customers obtained gas at a reliable price—all with Enron in the middle, profiting handsomely," stated one writer. To Sherron Watkins, "The Cactus SPEs funded Enron's volumetric products payment business, jump starting its trading operation."

The balance sheet solved, an income-statement complication emerged from the securitization. Buying VPPs was a current-period expense matched against future income under long-term sales contracts. The accounting mismatch created present-period losses (discussed later in this chapter), although the deal might be very profitable over the life of the contract under accrual accounting. Enter another accounting system championed by Jeff Skilling for gas merchandizing: mark-to-market, whereby future estimated income was booked in the present.

---

26. GE Credit's contribution, considered an equity investment by Enron, was treated as a loan by GE Credit because Enron was guaranteeing to purchase the SPE's gas in future fixed-price tranches. But as a loan, GE Credit would not be different from the banks' contributions, which would violate the 3 percent outside equity rule for the SPE to be independent of Enron. See also Internet appendix I.3, "Enron's Special-Purpose Entities: From 1991 to 1996, and Beyond," at www.politicalcapitalism.org/Book3/Introduction/Appendix3.html.

Reported Results

Enron's 1991 annual report highlighted EGS's 2.2 Bcf/d volume, up 38 percent from the year before. More than half (57 percent) of sales were long term. New long-term deals (*originations*) more than tripled to one trillion cubic feet.

Rather than four hubs as the year before, Enron was quoting prices at 50 locations for a variety of gas packages and was "one of the largest buyers and sellers on the NYMEX exchange." Combined with its other transactions, Enron was a top-four national gas seller behind majors Chevron and Texaco and eight-year-old Natural Gas Clearinghouse. With the pipelines and EGS, Enron handled 18 percent of the nation's natural gas.

Enron reported "a tremendous earnings increase" in 1991, partly owing to an accounting change from the accrual method to mark-to-market that, presto, increased the bottom line by $25 million from what would have been reported. Income before interest and taxes (IBIT) of $71 million more than quadrupled that of 1990.[27] A key link in the accounting revision, described in the next section, was an Arthur Andersen accountant turned Enron assistant controller, Rick Causey, who joined Enron that March.

Mark-to-Market Accounting

Ken Lay was in a big hurry to remake Enron into an energy giant. It was not only his persona; his upended industry invited it. New projects and whole new divisions were needed to retire high debt and fund the growth needed to become the world's first natural gas major, a vision Lay set for Enron in 1990. And with ENE holdings aplenty, Lay, Rich Kinder, and other top Enron executives needed another big year or two to solidify their financial futures. That year would be 1991—with the help of image over substance.

A major accounting change was explained in the back of Enron's *1992 Annual Report*. "Enron accounts for its price risk management activities under the mark-to-market method of accounting," read a footnote on page 50. "Under this methodology, forward contracts, swaps, options, futures contracts, and other financial instruments with third parties are reflected at market value, with resulting unrealized gains and losses recognized currently in the Consolidated Income Statement."

Market value for long-term contracts, unfolding over future years, the note continued, would be determined by objective factors and *management discretion*.

> The determination of market value considers various factors including closing exchange market price quotations, time value, and volatility factors underlying

---

27. Reported earnings before interest and taxes increased from $15 million in 1990 (and $13 million the year before) to $71 million in 1991.

the commitments, management's evaluation of future servicing costs and credit risks, and the impact on market prices of liquidating Enron's position in an orderly manner over a reasonable period of time under present market conditions.

Mark-to-market, the note concluded, was confined.

Enron's other activities (which are accounted for on a lower of cost or market basis) also enter into forward, futures, and other contracts to minimize the impact of market fluctuations on inventories and other contractual commitments. Changes in the market value of those contracts entered into as hedges are deferred until the gain or loss is recognized on the hedged inventory or fixed commitment.

———

The changeover had taken about 18 months. First, Lay signed onto the concept as a condition of Skilling's hiring. Skilling then persuaded his colleagues, and Enron's audit committee approved in May 1991. Its chairman and lead decision maker was Dr. Robert Jaedicke, an accounting professor turned dean of Stanford Graduate School of Business.

Arthur Andersen, Enron's outside auditor, was next, first with the Houston account team and then at Chicago headquarters. Enron's outside counsel, Vinson & Elkins, and advisers from Bankers Trust (then a partner of EGS) were at the table. Final approval came in January 1992 from the Security and Exchange Commission (SEC) in Washington, DC.

There had been pushback. Early in the process, Enron's David Woytek, a warning voice from the Valhalla oil-trading scandal a few years before, challenged Enron CFO Jack Tompkins about the liquidity of long-term gas contracts, which was needed for proper valuation. Mark-to-guess was not mark-to-market, Woytek argued, and thus income should not be realized in an accounting period unless money changed hands. Woytek also wondered about a growth wall, given that ever more deals were required for mark-to-market earnings growth.

Arthur Andersen had to get over the fact that oil and gas accounting had never been anything but accrual, with costs and revenues recorded as physically incurred. Not convincing its Houston office, Skilling presented to Andersen's top brass in Chicago, which gave the okay so long as the SEC went along. And when the SEC declined to approve after due diligence, Skilling made a presentation at the SEC's Washington headquarters to get the regulators to reverse. Letters followed, with Enron assuring regulators that its marks would be based on "known spreads and balanced positions" rather than being "significantly dependent on subjective elements."

The SEC verdict came in a January 30, 1992, letter to Jack Tompkins approving mark-to-market for natural gas beginning that month. A new chief accountant, Walter P. Schuetze, had just taken over at the SEC, and he believed deeply in the logic of mark-to-market. Allowing Enron to employ the technique would be a step forward.

(Unfortunately, Schuetze had worked only for accounting firms and bureaucracies. He had never served on the staff of an industrial corporation, and his philosophy of mark-to-market accounting depended on the fantastic assumption that companies would call in neutral experts to do their mark-to-market estimates. Post-Enron, Schuetze testified that mark-to-market accounting required "competent, qualified, expert persons or entities that are not affiliated with, and do not have economic ties to, the reporting corporate entity." The idea that Jeff Skilling would allow some outside, disinterested expert to come in and tell him what his assets were worth, regardless of what effect that might have on his numbers, was fanciful. As it was, Enron's revolutionary accounting method secured the safe harbor of an SEC approval, creating a staggering degree of moral hazard for investors, compared to an unregulated market.)

Tomkins's reply letter to the SEC mentioned that Enron would apply the accounting change retroactively to 1991 but that the effect was "not material." In fact, it was. Fast-forwarding earnings of long-term gas contracts executed in 1991 added $25 million to earnings, calculated by subjective factors in light of need and in the absence of price liquidity. The (new) net income of $242 million was 20 percent above that in 1990, which happened to be just the growth number that Enron had promised the Street—and preserved ENE gains that triggered executive bonus incentives.

The *discretion* was on. Champagne flowed on the trading floor with the news of the SEC's approval letter. Numbers met, Lay and Kinder gushed about Enron's "exceptional" financial performance in 1991, led by "strong results from Enron Power [the Teesside project] and Enron Gas Services units." This would be only the beginning, as Enron would go on to apply mark-to-market in new areas and for new purposes. The slippery slope was greased, and Enron was on it.

————

Enron's accounting windfall caught the eye of *Forbes* financial writer Toni Mack. In "Hidden Risks," she noted how Enron had been "the first and, at the time, the only nonfinancial public company to adopt so-called mark-to-market accounting." Gas contracts were not the sort of liquid financial contracts that could be rationally marked-to-market. Taking earnings now left future risks should new costs come in, such as a tax (Lay wanted a climate-related levy) or a transport-rate spike. Customers could default, too.

Mack duly presented Enron's side. Skilling noted how EGM required counterparties to be creditworthy and had built up a $49 million reserve to cover unexpected losses. Kinder dismissed the growth wall: "We think we can maintain a 20% or better growth rate each year."

Still, Mack's admonition hit a nerve. ENE uncharacteristically lagged the market, and Lay fired off a letter to her detailing the list of approvals (the argument from authority). Criticism of Mack by Enron-friendly Wall Street analysts was next.

"We regard the 'Forbes' recitation of risks as an inaccurate portrayal of the business and as showing a lack of understanding of the operations of the EGS unit and the industry," wrote Donaldson, Lufkin & Jenrette. "The article insinuates that mark-to-market accounting is some aberrant methodology that the SEC begrudgingly tolerates," argued Goldman Sachs. "In fact, it is the methodology endorsed by the [Commodity Futures Trading] Commission and is mandated for adoption over the next couple of years as it more accurately reflects the earnings and risks of futures and derivatives positions." (This begged the question of whether Enron's marking was in a *liquid* market—and whether Enron as market maker could make a market truly liquid.) Lehman Brothers dismissed Mack's piece as "misleading" and demonstrative of "a considerable lack of understanding." All reconfirmed their positive outlooks for ENE.

Skilling took his case for mark-to-market to Harvard Business School. A year later, a laudatory HBS case study on EGS stated on the opening page that Enron "could dismiss" Mack's concerns. But the article failed to think of Skilling's application in anything but a perfectly liquid market, using for its example a five-year deal where all parameters were known, EGS's reserve deduction gold, and Skilling impartial. A reality of less-than-liquid time periods or gaming was not raised.

Enron Business in 1994 addressed the issue for employees. "EGS's detractors call it aggressive accounting designed to make it appear as if Enron is making more money than it actually is by booking revenues prematurely from deals that look good today," the piece began. Skilling was quoted on how reality was being served and why Enron was the first to apply it to energy. "Because of the need to stabilize gas prices with the use of risk management tools," Skilling explained, "natural gas contracts today are more like financial instruments than the physically-oriented, highly-regulated documents they were a decade ago." Rick Causey was then quoted about how Enron got approvals internally from auditor Arthur Andersen and externally from the Securities and Exchange Commission.

Enron was being conservative, the article closed. Of the total calculated margin of a long-term contract, 30 percent was reserved for transportation, 10 percent for physical delivery, and 25 percent to cover discounting to a net present value. So a $2 million margin would have a current-year booking of $700,000, a 35 percent value (65 percent discounted).

Who knew of this methodology? Why was it not shared with Mack, if indeed it had not suddenly been hoisted into place? Management discretion was addressing the perceived shortcomings of management discretion—not a good

Figure 8.7 Enron Gas Services' use of mark-to-market accounting, announced in the 1992 annual report, was defended in the employee magazine after receiving negative press. Enron's Rick Causey would increasingly find himself lobbying his former employer, Arthur Andersen, for accounting liberties.

substitute for conservative accrual-based accounting principles for less-than-liquid markets.

———

The raison d'être of marking to market is *liquid, transparent pricing* for the commodity in question. Yet in early 1992, at the annual conference of the Cambridge Energy Research Associates (CERA), Skilling unwittingly blew natural gas out of the mark-to-market water. Between 95 percent and 98 percent of natural gas trades were "spot market or spot indexed," he told the packed ballroom, leaving few transactions to establish longer-term market values. "You need a lot of transactions for liquidity," he said, "and it's not in the cards for the next 5–10 years."

Why did Enron's gatekeepers pretend that natural gas was analogous to widely traded financial commodities? Why not tee up a *hybrid* whereby early-year liquid values were marked, leaving (illiquid) values to accrual accounting, at least until the out years ripened into mark-to-market? The SEC, of all parties, deferred to Enron, which proved to be an example of *government failure* in the quest to correct assumed failures of unregulated corporate accounting.

In the absence of external price signals (liquidity), Enron's discretion quickly turned mark-to-market into *mark-to-model*. Worse, Enron would arbitrarily import mark-to-market to wholly new fields, with nary a qualm from its internal or external gatekeepers (the regulators were all but removed). As it turns out, Enron's management was conflicted, as was Arthur Andersen. With stock rewards in the millions for Enron executives, client fees in the tens of millions of dollars for Andersen, and the SEC providing a safe harbor, a bad result was all but predestined.

Enron now had a tiger by the tail. Starting over every quarter of every year, remembered Gene Humphrey, left "no foundation ... to create any incremental earnings" in the out years of long-term contracts. Superaccelerated earnings set higher expectations for the reporting period, tempting both traders and management to use their discretion in increasingly shortsighted ways. Enron's "You eat what you kill"—every period being a start over—made Enron "a very, very exciting place to be," added Humphrey.

Second, money-in-the-door increasingly fell behind (paper) profits. "Cash flow was a real issue," remembered John Esslinger.

Third, with the huge deals generating an immediate lion's income, a conflict over compensation developed between the deal's originators and the trading desk. The deal makers got the contract signed, but the back office determined the deal's valuation. Model assumptions about future valuations of gas costs, transportation rates, and interest rates drove the net-present-value calculation.

Indeed, the mark-to-modelers, under Lou Pai, wanted a cut of the action. The result "went far beyond normal corporate infighting," one book on Enron found. "They turned into pitched battles over how much each camp—traders, marketers, and finance—got to claim from a deal's profits." Enron had an economic-calculation problem internally and externally. And with so much reported profit, bonuses "got way out of hand," Esslinger remembered.

As it was, EGS's accounting was an outlier for the industry. Coastal Gas Marketing under ex-Enron executive Clark Smith had little interest in what his superiors also saw as gimmickry. Still, CGM's cost of doing business jumped, given that EGS's compensation based on (soaring) present earnings was setting the market. Ditto for Natural Gas Clearinghouse, which was not interested in mark-to-market either.

Conclusion

Two years in, Jeff Skilling had transformed Enron's gas-merchant business. Gas Bank had turned into something much bigger, with physical on one side and financial on the other. Economies of scale and scope were at work. Contracts were being standardized, with firm commitments replacing interruptible supply even in a buyers' market. Enron was also keeping its reputational value high on both the marketing and the pipeline sides in the mandatory open-access era.

Enron Gas Services was a creative first mover in a new federally created business: the interstate wholesale market. (Retail marketing awaited open access at the state level of the local distribution companies.) But amid the creativity, Enron was bearing much risk and taking a promiscuous leap into present-over-future profit taking.

Enron had always been aggressive, with Ken Lay overpaying for the company in its parts (HNG Interstate) and in the whole (HNG itself, by InterNorth); tolerating the Valhalla trading operation; and gambling in a depressed commodity market. Now, wunderkind Skilling was testing the edges in his own Enron world. The mark-to-market affectation, in particular, was now essential to ENE as a *trust-us* momentum stock. Cash flow would lag reported profitability. Profit signals were falsified compared to accrual accounting. Compensation was skewing upward artificially. This accelerating treadmill would be hard to slow when it needed to be.

Taking a cue from Lay and Kinder, Skilling would soon indiscriminately apply mark-to-market to new areas, as discussed in the next chapters. Enron's well-regarded board of directors was also culpable in Jeff Skilling's turn from accounting conservatism to financial engineering.

9

Expanding Gas Marketing: 1992–1993

U nder financial-side Jeff Skilling and physical-side John Esslinger, Enron Gas Services (EGS) vaulted into rarified air in the two years under review. Building on its momentum of 1990–91, and utilizing the gas-futures market of the New York Mercantile Exchange (NYMEX), Skilling's enterprise would highlight the innovative side of Enron's history.

In 1992, EGS became Enron's second-largest earnings unit after the interstate pipelines, doubling income from the year before. "The significant growth in earnings can be attributed to a strategy that recognizes that the market is increasingly segmented and in search of customized products that fit individual needs," Enron stated. Profits of $147 million in 1992 would increase to $169 million in 1993. But unlike realized earnings elsewhere at Enron, mark-to-market accounting made some of this only paper profits on what was guessed to come. The resulting cash-flow problem required EGS to minimize liabilities on the balance sheet and self-finance projects.

With internal growth, external acquisitions, and asset reallocations within Enron, EGS ended 1993 as a large company within a company, boasting revenues of $6.1 billion, assets of $5.4 billion, and 1,100 employees. A huge hiring influx was under way, with talent coming to Enron from banks, smaller independent gas marketers, and gas utilities. Training programs were launched for college graduates (analysts) and those with graduate degrees and some experience (associates). The emphasis was on brilliance, and many were beginning their careers. In Enron's corporate culture, they would encounter many temptations, with little life experience to resist them.

While Teesside UK was the star project at Enron, Skilling's was the star division. Alas, Teesside would not be replicated, and hard-asset investments would be deemphasized, leaving gas commodification as the core Enron growth story into the mid-1990s.

Enron Gas Services: 1992

The year 1992 would be a breakout year—the *coming of age*—for Enron Gas Services. The year began with a record 20-year gas-sales contract and a reorganization adding two new divisions and ended with record volumes, revenues, and earnings. Organizational highlights included:

- Executing the largest gas-sales contract in the history of independent power generation and expanding Enron Power Services into gas sales to electric utilities;
- Rolling out a new slate of EnFolio products, which offered supply and price security for wholesale natural gas sales to gas utilities and electric utilities, out as far as 10 years;
- Centralizing and expanding short-term (30-day) trading and transportation into a new division, Gas Trading and Transportation (EGTT);
- Forming Enron Producer Services (as distinct from Enron Finance Corp) "to expand and reinforce our longer-term supply origination activities";
- Establishing EGS–Canada to have a North American presence;
- Purchasing Access Energy to integrate downstream into small-user gas sales;
- Forming Enfuels Corp. within Enron Ventures to commercialize the natural gas vehicle market;
- Legislatively setting the groundwork for Enron to enter into the unregulated wholesale electricity sales market;
- Establishing a McKinsey-type entry-level program for associates and analysts, while dismissing bottom performers as ranked by peer review.

Enron Gas Services, the go-to division at Enron, assumed the commercial operations of Houston Pipe Line and Bammel storage for "improved system-wide gas flow optimization and new/enhanced service design." Translated, Skilling's brain trust needed to find new ways for HPL/Bammel to improve margins for the commodity side, in order to supplement the low margins received in the overbuilt Texas market.

Risk control combined the pricing commitments of the Basis Book (pricing per delivery point) and the Index Book (pricing over time) with the influx of new talent. Also in 1992, long-term gas-purchase and gas-sales agreements were centralized to reduce risk and free capital.

Not all EGS initiatives would survive in the new merchant business. What Skilling described as "an absolute explosion of products and services" creatively destructed internally as well as externally. Hub pricing as a competitor to NYMEX failed to take hold, as described in the chapter 8. So did *Gas Trust*, a planned publicly traded company to buy and sell long-term gas contracts; and *Enron Gas Administrative Services (EnGas)*, an outsourcing option for gas-firm administrative services.

Still, there were many more hits than misses. A Harvard Business School study in 1995 listed five major areas of EGS leadership:

1. The largest nonregulated gas merchant in North America
2. The largest buyer and seller of natural gas in North America
3. Manager of the largest portfolio of fixed-price gas-derivative contracts in the world
4. Operator of the largest supplier of gas to the electricity-generating industry in North America
5. Operator of the largest pipeline system in Texas

Enron Power Services (Sithe Contract)

Enron's rebuilding of the market for gas to generate electricity took a major step forward in January 1992 when Enron Power Services (EPS) announced a 195 MMcf/d, 20-year gas agreement with Sithe Energies Group of New York—a $4 billion contract—to fuel a planned 1,000-megawatt plant in Oswego, NY. Most of its power would be sold to Consolidated Edison Company of New York, which pursuant to a 1978 federal law was obligated to buy the power at an *avoided cost* per kilowatt-hour had Con Ed built the plant itself.[1]

Enron guaranteed the delivery of gas at a fixed price for the first five years and a floating price thereafter. Still, completing the agreement would take another year, and gas finally flowed when the plant became operational on the first day of 1995.

Enron was betting big. Not all the promised gas was under contract. There were no partners. And using its newfound discretion with mark-to-market accounting, Enron superaccelerated the earnings, taking (paper) profits before any gas flowed and revenue was received.

"This project was originally conceived as a coal project, but due to the availability of a competitive firm long-term contract such as this, and due to a number of environmental, siting, and economic reasons, we decided to proceed with natural gas as the primary fuel for this facility," stated Sithe's press release. What Skilling called his "bell-cow transaction" integrated EGS's services (and profits) across units to redefine the gas industry's capabilities: gas sourced from various regions and delivered under a variety of transportation contracts, even

---

1. See Internet appendix 1.5, "Public Utility Regulatory Policies Act of 1978 (PURPA)," at www.politicalcapitalism.org/Book3/Chapter1/Appendix5.html.

some from to-be-built pipe. Risk-management tools hedged the risks where possible on the 240-month commitment. No fewer than eight internal EGS units were involved in what was easily one of the most, if not the most, complex commercial agreement in the history of the gas industry.

ENRON   BUSINESS

ENRON POWER SERVICES' COMMITMENT TO NATURAL GAS SUPPLY FOR ELECTRIC GENERATION

s Enron pursues its goal of becoming the world's first natural gas major, Enron Gas Services (EGS) is leading the pack in becoming the largest natural gas supplier to the electric power industry in the United States.

Paving the way was a Sithe Energies' project that received financing on January 27, 1993. The project is a 1,000 megawatt natural gas-fired cogeneration plant under construction in Oswego, New York. To an EGS subsidiary, Enron Power Services (EPS), the project translates into a $4 billion, 20-year gas supply contract for the company.

Figure 9.1 The 20-year, 195 MMcf/d contract to fuel Sithe Energies' 1,000 MW cogeneration project in New York State represented an extreme test for Enron Gas Services' capabilities. Three Enron principals were Mark Frevert (left), Dan McCarty (center, responsible for supply), and Ken Rice (right, in charge of sales).

This contract could not be hedged by Enron to cover the risk of spot prices rising above the promised delivery price. Liquid markets were only for the first few years at best. Enron assumed the risk between the spot price of gas and the price Sithe received for electricity (*spark spread*), itself based on an avoided cost of new generating capacity.

Enron's rosy up-front assumptions (resulting in immediately booked profit) were not always right, and liabilities began to accrue. But rather than report the losses on a current-period basis, Enron stretched its interpretation of mark-to-market accounting. The problem would be favorably resolved near the end of Enron's solvent life, but several hundred million dollars of liability that should have been reported in the interim were not.

Ken Rice, vice president of the Independent Power Marketing Group reporting to Frevert, was the primary deal maker behind Sithe. A chemical engineering major, Rice took an engineering position at InterNorth while earning an MBA. After moving to Houston, he sold gas to industrials before turning to electrical generation. Now, with the largest deal in EGS's history, Rice not only was in the money but also joined Jeff Skilling's inner circle with priority assignments ahead.

Government intervention that hurt gas and helped coal in prior decades was replaced by new regulation that made deals like Sithe-EPS doable. Consolidated Edison Company of New York, the anchor purchaser of the independent power, had to purchase Sithe's electricity at the utility's avoided cost, allowing Enron to arbitrage the deal with guaranteed gas. Mandatory open access (MOA) allowed Enron to deliver the gas from the Gulf Coast, Mid-Continent, and Canada to Independence Station, New York.[2] If access was not mandatory—if pipeline owners could refuse carriage—Enron would have had to pay more, bring in partners, or own more pipe to effectuate the deal.

———

In early 1992, the Electric Utility Marketing Group was formed to concentrate on the traditional utility generators. Geoff Roberts was named vice president and given a staff to broaden his efforts, paralleling Ken Rice's side, which was dedicated to independent power producers. Both reported to EPS head Mark Frevert.

Utilities and their regulators had to be cajoled, if not a bit shamed, to do the right thing for their customers. In 1991–92, Roberts and Frevert had private meetings, sometimes joined by Ken Lay or Richard Kinder, with more than 100 electric utilities.

"The coal industry is proving to be a very tough competitor in existing coal boilers," EGS's employee publication reported in early 1993. "Volatile gas prices and perceived unreliability of natural gas will make coal the more attractive fuel for many electric utilities subject to hindsight review of their fuel purchasing practices." But for new capacity, where gas could compete straight up, Roberts was closing deals. Florida Power & Light signed a 100 MMcf/d, 15-year contract in 1992, joined by smaller contracts with Texas Utilities and with Houston Lighting and Power.

The transmission and environmental pluses of gas played into these choices; coal was harder to dislodge in the Midwest because of better economics and friendly state regulators.

EnFolio Agreements

Ken Lay fought against low gas prices, even accusing the major oil companies of predatory pricing during the gas bubble, discussed in chapter 7. Jeff Skilling

———

2. Without regulation, an integrated utility might have built the power plant and arranged for shorter-term gas of its own making. But an integrated Enron might have still sold and delivered the gas to the city gate at wholesale.

declared himself an enemy of spot (month-to-month) gas. The answer to both was for longer-term gas deals that were more profitable than spot. Thus, EGS was given the task of executing long-term guaranteed contracts with higher prices and improved margins. Those began in late 1989–90 with Gas Bank, which took nerve when forward sales could not be hedged.

The evolution of Enron's merchant function, coupled with the integration of Houston Pipe Line into EGS, led to a highly marketed five-product offering in 1992. *EnFolio Gas Resource Agreements* were based on firm contracts for both gas and transportation: "things ... that we couldn't do six months ago," Skilling noted.

EnFolio 30 was an upgrade to spot market, where most of the nation's gas was transacted. In place of interruptible gas (price-majeure gas, as Skilling called it), EnFolio offered *firm* delivered gas at a fixed price for the upcoming month.

The other four offerings were longer term—where Enron really wanted the market to go. These EnFolio offerings were:

1. *GasBank*: For a term between 1 and 10 years, this contract could be priced at fixed or indexed levels (including seasonally) with various monthly volume obligations. The emphasis was on flexibility yet predictability compared to spot.

2. *GasBlend*: For a term of one, three, or five years, variable volumes with seasonal pricing.

3. *Indexed*: For any negotiated term, at 50 locations, priced at index or at a gas-equivalent alternative-fuel price (for example, the price of fuel oil, residual oil, unleaded gasoline).

4. *GasCap*: Winter service only (November–February) for up to three years with a price ceiling, with the price being the lower of the index or the cap.

Enron pitched "strength through a diversity of pricing structures," backed by a "superlative level of support." EGS's "full service" options included electronic nominations, transportation management accessing 61 pipelines, delivery confirmation per transaction, 24-hour emergency service, standard and customized billing, and a computerized consumption summary. Daily load balancing on Houston Pipe Line, the physical hub of EGS, kept the customer apprised of what gas flowed vis-à-vis its contractual obligation.

––––

The program was all about risk management. "EnFolio Gas Resource Agreements ... can help reduce or, in some cases, even eliminate future risk for you and your customers," EGS's glossy multipart brochure read. "They offer a unique way for companies like yours to build customized gas portfolios."

The "major uncertainties" were volume, deliverability, and price. Gas might not be available for contract, contracted-for gas might not be delivered as promised, and prices could spike. "How long will the bubble last," Enron asked. "Do we have adequate pipeline capacity—or not enough?" Are gas prices "going up, going down, or remaining the same?"

Spot was the bad boy. "See Spot. See Spot go out of control" warned EnFolio's advertising campaign, playing off the dog Spot of the Eric Hill illustrated children's books. Margins were low in the short-term market, which was well populated with competitors to EGS (Natural Gas Clearinghouse, Coastal Gas Marketing, etc.). Long-term, tailored products were where the money was— and more so because of mark-to-market accounting.

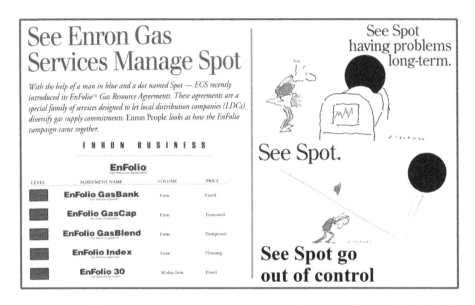

Figure 9.2 EGS's 1992 EnFolio advertising campaign, featuring Spot the big black dot, warned gas buyers about price spikes and reliable short-term gas. Long-term, fixed-priced firm contracts, assuming locked-in gas supply, could receive immediate profit recognition and separately securitized (monetized) with outside investors.

But Enron's executives were fork-tongued about the future state of the gas market, or business as usual. Ken Lay and Enron studies were bullish on gas-reserve additions for as far as the eye could see. Jeff Skilling told *Energy Daily* that pipeline availability would "increase dramatically" from FERC Order No. 636, just as deregulation freed up capacity in the airline and telecommunications industries. The gas bear was John Sawhill and McKinsey, whose pessimism was invoked to gin up interest in EGS's more profitable long-term fixed-priced gas.

EnFolio's sales pitch was for contract diversity for gas utilities serving captive customers and for electric utilities buying gas for power plants. "Purchasing all gas on the spot market or using spot-base [price] indices robs gas supply managers like you of important flexibility," the EnFolio brochure stated. "If Spot starts getting frisky, long-term, indexed and fixed-priced contracts [can] ... help insulate you and your customers from price increases."

EnFolio's sales effort ended by noting the guarantor behind its contracts: "Enron Corp. is America's leading integrated natural gas company, with more than $13 billion in annual revenues, $10 billion in assets, and almost 1.6 Tcf of gas reserves." Enron's 38,000-mile gas-transmission system, the nation's largest; Enron's 84 percent interest in Enron Oil & Gas, one of the nation's largest independent producers; and EGS's unparalleled producer, marketing, and risk-management services—all made EnFolio agreements the "truly stable, long-term alternatives to spot-based gas purchases."

———

EnFolio's national rollout in February 1992 required new capabilities at EGS. Branding, glossy brochures, PowerPoint presentations, advertising buys, and trade-show exhibits necessitated a new department: Marketing Services. One new hire was graphics specialist David Cox, who would become a Skilling favorite and, later, the Enron Broadband Services deal maker responsible for a mark-to-market fiasco.

Government Affairs needed beefing up. EnFolio was a sophisticated alternative to the default practice of regulated utilities depending on month-to-month spot purchases. But Enron's alternative could end up being very expensive if gas prices did not rise. This was not PURPA-sanctioned sales to power generators, in which long-term gas could be matched to regulatory-determined avoided cost. Gas utilities diversifying their portfolio with more expensive term gas needed to have the blessing of state regulators to avoid cost disallowances in future reasonableness reviews.

Educating state commissions was the job of Steve Harris, EGS's new director of Regulatory Affairs, as well as his boss, Leslie Lawner. Their task was not easy, because firm long-term contracts were priced at a significant premium—even double or triple the current spot price (say, $3.50 versus $1.30 per MMBtu).

Economists such as Robert Michaels of California State University, Fullerton, argued that the true market price was the going spot price, and prudent utilities should take their chances on price and not enter into near- or long-term above-spot-price obligations. Public-utility regulation precluded truly entrepreneurial long-term contracting, he argued. Besides, competition by rival marketing companies would prevent the very price spike that EnFolio was designed to avoid.

Another argument—not brought up by Michaels or anyone else—was the creditworthiness of the seller. In fact, Enron was now writing contracts for periods that would extend beyond its solvent life.

Enron Gas Trading and Transportation

A March 1992 reorganization created a new centralized organization within EGM. Enron Gas Trading and Transportation (EGTT) consolidated the short-term functions (one month or less) handled regionally and took over the current-month obligations of long-term contracts.

Six geographical divisions "with unique market/supply characteristics" were delineated: Western, Mid-Continent, Central, Texas, Eastern, and Northwest/Canada. Each was charged with its own gas purchases, gas sales, and related transportation. Midpoint prices for "firm, 100% take, baseload transactions" were established per location and time period. From this base, price quotes were modified for "monthly physical take options, daily swing provisions, delivery point flexibility, and transportation flexibility." Such tailoring to meet the exact needs of customers gave Enron a pool of contracts that could be matched and offset, creating economies that smaller marketers did not have.

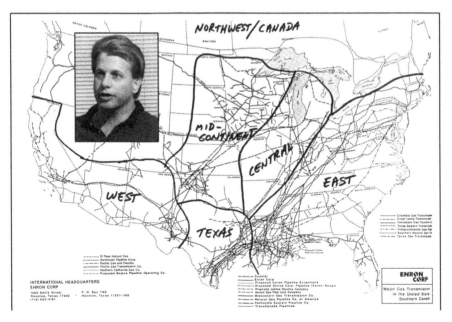

Figure 9.3 Enron Gas Transportation and Trading (EGTT), a new unit within Enron Gas Services, divided North America into six regions for short-term deal making. The sketched areas were attached to a March 1992 memo from Steve Smaby (inset) to EGS employees.

"We will work very hard to determine the lowest cost means to provide these services," explained Steve Smaby, vice president in charge. Pricing for transactions involving Houston Pipe Line, EGS's Texas hub, "are particularly complicated and still require more work," he added.

EGTT traders were assembled in one large open area at specially designed octagonal desks to share real-time information across regions. The open team atmosphere was also intended "to provide an inviting environment for the participation of other EGS personnel." Smaby personally invited all EGS employees to visit his area for "awesome" bid week.

———

Just months later, in what Skilling and Esslinger called "a very significant increase in our commitment to providing an absolutely reliable, nationwide physical delivery and transaction capability," EGTT assumed responsibility for all physical-delivery obligations for EGS, including those of newly integrated Houston Pipe Line. Transportation and Exchange (including long-term origination) was moved from Enron Gas Marketing to EGTT. An Information and Systems Management unit, headed by Melinda Tosoni, was formed to develop and integrate the *omicron* (intramonth, mainly daily) and *index* (multimonth, multiyear) function across EGS. Julie Gomez's Commercial Operations too was now in Smaby's unit. Within a year, total staffing for the unit would reach 168 positions, moving toward a target of 186.

A Physical Risk Management division was formed for not only short-term pricing but also multimonth and multiyear deals. The Basis Book (pricing per delivery point) was merged with the Index Book (pricing over time). Steve Harvey, who left the regulated-pipeline side to join EGS, as had his mentor Cathy Abbott two years before, was tasked with pricing omicron swing service, index services, storage options, and transportation. Harvey, in fact, was taking over for Abbott in important ways.

The new vice president of Physical Risk Management remembered his job as "developing positions to manage the physical risks of delivery using 'financial' market strategies." This was part of Skilling's goal, remembered Harvey, of explicitly managing all risks with a financial return on all risks taken. "This meant breaking fundamental risks into components, setting up 'books' for those risks ... and tracking their performance."[3]

But pricing to account for every penny of risk and/or to exceed calculated opportunity costs, as well as to make a return to cover EGS's costs (calculated at 1–1.5 cents per MMBtu), often put Enron deal makers at odds with the physical market. Competition was building, and EGS could not automatically get what the models said that it should.

Harvey's risk analytics unit was apart from Enron Risk Management Services, under Mark Peterson and Lou Pai. Still, at ground zero with paper deals

---

3. EGTT's five books were Regional Physical Trading, Index, Transportation, Omicron, and Storage. See Internet appendix 9.1, "EGTT Cost-of-Gas Pricing," at www.politicalcapitalism .org/Book3/Chapter9/Appendix1.html.

ripening into physical ones, EGTT provided crucial information for long-term contracting. ERMS, meanwhile, retained a Basis Book for its multimonth and multiyear agreements.

Risk Management

Enron Risk Management Services (ERMS) was formed within EGS in 1991 to quantify and manage the risk associated with gas merchandizing. Lou Pai, vice president, was tasked with pricing puts, calls, options, swaps, and sister products to reflect risk and profit margins. Given that he had more than 100 products (often bundled between physical and financial contracts) and given Enron's ability to "engineer virtually any type of financial contract its users demanded," Pai needed to understand the interplay of risk across products.

The result was a Lotus 1-2-3 spreadsheet that took 10 minutes or more to open—and then to save if modified. Users downloaded the file for their inputs, which became segregated from the master, which itself then had to be updated. And much was simply not modeled because no one knew how to—and there was no template elsewhere in the natural gas industry.

Enron's answer came in mid-1992. Vince Kaminski, a mathematics PhD and MBA working at Solomon Brothers in financial modeling, had been turned down on his initial interview by Lou Pai in New York City. ("I don't think he appreciated the skills that were required to take Enron to the next level," Kaminski remembered.) But the quant finagled his way to a second interview, this time with Jeff Skilling in Houston.

Skilling "came across as one of the most impressive people I've met in my life," remembered Kaminski. "He was low key, extremely bright, and had a vision." The feeling was mutual. Soon, Vince was at an open desk on the 30th floor, working alongside Pai and other notables, such as Kevin Hannon and Jeff Shankman.

Although nominally reporting to Pai, Kaminski was in his own orbit. The projects that Lou assigned the first day were soon usurped by trader-valuation requests. One of them was whether to buy gas storage, given expected future winter/summer price spreads that would encourage such new capacity in the market. Rigorous answers from complex optimization problems began to emerge for scenarios that were previously unapproachable. By the end of two weeks, Pai instructed his prodigy to hire staff.

The simple contracts given to customers might require multiple arrangements, even multiple contracts with other parties, in order to achieve viability. "Enron made it look easy," one author wrote. "In adapting options, swaps, and other investment tools, Enron stood on the shoulders of the financial community to build its trading business." This was new for natural gas (and forthcoming for electricity, led by Enron), creating a *before Enron* and *after Enron* for these two commodities.

————

An integrated holistic approach was needed, not bits-and-pieces modeling. Kaminski positioned himself between the programmers and the traders to devise software to integrate and quantify risk across Enron's merchant portfolio. The data of transactions and positions would be separate from the calculation and valuation engine.

By early 1993, a trader could get a quick answer to a scenario, or a programmer could tweak the engine to develop an answer. This was the first iteration of what became the *Value at Risk* (VAR) options model, the first of its kind outside Wall Street. VAR calculated the daily loss exposure at the 95 percent confidence interval, either in dollars or in a percentage of total company value. From this, exposure limits were set for each trader.

By 1994, VAR became the industry standard and made Vince Kaminski an in-demand expert at industry conferences and in print. The extremely intricate model of forward price curves and simulations would hold up well because of the expertise and realism embedded in them. But traders, wrote author Loren Fox, could violate their limits with tricks and receive a wink from their supervisor—so long as money was being made.

Mark Peterson, the first head of ERMS, was gone by early 1993. It was Lou Pai working on intertemporal bid/ask at different points in different time periods, along with Vince Kaminski's model, that integrated all the deals into a financial whole.

Enron assured investors that its trading operation was well managed, not rife with unknowns or open positions. "Each of EGS' operating sectors is managed internally with centralized risk management and logistics functions," Enron's 1993 annual report intoned. "EGS does not seek commodity positions and maintains a balanced position." Instead, "the company builds its business on the basis of competitive advantage and good people who can act on it." Deeper in the annual report, investors were assured that "net open positions" were monitored and managed to prevent "market fluctuations" from having "a materially adverse effect on financial position or results from operations."

A different reality existed inside the walls of Enron. Big bets and naked risks on projects were being made in the day-to-day market. "Even in the early 1990s," Fox wrote, "the trading operation had a reputation for making occasional big bets, or as some in the trading community put it, 'swinging a big bat'." An unrevealed big-bat blow-up in 1996, discussed in chapter 11, would demonstrate the difference of VAR in rule setting and trading in practice.

In 1992, the awards started coming EGS's way. Kaminski's work, coupled with the high profitability and newness of Skilling's operation, led *Risk Management* magazine to rank ERMS first in short-term and long-term gas swaps (to hedge against future price movements), as well as exotic products and structured transactions. ERMS was second in options, competing with the major trading houses on Wall Street and in Chicago.

Enron Producer Services

EGS's March 1992 reorganization created Enron Producer Services (EPS) to "complement and reinforce" Enron Finance and "expand and reinforce" long-term supply origination. EPS was tasked with contracting for supply for terms greater than one month, versus EGTT's one-month focus. EPS's function was also separate from EFC's producer-asset purchases and interface with major-account producers.

Mark Searles, vice president in charge, described its mission: to "create new and innovative deal structures targeted toward the producing community, which will allow the contracting of significant reserves paced to the phenomenal marketing success we have seen in Enron Power Services Inc. and Enron Gas Marketing."

EPS was marketing to wellhead sellers as vigorously as EGM and EPS were marketing to buyers. One program, EnVestor, offered independent producers the opportunity to invest in independent power projects put together by the other EPS, Enron Power Services. A less successful initiative was EnGas, which offered producers outsourcing services with administration and accounting, as well as with gas marketing itself.

Two departments—Independent Producers Gas Supply and Gas Supply–Majors—were established with regional divisions. A Canadian office was planned with a looming expiration of a stand-still agreement in that country.

Enron Finance

The challenge coming out of GasBank, as discussed in chapter 8, was securing enough long-term gas to meet the demand for fixed-priced gas to supply new electricity-generation capacity. One new financing concept was *volumetric production payments* (VPPs). That was Enron's response to the decline of reserve lending by the commercial banks in light of the stringent regulations enacted following the S&L debacle of the prior decade. Deals with Forest Oil and Zilkha Energy proved the concept in 1991. And in early 1992, EFC lent $42 million to a small, promising upstart, Flores & Rucks, to purchase and develop some south Louisiana gas prospects that seismic data revealed to be promising.

"There were no other financing sources at that time," remembered Billy Rucks. "The banks were getting hammered." The prospects, well vetted by Enron's reservoir engineers, led by Monte Gleason, came in above expectations. With call rights to the offshore gas, Enron made its money back and a lot more.

It was just the beginning. The next year, Enron fronted $118 million, all of which was highly successful for both Enron and for Jim Flores and Billy Rucks. Flores & Rucks would become a hundred-million-dollar company in just several years, with Enron making $20 million and, by some estimates, much more, through profit margins on sold gas, excess-production rights, and an ownership position.[4]

Overall, compared to $300 million in VPPs executed in 1990–91, Gene Humphrey's group originated $500 million in 1992 to solidify its position as "one of the largest entities arranging for capital to the independent oil and gas sector in North America."

———

In October 1992, a new unit was formed within Enron Finance to raise private equity to purchase and develop (but not operate) oil and gas reserves. ENGASCO, unlike VPPs, positioned investors as working-interest owners responsible for production costs. For Enron, such acreage offered not only future gas flow but also capital appreciation should additional reserves be found on the properties.

"We believe ENGASCO will give us significantly more access to the North American oil and gas reserve base than we currently have," Gene Humphrey wrote to EGS employees. Peter Forbes, a financial veteran with various Houston energy companies, was named vice president in charge.

Although a good idea, the unit ran into fiduciary issues, given Enron's ownership in Enron Oil & Gas Company. After two reserve acquisitions, ENGASCO was spun out of Enron Finance at year-end 1993 into a limited partnership. The reserves were profitably sold the next year and the successor entity dissolved.

EGM–Canada

In 1989, Enron signed preliminary agreements with Canadian producers to bring Arctic gas to the lower 48. Ken Lay mentioned taking an equity position in an export pipeline as part of the initiative, but all this went no further.

Enron did not have a marketing presence in Canada, because of a four-year noncompete agreement after the company sold Unigas Corp. to Union Energy in 1988. Upon its expiration, Enron Gas Marketing–Canada was incorporated. A Calgary, Alberta, office was opened August 1992. Vice president in charge was Glen Gill, hitherto head of gas marketing for Alberta Energy Company, the fifth-largest publicly traded oil and gas company in Canada.

Enron's reputation and aggressive compensation systems persuaded Gill to make this lateral move—and to an upstart, no less. He also had a big sales contract waiting for him: 113 Bcf with Unigas over 10 years, with gas flowing that November.

———

4. Flores & Rucks went public in 1994, raising $58 million in a one-third offering and retiring its debt to Enron. After Billy Rucks retired in 1997, Flores changed the name to Ocean Energy, which merged the next year with United Meridian and moved to Houston. In 2001, Ocean Energy was acquired by Devon Energy for $3.5 billion.

EGM–Canada's "aggressive" plan was to market 2 Bcf/d. Within months, Gill's staff of six exceeded 10 percent of its volumetric goal. In the same period, Enron purchased Canadian Gas Marketing Inc., already a 200 MMcf/d marketer. It was a good start for an effort to go from a national player to a national leader.

Enron Access: Getting to Retail
"Effective immediately, Dave Duran and Cliff Baxter shall be reassigned to Houston to develop an origination unit responsible for smaller end-user marketing," Jeff Skilling and John Esslinger announced in May 1992. "Their immediate goal is to significantly increase EGS's share of [this] market."

With Duran reporting to the Office of the Chairman, a major initiative was on. Hitherto, EGS marketed gas to large markets: wholesale to utilities and retail to electric generators and large industrials. Directly supplying commercial and residential users would require mandatory open access on the state level. Furthermore, only major aggregation (scale economies) could overcome high costs and low margins. These were two very big ifs to unlock a market with huge potential, not unlike the residential market for long-distance telephone service.

Would Enron start from scratch, enter into a partnership, or wholly acquire expertise in its new initiative? The answer came three months later with Enron's purchase of Access Energy Corporation of Dublin, Ohio, rumored to be at a cost of $10 million, maybe a little more.

Access Energy, the nation's first natural gas marketer, was the leading provider to small end users, with almost 10,000 customers in 34 states and in Canada.[5] The independent needed the "additional capabilities" of Enron, including risk management; Enron cited the two firms' complementary operations, necessary to profitably pursue the small-user market. A third reason for the transaction was Access Energy's low profitability, prompting majority stockholder Donaldson, Lufkin & Jenrette to put the company up for sale.

"The combined companies will be able to offer more products and services to more natural gas customers throughout the United States," the press release read. The new Enron Access would use the same staff and continue under the leadership of Lance Schneier.

"We are restructuring and adding considerable additional resources to our already able LDC Services team in order to position it to take advantage of the post–Order 636 world," reported Schneier in October 1993. The Western region was assigned to Bob Schorr to run from Houston. Newly hired Bob Laughman, previously president of Hadson Gas Systems, a competitor to Access Energy,

---

5. Access began in 1982 as Yankee Resources, the nation's first gas marketer (U.S. Natural Gas Clearinghouse began two years later).

ran the Eastern region from Dublin.[6] Other senior LDC-account executives were named, including junior rep Lynda Clemmons, who would go on to make a name for herself at Enron in weather derivatives.[7]

Although marketing to LDCs was primary, each office was set up to directly retail gas to small commercial and industrial end users. With the main office in Dublin, Ohio, and a secondary office in Houston, satellite offices were set up in Chicago, Pittsburgh, San Francisco, and Irvine, California. The new marketing was to commercial accounts, such as the Taco Bell outlets in Columbus, Ohio, and the churches in the Archdiocese of Chicago.

In 1993, the renamed Enron Access would be consolidated into Enron Gas Marketing, "providing value-added products and services to a broad spectrum of natural gas retailers and end users." Its new market, given Houston Pipe Line's longstanding presence, was "small industrials outside the Gulf Coast region and commercial businesses worldwide."

Enfuels (Enron Ventures)

"With positive rethinking and updated technology," *Enron People* told employees in early 1990, "the obstacles compressed natural gas once faced are considered benefits." The next year, Ken Lay told *Natural Gas Week* that he was a NGV "true believer," unlike several years before when he was "agnostic at best."

What changed? The Gulf War between August 1990 and February 1991 spiked gasoline prices—and anti-oil politics. Ken Lay saw an economic and political opening against petroleum, one of his two rival fuels. Natural gas for transportation was a new frontier to push consumption and thus help wellhead prices. Lay also welcomed the publicity that came with it.

Enter Enron Ventures in 1992, tasked with developing new markets for natural gas. One initiative, promoting natural gas cooling for industrial and commercial use, never took off. The other, promoting vehicles for compressed–natural gas sales, was politically correct and high profile. Both were part of leaving no stone unturned in Enron's quest to become "the first natural-gas major, the most innovative and reliable provider of clean energy worldwide."[8]

---

6. Hadson Corp. filed bankruptcy in October 1992 after incurring high debt from nonproductive nonenergy asset purchases. Five months later, GasMark filed Chapter 11, leaving Enron affiliates with $2.4 million in unsecured debt. Smaller marketers Centran, Endevco, and TransMarketing followed into bankruptcy.

7. EGS's associate/analyst training program, which would be run by Cathy Abbott after she completed her work in mid-1992 integrating Houston Pipe Line into EGS, hired a number of notables in the next year, including Greg Whaley and John Lavorato.

8. In 1994, Enron took a small position in fuel cell technology, which converted gas into electricity in micro-applications. The project ended without commercial success within two years of start-up. See chapter 13, pp. 548–51.

Enfuels was a consortium, led and operated by Enron as 50 percent owner. Tren-Fuels (Transco Energy) held 30 percent, and Entex (Houston's local gas distributor) held 20 percent. Its goal was to commercialize natural gas vehicles with a full suite of conversion services and a ring of public compressed–natural gas (CNG) stations around Houston, the nation's energy capital.

Fleet vehicles were targeted because they traveled in a defined geographical area and used more fuel than did regular vehicles. The passenger car market would have to come later because of multiple, reinforcing disadvantages: less driving range between fill-ups, longer fueling time at the pump, reduced trunk capacity from the fuel cylinder, and a lack of refueling infrastructure.

Enfuels' economic proposition depended on methane-for-oil fuel savings ($0.25–$0.50 per gallon) offsetting the initial conversion costs ($3,500 per vehicle). The math showed a 2.4-year payback assuming a $0.45 per gallon advantage for natural gas for a typical fleet vehicle. Conversion costs would be absorbed by Enfuels in return for a long-term operating-cost contract under which the savings could be locked in for the fleet yet a profit made by the originator. With Enfuels housed in Enron Gas Services, such outsourcing agreements would be hedged to account for a sudden increase in natural gas prices.

The plan was to perfect and apply Houston's model to Southern California (Los Angeles and San Diego) and New York City, each of them out of compliance with the Clean Air Act of 1990. Mexico City was also of interest. Emissions of nitrogen oxides (NO_x) and volatile organic compounds (VOCs), responsible for ground-level ozone, were reduced 80–90 percent with CNG compared to regular gasoline.

In mid-1992, Enfuels and Chevron opened the first public retail CNG station in Houston, the first of eight planned by the end of next year. The Enfuels Natural Gas Vehicles Technology Center opened for conversions soon after. In charge was Lee Papayoti, a veteran of Houston Pipe Line, with a passion for all things automotive.

Ken Lay predicted a 1.5 Tcf market for NGVs by 2015, displacing 750,000 bbl/day of oil to "make a big dent in the import and clean air problem." Enfuels planned to have 100 CNG-capable stations in Houston by this time—and many more elsewhere. "Enron's skills in financing and price risk management," as well as "CAA compliance without [fleets] having to make capital investments," was Enfuels' recipe for "a profitable, sustainable new gas market, helping the environment while mitigating domestic energy security concerns."

That was the plan—and hope. "By late 1993," remembers Papayoti, "it started becoming apparent that the opportunity faced insurmountable challenges." Despite the Clean Air Act of 1990 and tax incentives in the Energy Policy Act of 1992 (EPAct); despite Presidents George H. W. Bush and Clinton requiring federal NGV purchases; despite true believers (such as Texas Land Commissioner Gary Mauro) pushing NGVs, there wasn't enough incentive for fleets to sign up—at any rate, not enough fleets for Enron to approach scale economies. Things were too quiet at the Natural Gas Vehicles Technology Center, not to mention at the CNG pumps.

Convincing a Big Three automaker to mass-produce fleet trucks running on compressed natural gas, which could be paired with Enron's long-term turnkey contracts, was another front in the grand effort. But that fell short despite the best efforts of the gas industry in general and Ken Lay in particular. Automakers were lukewarm about creating a market that would only decrease the one they had.

————

Papayoti summed up the experience: "After some practical experience and significant high-level efforts (i.e., not just me), we reached the following conclusion: natural gas as a motor fuel is not a viable proposition in developed countries, but may be viable in certain developing countries that lack a refined [oil] product infrastructure, have native natural gas supplies, and are prepared to tilt the tax treatment in favor of natural gas."

Momentum was lost for several reasons. First, natural gas prices were going up and oil prices down, which increased the payback period.[9] Second, "the environmental advantages [of NGVs] became increasingly moot, as gasoline and diesel technologies (both vehicles and fuels) continued to reduce emissions at a lower cost than switching to alternate fuels," Papayoti's postmortem explained.

Third, "the domestic energy security issue also became moot" as "the diversification of US crude oil sources and increased liquidity in crude oil markets had rendered a repeat of the shortages and disruptions of the 1970s highly unlikely." And finally, Papayoti admitted, "there are still significant technology gaps in vehicle and station equipment."

Government subsidies (forced purchases, tax breaks), though substantial, were not enough. "We had hoped that the Clean Air Act and the EPAct would create an infrastructure in the government fleet sector ... [and] in the private sector," Papayoti remembered.

Theoretically, at least, greater mandates and incentives to buy and to convert could have kept the experiment going. But "there is no broad based political constituency for domestic energy security when refined product prices are low and have been low for a long time," Papayoti explained (ethanol's time would come later). And "private-sector fleets successfully lobbied against something

————

9. Between 1990 and 1993, compressed–natural gas prices increased 25 percent, while conventional motor-fuel prices held steady or declined, even with the advent of reformulated gasoline.

they (accurately) perceived to be uneconomic, and mandates for private sector fleet conversion were rolled back or abolished."[10]

Papayoti's in-depth postmortem explained why Enron ended its natural gas aspirations in transportation. Coal in power generation was the dragon to slay, and the sword was the global-warming issue rather than the energy-security issue. The United States was a net exporter of coal and a net importer of natural gas. So, coal had the advantage on national security grounds. But natural gas held a trump card when it came to the politics of global warming.

Enron exited Enfuels in 1995, having lost about $4 million in its overall NGV effort. CNG may have been the best alternative transportation source compared to propane, hydrogen, LNG, methanol, and ethanol, not to mention electric vehicles. But the real story was that gasoline and diesel fuel were not standing still. The internal-combustion engine was improving, (reformulated) gasoline was reducing emissions, and pump prices were down 20 percent from Gulf War highs.

Political Enron lost this one, as did gas utilities in nonattainment areas elsewhere. The best political efforts by the Natural Gas Vehicle Coalition—led for a time by T. Boone Pickens, who providentially wanted natural gas for vehicles but not power plants—were not enough in the mid-1990s. There would be other tries in the next decades (though not by Enron), with similar outcomes.[11]

Breakout Year

"The past year has been a highly successful one for the Gas Services Group," Jeff Skilling and John Esslinger informed employees as 1992 drew to a close. "Virtually all of our operating companies registered record profitability." In a difficult year for the industry, "our company has 'come of age'."

Volumetrically, EGS was the largest buyer and seller of gas in North America, the top seller of gas to power generators, and the top outlet for fixed-price contracts and risk management. "And almost unbelievably," they wrote, "through EFC we [are] one of the top 2 or 3 providers of new capital to the independent oil & gas industry in North America."

---

10. Papayoti's verdict was marketwide. General Motors identified 1993 as the year in which NGV demand "went away." American Gas Association executive Mike German stated in 1994 that $500 million spent in the industry to promote NGVs "has not been cost effective." *Natural Gas Week* editor John Jennrich the next year belittled the NGV effort as "much ado about 0.005% of Gas Demand." Still, some blamed the problem on "big oil" interests, not consumer fundamentals.

11. Enron stayed away from electric vehicles, which Papayoti described to management as having "appalling" economics, "marginal" environmental benefits, and far more practical disadvantages than NGVs for both passenger cars and fleet vehicles.

EGS's earnings were increasing faster than at any other Enron unit—and it was now Enron's second-highest profit generator, next to the Pipeline Group. But some sharp practice was behind these results. The 20-year agreement with Sithe Energy was just nearing finalization; gas would not flow for three years; and yet it had been marked-to-market to book immediate income.[12]

The report card then turned to human capital and EGS's "vision of how high-performing organizations should be structured." Flat organizational structures enabling decentralized decision making was one accomplishment; the other was merit-based compensation systems, rewarding, in particular, "unique, high-impact contributions." For talent, a forced ranking system weeded out the low performers, and an entry-level training program, under Cathy Abbott, hired top graduates, many with MBAs and some with relevant work experience.[13]

Promotions were announced. Andy Fastow was named one of seven commercial vice presidents. As "creator" of EGS's funding capability, the memo explained, he had closed financial transactions of more than $700 million that crucially provided long-term gas supply. "Andy is now moving to create a broader funding capability that will further enhance the services that we can provide to our customers," Skilling and Esslinger added.

In addition to Fastow, four other vice presidents were named on the commercial side.

- Dave Duran, a GasBank and Hub pricing veteran who had headed EGM's Eastern sales region before negotiating the purchase of Access Energy. Duran was embarking on a new division of EFC, Energy Ventures, to invest in natural gas vehicles, gas cooling, micro-cogen, and propane-air.

- Jere Overdyke, a "highly creative" VPP closer at EFC with Flores & Rucks and with EOG.

- Joe Pokalsky, the keeper of Enron's natural gas Risk Book, the largest anywhere.

- Geoff Roberts, the head of Enron Power Services' electric-utility sales, who was now integrating an emissions-trading capability for EPS.

On the noncommercial side, two executive promotions were announced. Rick Causey, the manager of most of EGS's accounting and control systems, was named vice president. "Rick was instrumental in acquiring SEC approval for mark-to-market accounting treatment, and has designed most of the structures that qualify for off-balance sheet treatment for our funding activities," Skilling

---

12. Enron's liability for the Sithe contract reached as high as $1.8 billion before its favorable resolution late in Enron's solvent life.

13. "The associate/analysts injected a whole new energy into the group," remembered Skilling, replacing "too conservative" staff veterans who were "killing ideas."

and Esslinger explained. Enron was a small world; just two years before, Causey had been managing the Enron audit as a partner with Arthur Andersen.

The other noncommercial VP, head of human resources and office services, was Sheila Knudsen, who helped develop and implement EGS's "unique performance review process and our compensation system." Unlike virtually everyone else, her career had been at Enron and its predecessor companies.

Another leader in EGS was Mark Haedicke, vice president of Legal. In a growth mode, EGS was hiring from top Houston law firms to staff four areas: Finance, Long-Term and Firm Gas Contracts, HPL and Short-Term Interruptible Gas Contracts, and Regulatory. Amanda Martin and Vickie Sharp from Vinson & Elkins, and Barbara Nelson Gray from Liddell, Sapp, were examples of the new talent coming to Enron. General Counsel of Enron was James Derrick Jr. (formerly of Vinson & Elkins), who replaced Gary Orloff in 1991.

It had been a good year. Houston Pipe Line had been merged into EGM. A number of asset restructurings and financings were completed. EGS had vertically integrated into the residential and commercial end-user market. And a major push into Canada made EGS a true North American operation.

Enron Gas Services: 1993

"Over the past several years, EGS has continued to redirect its business toward a range of natural gas products and services that provide high levels of supply reliability and price predictability," a recap to employees read. "To date this strategy has been very successful [making] EGS ... the leader in the nonregulated merchant business." But, Jeff Skilling and John Esslinger added, "we must continue to change and evolve to build on our past success."

EGS's aforementioned big year would scarcely slow in 1993. There were reorganizations where EGS, once again, assumed more of the commercial side of Enron's physical assets. There was entry into the air-emissions trading market, a major intrastate pipeline purchase, and a landmark investment partnership that was national financial news. Meanwhile, EGS continued to develop and define the long-term firm gas market.

EGS also capitalized on an Enron-driven provision of the EPAct, receiving a FERC certificate to trade power free of price and service regulation. This would be the new frontier for Jeff Skilling in the mid-1990s.[14]

AER*X Emissions Trading

In January 1993, EGS announced the purchase of certain assets of AER*X, an air-emission consultancy and sulfur dioxide (SO_2) allowance trading firm founded in 1984 in Los Angeles to serve a local broker market. Several million

---

14. Enron's push into wholesale electricity is discussed in chapter 11, pp. 469–472, and chapter 15, p. 590; retail electricity is discussed in chapter 15, pp. 594–608, 624–40.

dollars bought a large database on emissions per utility and per industrial site, historical air-permit trades, an expert staff, and consulting. No physical assets were involved.

AER*X was a creature of regulation. SO_2 emissions, associated with acid rain, were first regulated as a pollutant following the 1970 Extension of the Clean Air Act. The perverse incentives and inefficiencies of that law's New Source Performance Standards—an example of command-and-control regulation—gave way to a so-called market-based approach, emissions trading, in the 1990 amendments to the same federal law.

Recommended by regulatory economists, pushed by some major environmental groups, and championed by the Bush administration (with EPA Administrator William Reilly leading), the idea was to buy and sell pollution allowances under an aggregate cap that would require reductions. Firms able to reduce emissions cost-effectively would obtain credits to sell to firms less able to reduce SO_2. In effect, the latter paid the former for the right to continue to emit at prior levels. These so-called cap-and-trade programs had been tried before by EPA, with lead and chlorofluorocarbons.

Enron raised its voice as a company and through its trade associations to support emissions trading. This was a coal problem (natural gas emitted negligible SO_2 in relative terms), and higher costs for coal meant more markets for gas. Representing the Interstate Natural Gas Association of America (INGAA, where Lay was chairman) and the American Gas Association (AGA), Lay testified for SO_2 trading as "allowing utilities the broadest possible latitude to achieve the necessary emission reductions." The "freedom of choice approach" was economically efficient compared to per-plant requirements that controlled emissions through expensive rate-base additions, Lay explained.

The natural gas industry applauded the 1990 legislation. Said the AGA: "The flexible, free-market approach adopted by the administration will enable the nation to take full advantage of its increasingly optimistic gas supply outlook and its comprehensive, in-place natural gas infrastructure." Gas co-firing was one option for utilities to reduce emissions at existing coal plants. For new capacity, including new plants, starting with gas rather than coal avoided emission credit costs.

Coupled with the Bush administration's pro-gas National Energy Strategy, the new emission requirements "will create demand for another two trillion cubic feet of gas a year," predicted Michael Baly of AGA. Still, this 10 percent increase just returned the industry back to 1981 levels (which would be reached in 1995). There was a lot of work to do for Ken Lay's Natural Gas Standard (see chapter 7).

———

The overall SO_2 cap would require net emission reductions, thus giving the air permits a monetary value. The first SO_2 auction (held just months after Enron's purchase of AER*X) was a beginning for utilities and large industrial customers to comply with the January 1, 1995, start date for required aggregate reductions.

Emissions trading could be part of long-term, firm-gas packages to sell to electric utilities—a new niche for EGS and a good fit with Ken Lay's natural gas environmentalism. And should cap-and-trade be legislated for carbon dioxide (CO_2), AER*X could replicate its capabilities. Enron and the Environmental Defense Fund (EDF) were already thinking about that.

"AER*X is an internationally recognized expert in the fields of SO_2 allowances and market-based environmental programs," stated Jeff Skilling in a press release announcing its purchase from Electronic Data Systems (EDS, Enron's IT provider and an ENE investor). "This acquisition will provide Enron Gas Services a strategic advantage in providing comprehensive price risk management services relating to the SO_2 allowance trading market."

Good publicity followed. As one trade publication put it: "Adding yet another twist to its sometimes unorthodox marketing style, Enron Gas Services Corp. is trying to make gas converts out of oil- and coal-burning utilities with an offer to buy or market their sulfur-dioxide allowances."

Using puts and calls on SO_2, not only gas itself, future costs could be locked in for utilities by Enron to make the gas option attractive when compared with other compliance strategies. A coal plant, for example, could create SO_2 allowances by converting to gas and then sell the allowances to help pay for the conversion. Or the utility might simply decide to install a scrubber or alter power generation between plants to buy fewer or sell more SO_2 allowances.

Geoff Roberts, head of utility marketing for EPS, explained the purchase in an all-employee memo: "Even though natural gas may cost more at the burner tip than a fuel switch to low-sulfur coal, natural gas creates an incremental advantage through the generation of SO_2 allowances." But given the uncertain price of such permits, the memo explained, utilities were seeking risk abatement from other parties (energy providers, equipment sellers). This is where Enron could now negotiate. Explained Roberts: "Using price risk management techniques, Enron can provide a comprehensive range of solutions to the problems faced by both buyers and sellers of allowances, including the bundling of SO_2 allowance hedges with gas supply and related services."

Retaining all five AER*X employees, EPS was in negotiations with a dozen electric utilities and equipment vendors on bundled gas-and-SO_2 hedging. The founder and president of AER*X, John Palmisano, in a consulting role with EPS as part of the purchase, would go on to become Enron's chief climate lobbyist, leading to an international agreement to reduce CO_2 emissions, the Kyoto Protocol, five years later.[15]

———

———

15. See chapter 13, pp. 552–53.

Regulating sulfur dioxide was controversial, with questions pertaining to both the extent of the acid-rain problem and the ability of mandated SO_2 reductions to address it ("a billion-dollar solution for a million-dollar problem," one critic stated). That aside, cap-and-trade regulation in 1990 replaced the less efficient approach of 1977, which involved "best available [control] technology" (a regulatory term). It was considered a success by its proponents. "Our cap-and-trade plan to reduce acid rain cut sulfur dioxide emissions in half, at a fraction of the expected costs," EDF would later report.

Supply-and-demand trading of emission permits, although a market transaction, was in a government-created market, not a free market. "A government agency still must determine the level of permits, and the permits do not force polluters to compensate those harmed by the pollution," stated Terry Anderson and Donald Leal. "[T]he political process determines the initial or optimal pollution levels, not the polluters bargaining with those who bear the costs of the pollution." Another emission-reduction strategy, debated more with CO_2 than SO_2, was an emissions tax.

Louisiana Resources Company

Houston Pipe Line and Bammel storage gave Enron Gas Services a competitive advantage in the Texas market. Seeking the same for Louisiana, source of one-fourth of US-originated gas and home of the national pricing point of Henry Hub, EGS opened a New Orleans office in 1992. Later that year, EGS's director of acquisitions, Cliff Baxter, approached Williams Companies about purchasing Louisiana Resources Company (LRC), a 540-mile intrastate 730 MMcf/d gas pipeline, along with the nearby storage and liquids facilities at Napoleonville.

The deal was consummated in March 1993 for $170 million. The rich sales price (the pipeline was only marginally profitable for Williams) reflected synergies that Enron could exploit but Williams could not. EGS gained a multi-access "header system" connecting with every major intrastate and interstate pipeline in the second-largest gas state in the country (after Texas). Gas could move to the Midwest on four pipelines; to the Northeast on four lines; and to the Southeast on three lines, including Florida Gas Transmission.

With a physical presence at Henry Hub, where LRC accounted for one-third of delivery capacity, Enron could take or deliver gas associated with futures contracts seamlessly. There was unused capacity on the pipeline at a time when EGS was paying to ship gas in the state. Enron Operations, furthermore, soon to be in charge of physical operation and maintenance, improved the system in ways the previous owner had not.

"LRC offers us an opportunity to provide physical services against financial contracts," explained Skilling. The company not only made transportation revenue but also exploited price differentials between Texas and Louisiana. It was also connected to Napoleonville for storage, and it opened a New Orleans office for marketing. Throughput surged from 600 MMcf/d to 750 MMcf/d. With line-pack and storage, EGS's huge east-bound volume (estimated at 2 Bcf/d) was now offered with improved customer flexibility to suddenly increase or decrease a nomination (so-called swing or no-notice service).

Figure 9.4 Louisiana Resources Company's 540-mile, 730 MMcf/d pipeline, delivering gas to industry along the Mississippi River between Baton Rouge and New Orleans, gave Enron a physical presence at Henry Hub, the trading center of the United States.

The LRC purchase was a highlight of 1993. Mission accomplished, the New Orleans office relocated to Houston the next year.

Meanwhile, Houston Pipe Line, the Texas hub of Enron's gas activities, long mired in low margins, was being intensely evaluated for synergies with Enron Capital & Trade Resources. (HPL, unlike the interstates, was virtually unregulated.) To this end, Cathy Abbott left Basis Management, where she had determined locational pricing, for a newly created position: vice president of Business Integration. What HPL could not make on traditional margins, EGS could make on price differentials in an arbitrage game in which Enron as market maker had informational and transportation advantages.

CalPERS and JEDI

"LRC is the first step in our goal to create competitive advantages for EGS through strategic asset acquisitions," stated Doug Krenz, vice president of Strategic Development. But Enron was capital-constrained; Enron Gas Services needed outside investors. The target for 1993 was $50 million.

While Baxter was busy on the LRC acquisition, Enron Finance's Andy Fastow was entertaining the entreaties of the California Public Employees Retirement System (CalPERS), the nation's largest investment fund, about a partnership to invest in North American natural gas assets. CalPERS liked

Enron's track record and was warm to Ken Lay's natural gas message. Chris Bower, founder and CEO of Pacific Corporate Group, an advisor to CalPERS, cold-called Jeff Skilling about their interest. At first, Skilling thought it was a prank call, too good to be true. But the result was a $500 million, three-year investment, half in Enron stock and half in cash from CalPERS.

Potentially, Enron noted at the time, leveraging with debt could provide as much as $1.5 billion for EGS to finance its own asset plays (such as VPPs) or to buy pipelines and storage. As it turned out, a $500 million revolving line of credit was arranged (with ENE as collateral), giving $750 million for investment by Enron Capital Corp.

As an unconsolidated entity, this partnership would not be on Enron's balance sheet. Enron's debt-to-capital ratio, in fact, could even fall if Enron's ENE stock appreciated from the partnership. The limited partnership was named Joint Energy Development Investments (JEDI, later JEDI I). EGS was the operator, targeting projects with growth rates of at least 15 percent. The goal was to invest in future opportunities like LRC, but none would prove to be so spectacular.

JEDI was described in Enron's *1993 Annual Report* as "a defining transaction for EGS in the future." Ron Burns, the new cohead of EGS stated: "Over time, this has the potential to change the nature of our business in the same way that the first long-term fixed-priced contracts changed our business in 1989."

ENRON   BUSINESS

ENRON AND CALPERS JOIN FORCES TO INVEST IN NATURAL GAS

W hat do one of the nation's largest pension funds and Enron have in common? Try the natural gas industry and a targeted annual growth rate of at least 15 percent. And with this basic premise, Enron Capital Corp., a subsidiary of Enron Gas Services (EGS), and the California Public Employees Retirement System (CalPERS) have formed a joint venture to invest in natural gas assets and projects across North America.

> "It's a win-win situation for everyone. We are proud that CalPERS has chosen Enron for its flagship investment. It's a vote of confidence in the Enron story."

Figure 9.5 The unsolicited interest of the California Public Employees Retirement System (CalPERS) in energy investments by Enron was a corporate highlight of 1993. Equally funded by Enron, Andy Fastow–led Joint Energy Development Investments (JEDI) was capitalized at $500 million to fund Enron projects and outside ventures.

CalPERS, one of the largest common-stock holders in the country, with $75 billion in assets, was giving Enron a huge vote of confidence. "We are proud that CalPERS has chosen Enron for its flagship investment," Rich Kinder told employees. "It's a vote of confidence in the Enron story."

The manager of the joint venture was accountant and Andersen-ex Sherron Smith (later Watkins). "JEDI's gatekeeper" carefully reviewed numerous investment proposals from Enron units hungry for capital. Reporting to Andy Fastow, she would be at the epicenter of not only EGS but, later, on-the-edge accounting and financial practices that would engulf Enron.

Reorganization—and Promotion

In mid-1993, an Enron-wide reorganization further promoted Enron Gas Services within Enron. The year before, the addition of Houston Pipe Line gave Skilling a physical presence to complement EGS's trading function. Now, natural gas liquids and MTBE facilities joined EGS. But this was for commercial activity only; the physical operation of HPL, Louisiana Resources, gas liquids plants, and MTBE facilities was turned over to the newly created Enron Operations Corporation.

Lay and Kinder noted that the physical versus commercial split was "a departure from our existing business structure," but they claimed that it played to the comparative advantages of two very different parts of Enron. However, the rest of the story was that a troubled division, Clean Fuels, had been put in EGS's lap. EGS was a big profit center and intellectual hub that could deal with lemons—and maybe even make some lemonade.

The reorganization reached the top. Ron Burns was named cochairman with Jeff Skilling, with both reporting to the parent's Office of Chairman, Lay and Kinder. John Esslinger remained president. "Ron, Jeff, and John all believe that a team approach can give EGS the edge it needs to maintain its premier position in the industry and to capture the growth potential afforded by the changing gas and electric industry environment," Lay and Kinder wrote.

Why appoint Burns, who had previously headed the interstate pipelines and liquids operations? First, it could be said that he was just moving with Liquids to EGS. Second, Skilling was contemplating working half-time at half-pay to address domestic issues. Jeff needed operational help, and Burns was proven enough to require equal title.

Ron Burns had earned his spurs with Northern Natural Gas's transportation and exchange function and then as head of Northern Gas Marketing. But that was physical; EGS was whiz-kid financial. There was also something else that Ken Lay knew best. Ron was a *people person* and a regular-guy contrast to Jeff Skilling. There were corporate-culture issues at EGS that Burns could balance and so reduce the gulf with the rest of the corporation.

Skilling reputedly thought that his cochairman was out of place. After all, Ron was not a financial technician ("he never understood what was going on," remembered Esslinger). Lou Pai did not like the insertion of someone between himself and Skilling. But when Burns left Enron in mid-1995 to become president of Union Pacific Railroad, EGS would lose part of its human side. He would be missed.

———

A six-page memorandum from Ron Burns, John Esslinger, and Jeff Skilling (Office of the Chairman) to EGS employees in July 1993 detailed eight "significant organizational and staff changes," effective immediately:

1. *Creation of a North American Power Business.* The new unit, Enron Power Marketing, headed by Ken Rice, was tasked with creating a merchant business for electricity as had been done by EGS for natural gas.

2. *Realignment of Enron Clean Fuels.* Steve Smaby, previously head of Gas Transportation & Storage (GT&T), was tasked with creating a merchant business for MTBE and associated products, a particularly weak spot in Enron's asset portfolio.

3. *Restructuring of the ERMS/GT&T Interface.* Enron Risk Management Services and GT&T were merged to create Enron Risk Management and Trading (ERMT). Reporting to Lou Pai were Kevin Hannon (trading and risk) and Julie Gomez (physical transportation logistics).

4. *Assimilation of Field Producer Services.* Under Doug Krenz, Enron Field Services was formed to operate gathering systems, run gas processing, and oversee producer aggregation.

5. *Restructuring of Producer Contact Organizations.* With Mark Searles taking over EGM–Canada, independent and major producer relations were moved to Enron Finance.

6. *Consolidation of Interstate Marketing Activities.* Under Lance Schneier, Enron Access—in Dublin, Ohio—would market gas to local distribution companies, commercial and industrial users, and residential customers.

7. *Other.* Cathy Abbott, in charge of the analyst-and-associate program, was named head of Human Resources. Mark Haedicke, General Counsel, was also named Chief Control Officer with responsibilities for EGS's legal, credit, and trading risks.

8. *Promotions.* Ron Burns was chairman and CEO of Marketing and Supply; Jeff Skilling was chairman and CEO of Risk Management and Power; and John Esslinger was chief operating officer. Eight presidents were listed: Enron Power Services (Mark Frevert); Enron Finance (Gene Humphrey); Enron Field Services (Doug Krenz); Enron Hydrocarbon Services (Mike McNally); Enron Risk Management & Trading (Lou Pai); Enron Power Marketing (Ken Rice); Enron Access (Lance Schneier); and Clean Fuels (Steve Smaby).

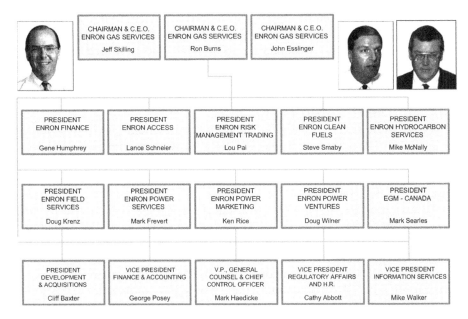

Figure 9.6 A mid-1993 organization chart showed the top 18 executives of Enron Gas Services Group. With Ron Burns joining Skilling and Esslinger at the top, the triumvirate presided over 11 presidents and 4 vice presidents.

Gaming Clean Fuels

The full-scale, retroactive use of mark-to-market accounting for long-term contracts was indiscriminate. Yes, Enron Gas Services discounted some two-thirds of the estimated future profits for present earnings, as discussed in chapter 8, but that was a judgment call that could easily be manipulated. A reality-based approach, reflecting accounting logic, would have retained accrual accounting for illiquid time periods (which would have been considerable).

If the gaming mentality of early EGS was in doubt, what happened next was sign of a wildcat mentality. Soon after EGS was assigned Enron's unprofitable MTBE and methanol business,[16] Skilling set out to (in effect) demote reality with his newly acquired discretion within the (loose) bounds of generally accepted accounting principles (GAAP). What Valhalla's oil-trading crisis of 1986–87 was to Ken Lay, mark-to-market artifice of Clean Fuels was to Jeff Skilling, given Enron's ultimate fate.

---

16. See chapter 6, pp. 298–300, for market and operational problems that plagued Enron's transportation-side environmental bet. The MTBE plant would be shuttered in 1997 after a $75 million charge was taken to earnings.

Skilling poached Ken Rice from Enron Power Services to figure out how to make MTBE profitable. Rice knew nothing about this territory, but Skilling gave the orders. Rick Causey assigned an accountant who proposed that the two profitable long-term contracts of Enron Fuels be rejiggered to manufacture a mark-to-market situation, so that the money-losing spot contracts could be offset. The trick was to increase liquidity—or just create a *rudimentary marketplace*—to get the new accounting treatment.

A few contrived deals later, the artifice was presented to Arthur Andersen for approval. The (client-captured) auditor approved, and immediate earnings were recorded for the two contracts—never mind that cash flow was absent, the rest of the business was lackluster, and there could be no more recorded profitability of the two contracts.

All was good on paper, with Clean Fuels reporting a year-to-year earnings increase from higher volume and "the impact of reflecting contractual commitments at market value." There was more. "During 1993," Enron's annual report added, "EGS significantly reduced its MTBE commodity price exposure by signing long-term fixed-priced contracts." But MTBE margins were weak and future profit taken. As in other areas, there would be a future price to pay for the fixation on the present.[17]

Power Marketing

The mid-1993 reorganization set up electricity marketing as a major growth area. Ken Lay and Rich Kinder wrote to employees: "With the addition of power, EGS will be able to offer a uniquely wide range of products and merchant services, from the wellhead to the busbar, to all of its customers across North America. Particularly through the addition of electric products and services, EGS should be able to significantly expand the potential market for the contracts and finances structures that the company has developed for the gas industry."

Could transmission access create a spot market in electricity? Natural gas offered a precedent, not to mention long-distance telephony that got all the way to individual users. As early as 1988, a group of MIT and other Boston-area academics, including future EGS consultant Richard Tabors, offered "a theoretically sound, yet practical foundation for the implementation of [electric] utility-customer transactions based on today's needs." Four criteria could be met: freedom of choice, economic efficiency, equity, and utility operational control. Better microelectronic technologies were required, however.[18]

---

17. See chapter 11, pp. 466–67.

18. The authors stated: "A spot price based energy marketplace has many benefits for both the electric utility and its customers. These benefits include improvements in operating efficiency, reductions in needed capital investments, and customer options on the type (reliability) of electricity to be bought."

In 1993, pursuant to the Energy Policy Act of 1992, EGS received FERC certification to provide "an intermediation function to the power industry in much the same way that it has in the gas business." The first order of business was for Skilling's power marketers to sign transmission agreements at power interchanges and establish dispatch operations to be able to execute transactions.

Hopes were high for a market two to three times larger than that for natural gas. As a national marketer contracting with wholesaler and retailer customers, however, Enron Gas Marketing and Enron Power Services ran afoul, potentially at least, of an arcane Insull-inspired New Deal law intended to prevent multiform holding companies in natural gas and in electricity: the Public Utility Holding Company Act of 1935 (PUHCA). A determination by the Securities and Exchange Commission, joining FERC's certificate, put Enron Power Marketing in business.[19]

Regulatory Issues

Under its blanket certificate, Enron Gas Marketing was not regulated by FERC, despite the fact that most of its buy/sell transactions traversed state boundaries. But this hardly meant that EGS did not have a government-affairs function. State and federal regulation was of great importance to Jeff Skilling on six fronts: four at the federal level and two at the state level.

First, seamless access to interstate gas transmission under federal rules was imperative for EGS's merchant business. This issue had been core before Skilling arrived in 1990 and remained so.

Second, the Commodity Futures Trading Commission (CFTC), founded in 1974, debated regulating EGS's derivative products. That would mean, in all likelihood, restricted volumes and/or tighter margins—not good for a mushrooming product slate. Here, defense was offense.

Third, a federal open-access law for electricity on the model of natural gas was needed for Enron to tap into a new, bigger energy market. The utilities were interconnected enough that sales at the city gate (wholesale) were considered interstate and thus under FERC jurisdiction. Cynthia Sandherr and Joe Hillings in Enron's Washington office were on the ball there.

Fourth, a priority was regulatory encouragement of the motor-fuel oxygenate MTBE (methyl tertiary-butyl ether), both absolutely and relative to ethanol. Margins were poor because of lagging demand, something that EPA instruction

---

19. On January 5, 1994, the SEC ruled that Enron Power Marketing was not an "electric utility company," because its purchases and sales of power were apart from ownership or operation of "facilities used for the generation, transmission, or distribution of electric energy for sale." Thus, the SEC found that PUHCA did not apply to EPM's "contracts for the purchase and resale of electric power and for transmission capacity in connection with power marketing transactions as described in your letter."

could help (or at least not make worse). Enron would not have much success in this area, given the locked-in laws that preceded Enron's ill-fated investment in motor-fuel oxygenates: the 1990 Clean Air Act Amendments and the 1992 Energy Policy Act.

Two issues were state level. First, Enron sought to replicate at retail what it had done with gas at wholesale, which would require state commissions to require local utilities to unbundle the commodity from transmission to homes and businesses. There was no beachhead here; each state commission was well captured by its in-state utilities, and they were not interested in an Enron making commodity sales. In other words, no state had introduced the equivalent of FERC's Orders No. 436 and No. 636.

Second, to the extent that gas utilities remained in the merchant function, state commissions needed to bless long-term purchase contracts that were priced at a premium to the then-going monthly spot index. Steve Harris and Leslie Lawner were focused on this for EGS in 1992.

Federal Regulation

Enron Gas Marketing's blanket certificate of public convenience and necessity allowed sales-for-resale at negotiated (nonregulated) rates in interstate commerce. Seen another way, FERC considered free-market commodity pricing as competitive, satisfying the just-and-reasonable standard under the Natural Gas Act of 1938.

But for Enron's pipelines, as for the rest of the industry, gas transmission across state boundaries remained rate regulated under federal authority. Unregulated EGM wanted it that way for the regulated pipelines, believing that what was monetarily denied in transmission would be theirs to capture in part or in whole. EGM's gas transportation, in other words, would be cheaper under MOA and cost-based regulation (based on depreciating original cost) than if negotiated with interstate pipelines in a free market.

EGM's rationale was arguably true only for existing conduits—and in the short run. Over time, regulated profits for transmission would discourage *new* transmission capacity (at least the high-risk portion of the market) and so diminish, or even reverse, EGM's rent-seeking gain.[20]

"We fully intend to remain a nationwide, largely unregulated marketer of natural gas," Ken Lay emphasized in the trade press. Enron's self-interest as the nation's leading gas merchant involved mandatory open access for transmission. Natural Gas Clearinghouse, the other large gas merchant in addition to

---

20. Ken Lay favored rate liberalization, not cost-of-service price maximums, for Enron's interstate pipelines and the rest of the industry (see chapter 6, pp. 265–66, and chapter 7, p. 309). EGM/EGS quietly favored FERC's cost-based regulation, while not challenging Lay.

Enron, was also busy working on the issue under FERC Orders No. 436 and No. 636, seeking ease of access and cost-based rates.[21]

Enron Gas Marketing routinely intervened in interstate pipeline FERC matters (rate cases and restructuring proceedings) to ensure streamlined access. (Intrastate pipelines, such as HPL, were not open-access-regulated by state authorities.) By early 1993, EGM had intervened in 58 pipeline proceedings, involving virtually all the interstate pipelines. Whether inside (Enron's interstates) or out (others' pipelines), transmission comparability allowed EGM to employ a hundred pipelines to move 2 Bcf/day in 37 states.

————

The newly competitive business created by MOA allowed Jeff Skilling to transform natural gas from a physical product into a financial one. Options, swaps, collars, and combinations thereof—*derivative products* based on the underlying physical commodity—had not existed with natural gas, as they had with oil, because of pervasive regulation, whether federal price and allocation regulation or state-level public-utility regulation of gas utilities.

Deregulation and regulatory change commoditized interstate natural gas beginning in the 1980s. In time, many dozens of products existed where a very few had existed before. This attracted the attention of the CFTC, which had jurisdiction over derivatives in virtually every other area and regulated them, ostensibly to protect consumers.

Derivatives in natural gas, as elsewhere, had a public purpose: to reallocate risk from risk avoiders to risk seekers. By lowering uncertainty, borrowing costs improved for capital-intensive, long-lived projects. Price certainty out 5, 10, or 15 years with gas purchases was important to a power plant. It could lock in gains by having one power-sales contract with a utility (or independent producer under a PURPA arrangement with a utility) and another contract with an industrial customer. Enron Power Services used derivatives to execute back-to-back contracts to lock in profit.

Unlike the same trades at J. P. Morgan or Morgan Stanley or Bankers Trust, Enron's trades on the New York Mercantile Exchange or the Chicago Board of Trade were not regulated by the CFTC. Enron did not have a securities license from the SEC; nor was Enron subject to the rules of the New York Stock Exchange. "Enron could set its own standards, a fact that would allow it to become one of the key players in the burgeoning multi-trillion-dollar over-the-counter derivatives market."

In November 1992, Enron and other energy companies petitioned the CFTC to exempt energy derivatives from regulatory control. CFTC commissioner

————

21. "We were pushing comparability of service long before FERC issued the Mega-NOPR, the proposed rulemaking that became Order 636," remembered Ken Randolph, head of regulatory affairs for NGC.

Wendy Gramm, a free-market PhD economist—and the wife of like-minded economist and US Senator Phil Gramm—championed the exemption and persuaded the majority. To populist critics, distrusting market governance, this exemption was characterized as "irresponsible," "blatant," and a "dangerous precedent."

Just weeks after leaving the commission in 1993, Wendy Gramm joined Enron's board of directors, a relationship that would net her nearly $1 million by the time of Enron's demise. To Robert Bryce, this (and the subsequent political support of Phil Gramm by Ken Lay) made the couple, "a wholly owned subsidiary of Enron Corp."

Yet Wendy Gramm was following her philosophy at the CFTC. Jeff Skilling's huge operation, both before and after this regulation debate, met the needs of the marketplace as if, to use Adam Smith's term, led by an invisible hand. There was no derivatives scandal at Enron, much less one that the CFTC could have prevented, so any might-have-been activism would have had few benefits to offset the costs of regulation, including restricting product development and the market's discovery process.[22]

One of Enron's most consequential lobbying efforts resulted in two provisions in the 1992 EPAct. That law amended the 1935 Public Utility Holding Company Act (PUHCA) to allow Enron to build power generation both in the United States and abroad, as well as to market power, without becoming a public utility in the eyes of the law, thus triggering strict ownership limits. The newly created Exempt Wholesale Generator category in the 1992 law freed Enron and like developers and marketers to build and supply multiple plants in different locales.

Enron's lobbying, along with that of other companies, such as Pacific Gas & Electric, proved crucial in PUHCA reform. "We conducted two Member/staff trips to Teesside/London.... We testified several times before Congress.... We met with countless staffers and Members.... We sent letters, made phone calls, etc.," remembered Cynthia Sandherr of Enron's Washington office.

A second EPAct provision opened up a new trading opportunity for Enron: wholesale (interstate) power trading. The Federal Power Act of 1935 was amended to require electric utilities to offer MOA to independent power marketers to make sales to industrial or power plants.

The large majority of utilities were against MOA on the wholesale level, fearing that it would be a precursor to retail wheeling. "I'll never forget Texas Utilities' (TXU) lobbyist saying that our language was 'the camel's nose under the tent'," remembered Sandherr. "He feared that it would lead to complete

---

22. In 2000, Enron dodged another regulatory bullet with the "Enron exemption" in the Commodity Futures Modernization Act.

transmission open access and that, heck, 'it was like someone dancing in your living room uninvited'." And by early 1993, the battle was on. "Soundly whipped in the battle over mandatory transmission access," a lead article in *Inside FERC* began, "the 'just say no' utilities may have yet to see the worst as competitive forces unleased by the Energy Policy Act appear to be moving inexorably toward some form of retail wheeling."

Said Section 721 of EPAct, amending Section 211 of the Federal Power Act of 1935: "Any electric utility, Federal power marketing agency, or any other person generating electric energy for sale for resale, may apply to the Commission for an order under this subsection requiring a transmitting utility to provide transmission services (including any enlargement of transmission capacity necessary to provide such services) to the applicant." With discretionary authority, FERC moved to fashion an order for 166 electric utilities akin to FERC Orders No. 436 and No. 636 for natural gas.

Case-by-case wheeling orders ceased in 1996 under the generic rules of FERC Orders No. 888 and No. 889. Enron, which began power trading in 1994, immediately became the top nonutility wholesale marketer and in 1995 set its sights on MOA to reach the utility customers (retail wheeling). In fact, the lofty goals of Enron 2000, which promised to double the size and profitability of the company between 1996 and 2000, was premised on a huge jump in Skilling-side revenues from power trading, a market more than twice as large as that of natural gas.[23]

State Regulation

EGM's wholesale gas business was created from federal MOA policy. State utility regulators could do the same at retail, where last-mile mandatory open access would allow independent marketers to sell gas to residential and commercial users in place of local distribution companies (LDCs). "Expand [FERC Order No.] 636 to States?" read a mid-1993 headline in *Natural Gas Intelligence*. EGM purchased Access Energy to capitalize on just that.

Retail open access would be a state-by-state matter, meaning that Enron Gas Services had to expand its Regulatory Affairs department in order to lobby public-utility commissions (PUCs) to get their LDCs out of the merchant function. But this was for the future; for now, Enron's long-term contracts with utilities needed regulatory blessing, given that LDCs were subject to reasonableness reviews and possible disallowance. This fell to EGS's Regulatory Affairs and Marketing Services Group, headed by Paul Wielgus.

———

As it was, LDCs were living off 30-day, interruptible spot supply in a buyer's market. For sellers, margins in the short-term market were thinned by

———
23. See chapter 15, pp. 589–90, 594–608, 624–27, 628–33; and Epilogue, pp. 655–58.

competition; EGM eagerly sought fixed-price medium-term (2–12 month) and long-term (1–10 year) commitments that had much higher margins. Spot gas was cheap compared to the fixed-priced pipeline contracts they replaced, and there was not much reason to believe that a buyer's market would disappear. The 1970s price spikes, after all, Ken Lay explained time and again, were from price and allocation regulation, not an aging mineral resource base.

The most powerful PUC was the California Public Utilities Commission (CPUC). The major natural gas state had the nation's largest spot market. The CPUC was the most proactive agency in the land in prudence reviews and integrated resource planning for its investor-owned utilities. And its consultant, Arlon Tussing, the most respected gas economist and gas advisor of his generation, concluded that spot gas was the way to go, not higher-priced gas for later delivery locked in today.

Enron demurred. Wielgus pleaded in a filing: "Fixed price contracts *cannot* and *should not* be evaluated against spot prices. They should, however, be judged against comparable gas purchase proposals available at the time of the contract negotiation." Utilities should take a "vintaged portfolio" approach, supplementing short-term commitments with longer-term agreements, he argued.

Taking issue with Tussing, EGS argued that the 30-day market be seen as a "residual activity that serves to clear the market," not "the whole market itself." Prudence, and thus leeway in prudence reviews by the CPUC, should favor "a balanced portfolio of fixed prices and market-responsive price contracts."

EGS warned that month-to-month (spot) reliance assumed that future supply would be similarly available in both price and delivery. Should transportation not be available on the monthly market or if prices spiked, (captive) utility customers without options to protect themselves would pay the price. EGS also cited the decline rates of gas fields—7.5 percent per year onshore, 20 percent per year offshore—as reason to diversify purchase choices. To give California gas consumers "the best of all worlds, reliable and abundant energy at extremely competitive prices," the CPUC should permit, if not encourage, fixed-priced firm gas for longer terms than one month.[24]

Rejecting Enron's argument, the CPUC sided with total spot-reliance purchases over partial long-term fixed-priced contracts. Other state commissions would challenge (higher-priced) term contracts. These regulators referred to the robust gas-reserve estimates, which had resulted from the technological improvements of Forrest Hoglund's EOG and others. "We have a 35-year

24. EGS made the same arguments for "a managed portfolio of fixed, spot and indexed supplies" (in contrast to a "'spot standard'") to the US Department of Energy, which invited comments on state policies affecting the gas industry.

supply of gas and ... low prices," stated one Delaware commissioner. Ken Lay could not have said it better in his natural gas campaign. In this as in other areas, Enron had trouble trying to have it both ways.

Competition and Pressure

"Selling natural gas is getting to be a real business, like selling washing machines," Jeff Skilling lectured at Harvard Business School. "We are taking the simplest commodity there is, a methane molecule, and we're packaging and delivering it under a brand name, as General Electric does."

This was quite an oversimplification, although the general point was that there were many buyers and sellers in a short-term market. And gas merchandizing, at least on the wholesale level, was getting *standardized*. With this came lower margins as other gas merchants imitated Enron Gas Services, often with former Enron talent. (Retail competition in place of bundled LDC provision was not of political age.)

As 1993 drew to a close, Enron's heralded merchant-gas business, a thousand employees strong, was creative but less profitable than the numbers would suggest. Mark-to-market accounting overstated net income. The contrived liquidity from Enron's troubled MTBE and methanol contracts (for mark-to-market accounting treatment) was a leap into perceptionism. Rich Kinder and Ken Lay, as well as Enron's board of directors, were culpable in this regard. Giving the wounded assets to Jeff Skilling's smartest-guys-in-the-room was an expedient that only postponed the inevitable.

The accounting facade was good for Enron's story but troublesome otherwise. Cash flow did not reflect reported net income. Compensation systems were thrown out of kilter. A treadmill was started that Enron would not be able to stop. ENE as a momentum stock was running, in part, on hot air.

Competition was intensifying. Trading desks at Natural Gas Clearinghouse, Coastal Gas Marketing, El Paso Gas Marketing, and elsewhere were shrinking Enron's margins. The hare's first-mover advantage was yielding to the march of the tortoises. Price discovery with NYMEX meant that mid-to-late 1980s margins of $0.50 to $0.75 per thousand cubic feet were now a nickel or two, "grocery store type margins," remembered Esslinger. Banks, too, were getting back into energy lending, forcing tighter deals in long-term gas for Gene Humphrey and the VPP origination group.

————

From a broader political-economy perspective, there is the overall question of reconstituting the gas merchant or sales function, the fourth segment of a highly regulated industry that hitherto had been balkanized into production, transmission, and distribution. In a true free-market environment, without state-level public-utility regulation and without the federal Natural Gas Act, the merchant function that Enron did much to create would have been in the domain of integrated producer-transmission-distribution companies. Enron Gas Services Group was a stand-in, so to speak, for an *integrated* natural gas major that would have complemented its physical infrastructure with (bundled) gas marketing (as Houston Pipe Line did in the unregulated Texas market).

As it was, EGS benefitted greatly from federal regulation in three ways: mandatory open access; PURPA rules for independent power generation; and a highly regulated, highly constrained banking system that (for several years after the S&L collapse) could not effectively capitalize gas drillers.

"In many ways, the natural gas industry has been its own worst enemy," Ken Lay would say. But, as he stated elsewhere, a surplus of regulation, not a geological shortage of gas resources, plagued interstate markets in the 1970s, an event that was not forgotten by major customers in the 1980s. Regulation elsewhere, including the anti-integration PUHCA, blocked structural market efficiencies.

Regulation giveth and regulation taketh away. In the case of gas marketing, Enron was provided with a once-in-a-generation opportunity to exploit a whole new market. In a world of second-best (or least-worst) public policy, Enron shone with entrepreneurial vigor in a regulation-enabled business arena.

Part V

Expanding Enron: 1994–1996

Introduction

In the mid-1990s, Enron was composed of five businesses: international energy infrastructure development, gas and oil exploration and production, interstate natural gas transmission, natural gas liquids, and natural gas and electricity marketing. Power generation, a stand-alone US-side business during the PURPA-driven boom, was reduced to an engineering division offering worldwide construction and operating services for power plants and pipelines.[1]

Ken Lay's company had two orientations. Iron-in-the-ground, traditional Enron was rooted in the old Houston Natural Gas Corporation, its 1984 acquisitions, and its 1985 merger with InterNorth. The 1980s Enron was a well-defined upstream-midstream energy company of wells, pipelines, storage, and gas liquids facilities, joined by gas-fired cogeneration plants and an emerging gas-marketing operation.

Liquids, once a stand-alone division, was now part of Enron Capital & Trade Resources (formerly Enron Gas Services). Included in Liquids were the troubled MTBE and methanol plants, expensively purchased from Tenneco in 1991. In 1992, the bulk of Enron's liquid pipelines, also part of Enron Liquids Fuel Company in the Mike Muckleroy era, were spun off in the first public offering since Enron Oil & Gas (EOG) three years before.

After Enron Liquids Pipeline (ENP), Enron monetized assets by selling fractions of Northern Border Partners (stock symbol: NBP) in third-quarter 1993; EOTT Energy Partners (stock symbol: EOT) in first-quarter 1994; and Enron Global Power & Pipelines (stock symbol: EPP) in fourth-quarter 1994. Operating agreements for all these assets provided service income to part-owner Enron.[2]

The 1990–96 era heralded two new large profit centers. Beginning with Teesside UK, Enron was now in 20 countries, many in the developing world, building gas and power infrastructure. (The oil majors had a petroleum focus.) Additionally, Enron was first, biggest, and best in the wholesale marketing of

---

1. With the PURPA boom coming to a halt, Enron marketed gas to electricity generators rather than building new capacity itself.

2. Enron's ownership at year-end 1996 were: EOG, 61 percent; ENP, 15 percent; NBP, 13 percent; EOT, 49 percent; and EPP, 52 percent. Enron also held a half-interest in Florida Gas Transmission (via Citrus Corp.) with Sonat Inc. owning the other half. In first-quarter 1997, Enron would sell its natural gas processing and liquids operations in Louisiana (Enron Louisiana Energy Company), as well as its wholesale propane business.

natural gas and electricity. Venture capital investing was also a growing part of
EGS/ECT.

———

Although not in gas distribution (Peoples Natural Gas Company had been sold
by HNG/InterNorth in 1985), Enron was the most integrated major natural gas
company in America. The self-proclaimed *natural gas major* was organized to
profit "by adding value to the gas molecule every step of the way from the time
it is produced at the wellhead to the point at which it is delivered at the burner
tip."

Enron benefitted from synergies. One was a premium-priced long-term contract between Enron's Texas City cogeneration plant and EOG, described in
chapter 5. EGS's Gas Bank contracted with EOG reserves, and Skilling's side
looked to EOG as a backstop for its nonhedged sales commitments.

Synergies were otherwise modest within Enron's natural gas chain. The five
aforementioned entities that became public companies were, at least nominally,
independent from Enron.[3] FERC regulation functionally separated interstate
transmission from gas commodity sales, precluding the most natural would-be
integration with Enron's two largest wholly owned divisions.

Office of the Chairman was the common denominator of the dozen or so
Enron divisions and spinoffs. Ken Lay was the visionary, image maker, and del-
egator. Performance was the responsibility of Richard Kinder, who was the conscience, the last line of defense, the brake for the whole corporation. But when it
came to making the numbers, specifically the 15 percent annual earnings growth
promised by Ken Lay, Kinder was also the accelerator, even corner cutter.[4]

Lay had two divisional heads who vied as Enron's number three. (Forrest
Hoglund of EOG was ensconced in his own public company.) Jeff Skilling, the
wunderkind of Enron Capital & Trade Resources, worked well with Kinder and
was prized by Lay. Rebecca Mark of Enron International/Enron Development
had wide license and high confidence from Lay, but Kinder (and Skilling) were
less confident about her mission and abilities.

In the upper chain of command, Ken Lay had the allegiance of the board of
directors and Richard Kinder. Skilling had the allegiance of Kinder and Lay.
Rebecca Mark had the allegiance of Lay. Rich Kinder had the allegiance of
everyone else, in addition to respect from above.

———

———

3. Enron Global Power & Pipelines, sharing management with Enron, developed conflicts
with the parent when its personnel tried to protect the interests of minority owners. It was
brought back inside Enron in 1997, discussed in chapter 12, pp. 509–13.

4. See Preface, pp. **xii–xiii**; Introduction, pp. 20–21, 24–25, 27, 62; and Epilogue, pp. 648–49,
668–701.

Chapter 10 describes traditional Enron in the mid-1990s. Enron Oil & Gas operated apart from Enron and was being sold down (it would completely divorce from the parent in 1999). The interstate natural gas pipeline group—Northern Natural Gas, Transwestern Pipeline, and (half-owned) Florida Gas Transmission—was the other major bedrock. Oil transportation and trading, accounting for half of Enron's total revenue, was deemed noncore and spun off as EOTT Energy Partners in 1994.

EOG and the interstates, under Forrest Hoglund and Stan Horton, respectively, were steady, profitable, and built to last. There were no accounting tricks or financial engineering, just old-fashioned planning and execution. These assets produced the cash flow that largely funded Enron's aggressive, even imprudent, ambitions in the 1990s.

Chapter 11 chronicles Enron Capital & Trade Resources. ECT was rapidly growing amid an industry-wide consolidation that saw its competitors drop by half. ECT was centered on wholesale marketing of natural gas, then electricity, enabled by federal regulation establishing nondiscriminatory access to the nation's interstate transmission systems.[5]

In Europe, ECT introduced large-scale natural gas and electricity marketing centered on Teesside, the world's largest cogeneration plant. From the physical base constructed and run by Enron Power, an ECT-like trading operation sprang up in the United Kingdom, a model for other West European centers.

Chapter 12 describes Enron's international ambitions. Rebecca Mark and Joe Sutton were bringing "project development, fuel supply, and financing" to underserved, capital-poor markets, part of Enron's wider effort of "providing integrated energy solutions worldwide."

Enron had power plants in India, China, Guatemala, the Philippines, and the Dominican Republic; pipelines in Argentina and Colombia; and a raft of other developing-nation projects in "final development." And Mark was promising Lay 20 percent earnings growth in the years ahead. The new Enron International (absorbing Enron Development) was just part of Ken Lay's global reach, with EOG and ECT expanding afar with their core competencies.

———

At mid-decade, Enron was on a steep growth trajectory with hardly a Plan B. The years 1984–85 were about creating a megacompany; 1986–87 involved adjustment and survival; and 1988–89 focused on recovery. The period 1990–93 witnessed division-by-division progress and breakout profit centers. In 1994–96, North

---

5. While having four such federally regulated pipelines, Enron had no power-transmission assets other than those of newly acquired Portland General Electric, which were reserved for PGE's core customers.

America's most integrated natural gas company was redefining its energy sphere and building energy infrastructure worldwide.

Enron enjoyed a reputation as innovative, well managed, and focused. It was championing the right fuel at the right time, the press proclaimed. Vision was complemented by operational excellence. The risk taker was an able risk manager—by all appearances. Enron was a *different* energy company, making higher returns. And what better place to work if you were in the energy industry or at a law firm or an investment bank related to energy? Ditto for a student from a top business school looking to begin a career.

But a closer look reveals a different Enron in the mid-1990s. With accounting and finance trickery here and special government favor there, dressed up with political correctness in the socioeconomic mixed economy of political capitalism, contra-capitalist Enron—while depending on a solid upstream-midstream base—was beginning to fool many, and even itself.

10

The Steady Side

I t's a Great Time to be in the Gas Business," John Jennrich editorialized in a 1996 column in *Natural Gas Week*. Supply abundance was "nearly a given." Pipeline adequacy was a nonissue. Wholesale gas marketing (the subject of chapter 11) was being rationalized. Enron was in the middle of all this success.

Enron's interstate pipelines were modernizing and expanding, which allowed earnings to increase despite federal rate ceilings and rate discounting. Costs were being significantly pared, specifically, and new capacity backed by firm transportation revenue was coming online. Stan Horton led this effort, and he would continue to lead the interstates, profitably and without incident, for the rest of Enron's solvent life.

Forrest Hoglund's Enron Oil & Gas (EOG) was pacing the upstream independents with strong, growing earnings and cash flow, making a successful transition from its tax-credit-driven business in the early 1990s to tax-neutral, low-cost production. By more than replacing its proved reserves year after year, EOG became the definition of a sustainable company. EOG was "the real cash cow: even in bad times," as noted at Enron's 1995 management conference.

Hoglund, his reign dating from 1987, would find his heir in Mark Papa. It was Papa who would lead EOG's complete divorce from Enron in 1999, the year Hoglund retired, and successfully run the company until his own retirement in 2013.

Gas liquids were in transition. Some assets were sold, others moved to Enron Capital & Trade Resources (ECT). Enron Oil Transportation & Trading, whose assets were about as old as the original assets of Houston Natural Gas and of InterNorth, was spun off as EOTT Energy Partners in March 1994 on the strength of financial guarantees from Enron. This separation of the oil side of the "world's first natural gas major" would cost Enron more in the next years than if it had simply sold the division and taken a loss.

Interstate Pipeline Progress

Enron was growing in nontraditional areas, but traditional natural gas transmission remained foremost in terms of quality earnings. Intrastates Houston Pipe Line and Louisiana Resources Company were housed in ECT as complements to the division's unregulated gas sales.[1] But the interstates, regulated by the Federal Energy Regulatory Commission (FERC), were part of Enron Operations (1993–95) before being separated out in 1996 as the Enron Gas Pipeline Group.[2]

Enron's interstate systems were wholly owned Northern Natural Pipeline and Transwestern Pipeline; half-owned Florida Gas Transmission; and minority-owned Northern Border Pipeline (9 percent). Enron operated all four systems, the latter two through a management contract with the other owners. In all, Enron was responsible for $3.6 billion in net plant value, with ownership of $2.1 billion.

This asset group was the first described each year in Enron's annual report, at least until Jeff Skilling took over as COO.[3] No wonder. The interstates' nearly $300 million in annual net income made up half or more of Enron's total. Interstate earnings were consistent and high quality, *not* marked-to-market. In contrast to ECT's procedure, income guaranteed to the pipelines under long-term contracts was recorded as received, not summed and taken in the current quarter on the basis of a legal obligation.

Favorable rate cases and expert management consistently generated double-digit rates of return on capital invested for the interstates. Adding depreciation expense to accounting profit, cash flow was even better, prompting the

---

1. The intrastates were under relatively light regulation by state commissions compared to FERC's interstate regulation. An attempt in the mid-1990s to introduce cost-of-service regulation to Texas intrastate gas pipelines, including Houston Pipe Line, was unsuccessful.

2. Enron Operations was also home to Engineering & Construction, which booked income from "the construction, management, and operation of assets worldwide." These projects included gas-liquids facilities, power plants, and international gas pipelines, as well as the technical side of Houston Pipe Line, Louisiana Resources, and the four interstates.

3. Interstate pipelines highlighted the cover of Enron's annual reports from 1985 through 1988, were mentioned first among major divisions in 1989 through 1996, mentioned second (after Enron Oil & Gas) in 1997 and 1998, and mentioned last in 1999 and 2000 (pages 22 and 18, respectively).

appellation "cash cows" for the FERC-regulated assets.[4] Taskmaster Richard Kinder tried to set the bar high, and Stan Horton's unit was making its goals for net income and cash flow.

Start-up, highly entrepreneurial units within Enron, and none more that ECT, belittled the rate-and-service–regulated interstate side as old school and stodgy. When offered the pipeline division, John Wing had said dismissively: "I divide the world into two parts: creators of wealth and custodians of assets, and pipeline people are custodians to the nth degree." But profitable pipelining required attention to detail and alertness to opportunity, given competition from other pipelines, existing and potential—not to mention competition from alternative fuels.[5] Interstate pipelining was a core competency at Enron; industry surveys confirmed Horton's group as Best in Class, and *Fortune* magazine named Enron first in its Pipeline category as part of its annual America's Most Admired Companies listings.[6]

Creditworthy long-term shipper contracts were necessary for long-lived, capital-intensive mainline expansions. Three-year rate cases negotiated with customers and other parties before FERC had to be done artfully to create opportunities to meet, and even exceed, the authorized rate of return (*beat the rate case*, in pipeliner lingo).

With a declining rate base upon which the rate of return was calculated— original cost less accumulated depreciation—each interstate needed to reinvest, if not expand, to maintain its physical capital for steady profit. In fact, as Enron explained at its annual analyst conference in Beaver Creek, Colorado, the strategy was to "target pipeline CapEx [capital expenditure] to DD&A [depreciation, depletion, and amortization] levels."

In the late 1980s and early 1990s, Transcontinental Pipe Line (once run by Ken Lay) was not making its authorized rate of return, much less surpassing it.[7] Bankrupt Columbia Gas Transmission (1991–95) was a woeful story of failing under changed federal regulation. In particular, these pipelines were plagued by take-or-pay costs as they made the transition (under FERC Orders No. 436 and

---

4. Compared to state-regulated rates of return of 11–12 percent for (less risky) gas-distribution companies, interstate pipelines lobbied FERC for a higher return of 15–18 percent, the average of unregulated Fortune 500 companies. Year-to-year earnings *growth*, however, was much less than the percentage return on invested capital in any one year.

5. Although market areas could fail FERC's quantitative test of so-called workable competition, real-world competition made a case for deregulation. See Internet appendix 10.1, "Competition: Real World versus Theoretical," at www.politicalcapitalism.org/Book3/Chapter10/Appendix1.html.

6. *Fortune* began the category for pipelines in 1994, and Enron was first, Williams second, and Panhandle Eastern third in the first year, 1995, and for 1996.

7. See Bradley, *Edison to Enron*, pp. 353–64.

No. 636) from merchants to open-access transporters. Enron, by contrast, undertook proactive settlements of problem contracts. Ken Lay's early-settlement philosophy, a highlight of his Enron career, unshackled his pipelines for success.

High throughput, each pipeline's goal, required congruent gas-in and gas-out. Pipelines had to court producers with gathering lines to their wells in the field, as well as interconnect with other pipelines to secure needed supply. Pipelines had to be shipper friendly with high take-away demand at the terminus.

Well-designed rate cases provided upside for extra profit if the interstate could reduce cost and/or increase revenue past the FERC-assigned return. (The only downside was a stricter baseline inherited for the next rate case.) With rate ceilings but not rate floors, and without the legal authority to make up discounted tariffs by charging higher-than-regulated rates later, the challenge was to keep throughput high.

The good news for open-access pipelines was FERC's new rate-design policy, which shifted more costs to the fixed (demand) charge that customers had to pay and less to the volumetric rate that could be discounted from its maximum or be wholly uncollected with idle capacity. Straight fixed variable (SFV) rate design reduced risk for pipelines, which was good for investors and a fact of life for shippers in the MOA era.

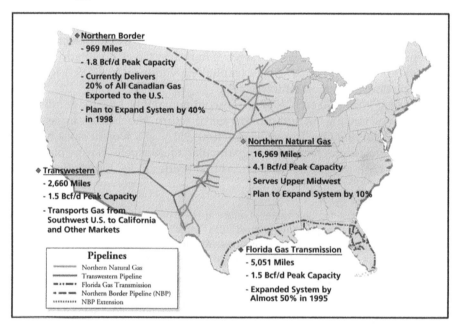

Figure 10.1 Enron's interstates had a peak-day delivery capacity approaching 9 Bcf/d in 1996, a nearly one-third increase from a decade before. In addition to wholly owned Northern Natural and Transwestern, Enron held a 50 percent interest in Florida Gas Transmission and a 9 percent interest in Northern Border and operated all four.

Gas demand was growing in California and Florida, less so in the Midwest. The jump in Enron's interstate investment (after depreciation from its original costs) from $2.8 billion in 1993 to $3.6 billion in 1994, the largest increase since 1991's 17 percent (to $2.5 billion), resulted from expansions anchored by shipper contracts requiring payment whether the (reserved) capacity was used or not (ship or pay).

New investment in net plant (rate base) was key to Enron's maintaining and increasing earnings in its biggest segment. But profit *growth* could hardly match Enron's target for newer divisions, where 15 percent or more per annum was expected.[8] The interstates could make 15 percent in earnings but not 15 percent earnings *growth*; growth of 5 to 10 percent was doing well.

Cost Reduction: Staying Competitive

"The four companies have launched an offensive to identify better, faster, simpler—and more profitable ways to do business," Enron's employee magazine reported in Spring 1994. Necessity beaconed. Costs had to fall in an environment where actual revenues were below theoretical cost-based maximums from some combination of discounted rates, low throughput, or no-longer-collectable demand charges. This was no longer the easy game of padding expenses and maximizing the rate base and letting the gas sell itself. "Just maintaining the status quo wasn't an option," remembered Tom White, one of Enron's top two executives overseeing the project.

One focus was substituting labor with fixed investment. Automation and modernization increased the rate base upon which pure profit was made, replacing dollar-for-dollar labor costs that earned nothing. *And* reduced expenses improved transportation economics in the open-access world.

One target was vintage compressor stations—the oldest of which dated from the 1930s on Northern Natural—that were manually operated by crews of four or five. New automation technology allowed Gas Control from Houston (Floor 42 of the Enron Building) to operate the stations remotely. The same was done with a redundant system in Omaha, the home of Northern Natural, should Houston's operation ever become incapacitated.

At the same time, management layers in the field were reduced under each vice president of operations as self-directed work teams were trained and skill-based pay implemented. A thorough inventory of work skills per person resulted in combined duties and pay increases for some and terminations or buyouts for others. "We found out all sorts of interesting things," White

---

8. One threat to Enron's simultaneous expansions was a shortage of domestic steel plate used in pipelines, which stemmed from federally imposed tariffs against imported supply. In 1989, "Enron succeeded in inserting language into the law that created a short-supply relief mechanism," but with this provision's expiration in 1992, the lobby effort had to be repeated by Enron's Washington office.

remembered from the skill assessments. One was literacy; some in senior positions could not read and depended on staff.

The results were dramatic. Enron's interstates pruned just over one-fifth of their workforce in the first half of 1993 alone. By the end of the process, approximately 40 percent of the interstates' overhead was gone. Reliability went up, as the gas moved per employee rose fivefold.

Field employment of Enron's interstate pipelines fell from 130 to 19. One of Northern's vintage compressors was relocated to a museum in Omaha. "I joked with Stan [Horton] that in 20 years there would be one man and one dog left at Clifton [Kansas]," Tom White recalled. "The man would be there to feed the dog, and the dog would be there to see that the man doesn't touch any of the controls in the compressor station."

Another cost initiative in 1995, the Performance Improvement Process, had cross-functional teams (about 40 across Enron's pipelines) set cost-reduction goals. The "cultural change" removed the last remnants of the old cost-passthrough mentality. "Before, if people figured they needed something, they just bought it," said one field leader. "Now they have to decide if they really need it, and then they have to check the money to see if they can afford it."

Hundreds of thousands of dollars in savings were achieved in the first months alone from these different practices. Expenses per facility were consolidated by region and put out for bid. "Nit-picking' expenses" were tracked for the first time. Legacy costs were eliminated ("Some locations were being charged for [phone] lines that were no longer in service—including a few dating back to the 1940s.") Operations were conducted "a little closer to the edge" without compromising safety.

The cost-savings efforts were led by Horton, cochairman and CEO of Enron Operations, along with White, head of engineering and construction. (In 1996, EOC split into two parts to leave Horton as chairman and CEO of the Enron Gas Pipeline Group.) An expert at rate-case nuances and with operational smarts, Horton favored expansions based on sound economics, not what Enron criticized as a "strict rate-base mentality." Enron's markets were quite rivalrous, although FERC's quantitative measurement of "workably competitive" (a controversial theoretical standard) said otherwise.

Transwestern Entrepreneurship

Transwestern Pipeline faced two major challenges in the 1990s. One was a pronounced capacity surplus to California from the entry of Kern River Gas Transmission, as well as expansions to the state by all three existing out-of-state suppliers, including Transwestern. The result was 7 Bcf/d of capacity chasing 5 Bcf/d of gas demand—a 30 percent surplus, one exacerbated by a regulatory distortion.[9] Rate discounting—and empty space on El Paso and Transwestern, in particular—was predestined.

The second challenge was a provision of FERC Order No. 636 (1992), which sanctioned the permanent release of unneeded capacity by local distribution companies (LCDs) to their interstate supplier. With the capacity surplus all but eliminating the value of such first-call rights, Southern California Gas Company (SoCalGas) notified Transwestern that it would turn back its capacity effective November 1996 pursuant to the expiration of its age-old contract.

As Transwestern's largest customer with firm capacity of 457 MMcf/d, or 60 percent of the pipeline's historic capacity to the state, SoCalGas would be freed of its $51 million annual payment to Enron. It would pay only for volumes actually transported, not a cent in reservation fees, whereas before, Transwestern (and El Paso) had had an open-ended agreement that SoCalGas would pay demand (fixed) charges on 60 percent of its historical contracts.

Transwestern Pipeline had to execute a business strategy that few interstates ever had to employ in the entire history of the Natural Gas Act of 1938.[10] The result was a "landmark settlement" that gave Transwestern partial relief, while implementing incentives to potentially secure more revenue. In return for SoCalGas's continuing to pay a reduced demand charge for 5 years, Transwestern agreed to a maximum indexed rate for 10 years (the first ever approved by FERC) and removed gathering-line assets from the rate base with customer credit. Transwestern also got the right to resubscribe the relinquished capacity rights (by SoCalGas) for its own account.

The highly negotiated, virtually uncontested global settlement, another first for FERC, left Transwestern free of (three-year) rate cases until 2006, a 10-year window in which cost cutting and other efficiencies could bring incremental revenue to its bottom line. The agreement was *regulation by contract*, not *regulation by FERC*—what a pair of Enron thinkers several years before called a "'social compact' where long-term contracts among the affected parties set price and service terms" to displace regulatory expense and motivate greater entrepreneurial alertness for efficiency.[11]

---

9. The California Public Utilities Commission (CPUC), as well as California's major gas utilities, successfully lobbied to delay new pipeline capacity to the central California enhanced-oil-recovery market. The multiyear delay prevented a more rational capacity increase in response to market demand and also caused periodic gas curtailments in the state beginning in late 1987, three years after new capacity was first proposed.

10. Transwestern's earlier entrepreneurship in the face of regulatory change is described in chapter 2, pp. 140–43; chapter 3, pp. 158–61; chapter 5, pp. 227–28; and chapter 6, pp. 262–63.

11. "I wouldn't be surprised to find that the combined cost of state and federal regulation is equal to one-half of Transwestern's [firm transportation] rate," commented then-president Terry Thorn.

TRANSWESTERN AND ITS CUSTOMERS CELEBRATE VICTORY WITH LANDMARK SETTLEMENT

Figure 10.2 Transwestern Pipeline's global agreement with its customers, led by SoCal-Gas, created a de facto 10-year unregulated period in which cost improvements and revenue enhancements could be brought to the bottom line. Deborah Macdonald, Transwestern's president, is shown along with a celebratory picture of other project team members.

Compared with the default capacity turnback, Transwestern gained a guaranteed revenue stream until the state's surplus could be worked down to give firm transportation rights economic value again. With low-cost Canadian gas coming into California, gas flows had to move east, which inspired three Transwestern initiatives: a 340 MMcf/d lateral expansion into the prolific San Juan basin of New Mexico for new supply, making its two Texas laterals bidirectional, and offering a joint Transwestern–Northern Natural transmission rate.

By 1996, the new Transwestern had 1.5 Bcf/d of capacity to the Golden State and, compared to little before, 1 Bcf/d of business east of California. Contrast this to when Enron bought the line in 1985: 750 MMcf/d west and 250 MMcf/d east. Ken Lay was correct when he told stockholders 11 years before that Transwestern "has the potential to increase its sales and transportation significantly during the next decade."

Better yet, profitability was preserved and better opportunity created amid an unprecedented buyers' market. The little sister in Enron's interstate stable had tripled in size and was arguably the nation's most entrepreneurial pipeline.

Florida Gas: Forestalling Entry

Incremental expansions on Florida Gas Transmission (FGT) in 1987 and 1991, each for 100 MMcf/d, just kept up with the market. Phase III, filed with FERC in late 1991, and facing potential entry from a new pipeline project cosponsored by United Pipeline and Coastal Gas Transmission (it would finally enter service in 2002), was much bigger.[12]

With existing capacity of 925 MMcf/d, FGT proposed to add 800 miles of new mainline and two new compressor stations, as well as upgrade existing compressors, for an additional 875 MMcf/d. The $940 million proposal was estimated to enter service in late 1994.

In early 1995, with the expansion scaled back to 530 MMcf/d (Phase IV six years later would make up the difference), FGT became a 1.45 Bcf/d, 5,275-mile system at a cost of approximately $1 billion. The sole gas provider to the Sunshine State was trying to stay that way with timely expansions, while building in cost advantages for future capacity growth. Cost escalation from environmental matters required prudency too.

The expansion was anchored by a firm transportation contract with Florida Power and Light, which was eager to both convert existing power plants from oil to gas and build new gas-fired capacity. Twenty-nine customers accounted for 99 percent of the new expansion, increasing Florida Gas Transmission's sure-money revenue (demand charges, paid whether or not the customer shipped gas) to 90 percent from 19 percent back in 1990. Straight-fixed-variable rate design, shifting transmission fees to the must-pay side, instead of volumetric payments as gas was actually shipped, accrued to the benefit of Citrus Corp., half-owned by Enron and half-owned by Sonat, and run by Enron's Bill Allison.[13]

Although the Phase III expansion was cut by 40 percent, costs did not fall proportionately. Unprecedented environmental requirements, in particular, added expense and time to the project. Some 2,300 gopher-tortoise "citizens" living near the mainline required "one of the largest relocations of a protected species ever attempted by environmental specialists." And for the first time, FERC required planting trees and shrubs instead of natural revegetation along the right-of-way.

"It's the right thing to do," remarked one Enron official. But it was also legally required—and good business for regulated rate setting. The extra cost went into the rate base for a rate of return, and would-be pipelines that might enter FGT's territory would be held to the same standard, increasing the cost of entry.

---

12. FGT's previous expansions are discussed in chapter 3, pp. 161–64; chapter 5, pp. 231–32; and chapter 6, pp. 263–65.

13. The proactive, innovative contract between Florida Gas and Florida Power both shut out oil and coal and forestalled a proposed new pipeline to the state.

Northern Natural: Incremental Growth

With more than one-half the overall mileage of Enron's interstates, Northern Natural Pipeline was the dominant supplier to the Midwest market, as it had been since its construction in the early 1930s. Northern's expansive, dispersed market was mature compared to that of high-growth Florida and California.[14] Still, as Enron stated in its *1994 Annual Report*, Northern Natural's "stable rate base, volumes, and margins have positioned it to produce consistently strong earnings and cash flow."

Small expansions maintained the all-important rate base in the face of depreciating original cost. Two 100 MMcf/d increases were completed in 1996: one in Iowa, Illinois, and Wisconsin; the other, in Minnesota. Capacity of 4.1 Bcf/d was almost as much as Enron's other three interstates combined.

Rate-case settlements before FERC were essential for Northern Natural's profitability, as for every other interstate. A resolution was reached in March 1996 when a rate increase was withdrawn in return for customer agreements extending (expiring) firm capacity by two years, giving Northern much-needed firm revenue. Another rate case was obligated sooner than the usual three years to deal with an unresolved proposal for Northern to price capacity seasonally (rather than annually, which was the FERC norm) in order to better match demand and supply should LDCs unbundle and allow end users to buy their own gas. (LDCs would continue to hold transmission capacity.) As elsewhere, Enron was pushing the regulatory envelope at the state level as well as at the federal level.

In 1996, Northern Natural announced a $105 million plan to increase firm capacity by 350 MMcf/d, concentrated in the upper Midwest, between 1997 and 2001. While small by Enron standards, Peak Day 2000 was Northern's largest expansion in 30 years. Every little bit counted; adding customers and capacity increased the rate base and allowed Enron's largest cash cow to keep giving whole milk.

Northern Border: More from Canada

Operator Enron held a 9 percent ownership in Northern Border Pipeline, a 1.7 Bcf/d, 970-mile line bringing Canadian gas to the US Midwest. Of this amount, 70 percent was delivered to Northern Natural Pipeline at Ventura, Iowa, for redelivery to various Midwest markets.

"The largest deliverer of natural gas from Canada to the U.S.," with a market share of 20 percent, applied to FERC in early 1995 to increase capacity by 15 percent for $700 million, mostly to bring more Canadian gas to the Midwest. This proposal was enlarged 40 percent to 700 MMcf/d with a new plan to reach Chicago, putting Northern Border in competition with existing suppliers

---

14. NNG's history is discussed in chapter 1, pp. 103–4; and chapter 2, pp. 105–18.

Natural Gas Pipeline of America and ANR Pipeline, as well as a potential supplier (Alliance Pipeline) that had an entry proposal before FERC. The $837 million expansion, the largest such project under way in the United States, would come on stream in 1998.

Since its 1981 beginning, Northern Border employed a cost-of-service tariff, while Enron's other interstates set rates under a fixed-variable rate design that allocated (mostly fixed) cost to the firm rate (demand charge) and other (mostly variable) cost to the interruptible rate. Northern Border's methodology required firm shippers to pay *all* their transportation charges as a fixed cost, leaving the incremental cost of actually moved volumes at nil. (This rate design, which was common among transnationals moving Canadian gas to the United States, and which virtually eliminated risk for the builder, would be replaced with SFV in 2000.)

Firm customers fully utilized Northern's capacity day in and day out. ("Since 1988, Northern Border has been transporting volumes at or near its maximum capacity.") Under FERC Order No. 636, however, the contractual shipper could relinquish its firm space to a third party for credit (payment).

Enron's interest in Northern Border was through its 13 percent ownership of Northern Border Partners LP (Partners), the other owners being Williams Companies, Panhandle Eastern, and TransCanada PipeLine. Partners, which owned 70 percent of Northern Border Pipeline, went public in 1993 as a Master Limited Partnership (MLP). Enron realized $217 million to help reach its corporate-wide earnings goal of 15 percent and "to repay debt and to fund projects that give us a higher rate of return and faster growth." Enron remained operator and general partner for fee income, while maintaining the "synergistic benefits" of Northern Border for Enron's other interstates and Canadian marketing office.

The MLP ownership structure, enacted by Congress in 1987 for natural resource and mineral companies, avoided the corporate income tax by issuing dividends straight to the owners. This meant that a full dollar was received compared to a full-tax-paid return of 60 cents. The three US owners of Partners were part of the MLP.

Enron Transportation & Storage

Enron's heady vision back in 1987 of a "single networked system" was more hype and hope than fact, although the five-pipeline intrastate-and-interstate system experimented with centralized functions and produced some two-pipeline synergies.[15] Florida Gas Transmission and Transwestern, in particular, combined their accounting, finance, and rates functions for a time.

---

15. Enron's pipeline-centralization efforts are reviewed in chapter 3, p. 157; chapter 5, pp. 225–26, 232; and chapter 6, p. 261.

Grid advantage was largely neutered by system-specific federal rate-and-service regulation, not to mention the MOA rules for pipelines. Gas Control on Floor 42 of the Enron Building showed a lighted screen of the five connected systems that Enron operated, but they were not functionally integrated. Still, there was much thought on how to "'Enronize' the pipelines."

A few cross-country transactions utilizing displacement-and-exchange to eliminate physical transportation made the news, such as a Transwestern to Northern Natural to Florida Gas deal in 1994. Such deals were more for show than dough, but significant intersystem synergies emerged with Transwestern's east-side expansion, which overlapped with the southern end of Northern Natural Gas Pipeline.

––––––

Effective March 1, 1994, Deb Macdonald and Bill Cordes, the respective heads of Transwestern and Northern Natural (both wholly owned by Enron) announced an integration to increase revenues and reduce costs. "Transwestern and Northern Natural Gas are combining revenue targets, business strategies, transportation services, and new product lines," they stated. Other units of the two were also exploring joint optimization for their geographical overlap. The combination was tagged Enron Transport and Storage (ETS).

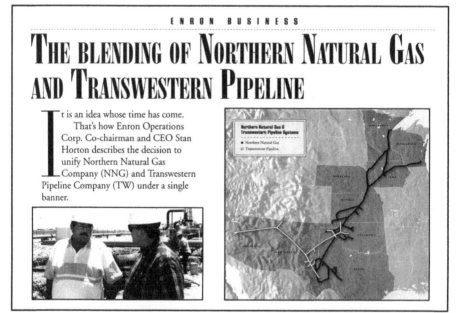

ENRON BUSINESS

THE BLENDING OF NORTHERN NATURAL GAS AND TRANSWESTERN PIPELINE

It is an idea whose time has come. That's how Enron Operations Corp. Co-chairman and CEO Stan Horton describes the decision to unify Northern Natural Gas Company (NNG) and Transwestern Pipeline Company (TW) under a single banner.

Figure 10.3 Enron integration strategy for its interstate pipelines encountered regulatory and ownership obstacles. But one opportunity (in 1996) was combining the southern part of Northorn Natural's system with the eastern end of Transwestern into one entity

This experiment was taken to the next level in September 1996 when the eastern end of Transwestern and the south end of Northern Natural were merged into a new entity, Enron Transportation & Storage (ET&S). Both pipelines remained separate legal entities, with ET&S being an "umbrella organization" to "give new identity" to that part of Transwestern and of Northern.

A single marketing force now served the overlapping markets. Scheduling and billing were merged for "seamless service." The goal of employees was to maximize profit for the new entity, not for one pipeline or the other, which was more money for Enron from fewer transaction costs.

Several factors made the de facto combination possible. Both pipelines had resolved their take-or-pay problems, were full open-access transporters, and had spun down their gathering systems (see pp. 445–46). Both had recently settled rate cases to provide some years of lightly regulated operation during which savings could flow to the bottom line. But most of all, the integration reflected the overlap of systems in West Texas and the Panhandle area of Texas and Oklahoma.

Stan Horton, the cochairman of ET&S along with Northern president Bill Cordes, saw the new entity as part of a "normal evolution of our industry." Indeed, the Gas Industry Standards Board (GISB), empowered by FERC, was well along in codifying best standards to facilitate virtual integration in common company areas.[16] But Horton's observation touched upon another fact: gas-transmission synergies were undoing the regulatory balkanization of the industry.

Deregulation Not

Enron was a fount of action for lightening FERC's regulatory hand. Under Jim Rogers, there were proposals for zone-of-reasonableness rates (1985); a gas supply reservation charge (1986), which later became the Gas Inventory Charge (1987–88); off-system interruptible sales service (1987); and flexible-purchase gas adjustments, or flex PGAs (1986, 1988). Monthly pricing within a cost-based framework was proposed by Rogers protégé Rick Richard at Northern Natural (1989). After securing FERC and CPUC approvals, Transwestern (1986) was the first interstate pipeline in California to bypass the local gas-distribution company and sell gas directly to a customer, thereby displacing residual fuel oil with gas at an electric power plant.

Transwestern and Northern Natural were the first interstates to declare for open-access transportation (1986). Transwestern became the first transportation-only pipeline three years later. Transwestern and Northern also filed deregulation proposals for released firm capacity, under which such capacity was

---

16. In March 1996, GISB, represented by producers, pipelines, marketers, and LDCs, came up with 140 standards concerning nominations, allocations, and invoicing. After further work, FERC adopted the GISB consensus as regulation the next year.

turned back by the original holder and was (re)contracted to the high bidder in an open market.

Transwestern successfully pushed for expedited transportation for new interstate capacity in the wake of the Iraq war of 1990, the rationale being to displace (unreliable) foreign oil. Ken Lay lobbied FERC to adopt fair-value rate-making for interstate gas transmission under which cost-based rates included (higher) replacement costs, not original depreciated costs, which was the way the agency treated interstate oil pipelines.

Rate cases were typically the vehicle for Enron pipelines to push against traditional regulatory boundaries. In addition to the preceding examples, proposals in 1991 for incentive ratemaking from both Florida Gas and Northern Natural were part of such three-year applications.[17]

But simply deregulating natural gas pipelines was not of interest to policy makers, however. The Bush administration's National Energy Strategy (NES), released by the Department of Energy in 1991, advocated rate decontrol only where "pipelines do not possess market power." The NES's "magic of the marketplace," in George H. W. Bush's words, did not apply in midstream interstate gas markets unless a special quantitative finding was made by regulators.

This was the entrenched industry position affirmed by producers, marketers, local distribution companies. It was regulatory inertia, and not many regulators are inclined to deregulate. All this made the interstates shy about pushing generic decontrol on the rest of the industry despite the successful precedent of light-handed state-level regulation for intrastates (as in Texas).

Enron, looking for the practical, endorsed "a combination of cost-based rates, incentive rates, and/or market rates based upon the particular service and particular market." Some free-market economists and libertarians associated with the Cato Institute and the Institute for Energy Research (IER) thought otherwise. In their eyes, full deregulation—with or without a phase-in—was workable.

While previously advocating relaxed regulation within a cost-based just-and-reasonable framework, Ken Lay endorsed full decontrol at a Cato-IER conference in 1993, becoming "the first chair of a major pipeline company to openly consider deregulating interstate transmission." At the same time, and even in the same speech, however, Lay advocated government intervention in energy markets, also for Enron's competitive gain.[18]

———

17. See below, pp. 444–45. See also chapter 6, pp. 265–66; and chapter 7, p. 309.

18. See chapter 7, pp. 318–19, 342–43. Lay advocated a Btu tax that would disproportionately hurt oil and coal relative to natural gas and so advantage Enron. The funds from the tax would underwrite crude oil purchases for the Strategic Petroleum Reserve.

Lay's self-interested position had a storied theoretical basis. FERC's quantitative test of "workable competition" in light of an interstate's "market power" was a methodology that assessed market-share ratios as calculated by the Herfindahl-Hirschman Index. HHI viewed competition and efficiency in *static* terms. It was an equilibrium analysis.[19] Yet competition, as economists from Joseph Schumpeter to F. A. Hayek had stressed, is a dynamic, unfolding process, not a snapshot (or at-the-moment measurement) of current industry structure. The gains from *entrepreneurship* cannot be captured in FERC's structure-conduct-performance model, because innovation is not a predictable, measurable action.[20] Yet *dynamic efficiency* was as or more important than *static efficiency*.

Opponents chided a market-process, qualitative view of competition. "A determination of sufficient competition cannot be made on an industry-wide basis, based upon anecdote, supposition, or Aristotelian Logic," said a brief for the producer trade groups Natural Gas Supply Association (NGSA) and Independent Petroleum Association of American (IPAA). The nonintegrated gas industry, created by regulation, in turn created this (pro-)regulatory conflict.

"Slow-moving traditional regulation cannot respond to the quick changes that have resulted [from] ... the expansion of competitive forces within gas markets," stated one Enron consultant. "Rates generally misprice services: in peak periods services are not allocated to the highest valued uses, in off-peak periods the pipelines are not used as fully as they could be, and administratively set rates fail to provide proper signals for entry and exit decisions."

Imperfect competition, as defined, moreover, cannot be policed and solved by immaculate regulation; there is *government failure* in the quest to address *market failure*. Opined Lay in his Cato-IER keynote address, "Imperfect markets are often better than perfect regulation," implying that even the best government action is often worse than government inaction.

In 1996, an internal Enron task force envisioned what a new set of free-market FERC commissioners might propose to reinterpret the Natural Gas Act's just-and-reasonable standard regarding market substitutes for regulation. The Deregulation Notice of Proposed Rulemaking (D-NOPR) hypothesized a free-market FERC replacing cost-based regulation and entry-and-exit authority with "market reliance and self-regulation through Commission-sanctioned settlement contracts."[21] The inspiration for this new thinking came from Transwestern's global settlement, under which the parties, with FERC's

19. See Internet appendix 10.1, "Competition: Real World versus Theoretical," at www .politicalcapitalism.org/Book3/Chapter10/Appendix1.html.

20. See Internet appendix "Entrepreneurship in Economics: From Unknown to Missing," at http://www.politicalcapitalism.org/Book1/Chapter4/Appendix2.html.

21. See Internet appendix 10.2, "Enron Memos on Natural Gas Transmission Deregulation," at http://www.politicalcapitalism.org/Book3/Chapter10/Appendix2.html.

blessing, entered into a contract that essentially replaced federal regulation with a long-term contract. Regulation was, in a sense, privatized—with lower costs and legal certainty.

———

Given FERC's guiding philosophy of guilty until proven innocent, Enron's interstates continued to push for lightened, market-conforming regulation in the mid-1990s. Some fell short from upstream and downstream opposition. These opposing parties saw stringent cost-based rates as a wealth transfer from the regulated party to themselves—a zero-sum view as opposed to the dynamic view that greater product choices and new entry would be encouraged by free-market incentives.

As it was, FERC talked big about market reform but was never comfortable about voluntary negotiations and let-the-market-decide. Not even incentive regulation, a stated priority of FERC from the late 1980s through the mid-1990s, got off the ground.

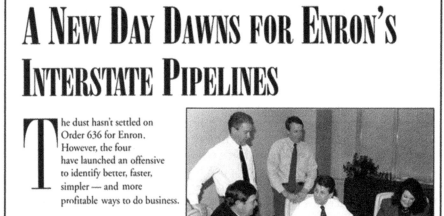

Figure 10.4 Enron's interstate pipelines practiced entrepreneurship under regulatory constraints. Under Stan Horton (bottom center), CEO of Enron Interstate Pipelines, the four pipeline heads were (clockwise) Deb Macdonald (Transwestern), Larry DeRoin (Northern Border), Bill Cordes (Northern Natural), and Bill Allison (Florida Gas).

Transwestern's global rate settlement in 1995 left the pipeline virtually deregulated until its next obligatory rate case ten years later. In the same year, Florida Gas proposed to index its cost-of-service rates to inflation for a five-year period and otherwise offer customers the option of negotiating rates and service different from the regulated default (the recourse option). What ended up being chosen under this "market matching program" depended on "the creativity of shippers trying to match their unique market circumstances in order to maximize flexibility, efficiency and value." Like a similar proposal by Florida Gas back in 1991, this proposal fell short of FERC enactment.

In 1996, Northern Natural pitched its Skyline proposal, under which shippers paid market-sensitive seasonal rates so that (other things equal) rates would be higher in the peak winter season and lower off-peak. Such scarcity pricing would be within an overall cost-based revenue ceiling under which higher-than-regulated rates would be balanced by lower-than-regulated rates within the same year.

Gathering Deregulation
While mainline interstate-pipeline markets were not considered "workably competitive" by federal regulators, gas pricing at the wellhead and at market hubs were. Producer price controls had created natural gas shortages in the 1970s, a black mark on administrative regulation under the Natural Gas Act of 1938. Federal legislation in 1978 and in 1989 removed all price ceilings with little effect because of the gas surplus.[22]

This left gathering lines, the small diameter pipe that was included as rate base under FERC public-utility regulation—and complicated interstate pipeline rate cases as such. Regulated systems subject to cost-based tariffs composed one-third of the market, which left most of the market as nonregulated competition. Regulated ratemaking also cross-subsidized poorer wells at the expense of lower-cost production.

Should FERC continue such regulation post–Order No. 636—given that gathering systems were being unbundled by their regulated pipeline owners? After all, nonaffiliated gathering was not regulated from Washington. To address these questions, FERC initiated a rulemaking in 1993.

"The threat of federal regulation posed by the 'regulatory string' with respect to affiliated gatherers places them at a competitive disadvantage vis-à-vis non-regulated competitors," Enron pleaded in the rulemaking. Other interstates with regulated gathering, represented by the Interstate Natural Gas Association of America (INGAA), which Enron's Rich Kinder happened to chair at the time, sought parity and entrepreneurial freedom.

Producers, independents and majors alike, lobbied for the status quo: FERC-established rate maximums. "Gathering competition at many wells is illusory," the chairman of the Independent Petroleum Association of America (IPAA) told FERC. Representatives from Conoco, Amoco, Anadarko, and the NGSA were opposed to gathering decontrol and even existing light-handed regulation.

---

22. This historic regulatory failure is described in Bradley, *Edison to Enron*, pp. 504–8.

The ruling came in May 1994. "The Commission will not regulate gathering facilities if a pipeline applies to 'spin-down' those facilities to a corporate affiliate or 'spin-off' those facilities to another company." Philosophized one FERC commissioner: "We would be in error if we overregulated that sector of the industry." Transition rules were set in place, and FERC passed jurisdiction to state energy regulators to step in as necessary.

———

This nod to free markets was a victory for interstates and for Enron. "We applaud the Commission for taking a very, very balanced approach," stated Stan Horton." There were safety nets, he noted, and "the abuse the Commission is worried about does not exist here at Enron." Producers, after all, were *customers*; without supply, and good relations going forward, there could be no sales.

It was time to spin down or spin off gathering.

"Our internal analysis, coupled with unsolicited offers from interested parties," stated Horton several months later, "indicates that the gathering assets on Transwestern Pipeline and Northern Natural gas may be more valuable to others." Sales ensued, which reduced the mileage of Transwestern and Northern Natural by 28 percent and 40 percent, respectively. Cash in the door—the interstates had done it again for Enron.

But Enron's gathering moves did not escape the long arm of government. The Federal Trade Commission intervened against a gathering system sale to Phillips Petroleum, requiring Enron to exclude one-third of a proposed 2,300-mile transaction in the Texas-Oklahoma Anadarko area. And Texas, among other states (including Oklahoma and Kansas), would assert jurisdiction and set up a complaint procedure for producers who felt discriminated against or abused by a gatherer through either rates or terms of service. Such light-handed regulation, however, was a far cry from the prior rate-based regulation for what had been part of interstate pipeline operations.

Enron Oil & Gas Company

The hiring of Forrest Hoglund in 1987 to rejuvenate Enron Oil & Gas Company was a highlight of Ken Lay's tenure at Enron. By 1990, EOG was strongly cash positive, thanks in part to John Wing's PURPA contract. The next years prospered from tax credits for tight-sands gas production, which accounted for 40 percent of the company's net income in 1992 and 1993. (EOG had labored to reinstate this expired provision in the federal tax code, as described in chapter 6.)

But far beyond rent-seeking, Hoglund was doing the right things to create competitive advantage. While other firms were reducing costs by consolidating division offices, EOG pared back Houston to set up regional offices. Staffed to be autonomous, each EOG division was its own profit center. The companies-within-a-company aggressively cut drilling and operating costs, helped by new technology, particularly 2D and 3D seismic and horizontal drilling, in industry-leading fashion.[23]

Natural gas prices that fell by half between 1985 and 1987 would not recover, but Hoglund bragged about an operation, self-helped by hedging, that was positioned for any industry conditions.[24] Unlike Enron, EOG was a low-cost operation, the "Southwest Airlines" and "Walmart" of its industry. Also in contrast to the parent, EOG maintained an "extremely conservative" balance sheet. Unlike Enron Gas Services, the nation's fifth-largest independent producer used no accounting legerdemain that borrowed from the future. ("We're not playing the easy type of game," Hoglund would say.) So it was not surprising that EOG, generating a half-billion dollars annually in cash flow, would increasingly go its own way to best monetize Enron's investment.

In 1989, Enron placed 16 percent of EOG on the public market, confirming an enterprise value that was greater than the rest of Ken Lay's company. Enron reduced its holding to 80 percent in 1992 and to 61 percent in 1995, realizing $110 million and $161 million, respectively. Also in 1995, Enron obligated itself to a year-end 1998 conversion to reduce its interest to 53.5 percent. (Full divestment would come the next year.) The New Enron was being financed, in part, by EOG.

With the tax credit expired for new drilling, EOG in 1993 shifted to tax-neutral strategies between adding low-cost deliverability, disposing of marginal properties, and acquiring strategic reserves. The period 1994–96 marked steady progress and foundation-building for more good years, even great ones, to come. There would be no unhappy ending for low-cost, low-debt, transparent EOG as there would be for Enron.

Low-Price Profitability

"Prosperity at home and abroad" was EOG's message entering 1994. International operations were beginning to contribute, but North America's seven district offices were the moneymakers. The most activity was in Big Piney (Wyoming), with other divisions covering South Texas, East Texas, West Texas and New Mexico, Oklahoma, the Gulf of Mexico, and Canada.[25] Natural gas

---

23. EOG's earlier history is described in chapter 3, pp. 174–77 (1986–87); chapter 5, pp. 216–20 (1988–89); and chapter 6, pp. 285–93 (1990–93).

24. "Up until last year," Hoglund joked, "we had thoroughly convinced everybody that we could continue to grow earnings with decreasing gas prices. The big challenge in 1993 was to show them that we also could grow earnings with an increase in gas prices."

25. The Department of Interior regulated EOG operations on federal land, specifically the Bureau of Land Management onshore (Big Piney) and the Minerals Management Service offshore (Gulf of Mexico).

accounted for 93 percent of reserves, although the company dropped its former tag line, *America's natural gas play*, because of growing international ambitions.

The mini-gas-price recovery of 1993 reversed in 1994, with average well-head revenue falling 16 percent to $1.62 per thousand cubic feet, prompting voluntary shut-ins (as much as 25 percent of EOG's deliverability) and a capital reallocation away from infill drilling towards reserve additions. Hedging and cost reductions, as well as (regulatory enabled) prior deals executed at premium prices, made for record earnings in 1994—and a two-for-one common stock split from the public company. Indeed, the market valuation of EOG since going public in 1989 had grown from $1.8 billion to $3.8 billion, annual compounded growth in excess of 15 percent. Total return to shareholders exceeded 100 percent, double that of S&P 500—and far, far above the 5 percent *negative* return for its peer group in the five years.

Reserve replacement in 1994 was 177 percent, another record. Finding costs were down to $0.88 per thousand cubic feet (Mcf). Tax benefits from grandfathered tight-sands properties added $21 million in the year, which gave EOG a 4 percent effective tax rate from its 35 percent statutory rate.[26]

"I don't think there is anyone in the industry who can stay with us on drilling costs," Forrest Hoglund boasted. A report by Goldman Sachs agreed, estimating EOG's cash operating cost per unit of energy produced far below its peer group. Improved three-dimensional models to target drilling, in addition to new applications of enhanced well-competition technology, were resulting in more gas at less expense. *Enron Business* told employees that drilling times fell from 24 to 17 days in one field and from 13 days to 7 in another.

———

With wellhead gas prices hitting a new low in 1995, EOG faced what Forrest Hoglund called "probably the toughest year in our company's history." EOG earnings were flat but impressive in what Hoglund called "an outstanding year."

The self-styled "low-cost independent" had to make money in new ways: "increased crude oil and condensate products, other marketing activities including commodity price hedges, and the sale of selected oil and gas reserves and related sales." Discretionary cash flow remained north of a half-billion dollars, and stockholder returns of nearly 30 percent for the year were more than double those of EOG's peers.

A 20 percent fall in gas prices and voluntary curtailments of 105 MMcf/d (14 percent of EOG's North American deliverability) shifted capital from drilling to reserve acquisition in 1995. Netted with property sales, EOG wound up the year

———

26. In 1992 and 1993, with tight-sands credits of $43 million and $60 million, respectively, EOG's effective tax rate was *negative* 22 percent and then 23 percent. Enron paid EOG a check for the tax savings on the consolidated tax return.

with higher reserves, more strategic properties to existing operations, and profit—"our best acquisition year ever." Doubled reserve replacement in the year set up the future.

EOG had a political moment during the price-stressed year. EOG wanted to turn its voluntary curtailment into a mandatory one to require its fully producing competitors to cut back too—all in the effort to buoy prices. Hoglund's bunch wanted help from any state commission that would issue mandatory proration orders. The Oklahoma Corporation Commission (OCC) was curtailing the state's 28,000 wells, just as EOG's state division head Leland McVay wanted. But other producers were doing what was natural: making up with volume what they were losing on price. The OCC watched helplessly as oil states Texas, Louisiana, and Kansas chose not to prorate and increased output. Competition was hurting the prorating state, and government was not able to plug the dike as had been done in past decades with crude-oil proration in the oil states and federal oil import restrictions.

Enron cashed in on EOG's strong stock price at year's end, selling 31 million shares of common for $650 million, earning $367 million ($161 million after-tax). Additionally, Ken Lay and Rich Kinder told shareholders in Enron's annual report: "Primarily, as a result of the successful completion of an EOG debt offering in December 1995, we reduced our debt to total capitalization ratio to about 40 percent and achieved a key credit rating upgrade to BBB+."

Proceeds from EOG "will expand business opportunities at ECT and Enron Development Corp," Lay and Kinder wrote. Forrest Hoglund welcomed "the increased liquidity in EOG stock [allowing] existing investors to significantly increase their positions while also attracting new investors." Hoglund was Enron's top division head, with consistent, high earnings and increasing enterprise value.

It was a story of the fishes and loaves. Prior to becoming a public company, EOG was worth an estimated $880 million to Enron. After stock sales generating $2 billion for the parent, Enron's 53 percent retention going into 1996 was worth $1.9 billion. And these were not easy times in the oil industry. Yet Ken Lay, fussing about low prices and once (in 1991) accusing the majors of predatory pricing, had wanted more.

————

EOG was part of a macro story of how the industry was performing for consumers, as if led by an invisible hand. The familiar warnings that "the easy stuff has been found" or "only the high cost supplies remain" were refuted early and often at EOG and across the United States.

"New technology and smarter management are prolonging the decade-old gas glut," Toni Mack wrote in *Forbes* in late 1994. "Oilmen have learned to squeeze costs, turn a profit, and produce more gas, even when prices stay low." The resulting supply was keeping prices down, and new technology, apparently without diminishing returns, was making what had been high-cost gas into low-cost gas. The marginal cost of so-called depletable natural gas was falling, just as predicted by Julian Simon and a few others in defiance of the mainstream fixity-depletion (neo-Malthusian) view.[27]

Information technology was replacing "dumb iron" to find natural gas. What was true at EOG was industry-wide (although Hoglund's results were above his peer group's). "The exploration dollars are shifting from drilling to 3-D seismic," said one Houston drilling consultant in 1995. "Three-D seismic gives a large overall picture while drilling gives you a single data point." Seen somewhat differently, "the reservoir will have wells drilled, produced, and eventually depleted by computer under a limitless number of varying scenarios before additional wells are actually drilled."

Not everyone was happy. As mentioned, Forrest Hoglund asked state regulators to help prices by prorating (curtailing) output between wells and fields. Ken Lay was of two minds after being heavily criticized for his predatory-pricing insinuation against major oil companies several years before. And pugnacious Oscar Wyatt urged the Texas Railroad Commission to curtail gas production between 20 and 30 percent during peak periods to increase prices to $2.50 per MMBtu (Mcf), a 50 percent jump from then-average wellhead prices. "We have freely chosen to flood the market with a premium fuel at disaster prices," the Coastal Corp. chairman complained about the natural order of things.

If the point of production was consumption, and if the welfare of consumers trumps that of producers, the natural gas sector was doing its job. Between 1985 and 1994, inflation-adjusted gas prices fell by more than 20 percent for LDCs and industrial customers, were steady for commercial users, and rose slightly for residential users.

There was something else. With more efficient midstream operations in the open-access era, whether at a pipeline or storage facility, less gas-production capacity got the same job done for consumers than before. (Open access was "ruining the pipeline construction business," stated John Jennrich, tongue in cheek.) Price volatility was certainly higher for those oriented to the spot market, but that was scarcity pricing in action, and risk products were available too. "The market really works," commented Joe Foster, formerly head of Tenneco's production side and now head of Newfield Exploration.

———

"In 1996, EOG will continue its strategy of increasing shareholder value regardless of market conditions," Hoglund wrote in the first quarter. But success would have to come without price hedges, which generated $107 million in 1995 and $54 million the year before. Open positions had been closed in anticipation of a price recovery.

---

27. See Bradley, *Capitalism at Work*, pp. 187, 240, 268–70, 271–80.

EOG bet right. North American prices jumped 43 percent in 1996 to $1.92/ MMBtu, which also increased volume sold with the end of voluntary curtailment. Yet net income was little changed from the year before, reflecting a $100 million drop in hedging profit compared to 1995, a large decline in property sales, a 13 percent increase in operating expenses (higher wellhead prices did that), and higher income taxes without new tax-credit-eligible gas production.[28] Still, higher wellhead prices were desired with every dime change at the wellhead altering cash flow by an estimated $13 million.

"EOG is stronger than ever and is committed to continuing to be a leader in the use of technological advantages and low-cost, fast-track performance to enhance future profitability," the 1996 annual report stated. Level earnings and cash flow since 1993 masked the true progress of the company from the time it went public in 1989, as well as its robust prospects for the future. In the eight years of EOG's public life, net income and cash flow had tripled to $543 million; deliverability had more than doubled for both gas (to 830 MMcf/d) and liquids (to 22,000 barrels per day). EOG now had an international presence. All this had caused a stock share of EOG to more than double in value since the company went public—and generate quarterly dividends from twice as much stock.

Nine consecutive years of increased proved reserves after production left the company with four trillion cubic feet (gas equivalent), a 60 percent rise from when EOG first went public. This reserve figure was 92 percent natural gas and 83 percent in North America. The debt-to-capital ratio increased to 27 percent from 20 percent, however, owing to a major increase in drilling programs in North America, India, and Trinidad.

International

Forrest Hoglund reported to Ken Lay and Rich Kinder. Enron's board of directors controlled EOG's board, which included Lay and Kinder. So the parent's keen international ambition was part of EOG's DNA. "If Enron Corp. is to become a natural gas major," Hoglund stated in 1994, "EOG must expand its exploration and production expertise globally."

EOG's international entreaties were good talk for investors and the parent. The philosophy was to pursue "selected conventional natural gas and crude oil opportunities outside of North America ... particularly where synergies in natural gas transportation, processing, and power generation can be optimized with other Enron affiliated companies."

Little came of discussions, agreements, tract purchases, or drilling undertaken in 12 countries: Australia, China, Egypt, France, Kazakhstan, offshore Malaysia, Russia, South Sumatra, Syria, UK North Sea, Uzbekistan, and

---

28. Compared to its statutory rate of 35 percent, EOG's effective tax rate in 1996 was 27 percent, just above 1995's 23 percent and well above 1994's tax-credit-driven 4 percent.

Venezuela.[29] Much-anticipated LNG projects in Qatar and Mozambique with parent Enron did not reach commercialization either.

The story was different in Trinidad, where fast-track production began in 1993. Production of 63 MMcf/d in 1994 reached 124 MMcf/d in 1996, accounting for 15 percent of EOG's total. Trinidad exceeded volumes generated out of EOG's Calgary (Canada) division, a niche play for many years because of low gas prices and limited transmission access.[30]

Joe McKinney and Dennis Ulak, the successive presidents of EOG's international operations, took many long trips and laboriously negotiated with state companies, all in competition against the oil majors. Their reward was Trinidad and some oil and condensate output in India, where EOG became the first foreign-owned company to win drilling rights. The plan for the world's "first low-cost, fast-track exploration and production company" was to double the percentage of foreign production to 25–30 percent of EOG's total. As it would turn out, in 1999, the year that Enron Oil & Gas split from Enron to become EOG Resources, the percentage outside North America was half of that, comprising Trinidad and not much more.

Forrest Hoglund often spoke of EOG's challenge to overcome the "political or cultural environment" in distant lands, no matter how hydrocarbon rich they might be. Hoglund was wary of political risk. Who could forget the Peruvian nationalization of 1985, which Enron finally settled in 1993? EOG's philosophy was "layering of moderate risk growth potential outside North America on top the company's steady North America growth profile." Trinidad, EOG's international bell cow, in fact, was made risk tolerable by a $100 million insurance policy courtesy of the US taxpayer-funded Overseas Private Investment Corporation (OPIC).

In India, a $200 million OPIC policy was secured as part of EOG's $1.1 billion offshore Bombay project, whose production was forecast to reach 280 MMcf/d in several years (it would turn out to be much less).[31] But in 1996, it was all-go with the Panna and Mukta oil fields and the Tapti natural gas play with drilling platforms and seismic surveys.

---

29. Ambitious, publicized plans to export expertise in coal-bed methane recovery from the San Juan Basin (United States) to Australia, China, the United Kingdom, and France, touted in EOG's 1995 annual report, were not heard about again.

30. Enron Oil Canada Ltd., facing wellhead prices around $1.00/MMBtu, contributed 30 MMcf/d in 1992. Doubled wellhead prices the next year increased production to 70 MMcf/d. In 1996, production of approximately 100 MMcf/d made Calgary an important office.

31. This project was separate from Enron's taxpayer-backed two-phase power plant at Dabhol, India, which began with $400 million in OPIC and Export-Import Bank support. In the 1999 spin-off to become independent, the renamed EOG Resources assigned Enron its Asian properties, the most valuable of which was the Tapti Field in India.

Mark Papa Joins In

Chairman, President, and CEO Forrest Hoglund was a man to keep. His original five-year contract was renewed in 1992 for three years. With a year to go on his second contract, the high performer was inked through 1998. Very few of EOG's 800 employees were anything but happy to retain their affable leader.

"Substantially all of Mr. Hoglund's future compensation in excess of his base salary is at risk and tied to the performance of Company's Common Stock," EOG reported to shareholders. Indeed, Hoglund eschewed raises and monetary bonuses in his contract. Incentives, not base pay, got Hoglund to Enron, and incentives, now totaling several million shares of stock, were keeping him there. Enron's stock price was rising more than EOG's, thanks to Enron Gas Services' valuation in particular—a good thing for retaining top executives such as Forrest Hoglund.

A stock sale in 1994 produced a $19 million compensation year for EOG's leader, which was tops for Houston's entire business community. "There's not a CEO of any major oil company in the country that made nearly that much," Ken Lay gushed. But it was well deserved, Lay explained, with EOG's 15 percent rate of return dwarfing the 5 percent typical of many of its competitors.

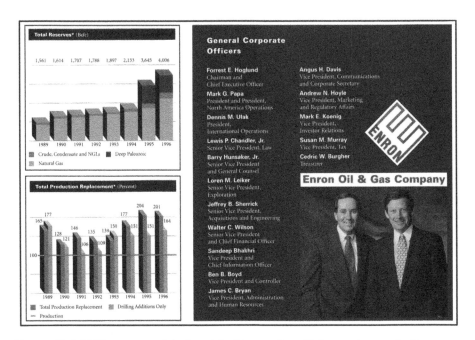

Figure 10.5 EOG was a model of sustainable growth, with increasing production, earnings, and reserves, year after year. Forrest Hoglund (right) was atop this performance, as was Mark Papa (left), who would take over from Hoglund in 1999, the year that EOG fully separated from Enron to become EOG Resources Inc.

The Letter to Stockholders in the 1996 annual report pictured two executives, not just Forrest Hoglund as before. EOG's new president was Mark G. Papa, who had been president of EOG's North American operations, and who retained his old title alongside his new one. Hoglund, now 63, had chosen his heir apparent.

The 50-year-old Papa had been with EOG since its inception and with EOG-predecessor Belco Petroleum since 1981. The engineer began his career in the field and then at headquarters with Conoco in Corpus Christi. After several years in Dubai, and having gained an MBA from the University of Houston, Papa joined Belco and in two years was named vice president of drilling and operations. At EOG, he was Senior Vice President–Operations before heading the company's North American operations, which encompassed onshore and offshore operations in the United States and Canada.

It would be Papa who succeeded Hoglund as CEO in 1999, the year that the two negotiated a full split from Enron. Papa would go on to build the renamed EOG Resources Inc. into one of the very top oil and gas independents and financial performers, until retiring in 2013.[32]

Enron redeployed its EOG proceeds to international and to gas marketing, the start-up businesses that Lay saw as crucial in the mid-1990s. EOG stock sell-downs gave Enron cash during vulnerable times. But more than this, Forrest Hoglund and EOG were a *model* for Enron: a conservative company with a much lower tolerance for risk and better cost controls than its parent.

While going its own way from the parent, EOG had richly benefitted from "four mutual synergies: product development and marketing; multiple international presences; tax credit utilization; and financial flexibility." EOG, too, had been the physical backup (the hedge) for early gas trading by John Esslinger's Enron Gas Marketing.

Price-rich EOG gas contracts pursuant to Enron's PURPA-driven power plants, in addition to the tight-sands tax credit, were part of this synergy. Upstream, as in the midstream and downstream, special government favor was a major theme of Enron's rise to preeminence.

Enron Oil Transportation & Trading (EOTT)

In the early 1990s, Enron Oil Transportation & Trading (EOTT) was housed within Enron Liquid Fuels (ELF), a five-division unit run by Mike Muckleroy. EOTT's sisters were Enron Gas Processing Company; Enron Gas Liquids Inc.; Enron Liquids Pipeline Company; and Enron Americas Inc.

---

32. Edmund Segner, number two to Papa as president and chief of staff, had been executive vice president and chief of staff at Enron before joining EOG in 1997.

Although rarely newsworthy, Mike Muckleroy's unit was profitable for a parent lacking in quality earnings. Liquids processing and transportation was a midstream business, complementing natural gas transmission and storage. As one of Enron's five major divisions, ELF operated alongside exploration and production (EOG), gas transmission (HPL and the interstates), electric generation (Enron Power), and gas marketing (Enron Gas Services).

Run by Charles Emel, EOTT was Enron's lone oil-dominated division. Less than one-tenth of EOG's reserves were crude oil, after all, and Enron never ventured into oil refining, just methanol and MTBE refining.

EOTT margins were more volatile than the margins of ELP as a whole. New lease acquisitions were key to its growth given that the company expected a 3–5 percent decline of North American crude oil annually.

EOTT always seemed to be in an industry-wide cycle, part of the nature of a highly competitive, short-term market. In terms of profitability, 1989, 1991, and 1993 were strong; 1990 and 1992, tough. In terms of revenue, however, EOTT was a huge business, accounting for approximately half of Enron's total. EOTT purchased crude oil from approximately 23,000 leases in 17 states, as well as from Canadian leases. Most of the approximately 250,000 average daily barrels was transported by EOTT's fleet of 333 trucks and 1,036 miles of gathering pipeline, mostly intrastate but some interstate.[33] Another 34,000 barrels per day of crude oil were imported for sale in 1994.

Storage capacity in trucks and in owned or leased storage tanks was nearly 300,000 barrels. Another 250,000 barrels of capacity was at four barge facilities in Louisiana and Texas. EOTT facilities also blended and upgraded crude oil in processing agreements with refiners and sold refined gasoline in 15 states.

There were few fixed-priced, long-term contracts and few open positions, just short-term back-to-back (buy and sell) deals. EOTT purchased crude oil at the lease and made a simultaneous sale to a refinery—with a positive differential to cover transportation. Sometimes the sale was to a third party that moved the oil farther downstream; sometimes a purchase was balanced by a sale on NYMEX for a future month.

Profit maximization was defined as the ability "to deliver the crude oil to its highest value location or to otherwise maximize the value of the crude oil controlled by EOTT." In contrast to Jeff Skilling's world, EOTT's policy was "not to acquire and hold crude oil, other petroleum products, futures contracts or other derivative products for the purpose of speculating on price changes."

---

33. Interstate oil pipelines were regulated by FERC but under statutory authority different from that governing natural gas pipelines. Consequently, FERC regulation of oil pipelines was more light-handed than its regulation of natural gas pipelines. See Bradley, *Oil, Gas, and Government: The U.S. Experience*, chapter 14.

Without government barriers to entering the field, margins were thin. Points of purchase shifted more than the destinations. It was a knowledge business in which just about everyone knew what everyone else was doing. In contrast to natural gas and electricity and (to a lesser extent) gas liquids, there was no particular Enron angle or house advantage. Still, "EOTT believes that new market services such as risk management and financial services will become increasingly important parts of the industry's service portfolio."

―――

"As we pursue our goal of becoming the world's first natural gas major, the crude oil related business functions of EOTT do not fall within the scope of our overall corporate direction," Ken Lay and Rich Kinder informed employees in fourth-quarter 1992. "We are planning to spin off Enron Oil Trading and Transportation to Enron Corp. shareholders," in order to form "a new, separately traded public entity completely independent of Enron Corp." Only employees of Multifuels, the risk-management section of EOTT, would remain with Enron by joining ECT.

McKinsey was hired to formulate a new business plan for the proposed public company, not a good sign. Before the year was out, 160 layoffs were announced, many involving the planned spin-off. But what was expected to take place in the first quarter of 1993 would be a year late. In the meantime, Mike Muckleroy, heading the transition, and expected to head the new company, had left Enron.

EOTT Energy Partners LP (EOT) went public in March 1994.[34] Raising $186 million from a 58 percent distribution, Enron recorded a $15 million pretax gain. The fourth of five such monetizations, EOT was Enron's third master limited partnership (MLP), joining Northern Border Pipeline (NBP, 1993) and Enron Liquids Pipeline (ENP, 1992), whose earnings were distributed to shareholders to avoid federal corporate taxation. (Enron Global Power & Pipelines and Enron Oil & Gas went public in regular corporate form in 1994 and 1989, respectively.) All five monetizations were in the service of improving the parent's balance sheet and increasing the price of Enron's stock.

The good news was that EOTT's offering increased Enron earnings in 1994. The bad news was that the $20 per share price to realize this gain (when there would otherwise have been a loss) required Enron to backstop the new firm's performance. MLPs worked best when cash flow was stable, and EOTT's was not.

―――――

34. Technically, EOTT Energy Corp., wholly owned by Enron, traded its crude oil marketing and transportation assets for stock in EOTT Energy Partners LP, as well as a 2 percent general partnership interest. Enron retained seven million subordinated units of EOT, a 42 percent ownership interest.

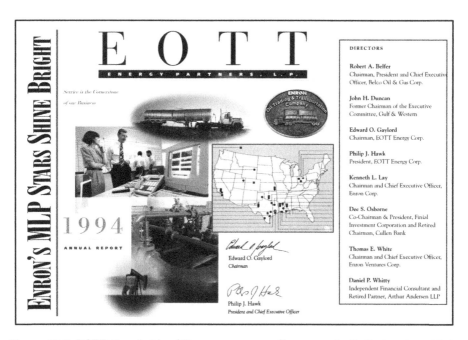

Figure 10.6 EOTT, the oil side of Enron, was spun off as a master limited partnership in 1994 with Enron guarantees to support the stock price and see that the partnership would meet its required quarterly distributions.

Specifically, Enron entered into an auxiliary agreement to ensure EOTT's cash distributions if cash flow (which by law had to be distributed to investors within 45 days of the close of each business quarter) could not support the stated payout of $1.70 per common share, an 8.5 percent return. Enron was pledged to guarantee such support through the first quarter of 1997. This would result in tens of millions of dollars in support and hundreds of millions of guarantees in the next several years.

As General Partner, Enron retained 42 percent ownership and operated EOTT for a fee. EOTT Partners described itself as a "value-added intermediary that seeks to create its profit margin from the services it provides to its customers," including "traditional trading, marketing, and transportation activities, as well as emerging risk-management services." Competing against Scurlock Permian Oil, Koch Oil, and Texaco Trading, EOTT Partners had about 4 percent of the market. Together, these four companies held about 25 percent of the lease crude oil market, with the major oil companies accounting for 40–45 percent more.

EOTT's three divisions were North American Crude Oil, West Coast Operations, and Refined Products Marketing. In December 1994, Philip Hawk was named CEO, reporting to board chairman Edward Gaylord. Rich Kinder and Ken Lay were board members, as well as John Duncan and Robert Belfer, indicating a remaining link between the former full owner and the now General Partner.

———

The first nine months as a public company were strong, joining a "much improved" 1993 that had been marked by "expansion of the company's strategic base, exiting unprofitable activities, and putting a new management team and business strategy in place." Earnings of $19.7 million ($1.13 per unit) in 1994—16 percent above 1993's $16.9 million ($0.97 per share)—supported a net cash flow sufficient to cover the investor distribution without special Enron help.

EOTT was not going to lose money in its basic buy-sell function with leasehold crude. The real risk was elsewhere. "The profitability of EOTT's processing agreement is significantly influenced by the crack spread, which is the difference between the sales price of refined petroleum products and the cost of feedstocks (principally crude oil) delivered to the refinery for processing," investors were informed in the company's first Form 10-K.

In first-quarter 1995, the lowest margins in a decade ruined the economics of EOTT's major processing agreement with a California refinery, which did not have hedged sales to go along with a locked-in refining fee. A bleak outlook for "crack spreads" led EOTT to terminate its West Coast processing and asphalt marketing business and take a $46.8 million write-off, equating to $2.70 per unit, in third-quarter 1995.

First-quarter losses required a $4.25 million cash distribution by the General Partner (Enron) from its authorized $19 million backstop. Second-quarter problems required another $4.8 million to support what now was a $1.90 per share distribution.

Enron in 1995 also increased its support obligation by $10 million (to $29 million) with its quarterly support extended one year (through the first quarter of 1998). Still more, Enron had $450 million in trade guarantees, letters of credit, loans, and letters of indemnity, through March 1996, to support EOTT day-to-day business.

Beginning at $20 per share, EOT increased slightly before falling below $15 later in 1994. Next year's woes sent the stock to $12.75 before Enron's $15 million stock repurchase plan buoyed EOT to a high of $18.50.

A year of relief followed. "We are proud to report that the partnership achieved record earnings in 1996," Edward Gaylord and Philip Hawk announced. "The steps taken in 1995 to exit the West Coast processing arrangement, the favorable impact of ongoing acquisitions, our continued focus on aggressive business building initiatives, plus favorable market conditions, all contributed to this success."[35] EOT increased from $18.25 at year-end 1995 to $21.875 per share at year-end 1996.

Quadrupled earnings from depressed 1995 were enough to support the $1.90 per share distribution in 1996. At the close of 1996, Enron guaranteed $182 million of EOTT's letters of credit, as well as $424 million in EOTT otherwise. "Enron is committed to provide support for EOTT's common unit distributions, if needed, up to a total of $29 million through March 1998 through the purchase of Additional Partnership Interests."

In fact, Enron would increase its ownership to 50 percent before ending 1996 at 49 percent, up from the 42 percent at the time of the public offering. In 1996, EOTT sold its Arizona asphalt terminals for $3.2 million to completely exit that business.

Cash infusions, credit guarantees, and "enormous management intensity": all for a $15 million pretax gain in 1994 and subsequent fee income as general partner. In retrospect, it would have been far better to sell the unit in whole or in its parts and exit the business rather than try to manage an MLP structure as if it was an "Enron bond."[36]

More challenge would come. EOTT's "very difficult" 1997, with losses of $14.4 million, or $0.75 per unit (versus its payout of $1.90), led to the ouster of Philip Hawk. Losses of $4.1 million followed in 1998, under Michael Burke as president and CEO, a year in which EOTT added "economies of scale" and "cost synergies" with the $235.6 million purchase of a crude oil gathering and transportation system from Koch Industries Inc.

The next year's loss of $2.2 million led to another management change with Dana Gibbs as COO and Stan Horton as CEO. Year 2000 rebounded to a $13.8 million profit from "increased scale, improved geographic diversification, and strategic application of technology."

Conclusion

The mid-1990s operation of three of Enron's most traditional units—pipelines, exploration and production, and the oil side of the liquids operation—showed contrasts. While the largest in terms of revenue, EOTT's earnings were the most volatile and unpredictable. Its spin-off in 1994 was a short-term palliative that would not be justified by future success. The other two units were the most economically profitable (in terms of cash flow, not just accounting profit). Over-

---

35. The most notable acquisition in 1996 was 614 miles of pipeline and other assets from Amerada Hess Corporation.

36. "Only those businesses which have the prospect of stable and predictable cash flows over the long-term are candidates [for MLPs]," stated Lou Potempa, Enron's vice president of corporate development. Yet this *Enron Business* article failed to mention that EOTT did not fit this mold and required special provisions.

all, the upstream and midstream of Enron were steady and sustainable compared to Enron's newer, sexier divisions.

Enron Oil & Gas and the interstates would thrive later in the decade as other Enron divisions faltered. EOG was a wholly separate company at the time of Enron's bankruptcy, and the interstates would prove to be the most valuable of Enron's assets during the liquidation process.

Forrest Hoglund would retire to other energy ventures, with Mark Papa presiding over his own streak of success at the renamed EOG Resources. Stan Horton, post-Enron, would go on to manage multiple interstate natural gas pipelines for various companies, among other ventures.

Steady Enron, the Enron *foregone* (in terms of what a CEO Rich Kinder would have likely cultivated), was a company driven by hard assets. Its next chapter under Kinder would have been asset purchases, not unlike those accumulated at Kinder-Morgan under an MLP structure. Kinder, Hoglund, and Horton would be remembered as the best of Enron.

11

Enron Capital & Trade Resources

By the early 1990s, Enron Gas Services (EGS) had transformed the buying and selling of natural gas. Although federal regulation enabled this (wholesale) commodity market for America's second-most-used primary energy, the transformation was accomplished by profit-driven entrepreneurship.

In 1994, the renamed Enron Capital & Trade Resources (ECT) continued to refine risk-management options that turned vanilla and chocolate (firm and interruptible contracts; short- and long-term contracts) into 31 flavors. ECT marketed itself with a Peter Drucker statement: "Losses based on fluctuations of commodities or currencies are no longer permissible, any more than it is permitted to have a factory burn down without insurance coverage." To help companies obviate such losses, the Jeff Skilling side of Enron marketed swaps, basis-risk hedges, caps and floors, collars, and hybrid strategies ("exotic options," in the terminology of Vince Kaminski and Stinson Gibner). These products could apply to currency and interest-rate risks, not only to energy commodities.

Electricity marketing, sparked by an Enron-sponsored provision in the Energy Policy Act of 1992, would come next, with ECT quickly becoming the national leader. But unlike gas utilities, electric utilities generated and moved most of their own power. Under incentives from the Public Utility Regulatory Policies Act of 1978 (PURPA), independent generators (including Enron) built capacity to challenge such vertical integration. Otherwise, there was business to get in this $91 billion market. "The myriad of skills, capabilities, computer systems, and product structures that EGS created and perfected for natural gas," Enron noted, "are directly applicable to the electric business."

By 1997, ECT was marketing and providing risk services for more than 25 commodities throughout North America. Amid a multitude of rivals, Enron stood apart. "Because of the economies of scale needed to provide energy merchant services, [our products] create formidable barriers against new entrants to the multicommodity market," ECT executive Ken Rice stated at the time.[1]

Retail, not wholesale, was a whole new profit area for natural gas and power if an independent could profitably poach and aggregate enough users from a utility. Job one was to gain access to the utility's so-called *last mile* of transmission. That meant *retail* mandatory open access (MOA), which required a vast state-by-state lobbying effort, short of a new federal law.[2]

ECT went international in the mid-1990s to replicate its North American model. The United Kingdom was its most prized market, with the neighboring Continent in view. An office in Buenos Aires, Argentina, sought to do the same in the Southern Cone. Heady plans for merchant globalization of gas and electricity was good talk for momentum-driven ENE, but results would prove slow.

———

Jeff Skilling's side was key to Enron's promise of 15 percent annual earnings growth. In 1994, ECT's income before interest and taxes (IBIT) jumped to $225 million, one-third higher than a year before. IBIT of $232 million in 1995, although only a 3 percent increase, represented nearly one-quarter of Enron's after-tax earnings. (That year was hurt by a write-off from the troubled liquids and MTBE operations, which Ken Lay and Richard Kinder had dumped in ECT's lap.) Earnings of $280 million in 1996, a 21 percent increase in earnings increase from 1995, represented 23 percent of the parent's IBIT.

The overall three-year increase of 66 percent easily led all Enron divisions.[3] The not-so-good news was that gains that would accrue in future years had already been taken under mark-to-market accounting. Every year, ECT had to start all over and make its ever-increasing numbers in an increasingly rivalrous market.

———

1. This was the beginning of what several years later was hailed as the "emerging and converging markets" of "emissions, telecommunications, broadband, and weather trading." This hyperbolic business model would die with Enron.

2. For Enron's unsuccessful effort at federal MOA legislation for retail electricity sales, see chapter 15, pp. 589–90, 602–3.

3. Liquids, which was absorbed into ECT in 1993, swung from a profit of $28 million in 1993 to a loss of $23 million in 1994, owing to lower margins and an explosion at Enron's 420,000 gallon/day methanol plant in Pasadena, Texas.

Short-term marketing was a solid moneymaker. Income from long-term originations, strong in 1994 and 1995, declined notably in 1996, revealing the downside of mark-to-market accounting, under which prior years had no more profit to give. Meanwhile, small but growing loan-origination income contributed to ECT's overall profitability.

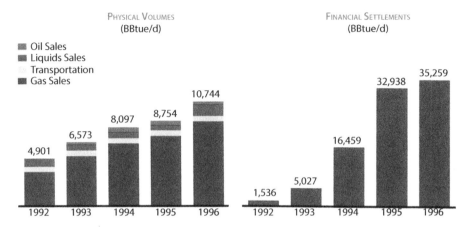

PHYSICAL VOLUMES
(BBtue/d)

FINANCIAL SETTLEMENTS
(BBtue/d)

Oil Sales
Liquids Sales
Transportation
Gas Sales

Figure 11.1 Physical volumes and financial settlements at EGS/ECT increased dramatically between 1992 and 1996. But the overall growth rate was slowing, and increasing competition and maturing markets were reducing margins.

ECT's volumes were rising more than income. Financial settlements, in particular, took off in the three-year period under review. But *profit margins per unit of sales were falling*, the result of steadily increasing competition from large and small companies, many with Houston offices that could pick off Enron employees. There was "energy store" NGC (formerly the U.S. Natural Gas Clearinghouse, later Dynegy); Hadson Corporation; El Paso Marketing Company; Coastal Gas Marketing Company (headed by Enron-ex Clark Smith); ANR Pipeline Company; Williams Trading Services; Transco Gas Marketing Company; Texaco Natural Gas ("air traffic controllers for your gas transactions"); Tenneco Energy Resources Company; Westcoast Gas Services; Brooklyn Interstate Natural Gas Corporation; and others.[4]

Jeff Skilling knew that continual innovation was necessary to escape normalized returns—and clear the bar set very high by his accounting method. The mantra was first-mover gains. "We don't accept the status quo," Skilling

---

4. Smaller competitors included Polaris Pipeline Company, Eastern Group, Paribas Futures, Grand Valley Gas Company, Gerald Energy, Hesse Gas Company, GPM Gas Corporation, and brokers BCMG and Capacity Central.

emphasized. "We're always rethinking what it will take to achieve our vision and how we can continue as a premier player in the marketplace."

Creative destruction applied internally, not only externally. Skilling required ranking employees, with termination of the lowest tier. Good was relative— much like a zero-sum sporting event. Yet on another level, ECT advertised itself as *tolerating failure*. "So, we have to allow people to make mistakes, and when they do, we have to encourage them to try again," Skilling told his thousand-plus workforce. There would be no rest for the weary.[5]

ECT's three major profit centers were *cash/physical* (gas contracts of one year or less), augmented by its intrastate pipelines and gas-storage facilities; *risk management* (gas contracts greater than one year); and *finance* (primarily to gas producers). Physical trading was tied to gas-futures trading, which began in 1990 on the New York Mercantile Exchange (NYMEX). Multiyear fixed-priced (risk-management) contracts were pioneered by Enron Gas Marketing in 1989–90 with Gas Bank. Volumetric production payments (VPPs) to producers were inaugurated in 1991.

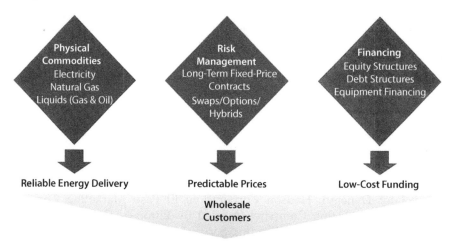

Figure 11.2 Enron's capabilities expanded from marketing and risk management of physical commodities (including, most recently, electricity) into project financing in the mid-1990s. EGS/ECT's tripartite pitch was supply reliability, price certainty, and a lower cost of capital.

Finance was enabled by Joint Energy Development Investments (JEDI), an Enron-operated venture half owned by the California Public Employees

---

5. ECT's corporate culture deviated from the rest of Enron. Skilling and Pai were closer to hard-guy Kinder versus softer Ken Lay. Over time, Lay worked to moderate ECT's indelicacies, including instituting a no-profanity policy in Skilling and Pai's domain.

Retirement System (CalPERS), the nation's largest investment fund. Theoretically, as Enron noted, the $500 million, three-year venture had the potential for being leveraged with $1 billion in debt, which would mean $1.5 billion in investment money for EGS to finance its own asset plays (such as VPPs) or invest in outside ventures. Moreover, JEDI was an independent special-purpose entity (SPE) that did not add debt to Enron's balance sheet.

Enron contributed its half of JEDI's $500 million capital in ENE stock. Thus, when a $500 million revolving line of credit was arranged (with ENE as collateral), the SPE had only $750 million for actual investment. Still, JEDI was a crucial part of ECT's $1.1 billion 1995–96 investment, making this division "a full-service provider of various types of capital, including leveraging existing assets, restricting existing debt, building equity partnership, and arranging producer funding through volumetric production payments."[6]

"We are at the beginning of massive change," Jeff Skilling stated in 1994. Actually, that statement for electricity had been as true a decade before for natural gas, when the marketing sides of InterNorth and Houston Natural Gas took off with FERC orders implementing wholesale MOA.[7] Now, Skilling's *massive change* applied to electricity, a prospective market three times that of natural gas. This "once in a hundred years" opportunity was "déjà vu all over again," Skilling quipped.

In 1994, ECT geared up to become *a full-service electricity merchant*. Natural gas was Enron's past and present; electricity marketing was its future. By 1996, Skilling was declaring that Enron's early bet on electricity was "dead on" at a time when "the general perception was that the market was still premature, and it was a little risky to go out on a limb like that."

In fact, as documented in chapter 15, Enron's electricity initiative and its retailing push more generally were not well grounded. The plan to sell gas and power to millions of households was halted in 1995. In 1996, a new and quite unproven plan was launched, offering *total energy outsourcing* (TEO) to large business and industrial sites (retail in a narrower sense).

Enron Energy Services (EES), the TEO subsidiary of ECT, would also employ mark-to-market accounting to claim profits and success on paper. Economic profits, signified by positive cash flow—an excess of money-in over money-out—was another story, one that in several years would help usher Enron into insolvency.

-----

6. ECT Finance's investments were mainly upstream (Flores & Rucks, Coda Energy, Hanover Compression) but also in energy-intensive industries seeking "integrated solutions" (Qualitech Steel Corp.).

7. See chapter 3, pp. 177–78; and chapter 5, pp. 232–38.

By 1994, Enron Gas Services was a large, growing stand-alone company within a company. It could easily have gone public in part or whole to great fanfare and profit to Enron—as Enron Oil & Gas had in two partial public offerings. But two factors kept that from being seriously considered. One, EGS/ECT needed Enron's corporate guarantee for some of its biggest deals, something a stand-alone company would not have. Second, EGS/ECT earnings had a very high value for ENE, as much as a 25 price-earnings ratio. A stand-alone company would probably be valued closer to eight times earnings, in line with other trading houses.

As it was, wholly owned EGS was the earnings engine and growth story within Enron, offering double-digit returns compared to the single-digit growth of the interstate pipelines. And EGS/ECT was much better than most everything else that was wholly owned and new, including Enron International. The human capital of Jeff Skilling's side was Ken Lay's ace card.

"Our number one priority," Jeff Skilling told Enron employees in February 1994, "is to continue the growth and earnings momentum that we've achieved in EGS." Volume growth in physical and notational (derivative) deals was expected. The financial arm, once dedicated to wellhead lending for gas supply, was now investing in midstream and end-user projects via JEDI. "Last year we went over the $1 billion mark," remarked Skilling regarding Enron Finance, "and we believe we have just scratched the surface."

The major challenge was natural gas liquids. Margins for such products as ethane, propane, normal butane, isobutane, and natural gasoline fell in 1994 and again in 1995, before recovering in 1996. But EGS/ECT's bigger problem stemmed from an ill-fated $632 million "top dollar" purchase of an MTBE plant and other facilities related to producing oxygenated (reformulated) gasoline.[8] Enron's "clean fuel" bet, pursuant to a mandate in the Clean Air Act of 1990, proved errant.

On the demand side, the US Environmental Protection Agency allowed localities and states to opt out of the clean-gasoline standards, lowering demand by one-third in the mid-to-late 1990s. Ethanol, an agricultural-based fuel favored as a form of renewable energy, came on the scene to Enron's displeasure.

On the supply side, other companies were rushing in with new capacity. The result? "The demand for reformulated gasoline and oxygenates such as MTBE failed to keep up with supply, forcing prices down to variable cost," and causing Enron "a significant loss of economic value in the hundreds of millions of dollars."

"We are rethinking our strategy in our liquids business," stated Ron Burns, EGS cochairman (with Skilling) in early 1994. Novel contracting and risk-management practices would result that were more about financial engineering

---

8. See chapter 6, pp. 295–300.

than about market realities. The problem was postponed, not solved. And things worsened in first-quarter 1994 when an explosion at the company's Pasadena, Texas, methanol plant eliminated 420,000 gallons of output per day, half of which supplied Enron's MTBE plant. Service was not restored until mid-1995.

As it turned out, three charges to earnings wiped out Enron's investment: $75 million in 1995, $100 million in 1997, and $441 million in 1999. Enron's expensive foray in energy for the transportation market was over.

New Name, Organizational Change

The old Northern Natural Gas Pipeline (NNGP) was marketing gas decades before a spot market developed. NNGP's "spaghetti lines" in the sparsely populated Midwest required a lot of phone calls and office visits to gain connections and extend pipe. The joke went that this quest to add rate base "connected the last outhouse in the area."

The old Houston Pipe Line Company in the ultracompetitive Texas Gulf Coast market was not far behind. But theirs was true free-market competition, a far cry from the FPC/FERC public-utility regulation that governed NNGP. Not regulatory profit maximization, but the basic economics of marginal cost versus marginal revenue drove HPL's decisions to add capacity.

In 1978, Northern Natural began a transportation-and-exchange function in response to new federal regulation, described in chapter 2. Talent began to migrate to an area in which there were a variety of opportunities for minimizing costs and (with rate-case incentives) making profits. Before long, a youthful Ron Burns was general manager of NNGP Transportation & Exchange, which was the forerunner of Northern Gas Marketing (formed in 1983). NGM became the guts of HNG/InterNorth Gas Marketing two years later, renamed Enron Gas Marketing (EGM) in 1986.

Given the makings of the best marketing division in the industry, including Gerald Bennett from the HNG side, Ken Lay hired Claude Mullendore and John Esslinger from Transco to work at EGM. With a blanket certificate from FERC, EGM was building up a national capability second to none to serve the wholesale gas market.

In 1988, federal regulation required interstate pipelines to divest their marketing affiliates, meaning that EGM took over PAMI (Transwestern), Northern Gas Marketing (Northern Natural), and Panhandle Gas (HPL). (Citrus, half owned by Sonat, set up its own independent marketing affliliates to market gas, primarily in Florida.) It was this powerhouse that Jeff Skilling—first as a consultant and then as an employee—was trying to get to the next level. Joining Enron in 1990, Skilling was the architect of Enron Gas Services (EGS), housing Enron Gas Marketing and Enron Gas Supply.

———

"We've spent the last four years changing the way you see the energy industry," read an Enron brochure mailed to thousands of energy clients in October 1994. "Now we're changing the way you see us." The news? "Enron Gas Services is now Enron Capital & Trade Resources."

Twelve North American offices and four international offices were listed in the six-page glossy. EGS had outgrown North America, not to mention natural gas, it was explained. ECT was *an energy company with global vision*. Physical capabilities, risk-management services, and financial commitment also encompassed gas liquids and electricity—and were reaching Europe and even South America.

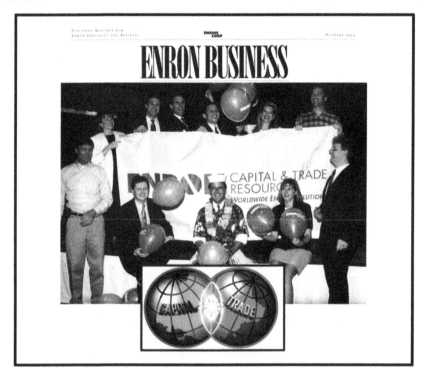

Figure 11.3 The name change to Enron Capital & Trade Resources, the cover story of *Enron Business* (October 1994), was cause for celebration for the former Enron Gas Services Group.

The name change was "catching up" to the existing business, not to mention what was ahead. Three months earlier, the old EGS had traded its first electron; now ECT had "a power marketing group that trades electricity 24 hours-per-day, seven days-per-week." Just a month before, Enron International's marketing side had merged with EGS North American, a nod to Skilling's growing favor within the company, as well as Rich Kinder's concern about EI's far-flung projects.

The final pitch in the promotion was to Enron itself—"a leading integrated energy company in North America with $11.5 billion in assets"—grounded by 3,500 megawatts of electric generation and 44,000 miles of natural gas pipeline. After all, the parent was the corporate guarantor in ECT's trading relationship.

Wholesale Electricity Marketing

Enron Power Services (EPS) was formed in 1991 to market natural gas to independent power producers (IPPs), a niche created by PURPA. Mark Frevert and marketing vice president Ken Rice had immediate business, none greater than a long-term contract signed with Sithe Energies, described in chapter 9.

In 1992, EPS began marketing gas to electric utilities. The pitch was to choose natural gas for new power plants and even introduce gas in existing coal plants by co-firing or conversion. Geoff Roberts led this effort, backed by the straightforward economic and environmental case presented in Enron's Natural Gas Standard.[9]

Other than being an IPP developer and operator of gas-fired cogeneration, Enron was not in power marketing. Enron did not own transmission lines, and utility owners had no interest in letting a competitor use their lines to access their service territory. *Forced access* via legislation or administrative regulation was required.

In 1992, an Enron-placed provision in the Energy Policy Act (EPAct) amended Section 211 of the Federal Power Act to require utilities to provide nondiscriminatory access to outside parties to conduct sale-for-resale (wholesale) transactions. MOA for local (in-state) distribution, known as *retail wheeling*, was expressly not mandated by the new law.

Thus, EPAct advanced what PURPA had begun 14 years before. Independent (nonutility) generation now had a way to reach interstate markets. Independent marketers, too, could buy electricity in one state and sell it in another at wholesale. The first FERC certificate was approved for Louis Dreyfus in December 1992, with Enron receiving the second the next year.

FERC wheeling orders in 1993 put Enron in a new business.[10] "'Power meetings' have taken on a whole new meaning at Enron Gas Services (EGS) following a reorganization that added the North American power business to EGS's portfolio of activities," *Enron Business* reported. While Enron continued to market natural gas to electric generators via Enron Power Services, the new entity was Enron Power Marketing, headed by Ken Rice.

---

9. See chapter 7, pp. 324–27; and chapter 8, pp. 373–75.

10. In April 1996, a final rule (FERC Order No. 888) replaced case-by-case approvals. Federal MOA for wholesale transactions required nondiscriminatory access to the transmission systems of 166 electric utilities.

"One of Enron Corp.'s most pressing growth areas this year is electric power marketing," an early 1994 cover story in *Enron Business* read. "Spearheading this effort is Enron Gas Services Chairman Jeff Skilling and a team of powerful executives whose goal is to establish a merchant business for electricity, similar to EGS's existing service for natural gas." This was not only a market effort—establishing a new retail business—but also a legislative and regulatory one, led by Terry Thorn, senior vice president of government affairs and public policy.

The business plan for 1994 was "creating an active spot trading function for electricity, structuring and marketing some power derivative instruments and consummating at least two sizeable supply and marketing arrangements for electricity." Heady ideas of *full-Btu marketing* on open gas and electric grids became part of Enron's lexicon for a future of new opportunity. "If we move gas by pipeline and convert it into electricity at a different location," Jeff Skilling suggested in 1993, "then we have effectively done the same thing as moving electricity a long distance."

"We think the electricity business today is where the gas industry was 10 years ago," ECT's Ron Burns told employees in February 1994. In June, Enron executed its first power trade. But between these months, something profound occurred outside the walls of Enron. The California Public Utilities Commission (CPUC) proposed to legalize retail wheeling, meaning that the investor-owned utilities—Southern California Edison, Pacific Gas & Electric, and San Diego Gas & Electric—would be required to open their distribution lines to third parties to reach final users.[11]

CPUC's Blue Book proposal of April 1994 led other states to begin investigating retail access for electricity (natural gas retailing was less urgent). Just two years after the EPAct, and sooner than anyone expected, retail was game-on. Not only electric utilities but also consumer groups, environmentalists, labor unions, and independent marketers increased their lobbying budgets. Major change meant winners and losers in a big way, the subject of chapter 15.

———

"Change Is Imminent for the Nation's Electric Industry," a headline in the July/ August 1994 issue of *Enron Business* read. "Imagine consumers selecting electric power service providers the way they now choose long-distance telephone carriers," the article began. A national map coded the wide discrepancy of industrial rates between states and between regions within states, indicating arbitrage opportunities. Jeff Skilling excitedly explained how high electricity rates would be brought down by competition and a futures price established for power. Better yet, this market was three times larger than the market for natural gas.

———

11. See chapter 15, pp. 598–600, for a lengthier discussion of California's historic proposal and its national implications.

EGS was busy in wholesale and readying for retail. Floor 31 of the Enron Building housed 100 power traders and a 24/7 dispatch center. From computers to products, the gas model was being lateralized to electricity. Skilling's own office was downsized and relocated to the middle of the new trading action. A 50 MW power agreement was executed with San Diego Gas & Electric (SDG&E), and buy/sell agreements were in place with the Los Angeles Department of Water and Power (a municipal utility) and with investor-owned utilities in Washington and New York.

"There is good reason to believe the transition process will move quickly," Skilling closed the above article. "When it does, Enron will be at the forefront." True, but a massive, unprecedented lobbying effort would be required to get the open-access rules right and into law in California and the rest of the lower 48. For now, wholesale power's $91 billion market was the prize.

"Continue to lead restructuring of the U.S. electric generation industry and to apply strong marketing capabilities and competitive advantages to this evolving market," Enron promised investors heading into 1995. With "the industry's recognition that a power contract can provide more flexibility than a power generation asset," long-term agreements were executed, including "the first functional de-integration of a major power system" (Tennessee Valley

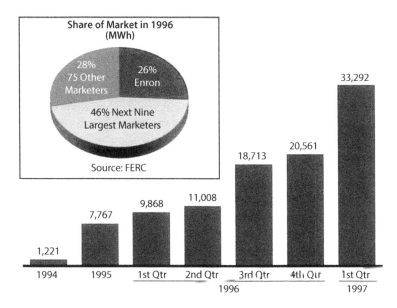

Figure 11.4 ECT's share of the wholesale electricity market dwarfed that of its closest competitors. But profit margins, a closely guarded secret, were falling from the early days of mandatory open access for natural gas. Volumes (in MWh) grew steadily.

Authority). This emerging *term market* from ECT's "sophisticated high value products and services" added to a short-term cash market. Another year-leading deal was executed with the largest electrical cooperative in Georgia.

Marketing electricity "in every region of the lower-48 states," ECT finished 1995 with a 29 percent share of the national wholesale trading market. Forty independents shared the rest. A year later, ECT registered 26 percent with volumes increasing almost eightfold (to 60 million MWh). The next 9 power marketers shared 46 percent, and 75 others accounted for 28 percent.

A big story was being told to investors about Enron's information technology (IT) push to arbitrage and rationalize markets wherein dispatched generation varied between 2 and 14 cents per kWh. A $250 million IT expenditure in the last five years, led by 1996's $70 million, was budgeted to "accelerate dramatically" with the impending acquisition of Portland General Electric's trading operation.[12] The strategy was to master wholesale and lead in the bigger retail market. That was the plan, anyway.

International

"Together with Enron International," read a March 1994 All Employees memorandum, "we have concluded that it is critical to begin deploying EGS merchant type products and services in the international marketplace." The entry point was the United Kingdom, where Enron's Teesside facilities generated electricity and gas liquids, and where the "unregulated nature of the gas and power markets" offered opportunity. But much lobbying and client development would be necessary to reach consumers through the transmission systems of incumbents such as British Gas, a company hardly friendly toward the foreign interloper.

"Mark Frevert will be leading a scout team to London to determine the market opportunity for our products and services and the scope of the operation that we should establish in the UK," this memo read. Specialists from EGS businesses would "determine how the merchant services role can best be integrated into the existing asset and development organization in London." The Delta Force of about 10 spent several weeks looking for entry points but saw little. Teesside's power was all but spoken for, and a merchant market for gas was deemed "several years away."

Jeff Skilling was ambivalent about taking a flyer in Europe. He had his hands full in North America, and some of his best talent would be diverted without immediate profits. The opportunity needed to ripen, he thought. Frevert's answer was good enough for him. But Enron's Office of the Chairman thought otherwise. Rich Kinder knew that the Enron's problematic J-Block UK gas contract needed EGS expertise. "It was on his 'top 10' things to fix at Enron that he

---

12. See chapter 15, pp. 618–24, for the PGE acquisition, announced in 1996 and completed in July 1997.

kept in his pocket." In fact, Enron's massive out-of-the-money position needed Vince Kaminski and other ECT talent to renegotiate. J-Block's eventual settlement (in 1997), indeed, left Enron to market the same gas at the best prices it could muster.

Five months after the UK announcement of March 1994, Enron International's marketing business was merged into EGS. Rod Gray, the head of EI, became the managing director of EGS's new "international merchant business," defined as energy marketing outside North America.[13] Gray was also tasked to coordinate the international work of Enron Oil and Gas and Enron Operations. All international gas-liquids activity was also brought within EGS. Remaining separate from EGS was the Enron Development Corporation under Rebecca Mark, who would report to Kinder and Lay.[14]

Jeff Skilling, contemplating a reduced role at Enron, was coequally titled with Gray and Burns as managing director at this time. But as head of new-product development, Skilling was keenly interested in new products in new markets. One reorganization later, Skilling, not Gray, would again be responsible for international merchant activities.

Rebecca Mark's aggressive projects in risky areas of the world worried Skilling and Kinder. Enron's bread-and-butter trading function depended on Enron's good credit and counterparty confidence. Bad international bets could compromise both. "Enron must continue to improve its balance sheet and credit rating," Skilling insisted. So EGS involved itself in Mark's domain.

"EGS is the sole funding entity for Enron's equity portion of all projects that [Enron Development Corporation (EDC)] brings to the table," explained Gray at the time of the merger. Enron Development was responsible for originating projects and attracting financial partners—but not more. After project completion (by Enron Development), gas or power marketing went to EGS, which vowed to replicate its North American model. Enron Development, meanwhile, would initiate new infrastructure projects.[15]

Just months after the integration of EGS and EI, Enron created Enron Global Power & Pipelines (GPP) as a separate public company to take over Enron Development's projects at the commercialization stage. Rod Gray was named president and CEO, with Rich Kinder as chairman. Skilling's checks on Enron Development were part of Kinder's plan for GPP.

---

13. Gray's role included coordinating Enron's other international activity emanating from Enron Oil and Gas and from Enron Operations.

14. See also chapter 12, pp. 490, 515.

15. The Kinder-Skilling check on Mark continued two years later with the creation of ECT's Joint Venture Management Group to review Enron Development's deals at the contractual stage. See chapter 12, pp. 509–10.

With Gray gone and Frevert's exploratory work done, Geoff Roberts was tapped to lead the London expansion for Enron Gas Services, now renamed Enron Capital & Trade Resources (ECT). Mike Morgan (Argentina) and Andy Lowenstein (Moscow) were also assigned territory in the "mini ECT" effort abroad.

———

ECT North America was the template for operations abroad, which Skilling described as 90 percent of the world. Enron's futuristic push for a "global merchant services business" began in 1994–95.

ECT's "three-pronged" international strategy was "building ECT core businesses in countries where Enron currently holds a presence, providing fuel supply and risk management services to projects developed by Enron Development Corp, and delivering fuel supply and risk management services to third parties worldwide." Enron's *1994 Annual Report* also stated: "ECT is providing a range of physical and risk management services for gas and electricity customers in the United Kingdom, Germany, Eastern Europe, and the Nordic Region."

Enron's *1995 Annual Report* gave investors the same report, verbatim. Enron's 10-K added: "ECT has established commercial marketing offices in London and Buenos Aires to offer the same type of physical commodity products, financial services, and risk management services currently available through ECT in North America."

Enron's *1996 Annual Report* stated: "ECT offers a full range of physical and financial natural gas and power products in the U.S. and Europe," with new power trading beginning in Norway and Sweden. South America was not mentioned. Behind the scenes, new emphasis was placed on Eastern Europe and the former Soviet Union to develop, in the words of Ken Lay and Rich Kinder, "the many significant opportunities that exist for Enron in this region." William Shoff, reporting to Geoff Roberts within ECT, would develop and coordinate projects for three other Enron subsidiaries (Enron Development Corp., EOG, and Enron Operations), as well as manage the nascent GAZPROM relationship.[16]

Later in the decade, EI and ECT schemed to create regional integrated energy companies in developing nations where physical assets (EI) would be joined by a merchant function (ECT). This failed, remembered one principal, because emerging markets were "too illiquid" and "without solid regulatory structure, modern bankruptcy laws, credit worthy counterparties, and multiple counterparties on all sides of the chain."

---

16. Eastern Europe and the former Soviet Union (FSU) would provide little reward despite much Enron effort and bullish press releases about early progress. See chapter 12, pp. 504 8.

ECT–Europe

Mark Frevert was Rich Kinder's choice to open a full-time London office in 1994. Frevert demurred, recommending Geoff Roberts. Kinder agreed so long as Roberts reported to Frevert, making the latter ultimately responsible for Europe.

ECT–Europe had four tasks: develop an energy merchant business in Europe, originate and purchase strategic assets, manage Enron's half ownership of the power plants at Teesside (the United Kingdom) and Bitterfeld (Germany), and address the ongoing J-Block issue. The first item alone was extremely challenging, creating "a global trading and risk management function ... that operates 24 hours a day in all major world markets." It was start from scratch: UK regulatory reform allowed Enron some room to sell gas to industrials, but there was no liquid spot market. Enron traders had to create bid/ask forward curves, and regulatory specialists had to lobby for access rules to compete against the establishment—and against no one more than British Gas (BG).

Roberts counted 24 countries, mostly on the European side of the Mediterranean Rim, where "long-term exponential growth" could be expected. Part of the job was to coordinate Enron's activity in that area, whether a project originated with Enron Oil & Gas or with Enron Operations. Enron Development Corp. and Gray's GPP, tied to emerging markets, were a world away.

"Geoff and his team are seeking innovative ways to work through the institutional barriers and create new opportunities," *Enron Business* reported. Skilling alluded to open markets awaiting Enron, but the United Kingdom's "traditional spot market" needed reform. The local UK gas and power market, about the same size as Texas's, had limited liquidity. Regulatory access to enable Enron and others to create a transparent spot market required a major advocacy effort with a wide range of constituents in the United Kingdom and on the Continent. That was the job of Tom Briggs, vice president of regulatory affairs under Roberts.

Teesside's extra electricity was bid into a central pool, priced in half-hour increments in a market dominated by two recently privatized UK electricity companies, National Power and Powergen. Gas was being sold by independents to industrial and larger commercial users. (By law, residential customers were inaccessible.) Enron's modest liquified petroleum gas (LPG) marketing activity from the Belgium coastal town of Zeebrugge, a small profit maker, was now under Roberts.

How to defray all the start-up costs—from salary bumps for expatriates, sophisticated information systems, and a prime business address? The short answer was: sell down legacy assets. "The history of Enron Europe is that I only made money when something was getting monetized," remembered Roberts. "There was not much origination effort."

In 1994, Roberts sold 7.5 percent of Teesside, producing IBIT of $25 million for the year. Earnings otherwise were negative, as expenses accrued from the regulatory, legal, financial, and operations platform for subsequent gas and power origination and trading.

Figure 11.5 A year after the Teesside cogeneration plant opened, Enron launched a UK-based European operation. Geoff Roberts (center, bottom-left picture) built the initial organization in 1994–95 (bottom right). In 1996, Mark Frevert's "second wave" expanded Enron Europe at 40 Grosvenor Place in Westminster, London (upper right).

After approximately nine months, the first natural gas trade was executed in April 1995. Merchant profits turned positive in the second half of 1995 under the 26-year-old gas-trading head, Louise Kitchen. That helped to produce IBIT of $50 million for the year.

Power trading under Richard Lewis, with forward markets and new product offerings, emerged the next year, highlighted by a 10-year power swap executed in March 1996. In 1997, the 819 MW Sutton Bridge power plant project increased liquidity and spot-power trading to further propel the UK market.

Trading and origination activity; a second Teesside selldown (14.5 percent, leaving Enron with 28 percent); and the financially completed Sutton Bridge gave Enron Europe a $125 million pretax profit in 1996. Better yet, Sutton Bridge traded its surplus power profitably, which contributed to an overall project whose earnings were estimated to be triple that of a traditional power plant.[17]

---

17. At a traditional plant (such as Teesside), gas inputs and power outputs were contractually secured to win arbitrage profit, subject to the physical operation of the plant. By contrast, Sutton Bridge provided a financial hedge for trades (backstopped by physical supply), exploiting lucrative gas/power differentials on a day-to-day basis.

But asset monetization elsewhere left skinnier assets on Enron's balance sheet—and less future profit.[18] Like mark-to-market, selling assets and thus eliminating future revenue streams was another form of consuming one's seed corn, all in the name of defraying start-up costs and meeting the parent's stringent profit goals.

In early 1995, Enron Europe began to participate in the broader European energy markets. That autumn, ECT became the first company not Nordic based to participate actively in Nordpool, the Nordic power market. It would be slow going in the next years; the balance of Europe was entrenched in favor of the incumbents protecting their core businesses.

———

Roberts got Europe off the ground. Trading profits were small, but Continental Europe was liberalizing, and its combined market approximately equaled that of the United States.[19] New scale and emphasis were needed for Continental Europe and the British Isles to become a mini-ECT.

Mark Frevert was ready when Jeff Skilling asked him in mid-1996 to take over London from Roberts. A two-year commitment beginning that November would turn into four, at which time Frevert would return to Houston as CEO of ECT North America. As part of that exit, Frevert retained jurisdiction for Europe, one reason being the synergistic cross-learning between the two continents' wholesale divisions that began in 1995 and accelerated thereafter.

Frevert's "second wave" of talent brought the US-side expatriate count to 60. Leading the charge to London were several notables. Greg Whalley would become head of Enron Wholesale Services before becoming Enron's president and COO in Enron's last year. John Sherriff would succeed Frevert as head of Enron Europe. Dan McCarty would become the chief commercial officer for Enron's interstate pipelines, bringing ECT ideas to FERC-regulated assets.[20] Frevert himself would be vice chairman of Enron in August 2001, number two to Whalley, joining the diminished Ken Lay (still chairman and CEO) in Enron's last months of solvency.

As time went on, US talent returned home, and a localized workforce was hired and trained. By the time Frevert returned in May 2000, only a half-dozen

———

18. "The investment banks allowed a restructuring approach that effectively hard-wired the equivalent of a mark-to-market outcome," remembered Roberts. Any operational problems in such situations were Enron's liability, leaving "incredibly cumbersome and commercially 'fragile' or 'brittle'" assets on Enron's balance sheet.

19. The Enron-influenced European Union's Electricity Directive of 1997 and Gas Directive in 1998 facilitated wholesale trading for Enron to capitalize upon.

20. Jay Fitzgerald was another notable expat in Frevert's initial group from Houston. Louise Kitchen, who came over from PowerGen, would later participate in developing Enron Online, which went live in November 1999 to much fanfare.

expats remained. The UK operation, alone, had become not only a mini-ECT but also a provincial one.

ECT–Canada

A 1992 start-up, EGS–Canada was centered in the Houston of the Great White North—Calgary, Alberta. Enron activity, if not synergies, abounded. Northern Border Pipeline Company, operated and partially owned by Enron, exported 20 percent of all the Canadian gas going to the lower 48. Nearly one-fourth of Enron Oil & Gas's reserves were in Canada, mostly in Alberta. Alberta was new territory for volumetric production payments (VPPs), perfected by Enron Finance for the Gulf Coast. And in the mid-1990s, an ECT investment vehicle, Caribou, was investing in Canadian energy projects off-balance sheet.

"ECT–Canada is capable of representing all the products that are marketed by ECT's Houston office," stated president John Gorman in 1996. "The only difference is that we customize our products for the local market." Five employees at start-up now were 55; volumes of 2.2 Bcf/d exceeded the group's "aggressive" goal of 2 Bcf/d made four years before. Mirroring Houston, ECT–Canada's Commercial Group was composed of Integrated Solutions, Trading and Risk Management, and Capital and Finance. A Business Support Group was operating as well.

In early 1997, Gorman's unit added 200 MMcf/d from integrated producer Suncor Inc. under a five-year, nonexclusive outsourcing agreement. The future was bright despite some growing pains.

John Gorman, a native Canadian, was ECT–Canada's fourth president. Native Glenn Gill was first, followed by Houston exports Mark Searles and Tom Glanville. The unit was a talent incubator, as shown by two of Gorman's executives. Dave Delainey, head of integrated solutions, would go on to run Enron Energy Services; John Lavorato, vice president, trading and risk management, would head ECT's North American trading.

ECT–South America

"ECT will be the leading provider of energy services to the emerging Argentine market," stated Mike Morgan, ECT's vice president for South America in 1995. "Our opportunities will increase as the southern cone of South America becomes a regional integrated system." Acquisitions, development, risk-management services, and gas and power marketing were on Morgan's to-do list.

Transportadora de Gas del Sur (TGS)—a 3,800-mile, 1.7 Bcf/d system serving southern Argentina—was the beachhead for Enron's Southern Cone strategy, akin to Teesside for ECT–Europe. But Morgan's plan would be long on hope. Private ownership was less prevalent than in Western Europe, and Latin countries were not interested in privatizing and then implementing the regulatory regime of mandatory open access. So, despite hardware projects, Enron would not have midstream and downstream access to industrial and commercial users, much less to residential customers.

In mid-1995, Morgan returned to Houston. Doug Hurley relocated to Buenos Aires as head of ECT–South America, with a specific mission to market financial products to producers. Enron had a growing physical presence, beginning with TGS and continuing with Centragas (a 357-mile, $215 million, 115 MMcf/d pipeline in Columbia [1996]) and Transredes (a 3,093-mile, $2 billion, 320 MMcf/d pipeline serving Bolivia [1997]). But that would not lead to a merchant function for Enron.

Buenos Aires was Enron's second international hub, after London, but it was a distant second. Canada was a US-like outpost for ECT. Mexico, geographically ideal and energy rich, was a statist black hole of all talk and no action, much like Russia and the rest of the former Soviet Union. Jeff Skilling's exhortation that "90 percent of the world lies outside the U.S., which means huge business opportunities for Enron" was just a dream. To make it real would have required nation-by-nation denationalization, competition, and capitalist institutions. ECT was ready for the world, but the world was not ready for ECT.

Risk Management, Corporate Culture

Enron Gas Services identified itself as "a mark-to-market company." "If our employees don't perform, we can't rely on an asset to carry us," Ron Burns said. Long-term contacts were year-one-and-done, in terms of profitability. "If we miss a beat and fail to contribute as expected, Enron won't have the performance that it needs," all were warned.

"You eat what you kill" was the philosophy of EGS/ECT, meaning that for compensation purposes, all of a deal's future profits were credited to the current team. It was motivating, no doubt, but it meant a lack of stored (out-year) profits. Jeff Skilling described such pressure as "a fascinating process" by a "cutting edge" enterprise, but it was a dangerous way to live. As the competition caught up and normalized returns, new products were always required for earnings growth. "The things we are doing are the things that our competitors will be doing two or three years from now," Skilling would confidently state.

Did this pressure mean inordinate risk taking in the company's trading? *No,* Enron assured investors. "It is Enron's policy to prohibit speculation on market fluctuations and EGS's objective to maintain a balanced portfolio," stated the 1993 annual report (dated March 1994). With "net open positions" being an inherent part of trading, "EGS closely monitors and manages its exposure to market risk," with policies limiting "the amount of total net exposure … for each commodity traded and all traded commodities combined."

Through "real-time monitoring" of commitments, as well as "daily reporting" of risk positions for compliance, "Enron does not anticipate a materially adverse effect on its financial position or results of operations as result of market fluctuations."[21]

---

21. Enron's *1992 Annual Report* (dated March 1993) described mark-to-market accounting's methodology but did not get into Enron's risk-management strategy.

A year later, ECT reiterated its guideline: "It is Enron's policy to prohibit speculation on market fluctuations." But new specifics were added: "Market risks are actively monitored by an independent risk control group to ensure compliance" at both the corporate and the subsidiary levels. A new calculation was introduced, *value at risk* (VAR), defined as "the potential loss exposure from adverse changes in market factors over a specified time period, with a confidence interval." According to Enron's models, developed by Vince Kaminski, less than 2 percent of the parent's IBIT was at risk at the 95 percent confidence interval on any day. Kaminski, whose continual questioning of traders to get information was initially greeted with suspicion, developed a rudimentary model of risks within and among commodities in 1992–93 and presented a full model in 1994–95.

In the next years, audits and real-world application would not find major problems in what would be fine-tuned by Kaminski, Stinson Gibner, and Corwin Joy, among others.[22] Traders, too, became appreciative of a macro model to help them understand, assess, and justify risk on their deals, separately and together.

———

Jeff Skilling, with close prodding from Rich Kinder, emphasized risk measurement and control within EGS/ECT. Risk management was the "tight" within his McKinsey-inspired "tight-loose" philosophy, at least as it was set up and championed publicly. Investors, after all, were wary of what could go wrong in large trading houses—like Enron's own operation in Valhalla. Enron's UK J-Block contract, a naked bet on gas prices that was hundreds of millions of dollars out of the money, was a well-known embarrassment. From just about any viewpoint, tight risk controls had to accompany Enron's licentious mark-to-market accounting.

In October 1994, EGS Global Credit Group was established under Jeff Kinneman for dealmakers at home and abroad to "assess credit risk [of Enron's counterparties], better monitor the overall EGS relationship with each customer, and increase the level of support to the commercial groups." Four units reporting to Kinneman were Gas, Power, Liquids, and Finance. Originators and traders had to receive approval from Global Credit for deals of $500,000 or more.[23]

———

22. Kaminski's VAR checked the risk-management services that Enron was providing for the outside market via Enron Risk Management Services (ERMS), which became Enron Risk Management and Trading (ERMT) in 1993. Kaminski was within ERMS/ERMT, first reporting to Lou Pai and later to Gene Humphrey.

23. International deals by Rebecca Mark were separately checked by Amanda Martin's Joint Venture Management Group, which worked to make sure that Enron's legal obligations, after construction, were properly aligned with counterparties for efficient and profitable operation. See chapter 12, pp. 509–10.

Global Credit, which was run by chief control officer (and vice president and general counsel) Mark Haedicke, took over the duties of EGS's Control Group (as part of a Global Risk Controls Group). Kinneman, in fact, had been overseeing credit under Haedicke's Global Credit, applying a risk-adjusted return on capital to trades and projects as modeled by Kaminsky. But Global Credit was separate from Enron Risk Management Services, later renamed Enron Risk Management and Trading.

In 1995, Global Credit became renamed Global Credit and Risk Adjusted Return on Capital (RARC) under Rick Buy, chief credit officer. RARC was renamed Risk Analytics two months later, responsible for project, credit risk, and trading-risk analytics. Buy was promoted to vice president the next month, August.

In 1998, Buy would become Enron's chief risk officer, a position much more complex than credit. Vince Kaminski could only wonder how his boss could add value to and direct a function that he was not trained or suited for. This development would contribute to Enron's ultimate demise.

———

Was Enron's "policy to prohibit speculation" an inviolate principle? Or was it a *stratagem*, a guideline? The precedent of mark-to-market accounting, not to mention Enron's overall growth imperative, suggested that *making the numbers* would win out, quite unlike a situation with real trading limits such as prevailed at Mike Muckleroy's EOTT some years before, where limit violations meant you fired yourself.

Another clue to the future came in Enron's 1995 annual report. In contrast to 1993 and 1994, Enron's "policy to prohibit speculation on market fluctuations" was absent. The new language read: "ECT has defined a set of portfolio management principles managed through risk limits and controls approved by Enron's Board of Directors." Translation? Enron was now speculating on market fluctuations regularly but under limits set by the nominally independent board of directors. *Trust us*, in other words, just as with mark-to-market accounting.

Jeff Skilling's characterization of ECT as a "logistics company" was tenuous at best. There was still radical uncertainty (unquantifiable risk), even if Enron was in full compliance with its stated policy (at least the statements of 1993 and 1994), and even if Enron's modeling was sound to historical variances (it was, capturing relationships between historical and forward markets). The oil-trading giant MG lost $1 billion in 1993–94 from unprecedented events. Several years later, Long-Term Capital Management lost several billion dollars and eventually liquidated when its vaunted financial models were falsified by unanticipated events.[24]

———

24. Roger Lowenstein's book on LTCM, *When Genius Failed: The Rise and Fall of Long-Term Capital Management* (2000), was popular reading within ECT both before and after Enron's collapse in late 2001.

"People caught in such financial cataclysms typically feel singularly unlucky," one chronicler of such cycles wrote, "but financial history is replete with examples of 'fat tails'—unusual and extreme price swings that, based on a reading of previous prices, would have seemed implausible."

To its credit, Enron fared well in late 1995 and early 1996 when a so-called basis blowout falsified historical price relationships.[25] On December 22, a volatile gas-futures market spawned rumors that Enron was taking heavy losses. ENE fell 8 percent to $35 per share, bad news for a stock that was already flat. Lay, Kinder, and Skilling fought back, explaining that ECT's profits were *positively* correlated with volatility, not the reverse. Enron began a stock buyback the next day, and ENE rebounded. The final answer apparently came one month later when Lay announced 1995 earnings of $520 million, a 15 percent increase from the year before, exceeding many analysts' expectations.

Enron, it seemed, had all its systems in place as the market leader in the buying and selling of natural gas in the United States. "Enron has such extraordinary risk-management capabilities that we look at them differently," said one analyst. ENE was priced (in terms of a higher price/earnings ratio) as an *arbitrage trader* (which it was not) rather than as a position taker (which it was). As Bethany McLean and Peter Elkind noted, "This was Enron's dirty little secret," one that "Skilling and his lieutenants stuck to ... long after it had become demonstrably false." But Wall Street believed that they were the smartest group in the industry, not only smartest guys in the room, thus giving ENE premium value.

"RAC existed to keep analysts happy, to keep the story alive," remembered one participant. But behind the scenes, Enron was not always winning on its bets, despite having a meteorologist on staff and arguably having more knowledge at its disposal than any other energy-trading firm.[26] To smooth out speculative earnings, which Vince Kaminski wanted to budget at zero expected value, ECT transferred $70 million from 1995 to 1996. This in itself was deception to support the logistics narrative.

This transfer was not enough when trading losses in 1996 turned a budgeted $100 million profit into a $90 million loss—a $190 million deficit. In what Malcolm Salter called "a defining moment" in Enron's culture of deceit, emergency meetings produced an accounting offset whereby the value of ECT investments (from JEDI) was assigned a "fair value" (higher than purchase price) under a

---

25. During an extremely cold period in the Northeast, a disproportionate increase in gas flowed to that region, while prices languished in the markets of Texas, the Midcontinent, and the West. Up-ended price relationships between Henry Hub (NYMEX) and regional spot markets led to new hedging and trading strategies across the industry.

26. "Even with all the market knowledge that we had," remembered John Esslinger, "we still could not figure out the market." A large investment in weather prediction, he added, failed to "get any better information than you get when you listen to the radio."

"resale" interpretation of mark-to-market accounting. Suddenly, an asset purchased for $95 million was valued at $140 million two months later, and an asset bought for $30 million was worth $45 million 27 days later. Sherron Watkins, manager of the JEDI investments at issue, could only describe the revaluations as "cuckoo." Worse, introduction of the so-called fair-value ruse allowed RAC to subjectively value assets to produce (paper) profits—a temptation that overwhelmed the function of RAC to block bad deals.

The ruse to offset trading losses with asset inflation worked—at least for then. Rich Kinder wanted it. Arthur Andersen, conflicted by Enron's high and mighty dollars, went along. So not only did ENE keep its premium, but also Jeff Skilling received a bonus of nearly $6 million for meeting his unit's goals. A higher bonus also went to most everyone else in ECT as a result of financial engineering.

———

The quality of models was one thing; obeying the limits set by Enron was another. "Even in the early 1990s," Enron author Loren Fox found, "the trading operation had a reputation for making occasional big bets, or as some in the trading community put it, 'swinging a big bat'." VAR limits were "loosely enforced," he added. "Even as late as 1996, though, a good trader who was making money at Enron could violate the VAR rules without consequences more serious than a winking reminder of the VAR limits." Fox quoted a trader: "If you went over the VAR limit and made money, they wouldn't ask questions. As you got cold, they asked you questions." Executive John Esslinger characterized EGS/ECT's philosophy more generally: "People at Enron didn't ask how you made your money but only why you didn't make your money."

There was a deep irony here. "Skilling made a name for himself by promising to reduce risk," noted Sherron Watkins, an Enron employee (and later author, with Mimi Swartz), "but it wasn't long before Enron Capital & Trade was making the bulk of its money from very shrewd trading." Lou Pai, who was at the center of EGS/ECT's risk efforts in the mid-1990s, acknowledged the mentality. "We're bookies," he said in a private moment. "We're making bets." With superior information and guts, Enron won more than it lost on speculation, a practice that it stopped denying by March 1995.

What if ECT's customers rejected its long-term products, described in chapter 9, and instead bet on the spot price as the market price, thus avoiding an up-front premium (above then-spot prices)? Would the customers be increasing risk, as Enron told them? Or would they just be accepting a winnable risk, particularly given that Enron's own gas-supply studies were bullish on future supply (and would be proven correct).[27]

———

27. In cases of locked-in prices for long-term gas enabling project financing (as part of a fixed long-term power purchase agreement), EGM/EGS/ECT contracts filled a market niche. But PURPA-related contracts were artifacts of government intervention, not the free market.

From the mid-1990s on, naked trading at Enron only grew. The business was less about origination, or working with customers for long-term supply as in the old days, a relationship business that John Esslinger cultivated before his retirement from ECT in 1996–97. "Customers" became faceless "counterparties" in the post-1996 Skilling era.

ECT's risk-control group—reaching 150 employees with a budget of $30 million per year monitoring 8,000 counterparties representing $20 billion in revenue—had various procedures in place. Deal-approval sheets (DASH) were inputs for RiskRAC, which analyzed more than a thousand trading scenarios based on the commodity, time frame, price, location, and interest rates each day. "You get fired if you do something that doesn't go through RAC," Skilling assured stock analysts.

But in the final analysis, ECT's risk control was "remarkably weak," concluded Harvard business professor and Enron author Malcolm Salter. The fault was less with Vince Kaminski or with trading-limit enforcement, which got better after 1997's J-Block write-off was ordered by Enron's board of directors. It was the dealmakers and the need for earnings that compromised the deal-approval methodology and neutralized the soft-natured, malleable Rick Buy (Enron's "top cop"). Incentives were key not only to the traders but also to making Buy's group back down when confronted by dealmakers. Approvals meant that everyone made more money come performance reviews.

As 2000 turned into 2001, the control system had all but broken down, a cumulative process that was predictable from Enron's long-standing risk-related actions. Throughout it all, Arthur Andersen, Enron's outside auditor, was not a brake but an enabler to its client.

Talent Evaluation and Infusions

Jeff Skilling sought to create a meritocracy in his heralded start-up. A regime of open information flow, delegated authority, and performance-based compensation—not unlike that at McKinsey or an investment bank—was established to nurture and motivate the high performers and superstars. At the opposite end, EGS needed to pare from its newly acquired divisions inherited employees who were coasting on seniority and accommodation.

Skilling wanted a tough, thorough evaluation system to reward superior performance and end cross-subsidized mediocrity, all beyond Enron's pay-for-performance system. In the early 1990s, ECT's Performance Review Committee (PRC) implemented a "360-degree" peer review that required the ranking of employees, with grades between 1 (best) and 5 (worst) and with a predetermined distribution: 5 percent "outstanding," 25 percent "excellent," 25 percent "strong," 30 percent "satisfactory," and 15 percent "needing improvement."

Level 5 performers were at risk. About half were terminated in the program's first iterations. As the quality of employees improved, "rank-and-yank" was relaxed to retain more level 5s on a probationary basis. Severance packages, based on years of service and salary at the time of termination, provided transitional help for those dismissed.[28]

By the mid-1990s, the fat-tailed bell curve became more of a goal and less of a requirement. But that evolution was about the only positive aspect; the PRC process became more burdensome and compromised as time went on, a victim of ECT's supercharged, deceptive corporate culture.

As many as two-dozen peers evaluated and reviewed each employee on paper. Then the managing directors engaged in days of "hairsplitting debates" offsite. In consequence, a sizeable amount of time was lost from traditional moneymaking. Worse, PRC turned into an "institutionalized popularity contest" in which each employee and appointed advocate ("daddy") competed against other employees and their advocates. "Performance gave way to relationships," remembered one participant.

The process became "a management tool for rewarding loyalists and punishing dissenters." The committee process "perverted" RAC, in particular, as the hunger to get deals approved by division heads and dealmakers overwhelmed risk controls. Profitable, completed (paper) deals were overvalued relative to their operational performance, a problem also experienced with Enron's developing-country projects.[29] Traders who hit big profits at the right time could benefit more from the performance review than did steadily profitable traders.

Compensation did little to "reward the grinders," those who made sure the trains ran on time, as opposed to the originators and traders. Bonuses in hand, high performers jumped to the newest hot area, leaving others to deal with postdeal issues. (The problem became acute beginning in 1998 with major new Enron divisions that were more hype than substance.)

Teamwork in the day-to-day workplace suffered in the face of zero-sum-game pressures. Debased processes created bad incentives that led to a culture of internal gamesmanship and external deceit. Enron's performance-compensation system, concluded Malcolm Salter, resulted in "a gladiator culture in which increasingly risky gambles found support, personal opportunism ran rampant, and risk management processes broke down at the most inopportune times." Worthy ideas could hardly see the light of day as time wore on.

————

28. The formula was two weeks' pay for every year of service and for each $10,000 of salary, which might sum to nearly a year's base pay for Enron's average employee. But that was undone by 2001's bankruptcy, when 4,000 dismissed employees received a court-approved severance of $4,500, with future payments uncertain.

29. See chapter 12, pp. 509–10.

Impressive talent was coming in to staff growing areas as poorly graded performers left. The Analyst and Associate program, which Jeff Skilling called "the source of Enron's competitive advantage," was a prized part of ECT. This program was run by Cathy Abbott between 1992 and early 1994, Ken Rice in an interim role, and then Paul Trieschman (hired from Texas Commerce Bank down the street). The program made many productive hires, such as, in the summer of 1994 alone, Luke Clemente, Joe Gold, Joel Hirl, Sean Holmes, Paul Racicot, and Jim Steffes.

The *Analyst Program* was a one- to two-year training regime with quarterly rotations between four areas: trading and risk management; origination (LDC and industrial marketing, power marketing, power services, consumer services, liquids, and structured finance); finance and strategic ventures (Enron Capital, Enron Strategic Ventures, Corporate Development); and specialized or elective (credit, contracts, regulatory, finance and accounting, legal, and commercial operations). "The EGS Analyst program will continue to provide the bulk of EGS financial, market, and industry analysis for the commercial units and some commercial support units," an internal Enron memorandum read.

The *Associate Program* was an entry-level program above Analyst for new hires with MBAs and work experience, as well as promoted Analysts. (Unpromoted Analysts had to leave the company.) Associates were expected to "make a measurable contribution in the various commercial processes such as product development, customer contact, deal structuring, etc." With dedicated placement instead of scheduled rotations, the commitment was for two years.

Incubating next-generation talent, many Associates would rise to the top of Enron's hierarchy. Greg Whalley, for example, was hired in one of the first classes. A graduate of West Point, he spent six years in the army before obtaining an MBA at Stanford University. Joining Enron in 1992 and rising quickly, the consummate trader would become the leader, the "union boss," for the entire trading floor. Whalley would go on to become Enron's president and COO in the company's last solvent months, making decisions for an increasingly ineffective Ken Lay.

———

In contrast to top-down job placement, EGS/ECT sought a "free market" wherein employees would seek out positions around the company. Promotions and compensation changes did not accompany such "voting with your feet" (that came in annual performance reviews), and each employee had "an obligation to notify his current manager early enough in the process so that transitions can occur in an orderly fashion."

Lateral transfers were prized over external hires, but external talent was coming in from banks, law firms, energy companies, and utilities. One such hire, previously head of corporate sales for Pacific Gas & Electric and more recently with a small gas marketer, joined Enron in April 1994. John Sherriff, one of many West Coast energy specialists who would join Enron in the mid-to-late 1990s, would head Enron Europe's trading operation just two years later.

ECT's vice presidential elections in the first quarter of 1995 indicated the range of pre-Enron employments. Six (of the 15) had these backgrounds:

- Brian Barrington: First Boston Corporation, where he worked in corporate finance and mergers and acquisitions

- Don Black: Kidder Peabody in New York, where he established their energy derivatives trading practice

- Stinson Gibner: California Institute of Technology, where he was a research assistant

- Jeff Kinneman: Phibro Energy, where he managed long-term derivatives

- Mike McConnell: Excel Resources, where he was in gas supply and marketing

- Eric Van der Walde: American Airlines, where he was financial-risk manager

"We hire very smart people, and we pay them more than they think they are worth," boasted one ECT executive. With superior compensation and a reputation for delegated authority and entrepreneurship, Enron was *the* place to work for many energy professionals. The term "Enron Premium" came to describe the advantage that Enron employees gained from superior information, cutting-edge techniques, and liberal responsibility relative to the competition.

Conclusion

"Congratulations!" a year-end 1996 memorandum to ECT's North America employees began.

> In addition to exceeding our original 1996 operating plan by 39%, we have:
>
> - Further established ECT as the leading non-regulated natural gas and electric power merchant in North America;
>
> - Profitably managed the physical and financial gas trading business through an extremely volatile period;
>
> - Become the second largest wholesaler of electricity in North America;
>
> - Continued to evolve our origination function to adapt to changing market conditions by incorporating more finance, power, and transportation structures within an increasing focus on new product development;
>
> - Added key strategic assets and skills through our merger with Portland General Corp.

The five-member management committee for ECT's North American Energy Group (NAEG) was poised for a bigger 1997 with these responsibilities and units under Ken Rice:

- Ken Rice: Overall unit coordination with focus on strategic market development, origination, and assimilating Portland General
- Bill Butler: Middle market origination and power trading, coal trading (a new area), and risk management
- Kevin Hannon: Gas trading and global risk management
- Amanda Martin: Gas and power origination with investor-owned utilities, independent power producers, municipals, cooperatives, and local distribution companies
- Eric Gonzales: Industrial origination, coal business development (a new area)

Four additional NAEG units (making eight in all) were Canadian Origination (under Dave Delainey), Regulatory Affairs (Steve Kean), Special Projects (John Stokes), and Research (Vince Kaminski).

Heady thoughts surrounded ECT's push into wholesale electricity. A gas-and-electricity convergence was advertised, inspiring visions of systemwide synergies and an intrinsic knowledge advantage to blur the distinction between speculation and arbitrage. Hubs and market centers were now graduating to network economies and full-Btu marketing. The old function of off-system transportation-and-exchange for one party was now on-system for national marketers.

Still, profit arbitrage was at work, with imitation following innovation, bringing margins down. Mark-to-market accounting allowed little cushion going forward. ECT's physical assets were being monetized by stripping out revenue streams for third-party sale. And to keep the profit streak going, ECT assets were artificially marked up with appreciation reported as earnings. Present-period earnings was the mantra at Enron—and nowhere more than at the accounting-profit engine of Enron Capital & Trade Resources.

12

International Ambitions

G lobal energy projects—big or small, integrated or stand alone, even natural gas or not—were integral to Enron's vision of becoming a *new energy major*. Ken Lay's model for a natural gas major looked to the example of the so-called oil majors, which he defined as "integrated companies that are able technically and financially to do virtually any and all aspects of the oil business anywhere in the world."

By the mid-1990s, Enron pointed to its power and pipeline projects in Western Europe, South America, and India as "beachheads" for further development. Upstream integration could involve Enron Oil & Gas Company (EOG), then in Trinidad and India, with negotiations to drill in Venezuela, Mozambique, Qatar, Uzbekistan, and China. Enron Capital & Trade Resources (ECT) could develop a merchant business of buying and selling spot and term gas. And Enron Engineering & Construction (EEC) was ready to design, build, and operate anywhere. Enron Renewable Energy Company, first offering solar and then wind, could participate too.

Enron International (EI) was by all appearances a successful new business line for Enron. Income before interest and taxes (IBIT) increased from $33 million in 1992 to $132 million in 1993, $148 million in 1994, $142 million in 1995, and $152 million in 1996. Compared to 1989, when approximately 2 percent of Enron's earnings came outside of North America, International in 1996 accounted for 12 percent. But asset selldowns and spin-offs, not profit from continuing operations, were maintaining the numbers. Large profitable *new* projects were required.

Twenty percent annual earnings growth was expected from EI in the next years, a key component of Enron's aggressive promise to Wall Street of 15 percent growth for the corporation as a whole. With ECT's growth under stress from previous years of mark-to-market accounting, negotiated high-margin deals with developing countries were sought by Lay, although less so by Richard Kinder.[1]

Enron International, which had "a portfolio of development projects ... valued at $20 billion," was a large part of Enron's first-quarter 1995 declaration as "the world's first natural gas major." EI's major asset (completed in first-quarter 1993) was a 1,875 MW cogeneration plant (the world's largest) located in Teesside, in northwest England (called Teesside I to distinguish it from a planned venture in the same locale). Somewhat earlier, in mid-December 1992, Enron acquired a stake in the southern half of Argentina's newly privatized natural gas pipelines: the 3,800-mile, 1.7 Bcf/d pipeline of Transportadora de Gas del Sur (TGS), Argentina's largest. In 1993, both Teesside and TGS were fully operational and profitable.[2]

In 1993, EI also operated a half-dozen electric-generation facilities totaling 484 MW, three-fourths of which it owned.[3] A bevy of other projects were in advanced negotiations—and none greater than the two-phased, 2,014 MW power plant in Dabhol, India, the work of EI's "strongest product line" Enron Development, headed by Rebecca Mark.

As it turned out, EI's first-generation projects—entering service in 1993–94—would be the high-water mark for EI. Teesside I and several other power plants exceeding 2,300 megawatts, combined with Enron's winning bid for TGS, was a solid and profitable beginning. But it would not be replicated. Large disappointments lay ahead with regions, business lines, and individual projects.

––––

Behind International's big numbers and happy talk at mid-decade lay a somber story. Teesside's second phase (Teesside II) was a big bet going awry. The Dabhol megaproject was contractually solid but a political tinderbox, with a fragile government entity as the sole counterparty. And despite liberal taxpayer aid, many projects in developing (*undeveloped*) countries—all hostile toward capitalist institutions and suffering from statism and corruption—would either not

––––

1. Enron "saw a huge margin in the emerging markets, so we went after that," remembered one principal. The challenge, Jim Hughes added, was that these countries had "lots of economic activity and no money."

2. Enron had 50 percent ownership in Teesside I and 17.5 percent ownership in TGS. By 1996, Enron's Teesside I interest was reduced to 28 percent.

3. These projects were Batangas (105 MW) and half-owned Subic Bay (116 MW) in the Philippines; two leased plants at Subic Bay (28 MW); half-owned Puerto Quetzal (110 MW) in Guatemala; and Bitterfeld (125 MW) in Germany. Except for the last plant, all were oil-fired rather than gas-fired, a fact kept quiet at Enron, the natural gas major.

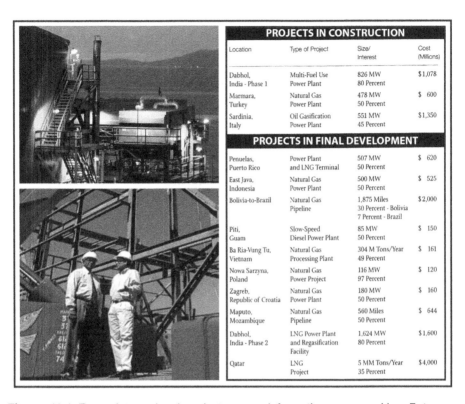

PROJECTS IN CONSTRUCTION			
Location	Type of Project	Size/ Interest	Cost (Millions)
Dabhol, India - Phase 1	Multi-Fuel Use Power Plant	826 MW 80 Percent	$1,078
Marmara, Turkey	Natural Gas Power Plant	478 MW 50 Percent	$ 600
Sardinia, Italy	Oil Gasification Power Plant	551 MW 45 Percent	$1,350
PROJECTS IN FINAL DEVELOPMENT			
Penuelas, Puerto Rico	Power Plant and LNG Terminal	507 MW 50 Percent	$ 620
East Java, Indonesia	Natural Gas Power Plant	500 MW 50 Percent	$ 525
Bolivia-to-Brazil	Natural Gas Pipeline	1,875 Miles 30 Percent - Bolivia 7 Percent - Brazil	$2,000
Piti, Guam	Slow-Speed Diesel Power Plant	85 MW 50 Percent	$ 150
Ba Ria-Vung Tu, Vietnam	Natural Gas Processing Plant	304 M Tons/Year 49 Percent	$ 161
Nowa Sarzyna, Poland	Natural Gas Power Project	116 MW 97 Percent	$ 120
Zagreb, Republic of Croatia	Natural Gas Power Plant	180 MW 50 Percent	$ 160
Maputo, Mozambique	Natural Gas Pipeline	560 Miles 50 Percent	$ 644
Dabhol, India - Phase 2	LNG Power Plant and Regasification Facility	1,624 MW 80 Percent	$1,600
Qatar	LNG Project	5 MM Tons/Year 35 Percent	$4,000

Figure 12.1 Enron International projects ranged from the moneymaking Batangas power plant in the Philippines (upper left) to the non-revenue-generating Dabhol plant in India (lower left). Half of the 10 projects in "final development" in Enron's 1996 annual report would not be completed.

reach commercialization or would underperform after completion. Enron's high-return deals were threatened by high risk, which Ken Lay attempted to ameliorate through the political means.

Apart from Teesside, *taxpayer help was needed for virtually all of Enron's international ventures*, including Enron Oil & Gas's Trinidad project (1992).[4] Loan commitments and/or loan guarantees from the Overseas Private Investment Corporation (OPIC) and the Export-Import Bank (Ex-Im) were increasingly

---

4. Enron's involvement with OPIC and Ex-Im is reviewed in chapter 6, pp. 274, 282–84; and below, pp. 498–99. Enron's Washington, DC, office not only worked to preserve such aid but also lobbied against US-imposed sanctions against host countries. This work required Enron to be a member of or otherwise support 16 US-based foreign organizations.

necessary to finance Enron's power plants and pipelines. There was a reason that the oil majors, with very strong balance sheets, were much slower to venture into the countries where Enron saw gold. But Ken Lay, the inveterate optimist in a big hurry, went where the competition was the thinnest in order to get the highest rates of return: "somewhere in the twenties," Rebecca Mark testified at a US Senate hearing in 1995. Lay even bragged that Enron went where the analysts said not to go.

While assuring investors about prudence for the long haul, EI was fixated on making its current-year number to help Enron please the Street. As much as possible, income was recorded during construction. The costs of failed efforts were not written off but rolled into the capital accounts of still-viable projects. This produced an ever-increasing "snowball," as it was called, which began in the tens of millions ($90 million) and reached as high as $200 million, attracting dissent inside the walls of Enron. But ENE had become a momentum stock; the show had to go on.

EI's future-is-now philosophy was akin to Jeff Skilling's mark-to-market accounting treatment of long-term contracts. EI was quite unlike Forrest Hoglund's Enron Oil & Gas and Stan Horton's interstate gas pipelines, where each earnings period stood on its own (accrual accounting), and major asset selldowns were absent.

Early Successes

In spring 1994, a *Wall Street Journal* front-page article was headlined "Natural-Gas Industry Is Reinventing Itself by Going International." The subtitle: "Enron Is Racing British Gas in a Global Expansion Aimed at Big Oil's Empire," and a third line: "Pitching Clean Air in Asia." In the feature, Daniel Yergin commented about how Ken Lay had presciently challenged him about how the Age of Oil was giving way to a new age of natural gas. "And he's proving himself right by creating a new gas industry as he goes along," Yergin stated.

"Enron and British Gas are the new paradigm of the surging, $120 billion-a-year global gas market, racing across five continents to plant their corporate flags in a flurry of ambition that had been unheard of in their stay-at-home industry," the article explained. "They are reinventing themselves as the first international gas utilities." The article's authors added that ENE had outperformed the stock price of the world's top seven oil companies, not only the stocks of natural gas companies back home.

Great press about flashy high-risk plays was a public relations coup. Enron painted its international forays as pioneering and humanitarian ("to bring electricity to ... children and schools and hospitals"); well managed for risk ("solid legal contracts"); synergistic ("turnkey construction operator agreements, fuel supply, and fuel management contracts"); "geographically diverse"; "integrated market-led"; increasingly selective; and *profitable.*

Enron Development Corp. described its mission as "selecting projects that have the greatest chance of succeeding" and "pursuing projects that will offer the highest long-term value to shareholders." To this end, "risk analysis and management" were "key components of EDC's development projects."

All bases were covered, Enron assured investors. Project financing limited liabilities to a particular project without recourse to other corporate assets. Long-term contracts at known rates, denominated in US dollars, locked in margins. The creditworthiness of power purchasers and pipeline shippers was carefully vetted. Sovereign guarantees and letters of credit were executed, as needed. And political risk was mitigated via loans and loan guarantees from OPIC and Ex-Im (Department of Commerce), as well as the International Finance Corporation (World Bank).

Problems? Enron's burgeoning liability with its J-Block (Teesside II) UK contracts "will not have a materially adverse effect" on earnings. Dabhol's contract cancellation and construction halt in 1995 was a blessing in disguise as a renegotiation resulted in a larger project and restart the next year.

Kudos was common in the period under review. Yergin's Cambridge Energy Research Associates (CERA) ranked Enron tied for first in global project development in the 1991–94 period. Ken Lay touted his company as "the market leader in creating energy solutions worldwide." Rebecca Mark wowed her audiences with such zingers as, "We recreate ourselves, our definition, and our mission in the marketplace on a regular basis." Enron International, in fact, was one reason that *Fortune* ranked Enron as America's "Most Innovative" company in March 1996.

Developing Problems

EI emphasized its mission as creating sustainable value through careful vetting and taking the long view. Yet aggressiveness and risk taking were evident in most EI projects. Teesside II, Dabhol I, and Dabhol II were problematic from the start. A few projects encountered design and operational problems that never occurred at home. But high corporate overhead, beginning with EI's lavish Houston headquarters across the street from the Enron Building, not to mention over-the-top events for employees, were just part of the optimism amid the imaging of a global Enron.[5]

Enron's rent-seeking in the far corners of the world took on a macabre quality in April 1996 when Ron Brown, the Clinton administration's Secretary of Commerce, died in a plane crash on an Enron-related trade mission in Croatia

---

5. Among the "outrageous skits" was a live elephant rented by Enron's Africa team in competition with the acts from the other regions. "Everything Enron did had to be better and flashier," it was later written, "and no gesture seemed too lavish."

(formerly part of Yugoslavia).[6] Brown was a top EI booster, reflecting the help that Enron received from his department's lending agencies. He was present at some of Enron's most high-profile contract signings, including at Dabhol.

Teesside II (J-Block)

Teesside I's commercial launch was just weeks away in early 1993, with the power plant and liquids plant fully supplied with gas from the Everest and Lomond fields. Mission accomplished, Enron was thinking ahead to bigger, grandiose things. More gas and associated transportation *could* fuel new facilities that Enron would build and operate—and launch a gas-merchant business along the lines of Enron Gas Marketing in North America. A "mini-Enron" for the United Kingdom and Continental Europe was in the works.[7]

Enron believed that indigenous gas was limited and should be locked up if the company was to be in the driver's seat. A bigger transportation contract was also needed to anchor a major transmission system that could get the offshore gas to Teesside. Negotiations were going along well, it seemed, for Enron to construct a second power plant and liquids facility at Teesside (Teesside II).

Enron in March 1993 entered into a life-of-field take-or-pay contract, estimated to be 15 years, for 300 MMcf/d of gas from the J-Block area in the Central North Sea (Judy and Joanne fields). A minimum physical take of 260 MMcf/d was intended to ensure that the associated oil and condensates were produced each and every day of commercial operation. One annual payment was stipulated for any take deficiency under the contract.

Enron also executed a 300 MMcf/d ship-or-pay contract with the Central Area Transmission System (CATS), operated by Amoco, to transport the gas from the offshore platforms to Teesside. The CATS agreement, one-half held by Enron and the other half with Imperial Chemical Industries (ICI), "had just as many issues and complications as the J-Block agreements." In particular, the transportation contract's commencement date was not lined up with the J-Block contract, with deficiency payments due quarterly for transportation rather than due annually as with J-Block production. Gaming and legal battles ensued.

All the contracts—11 agreements with 130 supporting documents—made Enron's obligations "extremely firm." There were no market outs or regulatory outs in the face of changed conditions; only acts of God could legally block contract performance.

---

6. Enron representatives were not aboard the plane that killed all 35 passengers, including executives of ABB, Enserch International, and Foster Wheeler Energy Group. Joe Sutton, number two at EI behind Rebecca Mark, was on an Enron jet that landed safely just ahead of Brown's converted military Boeing 737.

7. See chapter 11, pp. 472–79.

"At the time Enron must have really wanted this gas supply," thought Mike McConnell, tasked by Enron Europe CEO Geoff Roberts to renegotiate the problem contracts, "because not only was the price very high but also every paragraph in the agreements was in Phillips' favor." But Phillips Petroleum, British Gas, and Agip UK, equal partners in J-Block, needed such surety to underwrite a billion-dollar project, as much as Enron might like to have had more flexible terms. Iron-clad preconstruction contracts were basic protection in a thin market, akin to Enron pipelines inking firm shipper contracts before construction. It had been fair enough for the producers, but Enron got ahead of itself in the worst way.

———

"Additional natural gas supply from the North Sea," Enron announced at the time of the agreements, will "supplement our supplies in 1996 and beyond for additional power projects and gas marketing activities in the U.K." After all, the United Kingdom was in a "dash for gas." *But where were the markets?* The magic moment for Teesside I was the *simultaneous* execution of multiple congruent gas-demand and gas-supply agreements. John Wing was no dummy, and Robert Kelly (who was now in charge of Enron Europe) knew the drill. But Kelly had been summoned back to Houston, and Claude Mullendore (late in his career and perhaps having too good a time between negotiations in London town) was up against the reputed King of Gas, Phillips Petroleum's Bill Van der Lee. "Amazingly," McConnell could only say, "the UK and US office didn't communicate well." But the communications might have been just fine; Enron's long bet on gas was not unlike what it was repeatedly doing in other venues.

In first-quarter 1992, Enron reported an "agreement" to build a 380 MW power plant near Teesside. "Pending regulatory and governmental approvals," construction was forecast to begin by early 1993. But a year later, there was no mention of this project or any other at Teesside, just the supply and transportation deals "for additional power projects and gas marketing activities in the U.K."

Enron's *1993 Annual Report*, released in first-quarter 1994, was silent on any power plant but mentioned a second liquids plant at Teesside: "Phase II construction is expected to begin soon in order to be on line by 1996 when additional natural gas volumes from the J-Block field in the North Sea come on line." Negotiations, however, were going on with a "half-baked" project named Park Lane, which was conceived to be 1,000 MW, even larger. But some parties to that project were taking less-than-loved Enron for a ride.

Enron's *1994 Annual Report* was completely silent on *any* projects that would either burn the gas or strip the liquids. The 300 MMcf/d J-Block and CATS commitments went unmentioned as well. The first required take nomination, by October 1, 1996, was still some time away. "The gas contracts were put in a drawer to be addressed later," McConnell noted.

In fact, Enron was in trouble and scheming. There were virtually no markets for Enron's gas in the receiving area, much less at Enron's fixed, escalating, *above-market* price. New discoveries in the North Sea had foiled Enron's lock-in strategy, and demand growth was not going Enron's way. Open-access transmission of electricity, needed to jump-start Enron's merchant services for the United Kingdom, was years away, too.

Negotiations began shortly after McConnell's relocation to London in early 1995. The situation was bad—and worsening. J-Block's locked-in price was the highest from the North Sea, which gave producers "a super incentive to develop technologies or find ways to put the maximum amount of gas into our contract and not have any decline rate at all," remembered McConnell. And if Enron did not take the gas, send-or-pay liabilities would accumulate on CATS.

At $0.60/MMBtu, the J-Block stalemate accrued a quarterly liability of $15 million in transportation alone. CATS claimed readiness to set the contract commencement date at November 1994, later changed to May 1995, but still well ahead of J-Block's readiness. Litigation was next.

———

It was ironic. This was the very scenario that had whipsawed the interstate pipelines in the 1980s in the United States. Had not Ken Lay and Claude Mullendore struggled with just this back at Transco? Enron had smartly settled its take-or-pay contracts ahead of the competition, vowing never to enter into market-insensitive agreements again. Richard Kinder, on watch from Houston, should not have approved such naked risk. But he did—and Lay, with board in tow, did. Enron now had a $1.2 billion problem on its hands, quite material for a company with total shareholder equity of $3.2 billion.

In June 1995, Enron made its first settlement proposal to J-Block (CATS would be on a different track). Enron would pay the producers $100 million upfront and commit to firm takes under six different "market based" indexed pricing structures, a novel concept imported from Enron's US side.

Phillips summarily declined the offer. The continuing slide in the spot price by year end (by more than 50 percent) left Enron's firm J-Block contract price at 18.50 pence per therm deeply out of the market, with no prospect for improvement.

The producers were less interested in renegotiation than in contract performance. "In this business, traditionally the producer takes the upfront risk of production and the purchaser takes the market risk," stated Wayne Allen, CEO of Phillips Petroleum, the operator of J-Block. The contract Enron signed "was competitive," he added. "We could have sold the gas to several other people." Allen's speech, widely reported in the trade press, signaled a long fight, "the World War II of the business world" to the Enron side.

Enron's *1995 Annual Report* discussed the problem contracts for the first time with some facts and little worry. Enron notified J-Block sellers in September 1995 that its nomination would be zero for the first contractual year (October

1996–September 1997) with no nomination for the next. Without markets for the gas and with "the contract price for such natural gas ... in excess of current spot market prices in the United Kingdom," settlement negotiations were under way to "develop mutually beneficial solutions regarding pricing terms so that production from J-Block can begin as soon as possible."

Amid the legalese, Enron also mentioned "potential prepayments for gas to be taken in future years," the "favorable" long-term demand for North Sea gas, and the immateriality of the dispute on its financial position. In any case, "there are alternative markets for such gas should the gas not be taken by Teesside."

Enron was not going to take gas that could be sold only at a large loss. There was no room, given Enron's commitment to 15 percent annual earnings growth for that. Meanwhile, J-Block—connected to CATS and ready to ship gas seven months ahead of Enron's first nomination due date—installed gas-reinjection equipment for $82 million in order to produce and sell the associated crude oil and condensate without having to remove the natural gas.

A second proposal from Enron in early 1996 doubled the up-front payment to $200 million and offered free transportation on Enron's CATS capacity, among other enticements, reducing Enron's liability by $1 billion compared to the original contract obligation. This was going in the right direction—but not enough for closure. Even putting the economics aside, upstart, market-invading, contract-reneging Enron was not the favorite company of anyone on the other side of the table, particularly not British Gas, the former monopolist in the United Kingdom.

———

With J-Block in stalemate, Enron's London team turned its attention to the transportation side of its North Sea imbroglio. CATS seized on loose language in the agreement, claiming that notification, not ability to physically deliver, activated the contract, triggering ship-or-pay. Enron filed suit against CATS, claiming nonperformance.

March 1996 was active on all fronts. Enron bought out ICI's half-ownership in Teesside Gas Transportation Ltd., the holder of the capacity reservation and transportation agreement, and made its first settlement offer to CATS. Phillips asked a British court to interpret the terms of the General Sales Agreement to spur Enron to take or pay up.

Enron filed suit in hometown Harris County, alleging contract nonperformance by CATS because of leaks, mercury contamination, and other problems with the new capacity. "Can't get the gas in and can't get the gas out," Enron argued. This argument would have legs compared to the producer contract.

Enron also sought to enjoin J-Block's reinjection on grounds that the gas fields, dedicated entirely to Enron, could be harmed. Soon, six lawsuits were in motion between Enron on one side and the producers and CATS on the other.

Enron Capital & Trade Resources, and Jeff Skilling personally, entered the negotiations. Vince Kaminski's high analytics were behind the scenario analysis that ended as proposals from McConnell's team, combining price, volumes, transportation, and cash.

A third proposal to J-Block was made in late 1996, offering $350 million up front. Some lawsuits were finally going Enron's way. The final resolution, for $675 million, coming the next year, required Enron to take its worst earnings charge of all, eclipsing the write-offs of Peru ($218 million) and Valhalla ($142 million) combined.[8] (CATS played out longer, until a UK court ruled against Enron in 2001, resulting in a payment from Teesside Gas Transportation to British Gas et al. of $140 million.)

Rich Kinder never wanted to take a hit like that. It ruined the year and laid waste to the Enron 2000 goal of 15 percent annual earnings increases. Of course, in accounting terms, it was *extraordinary*. But that was no longer his problem; Kinder resigned from Enron at year-end 1996. A new regime, headed by Jeff Skilling, would lead Enron alongside founder and chairman Ken Lay.

Dabhol I, II

In the same year that Teesside became operational, Rebecca Mark of Enron Development inked a $2.8 billion, 2,014 MW combined-cycle power project with India's Maharashtra State Electricity Board (MSEB).[9] Years of laborious negotiations culminated in financing in early 1995, and construction began that March on the 695 MW, oil-fired first phase—with more than 2,000 workers soon on site.

"Financing for Indian Plant Secured," the *Houston Chronicle* told Enron's hometown. "Two federal agencies have agreed to lend nearly $400 million to an Enron Corp.–led group to build a $920 million electric power plant in India," the article began. The Clinton administration's Secretary of Commerce, Ron Brown, was quoted from India, where he, Ken Lay, and other business leaders were on a trade mission.

This was a big government play. OPIC had come on board with $100 million in loans and then thrown in another $200 million for political-risk insurance. But Ex-Im officials, aware that the project had been turned down by the World Bank, had to be browbeaten into putting up $302 million in direct loans. Wrote one staffer in an email: "I have been involved in a lot of transactions and come in contact with any number of poorly behaved people, but I think that Enron's attitude and demeanor in this transaction has been extraordinarily bad and very counterproductive." But Enron got its way, and the Commerce Department was involved in more than 40 percent of the total financing, versus Enron's

---

8. See also chapter 6, pp. 271–73.

9. See chapter 6, pp. 280–82.

equity contribution of $270 million as 80 percent owner (builder Bechtel and turbine maker GE owned 10 percent each). Ron Brown's agency's commitment was also larger than the combined capital from US banks ($150 million) and Indian banks ($100 million).

"In a place like India, you never know," one analyst told the *Houston Chronicle*. As if to shrug, Larry Crowley figured that some "new sort of economic, business understanding" came out of "the political hoopla." Projects there, he warned, "had a way of getting bogged down in the bureaucracy, to the detriment of what is good for the economy and the business environment of the emerging economy." This explained why so much government risk insurance was required.

Forbes asked, "Is India a risk-free investment?" only to answer, "Not on your life." The article explained how most private-sector firms were "leery about the ability of [state-run electricity] boards to pay their bills," given that one-half of their distributed power was "lost in transmission, stolen, or given away as subsidies to farmers." Indeed, the World Bank had removed a $750 million line of credit for Indian power projects because of this very problem.

———

Why worry? With strong equity partners (Bechtel, GE), major government risk insurance, and a rate of return estimated at 25 percent, Rebecca Mark's project on the west coast of India was Enron's new Teesside, on paper at least. Chickens counted, Enron awarded Mark and team a $20 million bonus pool upon Dabhol's financial close.[10]

But India was hostile to Western corporations and capitalism. The Indira Gandhi era (1966–77, 1980–84) was one of extreme nationalism, just the opposite of the internationalism that Adam Smith saw as the wealth of nations. Companies had been asked to leave or simply prohibited from coming in the first place. The December 1984 Union Carbide Bhopal disaster, moreover, in which a gas leak turned into the worst industrial accident on record, was just a decade removed from Enron's negotiations.

Most important regarding Dabhol, the MSEB was an impoverished socialist entity with a chronic account-receivables problem. Need and want were quite different from *ability to pay*. The "excruciatingly slow" negotiations, with days spent on a single item, reflected a Third World understanding of contacts, incentives, obligations, and outcomes on the part of the buyer. (A key Indian negotiator likened the process to "learning to play a violin solo in public" where "every dissonant note gets heard.")

———

10. In accordance with Enron policy, this bonus was 10 percent of the project's calculated net present value to Enron upon closing, not after commercial operation. In Dabhol's case, that would make all the difference.

Dabhol's phased-in rate increases, starting at around $0.075/kWh, and for such large quantities, would surely inflame the masses—despite Enron's efforts to beautify the area and underwrite local social services. The contract allowed Enron to pass through fuel costs and be reimbursed for operating-cost increases. Payments were denominated in US dollars, eliminating the rupee's currency risk. "It is astounding, in retrospect," one analysis concluded, "that no one on the Enron side could envision the kind of resentment and backlash such a one-sided agreement would engender."

Enron's "can't-lose" agreement also bypassed an obvious issue: *Why were oil and gas chosen over the least-expensive indigenous fuel, imported coal?* The World Bank asked the same question in declining to join with the Commerce Department in financing.[11] But Enron was all about gas (or oil), including LNG, not coal.

Enron became a political target in Maharashtra. A Hindu nationalist coalition promising to "push Enron into the Arabian Sea" defeated the ruling Congress Party in March 1995, a surprise for India's Prime Minister Narasimha Rao, who championed modernization, foreign capital, and Enron's project. Phase I of Dabhol was immediately placed under review. Tensions were high, and a riot between villagers and workers at the site two months later made world news. Enron was becoming internationally known in a unique way.

Claiming "fraud and misrepresentation," the MSEB, now under the coalition BJP–Shiv Sena Party, cancelled its contracts for Phase I and Phase II. Allegations against Enron included a lack of transparency, unnecessary costs, and environmental risks. Enron's $20 million effort to educate Indians about capitalism and electricity was seen as worse than indoctrination. "The country would certainly like to discover the names of the politicians and officials who thus 'graduated' from the Enron School of Business," one political foe testified.[12]

Construction ceased three days later, August 8. More than a dozen lawsuits from the buyer side alleged bribes, corruption, and other misdeeds. ENE's price sagged and then languished with EI's white elephant. It was "the disaster that many people have feared." India was being India, at least where it mattered to the Enron-led Dabhol Power Company.

Enron filed for arbitration in London to recover incurred costs and foregone profits, calculated at $300 million. The ongoing cost of delay was estimated at $250,000 per day. "I'm in grief," Rebecca Mark told the press. The "Empress of

---

11. Other concerns in the April 1993 report included an inability of customers to pay, as well as the baseload (80–85 percent must run) nature of the contract, whereby other generation, including hydroelectricity, had to be backed off during nonpeak hours.

12. Enron was spared an accounting of the $20 million by Indian courts, which would have more precisely determined for what and to whom the payments were made.

Energy"—praised by Ken Lay, Daniel Yergin, and the dean of the Yale School of Management, among others—was looking quite pedestrian.

Mark and negotiators camped in India, reporting each day's progress to Rich Kinder on 8:00 a.m. conference calls in Houston. Clinton administration officials from Treasury, Commerce, and Energy lobbied Indian politicos to negotiate a solution to win back world confidence for their country.

"Enron came to India because it was invited to come to India," Ken Lay stated. "We are committed to be good, long-term corporate citizens of Maharashtra." There were no bribes, corruptions, or other irregularities, he stressed. "We only ask that the review be fair and objective, based on merit and not politics." But politics it had to be with the government as buyer, not to mention the public financing from the US side.

———

As stated by Manohar Joshi, the chief minister of Maharashtra, the cancellation "is not against the U.S. It is against the Dabhol Project." Actually, Enron-as-scapegoat was a winning political issue for the antireform party. But with Enron pushing arbitration and befriending the new political majority (new ground for Mark et al.), Joshi let it be known that a changed project with more favorable terms was doable.

Serious negotiations began in November. Rumors began to swirl, even enough to result in an ENE buy recommendation from Salomon Brothers, based in part on Dabhol's resurrection. Sure enough, a deal emerged the next month. A 20 percent electricity rate reduction from falling turbine costs and a better-scaled project (in terms of supply, not demand) was enough for Joshi's government. Phase II was now mandatory, unlike before. Enron also offered to reduce its share of the project to give the state of Maharashtra as much as a 30 percent interest.[13]

Nevertheless, pushback among radical groups continued. A second rate reduction, less than 2 percent, was agreed upon in January 1996 to seal the new deal—on paper. Arbitration proceedings continued in London, with the plant's restart awaiting both court rulings and a coming election.

Back home, Enron was all smiles. "While project review and renegotiation created delays," Enron's *1995 Annual Report* stated, "this project exemplifies the extent to which Enron shareholders benefit from solid contracts that protect Enron's investment and from the company's ability to work with its customers to create mutually beneficial solutions."

"I enjoy being a world-class problem solver," Rebecca Mark told the press after the renegotiation. "I'm constantly asking 'How far can I go? How much can I do?'"

———

13. Originally, Enron was going to sell a 20 percent interest to Entergy, but the project cancellation in August 1995 negated this obligation. The MSEB would end up with a 15 percent interest.

Such celebration was premature. Financing was redone, but a 600-page final order from the Bombay High Court did not come until December 1996, marking 16 months of suspension. Construction then resumed on Phase I with a new completion date of late 1998. Phase II, to bring the total to 2,450 MW, was set to use LNG from Qatar's North Dome Field (another Enron stretch project) in the year 2000.

Was the redo a savior or a still more perilous bet? The new rate, just under $0.06 per kWh, was still pricey for the locals—if they paid for electricity at all. The $30 billion (lifetime) commitment by MSEB was a prodigious sum for a fragile government entity to demand from the populace, even if the government was now a partial owner of the project.

It would not turn out well. Phase I would enter service in 1999 to the usual huzzahs ("We feel extremely proud to have proven them all wrong," Mark said) only to find the buyer unwilling to pay after less than two years of the twenty-year contract. Phase I became idle, while Phase II, with taxpayer support, began construction. All told, for $900 million in costs, Dabhol would never generate steady income during Enron's solvent life. But write-offs were precluded, partly because of earnings pressure and partly because Enron's board would have been irked, having been promised no more write-offs post-1997 (J-Block, MTBE).

The end would come only after Enron's own demise. A court document summed up the carnage:

> The Dabhol power plant sits idle; the Project operating company ('Dabhol Power Company' or 'DPC') is in receivership; the Project investors ('General Electric, Bechtel and Enron, collectively, the Investors') have lost their entire multi-billion dollar investment; the Project lenders (including the Bank of America) hold nearly $2 billion in worthless, non-performing loans, including direct loans totaling over $190 million with accrued interest and costs made by the Overseas Private Investment Corporation ('OPIC'), a U.S. Government agency; and OPIC, as Project insurer, has paid out over $110 million on political risk insurance policies covering the Investors and the Bank of America against the risk of expropriation of their interests in the Project.

Enron's estate would receive just $20.4 million, in 2004.

"You have to stay in touch with the politics in the country, and we didn't," lamented Joe Sutton of Enron Development about his problem child. Rebecca Mark felt that more personal attention when Phase I came on line would have helped ensure the commercialization phase. But another Sutton observation was probably best: "You have to be very careful about ending up trying to do a deal that shouldn't be done, or can't be done."

San Juan Gas Company
Enron had some small Caribbean businesses inherited from InterNorth dating from when Sam Segnar purchased Belco Petroleum in 1983. Marginally profitable, these stragglers were not sold by Mike Muckleroy after the 1985 merger

between HNG and InterNorth. The same assets were not divested in the early 1990s either.

The thinking was that a far greater South American presence would emerge. "Enron Americas plans to capitalize on its historic presence in the Caribbean area to take advantage of significant potential power generation opportunities in the area," Enron told investors. But there was another reason that Enron remained in this distant mom-and-pop arena: Rich Kinder reputedly did not want to take a small write-off from a sale, estimated to be $1 million or $2 million.

Enron Americas had two businesses in Venezuela. Industrias Ventane (Ventane, also known as Vengas), founded in 1953, was the leading transporter and distributer of natural gas liquids in Venezuela (bottled propane, mainly). Enron was also part owner (with General Electric and locals) of the leading manufacturer and distributor of washing machines in the country, a business that just needed, so the joke went, a second Mother's Day to improve profitability.

In Jamaica, as in Venezuela, Enron Americas had a bottled-gas presence. But a third similar business in San Juan, Puerto Rico, would be much more consequential. San Juan Gas Company became notorious in November 1996 when a massive explosion destroyed a six-story building in the commercial section of Rio Piedras. Thirty-three were killed and 80 injured in what was one of the worst industrial accidents in the history of the region.

San Juan Gas did not serve the building, but a propane leak from a nearby underground line of the company was eventually implicated. "San Juan Gas Company's Inadequate Training of Employees and Government Deficiencies led to Building Explosion," concluded a study by the US National Transportation Safety Board (NTSB) in 1997. "Contributing to the loss of life was the failure of San Juan Gas Company, Inc. to inform adequately citizens and businesses of the dangers of propane gas and the safety steps to take when a gas leak is suspected or detected," the full accident report found. Eight hundred plaintiffs filed 500 lawsuits against six different Enron subsidiaries.

Enron denied its involvement until 2000. In what would be its final annual report, Enron stated that "numerous claims have been settled," a fund had been established to cover future settlements and awards, and the final outcome "will not have a material adverse effect on its financial position or results of operations." At the time of Enron's bankruptcy, about $60 million had been paid, covered by indemnity insurance. Another $50 million in payments were expected. All this from a meager asset with small profits in the best of times.

Expertise could have prevented the accident; as it was, numerous visits to the building by San Juan employees failed to pinpoint the leak because of a lack of proper training. Best practices by Enron in North America were not in place in Puerto Rico. Enron knew that San Juan's operations had been out of compliance since 1985, the NTSB concluded, but a correction of deficiencies "was neither timely nor sufficient." In fact, 40 percent of San Juan's service lines were

Figure 12.2 Enron Americas, led by Mike Dahlke, was a little-known part of Enron until a gas leak from a pipeline in San Juan caused a human disaster. Only a lack of immediate linkage to San Juan Gas Company and Enron's later implosion saved Ken Lay from a great embarrassment.

inactive, a reason behind the company's unaccounted-for gas problem, Enron's affiliate was told in a year before the explosion.

"The pipeline was in terrible condition," said Enron's top infrastructure executive, Tom White, in 2001. "We had done leak surveys and were working hard to fix it up." But the unthinkable happened. "Every once in a while, we get too clever by half by ignoring operational risk," he added.

Unfulfilled Aspirations

Enron International brought home a string of successful first-generation projects. But the next wave would prove to be a step back from the Teesside-led successes of 1993–94. Whole business lines did not materialize (global liquid marketing; global LNG). Major regions did not produce profits, despite early-in years of effort: Russia, Mexico, the Middle East, Africa, and China. The same proved true for the developing nation of Enron's greatest aspirations, despite Lay's assurance that "we're planning to be in India for the long term." In these and other nations, many touted projects would quietly fade away.

"Execution to date has been difficult," Rebecca Mark told the Senate Committee on Foreign Relations in 1995. Privatization was "politically unpopular" where "the government uses the infrastructure bureaucracy to create thousands of jobs," she added. Developing countries' "fleeting" interest in privatization and "see-saw politics" were barriers, as was unstable currencies. What Daniel Yergin and Joseph Stanislaw's *The Commanding Heights* termed (in its subtitle) *The Battle Between Government and the Marketplace that Is Remaking the Modern World* was a struggle for Enron in some of the most inhospitable areas of the world.

Risk mitigation was key. Mark stressed government funding and guarantees as a difference maker: "One of the big issues that helps us and/or can hurt us is the access to capital, particularly from US EXIM and OPIC." Indeed, for India's Dabhol project alone, $400 million in direct funding and $200 million in equity insurance got the financing done—and to everyone's detriment.

Many well-announced projects would terminate with nary a mention. These included proposals to build power plants in East Java, Indonesia (500 MW, $525 million, 50 percent owned), and in Poland (116 MW, $120 million, 97 percent owned). In the Republic of Croatia, where Ron Brown's Enron-related trade mission had ended tragically, a 180 MW, $160 million project, scheduled to begin construction in 1997 with completion two years later, did not get off the ground.

In Mozambique, reputedly the poorest country in the world, Enron garnered great press for its proposed 560-mile gas pipeline project that would market gas from the country's Pande Field (a potential EOG project). DOE Secretary Hazel O'Leary, who led a trade mission to South Africa in 1995, was present for the $700 million signing. Enron's half-owned project, however, would not materialize.[14]

The Middle East was also part of Enron's ambitions. Rebecca Mark wanted to sell liquefied natural gas to Israel from Qatar, breaking what otherwise was an impasse between the two countries. (There was irony in Enron's attempt to do business in the very region of the world whose instability Lay cited as a reason for the United States to move from oil to natural gas.) The $4 billion mega-

----

14. The country's minister of energy resources complained about the political pressure coming from Washington to close the Enron deal and, in particular, being told that "other aid to Mozambique might be in jeopardy" otherwise.

deal ("so big that it will raise us to a new plateau when it comes on stream," Lay told the press) never got done.

There was a proposed $161 million natural gas processing plant in Vietnam that did not reach fruition. All told, 5 out of 10 projects listed as "in final development" in Enron's 1996 *Annual Report* would be terminated.

The ones that made it had their own issues. On the island of Sardinia, for example, a 551 MW power plant that would turn residue from Italy's largest refinery into electricity, described over two pages in Enron's 1996 *Annual Report*, was way late. The $1.35 billion project, 45 percent owned by Enron, began construction in August 1997, with commercial operation set for two years later. In 1998, Enron postponed the in-service date to first-quarter 2000. Finally, in 2001, in Enron's last months of solvency, the refigured integrated gasification combined-cycle plant began operations.

———

The problem went beyond individual projects to whole divisions, business lines, and regions. A division of Enron International, Enron LNG, formed in early 1993, never got a deal done despite numerous well-publicized project negotiations. The cover story of a 1996 issue of *Enron Business*, "EDC Takes LNG to the Middle East and Beyond," touted the prospects of the "proven" technology being "the fuel of choice in developing nations that have no indigenous gas supplies or limited pipeline import capacities." Africa, Middle East, Russia—whole regions where Enron rolled the dice in the quest to become "the premier international global" resulted in snake eyes. Same for an LNG import terminal in Puerto Rico with Kenetech Corp., a soon-to-be bankrupt wind developer.

International liquids marketing reflected Enron's own liquids and petrochemical production. But finding a "market niche to provide us with some competitive advantage," as stated by EI head Robert Kelly in 1993, was never solved. This would require becoming the low-cost provider à la Enron Oil & Gas, added Kelly. That did not and probably could not happen; asset-rich incumbents, including the oil majors, were ensconced in that field.

Big plans for China, begun in 1990, produced one project that Enron would have been better off without. A purchased power agreement for the $130 million, 150 MW Hainan Island, completed in 1996, was a "debacle," remembered one principal. "The economy turned south, didn't need the power, and they stopped paying us," said Jim Hughes, who was assigned the cleanup.

Russia was another mega-target for Enron and Ken Lay. On the "historic morning" of August 30, 1993, Gazprom Chairman Rem Viakhirev signed a "major agreement" to supply natural gas to prospective Enron power plants in Greece, Italy, Turkey, and Germany. Along for the signing were Russian Prime Minister Viktor Chernomyrdin and US Energy Secretary Hazel O'Leary. Lots of press resulted from the highly choreographed event.

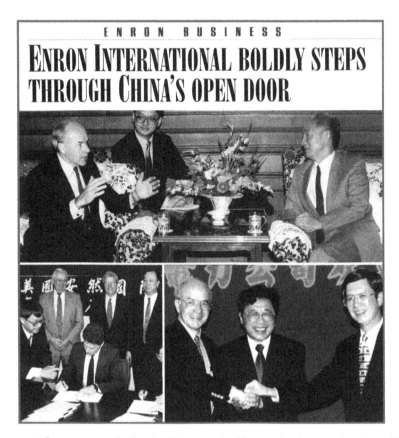

Figure 12.3 Seven years of effort in China resulted in one (problematic) project, Hainan Island (1996), signed and celebrated by Ken Lay. An earlier agreement signed by Enron to develop an LNG project in China (lower left) did not reach fulfillment.

Actually, this was a second beginning between the two parties. Gazprom had just nixed a several-year effort by Enron to enter into a contract to rehabilitate Russian pipelines. And as it turned out, Gazprom did not want to enable a competitor, and a capitalist one at that. Why would the world's largest gas company with reserves of 1,700 TCF—nearly a thousandfold that of EOG—want to give a hyperaggressive US company a beachhead in Europe and in Russia itself?

Enron got some scraps. Fifty-four Russian pipeliners had been trained at Northern Natural Gas's facilities in Nebraska. Also in 1994, Enron Operations helped Gazprom with document management. The next year, Gazprom turned to EOG to jointly develop and market gas reserves in Uzbekistan with Uzbekneftegaz. In neighboring Latvia, the former Soviet republic utilized Enron's expertise in storage field equipment and operation. A compressor station was refurbished in St. Petersburg.

But the bigger things midstream or downstream—with transmission, marketing, or sales—were no-gos. "Gazprom did not want to liberalize markets," one Enron principal remembered. "They truly believed that letting Enron into this particular spot was a taste of something they didn't want."

Figure 12.4 A framework agreement was signed with Gazprom in 1993 in Enron's 50th-floor boardroom. Witnessed by dignitaries from both countries, the signing did not result in major projects. The world's largest gas entity was not interested in enabling a capitalist competitor on its home turf.

———

The off-limits country just to the south of Enron—rich in minerals, people, and climate—stood ready to be a Canada or even a new Texas with private ownership, voluntary exchange, stable money, and the rule of law. But Mexico, lurching between crisis and recovery (euphemistically referred to as "a transition period"), kept Enron on the sidelines, as it did the whole of US industry.

There was always hope. The North American Free Trade Agreement (NAFTA) was seen as a wedge capable of increasing gas exports from the United States to Mexico sixfold by 2000—not to mention increased Mexican demand for energy infrastructure. The American Gas Association and Interstate Natural Gas Association of America (INGAA), both with Mexican membership, made it their top legislative priority, and Ken Lay personally testified in favor of the trade bill. Another upside was that NAFTA, in the words of *Natural Gas Week*, "undoubtedly will serve as a model for other agreements throughout Central and Latin America."

Mexico, meanwhile, talked a good game about opening up its natural gas market to imports, foreign capital, and even open access to transportation and storage facilities. "We're aggressively looking for opportunities in Mexico," stated Jeff Skilling in 1993. "NAFTA is obviously a plus from a long-term standpoint," he added.

Hard-fought NAFTA became law on the first day of 1994. DOE Undersecretary Bill White directed a trade mission to Mexico in mid-1995 to "promot[e] U.S. energy, environmental, and technological interests in Mexico's expanding and emerging markets," inviting Enron representatives from various business units and from government affairs. It was such a natural with Houston Pipe Line reaching Mexico's border.

Infrastructure opportunities were certainly there. At an INGAA-sponsored event, the head of the gas pipeline division of Petróleos Mexicanos (PEMEX) rejected any move toward privatization or open access. But he predicted that Mexico's new Energy Regulatory Commission (enabled by November 1, 1995, legislation) would modernize what was currently a manually operated system, characterized by once-a-week readings instead of automatic metering controls and daily balancing.

Mexico business was not to be, despite much effort by Enron. The peso crisis in late 1994–95, remarked James Steele of Enron Development, was just the sort of political risk that made financing unavailable for the socialist, quasi-corrupt, impoverished country. "The experts don't know what will happen; the equation is constantly changing," he lamented.

Enron Global Power & Pipelines

The chairman and CEO of Enron International in 1994, Rod Gray, had the difficult task of presiding over a global start-up and, in particular, the whirlwind Rebecca Mark. Mark, head of EI's Enron Development Corp., was a John Wing protégé turned Ken Lay confidante. Combining Wing's drive and toughness with Lay's incurable optimism, Mark saw few obstacles that she felt she could not overcome.

EI's goals in 1994 went beyond finding markets for Teesside II's gas and getting Dabhol to financial close. Gray saw a basic need to better coordinate EI's far-flung operations in order to improve information flow and teamwork.

As Gray grappled with pulling the team together, Jeff Skilling and Rich Kinder worried about Enron Development. With Mark's acquiescence, and to Gray's relief, the Joint Venture Management Group was formed within ECT to compare actual performance to contractual obligations and financial projections. The auditors were led by Amanda Martin, a lawyer who had come to Enron in 1991 from Vinson & Elkins. Second in charge was Darrell Kinder, recently discharged from his troubled gas liquids and MTBE operations. With an eye for numbers, in addition to her other strengths, Martin would become ECT's first female managing director in 1996.

"Our mandate is to look at each project from the perspective of the owner," Martin explained to Enron employees. "We're not looking at a deal as a developer or as a turnkey operator." The goal was to have the legal foundation to ensure "that a good project is developed that is viable for the duration of the asset's life cycle in this competitive marketplace," she added. Only then, added Lou Pai, would developing-country projects "make a major contribution to Enron's global expansion."

But the horse was out of the barn. Martin uncovered operational issues that would have embarrassed Enron back home, from a leaky pipeline to an infested water intake at a power plant. Cost estimates, profit forecasts, and risk analyses were dicey. Because of the timing of their bonuses, the people in Mark's deal shop turned out to be far more interested in financial closure than in actual operations.[15]

What was needed, Rich Kinder et al. concluded, was a new stand-alone organization dedicated to developing-country operations. Also, to the extent that a project's market value (as revealed by the public offering) exceeded the project's book value, Enron wanted to monetize the investment to keep earnings growth high, reduce debt for a strong credit rating (of great benefit to Skilling's side), and capitalize other priorities. Investors, too, were more interested in operating projects than in taking development risks. A step toward a credit-rating upgrade, of great benefit to Skilling's side, in particular, was welcomed too.

Four times already, Enron had taken a wholly owned subsidiary public: EOG (1989), Enron Liquids Pipeline LP (1992), Northern Border Partners LP (1993), and EOTT Energy Partners LP (March 1994). A fifth time would attract capital for emerging-market projects, while offering Enron investors a new play. The company could also bring dividend earnings to investors.

The result was Enron Global Power & Pipelines LLC (EPP), which went public in November 1994 with Rich Kinder as chairman, Rod Gray as CEO, and Jim Alexander as Chief Financial Officer (CFO). Just five months before, EI had been merged into ECT, with Gray joining Ron Burns and Jeff Skilling atop management. Now, Rebecca Mark of Enron Development reported to Kinder and Lay, with her projects designed to be turned over to EPP for operation. EI, meanwhile, a shell of its former self, was ECT-focused to create liquid markets for gas and electricity abroad.

---

15. "We were not very good at execution," Tom White later recalled. "We were great at putting deals together, but then someone would say, 'Oh my goodness, we have to build or run this place now!' as kind of an afterthought." White's Enron Operations Company "pushed hard to develop our execution capability so we wouldn't lose our shirts as we tried to make some money out of the project."

Although EPP was a publicly traded company, Enron as majority owner created complications. "Enron will control the Company and will have extensive ongoing relationships with the company," the prospectus read. "Certain conflicts of interest exist and may arise in the future as a result of these relationships." To arbitrate, Enron-EPP deals would be reviewed by three independent members of the board of directors, two of them being George Slocum (the ousted head of Transco Energy and now a consultant) and General Brent Scowcroft (the former national security advisor to Presidents Ford and George H. W. Bush).

EPP would own and operate Enron's power plants and pipelines located outside North America and Western Europe, that is, in the developing world. The new public company began with Transportadora de Gas del Sur, as well as ED's two power plants in the Philippines and one in Guatemala, all of which were strong enough.[16] Further assets would come from a Purchase Right Agreement whereby Enron promised to sell, "at prices lower than those available to third parties," its developed interests in like assets through 2004. Similar commercial assets from outside parties could also be acquired in the same geographical region, investors were told.

———

Ten million shares, representing 48 percent of the company, were placed at $24 per share, raising $225 million for Enron. The year-end cash-out helped Enron make its 1994 numbers and provided an instant valuation for Enron's remaining 52 percent share.

EPP would acquire new assets from Enron right after they had achieved commercialization. In second-quarter 1996, EPP purchased Enron's 49 percent interest in Centragas, a 357-mile, 110 MMcf/d pipeline in Colombia, anchored by a 15-year shipper agreement with state-owned Ecopetrol. The next month, EPP purchased Enron's 50 percent interest in a newly commercialized 185 MW barge-mounted power plant in the Dominican Republic, anchored by a 19-year power purchase agreement with the public utility of the country. (This project was a fiasco on many fronts, negating returns on its $95 million cost.) The missing asset, however, was the grandest one: Dabhol. Just the prospect of restarting the project in 1995 moved EPP's stock.

Predictable problems developed as EPP management's fiduciary duties to their minority shareholders bumped into the concerns of Enron, which was why the accounting rules discouraged such arrangements in the first place.

---

16. EPP began by purchasing Enron's net interest in TGS of 17.5 percent. In 1996, EPP increased its interest to 23 percent, while Enron purchased an additional 11.6 percent interest. TGS, with a return on investment of 19 percent, was a solid investment as "an American pipeline ... just way down south," at least in these years.

Figure 12.5 Enron Global Power & Pipelines, under Rod Gray, was Enron's attempt to monetize its investments in developing-country projects. EPP's problems in navigating between majority-owner Enron and minority owners resulted in Enron's taking the unit back after less than three years.

Enron spent $2 million with lawyers and accountants to find a way to be in control, but technically not be, in order to book profits by taking EPP public.

Selling high and buying low was a tough mix for two public companies committed to 15 percent earnings growth. It was a classic conflict of interest. And soon, EPP's CFO Jim Alexander was at loggerheads with Rich Kinder over valuation. To Alexander, Enron's assets were being sold to EPP at cost, not market, not good for EPP given Enron Development's high-cost, low-value propositions.[17]

---

17. "Had Global Power shareholders known what Alexander knew about overpaying for acquisitions, Alexander would have been subject to legal action," said Malcolm Salter of Harvard Business School.

In addition to Kinder, Alexander fussed with his boss, Rod Gray, over Enron's cost assignments, such as the snowball. Alexander met with Ken Lay to voice his concerns only to have Lay return the issue to Kinder. When Alexander's accounting function was outsourced to ECT, it was a signal to resign. (ECT had assumed scaled-down EI in August 1994, five months before EPP went public.) He did, as did EPP's general counsel Jennifer Vogel and controller Jeffrey Spiegel. "I am not going to sign any SEC documents unless I have control over the numbers," Spiegel insisted.

Gray remained as CEO, and Stan Horton was brought in along with other Enron-side executives in the makeover. Only Alexander's resignation was announced. It was time for Enron to end the experiment and the conflict-of-interest imbroglio, by either selling its 52 percent to EPP or buying out EPP shareholders' 48 percent.

The latter option was chosen in August 1997, with EPP's owners receiving ENE at $35 per share of EPP, effective November 1. It had been less than three years from the partial spin-off. EPP shareholders exited with a 14 percent annual return on their investment. Enron admitted it paid a "premium price," part of a bigger cause of assuring "Wall Street that its investments were stellar." The assets were redeployed within Enron Capital & Trade Resources, which was already managing the commercial side of Enron's domestic power plants.

Authors Bethany McLean and Peter Elkind described the short-lived arrangement as "a remarkably sleazy solution," a paean to the present at the expense of the future, not unlike the all-in use of mark-to-market accounting elsewhere at Enron. "This story again reveals Lay's (and Kinder's) failure to address serious conflicts of interest," noted Harvard Business School professor Malcolm Salter. In 2002, Alexander would tell the *New York Times:* "We were the dead canary in the coal mine."

Enron Engineering & Construction

Formed on the fly to design and build the 1,725 MW Teesside cogeneration plant, Enron Power US was an immediate profit center that generated $100 million during 1991–93, a 7 percent margin on a $1.4 billion project.[18] Originally housed within Enron Power Corp., this unit was "responsible for design and construction aspects of worldwide power development." In addition to Teesside, the unit got busy on Enron International's "fast-track and integrated projects," several of which were completed in 1993–94.

With a track record of "high quality construction on time and under budget," Enron Power US—now housed within Enron Operations Corp. (EOC)—was "building, managing and operating all of Enron's assets around the world,"

---

18. See chapter 6, pp. 269–71.

excepting those of EOG. The self-described "best in class builder and manager" sought third-party business as well to be "a growth area for EOC." But how could this division grow beyond the captive business of its parent to help Enron become a new energy major?

In first-quarter 1994, EOC head Tom White announced Project Mid-1990s, "a bottom up review of [our] engineering and construction services." McKinsey & Company, still Enron's favorite, would facilitate and summarize the proceedings for 70 task force heads and members.

The result was a new division, Enron Engineering & Construction (EEC). Six months of feedback from "internal and external customers, benchmarking against competitors, and an in-depth review of current practices," defined EEC's purpose as undertaking "major construction projects in support of business developers in Enron International and Enron Gas Services [and] ... major 'rate base' projects for our pipeline companies." The leader of EEC was Linc Jones, at that time head of Enron Power Corp. Larry Izzo, the hero of Teesside, was vice president of project management—and soon to take Jones's place as president of EEC.

"Through the end of the decade," Enron's *1995 Annual Report* read, "EE&C is negotiating turnkey contractor and engineering services for approximately 30 projects throughout the United States, Asia, Latin America and Europe with total capital costs of approximately $15 billion." With international starts slow, however, EEC turned to home projects, such as Northern Natural's East Leg expansion and a small intrastate pipeline for a Midwest gas utility.

Net income of $47 million in 1994, driven by EI projects, flatlined at $44 million and $46 million in 1995 and 1996, respectively. Third-party work was the exception, and mixed results made Teesside's triumph a fading star. Operational problems with several EI/ED projects—the 185 MW Puerto Plata project in the Dominican Republic being foremost—reflected design and building issues. Cost-plus contracting between affiliates created malincentives, and fiefdom-like problems grew over time. "Army mafia" was a term coined by critics of EEC, including Jim Alexander of EPP.

————

EEC pitched itself as "the low-cost provider" with "depth and breadth of experience, leading-edge technology and excellent safety and environmental records." A backlog of $3–$4 billion was trumpeted in Enron's 1996 annual report. But third-party business was going to Bechtel, Black & Veatch, and Foster Wheeler, among others. (Bechtel, in fact, was building Enron's Dabhol power plant in India as part owner.) EEC did not even have a sales force to pursue outside projects, hardly a sign of confidence.

The growth strategy turned to acquisitions. Now housed in Enron Ventures (the expanded successor to Enron Operations), EEC bought National Energy Production Corp. (NEPCO) from Zurn Industries in 1997 to "help Enron meet its goal of becoming the world's leading energy company." NEPCO, headquartered in Washington State, had a full book of business to add to its 45 completed power plants. More business was envisioned from a restructured electric industry.

As it turned out, EEC's appetite outraced its capabilities in the next years, as NEPCO accumulated a multibillion-dollar liability from violated performance agreements. NEPCO would file for bankruptcy six months after Enron. "The recklessness surrounding the acquisition and development of NEPCO is noteworthy because it shows the pervasiveness of Enron's commercial naïveté, deal orientation, and lack of financial discipline," wrote Malcolm Salter. Larry Izzo, meanwhile, on whose watch the unreported liabilities accumulated, was now CEO of Calpine Power Services.

Conclusion

Enron's international effort failed to sustain its fast start. In 1992, income before interest and taxes was $33 million; in 1993, $132 million. But there it plateaued. The absolute level of IBIT remained high: $148 million (1994), $142 million (1995), $152 million (1996). But asset sales and one-time project bookings, not annual cash flow from operations, made these earnings transient.

In 1995, Rebecca Mark and Joe Sutton told investors: "By the year 2002, Enron's international projects could total 14,000 megawatts of generating capacity and 6,000 miles of pipelines." By the time Enron deemphasized international infrastructure development (in 1999), with less than 4,000 megawatts and with 10,000 miles of pipe (all in South America), the entire international portfolio was for sale. Rebecca Mark and Joe Sutton left Enron in 2000, and by the end of 2001, Enron was insolvent.

It began so promisingly with Teesside I. But that harrowing project was diminished by Teesside II and would not be replicated in countries and regions less capitalistic than the United Kingdom.

The mixed bag of International was, no doubt, plagued by a lack of capitalist institutions that kept country populations away from energy prosperity. Enron was ready with capital and expertise to perform around the world. But execution was marred by hubris (rather than humility); hope (rather than prudence); illusion (rather than substance); promise (rather than results); signings (rather than operations); postponements (rather than admissions); politics (rather than markets).

In this regard, contra-capitalist Enron International was not unlike its parent. In fact, the financial drain from EI contributed to the decision of capital-starved Enron to double down on financial shenanigans in the late 1990s.

Rebecca Mark, a "New Age corporate diva" to her critics, proved to be too confident in her ambition, too inattentive to the marketplace, too trusting in government. Heart-over-head, she was a Lay-like *gambler*. Talented, and with many successes in her earlier corporate life, her flameout would come with Azurix, a water company she founded at Enron in 1998.

Part VI

Restless Enron: 1994–1996

Introduction

Ken Lay was impatient. His new goal was to double Enron's size and earnings in five years, a mere waystation on Enron's march to become the world's leading energy company. Wholly new profit centers had to be created, building upon the Enron described in Part V: exploration and production; gas transmission; gas liquids; gas marketing; international infrastructure development; and operations management.

The future Enron was taking shape. The rechristened Enron Capital & Trade Resources (ECT, formerly Enron Gas Services) was marketing electricity and raising outside capital to invest in different energy areas.[1] And three new businesses were in process that would become new Enron divisions in 1997.

An entry into solar power in 1995 (via half-owned Solarex) was followed by a major wind power purchase (Zond Energy Systems) to form Enron Renewable Energy Corp. The smallest of the three new businesses, EREC, a political bet, was foremost in issuing press releases. Enron also redefined itself as a *new energy major* by launching Enron Energy Services, as well as acquiring the Oregon public utility Portland General Electric.

Enron was going beyond its original natural gas mission, even its core competency. "Clean" and "green" energies were offered to the stationary market (renewables to generate electricity) and for transportation (MTBE to reformulate gasoline).[2] Ventures completely outside the field of energy—broadband (begun in 1997) and water (begun in 1998), both failures—would be next.[3]

Chapter 13 reviews Enron's entry into solar power and then wind power, a political and public-relations play dependent on special government subsidies to compete against cheaper and more reliable fossil-fuel generation. Wind power, the larger acquisition, was made "to further position Enron as a world

----

1. By the end of 1996, Enron was managing a special-purpose entity, Joint Energy Development Investments (JEDI). It was funded with equal $250 million contributions from the California Public Employees Retirement System (CalPERS) and Enron. CalPERS put up cash, while Enron gave only stock.

2. Enron's small, failed experiment with natural gas vehicles ended in 1995 (see chapter 9, pp. 400–403), which left the far larger but also troubled investment in the gasoline oxygenate MTBE.

3. PGE's start-up FirstPoint Communications was retained by Enron rather than sold, as had originally been planned in 1996–97. With growing Enron investment, the division became Enron Communications in 1999 and Enron Broadband Services the next year.

leader in the renewable energy market." Chapter 13 also overviews Enron's interest in other alternative-energy technologies—and Ken Lay's political leadership in government energy and climate policy.

Chapter 14 delineates Enron's ever-growing visions and aspirations, as defined by Ken Lay and enforced by Richard Kinder. In 1995, Enron announced its "most aggressive vision to date," namely, "to become the world's leading energy company—creating energy solutions worldwide." That superseded the prior fuel-constricted vision: "To become the first natural gas major; the most innovative and reliable provider of clean energy worldwide for a better environment."

This third vision was accompanied by Enron 2000, which promised investors a doubling of revenue and profit in five years. Fifteen percent annual growth, nominally achieved in each of the prior eight years, was set as a five-year average for 1996–2000. In fact, this vision-within-a-vision would be all but forgotten after major write-offs in 1997.

Chapter 15 describes Enron's expansion from wholesale to retail marketing, with natural gas and particularly with electricity, a bold incursion into the domain of public utilities. Throwing down the gauntlet, Enron challenged the utilities—those "scaly dinosaurs of yore"—to allow "deregulation," so that commodity providers (and no one more than Enron) could reach the final user. In fact, what Enron called deregulation was just a different structure of regulation—*unbundling* via governmentally mandated open access.

But Ken Lay and Jeff Skilling's "grand plan" to profitably reach millions of households had to be cut short, very short. With losses mounting and investors promised megaprofits, Enron quickly turned to a new retail concept: *total energy outsourcing* for large commercial and industrial users, itself an unproven business in terms of economies of scale and of scope.

Enron was expanding quickly and dangerously. To outsiders (and to Enron itself) the company appeared to be building a unique energy franchise, with intrinsic competitive advantage. But under the hood was an engine partly dismantled, partly malconstructed, and running too hard.

Ken Lay's unrelenting earnings goals were too high for the company to describe realistically or reach prudently. There was a large and growing out-of-the-money gas position in the United Kingdom. A major acquisition of MTBE facilities was sour. Mark-to-market accounting had claimed a lot of future earnings. Long-lived revenue streams were being sold for current income (monetized). The Dabhol power plant in India was turning out to be all cost and no revenue.

Nevertheless, according to Enron's founder, chairman, and CEO, the company was going to be a different kind of energy major. Exxon (soon to be Exxon-Mobil) was old and traditional; Enron was new and revolutionary. Lay's

50th-floor office looked over the very building where, 30 years before (back when Exxon's Houston presence was Humble Oil), Lay had been a corporate economist. The Enron Building was newer and taller than that of Exxon USA at 800 Bell Street. Ken Lay felt newer and taller too.

The period covered by Part V and Part VI ends with the resignation of Rich Kinder and the ascension of Jeff Skilling, named Enron's president and chief operating officer effective January 1, 1997. CEO Ken Lay would increasingly turn his company over to Jeff Skilling and to Skilling's preferred businesses. The Epilogue describes the consequential leadership change of Skilling for Kinder, the continuance of some Kinder-era business directions, and the new bets by restless Enron.

13

Alternative Energies

E nvironmental policy was Ken's baby," remembered Bruce Stram, Enron's chief economist for many of his 17 years at the company. "Per Ken Lay, Enron was the only natural gas company that clearly understood that environmental regulations, if properly implemented, were good for gas—and acted on it."

Enron turned natural gas into a clean-energy play. From Lay's first annual report in 1984 to the annual reports of the mid-1990s, methane energy was the emphasis, reflecting the relatively small scale of petroleum operations at the company. And in terms of vision, "the premier integrated natural gas company in North America" (1987–90) became "the world's first natural gas major, the most innovative and reliable provider of clean energy worldwide for a better environment" (1990–95).

Enron's clean-energy differentiation, which included a foray into compressed gas for vehicles, was expanded to solar power in 1995 and to wind power in 1997 at modest cost (several tens of millions of dollars). In first-quarter 1997, these efforts were consolidated as Enron Renewable Energy Corp. (EREC), which nominally became the company's fifth division despite its meager profits. Sales of both the division's units—solar to BP in 1999 and wind to GE in 2002—would make for profitable endings despite operational struggles during five years and six years, respectively.

———

EREC, backed by Enron's lobbying and messaging, was central to the political economy of energy in the formative era of climate-change policy. Ken Lay's was "the company most responsible for sparking off the greenhouse civil war in the hydrocarbon business," an ex-Greenpeace executive recalled. Enron's entry into solar came when the big oil companies were going the other way. Jump-starting Amoco's lagging solar business gave new life to this sector, although Enron's grand plan for utility-scale plants failed, leaving the rooftop market.

Enron's next environmental energy play was bigger, financially and other-wise. As noted by Daniel Yergin, "the company that actually put wind back in business in the United States was Enron." Small wonder, then, that this new energy major became the political establishment's favorite in the 1990s, with fawning business features in major publications, a special relationship with the Clinton administration, and praise and awards from Left environmental groups.[1]

Enron's push into renewables changed economics and politics in the natural gas industry too. Government-enabled wind and solar power reduced gas demand in electric generation, making the gas industry a natural opponent of such nonmarket favoritism. Had not Jeff Skilling once said: "Going back to more long-term [gas] contracts and relationships can only help our ability to outperform the alternative fuels of the future"? But when the Natural Gas Sup-ply Association (NGSA) lobbied against renewable energy subsidies in 1997, particularly state-imposed quotas (aka Renewable Portfolio Standards), Ken Lay, chairman of the (Enron-founded) Business Council for Sustainable Energy (BCSE), urged NGSA to be part of "a cooperative effort to promote the eco-nomic and environmental advantages of clean fuels ... as we address the critical issues of industry deregulation and climate change."[2]

BCSE included not only natural gas and renewable companies but also firms profiting from mandates to reduce electricity usage. Nonmarket conservation (*conservationism*) came at the expense of the swing fuel in power generation, which typically was natural gas. Nevertheless, Enron Energy Services (EES), created in March 1997, touted conservation(ism) as part of its outsourcing ser-vices for large commercial and industrial customers. Ken Lay, in short, was playing three sides against the middle.

———

The birth of wind power as commercial energy began in California in the early 1980s. The winds were no stronger than before, but government largesse kicked

———

1. In 1996, Enron received the Corporate Conscience Award for Environmental Leadership from the Council on Economic Priorities, a left-of-center group. After receiving multiple awards in Kyoto, Japan, the next year, Enron was awarded the EPA's Climate Protection Award in 1998.

2. BCSE, founded in 1992 as the Business Council for a Sustainable Energy Future, was organized by Bruce Stram, then Enron's vice president of corporate planning. NGSA repre-sented the domestic upstream interests of the integrated oil companies, which could have different viewpoints from those of independent producers, represented by the Independent Petroleum Association of America (IPAA).

in as a response to the energy crisis, a time when oil and gas shortages turned attention to renewables as the energy future.

On the demand side—very important, since wind electricity was expensive, intermittent, and unproven—were California's "most cooperative utilities in the nation," which entered into long-term purchase contracts pursuant to the Public Utility Regulatory Policies Act of 1978 (PURPA), as interpreted by state commissions under the eye of the Federal Energy Regulatory Commission (FERC). On the supply side, California—a "nation within a nation" by size and philosophy—"offered lucrative incentives to match those of the federal government," virtually doubling the federal 25 percent tax credit.[3]

This confluence resulted in "an avalanche" of capital into California, "including wind and solar power plants as well as solar water heaters." Eclipsing Denmark's 30 percent tax credit, California "almost overnight" became the center of the world wind industry, with 50,000 investors pouring $2 billion into projects. Amid this government-created Spindletop (the 1901 oil gusher that launched the Texas oil industry), quick money was made. But a boom-bust cycle resulted from the end of tax subsidies in the mid-1980s, when a surplus of oil and gas dimmed the energy-crisis rationales for renewables: depletion and energy secutiry. (The global-warming issue was not yet in play.)

Major federal laws commercialized solar- and wind-generated electricity for the grid. Significant government research and development aid under President Carter, diminished under Reagan but resurrected by George H. W. Bush, was not enough. As intermittent resources with concentrated up-front capital costs, solar and wind needed contractually secure long-term sales and a known investor payback. The aforementioned PURPA (1978), enacted when the prevailing wisdom was that oil and natural gas were running out, as well as the Energy Policy Act of 1992 (EPAct), created that certainty as a reward to the renewable-energy lobby, consisting of involved businesses and environmental groups in the Bootleggers-and-Baptists tradition.[4]

Section 210 of PURPA, which made a market for independents to compete against hitherto monopolistic utility generators, was crucially shaped by a waste-to-energy firm, Wheelabrator-Frye Corporation, as well as its trade association, the 48,000-member Solar Lobby, representing not only solar-panel companies but also biomass, hydro, and wind enterprises. Electric utilities were

---

3. Christopher Flavin (of the Worldwatch Institute) was moved to say: "Southern California is doing more to challenge the world energy economy than any single national government is."

4. This phrase takes its name from the noticed lobbying partnership between business (the Bootleggers) and public-interest groups (the Baptists). Enron and environmental groups worked together in Bootleggers-and-Baptist fashion with natural gas and, later, with renewable energy and conservationism.

required to buy power from "qualifying facilities" at a rate up to "the incremental cost to the electric utility of alternative electric energy."

Importantly, incremental cost was not the marginal cost of operations; nor was it to be determined in a competitive least-cost bid process by the purchasing utility. Intended to promote renewables (and cogeneration, which became a whole business for Enron, run by John Wing and Robert Kelly), "total avoided cost" was determined by the state utility commission with blessing from FERC. The resulting avoided-cost determinations, at least as interpreted in the (gravy-train) 1980s, were a bonanza for independent (nonutility) generators such as Enron but a burden for ratepayers.[5]

The second law, EPAct of 1992, introduced the Renewable Electricity Production Tax Credit (PTC) of 1.5 cents per kWh, representing a good half of the going price of electricity at the power plant (busbar). The 10-year provision was inflation-adjusted, which in Enron's lifetime would increase the price to 1.8 cents per kWh. Multiple extensions of the PTC, the first during Enron's last year of solvent life, would keep the subsidy alive as of 2018, with its current inflation-adjusted amount at 2.4 cents per kWh.[6]

Big Thoughts, New Bets

"To develop long-term strategic alternatives for Enron and to thoroughly evaluate the many opportunities that come before us," Ken Lay and Richard Kinder announced to employees in mid-1993, "we have created the new position of executive vice president and chief strategy officer for Enron Corp." This position was created for Robert Kelly, a former economics professor and combat veteran who had just returned to Houston from London, where he oversaw the operation of Teesside I and was negotiating Teesside II as head of Enron International.[7]

"Bob brings the perfect mix of experience and intuitive knowledge to this new position," Lay and Kinder noted. Working under John Wing, Kelly had negotiated gas contracts and other aspects of Enron's cogeneration projects. The nuclear engineering undergraduate and Harvard PhD economist was a big thinker too.

---

5. See chapter 1, p. 101; chapter 2, p. 131; chapter 3, p. 166; and chapter 4, pp. 203–20.

6. The original EPAct credit expired at year-end 1999. Legislative extensions followed in 2000, 2002, 2004, 2005, 2007, 2009, 2012, 2014, and 2015.

7. Enron entered into firm, price-certain gas-supply contracts before executing gas-purchase contracts to cover both supply and price. The naked bet by Kelly et al. turned out badly: Enron could not profitably sell its gas and took a $675 million write-off in 1997. See chapter 6, pp. 271–73; and chapter 12, pp. 494–98.

The plan was for Kelly to join an operating unit in Houston. But the divisions "were well staffed internally," he remembered, and "it was Ken's idea to explore our options with renewable energy." Kelly formed Enron Emerging Technologies Inc. (EET) to evaluate alternative-energy technologies with high-growth potential.

Kelly had two key advisors in his new role. On behalf of Ken Lay, John Urquhart, a former top GE executive who was vice-chairman at Enron, would oversee the venture from the office of the chairman.[8] Corporate Strategy and Planning, headed by Bruce Stram, another PhD economist, would report to Kelly, with Stram's new title soon to be senior vice president of EET.

From "day one," renewables topped the list. "In particular," remembered Kelly, "two of the things that we were going to look at were solar and wind power." Biomass was only of cursory interest, and hydroelectricity was not considered an alternative technology. Stram was put on fuel cells, a distributed-generation technology using natural gas. Natural gas vehicles, another environmentally connected technology play, were already being pursued—but would soon be abandoned.[9]

Why invest in renewable energies when supply forecasts for conventional energies were robust, especially at Enron? Why bet on renewables when technology was reducing overall pollution despite growing use of oil, gas, and coal? Ken Lay himself considered natural gas as more akin to renewables than to the other fossil fuels, a theme underlying his September 1995 address, "The New Worlds of Natural Gas," to the Pacific Coast Gas Association.

In that speech, Enron's chairman opined that "the environmental preference of renewable energy over natural gas is getting somewhat blurred" and that "natural gas resources—just like renewable energy—are virtually unlimited." He added: "In many cases, a state-of-the-art controlled-burn gas-fired combined cycle plant may be environmentally preferred to a wind farm in a heavy bird population center or a new hydroelectric facility located in a salmon spawning area."

But Enron saw green in green energy. Wind and solar as primary energies had new public policy rationales and powerful political constituencies. Specifically, global warming from fossil-fuel usage via the enhanced greenhouse effect was the new neo-Malthusian scare, and post–Gulf War concerns over energy

8. After graduating from Virginia Polytechnic, Urquhart joined General Electric as an engineer in 1949 and rose to run GE's Gas Turbine Division in 1974 and Gas Delivery Group five years later. In 1982, he became GE's "top international executive" in charge of a $10 billion business.

9. See chapter 9, pp. 400–403. Enron invested in MTBE and methanol but not ethanol, and it never invested in electric vehicles beyond a few owned by Portland General Electric (which Enron purchased in 1997).

security put petroleum on the defensive. Even more than this, renewables had public cachet for an energy company, particularly one that prized publicity and promoted a momentum stock.

Environmentalists—habitually hostile toward oil and coal as depleting, polluting energies—looked to wind and solar first and natural gas as a "temporary buffer," a "bridge" fuel, to that sustainable future. Nuclear power, once hailed as cost-effective and environmentally benign, was seen as neither after Three Mile Island in 1979 (and, later, Chernobyl).

"In the midst of the mounting energy-related difficulties confronting the United States," the Union of Concerned Scientists concluded in 1980, "one clear solution emerges: an aggressive strategy emphasizing improvements in energy productivity and the implementation of a variety of attractive solar technologies that can lead us out of the morass and onto the road to a sage and sustainable energy future." Several years earlier, Amory Lovins had popularized the idea of the *soft energy path* in contrast to the fossil-fueled central stations first championed by Thomas Edison and Samuel Insull a century earlier.

Distributed generation would be powered by a natural flow of energy, not resources that had to be mined and combusted. More-the-better conservation, or conservationism, was seen by Lovins as an energy source (*negawatts*, to join megawatts). Enron, too, jumped on the idea of mass energy savings via outsourcing by forming Enron Energy Services, a foray that would prove exaggerated (*economical* conservation proved to be significantly less than *technical* conservation).

————

Energy scholar Vaclav Smil found himself at odds with the energy romanticists, who saw an easy answer in the free, always-out-there flow of the sun. In the 1980s, he explained the "irremovable mismatch" between energy supply and demand of flow-versus-stock energy.

Industrial processes required energy flows of between 10^2 and 10^7 W/m^2, and large cities consume energy at levels between 10^1 and 10^2 W/m^2. Solar power came in densities of between 10^0 and 10^1 W/m^2 and required costly "storage to overcome random flows." Wind power, also needing storage to provide continuous service, was more dilute at 10^{-1} W/m^2. Enter fossil fuels, whose 10^3 W/m^2 power density, "matching much more easily the needs of industrial civilization," was continuous—and came "without exorbitant land requirements."

Smil was hardly the first to note the paradox. In 1878, inventor John Ericsson lamented the fact that "although the heat is obtained for nothing, so extensive, costly, and complex is the concentration apparatus that solar steam is many times more costly than steam produced by burning coal." Practical attempts to harness the sun predated the fossil-fuel era, in fact, and it was fossil fuels that made utility-scale solar unnecessary by the late-nineteenth century.

Relative power density explained why solar ventures in population and industrial centers were few and in perpetual need of special government favor. But Ken Lay did not read Vaclav Smil. Enron's CEO was more attuned to energy fads and public policies, although Lay's PhD dissertation demonstrated a technical proficiency to comprehend energy physics.[10] Lay preferred the energy and climate writings of Christopher Flavin of Worldwatch Institute. But Flavin, like Lay, was fixated on trends and policies rather than on the underlying technical fundamentals that explained why some energies were commercially viable and others government dependent.

Enron's CEO saw where energy policy was going—and where energy activists were saying it should go. The large tax credit and accelerated depreciation for qualifying renewables in the Energy Policy Act of 1992, signed by George H. W. ("all things to all people") Bush, restarted the push. And Bill Clinton was all-in with wind and solar, in addition to natural gas.

The Clinton administration's Department of Energy appointed an Enron friend, Deputy Secretary William "Bill" White. As second in charge at DOE, this Houstonian and former trial lawyer would assist Enron on a variety of fronts. A reelected Bush would have offered Enron a lot (and maybe even a cabinet post acceptable to Lay), but Clinton certainly offered Enron the opportunity to expand its green image beyond gas, as Greenpeace and other environmental pressure groups wanted.

There was something else that Enron's forward-looking chief might have grasped: that renewable energy would give Enron a powerful card to get what environmentalists did not want: the ability of rival power sellers, like Enron, to sell electricity to the retail customers of electric utilities, thereby driving down rates, increasing usage, and reducing self-interested conservation.[11] Coupling a renewable mandate with mandated open access (MOA) power transmission would prove crucial to an Enron-driven 1999 Texas electricity restructuring law that would all but restart a stalled domestic wind industry.

Lay, Kelly, and Stram—all PhDs attracted to the climate issue and yearning to get beyond business-as-usual—were true activists for energy transformation. Under Lay's direction, Enron would *restart* the solar industry, *rescue* the US

---

10. Lay's 178-page dissertation, "The Measurement of the Timing of the Economic Impact of Defense Procurement Activity: An Analysis of the Vietnam Buildup" (1970), employed a theoretical and statistical (econometric) model to "estimate changes in economic output resulting from changes in the demand for defense procurement items."

11. By replacing standard utility service, multifirm competition for electricity sales to homeowners or businesses promised lower prices, increased usage, and the cheapest way to generate more power. This "nightmare," to use Christopher Flavin's term, would discourage renewable energy and demote the utility's "service" of demand-side management (ratepayer-subsidized conservation programs).

wind industry, and help *legitimize* the climate issue. Stram's 1995 essay for the Harvard Global Environmental Policy Project, "A Carbon Tax Strategy for Global Climate Change," added to his in-house work. Post-Enron, Kelly would publish *The Carbon Conundrum: Global Warming and Energy Policy in the Third Millennium* (2002), siding with the market-failure/government-activism approach. Numerous other employees would also continue to labor in the energy-environmental area post-Enron, a legacy that had roots in Robert Kelly's new policy directions of 1993–94.

Solar Power

The photovoltaic (PV) effect, discovered in 1839, used the energy of sunlight to eject electrons from simple materials and, much later, from semiconductor chips. In 1954, Bell Telephone Laboratories introduced the PV method of generating electricity from silicon. But capturing and concentrating dilute rays of energy was capital- and land-intensive, compared to using the energy stock from the sun's work over the eons, embedded (stored) in oil, natural gas, and coal. Solar as flow energy is also intermittent (the sun is not always visible, and storage capability was limited) compared to the embedded energy of fossil fuels.

Nonetheless, solar had a niche far away from the reach of a utility's wires. Putting PV panels in space was the opening application from which a new industry emerged. Offshore oil and gas platforms became the next market, offering an energy alternative to huge batteries that were transported to sea, used up, and tossed overboard.

Other uses emerged as costs dropped: navigation aids (buoys, call stations), remote military applications, and off-the-grid living where propane gas was unavailable. The major on-grid use for solar was water heating, which became common after World War II in California, Florida, and other sunny regions.

A Flashy Proposal

Robert Kelly had scoured the field to locate a partner to enter the solar business. But before this was completed, Enron went into full proposal mode in response to a solicitation by the Department of Energy for bids to build a solar farm in Nevada. Utility-level solar was just what Kelly had in mind to launch his business plan based on scale economies. Top experts were retained and quotations gathered from existing providers. When completed, it was an Enron PR moment heard around the political-energy world.

"Solar Power for Earthly Prices," read a November 15, 1994, headline in the *New York Times*, replete with a photo of Kelly holding a panel to the bright sky. Subtitled "Enron Plans to Make the Sun Affordable," the business feature described Enron's proposal to deliver electricity to the federal government in two years at $0.055 per kWh, a year-one rate that would escalate 3 percent annually for 20 years. This quote was unheard of: it was only a fourth of the $0.20 per kWh estimate, give or take, quoted by Worldwatch Institute.

"Grand promises in the late 1970's about the potential of virtually pollution-free, endlessly renewable energy sources like solar energy faded into an embarrassed hush," the article allowed, but Enron's optimistic goal was described as "probably reachable." Unit costs had "quietly" declined by two-thirds, it was explained. What Enron was proposing—a $150 million, 100 MW manufacturing plant—would provide the scale economies that were hitherto missing.

"If a good group of people puts a plant of that scale in, it will have a real consequence on costs," a Princeton electrical engineer opined. "It's not going to go down by just a little bit, but by a factor of two." Another endorsement came from DOE Deputy Secretary White. "I'm confident we can make some commitment for a Federal entity to purchase or at least broker some purchase of solar power."

Tony Catalano, director of DOE's PV division, stated: "This is going to be very competitive in the U.S. and lots of other places in the world." Added DOE's solar-energy director: "This establishes the benchmark we want and restarts a stalled solar industry." In fact, Enron's proposal might not even need "expensive federal aid."

The article explained the new technology and referenced a solar manufacturer and a consultant working with Enron. "Yes, it can be done," said one. "It's the dream we've all had: that someone would take the risk of building a very large factory." In fact, this new plant would be *12 times larger* than anything then in existence.

A confident Robert Kelly explained how producing solar power followed from Enron's experience with gas-fired generation. The article closed: "Asked how soon solar power could generate earnings, [Kelly] said: 'Now. We're a very impatient company in terms of profits'."

It was as if Enron had written the article. But the author was Allen R. Myerson, the *Times*'s Dallas-based energy reporter. Enron was raking in what the trade called *earned media* (versus paid-for, or unearned, media). Myerson would continue to wax enthusiastic about Enron until the company's demise in December 2001; in August 2002, he jumped from the *Times* building to his death.[12]

This project, situated at a nuclear test site in southeast Nevada, was highly speculative. The government had not decided to buy power from Enron or anyone else. The electricity would be available only during the day when the sun was visible. The price depended on a raft of special favors and obligations—local, state, and federal—and a 20-year fixed-priced commitment, something

___

12. Myerson's suicide, attributed to marital and financial woes, drew association with the suicide of Enron's Cliff Baxter earlier that year and with the suicide two years earlier of Agis Salpukas, another *Times* reporter covering Enron.

the electricity market was otherwise moving away from. And Enron had never built, installed, or owned a single solar panel. Kelly only revealed that Enron had an undisclosed partner that would produce the solar cells.

Two years later, DOE chose a scaled-down 10 MW proposal from Enron. But it was not an executed deal. The "award" was the right to "finalize a definitive power purchase agreement by mid-1997," with construction of the would-be largest solar facility in the United States in the next year. The same Enron press release mentioned two other solar-farm deals that were in process. But none of the three would be undertaken.

An Unlikely Partner

Kelly and Urquhart's mission to find a viable entry point into the new business of solar energy had been under way for about a year when they came up with a seemingly unlikely partner: the oil major Amoco, which had evolved out of the Standard Oil Company of Indiana, and ultimately out of John D. Rockefeller's Standard Oil trust. Why had such an old-line oil company gotten into solar power? The story began in the early 1970s.

Like other cash-rich oil majors, Amoco had been whipsawed by oil and gas regulations that triggered and prolonged the 1970s energy crisis. Then, too, the executives of Amoco genuinely feared the depletion of oil and natural gas. Under the circumstances, this Chicago-based company began looking to non-traditional lines of business as a hedge.

"We believe a prudent management should seek out and develop alternative investments outside of the oil and gas business to hedge against proliferating government interference and controls which will inhibit our ability to operate profitably in the petroleum business," Amoco informed industry analysts in 1976. Green bona fides were also prized for petroleum-marketing purposes; Amoco's "quest for environmental leadership in its industry" went only so far with compressed natural gas as an alternative to gasoline and diesel at the pump.

In 1979, President Jimmy Carter told the world: "There is no longer any question that solar energy is feasible and cost effective." Whether or not they believed him, Amoco executives that year purchased 30 percent of a leading manufacturer and distributor of solar cells, Solarex, located in Rockville, Maryland. The balance was bought four years later for total ownership.

One of Amoco's early initiatives was the nation's first solar-powered gasoline service station. Formed in 1973, Solarex introduced the use of polycrystalline silicon in solar cells in 1976 and marketed thin-film amorphous silicon modules three years later. Still, a large cost premium remained for distributed solar, limiting its niche applications and obviating any role in a power grid.

Despite federal grants, more than 90 percent of which "ended up in the coffers of the largest corporations in the United States," a graveyard of private efforts resulted from President Carter's vision. In the 1970s and 1980s, failed solar investments were made by Texas Instruments, General Electric, IBM, Polaroid, RCA, and Westinghouse; Sanyo, Kyocera, and Sharp of Japan; and the energy majors Arco, Exxon, Mobil, and British Petroleum. Exxon exited the business in 1984 after 15 years and $30 million in losses. Arco Solar would be sold to Siemens in 1989 after 12 years and $200 million in deficits.[13] Mobil Solar Energy Corporation was purchased by Applied Solar Energy (ASE) in 1994.

That left one major domestic player, Amoco's Solarex, the largest US-owned manufacturer and distributor of PV modules and systems. In 1987, Solarex was placed within Amoco Technology Company with a mission to reduce costs in order to increase sales, as well as improve production economies. Its largest facility was increased to 5 MW (annual capacity of produced solar panels). But profits were inadequate for further expansion to utilize new-generation technology. Solarex needed fresh capital, better marketing, and a new business plan.

Amoco/Enron Solar (Solarex)

"Amoco Corporation and Enron Corp. have agreed to form a new general partnership to manufacture photovoltaic (solar electric) modules and develop solar power electric generation facilities," an Amoco press release announced December 19, 1994. The 50-50 partnership, representing a $20 million Enron purchase, obligated each partner to contribute $15 million to complete construction of a thin-film manufacturing plant capable of annual production "in excess of 10 MW of large area, multijunction amorphous silicon modules." This new technology, the press release noted, was developed in conjunction with the Department of Energy.[14]

"Amoco gained a partner that was a fast-growing leader in power generation and sales and had a hard-driving, entrepreneurial culture well-suited to the rapid expansion of Solarex," explained a scholarly corporate history of Amoco offered by Joseph Pratt. "For its part, Enron gained a share of one of the largest solar cell manufacturers in the United States."

Amoco/Enron Solar assumed the assets of Solarex effective the first day of 1995. Headquartered in Frederick, Maryland, Solarex would become the name for a unit of Amoco/Enron Solar that was responsible for production, research, development, and system design. With a manufacturing plant in Australia and

---

13. Exxon began researching solar in 1969 and formed Solar Power Corporation in 1973. In 1984, losses and limited prospects led the world's largest energy company to shut the division down. ARCO Solar, formed in 1977 with a goal to become "the General Motors of the photovoltaic industry," was sold to Siemens A.G. of West Germany in 1989.

14. This third-generation technology, in the experimental stage, came after silicon wafers and thin-film amorphous silicon.

an assembly facility in Hong Kong, Solarex was now building a second-generation PV plant outside Newport News, Virginia.

The partnership had a second subsidiary. In addition to Solarex, Houston-based Amoco/Enron Solar Power Development, headed by Robert Kelly, was responsible for marketing, financing, and subsequent operations. Kelly's grand strategy was to build large grid-connected solar farms, creating scale economies for panels to capture the rooftop market.

"Our joint venture with Amoco builds on Enron's strategy of providing clean energy to the world economy," stated Enron's vice-chairman Urquhart. "This is the technology that will allow us to provide solar electric power at competitive prices, both in the United States and in other areas around the world." Amoco hailed the joint venture as providing "the missing link in PV—lower costs through high-volume production enabled by sales into grid-connected markets."

Enron was now in a wholly new business. Ken Lay had added renewables to Enron's list of "energy solutions worldwide." Kelly was coupling the expertise of ECT and Enron International to rapidly improving technology that between 1986 and 1994 had reportedly tripled solar's energy yield per dollar. High volume and big profits were envisioned by Enron in a carbon-constrained world.

Imaging versus Reality

The one-year anniversary of Enron's Amoco partnership was marked by a cover story in *Enron Business* describing the work of the six-member Amoco/Enron Solar Power Development team under Robert Kelly, CEO and cochairman of the Amoco/Enron Solar Managing Board. The partnership was "right on track," Kelly reported. "We're currently number two worldwide in the production of photovoltaic cells." Better yet: "We expect to be number one by the end of the century, and by a wide margin, because we have certain growth opportunities that our competitors don't have."

The most exciting development was "the go-ahead to build the world's largest solar electric generating plant in northern India." But the 25-year power contract to underwrite this $100 million project was not quite final. In the post-Dabhol environment, the Rajasthan State Electricity Board said that it needed to bid out the 50 MW solar-and-gas project. Facing stiff competition, Enron applied to the Indian Renewable Energy Development Agency for low-interest financing. (Turned down, Kelly's project died in December 1997.)

In addition to the Nevada project, Enron was working on solar farms in southern California and in West Texas. Internationally, publicized project negotiations included China (150 MW), the aforementioned India (50 MW), Greece (50 MW, part of the Greenpeace Solar Campaign, described in the next section), and the Middle East. A $1.14 million DOE grant to build a 4 MW solar farm in Hawaii did not result in construction.

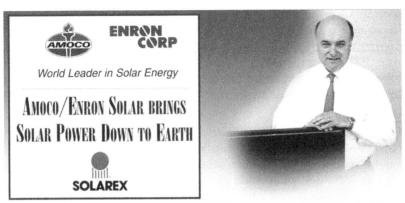

Figure 13.1 Enron's partnership with Amoco was a quick entry into the international solar market. Robert Kelly (top right) oversaw a staff of five to market solar farms and to place large orders for rooftop panels. After troubled sales, Enron's half-interest was profitably sold to BP (which purchased Amoco) in 1999.

Central arrays feeding the power grid was what Kelly saw as the main story, but Solarex was a big player in rooftop solar. Amoco/Enron Solar was the world's second-largest manufacturer of panels and the largest US maker, with plants in Frederick, Maryland; near Newport News, Virginia; and in Australia, Hong Kong, and Japan.

Sales in 70 countries were a mix of "solar farms, rooftops, village electrification, water pumping, telecommunications, and other industrial and consumer products." One venture in Japan, helped by $25,000 government grants, offered residents the world's first "zero-energy house," where solar and efficiency investments eliminated the monthly oil, gas, and electric bills.

Rooftop solar was profitable. But what hurt earnings were research and development expenses by Amoco/Enron in their attempt to commercialize solar farms. It was distributed generation or bust for now, a subsidy play helped by a raft of special government favors, capped by the Clinton administration's Million Solar Roofs Initiative, which Solarex head Harvey Forest predicted would help "stimulate a domestic market here in the United States."[15]

———

While sunshine produced little electricity, Enron's effort generated warm feelings from environmentalists. To get beyond carbon-based energy, it was not enough for natural gas to take market share away from oil and coal. The green dream was wind and solar—and electricity from renewables to power motor vehicles. Enron was at least partly on their side.

"I needed to know more about Enron's solar push," recalled Jeremy Leggett, director of Greenpeace's Solar Initiative, who visited at length with Robert Kelly in April 1995. "It seemed genuine, but I had to be sure." Leggett explained:

> Here was the biggest gas company in the world, with oil interests as well, joining up with Amoco, one of the Seven Sisters, to launch a venture which could provide the catalyst for the take-off of the solar-photovoltaic market. Was there something I was missing?

He recalled how Kelly saw solar as "the future," not only for business reasons but also because of "the global warming threat."[16] Leggett left convinced, a story he recalled in his 1999 book, *The Carbon War: Global Warming and the End of the Oil Era*.

Enron was now establishing good relations with the far side of the environmental movement that was otherwise against natural gas. Greenpeace, which Ken Lay took to task in 1994 for rejecting natural gas as part of the environmental equation, finally has something good to say about a natural gas company.

Robert Kelly's business plan for Enron's $35 million investment centered on production economies, which solar engineers assured him lay on the other side of higher sales. The solar *farm* of thousands of aligned panels was key; large arrays would not only reduce unit costs (with fixed costs spread over more vol-

———

15. The $600 million federal loan program, as proposed by the Solar Energy Industry Association, involving a constellation of government agencies, would provide "buy-down" subsidies for one million installations of solar water heaters and PV equipment by 2007.

16. Kelly claimed resistance within Enron for pushing the global-warming threat. "I may be muzzled on this, but I'm also a bit independent. I need a logical argument to shut me up," he told Leggett. In fact, Enron and Ken Lay were on board with the climate issue beginning in 1988, and Enron would never waiver in its quest for US and international energy policy predicated on limiting carbon dioxide (CO_2) emissions.

ume) but also capture the rooftop market for Solarex from better pricing. True, the Nevada proposal was languishing, as were the others. But one proposal seemed to be falling into place, and Enron was right there.

The Crete-Greenpeace Proposal

In October 1995, Greenpeace launched the Solar Crete campaign to halt the construction of a 50 MW diesel-fired power plant. With the island's average and peak power demand increasing at twice the rate of Greece as a whole, Greenpeace demanded a completely new approach to supply. It was "the fight of oil versus the sun and wind," an Athens magazine noted.

Solicitations were sought. One serious proposal emerged in mid-1996 from Amoco/Enron. An industrial facility would also be considered to manufacture an estimated 528,000 modules holding nearly 50 million solar cells generating the necessary 50 MW. Kelly opened a Greece subsidiary, IWECO Solar, to work toward a final agreement on what was (on paper) 15 times larger than any solar farm in the world.

The $120 million project, with $2 million per year in estimated operating costs, needed a lot of help even to be considered by the authorities. Although advertised to be substantially less than the global average of grid-connected solar, costs were still prohibitive. A phase-in of this capacity would be required in any case.

In mid-1997, Enron announced a $10 million grant from the European Union to build an $18 million, 5 MW solar farm in Crete, also helped by a tax break that reduced the cost by 30 percent. "This project will serve as the centerpiece for opportunities we are pursuing in a Mediterranean region that has excellent solar resources," said Amoco/Enron's area representative. The plan was to build the first 5 MW by year-end 1998 and add 9 MW per year to reach a total of 50 MW by 2003, a $180 million proposition.

The official news came in a Greenpeace press release dated June 12, 1997: "Solar power today enters a new era with Greek Government's decision to begin the construction of the world's largest photovoltaic (PV) power station on the island of Crete." For $17.75 million, with 55 percent of the capital pledged by the European Union and the Greek government, Enron would build a 5 MW facility, eclipsing the then largest solar array of 3.3 MW in Italy.

"This smashed conventional assumptions on solar power in terms of scale and costs," a solar enthusiast stated in Greenpeace's press release. It was Robert Kelly's virtuous circle of market-pull and technology-push, where higher demand lowered cost to increase demand, ad infinitum.

Greenpeace's Mediterranean Campaign saw Crete as the "show case" for a regional move to "the solar power revolution," which would help provide "the solution to global warming." It was all so simple (but postmodernist): "All we need is that governments believe in the region's potential and have the will to seriously consider their renewable energy future after coal, oil, and gas are over."

The project was not to be. Greece's Public Power Corporation could not afford the power, much less plan around solar's intermittency, which made the array's real dispatch a fraction of its nameplate capacity. The Association of Industries and Commerce was against even the starting tranche of the grand experiment. The "lowest price on record" was cost-prohibitive—and for an inferior product compared to 99 percent of the island's other (fossil fuel) sources. Adding storage to allow solar to achieve grid-parity, not part of the project, would have *doubled* its cost.

A Graceful Exit

Enron's public relations bonanza from solar would not be matched by executed projects or profitability. The Virginia thin-film plant was behind schedule and over budget, leading to a management shakeup by Amoco. Declining sales meant that Enron's investment was not making money, just garnering earned media. Enron Wind Corporation would soon become the center of attention for Kelly and Enron, but a fortuitous ending for Enron's solar effort was just ahead.

Effective January 1, 1999, British Petroleum, now just BP, purchased Amoco for $48 billion to form BP Amoco. The year before, BP CEO John Browne was the first major oil company executive to declare carbon dioxide emissions from burning fossil fuel to be a climate threat. Invoking the precautionary principle, Browne cited the scientific work of the Intergovernmental Panel on Climate Change (IPCC) to conclude that "to be sustainable, companies need a sustainable world," a *carbon-constrained* world.

Regarding Browne's speech, Stanford climate scientist and activist Stephen Schneider said: "They're out of climate denial." But even while Browne endorsed climate action, he noted the essential role of fossil fuels in modern life and the continuing need for profit-driven oil and gas enterprise. "Real sustainability is about simultaneously being profitable and responding to the reality and the concerns of the world in which you operate," he opined. "We're not separate from the world. It's our world as well." Still, Browne pushed back against the end-fossil-fuels-now movement.

> I disagree with some members of the environmental movement who say we have to abandon the use of oil and gas [because] … that view underestimates the potential for creative and positive action. But that disagreement doesn't mean that we can ignore the mounting evidence and concern about climate change. As businessmen, when our customers are concerned, we had better take notice.

Ken Lay's decade-old interest in climate action was a play of natural gas against the higher CO_2 emissions of oil and coal. Browne's climate strategy flew in the face of his company's producing, transporting, refining, and marketing of petroleum. Still, BP with Amoco added was natural gas heavy, offering benefits for climate-policy activism. There was also a petro sales strategy ("greenwashing" to its critics) in being environmentally preferred at the service station to Lee Raymond's Exxon, if not other rivals.

Enron's half-ownership in Solarex created a conflict of interest for Amoco's new owner, given that BP Solar (established 1981) was bigger than the unit it was buying. Redundancies could be eliminated, and BP's new branding was to be the world's *green* petroleum marketer, not unlike Amoco's aspiration a decade before. Thus BP (now standing for "beyond petroleum") became the largest solar-panel manufacturer in the world, effective March 31, 1999, by purchasing Enron's half of Solarex for $45 million, a rich sum for a money-losing unit. Enron happily recorded an after-tax gain of $6.5 million for its otherwise unsuccessful foray.

Enron's exit came with a discouraging report card. "None of the proposed solar farms ever got built," Sarah Howell of Solarex told the press, referring to a dozen projects touted by Kelly and Enron. "We are concentrating on the more viable grid-tied [that is, urban rooftop] systems." This was the business that everyone else was after too.

———

"All the world's energy could be achieved by solar many thousands of times over," Shell's renewable-energy chief opined in 1995. "Amoco/Enron Solar aims to power the earth by harnessing the energy of the sun—at a price that is competitive with fossil fuels," *Enron Business* stated in 1996. And Greenpeace said: "1997 is being viewed as a turning point in the fortunes of solar photovoltaics as global demand is 'poised to soar.'"

But was scalable solar achievable in the real world?

In the mid-1990s, Solar Two, a $55 million, 10 MW solar thermal demonstration project in the Mojave Desert, led by Southern California Edison, began producing (intermittent) power at between $0.18 and $0.22 per kWh. (Solar One, a 10 MW project built in 1981, had been destroyed by fire in 1986.)

"Solar Two looks good on paper, and it is expected to provide steady baseload electricity as well as late afternoon peaking capacity, but the future of all the central solar generators is in doubt," opined Christopher Flavin and Nicolas Lenssen in 1994. "They are expensive to build, their very scale escalates financial risks—as with nuclear power—and their massive height (in excess of 200 meters) may attract opposition." They were right. Solar Two's 130-acre computer-controlled mirrors, reflecting sunlight to a central tower, ceased operation in 1999 and were demolished a decade later.

Solar Two was "a technological success, but not economically ready for prime time," the editors of the *Electricity Journal* concluded. BP's John Browne was correct; solar energy produced peak-demand power at about double the competitive rate.

But, just perhaps, direct solar was less the energy answer than *indirect* solar from wind, itself the result of differential heating of the earth and the atmosphere.

Wind Power

Enron's expansion into wind-turbine manufacturing and sales—and the designation of renewable energy as the company's fifth core division—reflected a government-created opportunity. Wind turbines, like solar panels for grid electricity, were generously subsidized at the federal level and in California, with other states to follow. Wind and solar were politically correct to the powerful environmental establishment. Hydroelectricity and biomass were less so, and nuclear power (the largest emission-free energy source) was not. Enron did not invest in these latter areas.

The new US leader in renewable energy had taken a leap beyond natural gas. Enron was differentiating itself in its quest to become the world's leading energy company. It was good timing, too, with Bill Clinton and Al Gore ensconced in the White House.

Ken Lay became *the* progressive energy leader to politicians and environmentalists. He was a new friend of Bill's despite having done many years of work for the Republicans. Was not this the CEO who helped persuade President George H. W. Bush to attend the United Nation's Earth Summit in Rio de Janeiro to advance the global-warming, social-justice cause? Now Enron's chief was speaking Greenpeace's language of a post-fossil-fuel world, although for the distant future.[17]

Still, wind power was barely viable. There was competition for projects and warranty issues with new technology. For Enron Renewable Energy Corporation, losses were registered. But tax credits for the parent were utilized, and the green theme helped keep ENE a momentum stock in the mid-1990s.

Wind Energy in History

Windmills represented an early use of mechanical energy, predating the fossil-fuel era by centuries. Turning wind into electricity had an 1887 beginning in Thomas Edison's neighborhood and a business push in Denmark a decade later.[18] American companies picked up the pace in the 1920s. During World War II, the 1.25 MW Grandpa's Knob wind turbine distributed electricity to Central Vermont Public Service Corporation, an experiment that led the Federal Power Commission to estimate the potential of domestic wind power in 1945.

The energy crisis, which began with natural gas shortages in the winter of 1971–72 and oil shortages two years later, revitalized interest in wind power in

---

17. "I would guess that, within a century of so, we are going to see a big share of our total energy needs served by renewable energy," Lay stated in 1993. "And certainly the day could come when virtually all of our energy needs could be served with renewable energy."

18. To compete against coal-fired power lighting his home, Charles Brush, a rival to Thomas Edison, erected a 60-foot windmill, a dynamo, and batteries to capture the current. Soon, Brush connected to central-station electricity, Edison's model, which was cheaper and more available than intermittent, distributed power.

the United States. The American Wind Energy Association (AWEA) was formed in 1974; six years later the nation's first wind farm was constructed in Vermont, consisting of 20 turbines generating 600 kilowatts (0.6 megawatts) at its peak.[19]

"Wind power may be a breath of fresh air on the world energy scene during the eighties," wrote Christopher Flavin in *Wind Power: A Turning Point* (1981). "Pacific Gas & Electric and Southern California Edison seem to be playing a game of leapfrog as each attempts to one-up the other in a fight for leadership and public recognition in wind-energy development." In fact, via PURPA-qualifying sales contracts, captive (utility) ratepayers joined unwitting taxpayers in launching a new domestic industry.

———

Zond Systems was founded in 1981 by Jim Dehlsen in a mountain town with whistling winds, Tehachapi, California, located between the San Joaquin Valley and the Mojave Desert. "One of the most important and committed pioneers" of his industry, Dehlsen spent that New Year's Eve on a dangerous ridge in Tehachapi Pass, struggling to get his turbines operating to qualify for an expiring state tax credit. Humbled by the unrelenting winds, he began importing turbines from the Danish wind company Vestas, itself helped by a government-funded research institute near Copenhagen.[20]

Zond would prove to be the major survivor of "California's extraordinary wind rush," which produced "an eyesore of broken and twisted blades," "PURPA machines," and "tax farms" in return for little electricity. To break out of the pack, Zond in 1993 hired a Danish turbine designer, Finn Hansen, to remake its technology. A million-dollar grant from US Department of Energy helped this effort. Major projects, such as the 342-turbine Sky River Project in California, made Zond a US leader.

Times turned tough by mid-decade. Lower gas prices dropped the avoided-cost assignment from regulators pursuant to PURPA. Some in-state subsidies expired. A revenue stream from a small ownership interest in each project proved just enough for Zond to, in the words of Dehlsen, "survive until the next stage."

Major Issues
Wind-generated electricity was not for the rooftop or yard. At scale, it was not a distributed energy, as was a solar panel away from a utility grid. But power from large wind turbines was far cheaper than power from a large array of solar

———

19. The secondary status of wind was evident in President Jimmy Carter's 1977 National Energy Plan, which emphasized solar energy, nuclear fusion, synthetic fuels (from coal), and municipal waste.

20. "Risø [National Laboratory] was critical to the rise of the Danish industry," summarized Daniel Yergin. "So were subsidies from the Danish government."

panels. Still, for new, on-grid capacity, wind power was uneconomical and less reliable than conventional sources. Further, the huge turbines with blades larger than a 747's wing were a hazard to avian wildlife and a nuisance to neighbors prizing tranquility.

Free energy spun the turbines, but electricity conversion was material- and capital-intensive. Like solar, wind power was intermittent. An 1883 article in *Scientific American* noted wind's unpredictable, unsteady flow and asked how the output could be stored from "gathering it at the time we do not need it and preserving it till we do."

The first opus on energy, published in 1865, did not consider wind a substitute for "our cheap supplies of coal," because of the former's "irregular" availability and siting limited to "open and elevated situations." In contrast, explained W. S. Jevons, coal was plentiful, portable, storable, and dependable— attributes that would carry over from its industrial use to the generation of electricity.

"Even energy from wind—seemingly the freest, most renewable energy source imaginable—isn't environmentally perfect," a 1978 *Wall Street Journal* story reported. "Giant windmills interfere with television and radio signals, and their spinning blades can kill unwary birds." Furthermore, "the biggest problem is where to put the things: people in windy places like Cape Cod aren't eager to strew their picturesque landscape with immense metal structures." (A quarter-century later, a proposal to erect wind turbines off Cape Cod would encounter lawsuits from area residents.)

"Avian mortality" would become a notable issue, as Zond found out first-hand in 1989 with its rejected application to build a wind farm just outside Gorman, California.[21] A range of opponents, including the local chapter of the Sierra Club and the National Audubon Society, left Zond "to nurse $1 million in fruitless expenses."

Other issues—such as long transmission lines to get wind power from the wilds to urban areas—added to the challenge. But these drawbacks did not prove decisive to the industry as a whole. The environmental community, having little supply-side strategy otherwise, accepted wind power's shortcomings. The political will to subsidize wind power into commercial use would emerge by the early 1990s and not disappear in Enron's lifetime—or after.

———

The rumor inside Enron was that a second foray into renewables was imminent, the lack of profitability of solar notwithstanding. The company's director of public policy analysis (this writer) responded with a memo urging Enron to

———

21. "Zond's proposal and its dogged pursuit of the project through several public forums damaged not only its own image but that of the entire industry," stated wind historian and advocate Paul Gipe.

stay with its natural gas knitting. "Given Enron's consideration of entering the central-station windpower business, I must express my concerns from a public policy perspective as well as a pragmatic business perspective," began a November 1996 missive to Terry Thorn, Enron's Senior Vice President, Government Affairs and Public Policy. As a rule of thumb, the memo stated, the cost of electricity from new wind capacity was double that from gas-fired generation and triple the cost of spot electricity (surplus power available for immediate purchase). Wind was not economic even if natural gas was assigned a carbon tax, as recommended by environmental groups and Robert Kelly himself.[22]

"Wind has raised a number of environmental concerns, led by the 'avian mortality' problem that has led the National Audubon Society to call for a moratorium on new projects in bird sensitive areas," the memo added. "The Sierra Club has also been very mixed toward wind power." (In fact, during a dispute over a Zond project, Sierra's Los Angeles director coined a term that would be used against an Enron wind project a few years later: "Cuisinarts of the air.")

"It cannot be emphasized enough how both economically and environmentally, natural gas has changed the renewable equation." This writer's memo concluded:

> Fuel oil, coal, and nuclear are no longer relevant to the debate over renewables. Common sense dictates that renewables have no future in the U.S. without massive government subsidy, and renewable energy is a controversial investment internationally where natural gas is present, even accounting for environmental externalities.

This memo was written too late and at the wrong company. The Big Thought was that a diversified renewable-energy play could grow and be spun off (monetized) with an initial public offering, even with some biomass and hydro added. And, in fact, Robert Kelly had heady thoughts about just this.

Ken Lay was eager to go where the energy majors, including his old company Exxon, did not go. A lucrative tax credit for every sold kWh of wind-generated electricity could lower the parent's taxes now that EOG's tight-sands credit was running its course. And so-called green energy could help differentiate Enron from the traditional utility sellers to be a power retailer of choice to a mass market, producing the revenue and margins to achieve Enron 2000.

———

22. "Is the present or future price of windpower competitive with natural gas (or LNG internationally) after factoring a reasonable carbon-cost credit (say 2 cents per kWh for coal and 1 cent per kWh for gas, which is what the NRDC has proposed in their recent study, *Risky Business*)?"

Robert Kelly's vision of Enron as the global renewables leader included pushing public policy at the highest national and international levels. In late 1996, with the purchase of a major wind power company forthcoming, Kelly unveiled a master business plan to restructure China's energy economy with a 25 percent shift away from planned coal generation by 2005 (10 years) and 50 percent by 2015. Half of the substitution would come from natural gas, with the other half from renewables: 25 percent hydro, 15 percent wind, and 10 percent solar.

Kelly's self-described "aggressive but feasible action plan" would be "available and competitively priced for the Chinese consumer" to "not dampen Chinese growth aspirations." His presentation noted "barriers to implementation of the gas/renewable strategy," including the absence of long-term financing mechanisms and a "lack of understanding about the costs, benefits, and efficiency of renewable energy alternatives," as well as integrating renewables into the electricity grid.

Turning to public policy, Kelly proposed a "China Greenhouse Gas Marshall Plan" whereby the US government would loan or guarantee 75 percent of the capital costs of the conversion, estimated at $9 billion per year for 20 years, a total of $180 billion. The remaining 25 percent would come from Enron and other private sponsors. Such United States–to–developing-country projects, called Joint Implementation, was a negotiating item for the upcoming international climate negotiations in Kyoto, Japan.

Purchasing Zond Corporation

"Enron Forms Enron Renewable Energy Corp.; Acquires Zond Corporation, Leading Developer of Wind Energy Power." The January 6, 1997, news release announced that Robert Kelly would head the new Enron Renewable Energy Corp. and join Enron's 25-member management committee. Zond's then-CEO Kenneth Karas and Richard Barsky, CEO and chairman of Amoco/Enron Solar, would report to Kelly, who would be CEO and chairman of EREC. (In EREC's solar division, at this time, the big hope was still the Rajasthan State project, while Crete lay six months in the future.)

"Renewable energy will capture a significant share of the world energy market over the next 20 years, and Enron intends to be a world leader in this very important market," Ken Lay stated. The big news was Enron's purchase of Zond Corporation of Tehachapi, California. "We believe wind energy is one of the most competitive renewable energy resources, and we believe this acquisition clearly positions Enron as a leader in this business," Lay added.

The release described 15-year-old Zond as "developing, building, and operating wind power stations," with its Z-class turbines being "among the world's most competitively priced" and "capable of producing electricity at competitive prices." With 2,400 sited turbines rated at 260 megawatts, Zond's 1995 output of 600 million kWh earned a federal tax credit approaching $10 million. Unused tax credits, or so-called carry-forwards, were valued in Enron's purchase price of $80 million: $60 million in cash and the rest in debt.

"Enron Corp. is looking for EREC to provide a significant contribution towards Enron's growth over the next 5 years," Robert Kelly stated in a memo to the unit's employees. "During this period, we have an opportunity to emerge from the pack as the world leader in renewable energy and to lead the transition towards a sustainable energy future." After describing the organization and responsibilities, Kelly hinted at more ventures. "Other renewable energy interests pursued by EREC will include activities jointly coordinated with Enron Capital and Trade ("ECT") and Enron International ("EI") in hydroelectric power and the sale, through ECT's power marketing activities, of green power, or electricity produced from sources which do not directly generate CO_2, SO_x, NO_x, or other air pollutants." (No such joint ventures would materialize.)

———

"This action by Enron underscores the enormous worldwide potential for wind energy," stated Randall Swisher, head of AWEA, adding: "Clearly, Enron sees renewable energy as a necessary component of their operations—a component that will give them a competitive advantage in tomorrow's electricity market where consumers will be able to choose their power suppliers."

"We believe that utility restructuring holds tremendous promise for companies with 'green' energy sources, like renewables," stated Norm Terreri of Green Mountain Power Company, "because environmentally-conscious customers will prefer to buy their power from a clean source." Terreri mentioned opinion-polling research from New Hampshire where households were choosing their electricity provider in a pilot program led by Enron, discussed in chapter 15.

An *Enron Business* feature was nothing but bullish. A projected 50 percent increase in energy demand in the next 20 years "will put considerable pressure on conventional fuel supplies, like oil, coal, and natural gas," Robert Kelly opined. "That's why we believe that renewable energy sources, such as wind (and solar), will capture a significant share of the global energy market over the next quarter century and certainly a large portion by the year 2000."

Declines in cost, with more to come, were prominently cited. Compared to 13 cents per kWh in 1985, Zond's new technology (the Z-46 turbine) could generate power at 4.5 cents—and 3 cents with tax credits, Ken Karas stated.[23] This estimate was below the common range of between 5 and 7 cents per kWh. But *grid parity* with fossil-fuel-fired electricity could not be claimed given wind's intermittency, only that wind power was becoming "more competitive." In fact, Ken Lay gave a higher estimate at a Harvard University–sponsored conference the next year: "Wind energy today can be produced in the right location without

———

23. Several years earlier, Karas estimated the cost to be between 4 and 7 cents per kWh, adding: "I don't think we could ever build a project for $0.02 per kilowatt-hour."

any tax credits for 5–5.5 cents per kWh, attractive compared to coal-fired plants but not to IGCC generation, which has a cost of about 3 cents." (IGCC, or integrated gasification combined cycle, processes coal into a gas to fuel a combustion turbine to run a generator.) Cost aside, wind as an intermittent resource was unattractive when compared to power generated from coal, oil, gas, and nuclear—the *dispatchable* energies.

Electric industry restructuring—allowing Enron to sell electricity to households—presented an upside for wind, Kelly noted. Market studies purportedly showed that consumers would pay a premium for "green power," a niche that EREC was exploring with Enron Energy Services, the new electricity retailer. Global-warming concerns and energy independence made the quest a social cause, the article explained, given the absence of a social cost assigned by regulators to fossil-fuel's emissions.

Zond had a backlog of projects well beyond California that Enron would continue. Purchase-power agreements had been signed with Minnesota's Northern States Power (100 MW) and Iowa's MidAmerican Energy Company (112.5 MW). (Both projects were part of state legislative mandates requiring these utilities to buy wind in return for storing part of their nuclear waste.) A 5 MW Zond project in Vermont for Green Mountain Power was nearly complete.

In Crete, where Amoco/Enron Solar's proposal would become stuck, two wind projects totaling 15 MW were under way. Planned projects or turbine orders in Zond's book of business were reported for Ireland, Wales, China, and Korea, with active negotiations from Texas to Spain.

———

"We brought Zond back from the brink," recalled Robert Kelly. Zond was running low on cash and unable to monetize its huge tax credits. "We were hanging by a thread," Zond's James Dehlsen remembered. "It was a really grim story."

The domestic wind industry was in even worse shape. Kenetech Windpower, experiencing technical difficulties with its turbines, among other problems, had entered bankruptcy in June 1996, six months prior to Enron's January 1997 purchase of Zond.[24] A lack of competitiveness versus conventional sources was the reason, although wind advocates emphasized another culprit. "Managing a growing company in the renewable energy business [is] far more difficult than it should be," complained AWEA, which blamed "our government's

———

24. *Congressional Quarterly Weekly Report* cited Kenetech Corp.'s "horrible mechanical problems with its newest wind turbine, overly aggressive expansion, even environmental concerns arising from the mulching of federally protected birds by the company's windmills."

Figure 13.2 Enron turned to wind power, a more economical (but still problematic) form of renewable energy than solar farms. The purchase of Zond Energy Systems to begin 1997 had Ken Karas (pictured) reporting to Robert Kelly of Enron Renewable Energy Corp.

inconsistent policies and its overwhelming emphasis on short-term fixes to problems at the expense of long-term policies."

The company to be renamed Enron Wind Corporation would struggle to help Enron's bottom line in its first years. Lessons were learned about new technology on the fly. Kenetech's blade failures were avoided. Zond had done the proper testing and worked with a world-leading turbine manufacturer, Vestas, to address life-cycle blade integrity. The extra work paid off. Enron Wind, which the parent put up for sale in 1998, would fetch top dollar when it was sold to GE in 2002, the year after Enron's bankruptcy. By that time, Thomas White was heading EREC, Robert Kelly having exited Enron in mid-1997 for medical reasons with a nice severance agreement to give him time to, among other things, write a book about the alleged CO_2 threat.[25]

———

Zond entered Enron folklore for another reason. Under federal regulation, Enron's purchase of Portland General Electric made it a public utility. And

———

25. *The Carbon Conundrum: Global Warming and Energy Policy in the Third Millennium* (Houston, TX: CountryWatch Publications) was published the year after Enron's bankruptcy.

public utilities could not be a "qualifying facility" for PURPA's avoided-cost pricing, which would strip three Zond wind farms of their lucrative sales rates.

The first response was to seek outside buyers for Zond Windsystems, Victory Garden, and Sky River. But Andrew Fastow, senior vice president of finance, offered another plan akin to what he had recently done with Cactus, a special-purpose entity (SPE) for volumetric production payments.[26]

Under accounting rules, SPEs allowed Enron to control but not own assets, if at least 3 percent of equity was external and at-risk. Thus, a special-purpose entity with a minimum of outside involvement could own Zond and receive the bureaucratic designation "qualifying facility," so long as the FERC agreed (which it did). Fastow and his lieutenant Michael Kopper set up two SPEs, called RADR, to buy 50 percent of Enron's wind farms for approximately $17 million, 97 percent of which was an Enron loan with the balance coming from Fastow, his wife Lea (an heiress and Enron employee), and a few others, collectively called the Alpine investors.

Enron's internal audit concluded that this arrangement headed by an Enron employee did not meet the independence test under the SEC's rule. In response, Fastow and Kopper surreptitiously arranged to provide money to nonemployees and have them supposedly put up the external 3 percent. "With a little money laundering," concluded one writer, "Fastow had pulled off the very deal that the accountants had said couldn't be done—at least not legally."

This off-book partnership was reported but not forthrightly explained to, much less scrutinized by, Enron's vaunted board of directors. In fact, as Fastow would later testify, Jeff Skilling himself knew nothing of the deception. Neither did Fastow and his co-conspirators declare their high earnings for personal income-tax purposes.

EREC's Zond had unwittingly inspired Fastow's most pronounced move from *philosophic* fraud toward *prosecutable* fraud—and had become the opening act in a series of Fastow machinations that would be instrumental in bringing down Enron four years later.

Fastow must have felt confident about his subterfuge. Perhaps, as one learned interpreter posited, the government (in the form of FERC) was not schooled or really interested in arcane financial rules, only in ensuring that the PURPA-qualifying technologies were being used. Had Enron not fallen, little critical thought would have been trained on the sins of Zond's SPE ownership.

A Try at Fuel Cells

Bruce Stram earned his spurs working on a gas-supply model for Enron's *Outlook for Natural Gas*, first published in 1989, which accurately upped the existing forecasts of future supply. He worked on Ken Lay's early pipeline acquisitions,

---

26. See chapter 8, pp. 376–77.

as well as evaluating HNG's oil and gas exploration and production subsidiary that indicated areas of concern that would culminate with the hiring of Forrest Hoglund in 1987. Now, at the request of Robert Kelly (then of Enron Emerging Technologies), Stram was to investigate fuel cells based on natural gas.

Although not a renewable resource, natural gas fuel cells generated continuous direct current via a quiet plant with no moving parts, only a chemical conversion. The battery-like designs could be sited almost anywhere, even providing "power from the basement." Potentially, heat created in the fuel cell's secondary processes could be recovered for either water or space heating.

This technology was not new. The underlying principle—combining hydrogen and oxygen to create electric current and water—had been proven in 1839, and the modern version was developed at Cambridge University in the midtwentieth century. Fuel cells were first used in space vehicles, with Pratt & Whitney producing the modules for NASA. "Early fuel cells built for the space program cost from $100,000 to $400,000 per kilowatt; those used in military applications cost about $30,000."

By the early 1970s, nearly 50 companies, mostly in the United States, had invested north of $50 million (several hundred million in today's dollars) to commercialize the technology. Major firms were involved, including Exxon, Arco, and Westinghouse.

Fuel cells became popular discourse as part of the environmentalist dream of a postcarbon energy future. In this scenario, renewables would create hydrogen (via electrolysis of water) for the home or business or industry. Distributed generation would supplant the power grid.

"In the United States," Christopher Flavin reported in 1996, "the race is on." The leader was ONSI Corporation, a United Technologies unit that had just completed the world's first fuel-cell manufacturing facility to produce dozens of units annually at half the cost of earlier models. (Pratt & Whitney was a division of United Technologies.) Allied Signal, IBM, Dow Chemical, and Ballard Power Systems were also in the fuel-cell market, leading Flavin to predict that "a commercial takeoff for fuel cells is likely within the next decade."

———

United Technologies inspired confidence regarding reliability and warranty work. But it was selling a new technology, not electricity. Enter Enron: In 1995, Bruce Stram, running Enron Emerging Technologies within Enron Capital & Trade Resources (ECT), changed the equation to offer set-price, long-term electricity, with Enron-ONSI installing and servicing the equipment at no capital cost to the buyer. Enron would supply the natural gas that produced hydrogen in the outsourcing, as well as market and finance the deals.

ECT offered customers 20-year fixed power at around $0.08/kWh from the 10-foot high by 10-foot-wide by 18-foot-long cells. But minimum-purchase requirements made this *premium-priced baseload power* compared to what industrials could buy from their utility, even in a high-rate state such as California. Enron marketed the fuel as backup power, which would allow the user to switch from continuous flow for normal use to fuel cells for critical use, for example, in case of a blackout. Diesel backup, little used, had start-up risks for the user. Power from fuel cells, on the other hand, was continuous and reached full power within seconds of start.

An *Enron Business* cover story was bullish—and more. As with rooftop solar, Enron envisioned a niche market ready to explode via better technology and scale economies. "We're on the leading edge of a huge growth market," Stram believed, with as much as 50 percent of the power-generation market available for competitively priced distributed generation.

Enron was marketing ONSI's PC25C, a third-generation technology that had 60 purchases to its credit since 1992. In what was seen as an "entrée to a large national account," Enron was in advanced negotiation to place two units supplying 400 kilowatts to a California Health Maintenance Organization, the article reported.

But a decline in cost was necessary to truly commercialize electrochemical energy, estimated by Enron to be around \$0.06/kWh. (The average US retail rate for industrial power was less than \$0.05/kWh and falling.) But ONSI was not willing to take the technology risk to guarantee a decline in cost that would make even the \$0.08/kWh doable.

Enron's five-member team was not able to bring any deals to fruition. The partnership with ONSI was dissolved, and EET disbanded in early 1996. Stram's idea to sell a service rather than a fuel or a technology, however, would soon reappear in Enron Energy Services's total energy outsourcing concept.

There was an undisclosed emission issue with fuel cells, too. Although fuel cells produce virtually no nitrogen oxides (NO_x) or sulfur dioxide (SO_2), the use of natural gas to produce hydrogen yielded carbon monoxide (CO) and carbon dioxide (CO_2).

"In fact, if CO_2 becomes a regulated 'pollutant,' as environmentalists are demanding," one expert noted, "a 40% efficient fuel cell would look less appealing than a 55% efficient combined-cycle plant." Recapturing heat from the creation of CO_2 could raise the fuel cell's efficiency level, but that was a promise that Enron never put to a market test.

Enron's exit did not prove premature. "Fuel cells continue to face major challenges," summarized Daniel Yergin in 2011. "The fuel cells themselves—the device that converts hydrogen or another chemical feedstock into electricity—are expensive and will require substantial investment and breakthroughs for commercialization." As it was back in the 1970s, cost-effective chemical conversion competed against the improving efficiency of gas-fired combined cycle.

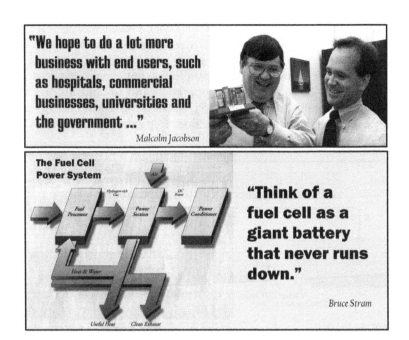

"We hope to do a lot more business with end users, such as hospitals, commercial businesses, universities and the government ..."
Malcolm Jacobson

The Fuel Cell Power System

"Think of a fuel cell as a giant battery that never runs down."
Bruce Stram

Figure 13.3 Enron's fuel-cell marketing began with high expectations and ended with no executed contracts, as ONSI Corp. was unable to install the units at a cost that allowed Enron to sell long-term electricity. Bruce Stram (left) led the 2½-year effort, assisted by marketing director Malcolm Jacobson (right).

Enron Environmental Services

In 1996, Enron created a profit center within Enron Capital & Trade Resources, Enron Environmental Services, to offer fully integrated environmental services to electric utilities seeking to minimize costs or maximize profits under regulatory constraints. (In Enron's words: "monetize Clean Air Act and electricity deregulation opportunities.") EES's mission statement read: "Optimizing environmental compliance through innovative technology, fuels, power, risk management, and finance." The next year, Enron Environmental Services was renamed Clean Energy Solutions Group (CES) to avoid confusion with the new EES, Enron Energy Services.

Under Chris Holmes, CES's staff of 13 stood ready to quantify and certify emissions reductions; offer insurance protection for international deal making (under Joint Implementation guidelines); place forward, put, call, and spot transactions with any traded emission; and finance projects. Emissions trading for SO_2 and NO_x (as well as the potential regulation of CO_2, whereby firms could receive credit for preregulation reductions), presented opportunities for a national market maker such as Enron, which had been in this business since 1993.[27]

With solar projects and wind facilities, Enron envisioned itself with a bank of emission credits to back a trading operation and to help utilities run their plants under emissions caps. Enron would also bring to the table its propriety technology, such as that from its $30 million, 15 percent investment in an emission-reduction technology for gas turbines.[28]

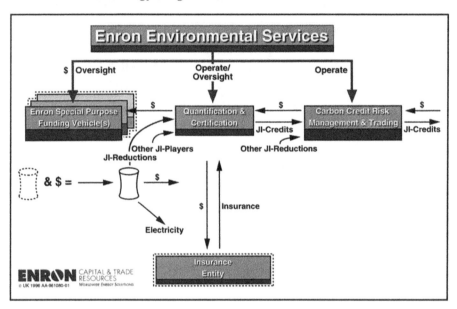

Figure 13.4 A schematic presented to electric utilities and others explained the range and interaction of services offered by Enron Environmental Services (later renamed Clean Energy Solutions). Growing regulatory complexity suggested a role for a specialized aggregator and outsourcer, but Enron was not able to execute outsourcing arrangements.

Central to Enron's new service was a prospective regulatory program for developed countries to plan and subsidize the greenhouse-gas reductions in developing countries: Joint Implementation (JI). The United Nations Framework

---

27. For the purchase of emissions trader AER*X in 1993, see chapter 9, pp. 405–8.

28. This late-1997 investment in Xonon Combustion Systems, to obtain an experimental technology, would become part of Andy Fastow's controversial partnerships that would help bring down Enron in 2001.

Convention on Climate Change, created in 1992, proposed a JI pilot program through the year 2000 at the first Conference of the Parties in 1995. Enron, lobbying for what would become the Kyoto Protocol of 1997, saw synergies for its business units from the program.

"The endorsement of joint implementation within Annex-1 is exactly what I have been lobbying for and it seems like we won," wrote Enron lobbyist John Palmisano in late 1997 from Kyoto, Japan. "A 'clean development fund' is included [to] … allow for emission offsets from projects in developing countries." With JI for "Annex-1, developed countries and the transitional economies," he continued, "Enron projects in Russia, Bulgaria, Romania or other eastern countries can be monetized, in part, by capturing carbon reductions for sale back in the US or other Western countries."

Clean Energy Solutions, one of seven profit centers tied to the global-warming issue (in the specific form of priced and rationed CO_2 emissions) never got off the ground. On one level, CO_2 regulation was slow in coming at home. And facing certain if not unanimous defeat, the Kyoto Protocol would never be submitted to the Senate for ratification.

As important, or even more important, utilities maximized their profits by keeping their environmental activities inside the company, where expenses could be passed through and pollution-control investment could create rate base for profit making. And why do business with Enron? The vitriolic electric-restructuring debate, described in chapter 15, put Enron on the utilities' black list. The environmental-outsourcing initiative of Chris Holmes would disband in 1998.

President's Council on Sustainable Development

Ken Lay coveted a second term for George H. W. Bush, who might ask Enron's chairman to join the administration as chief of staff, Secretary of State, or Secretary of Treasury. (Lesser plums, such as heading the Department of Energy or the Department of Commerce, were not of interest to Lay.) With a cache of ENE stock in excess of $20 million, and Rich Kinder poised to become CEO, Lay could leave on top.

At age 50, with his unique combination of smarts, people skills, and credentials, in addition to his storybook past, a new political chapter might lead to bigger things, even consideration for a Republican presidential ticket. But it was not to be. Ross Perot's third-party candidacy, plus some Bush stumbles, gave the election to Bill Clinton and Al Gore with 43 percent of the popular vote.

Enron was hardly deflated by the change of administration. Terry Thorn positioned Enron well during the campaign by being all things to Democrats. Natural gas was in favor across the aisle, and, as Enron's newsletter explained, "there probably will be a great deal of attention devoted to global warming and a stronger push for limitations or reductions in CO_2 emissions." In fact, the new

vice president's environmental manifesto, *Earth in the Balance*, published just
the year before, declared that the world must search "for substitutes for coal
and oil." Natural gas would be a bridge fuel to that new energy future.[29]

"With the Clinton Administration," the INGAA Foundation wrote, "the natural gas industry has its best opportunity in years to promote its fuel and stimulate gas consumption to breach 1972 levels." It had been a long 20 years, and
now a Democrat would help get them there. In fact, 1972's gas consumption of
22.1 Tcf, which had fallen 25 percent to 16.2 Tcf by 1986, had fully rebounded by
1995.

————

The 1992 Rio Summit had produced a 180-nation voluntary pact to pursue "sustainable development," which the UN-sponsored World Commission on Environment and Development (meeting from 1984 to 1987) had defined as
development that satisfies the needs of the present generation without compromising the ability of future generations to do likewise. Environmentalists had
wanted more from Rio in terms of targets and mandates, but this was as much
as President Bush would do. The United States was a laggard to some, but it
had been a close call to get Bush involved at all, as Ken Lay knew.

Agenda 21, a broad blueprint, also known as the Rio accords, became the
responsibility of the 53-nation, UN-sanctioned Commission on Sustainable
Development. At its first meeting in June 1993, Al Gore, promising "real leadership" from the US side, announced the creation of the President's Council on
Sustainable Development (PCSD), a 25-member commission of government
officials, friendly industrialists, environmental activists, and civil rights
groups.[30]

Free-market groups active on energy and environmental issues, such as the
Competitive Enterprise Institute (CEI), were not invited. PCSD was another
front to get beyond Bush policy in the wake of Rio, joining Clinton's recently
declared goal for the United States to reduce its greenhouse-gas emissions to
1990 levels by the year 2000, a pledge his predecessor would not make.

Established by executive order, PCSD was chartered to "develop and recommend to the President a national sustainable development action strategy that
will foster economic vitality." Purely advisory, the intent was to reach consensus

————

29. "Natural gas," Gore explained, "can replace coal and oil for many uses and supply the
same amounts of energy with only a tiny fraction of the unwanted by-products."

30. Cochairmen of PCSD were David Buzzelli, vice president of Dow Chemical Company,
and Jonathan Lash, president of World Resources Institute. All major cabinet secretaries were
represented, as were the heads of the environmental groups Natural Resources Defense
Council, Environmental Defense Fund, Sierra Club, Nature Conservancy, and National Wildlife Federation. The liaison to the Clinton-Gore administration was Kathleen McGinty, chairwoman of the Council on Environmental Quality.

on contentious issues and conduct "a public awareness and participation campaign" to further the new paradigm.

"It may not be a sustainable resource," one gas industry publication reported, "but natural gas nonetheless has been given a prominent voice on the [Council] established last week by President Clinton to advise him on economic and environmental policy." Ken Lay was one of the selected, along with the CEOs of two California-based energy companies: Chevron and Pacific Gas and Electric (PG&E).[31]

"America can set an example" for sustainability, Clinton said in a Rose Garden speech announcing PCSD, flanked by Lay and the other members. Al Gore challenged the group to "look long, be creative, and think big." From the private side, optimism abounded. "If we are to solve some of these environmental problems and do it in ways that are economically efficient," Ken Lay stated, "there has to be an increased dialogue between the private sector, environmentalists, and the government." Best of all, he noted, PCSD was empowered by Clinton "to come up with meaningful policy."

———

It was supposed to be a grand consensus, a collaboration, between environmentalists and industry. But there were no members who might define sustainable development differently, such as dialing back climate alarmism in favor of energy affordability and reliability, and looking to private ownership to better employ publically owned resources—a wealth-is-health approach.[32] As it was, PCSD's principles of sustainability and social justice were joined by a third: *economic growth*—insisted upon by the business side, and Chevron and Enron in particular.

"To achieve our vision of sustainable development, some things must grow—jobs, productivity, wages, capital and savings, profits, information, knowledge, and education—but others—pollution, waste, and poverty—must not," began the "We Believe" foreword of the final report, released in February 1996. "Economic growth based on technological innovation, improved efficiency, and expanding global markets," it added, "is essential for progress toward greater prosperity, equity, and environmental quality." But economic growth had to have the proper linkage with the other two ends. "A growing economy and healthy environment are essential to national and global security," read another principal point.

---

31. BP was not part of the PCSD until after John Browne's historic Stanford University speech of May 1997. Steve Percy of BP America Inc. became a new energy-industry member, as did the chairman of American Electric Power, E. Linn Draper, who replaced Richard Clark of PG&E.

32. See Internet appendix 13.1 "Sustainable Development: Two Views," at www .politicalcapitalism.org/Book3 /Chapter13/Appendix1.html.

This (minimal) business-side victory was joined by calls for "reducing disparities in education, opportunity, and environmental risk" pursuant to PCSD's three pillars of "economic growth, environmental health, and social justice."

Despite Enron's efforts, natural gas was not differentiated as a means for CO_2 emission reduction. ("If the risks of global warming are judged to be too great," the report stated, "then nothing less than a drastic reduction in the burning of coal, oil, and natural gas would be necessary.") Mandatory or tax-directed electricity conservation(ism), a major push, came at the expense of natural gas too, an internal Enron memorandum by this author pointed out.

Existing government subsidies for coal and nuclear were not specifically targeted for elimination. "Reading the final report," the present writer wrote to Terry Thorn, "I can only conclude that our energy input fell victim to the lowest common denominator, while the rest of the document was written by the environmental left."

Sustainable America: A New Consensus, the glossy final product published in February 1996, was portrayed by the mainstream media as a collaborative breakthrough between government, environmentalists, and industry. "After a year in which industry and environmental groups have been at war over Republican-led efforts to roll back Federal environmental regulation," the *New York Times* reported, "a Presidential panel with adversaries from both sides has reached a rare consensus that while the existing system can be improved, it must not be weakened." The report, "destined to serve as the environmental platform for Mr. Clinton's reelection campaign," was depicted as a rebuke against Republican-aligned business.

To be sure, the final report contained such buzzwords and phrases as "decentralized decision-making," "regulatory flexibility," "best available science," "market pricing," "market-based regulatory framework," "new market-based approaches," and "the use of market mechanisms." Homage was paid to "a free society," "unlimited human capacity," "technological progress," and "entrepreneurship, innovation, and small business." "Competitive advantage," "efficiency," and the "polluter pays principle" were other locutions in the high-sounding report.

But the document *assumed* rather than *analyzed* what was good and bad. Environmental ends were given; the science was settled; neo-Malthusianism was a fact; consumption trends and business-as-usual were therefore not sustainable. Carbon dioxide was viewed as bad, despite its well-known positive benefits for ecosystems and plant life. Market failure was seen as pervasive, but the other side of the coin, *government failure*, went unremarked.

The uncritical use of the precautionary principle, which sees stasis as safety in situations of scientific uncertainty, ignored the costs of inaction. Cost-benefit analysis was hardly mentioned in the report, and the historical correlation of wealth and health was ignored.

Market pricing, as used in the report, meant adding a government-determined social cost to the market price. The institutions behind true sustainability—private-property rights and contracts enforced by the rule of law—went unrecognized. To CEI head Fred Smith, *Sustainable America* was "a thinly veiled excuse for extensive government intervention into the market."

Chapter 6 of the report, "Population and Sustainability," harkened back to the limits to growth, the old $I = P \cdot A \cdot T$ equation of Paul Ehrlich and John Holdren, which maintained that negative environmental Impact was positively correlated to Population, Affluence, and Technology. "In an agricultural or technological society," Ehrlich and Holdren had written, "each human individual has a negative impact on his environment." PCSD's final report, consequently, mentioned the "overarching issue of consumption" and "changes in lifestyles."

The PCSD-friendly *New York Times* cited no sincere opponents who might dare to disagree. Quite the opposite. Disagreement was declared unpatriotic and un-American. "The environment is something that brings us together as a nation," the *Times* quoted Kathleen McGinty as saying. "It is a deplorable idea to use it to polarize the nation."

The report attempted to reposition the United States to engage and even lead on international climate-change activism—and just in time. The second conference of parties from the 1992 Rio Framework Convention on Climate Change was coming up in December 1997, in Kyoto, Japan.

―――――

After the final report, and with PCSD extended for a second term, news surfaced about a working group focused on the "deeply political" subject of fiscal issues, and none greater than pricing carbon dioxide through a tax or a cap-and-trade program. President Clinton's Btu tax proposal had gone off the rails just two years before,[33] and Democratic seats were lost in the 1994 midterm elections, explaining why *Sustainable America* left out specifics when advocating fiscal and subsidy reform, including revenue-neutral tax reform.

One member from the private side, Ken Lay, particularly wanted to regulate and/or tax CO_2. The result was the WRI [World Resources Institute]/Enron Working Group on a Fiscal Policy and Subsidy Commission. Teaming with Enterprise for the Environment, chaired by former EPA administrator William Ruckelshaus, the group explored what criteria a new commission could use to recommend concrete policy. It suggested eliminating subsidies and shifting taxes to promote sustainable development. "Environmental taxes" and (auctioned) "tradable emissions permits" were identified as key. "The [Working] Group feels further that a bipartisan, multi-stakeholder forum is a useful

―――――

33. See chapter 7, pp. 342–43.

mechanism to further the discussion of ideas that are difficult to discuss in other more partisan settings."[34]

In December 1996, a major PCSD meeting, in which Al Gore made a guest presentation, shared the efforts of the Working Group. While commending the effort, the Clinton administration, not wanting to inflame Congress and put Democrats on the defensive with an unpopular issue (new taxes), declined to establish a new commission.

Enron, meanwhile, was ready to disengage. Without cover from the Clinton administration, Enron feared that any sponsorship of CO_2 pricing could jeopardize the lobbying message for the corporation's number-one priority: restructuring the electricity market to allow it to enter at the retail level.

"We need to think hard about whether Enron continues to front an effort that does not have as much political cover as we would like or whether we work—just as hard—behind the scenes," a memo to Ken Lay from this writer stated. "The last thing we want is for [the Edison Electric Institute, representing investor-owned utilities] to accuse Enron of wanting to reduce electric prices through open-access and raise them with a carbon abatement program—all to make trading dollars." (In fact, CO_2 trading was in Enron's sights to join electricity trading.) A calculation followed in the memo: "A $20/ton or $30/ton carbon cost would probably undo the gains of [electricity] restructuring rate-wise (the rule of thumb is 1 cent/kWh for every $10/ton CO_2 cost)."

"You're raising all the right issues," Lay wrote back to Bradley. "Although we want to be helpful, we probably should try not to be too public."

As it turned out, a post-WRI/Enron task force within PCSD, the Climate Task Force (not joined by Enron) came out in late 1998 for a "voluntary ... incentive-based early action program" to reduce greenhouse-gas emissions that "encourages broad-based participation, learning, innovation, flexibility, and experimentation; grants formal credit for legitimate and verifiable measures to protect the climate; ensures accountability; is compatible with other climate protection strategies and environmental goals; and includes local, state, and federal government leadership." Al Gore stated in a PCSD press release: "I am pleased that this broad coalition of business, government and environmental leaders is calling for ... common-sense action to protect our environment and our economy from the effects of global warming."

The PCSD was extended in 1996 for a second three-year term. Ken Lay resigned by letter on March 5, 1997, although his name was kept on the membership list. At that point, it was not worth insisting upon formalities. Enron as

---

34. "CO_2 abatement is the number one issue, although it is not explicitly stated," an update from this writer to Ken Lay on the working group explained. "The general language is to correct [negative] externalities."

a company continued as a member, unlike PG&E, Chevron, Georgia Pacific, and others from the corporate side. PCSD continued with outreach and educational effort until its expiration in June 1999, six years after its creation.

What had been wrought? Although PCSD held no enforcement powers or grant-making ability, it was part of the Clinton administration's pushback against a Republican Congress. The collaborative effort elevated US support for climate action in the international community. It was an educational opportunity for neo-Malthusianism pushing against a Julian Simon view of the world.[35] For Enron, it was another step down the political road to promote natural gas, solar power, and wind power at the expense of oil and coal. For Ken Lay, it meant he was now a Friend of Bill.[36]

Conclusion

"As the energy revolution gains momentum, some of the largest gas and oil companies are beginning to support it," commented Lester Brown and Jennifer Mitchell of the Worldwatch Institute. "Enron, originally a large Texas-based natural gas company," in particular, "has made a strong move in the renewables field with its acquisition of Zond, the largest wind power company in the United States, and its investment in Solarex, the second largest U. S. manufacturer of photovoltaic cells."

Enron *was* the favorite energy company of many environmentalists who otherwise disdained fossil-fuel enterprises. Even so, Enron was in the crosshairs of environmental regulation and the US Environmental Protection Agency for its day-to-day pipeline activity. "Existing environmental regulations are sufficiently extreme to the point of nearly paralyzing the natural gas industry," complained one Enron environmental officer to Terry Thorn, "especially with respect to the construction of new facilities, additions and improvements to existing facilities, and operations in general."

But Enron could not do much to change that, and rival pipelines had the same problem. So, as long as FERC's public-utility regulation blessed environmental costs for ratepayer passthrough or allowed environmental infrastructure to be added to the rate base, Enron's profits were unaffected or even enhanced.

---

35. For the clash of these two worldviews in reference to energy, see Bradley, *Capitalism at Work*, Part III.

36. Two months after PCSD's creation, Lay was invited to play golf with Bill Clinton in a foursome that included former President Gerald Ford and championship golfer Jack Nicklaus. On the first tee, the media reported, Lay and Nicklaus shot straight, while President Ford missed the fairway right and Clinton left.

Enron's initiatives were not only about rent-seeking but also about favor-trading. With Enron's purchase of Portland General Electric hanging in the political balance (see chapter 15), Ralph Cavanagh of the Natural Resources Defense Council (NRDC) brokered a deal whereby environmentalists got projects funded by Enron ("a robust assortment of public benefits for the citizens of Oregon") in exchange for supporting the merger.

Cavanagh's testimony before the Oregon Public Utility Commission included a story about Enron's help in blocking the 104th Congress's attempt to undo some of the Clinton administration's environmental laws. "We appealed for help from the corporate community," he recalled, only to meet conspicuous silence. But not so with the "extraordinarily honorable—and initially lonely" Ken Lay, whose activism was "part of the reason why the bad guys ultimately failed at most of what they attempted."

"Can you trust Enron?" NRDC's energy expert asked rhetorically. "On stewardship issues and public benefit issues I've dealt with this company for a decade, often in the most contentious circumstances, and the answer is, yes."

Undoubtedly, not all of Enron's ventures in renewables were based on Bootleggers-and-Baptists cynicism. There was a bit of smarter-than-thou intellectual arrogance too. Robert Kelly saw the world's energy eras going from coal to oil to natural gas—and then, in the twenty-first century, to renewables. In his pronouncements, he even questioned, if not reversed, Bruce Stram's *Enron Outlook* for plentiful natural gas in the decades ahead.

History tells another story, however politically incorrect. The energy world had gone from renewables (before the industrial age) to a carbon-based energy era, with an expanding, changing mix of coal, oil, and natural gas. New technology and scale economics were making solar and wind power more economical, but the fossil fuels were improving too, in extraction, combustion, and steps between. The basic facts remained: Wind and solar were dilute, intermittent energies—and adding battery storage for reliability was prohibitively expensive.

———

Enron hardly profited from its solar and wind investments on an operating basis.[37] But lucrative sales of both units made for successful endings, and Enron got a green card to become the most politically correct energy major in the United States. Taxpayers and captive ratepayers were the ones to thank for Enron's years in renewable energy.

Enron's grand hopes that economies of scale and economies of scope would make viable so-called clean fuels—vehicular compressed natural gas, solar power, wind power, and fuel cells—greatly exceeded the eventual reality.

———

37. After recording a small loss in 1997, EREC lost $2.4 million in 1998 versus its profit goal of $21.3 million. The losses came despite earning $562,000 in taxes (tax credit) in 1998 and receiving federal research and development grants of $4 million in 1997–98.

(Enron's bet on MTBE for reformulated gasoline fell short too.) Although politically opportune, each of the four ventures was economically incorrect. There was simply too much cost and sacrificed quality in circumventing petroleum as a transportation fuel and in eliminating fossil fuels for electrical generation. And Enron's suite of environmental services anchored by a national and global CO_2 control program was, at best, ahead of its time.

Playing the environmental game for competitive advantage was a natural for Ken Lay's pliable means and ends, his *contra-capitalism*. Bootlegger Enron was enabled by Baptist environmentalists, who went beyond cleaner air and cleaner water to an agenda-driven, anti-industrial initiative (climate change in particular). Politicians, some reluctant and others committed, welcomed a new frontier of activism to give alternative energies a foothold. These beginnings would define energy policy for decades to come.

14

Visionary Enron

O mer Lay served as a lay Baptist preacher in rural Missouri. Son Ken became a pillar of First United Methodist Church of Houston. Although never Evangelical (Ken played to the middle in all things), he would occasionally bring in God and the Holy Word professionally. Enron's success was dependent upon employees using their "God-given talents" and "God-given potential," Ken liked to say.

Religion also influenced the corporate mission statement: "There's a Biblical phrase that says something like 'Without vision, the people will perish'," Lay intoned, citing Proverbs 29:18. "Well, I'm not sure the people will perish, but it's pretty certain that without a vision, they may wander around in the wilderness."

Ken always prayed for guidance for Enron's worldly endeavors. As his confidence grew in the mid-to-late 1990s, he came to see Enron as God's handiwork. In fact, false confidence derived from religion—a misapplication and overreach of faith in the realm of reason—would be a factor in overheating Enron's engines.[1] It led to a visionary approach heavy on grand plans rather than measured experimental discovery—and on perceived outcomes rather than capabilities. Both set a high-risk compass for Enron.

New Enron Visions

In a mid-1990s address at the annual Houston conference of the Cambridge Energy Research Associates (CERA), Ken Lay remarked how "the company of the 21st

---

1. For theological philosophers on this point, see Bradley, *Capitalism at Work*, pp. 86–87.

century must be vision-driven." Indeed, Lay embraced high goals and set ambitious corporate missions for his entire CEO life, from mid-1984 until early 2002.

Playing defense as the new head of Houston Natural Gas Corporation, Lay's message was about focusing on natural gas, repositioning for growth, and maximizing shareholder wealth.[2] "HNG's objective is to perform at the top of our industry in terms of earnings per share growth and return on equity," he wrote shareholders in October 1984. Two months later, Lay targeted increasing the company's percentage return on equity to the high teens or low twenties "by improving operating procedures and encouraging innovative entrepreneurship."

These were goals. Lay's initial vision came in the heady beginning of HNG/ InterNorth. Quickly contrived, the merged entity aimed to become *America's most successful energy company*. Amid the postmerger problems of 1985–86, this vision, as well as the tag line *America's Premier Energy Company*, were forgotten.[3]

Footing regained, Ken Lay established his first vision for Enron: "To become the premier integrated natural gas company in North America." Set in 1987, this vision was declared accomplished in 1990 and immediately replaced by another.

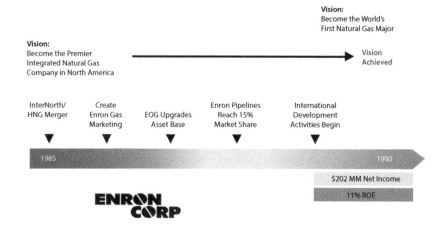

Figure 14.1 This slide (from Ken Lay presentations) highlighted several events that made Enron (in its own view) the premier integrated natural gas company in North America. The second major vision was set in 1990 (upper right).

Natural Gas Major

The new mission remained tied to natural gas. But with Teesside under way, the vision went international. What would prove to be Ken Lay's most memorable

---

2. See chapter 1, pp. 77–79.

3. See chapter 2, pp. 124–25.

vision was *"to become the world's first natural gas major, the most innovative and reliable provider of clean energy worldwide for a better environment."*[4]

Along the way, Enron declared itself "America's leading natural gas company" (1992), then, a few years later, "the largest full-service natural gas company in the world." Energy consultant Dale Steffes listed Enron as one of the "'Seven Brothers' of Natural Gas," the others being Tenneco, British Gas, Gas de France, Ruhrgas (Germany), Nova (Canada), and Gazprom (Russia). Steffes's term was a play on Anthony Sampson's book title *The Seven Sisters,* which referred to the top seven international oil companies.

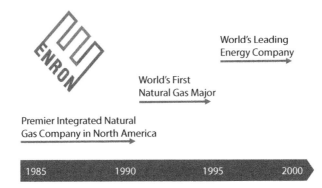

Figure 14.2 Enron's first three major visions went from natural gas and North America (1987) to natural gas and global (1990) to energy and global (1995).

In early 1995, Enron ended its five-year quest by declaring itself the world's first natural gas major. In a congratulatory note to employees, Lay and Richard Kinder gave the following (ten) reasons:

- The largest natural gas company in the largest natural gas market in the world;
- The most creative force, with the best people in energy worldwide;
- The operator of the largest natural gas pipeline system in the world outside of Gazprom in Russia;
- The leading and most reliable marketer of natural gas in the competitive world;
- The world leader in providing physical and financial natural gas products;
- A leader in restructuring the electricity industry in the United States, trading more electrons than any independent marketer, and generating significant electricity in both the United States and the United Kingdom;
- The most profitable independent producer of natural gas in the United States;

---

4. See chapter 6, p. 254.

- The developer of more natural gas-fired, independent power plants than any company in the world;

- The owner and operator of energy facilities in 15 countries, with projects under advanced stages of development in 12 additional countries;

- Providing consistent compound annual earnings per share growth, having achieved 20 percent annually since 1990.

Absent from this list was mention of compressed natural gas for vehicles, an opportunity Enron had touted just a few years before. Transportation accounted for one-fourth of all energy usage in the United States, and Lay had wanted in. As a matter of fact, Enron tried to breach petroleum's wall by jump-starting an NGV market in Houston, with other major urban centers to follow. But the Houston project bled money, and the math did not work for more attempts.[5] Gasoline and diesel, reformulated with oxygenates for better environmental performance (an alternative of which Enron was a part), won on the merits.

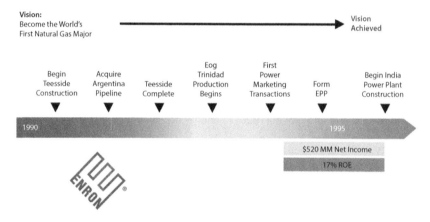

Figure 14.3 Another Ken Lay slide showed a timeline of events that made Enron (in its own view) the world's first natural gas major. But the steady growth of Enron's traditional gas functions, as much as or more than these seven milestones, underlay that designation.

Still, Ken Lay and Enron had filled the largest natural gas niche. Unshackled from past regulation, and now benefitting on net from federal policies, natural gas was fertile ground for electricity generation. Whereas gas accounted for about 5 percent of new capacity in this market in the early 1980s, it now claimed

---

5. See chapter 9, pp. 400–403. Lay, who had gone from "agnostic at best" to a "true believer" after the Gulf War pushed up oil prices, ceded defeat after Enron lost $4 million. "I am not as enthusiastic about natural gas vehicles as some people are," Lay stated in 1995. "[I]t will be a very small piece of the total U.S. or worldwide energy picture."

60 percent.[6] That was both the result of Enron's activism and a continuing opportunity.

Ken Lay's natural gas vision was a bit forced—and too confining for Enron itself. Money making, not fuel absolutism, was the real mission. Rebecca Mark's "market-led approach" to international development—defined as "finding solutions to a country's energy needs rather than selling a specific fuel or pushing a specific project"—resulted in several oil-fired power plants.[7]

Enron's coal play several years later would also testify to profits over fuel type. Assuring a newly hired coal executive that Enron was serious despite its green environmental image, CEO Jeff Skilling said: "Mike, we are a green energy company, but the green stands for money." Such deviations, even ironies, were ameliorated by Enron's third energy vision, the widest yet.

"The World's Leading Energy Company"

Ken Lay characterized Enron as not only the first natural gas major but also an "international 'energy major'." And with electricity a big new focus, as well as renewable energy, not to mention oil plays here and there, a broader vision was necessary. Lay wanted a new mission as ambitious as, or even more ambitious than, his previous one. Employee suggestions were invited, although the CEO really didn't need much help.

The 1995 annual report announced Enron's third vision: "Become the World's LEADING Energy Company—creating innovative and efficient energy solutions for growing economies and a better environment worldwide." Enron's new tagline for communicating that message was "Creating Energy Solutions Worldwide."

The new vision, Ken Lay and Rich Kinder emphasized, did not necessarily mean being the largest or most profitable energy company. It meant "providing leadership in creating the best energy solutions for customers on a worldwide basis." Enron, in other words, would be *the first company that customers would think of and come to for their energy needs, however complex.*

What Enron had done with natural gas would now be done with energy, broadly considered. The finest workforce just needed time, resources, and direction to achieve this boldest-yet vision. Explained Ken and Rich:

> Ambitious? You Bet. Achievable? Yes. Because we believe you are the most talented and creative work force in the world and that no company is better

---

6. Updating his Natural Gas Standard analysis from several years before, Lay estimated the levelized cost-advantage of a new gas-fired power plant versus a new coal plant at between 10 and 30 percent (and a 40 percent advantage over a nuclear power plant). The better economics was concentrated in on-front capital costs, where gas was 50 percent and 70 percent cheaper compared to coal and nuclear, respectively.

7. See Introduction, p. 30.

ENRON CORP

CREATING ENERGY SOLUTIONS WORLDWIDE

Interoffice Memorandum

To   All Employees

From   Ken Lay and Rich Kinder

Subject   New Vision

Department   Office of the Chairman

Date   3/7/95

As you are all aware, we have declared victory on Enron's vision of becoming the world's first natural gas major. It became a reality through your hard work and dedication. Congratulations once again to each of you on this major accomplishment. Just to reiterate, here's what you'll be reading in Enron's annual report and in advertisements later this month to support our claim of having become the world's first natural gas major. We believe we are:

- The largest natural gas company in the largest natural gas market in the world
- The most creative force, with the best people in energy worldwide
- The operator of the largest natural gas pipeline system in the world outside of Gazprom in Russia

There is a distinct possibility that each of us is in the early phase of a very major, international success story, but in today's competitive environment, we cannot rest on our laurels. We don't believe Enron will do that. In fact, 1994's accomplishments laid the foundation for significant growth potential. Together, we can and will translate that *potential* into *real* growth. It's part of our new vision of becoming *The World's LEADING Energy Company – creating innovative and efficient energy solutions for growing economies and a better environment worldwide.*

VISION

Become the World's LEADING Energy Company - creating innovative and efficient energy solutions for growing economies and a better environment worldwide.

VALUES

Your Personal Best Makes Enron Best
- Achieve your personal best.
- Every employee can make a difference.
- Enron will help you reach your personal best.
- Honesty and integrity at all times.
- Enron rewards individuals and teamwork performance.

Communicate: Facts Are Friendly
- Tell it the way it is.
- Trust and openness.
- Ideas are a good thing to share.
- When in doubt, ask.

Better, Faster, Simpler
- Do we need to do it at all?
- Do it right, do it now.
- If you are not sure who is supposed to do it, do it.
- Innovate.
- Break the mold.
- Simplify, simplify, simplify.
- Excess paper kills.
- Excess meetings kill.
- Don't be satisfied with the way it has always been done.

Excellence in Everything We Do
- Listen to the customer.
- Deliver value.
- Ethics, environmental responsibility and safety - uncompromised.
- Set the standard for others.

Figure 14.4 Enron's "Vision and Values" statement (1995) listed 4 values and 22 descriptions as part of the new goal to "become the world's leading energy company." Lay saw values as "the tools [employees] will use to stay on course."

positioned to take advantage of the opportunities that exist in our industry today than is your company.

Lay wanted Enron to be the company that the competition studied and emulated. And with this mission, Ken Lay needed employee and stockholder buy-in to make the grand vision seem possible, even inevitable.

Enron 2000

Soon after the new vision was announced, Ken Lay unveiled a "vision within a vision," described as "our first 'way-station' or 'check point' on the road to becoming 'the world's leading energy company' in the 21st century." Lay's gambit put positive packaging around the fact that much uncertainty surrounded Enron's ability to consistently best its high earnings growth.

Enron had a unique success story by the numbers. The 1995 annual report summarized the "outstanding" financial statistics since 1985—"unsurpassed in the industry"—as the foundation for Enron 2000:

- Net income (before extraordinary losses) increasing almost fourfold to $520 million;

- Earnings per share (from continuing operations before extraordinary losses) increasing more than fivefold to $2.07 in 1995;

- Market capitalization increasing fourfold to $10 billion;

- Average return on equity increasing to 17 percent (from 6 percent); and

- Debt-to-capitalization falling to 40 percent (from 73 percent).

Replicating this success quarter by quarter, year by year, however, was worrisome for management. The earnings bar from mark-to-market accounting; international issues such as the underwater J-Block contract in the United Kingdom; India's idled Dabhol plant; and the bad clean-fuels bet (MTBE) hung over Enron's growth story.[8] Even the earnings engine Enron Capital & Trade Resources (ECT) was "losing steam," recalled Jeff Skilling: Strong volumes were accompanied by falling profit margins, the extent of which Enron would not make public.[9]

ENE was a momentum stock with a virtually uninterrupted growth story. The Street's expectations had to be reoriented longer term. Specifically, 15 percent earnings growth for eight years running had to be promised not for 1996 or even 1997, but as an *average out to year 2000*.

---

8. These troubled investments are described in chapter 11 (MTBE and methanol, pp. 466–67) and in chapter 12 (the J-Block contract, pp. 494–98; and the Dabhol plant, pp. 498–502). Mark-to-market accounting's capture of future earnings for current income is explained in chapter 8, pp. 378–83.

9. Some serious earnings issues at ECT in 1995–96 were being papered over, as discussed in chapter 11, pp. 482–83.

Enron 2000 was highlighted in the 1995 annual report: "We intend to realize net income in excess of $1 billion in the year 2000, which would approximately double 1995 net income and result in a compound annual earnings growth rate of approximately 15 percent over the five-year period." Enron had doubled its income in the past 10 years; now the target was in 5.[10]

Enron 2000 sought to assure the Street that "Enron is a growth company, even more so than an energy company." Extending 8 years of 15 percent annual growth to 13 years was being pledged.

Becoming the World's Leading Energy Company

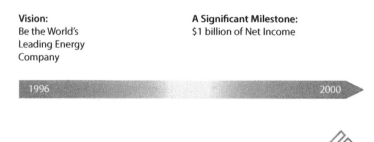

Vision:
Be the World's
Leading Energy
Company

A Significant Milestone:
$1 billion of Net Income

1996   2000

Figure 14.5 Enron's third vision (1995) contained a vision-within-a-vision: to double income (to $1 billion) by 2000. In what would be the company's final solvent year (2001), Ken Lay declared Enron as the world's leading energy company and announced a new vision: to become the world's leading company.

ESOP-laden employees were targeted with talk of a doubled stock price and greater career opportunities as part of the five-year plan.[11] A celebratory all-employee meeting, looking back and then ahead, was held at the Hyatt Regency's spacious ballroom. A commemorative gift was provided to everyone. That was the Ken Lay way.

———

10. Other Enron 2000 goals were cash flow of $2 billion or more; a credit rating of A or AA; market value of $20 billion or more.

11. A goal for 1996 was a ratings increase to B+++ (large agency) and A- (small agency). "In 1985, Enron was not an investment grade company," Lay remembered. "Today, we are a strong investment grade company headed toward an A- credit rating." The debt-to-total capitalization ratio fell from 73 percent in 1985 to 42 percent in 1995, although off-balance borrowing disguised Enron's debt.

The rollout included a presentation in Enron's 50th-floor boardroom by Ken Lay to local analysts and money managers on how Enron planned to double itself over the next five years. "The presentation was quite good and quite smooth, as most Enron road shows went," remembered John Olson, then with Merrill Lynch. "But it did gloss over some of the more mundane realities that hobbled the story."

It was time for questions from the approximately 20 guests. Most queries were soft and easily handled. But one question from Olson was probing, albeit obvious to real students of the company: If half of the projected earnings was coming from hard-asset businesses growing at 5 percent annually, then ECT must be projected at 25 percent. "Was that doable?" Olson asked Lay.

"Ken was usually affable and polite, but not that day," remembered Olson. "He had a way of turning red, and I could see the veins in his head start to bulge, so I sensed a blowup was coming." Without Kinder in the room (did he want to be?), Lay answered in we-did-it-and-will-do-it-again generalities. As the group departed, Lay turned to Olson "with some indignation and sneered that I 'really didn't get the message', and that I 'didn't understand Enron's great potential'."

But Olson the outlier was just doing his job: to objectively assess the state and prospects of the company for the general investor—"what I had been taught by my much better mentors." John Olson was not in the quid-pro-quo, conflict-of-interest business of helping the investment banking side get business from a convenient valuation. Yet Enron was all hardball. "Lay wanted Strong Buy recommendations from every analyst," remembered Olson. "If you didn't go along, he made sure that no investment banking fees went to your firm."

Coming out of the Enron 2000 pitch, Olson held out with a Hold—not a Strong Buy as some 15 other investment analysts rated the company. "That didn't sit well with Ken, because he knew that Merrill Lynch had tremendous buying power in its client base."[12]

Enron and Olson had, in fact, been going at it since at least 1990—and would continue to bump heads for the rest of Enron's solvent life. "Ken tried to get me fired three different times," remembered Olson. "The first was at First Boston in 1990, which prompted my move to Goldman Sachs; the second in April 1998 at Merrill Lynch, which felt that $45 million-plus of investment banking fees were a lot more important than a simple analyst—and so this analyst was 'whacked'."

---

12. Olson added: "My sense was that he was obsessed with the stock price as both a validation of his career, and because he wanted to get very rich in the process. Recall that even the elevators in the building had stock price quotations."

The third would be just several months before Enron's implosion when Olson was at Sanders Morris Harris.[13]

"If a stock price rises arithmetically, management's ego rises exponentially." John Olson's Maxim on Management would be part of his post-Enron talks at business conferences and at business schools. But his doubts had many times been greeted by a rising ENE and skepticism from the consensus—and derision inside the walls of Enron.

ENE rose by a fourth in 1995—and would climb 15 percent in 1996. That inspired another quotation used by Olson in his presentations: "Markets can remain irrational longer than you can remain solvent."[14]

———

"We are not using pie-in-the-sky assumptions to achieve Enron 2000," insisted Rich Kinder. He was right on a few things but not on others. Already planned selldowns of EOG, Northern Border, and EOTT were assumed and doable. But international projects, such as India Phase I and II and Qatar's massive LNG, were projected to be operational and profitable by 2000), and they would not be. That *was* pie in the sky. So, too, was the big political-capitalism bet that retail gas and electricity would become a major profit center. (As it turned out, Enron's reported year-2000 earnings of $979 million were lowered the next year to $847 million, and the bankruptcy examiner slashed the final accounting to $42 million. Other Enron 2000 goals would also be eviscerated.)

Trust us, we can replicate our outstanding past was the real pitch of Enron 2000. But what new, large earnings generator would be created? The most important by far was a new profit center within ECT—retail electricity marketing. But that *sure thing* was hardly certain. MOA on the state level for electricity, Kinder admitted, "puts enormous pressure on us at the corporate level but particularly on ECT to develop the right regulatory and political game plan to make this succeed." Political Enron would be even more so in the next years, as discussed in the Epilogue.

———

13. Complained Ken Lay to Don Sanders, the head principal at Sanders Morris Harris: "John Olson has been wrong about Enron for over 10 years. And he is still wrong. But he is consistent."

14. The original adage, "Markets can remain irrational a lot longer than you and I can remain solvent," was coined by financial analyst A. Gary Shilling in 1993. Olson misattributed it to John Maynard Keynes, who was famously wiser as an investor than as an economist.

New-Economy Enron (Gary Hamel)

Describing Enron's new vision and values, Ken Lay noted how trained, retained employee capital, less traditional physical infrastructure, was driving the energy industry. "It's not so much what we own, but how we maximize the use of our assets," he said. And Enron had unique *human* capital.

The IT revolution from desktop computing was only part of the story. ("We now have more PCs and workstations in the company than employees," Lay mentioned in 1996.) Enron's activity in energy was driven by MOA transmission creating a for-profit merchant function that gave brainy, savvy traders the ability to use the pipelines and the wires of other companies to create and master emerging networks. Wholesale gas was the first opportunity in the mid-to-late 1980s, joined by wholesale electricity by the mid-1990s. On deck were retail gas and far larger retail electricity markets for Enron's best and brightest.

New terms peppered Lay speeches and Enron promotional material at mid-decade. Some were general buzzwords from the management literature, such as the *knowledge economy* and *borderless company*. Some were Enron-centric terms: *network economies, virtual integration, energy megatrends, New Energy Major, Btu marketing,* and *full-service energy company*. One term was the holy grail of the environmental movement in which energy was central: *sustainability*.[15]

In the *new economy*, Enron was a *new-economy energy company*. Enron's model was different from the staid integration model of the hitherto dominant oil major, the messaging went. This differentiation would reach a pinnacle several years later when Jeff Skilling declared the coming end of the integrated oil major. "You will see the collapse and demise of the integrated energy companies around the world," he blissfully predicted, "into thousands and thousands of pieces." However wrong, the seeds of Enron's redefinition of *energy major* were in evidence with Ken Lay's third vision.

———

"The leaders' most important functions will be to inspire by articulating a clear vision of the organization's values, strategies, and objectives, and to know enough about the business to be the risk manager of risk managers." So read a paragraph of a 1994 *Fortune* article by reporter John Huey, "Waking Up to the New Economy," underlined by Ken Lay and labeled *trip file* for further review. Just a few months later, Lay discovered a management strategist who was articulating what Enron was all about without even knowing Enron.

Although influenced by Peter Drucker, Ken Lay was his own visionary until he read an advance draft of "Strategy as Revolution" and met its author, Gary Hamel, at a Florida retreat in early 1996. Returning home, Lay distributed this

———

15. Enron's role in the President's Council on Sustainable Development is described in chapter 13, pp. 553–59.

essay to his senior staff with a note, "This article is one of the best business management articles I have read in quite some time."

Soon, Lay's speeches incorporated Hamel's tripartite classification of *rule makers* (IBM, United Airlines, Merrill Lynch, Sears, Coca-Cola); *rule takers* (Fujitsu, US Air, Smith Barney, JC Penney, Pepsi); and *rule breakers* (Compaq or Dell, Southwest Airlines, Charles Schwab, Wal-Mart, Gatorade). The rule makers and rule takers practiced incrementalism, where cost and revenue improvements were made within a relatively stable industry structure. Rule breakers, the *revolutionists*, took a whole new approach to the business.

"Enron can probably be described as a 'rule breaker,'" Lay stated at Daniel Yergin's annual CERA conference in Houston. Enron received 40 percent of its income from businesses that did not exist in 1985, Lay allowed, and 40 percent of the income anticipated in year 2000 (Enron 2000) would be from businesses that did not exist in 1990.

Enron's upstart business lines were international LNG, electricity wholesaling, gas and electricity retailing, and solar generation. Three of these four, and maybe all four, were notably premised on government intervention and special government favor. Electricity wholesaling was enabled by an Enron-authored (MOA) provision in the Energy Policy Act of 1992. Gas and electricity retailing were state-by-state legislative (MOA) matters, into which Enron was pouring resources. Solar generation (soon to be joined by industrial wind-power generation in Enron's renewable-energy push) was dependent on generous tax credits birthed in the same 1992 federal law. Government loan assistance was also part of the discussion of international LNG.

This book has documented the Hamel-Enron theme of revolutionary change in terms of political capitalism and rent-seeking, the *political means* as distinct from the *economic means* to business profit and success.[16] Ken Lay's business model was predicated more on the vagaries of government energy policy than on a patent or a sustainable free-market competitive advantage.

———

"Let's admit it," the opening sentence of Gary Hamel's 1995 essay read, "we've reached the limits of incrementalism." He continued:

> Squeezing another penny out of costs; getting a product to market a few weeks earlier; responding to customer inquiries a little bit faster; ratcheting quality up one more notch; capturing another point of market share; surviving industry shake-out—these are the obsessions of managers today. But pursuing incremental advantage while rivals are fundamentally reinventing the industrial landscape is akin to fiddling while Rome burns.[17]

———

16. See also Bradley, *Capitalism at Work*, pp. 83–84, 101–3, 265.

17. "This book is not about catching up, it's about getting ahead," Hamel added to this paragraph in his book.

"Strategy as Revolution" would be published the next year in the *Harvard Business Review*, becoming one of the most reprinted articles in HBR history. This paper would be incorporated into the preface to the second edition of *Competing for the Future* (1994, 1996), coauthored with C. K. Prahalad. And it would result in speaking and consulting opportunities with Enron that resulted in high praise in Hamel's next book, *Leading the Revolution* (2000). "As much as any company in the world," Hamel would write, "Enron has institutionalized a capacity for perpetual innovation."[18]

But a *change-always* business model is execution dependent, given that others are trying to excel in the same competitive arena. "The more radical the change—the more radical the deviation from the customary path," one management strategist explained, "the more abstract will be the institutions necessary to change, create, or otherwise redirect concrete capabilities in an effective direction."

Enron in its entire life had lived somewhat abstractly and dangerously. The era of Rich Kinder at Enron, not only that of Ken Lay and Jeff Skilling, had engendered bad practices and unresolved issues. The year 1997 would *not* inherit a clean Enron from 1996—and before. The Enron revolution had issues from virtually the beginning.

Great Man, Great Company

Ken Lay, the natural gas industry's Great Man, was now in the conversation with such oil industry stalwarts as John Browne of BP (CEO: 1995–2007) and Lee Raymond of Exxon (CEO: 1993–2006). Enron was the company most followed and publicized in the industry. ENE was a momentum stock outperforming the oil majors. Lay reveled in his 1400 Smith Street 50th-story office, which peered down at the 44-story Exxon Building at 800 Bell Street, where he had worked 30 years before (when the company was called Humble Oil).[19]

Within the confines of America's preeminent integrated oil major, Ken Lay was a topic of conversation. "There were a number of senior managers in our company that were basically quite jealous of him," remembered Exxon economist John Boatwright, who worked with Lay in the mid-1960s and retired from Exxon in 1994. "They would say, 'Damn, Enron is doing this or Enron is doing that'."

Enron was a very *public* public company. Exxon did its work quietly; Enron seemed to inform the press at every stage of every new project. (Shell, BP, and

---

18. Enron's bankruptcy in late 2001 led to a "fully updated with a new introduction" re-release of *Leading the Revolution* the next year, wherein praise of Enron was deleted and the company's collapse analyzed.

19. See Bradley, *Edison to Enron*, pp. 291–93.

Chevron were somewhere in the middle of these two extremes.) The problem was that Enron's hyperbole set a standard that was difficult to maintain, much less increase on a compound basis. The earnings pressure was on Enron bigtime in the mid-1990s, as it had been since the very beginning. It was momentum or bust for Ken Lay.

Corporate Culture

Ken Lay's strategy for superior performance and company greatness revolved around the workforce. "With the support of employees," he emphasized, "Enron can achieve its goals and vision to become the world's leading energy company."

Enron's corporate culture was progressive. Time off for special needs; portable health care and retirement plans; a voluntary employee assistance program for personal problems; paid vacation and sick leave; a country-club-like health facility; on-site nursing services; on-site subsidized dining; proactive training programs (including college tuition reimbursement) and an emphasis toward advancement; generous severance agreements in the event of layoffs.[20]

"At the end of a hard day," Lay summarized, "I want employees to feel they've been fairly paid and are sharing in the success and upside of the company." But more than this, "I want them to know their efforts are recognized and appreciated." Supervisors who do not commend good work "are neglecting what I consider to be a fundamental component of management and leadership."

Enron's industry-leading compensation and perks were designed to attract and retain superior intellectual capital.[21] Lay praised Enron's unit-specific compensation systems relative to the oil majors' "hierarchical, one-size-fits-all compensation system that has been part of their culture." Merit pay, skill-based pay, pay for performance permeated the whole corporation, although it was pursued most ardently by Jeff Skilling at EGS/ECT (with decidedly mixed results).

In 1996, Lay proudly pointed to double-digit annual growth in average overall compensation for Enron employees, compared to the annual inflation rate of 3 percent. The result was that "virtually all Enron employees have significantly improved their standard of living during this [five-year] period." Employee stock ownership was a major contributor to this result.

"It really takes a unique compensation system to compete against the investment bankers or the entrepreneurs that are developing projects," Lay explained, pointing to ECT and to Enron Development, in particular. "I have been very

---

20. See also chapter 6, pp. 300–303.

21. Ken Lay had long declared his employees superior. "We are convinced that Enron's work force on all levels is the best in the industry," he wrote in his March 1989 chairman's letter for the 1988 annual report.

satisfied with the results of Enron's compensation program to date [1996]," he added. "We have lost very few of our key developers, traders, or executives we wanted to keep." Lay pointed to Forrest Hoglund, who two years before garnered $19 million in total compensation, mostly from exercising stock options, to out-earn even the CEOs of the major oil companies. Lay also boasted about the increased percentage of his workforce with advanced degrees: 14 percent in 1995 compared to 4 percent a decade earlier.

———

An employee survey released in late 1996 rated Enron relatively high in relation to large successful companies (all surveyed by Watson Wyatt & Company) in general satisfaction. Safety was considered a core asset. Enron had a strong sense of urgency, with stockholder welfare foremost. Compensation and benefits were highly ranked—with greater satisfaction levels than in Enron's last such survey in 1992. Enron's senior management was trusted and respected for future success, too.

There were some negatives, which a letter to employees from Ken Lay and Jeff Skilling (Rich Kinder had announced his departure) described as "unsatisfactory" and "unacceptable." Open communication (what Enron promoted as "facts are friendly") was the major negative. "We made little progress since 1992 to improve the quality of communications across Enron," Lay and Skilling wrote. "Many of you are still uncomfortable about openly voicing your opinions, and many of you believe that your managers and supervisors do not listen to your suggestions, much less act upon them." The significance of this employee feedback would be appreciated only in retrospect.

The other problem concerned workload, no doubt emanating from the Skilling side. "While, in most cases, you feel that you are treated with respect and dignity, there is growing concern about job security, workloads, and the impact of cost cutting on work quality which can affect what we deliver to our customers."

Lay and Skilling promised urgent action on the weaknesses "until we get it right." The missive ended:

> There is a lot that is good at Enron, and most of our competitors would be delighted with our survey results. However, good is not enough at Enron. We want to be outstanding in everything we do. We will continue to lead our industry in innovation and financial performance, but also in the way that we treat our employees and customers. Our goal is to excel in each of these categories. Our future depends on it and we ask your commitment to make it happen.

Corporate Ethics
Enron had high ethical standards—except when it did not. Desperate times required desperate measures to meet earnings expectations and trigger performance awards. "Our employee base and management team," after all, as stated in Enron's 1995 annual report, "have strong incentives to see the company succeed through their collective ownership of Enron common stock."

Short-term profit maximization, particularly at year-end—all to strengthen ENE—created extraordinary moments when what was *legal* was okay. Gaming the accounting rules or stretching the tax regulations were old hat at Enron by the mid-1990s. And later in the decade, this mentality found a new opportunity—gaming California's electricity regulations for extraordinary profits.[22] But what might be technically legal in the Golden State was not so in the court of public opinion, and even the judiciary gave more weight to fraudulent intent than regulatory punctilio (as US jurisprudence says courts should). Enron's massive paper profits proved uncollectable when Enron most needed the cash flow.[23]

Seeking and acquiring special government favor (called *rent-seeking* in the jargon of political economy) was legal and thus ethical at Enron. Had not iconic free-market economist Milton Friedman himself declared that the social responsibility of business was to make a profit? Enron's profit centers were government dependent for the most part. The company's free-market situations were fewer, but Ken Lay, in particular, interpreted regulation that was merely procompetition to be promarket—and none more so than MOA of interstate energy assets.

Then there was nepotism, part of the Great Man syndrome. This problem existed at Ken Lay's Enron from the beginning, as discussed later in this chapter.

———

Enron's major initiative beginning in 1996 was to become the nation's leading provider of electricity and natural gas to the homes and places of business. Electricity retailing, in particular, a $200 billion market, was the bet behind Enron 2000: the promise to double the size and profitability of the company in five years.[24]

As part of a national branding campaign to make itself a household name, Enron enlarged its community-affairs effort and redoubled its "green" energy image. Likable, soulful Ken Lay himself would be the voice of Enron, spending more time giving speeches and working with outside constituencies to boost the image of Enron and of ENE as a momentum stock.

In mid-1996, *Enron Business* published "a Message from Chairman & CEO Ken Lay" to the Enron community, including shareholders. "Corporate

———

22. Enron not only exploited the unintended opportunities created by California regulators but also bragged about it as electricity rates skyrocketed and shortages ensued. The 1999–2001 episode is recounted in chapter 17, "Gaming California," in the best-known Enron book, *The Smartest Guys in the Room*.

23. Enron's infamous gaming in the regulated environment of California resulted in paper profits of several hundred million dollars, which was not enough to rescue the company from its losses elsewhere.

24. See chapter 15, p. 594.

Citizenship: A Priority in the Enron Workplace" alleged the "moral obligation" of corporations to "employees, customers, and shareholders" to "share their success with others in the community."

"As Enron continues to expand its businesses globally, the responsibilities of corporate citizenship will expand as well," Lay stated. The effort began with good customer relations that produced value for shareholders. But customers too, Lay said, must see their Enron counterparts as "dedicated, caring professionals who have high ethical and moral standards—a company they want to do business with for a long time." To that end, "every transaction we undertake should be a win-win for all parties."

Figure 14.6 The fatherly Ken Lay expounded his emphasis on corporate stewardship in the July/August 1996 edition of *Enron Business*. Subheadings in the article were "Citizenship begins in the workplace," "Enron's external focus a priority," and "Enron's role in community moves into the spotlight."

The same must be true internationally, he continued. "For example, our success in bringing back the Dabhol power project back on line is due primarily to the hard work of many employees, underscoring, once again, the commitment we have to our customers and partners." (In fact, Dabhol, back under construction, would not profitably sell electricity in Enron's lifetime.)

Grants to education and the environment in 1996 of $5.7 million under-scored Enron's stakeholder commitments. "Our employees are aware that the business decisions they make can have a significant social and global impact in the areas where Enron operates," Lay closed. "So by striving to create energy solutions that promote a better environment for everyone, and by sharing some of their success with the community, our employees the world over are bolstering Enron's reputation as a responsible corporate citizen."

————

Ken Lay's views on corporate citizenship were also reflected in a business ethics essay in which he characterized Enron as a *heroic enterprise*, citing

> our role in helping to bring competition and customer choice to two traditionally public-utility industries, natural gas and electricity. Our effort has run the gamut from initiating fundamental regulatory reform to developing new products to meet consumer demand in the ensuing restructured industry.

In fact, Enron's do-goodism was about political correctness and rent-seeking, not only about real wealth creation, part of a quite nonheroic finale.[25]

Internally, Lay stressed *employee empowerment and trust* in a knowledge-driven business. "Our vision and values stress honesty, openness, excellence, and reward," he wrote. "The result is a dedicated, even passionate, workforce that we believe sets the industry standard."

Lay also believed that *heroic Enron* could find "profitable solutions ... to social problems" and practice "strategic philanthropy." The former included Enron's being "part of the solution to global climate change by making a market for carbon dioxide air emission permits." The latter meant deploying not-for-profit activity in ways that blended with Enron's for-profit entrepreneurship. Both initiatives would prove empty for Enron: The required government intervention never activated CO_2 emission permits, and Enron's venture into urban philanthropy (Enron Investment Partners) was a bust.

————

"Enron Corp. believes in conducting its business affairs in accordance with the highest ethical standards," began a letter dated November 30, 1995, from Ken Lay to Enron's business partners. The annual (anti) conflict-of-interest missive continued:

> Enron expects each of its vendors and contractors to maintain adequate records that document its work relationship with Enron. Enron's auditing department will routinely conduct business ethics compliance audits of certain vendors and contractors with whom Enron does business. Your recognition of our ethical

---

25. See Bradley, *Capitalism at Work*, pp. 309–10.

standards allows Enron employees to work with you via arm's length transactions and avoids potentially embarrassing and unethical situations.[26]

The letter reminded vendors that "employees of Enron and its subsidiaries are required to comply with Enron's Business Ethics Policy which requires an employee to conduct himself/herself in a manner which is not detrimental to the best interest of Enron or which could bring to the employee financial gain separately derived as a direct consequence of his/her employment at Enron." Yet slightly more than one year later, Andy Fastow would set up the sale of Zond wind properties to a group secretly funded by himself, ushering in a new era of conflicts of interest that would lead Enron to unanticipated insolvency.

Accolades
Enron was media hungry—for good news only. Ken Lay despaired of bad press and did not forget his contrarians. ENE, a momentum stock, was pumped by regular press releases announcing project beginnings, advances, and conclusions (if positive). Rule-breaker Enron had a lot of novel dealings, and the financial numbers looked strong.

The hard work of public affairs paid off in 1996 when *Fortune* magazine's annual survey of top US public corporations ranked Enron first in innovation. Old and new corporate icons Rubbermaid and Intel were second and third, respectively. For two years, Enron had been voted the most-admired energy company; now a new streak was started with a most impressive category. "America's Most Innovative Company" became a new tag line at Enron for years to come.

In March 1997, *Fortune* again ranked Enron first in innovation among 431 rated companies across 49 industries. (Mirage Resorts was second and Intel, again, third.) Enron was ranked the 21st-best company overall (up from 22 the year before) by the more than 13,000 experts choosing the top 10 companies in their field using eight criteria (listed in this chapter's Conclusion).

Among energy companies, Enron was ranked first, followed by Shell Oil (at 30), Mobil third (40), and Exxon fourth (44). Among pipeline companies, Enron was first for the second year, ahead of Williams, PanEnergy, and Sonat.

Enron was "a very different kind of power company," *Fortune*'s Brian O'Reilly explained in an accompanying article. Ken Lay was the star. "I was trained as an economist, loved free markets, and was convinced that government regulation was causing most of the problems in the gas industry," stated

---

26. Lay's letter invited anyone knowing of "variances from our policy" to contact Enron's general counsel James Derrick. Hired away from Vinson & Elkins, Derrick replaced Gary Orloff (who joined Enron in 1987 from the same firm), who left Enron under an undisclosed personal-ethics complaint in 1991.

Figure 14.7 In March 1997, *Fortune* magazine announced its poll results ranking Enron as America's most innovative company—and first among energy companies in the America's Most Admired category.

Enron's architect. Lay "viewed that national map of gas pipelines differently than just about everybody" by "pushing deregulation" [really mandatory open access], O'Reilly wrote. Explained Lay: "We changed the concept of how the natural gas industry was run—new products, new services, new kinds of contracts, new ways of pricing."

O'Reilly was impressed: "Gadgets, patents, doodads? At Enron, not a one. Nonetheless, Ken Lay has turned Enron into the most innovative power company in the country."[27]

Rich Kinder might caution against self-aggrandizement, invoking such locutions as not smoking one's own dope or drinking one's own whiskey. But the media, even the outside world, was increasingly imbibing Enron.

Nepotism

Did conflicts of interest apply to Ken Lay, the one employee who did not report to another Enron employee but only to the board of directors? Not quite; from

---

27. O'Reilly's characterization of Enron as a power company was superficial—and premature. Enron was primarily a gas company serving the power industry and a developer mostly of gas-fired power plants. Enron *wanted* to become a major power player via MOA, a goal set in 1994–95 and in full swing by 1996.

the beginning, as noted in chapter 1, Ken Lay directed company business to his sister Sharon's travel agency. (Lay was also a part owner of this business in its early years.) Lay's number two at Houston Natural Gas, Jim Walzel, thought this highly inappropriate. Nothing like that was proposed or slipped through the cracks under Robert Herring or M. D. Matthews at the old Houston Natural Gas, much less their predecessors Frank Smith and Bus Wimberly.

And there would be more. Ken's son Mark Lay cut deals with Enron between his two employment stints there, earning three proxy statement mentions. Daughter Elizabeth Lay would later work at Enron (at Azurix, the water subsidiary) but not have a proxy event.

To Ken Lay, business was personal, and the personal was business. "Since he was personally willing to devote 100% of his time, energy, and life to his employer, he felt that the distinction between his employer's assets and his own was a relatively meaningless distinction," remembered one confidant.

———

Travel Agency in the Park (TAP) offered volume savings for the company. Like her brother, Sharon Lay was smart, diligent, and congenial. Her company, in the estimation of many, provided "good service" to Enron. TAP scored well in audits and rebated part of its volume savings to Enron.

But the type of employees and business units that Enron fostered did not like to be told what to do in such areas. Some found deficiencies with TAP and made their own travel plans, even surreptitiously. For a company priding itself on open markets and competition, this was reason enough to leave things decentralized—if not formally brought in house or (competitively) outsourced to a firm or firms. Perhaps domestic and international travel arrangements would be sourced differently, for example.

But Ken Lay expected Enron to go to one place—a family place. Wasn't it his prerogative as a chairman adding so much value for employees and shareholders? Scale economies were cited, with TAP negotiating volume discounts with hometown Continental Airlines, for example.

Enter Jim Barnhart, the self-described "ad man," as in *administration man*. A Florida Gas Company veteran under Jack Bowen, Selby Sullivan, and then Ken Lay, Barnhart rejoined Lay when HNG purchased Florida Gas in 1984. "I was the head janitor, the head copy maker, the head mail boy, the head security guard," remembered the affable Barnhart. He was responsible for all building matters at 1400 Smith and other locales, as well as transportation (Enron jets, notably), and records administration—20 or more functions in all.

Barnhart's jurisdiction included corporate travel, which was pushed to Sharon Lay. Some years later, the law department determined that the relationship between the CEO and vendor had become "a proxy deal" under the Securities and Exchange Commission (SEC) guidelines, reportable under "Certain Transactions" in Enron's Notice of Annual Meeting of Stockholders.

Nobody wanted this disclosure, so the travel contract was put out to bid. Jim Barnhart hired the former head of the Travel Agents Association as a consultant to devise a specification sheet and to compile a bid list to solicit offers.

Major players, such as American Express, stood ready with their own economies of scale, if not economies of scope. Another option was to just decentralize travel, so that different Enron units decided what was best for them. Individual employees, too, might have a relationship or other connection that allowed them to get a good deal. (Online travel reservations were not yet in place, although hometown Continental Airlines' System 1 was part of TAP's service.)

Sharon Lay was worried—and told her brother about it during their Sunday night dinners at Ken's house in River Oaks. Barnhart began to hear things. He visited with Lay, only to be assured that things would be okay.

Bids were submitted. With apples and oranges, Barnhart passed the "hot potato" to Enron internal audit, whose decision came in a management committee meeting. The winner was ... Travel Agency in the Park. Barnhart was a bit surprised; his cursory examination had led him to expect a new travel vendor for Enron.

Legal returned to Barnhart the next year asking for a new bid-out on the travel contract. As Barnhart recounted:

> I said "Bullshit! What are you talking about?" They said, "Oh yes. We've got to put out this proxy every year." I said, "It's a multiyear deal." They said, "No, it's a one-year deal."

> I said, "I'll guarantee you it is a five-year deal." And by the time I went home that day, it was a five-year deal. I got it past [my] retirement [in 1996].[28]

In 1996, TAP earned approximately $1.6 million in commissions from Enron, as well as additional sums from third parties doing business with Enron, such as the Vinson & Elkins and Andrews & Kurth law firms. The Great Man knew about and appreciated their business.

———

Mark Lay was smart and cordial. He was a good guy, more reserved than stuffy. He had attended UCLA, where he had been part of the debate team and graduated magna cum laude and Phi Beta Kappa.

In 1990, after short stints with Drexel Burnham Lambert and Credit Suisse First Boston, Mark joined the company where his father was chairman and CEO. Enron was a great gig, and Mark caught a wave at Enron Finance, where Gene Humphrey was devising new approaches to fund natural gas production

---

28. After the five-year period ended, Enron Property & Services and TAP would enter into a long-term contract that was reported as a proxy item.

to contract supply for Enron's long-term sales contracts. Mark even made Enron's *1990 Annual Report*, a staged hallway work shot with his discerning master and erstwhile critic, Lou Pai.

After two years working on oil- and gas-production payments and otherwise learning the business, Mark left Enron to join AIG. As vice president of trading, he marketed crude oil, natural gas, and petroleum products, both physical and financial. After AIG, Mark went out on his own with different stakes in the fast-paced gas business. It was here that a potential conflict of interest occurred, one that was reportable as an Enron proxy item (the first of three for him).

In April 1994, Bruin Interests LLC, founded and 48 percent owned by Mark Lay, entered into a master storage agreement with Houston Pipe Line Company to inject and withdraw natural gas on an interruptible basis from the Bammel storage field, the largest such facility in the United States. (Firm capacity was reserved by Entex, the local gas distributor supplied by HPL.)

Bruin's deal aimed to inject during the low-demand months, when prices were relatively low, and withdraw during the high-demand months, when prices typically peaked. The injection was up to eight billion cubic feet during the April–August period, with withdrawal from December 1994 through January 1995.

A supplement to Enron's 1994 proxy statement announced the pending transaction. After detailing the payment terms and contract rights of the two parties, Enron stated that the transaction was "comparable to those available to unaffiliated third parties."

The next year, the proxy summary announced a renewal of the interruptible arrangement, this time with an injection fee (around $0.16/MMBtu) and transportation fee payable to HPL by Bruin. A minimum payment protected HPL by acting as a reservation fee. The quantity was six Bcf versus eight the year before.

HPL had never done such a deal in the 30-year history of Bammel, and the first was with the son of the chairman. The proxy statement added: "The Master Agreement and the initial confirmation were subsequently assigned by Bruin to a third party; HPL consented to such assignment." In other words, Mark Lay's company planned to assign the deal to another party—the one that had come up with the idea to arbitrage interruptible capacity.

Normally, the actual user of storage (the third party) would have arranged the deal with HPL. But evidently an entry fee was needed for getting inside Enron. Otherwise, it would have to be concluded that two cuts of profit outside of Enron still resulted in more money for Enron than if Skilling's own maestros had arbitraged the gas.

Enron's lawyers took it from there in the second go-around. "HPL believes that the terms of the existing Master Agreement are comparable to those available to unaffiliated third parties, and HPL does not intend to engage in or permit any affiliate to engage in any transactions with Bruin except on terms that HPL believes are comparable to those available to unaffiliated third parties," the proxy read.

"Nobody but Ken Lay's son or brother-in-law could have made a deal like that," one HPL official stated years later. "That's the only time we ever leased out Bammel." The scuttlebutt was that Jeff Skilling okayed the deal to curry favor with Mark's father; Lou Pai was nonplussed. A number of Enron insiders held their noses on this one, beginning with the proxy's introduction of Mark's deal as occurring "in the ordinary course of its business...."

————

Another proxy matter involving Mark was reported in 1996 (the third straight year he was a subject of disclosure). "In January 1996, ECT, United Media Corporation ('UMC') and certain other individuals, including Mark K. Lay, entered into a feasibility agreement providing for the performance by UMC and ECT of a feasibility study relating to the fixed price purchase and sale of certain paper products." ECT advanced $300,000, with an option to double this amount for work.

Enron's UMC contract included third-party outreach with potential paper suppliers. Should the project proceed to commercialization, UMC would receive an equity interest of up to 49 percent. "ECT has been informed that, if the project proceeds, Mark K. Lay would own 20% of UMC's interest in the project." Four months later, this deal was cancelled, which was followed by another contract from ECT for Bruin Interests (Mark Lay et al.) to study the iron carbide business.

The next year, another event concerning the chairman's son was reported. "In May, 1997, Mark K. Lay and certain other individuals ... who were formerly officers, directors, and/or shareholders of Paper & Print Management Corporation entered into employment agreements with ECT for the development within ECT of a clearinghouse for the purchase and sale of finished paper products," the proxy read. In return for "certain intangible property rights," ECT agreed to "reimburse PPMC $1,005,257.85 in expenses that were incurred by PPMC to a third party in conjunction with PPMC's prior business." In other words, lots of present money traded for the *potential* of profit.

Additionally, Mark received a three-year employment contract guaranteeing $750,000, with $100,000 up front. Enron's newest vice president had a minimum base salary and bonus per year of $150,000 and $100,000. Stock options were provided as well.

Was the retirement of debt and a sweet employment agreement a bailout for the chairman's son? Maybe so but maybe not, in that ECT wanted to go in the same direction. The establishment of long-term forward markets for pulp and paper products was innovative and made money—and seemingly provided a happy ending. But Enron would have to invest considerable sums in the process, leaving the verdict in doubt from the perspective of opportunity costs.

Conclusion

At the close of 1996, the company that Ken Lay christened the world's first natural gas major—and a company he declared positioned to become the world's leading energy company—was really a North American natural gas company with an uneven international project portfolio. Enron was borrowing from the future at every opportunity, major problems were festering, and the company's growth promise to Wall Street depended on a gigantic regulatory bet—MOA at the state level with electricity (retail wheeling by local utilities, the subject of the next chapter).

Yet mighty Enron and Great Man Ken Lay were atop the energy industry and certainly hometown Houston. Hadn't *Fortune* ranked Enron as top tier in innovativeness; quality of management; value as a long-term investment; community and environmental responsibility; ability to attract, develop, and keep talented people; quality of products and services; financial soundness; and use of corporate assets?

Did not *Fortune*'s hand-picked experts nominate Enron as the best of all energy companies, giving credence to Lay's new vision to become (astoundingly in retrospect) the world's leading energy company? Was not Ken Lay featured, and Jeff Skilling mentioned, as *masters of innovation* in *Fortune*'s America's Most Admired Companies issue of March 1997?

Houston was all but in Enron's hand. "Ken Lay was a good guy and Enron was a great corporate citizen, and Houston was all the richer for both," one book explained in the wake of Enron's demise in late 2001.

Such fawning and favor meant little when the harsh truth seeped out in Enron's last year of solvency. Many years of cultivated goodwill ended quickly. But the pathways to this shocking finale were already present in 1996—and in need of major, if not dramatic, midcourse correction.

15

Energy Retailing

Retailing gas and electricity to the home—a step downstream from wholesaling to utilities—was central to the goal of doubling the size and earnings of Enron between 1996 and 2000. Enron 2000, as that goal was called, was part of becoming *the world's leading energy company*, discussed in the previous chapter.

Ken Lay's new vision and Enron 2000 were very aggressive, even brazen. So was Enron's grand leap into energy retailing, which began in 1995 and was in full swing by 1997. The next year, however, a major strategy change was made: to shift from residential commodity sales to total energy outsourcing for large establishments and industry.

Enron's retail plan required scaling three peaks. First, a public policy change-over to mandatory open access (MOA) for utility transmission was necessary to allow independent providers (such as Enron) to reach residential users and commercial establishments. Enron, in fact, would have to create a movement in state legislatures and state commissions, an effort requiring dozens of full-time lobbyists and a war chest for political contributions.[1]

Second, Enron was unknown to the buying public. Brand-name recognition and trust were necessary to compete against established utilities. Consumers, although captive to their utility, were hardly rebelling, much less searching for an alternative supplier. Regulators and legislators were well tended to by the incumbents to help keep this status quo.

Third, Enron had little retailing experience. Mass marketing was quite different from business-to-business sales, Enron's niche. Ken Lay's was not a

---

1. This regulatory and legislative effort, which began with about 5 professional lobbyists in 1995, would expand to 30–40 in 1998–99 with an annual budget of $25 million.

low-cost, small-margin, boiler-room operation; Enron's best and brightest received industry-leading compensation and perquisites and were not schooled in humble labors.

Enron's three-part challenge—retail MOA, public branding, and retail sales—went to three senior executives, two newly hired. Government Affairs veteran Terry Thorn was assigned exclusively to opening retail markets for gas and power. Elizabeth Tilney was hired to lead advertising and outreach in order to make Enron a "brand" for mass consumers. Ashok Rao joined Enron to develop retail energy products for the home and business.

Ken Lay, meanwhile, was using his many forums to espouse the consumer benefits of competition all the way to the smallest home or business. Jeff Skilling, too, pushed MOA to reach final users as the commonsense, utilitarian policy to better America, while transforming and enlarging ECT.

Lay and Skilling were thinking big: 10 percent market share, $20 billion in sales, and a 2 percent margin for $400 million in earnings. But after 18 months of effort, the vision of a million-plus customers would evaporate. With fewer than 50,000 to show for $20 million of effort, and without enough open markets to pursue, Enron would return its customers to the local utilities and set out on a new retail path.

———

Enron's retail effort was early and all in. In December 1993, Enron Power Marketing Inc. (EPM) received a blanket marketing certificate from the Federal Energy Regulatory Commission (FERC), allowing sales of wholesale power at market prices. EPM executed its first wholesale power trade in June 1994, and by year-end, its 70-strong division was selling more electricity than all the other independents combined. With 80 interchange and unilateral contracts and 9 transmission agreements, Enron wholesaled power "in every region of the lower 48 states," creating, for the first time, however embryonic, a *continental marketplace*.

Enron's dominance would continue even with new entrants, such as Electric Clearinghouse (of NGC) and Applied Energy Services (AES). ECT's 26 percent share of the nonregulated (nonutility) market in 1996 was the fruit of being first in. (Enron's 17 percent share of the wholesale gas market, by contrast, was a decade's work in a mature industry.)

But what were the profit margins from power wholesaling? Enron would not say, but 87 active marketing companies (of more than 200 FERC-certified) were chasing less than 5 percent of the overall (wholesale) power market, making margins far less than those of early natural gas marketing. Like wholesale gas, wholesale electricity by 1997 was "fully competitive," noted EPM's Ken Rice.

Natural Gas

Enron was well ensconced in the business of wholesale natural gas by the early 1990s. But new opportunities were needed to increase ECT's earnings. Existing long-term deals had no more profit to give under mark-to-market accounting. Each new year was a do-over just to match the prior year's financial performance.

Gas wholesaling, estimated to be a $30 billion market, was a mature business with many competitors emulating Enron. The new frontier was *retailing* natural gas to customers who lay behind the local distribution company (LDC): commercial, industrial, and even residential. But far from a voluntary, free-market activity, retail competition was the downstream application of MOA within a century-old regulatory institution.[2]

What was next in the new world of natural gas, Ken Lay was asked in 1992. His answer? "Bypass." In that year, Enron purchased Access Energy Corporation of Columbus, Ohio, which sold natural gas to 10,000 small commercial users in 34 states and Canada. Renamed Enron Access, notable customers included Taco Bell in Columbus and the churches in the Archdiocese of Chicago.[3]

Households were another story. These small users were costly to aggregate and the least profitable to serve. In terms of rates, however, homeowners seemed to be a plausible target. Between 1985 and 1994, gas prices fell by more than 20 percent for LDCs and industrial customers and were flat for commercial users. But residential rates *rose* 5 percent. In 1996, houses, on average, paid $6.34 per MMBtu, 17 percent and 85 percent more than commercial and industrials users, respectively.

The national retail gas market was estimated by Enron to be $70 billion, mostly behind LDCs, which accounted for 71 percent of end-user sales. (Municipal distributors and co-ops, beyond the reach of FERC or state commissions, and thus MOA, accounted for the balance.) As the nation's leading gas wholesaler to LDCs, Enron in effect already served a portion of this market, so its actual available additional sales market (retail minus wholesale) was closer to $40 billion.

———

With federal MOA complete in the wholesale (interstate pipeline) gas markets by 1993, states started exploring retail unbundling. California, Ohio, Illinois, Massachusetts, Maryland, and New Jersey began LDC-bypass programs. Georgia opted for the most comprehensive statewide program when Atlanta Gas Light Company, the Georgia Public Service Commission (GPSC), and legislators hammered out the Natural Gas Consumer Choice Act of 1996,

———

2. The beginning of statewide public-utility regulation, under which the franchised monopolist sold a bundled product under cost-based rate maximums, is described in Bradley, *Edison to Enron*, pp. 86–88, 121–26, 172–76.

3. See chapter 9, pp. 399–400.

which was enacted the next year as the Natural Gas Competition and Deregulation Act.[4]

So-called LDC unbundling (separating out the delivery service from the commodity) had political life. But effective competition was limited as of 1996, notwithstanding Enron's 20,000 customers saving an estimated $50 million compared to their utility alternative in three states where access was furthest along: California, Illinois, and Ohio.

Before the GPSC and other state bodies, Enron elaborated a set of principles for "comprehensive unbundling" to allow its commodity-only service to compete in a new market. Enron advocated regulation for utility (delivery) service but not regulation for itself, excepting a minimum financial requirement to limit the number of commodity entrants to the strongest.

Utilities would be required to exit the merchant function—to end bundled service—and be subject to level-playing-field regulation from their public-utility commission. That way, any independent provider would not be disadvantaged against the utility. In fact, the utility would have to set up an arm's-length subsidiary, *with a new name,* to provide commodity service without special, advantageous rates or terms of service from the parent. "It is vital," Enron emphasized, "that the traditional monopoly seller—the local distribution company—not have preferential advantage to discourage the new commodity providers from effectively competing in the new retail access market."

Private contracts would replace the LDC's obligation to serve. Utilities, under Enron's proposal, would still be responsible for aggregating customers for the third parties, reading meters, and providing backup service. Utility rates for delivery and ancillary services would be cost based under traditional public-utility regulation. Incumbents would not be able to charge customer exit fees to discourage any transition from bundled to unbundled service.

That was Enron's ideal—*unless* it was in Texas, Louisiana, or a country where Enron itself was the bundling merchant, making money on both the transmission and commodity sale. And Enron was doing just that with Houston Pipe Line, Louisiana Resources Company, and Transportadora de Gas del Sur (in Argentina). As has been said: *Where you stand depends on where you sit.*[5]

––––

"Much in the way that the long-distance competition sprang up from the break-up of AT&T Corp.," the *Wall Street Journal* reported in Spring 1996, "natural-gas companies are competing in the wake of deregulation." Unbundling the commodity from delivery was much like Sprint or MCI using the

––––

4. A more accurate title would have been the "Natural Gas Competition and Restructuring Act," although the buying and selling of the commodity *were* deregulated for the first time.

5. On Enron's public policy contradiction, see Introduction, pp. 34–35.

transmission lines of the Baby Bells to reach the home or business, the article noted.

Enron Access was offering Energy Bucks and other promotions for new customers, the article continued. Branded natural gas, akin to the oil majors' gasoline, was one possible result. "One day we'll be able to send bills with Mobil's flying red horse on them," predicted Paul Anderson of PanEnergy, a large transmission company that teamed up with Mobil to market natural gas.

Was small-customer aggregation a profitable business? No one yet knew, but there were clearly obstacles. In terms of regulation, state-level unbundling was moving ahead, however imperfectly, despite limited utility support.[6] In terms of business, aggregating enough customers for scale economies was expensive, from solicitation to billing to collection. But in early 1997, Enron was going to try it all with a Toledo, Ohio, residential natural gas pilot program that offered a guaranteed double-digit discount for customers.

Enron's *Clean Start* signed up a small fraction of the eligible market. Retailing natural gas to the home, as opposed to commercial establishments and manufacturers, was just not ripe. As Ken Lay told FERC, "traditional suppliers have the advantage of incumbency, including brand name goodwill, proprietary marketplace information, and familiarity with the regulatory process." What was needed was for the LDC to unbundle—to separate transmission from the commodity—and to form a renamed stand-alone independent entity to compete for a margin that was previously just a dollar-for-dollar cost passthrough.[7]

Charles (Chuck) Watson, head of NGC (formerly the U.S. Natural Gas Clearinghouse, later Dynegy), rejected such retailing, although his company was well positioned to try it. Now teamed with Chevron as the largest gas marketer in the country (surpassing Enron), NGC's *Energy Store* would stay at wholesale, he told *Natural Gas Week*. With estimated annual profit of $25 per customer, independents could achieve profitability only in a market of millions.

Enron would find this out. "In Dublin, Ohio, where Access Energy used to be," remembered Tom White, vice chairman of Enron Energy Services, "we were selling gas contracts like hot cakes to people willy-nilly around the country." Without regard to cost or per-customer profitability, Enron was manually servicing accounts behind LDCs, each having its own tariff structure and service rules. White recalled that the account behind Amarillo Gas Company was serviced by two dedicated Enron employees. Simply eliminating the bottom

---

6. In 1998, 11 states had either legislation or PUC orders; 12 states had pilot programs; and 11 states were considering action. The remaining 16 states had no initiatives to allow gas sales to households.

7. The Georgia Public Service Commission required Atlanta Gas Light Company to use a different name for its (unbundled, for-profit) gas-retailing division: Georgia Natural Gas Services.

20 percent of gas customers by volume reduced the LDC count from 120 to 30, but years of waste and losses would not be recouped.

Electricity

The driving assumption behind achieving the goals of Enron 2000—a doubling of Enron's size and profitability in five years—did not so much involve natural gas, much less solar and wind power. It was not about biomass; ethanol, in fact, competed against Enron's large investment in natural gas–derived gasoline oxygenates. Enron had spun off most of what it had relating to oil. Coal was not of interest to Enron—yet.

The Big Bet was on the energy of energies, *electricity*, a retail market much greater than that of natural gas, hitherto Enron's bread and butter. "Enron has a grand plan here," noted investment analyst John Olson. "The strategy is in five to 10 years to have a national branded product … to become the Coca-Cola, the Proctor & Gamble" of power.

A McKinsey study commissioned by Jeff Skilling had outlined the huge possibilities of selling electricity to the home: a potential market share between 5 and 8 percent, and margins between 1 and 3 percent. That would be an incremental $300 million for Enron's bottom line.[8] Already, Enron Gas Services was all in with *wholesale* electricity marketing, executing deals in the second half of 1994. Jeff Skilling's new office, in fact, was centered amid 100 power marketers on Floor 31 of the Enron Building.[9]

In late 1995, the retail push began at both the corporate level (public affairs, government affairs) and within Enron Capital & Trade Resources. From a *business plan* to *product development* to *marketing strategy:* Everything was new despite a decade of experience in wholesale natural gas and a year of wholesale work with electricity.

In May 1996, Skilling and Lou Pai announced that the preliminaries were finished. "Over the past five months, the Retail Group has made substantial progress in defining new retail markets and developing business strategies." It was now "time to focus a significant amount of additional resources to the effort." All hands on deck: "Your efforts will be viewed as critical in positioning ECT to be the dominant energy merchant into the next century."

"Three discrete businesses"—Consumer, Commercial, and Specialty—would make up Retail Group, in anticipation of "[mandated] open access to

---

8. Natural gas retailing was less of an incremental market for Enron than was electricity. The gas market was smaller, and Enron already wholesaled the gas that would become its retail business with the LDCs leaving the merchant function.

9. See chapter 10, pp. 461–62.

retail gas and electric markets." Given the potential size of each ("as large an undertaking as ECT itself"), all three would report directly to ECT's Office of the Chairman. Meanwhile, Enron Power Marketing, created almost three years before, housed wholesale.

Tim Ballaglia and Lou Pai led *Specialty*, involving "customized, complex" contracts with institutional chains, such as hospitals and schools. *Commercial* was led by Dave Duran, who had developed the business with Access Energy in Dublin, Ohio, before his company joined Enron.

Consumer, the third area, had neither customers nor a business plan. "This business unit will be charged with developing a new 'company within the company' at ECT," Skilling and Pai stated, responsible "for development of products and sales for and marketing to consumer markets"—as well as be ECT's voice in "retail alliances, brand development and management, advertising and P.R. activities." Their final sentence: "The Consumer Group will be led by Andy Fastow."

How could Enron profitably serve the smallest of energy users with electricity, not to mention natural gas? Fastow had previously pulled rabbits out of the hat with finance; now, with a dedicated team, he was tasked with designing a plausible road to profitability.

Seven weeks later, changes were announced for two of the three divisions of the Retail Group. Only Duran's "middle market, single location business to which physical delivery is possible today," was unaffected.

Specialty—"the most immediate new business opportunity within retail for ECT"—was centralized with its own origination, pricing, and risk function. Change was positive there, with an increase of integrated functions.

That left Consumer, where whiz-kid Fastow was out. Rick Causey, formerly with Treasury, was now in charge of developing "a range of [retail] energy services ... as well as risk management, logistics, and rate analysis." Andy Fastow had not been able to chart expenses and revenue in a way that showed a viable spreadsheet profit. (His ideas about product differentiation certainly did not suit a generic product such as electricity.) But just perhaps what Enron's top leaders envisioned was not there to be had at all.

Fastow quietly rejoined Treasury. "Andy's significant experience in finance and capital markets will add greatly to Treasury's activities as well as continued growth of capital as a product for ECT," a memorandum read. Reassigned, and perhaps anxious for redemptive success, Fastow would stretch the boundaries of prudence in Enron's hothouse.

Causey worked the spreadsheets and accounted for minutiae, but the logistics of retail remained daunting. Who knew how many customers would leave the comfort of their existing supplier? What would it really cost to set up an account and subsequently bill that user? What would it take to retain that customer for future billing cycles?

After a few months, Causey too returned to Treasury.

The conundrum next went to Ray Bowen, who had worked right through the Fastow and Causey regimes. More and better detail went into the spreadsheets. But the numbers that a young Harvard MBA (Gustav Beerel) had put together early-on for Fastow stubbornly indicated a problem of high costs and low margins, necessitating a customer count beyond the available near-term market.

Jeff Skilling was getting nervous, but pilot projects to prove the concept (discussed below) were going ahead. A new leader, K. Ashok Rao, was hired from the outside to bring his experience fighting as an independent against AT&T's long-distance monopoly. (He would not last.)[10]

Public Policy Push

By the early 1990s, a competitive retail electricity commodity market was an idea waiting to happen. In 1982, Irwin Stelzer (later Ken Lay's top consultant for Enron) stirred the hornet's nest with an essay in *Regulation* magazine—"Electric Utilities—Next Stop for Deregulators?" FERC, the Department of Energy, and Virginia Electric & Power, Stelzer reported, were each studying alternatives to the industry's vertically integrated monopoly structure. He attributed this development to deregulation elsewhere (airlines, trucking, railroads, telecommunications), as well as to the recognized problem of utility overinvestment under the (mal)incentive of rate-base regulation.

Stelzer's logic led to a simple but foreign idea to "give distributors and their customers an opportunity to buy power from the cheapest sources." Power generation, after all, would be populated by many sellers, not the "natural monopoly" of one distribution provider (the company owning the wires).

In 1986, the head of the Illinois Commerce Commission, Philip O'Connor, proposed "requiring nondiscriminatory wheeling of power between individual consumers and producers to eliminate unjustifiable regional differences in price, thereby creating a national energy market." Utility generation could be deregulated and spun off to independents, O'Connor and two coauthors posited. Spot prices and futures prices could develop, and utility services—none greater than transmission—could be unbundled for separate pricing.

Enron started from scratch with its vision of retailing electricity. But the opportunity was set up by its Washington office, which sponsored a provision in the Energy Policy Act of 1992 to require utilities to provide nondiscriminatory access to the transactions of outside parties doing wholesale business (sale-for-resale). Mandatory open access for in-state distribution (referred to as *retail*

---

10. See below, pp. 626, 637.

wheeling) was expressly *not* required in the federal law. Enron could not dare ask for that—yet.

So, Enron had won the fight for interstate mandatory open access.[11] But at the state level, the integrated electric companies possessed much more clout with utility commissions and lawmakers. "Retail wheeling is bad policy," stated David Owens, whose Edison Electric Institute (EEI) favored "incremental competition." Debate and delay ("going slow") gave the utilities more time to recover their uneconomic ("stranded") costs from captive consumers, which they could not have done if cheaper power were wheeled in (short of a special surcharge in transmission rates). Only a few electrics favored retail competition—trusting the political process to provide stranded-cost recovery during the transition. One such company was Cinergy, headed by Enron-ex Jim Rogers.

What about the captives behind the monopolists? Consumers were not up in arms, much less organized, to champion retail access to gas or to electricity. Households and commercial users were accustomed to their rates and, short of a price spike, valued the personal time and energy that would be spent in switching. (Utilities proactively engaged in public relations for this inertia.) And wasn't commission regulation a substitute for competition, capping rates in the public interest, at least in theory? Still, with retail access in play, the utilities' contributions to Political Action Committees (PACs) tripled in 1995–96 from what it had been in 1994, and they got busier in almost every relevant political jurisdiction. Enron was in for a fight.

Environmentalists were not supportive of a changeover that promised to lower rates and increase consumption, which was the opposite of Amory Lovins's conservationist vision, called *negawatts*, and which was also opposite to utilities' demand-side management (DSM) programs. A Lay favorite otherwise, Christopher Flavin of the Worldwatch Institute called retail wheeling "a nightmare" because it would bring a low-rate ethic to power generators and to consumers, discouraging renewables. Environmentalists would go on to criticize Enron by name, favoring a total-energy-outsourcing approach ("offering energy-efficient light bulbs, water-heater insulation blankets, and tips on reducing energy use") in place of a commodity price war. Such a strategy would, in fact, fall short for Enron, as discussed later in this chapter.

Bootlegger Enron needed a Baptist, a public interest group touting its legislative and regulatory agenda as more than self-interested. "This is about

---

11. See chapter 9, pp. 418–19; and chapter 11, pp. 469–72. FERC would issue discretionary, case-by-case orders to petitions, while beginning the rule-making process to pass generic orders for 166 electric utilities akin to FERC Order No. 436 and FERC Order No. 636 with regard to natural gas. The result was FERC Order No. 888 and FERC Order No. 889, both for electricity in April 1996.

money," stated Don Jordan of Houston Industries (later Reliant, now NRG), the franchised electric utility serving Enron's home. To him, as well as the utility establishment (except for Ken Harrison of Portland General Electric, as discussed below), retail wheeling was a zero-sum game between the utility and the interlopers, without meaningful gains in economic efficiency.

There certainly could be net efficiency gains for consumers from a competitive industry restructuring, whether or not the captives were assigned a (transmission) rate surcharge to cover the utility's stranded costs. And that case for reform was put into play by the most progressive state utility commission in the nation.

A California Proposal. In response to a deep recession in his state, Governor Pete Wilson instructed the California Public Utilities Commission (CPUC) to address electricity rates, which were substantially above the national average. In April 1994, the CPUC proposed a regulatory restructuring that included "direct access" (retail wheeling) in a way Jeff Skilling and Ken Lay could have proposed but had scarcely lobbied for.

In response, Enron began a full-court press on both the lobbying and business fronts in its quest to become the nation's foremost provider of electricity (and gas) to households—and to double the size and profitability of the company in five years (Enron 2000). Spurred by Enron, a group of libertarian-leaning think tanks and advocacy groups sided with partial deregulation (of the commodity) and retail competition enabled by a new government intervention: mandated open access (MOA) for the distribution of gas and electricity to final users.[12]

"California's investor-owned utilities currently charge some of the highest prices in the country," the CPUC declared in its historic proposal. "This distressing fact prompts us to explore reasonable alternatives to the current framework." The *Order Instituting Rulemaking and Order Instituting Investigation* continued: "Our express objective is to establish a new framework" in place of the "traditional cost-of-service regulatory model governing vertically integrated, natural monopolies," which would do "a considerably better job of exerting downward pressure on the prices California's residential and business consumers must pay for investor-owned electric services."

California's average rate of 10.3 cents/kWh was *50 percent above the national norm*—and twice that of Oregon to the north. The proposal was to phase in

---

12. Open access was *mandatory*, a government intervention into the market, although the status quo was arguably marked by as much or more government intervention than MOA. True deregulation and free-market competition would void public-utility regulation (not to mention integrated resource planning) and not impose mandates on transmission owners, the utility or otherwise.

access to a different customer class every two years, taking eight years in all, with residentials finally eligible for direct access on the first day of 2002. No disallowance for stranded costs was proposed, and no rate reduction, consumer savings, or economy-wide benefit was forecast. The benefit of direct commodity competition spoke for itself.

The CPUC questioned its own integrated resource-planning approach, admitting that "attempts to predict, plan, or mandate a single electric future for California means more of the same—central planning and micro-management." A competitive, consumer-friendly regulatory regime was sought. Writing from Washington on all the commotion, John Jennrich titled his *Natural Gas Week* Perspectives column, "Creeping Capitalism Slithers Out of California."

The "Blue Book" proposal was a shot heard 'round the country. Stock prices fell by double digits for many electric utilities as investors contemplated whether the vulnerable could recoup their stranded costs, estimated at $150 billion nationally and $30 billion in California alone.[13] EEI assessed its members several million dollars to lobby against the maverick reformers, industrial users (organized as Electricity Consumers Resource Council, or ELCON), and Enron.

"What is taking place in California is analogous to what occurred over the last 10 years in the natural gas industry when the Federal Energy Regulatory Commission mandated open access on all interstate pipelines," Jeff Skilling explained to Enron employees in the wake of the CPUC proposal. Better yet, there would be a "broader impact" with electricity reaching residentials, in contrast to natural gas. With California being a trendsetter for other states, this "end step," Skilling noted, "will create a market three times the size of the one for natural gas."

The historic proposal was *not* deregulation, depoliticization, and cold water for the franchised monopolists. It was a rearrangement of regulation, what one economist called "regulator-imposed alterations in the structure of the industry," under which special interests were still dominant. Utilities wanted full recovery of stranded costs, and environmental groups wanted rate recovery and surcharges for their pet supply- or demand-side programs.

Sure enough, the CPUC's proposal would become more politicized as it made its way into legislation, finally passing as the something-for-everyone Electric Utility Industry Restructuring Act (AB 1890) and signed into law by Governor Wilson in September 1996.

The final legislative and administrative product would be anything but a clean retail-access regime, much less true deregulation, under which providers negotiated with consumers for commodities and services. There would be

---

13. This difference between undepreciated cost and expected revenue (from national retail competition) was estimated to be as low as $20 billion and as high as $300 billion. Moody's estimate was $135 billion.

implementation delays and a half-slave/half-free regime that would result in a full-blown electricity crisis in California several years later. Enron would be central to that story, and not in a good way.[14]

––––––

Enron developed a public-interest rationale for retail electricity competition in-house and through external studies. One approach estimated the savings from other deregulated or restructured industries; another formally modeled the price reductions in an industry where average (monopoly) costs were above the marginal (competitive) costs.

"Since deregulation began in 1984, there have been $83.7 billion in cumulative cost decreases for the natural gas industry," Skilling noted, "[compared] to $65.3 billion in electric cost increases for the same period."[15] Looking ahead, California alone stood to gain nearly $9 billion per year in lower electricity rates, he estimated, "enough money to pay down current debt, to double and triple the number of police officers and teachers in the state's largest cities, and still leave about $1 billion for discretionary purposes." In CPUC hearings, Jeff Skilling supported the Blue Book proposal as "on the right track" and a model "for the rest of the country."[16]

Arguing the Case. The potential consumer saving from retail competition was large, according to two Enron-backed studies. In May 1996, economists from Clemson University estimated that full electricity access would reduce rates by 13 percent near term and 43 percent long term, thanks to cheap new capacity and expanding consumption. These estimates repriced the utility's uneconomic generation to market; stranded-cost recovery was dismissed as "an issue of fairness, not economic efficiency." Such recovery (allowed or not) was outside of variable rates (but in a demand charge).

A press release from Citizens for a Sound Economy (CSE), the study's sponsor, put the annual near-term savings in dollars for maximum political impact.

––––––

14. Enron traders infamously gamed the complex regulations to increase wholesale electricity rates to unsustainable levels, which, coupled with retail price ceilings, caused physical shortages (brownouts) in major areas of the state.

15. This consumer savings of gas over electricity reflected lower wellhead prices and mature wholesale MOA for the former, bringing rates down at retail. Wholesale MOA for power could not be expected to have the same effect at retail, because most utilities generated their own electricity.

16. In March 1995, Enron's first commissioned study (by MIT professor Richard Tabors et al.) concluded that unbundling did not pose reliability problems (given that electricity could not be economically stored); bilateral transactions were feasible in place of centralized dispatch (Poolco, discussed later); and retail MOA could save an estimated $60–$80 billion annually (versus total stranded costs of $200 billion).

The numbers were $216 for households, $2,176 for commercial establishments, and $36,000 for large industrials.

In early 1997, another Enron-organized study, authored by Robert Crandall of the center-left Brookings Institution and Jerry Ellig of the free-market Center for Market Processes (now Mercatus Center) at George Mason University, estimated the consumer savings from other deregulated or restructured "network" industries to find double-digit savings, each growing over time. Airlines, natural gas, railroads, telecommunications, trucking—the analogy was made for electricity.

———

The utilities attracted less interest from think tanks for their agenda. But they found voice in legal scholar and economist J. Gregory Sidak, holder of a chair at the American Enterprise Institute (AEI), a respected old-line, center-right Washington think tank. In articles, books, and testimony, Sidak (along with economist William Baumol) advocated full stranded-cost recovery as a matter of precedent and law (the regulatory contract). The cost recovery that critics on both ends of the political spectrum called a "bailout" reduced most of the consumer savings from retail competition. Sidak frontally challenged the CSE study on these grounds.

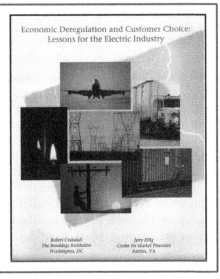

Figure 15.1 Two major studies organized and funded by Enron made a consumer case for retail wheeling of electricity. *Customer Choice, Consumer Value* (left) estimated the reduced cost and prices from MOA; *Economic Deregulation and Customer Choice* (right) estimated the price declines from other industries to suggest the same for electricity.

"I was surprised and extremely disappointed to see the American Enterprise Institute as being represented as a supporter of the lobby in opposition to a recent study by Citizens for a Sound Economy," one board member and donor wrote to AEI president Christopher DeMuth in mid-1996. "Please advise me if AEI's long-held, pro-competition beliefs have changed or been compromised."

In a lengthy response, DeMuth assured Ken Lay that AEI was not in the business of taking institutional positions, and full stranded-cost recovery was a legitimate position for debate. In fact, Enron would come to support stranded-cost recovery so long as the utility was out of the sales function, although this concession certainly reduced the consumer cost savings calculated in the CSE study.

Two new lobby groups in 1996 backed by utilities made a case for slow reform. The Alliance for Competitive Electricity and the Competition Policy Institute argued against federalization of electricity policy. Maximum flexibility, not one-size-fits-all, would best ensure reliability against blackouts or brownouts. Small consumers should be protected in any transition, given that "big dogs eat first" (referring to commercial and industrial users). Just-started natural gas pilot programs should be studied. And most of all, stranded costs should be fully recovered, not written off as a loss (as 25 percent of pipelines' take-or-pay costs had been under FERC regulation).

Federal Action. Enron needed a home run: federal legislation for near-term, date-certain MOA for each investor-owned utility. A few wording changes and new sentences amending Section 211 of the Federal Power Act of 1935 would do the work that otherwise would have to be done, expensively and slowly, state by state.

In early 1996, proposed legislation sponsored by J. Bennett Johnston (D-LA) mandated retail MOA by 2010, while allowing full cost recovery of stranded costs. The EEI bill was followed six months later by the so-called Enron Bill. The Electric Consumers' Power to Choose Act of 1996, introduced by Dan Schaefer (R-CO), set a date of December 15, 2000, a distant date intended to spur the states into action and set the stage for more serious debate in 1997.

"I must admit I'm a skeptic about major federal intervention on this," stated Slade Gorton (R-WA), a member of the Senate Energy and Natural Resources Committee. Federalization violated state rights, something to which conservatives were otherwise partial. But the bigger reason for Gorton was rate equalization in an opened market, under which his state's low-rate power (from hydropower, in particular) would be bid up by high-rate California.

Many more bills would be introduced in the next years, most with date-certain requirements and some with mandates (quotas) for renewable-energy generation (like the Schaefer bill). The Clinton administration's Comprehensive Electricity Competition Plan of 1998 specified a year-2003 opening, full-cost recovery, and a renewables mandate.

Federal MOA for retail would not succeed. That left much to do for Enron's dozens of lobbyists at an expense north of $10 million per year.

The great electricity debate was between the status quo and a new regulatory regime, not true deregulation. "Even the most ardent free-marketers don't suggest a complete pull-out by the government," stated an editorial in the *Wall Street Journal*. But there was one holdout. Although Enron persuaded several free-market think tanks to front the effort and perform studies aligned with MOA (at the time, the job of the present author), the libertarian Cato Institute demurred.

"Mandated access is a bad idea in part because it is a violation of property rights," stated Cato chairman William Niskanen, a noted economist and former acting head of Ronald Reagan's Council of Economic Advisors. "It isn't genuine deregulation." The PhD economist called for an end to rate regulation and legal monopoly, in order to allow distributed generation and new rights-of-way to compete against the franchised utility. Such bypass would avoid stranded-cost recovery too.

Niskanen's interest in the issue was prompted by Cato's director of natural resource studies, Jerry Taylor, who tenaciously fought against MOA by writing and commissioning studies and by participating in policy and lobby forums. He was the free-market skunk at the restructuring party who, over time, neutralized the free-market community by splitting it more toward total deregulation.

———

In March 1996, Ken Lay, Richard Kinder, and Ed Segner announced Enron's push for "a changed regulatory and legislative environment." Assignments followed. "Our success in effecting this change will depend on many individuals throughout ECT and corporate staff, and Terry Thorn will now lead this effort by devoting 100 percent of his time to these very important activities." The senior vice president for public policy reported to Jeff Skilling, leaving federal and state government relations to Segner, Enron's chief of staff.[17] Steve Kean and Kathleen Magruder, both lawyers, would cover California and other states opening markets to retail competition. And Enron's Washington office, led by Joe Hillings and Cynthia Sandherr, were on the job under Thorn's Houston direction.

Enron's pitch was straightforward: Rivalry in place of monopoly—*customer choice*—lowered rates and improved efficiencies. "This is not an Enron issue but a consumer issue," stated Skilling. "This is not an issue of states' rights," he added elsewhere. "It is an issue of individual rights." And on big dogs eat first? "Big dogs have already eaten.... The market needs to be open for the people [residentials] who can't negotiate a deal in a dark room with cigar smoke."

———

17. The same memo announced the hiring of Elizabeth Tilney as senior vice president over marketing and communications. Thorn's job was to achieve retail MOA, Ashok Rao to develop retail products, and Tilney to facilitate sales.

ENRON BUSINESS

ELECTRICITY RULING CLEARS PATH FOR WHOLESALE WHEELING

Figure 15.2 The legal right of Enron to access utility customers (MOA), first at wholesale and then at retail, was the job of Government Affairs. Terry Thorn and Cynthia Sandherr (left) led the Washington, DC, effort. Steve Kean and Kathleen Magruder (right) led the state effort. Top executives (center) were dedicated to the overall electricity effort: Jeff Skilling and Lou Pai (front, left to right) and Mark Frevert, Ken Rice, and Thorn (back, left to right).

"Cheaper electricity means economic growth and job creation," Lay intoned. "For example, a 1 cent/kWh decline in average consumer electricity prices would put an additional $452 per year into the pockets of an American family of four to save, invest, or spend in our economy."

Jeff Skilling regularly presented his case for electricity restructuring. His standard speech produced this quotation on the alleged impracticality of FERC Order No. 436 and the competition it would bring to the natural gas industry. "Given its capital-intensive nature, oligopolistic producing sector, monopolistic and vertically integrated transmission sector, and the exclusive nature of franchises," the American Public Gas Association had stated in 1985, "the industry is a textbook example of an industry that does not lend itself to the discipline of the free market." The point? A decade later, go-slow electric utilities were making the same argument against the practicality of retail wheeling.

Poolco Threat. As a product that could not be economically stored, electricity had to be consumed the moment it was produced. This engineering fact required *centralized dispatch,* coordinating all sources of supply with all demand on the grid. As such, come the restructuring debate, technical economists proposed a system wherein one price would be periodically determined from an aggregate bid process, akin to pricing on the New York Stock Exchange. The generated market-clearing price (occurring every 90 minutes, say) would allow participants to lock in prices via financial contracts ("contracts for differences"). Harvard economist William Hogan tirelessly presented the Poolco model to state and federal authorities for implementation, drawing inspiration from the United Kingdom's pool. Voluntary transactions between generators, marketers, and end users outside the pool were to be prohibited.

The alternative to Poolco was *bilateral contracting*, also called *direct access*, whereby each deal had its own terms, including price, although the electricity would still be centrally dispatched. Enron wanted the higher margins produced by separately negotiated contracts, just as it received for natural gas. Thus, Hogan's model was a policy risk for Enron within a retail-wheeling regime.

After six days of hearings from 140 parties on its Blue Book proposal, the CPUC in May 1995 ruled in favor of Poolco, described as "virtual direct access through a voluntary wholesale pool with retail competition through physical, bilateral contracts." Commissioner Jesse Knight issued a minority opinion, rejecting "a single, mandatory Poolco structure" in favor of "competing networks of commercial arrangements and institutions, with those bringing the greatest value to market participants winning the competition."

Ken Lay disparaged Poolco as a "threat" to customer choice and an "invented market where regulators force all transactions to be centrally dispatched from one regional pool." As a glorified wholesale market where many voluntary transactions were illegal, Lay warned about Poolco becoming the "next regulatory tar baby."

"The free market model, in contrast," Lay explained, "allows unilateral and multilateral contracting according to the market's infinite variety, while retaining central grid control for physical distribution to ensure system integrity." Regarding the grid, not one but rather multiple grid operators and control areas would promote, in the words of Ken Rice, "innovation, experimentation, and competitive adopting of the 'best transmission practice' (particularly if combined with incentives)."

And so, it came to pass that independent marketers and end users favored bilateral transactions, whereas utilities (burdened with uneconomic generation), environmental groups, and FERC welcomed one big market.

Economist Robert Michaels, who in another context was critical of the long-term, fixed-priced contracts that Enron was selling to monopolists, was a key expert against retail centralization. "Poolco is an attempt to do something no government has ever managed to do right—invent a market and force everybody into it to make trades according to rules imposed from above." Elsewhere, Michaels branded the design as "the monopolist's new clothes," suggesting that the utilities' interest in such centralization was to retain "continued retail monopoly with a more elaborate dispatch system."

Branding Enron

Enron was going to the individual home at full scale. The potential market was millions of gas and electricity customers, versus the hundreds of wholesale accounts long served by ECT and ten-thousand-plus commercial accounts arising from Enron's purchase of Access Energy in 1992.[18]

Enron 2000 was predicated on mass retailing to the hitherto captive customers of franchised utilities, a $200 billion market. Under traditional public-utility regulation, ratepayers bought a bundled product (the commodity plus its transportation). Under state-level MOA, Enron and other independents would provide the commodity—the gas and/or the electricity—leaving the utilities to provide the transmission, the so-called *last mile* of pipe or wire.

Enron's goal, as stated in the 1996 annual report, was to "become the largest retailer of electricity and natural gas in the country." Enron's plan to acquire 10 percent of this market, if not more, required a public relations effort far greater than the company's name change (in 1986) and the branding of natural gas as green (in 1989–90). The new challenge was to make Enron, and Ken Lay himself, recognizable at dinner tables.

Edmund P. Segner III, executive vice president and chief of staff, was tasked with expanding Public Affairs, which resulted in the March 1996 hiring of Elizabeth (Beth) Tilney to the new position of senior vice president of marketing, communications, and administration. Five months later, Enron announced its branding campaign with its first-ever daylong media conference.

"Enron Hires an Ad Agency for Campaign: Company Prepares for Move into Retail," a *Houston Chronicle* headline read. Ogilvy & Mather had been retained, a new logo was in the works, and an advertising buy of $30–$50 million was rumored. (Tilney, in fact, had worked at Ogilvy before becoming an executive recruiter for Russell Reynolds, from which she was hired by Enron.[19])

Step-outs in natural gas and electricity branding by other companies had already started. A natural gas marketing alliance between PanEnergy Corp. and Mobil Corp. was using Mobil's Pegasus logo. UtiliCorp's EnergyOne used direct mail and targeted ads to tout its "one-stop store for the customer," which began with the energy commodity but went to appliance repair, security systems, and carbon monoxide detection. NGC (later Dynegy), Southern Company, and Entergy, among others, were experimenting with name recognition.

Enron's branding was different. Eyebrows were raised because Ken Lay and Jeff Skilling's effort was in *anticipation* of a national market. Few retail MOA

---

18. See chapter 9, pp. 399–400.

19. Elizabeth Tilney's husband, Schuyler, an investment banker in the Houston office of Merrill Lynch, became involved with Enron and Andy Fastow beginning in 1998, a relationship that led to controversial financial engineering known as the Nigerian Barge case. Following Enron's collapse, the SEC prosecuted Tilney for fraud in a civil trial, a subject of Book 4.

pilots were under way. California alone had a statewide plan, but that opening was phased, political, and, in terms of profitably for the new independents, highly uncertain.

Yet Enron exuded optimism. The pioneers of natural gas were just going downstream to retail and sideways to electricity. Economies of scope today; economies of scale tomorrow. Enron's leadership in renewable energy, furthermore, would counter the utilities' *green pricing* programs intended to forestall retail competition.[20]

The media was Enron friendly. Why should Enron, *Fortune's* "most innovative" company, not get the benefit of the doubt? Enron could be "extraordinarily successful," one marketing expert stated. "In a market where there is no national brand, being the first one out is going to be important," another source told *Natural Gas Week*. "It is always harder to play catch-up." And in the august *New York Times*, Allen Myerson favorably described a company on its way to an annual ad buy of $200 million to create, in Ken Lay's words, "an AT&T for the electricity business."

But Enron's "Big Enchilada" depended on the political will of states to implement MOA—and getting those rules just right to overcome entrenched utilities. Enron's marketing, in fact, was intended to raise the political will. If regulators and voters knew and liked Enron, as well as Ken Lay, Mr. Enron, the incumbency advantage of utilities could be overcome. The aforementioned *Times* article by Myerson was clear on this.

There was a residual benefit too. "People saying 'Enron is getting out in front'," noted a marketing professor, "certainly doesn't hurt a stock." And ENE needed a tailwind. A yearlong dip in Enron's stock price (the company's underlying problems remained) had made Enron a potential takeover target in 1997.

The year of the brand at Enron was 1997. On January 4, a new logo, designed by the iconic Paul Rand, was ceremoniously unveiled for Enron employees. Rand's angled E, called the "Big E" by Beth Tilney, came with the trademarked tag line: *Natural gas. Electricity. Endless possibilities.*[21] The work, actually, had been done by Conquest, a sister company to Ogilvy & Mather, because of the latter's account with Shell.

There was one surprise, reminiscent of the aborted effort to rename HNG/InterNorth as Enteron. When photocopied or faxed, the tilted *E* (with its three

---

20. As an alternative to a costly, difficult generator-to-meter tracking scheme for each electron, Enron proposed a "green tags" program whereby the characteristics of the source generator for each kWh of eligible renewable generation could be separately traded from the electrons themselves. *Green tags* was the conceptual basis of what would become renewable energy credits (RECs).

21. Enron's logo, which became known as the "crooked E" after the company's collapse, was Rand's last logo project before his death in 1996 at age 82.

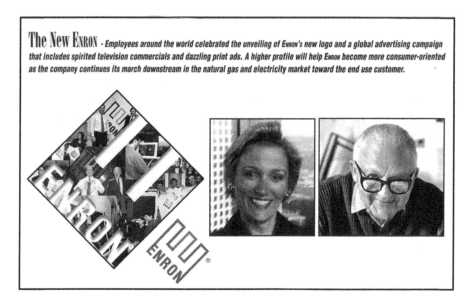

The New ENRON - *Employees around the world celebrated the unveiling of ENRON's new logo and a global advertising campaign that includes spirited television commercials and dazzling print ads. A higher profile will help ENRON become more consumer-oriented as the company continues its march downstream in the natural gas and electricity market toward the end use customer.*

Figure 15.3 Enron's branding, led by Beth Tilney (center), was highlighted by a new logo designed by Paul Rand (right). The unveiling of the New Enron in early 1997 was a company-wide celebration to get employees to take the effort to family and friends.

prongs in red, yellow, and blue) had a color missing (it turned white). The middle color was the problem. The easy solution (and the obvious one, in retrospect) was substituting green for yellow.

This mistake required a redo of marketing materials, from banners to brochures to letterhead, at a six-figure cost. But with that problem solved, advertising was purchased, and none more celebrated than 30-second airings in selected cities as part of Super Bowl XXXI, on January 26, 1997.

It was now time to, in the words of Ed Segner, "enhance the company's image the world over." An Internet Home Page was created to link Enron with customers, investors, and other constituencies. In Houston—company headquarters, the fourth-largest city in America, and the energy capital of the world—every employee was summoned to represent Enron "with integrity and respect for others in mind … in all of our activities."

New banners adorned the lobby at 1400 Smith Street. "The Wisdom of Open Markets" and "Being a Laboratory of Innovation" were among the "What We Believe" posters. Catch phrases included "At Enron, we're up to the challenge … down to the very last detail" and "they're not only talking energy, they're talking Enron." Words and phrases had never been so important at Enron, which was saying a lot.

———

Ed Segner had hired Beth Tilney to lead Enron's branding effort, and Tilney, in turn, approached Cindy Olson to take over Community Affairs, whose activities would be "a critical component in building Enron's brand." This department had been under Nancy McNeil in Ken Lay's office, but McNeil was leaving the company alongside her soon-to-be husband, Rich Kinder.

Cindy Olson (no relation to John Olson, the financial analyst) had just signed a three-year agreement to reconfigure the noncommercial ("back office") side of ECT's wholesale trading operation in order to prepare for retailing, with as many as *six million* customers envisioned. Olson was detail-oriented, creative, and personable enough to take on a task encompassing gas accounting, contract administration, financial accounting, and risk management. Annual cost reductions in the $20–$30 million range were promised from "all processes, systems, and headcount being reworked." It was an important job, to say the least.

Olson was not sure about the new opportunity. ECT was a core profit maker; this outreach work was mostly fluff, she thought. But a visit with Ken Lay sold her. "He wanted to have community relations basically re-engineered," she remembered. That meant leveraging Enron's charitable giving in new ways to maximize goodwill and publicity. And it meant creatively engaging Enron's thousands of employees, particularly in Houston and in Portland.

Every employee was a walking Enron, as well as an ENE holder. Each had a home life and a social life. Beginning in May 1997, the company magazine was sent to the home rather than distributed at work. "I hope you enjoy receiving your *Enron Business* at home," Ken Lay wrote. "We're doing it because we believe it's important that our families know and understand our business and community activities so they can support and share in Enron's success."

Community Affairs launched Enron Envolved to engage employees in benefits for the Downtown YMCA, Juvenile Diabetes, Ronald McDonald House, United Way, and other local organizations. Activities in Portland, home of PGE, were also emphasized, as were some events in Calgary, home of ECT–Canada. Ad hoc opportunities were pursued, such as Enron's hosting the Women's Leadership Conference in Houston in October 1996. "This is an exciting time for us because one of Enron's ultimate goals is to enhance its image as a responsible corporate citizen and increase visibility in communities where the company operates," Cindy Olson explained in *Enron Business*.

Community Affairs had a political side too. Much work was required to engineer a come-from-behind victory for a taxpayer-financed sports stadium in 1996, a key part of Enron's branding effort. Olson would work on all things stadium related, including fulfilling the construction-phase minority set-aside pledge that had been crucial in the referendum's victory, explained below.

Enron's branding aspirations were global, not just regional and national. "In my community role, I was also responsible for helping Ken with many of the efforts he got involved in around the world to promote Houston," Olson remembered. Ken Lay "firmly believed that if Houston was viewed as a world-class city, then we could attract the world-class talent we needed to work at Enron." Among other things, she traveled to Tokyo for economic-development meetings that Lay cochaired between the two cities through the Greater Houston Partnership.

Olson's time as vice president of community affairs was "the most fun I had ever had at Enron." Big budgets and over-the-top events were all in the name of a company on the upswing. "Our community programs were generating nearly $15 million in earned media or free media for Enron every year," she remembered about the heyday. (The party would quickly end in the second half of 2001.)

———

Ken Lay was graduating from Great Man of Energy to Great Man of Business. Enron's CEO was named one of *BusinessWeek's* top 25 managers of 1996—and one to watch in 1997. "Kenneth L. Lay has built Enron from a small pipeline company into the first natural gas major to rival oil giants in vertical integration and global breadth," the cover story read. And now "Lay is pushing abroad and barreling into the $200 billion electricity market at home with a $3.2 billion bid for utility Portland General."

Lay had won over the Clinton administration several years before by Enron's embrace of the global-warming issue.[22] Enron's new pitch concerned the benefits of retail competition, which "spoke directly to Ken Lay's missionary instincts." Enron's Great Man just needed positioning to join the greats of business, politics, and academia.

In the mid-1990s, the company set up an endowment at Rice University's James A. Baker III Institute for Public Policy to award the Enron Prize for Distinguished Public Service. The first recipient, retired general Colin Powell, would be joined by other major figures to raise the profile of Enron and Ken Lay in particular.[23] In the same period, The Houston Forum inaugurated the Kenneth L. Lay Lecture Series to feature nationally known PhD economists to local audiences.[24]

Ken Lay's commoner story, drawing from his modest beginnings in rural Missouri, was the basis for induction into the Horatio Alger Association. His 1998 admittance was preceded by much fanfare. "Enron Chairman and CEO Kenneth L. Lay Named to Horatio Alger Association of Distinguished

———

22. See chapter 7, pp. 338–40; and chapter 13, pp. 553–59.

23. The periodic award would also be given to Mikhail Gorbachev (1998), Eduard Shevardnadze (early in 1999), Nelson Mandela (late in 1999), and Alan Greenspan (2001).

24. Speakers included Senator Phil Gramm; Harvard economist Robert Barro; the former chairman of George W. Bush's Council of Economic Advisors Glenn Hubbard; and resource economist Julian Simon.

ENRON BUSINESS

PRESTIGIOUS ENRON PRIZE DRAWS SOME OF CENTURY'S GREAT STATESMEN TO HOUSTON

Figure 15.4 Situating Ken Lay as a world figure, part of Enron's branding effort, included extracurricular activities, such as establishing the Enron Prize for Distinguished Public Service, awarded at the Baker Institute at Rice University. The second recipient, Mikhail Gorbachev, attracted a Who's Who of American statesmen, such as Henry Kissinger and James Baker, both of whom consulted for Enron.

Americans. Award Recognizes a Lifetime of Achievement and Community Service," a November 1997 press release from the company was headlined.[25]

The son of a lay Baptist minister, Ken Lay always had a religious streak. This card was played when Lay told his story onstage at Robert Schuller's "Hour of Power" at the Crystal Cathedral in Garden Grove, California, a program broadcast in a number of foreign countries where Enron was active.

Lay's growing public appearances necessitated a speechwriter, which led Ed Segner to hire the present writer into corporate affairs in mid-1995. Industry events, public policy conferences, and business schools were common venues. A highlight was the annual World Economic Forum in Davos, Switzerland, where Enron's CEO participated in numerous panels with world-class business, government, and nonprofit leaders. In Enron's final year of solvency, Lay was involved in five presentations at Davos.

---

25. Ken Lay was scheduled to chair the association's 2002 events until Enron's collapse, after which his name was removed from the association's website.

The Road to Enron Field

How could Enron brand itself nationally? For a newcomer, obtaining the naming rights to a sports stadium was ideal. An ambitious electric utility based in Cincinnati, Ohio, did just this, with Riverfront Stadium becoming Cinergy Field in 1996. Former Enron executive Jim Rogers, a Lay protégé, was the decision maker there.

But Houston had a professional sports problem. Its National Football League franchise was abandoning the 30-year-old Astrodome for a new taxpayer-subsidized stadium in Nashville, Tennessee. Baseball's Houston Astros wanted out from the Dome too. The NBA Houston Rockets, in another aging facility (The Summit), might well follow in a few years.

With Houston and Harris Country budgets tight, taxpayer-backed bonds would be necessary to build any new stadium, much less three. Voters would have to approve such borrowing. But the idea of average citizens subsidizing wealthy owners and rich players was unpopular, particularly on the heels of the 1994–95 Major League Baseball (MLB) strike and the lackluster performance of the Astros. MLB was the least supported of the three major sports in Houston. Another problem: Not knowing what stadium might be built, the various professional teams were not unified for the referendum.

Informal polling said that Houstonians would defeat a public funding measure. Indeed, voters had rejected a $390 million school bond only six months before.

Facing few good options, Houston's popular mayor, Bob Lanier, had gone to Washington to explore the strategy of lobbying Congress to repeal the antitrust exemption for major league sports in order to increase the number of franchises. Lanier even lined up counsel to sue the National Football League (NFL) for triple damages for the cost of the lost franchise.

Enron had its eye on naming rights. Houston was the logical place.[26] A new stadium situated downtown could revitalize the area and be an easy outing for Enron employees on business or pleasure. The best and brightest that Enron was recruiting from elite business schools would embrace downtown living and nearby recreation. New York City, Chicago, San Francisco, and other top destinations for financial professionals had what Houston was in the process of losing.

Lanier was negotiating with Astros owner Drayton McLane Jr. to keep the team under a new long-term contract. Other markets, led by Washington, DC, were poised to erect a new stadium for McLane on terms that Lanier felt Houston voters would not match. "When the deal looked like it was about to slide

---

26. Enron also looked at naming rights for the new stadium to replace Candlestick Park in San Francisco, what became Pacific Bell Park, now AT&T Park. California was at the center of energy retailing, making this option of interest for Enron.

away," recalled Lanier, "Ken Lay came in." At midsummer, with the vote in November, it was now or never—or the Astros would likely go the way of the NFL Houston Oilers (soon to be Tennessee Titans).

Lay took on the task of closing the gap between what the city and county were willing to give and what the Astros wanted, as well as raising the money to finance a winnable referendum campaign. The amount that voters needed to approve was estimated at $180 million of the $300 million total, but the language on the ballot would be just for the *authority* to levy taxes to get the needed amount. With property taxes taken off the table for the referendum to be passable, the burden would fall on hotels and rental cars, aka visitor taxes, which would require a last step of approval from the Texas Legislature.[27]

When head of the Greater Houston Partnership, Ken Lay had impressed city officials. "He was a leader in the business community," Lanier remembered. "People would follow him." Optimism crept in. "I could sense we would move from leaving the deal to making the deal," Houston's mayor recalled. But Lay had one condition: The new stadium would be downtown, not near the Astrodome eight miles away.

———

After meetings to assess the situation, Lay spearheaded the formation of the Houston Sports Facility Partnership to provide a $35 million interest-free loan without any repayment until 10 years after the stadium opened. But in the fine print, what the media described as a "contribution" had the benefits of repayment with interest, purchase and leaseback rights to the stadium land, and first rights "to provide goods, services, advertising and naming rights to the new facility at competitive prices and terms." Announced in August, Enron was 1 of 14 companies to contribute. (The final draw would be $33 million, almost 12 percent of the total estimated cost of $265 million.)

Enron Community Affairs poured resources into the effort. Lay solicited Enron's vendors. About $1.4 million was raised, plus in-kind services, to mount an all-out election campaign.[28]

"Bringing world-class professional sports facilities to downtown Houston is one of the great opportunities that Houstonians have been thinking and talking about for quite some time," Enron's CEO editorialized in a *Houston Chronicle* piece, "Downtown's a Natural for Sports Arenas." Other notables who would

———

27. The language of Proposition 1 was as follows: "Authorizing Harris County to establish and operate new or renovated stadiums, arenas, and other facilities for professional baseball and football teams, provided that no county real or personal property taxes are spent to acquire, construct, or equip such facilities."

28. Enron directly gave $100,000, as did Compaq Computers, where Lay was a director. Shell (which was close to the new stadium) and the Houston Rockets also gave that amount. Arthur Andersen, under Enron's thumb, gave $25,000.

be the public face of the campaign were legendary Astros pitcher Nolan Ryan and George H. W. Bush. (Son George, now governor of Texas, stayed above the fray.[29]) Opposition came from a small pro-taxpayer group, the Houston Property Rights Association, led by Barry Klein, as well as influential local radio host Dan Patrick (later to become lieutenant governor of Texas).

"It's not just about sports. It's about the future of our community," a one-page flyer for Proposition 1 read. The pitch was about jobs ("retain or produce thousands of jobs"); no property taxes ("paid for by the team, private business, tourists, and the stadium users—not Harris County property taxpayers"); and downtown revitalization ("reinvigorating business, shopping, entertainment, and residential housing"). And passage would mean a done deal, with McLane and the Astros agreeing to a 30-year commitment to stay in Houston, as well as a chance for the city to win a new NFL franchise.

With just weeks to go, polling indicated that Proposition 1 was heading to defeat. The answer was an eleventh-hour strategy of increasing the minority set-aside so that black pastors, led by William Lawson of Wheeler Avenue Baptist Church, would preach Yes. Going above the regular 20 percent target for local public projects (which was not a legal requirement), Lay and McLane promised 30 percent, stating that their businesses would otherwise true up their pledge if the stadium work fell short. "So that kind of formalized it," remembered Lanier.

"Local Black Leaders Agree to Support Stadium Plan," a *Chronicle* headline read just days before the election. Another article the same day reported polling indicating defeat for the referendum. But a Sunday morning push was planned for the pews, and Hispanics and Asians were courted too.

A memo went to all Enron's Houston-based employees the day before the vote. "Proposition 1 is about more than just keeping the Astros in Houston," Ken Lay wrote. "It's about revitalizing downtown and making our central business district a popular destination for not only those of us who work here, but also for everyone in the areas, as has been proven by other cities around the country when new stadiums have been built." The Astros were ready to leave town, it was noted, having received "a deal in another city which is much more lucrative than the one proposed to keep them in Houston." Lay closed: "I hope you vote for the last item on the ballot—Proposition 1."

———

Proposition 1 passed—narrowly. With 51.1 percent for and 48.9 percent opposed, 16,400 votes made the difference. Mayor Lanier recalled Senator

———

29. George W. Bush had baseball baggage: In 1989, he led an investment group that purchased the Dallas-area Texas Rangers, after which a $193 million taxpayer-supported stadium—aided by an eminent-domain seizure—was completed in 1993.

John Kennedy's (1958) quip that his father was "willing to pay for a victory but not a landslide."

The come-from-behind victory needed everything: a 10-to-1 spending advantage, public figure support, relentless editorializing by the *Houston Chronicle* (the sports section sold many papers), and the minority set-aside sweetener in the home stretch. The Greater Houston Partnership was also all-hands-on-deck.

"The proposition pulled ahead as affluent and low-income residents inside the city countered middle-class suburban voters opposed to the proposition," the *Houston Chronicle* reported, adding: "Astros owner Drayton McLane Jr., who last Friday announced an affirmative action program to help minority contractors gain work at a proposed ballpark, thanked all supporters and especially minority voters for the win."

Ken Lay was pleased. "I want to thank all of you who voted for Proposition 1 in Tuesday's election," he wrote to employees.

> This was the first and very significant step toward building a new downtown baseball stadium and renovating the Astrodome for a new professional football franchise .... Had the proposition failed, it could have been years, and perhaps decades, before Houston would have had professional baseball and football teams again.[30]

"The baseball stadium passed in large part thanks to the African-American vote, and Ken's and Drayton's commitment to diversity," remembered Cindy Olson. "Ken called on three of his friends in the African-American community to help." They were Howard Jefferson, president of the Houston NAACP; Bill Lawson, who would be a rare public defender of Lay after Enron's fall; and Al Green, a Houston judge who would go on to become a US congressman.

Olson enforced the 30 percent target on the major contractor (Haliburton), which was trying to keep costs within budget. Enron significantly increased its own minority spending under her leadership, going from under 1 percent to 30 percent in 18 months, according to Olson.

Lay would be present for downtown baseball's groundbreaking in October 1997. The Ballpark at Union Station was renamed Enron Field in April 1999 under a 30-year, $100 million contract. In short order, newly formed Enron Energy Services announced a 30-year, $200 million energy contract to provide the gas and electricity, as well as heating, ventilation, and air conditioning

---

30. Taxpayer-subsidized stadiums in Houston next required a battle in the Texas legislature in Austin, which put Enron back in full advocacy mode. A downtown rally in May 1997 prompted a memo from Lay: "Enron employees are encouraged ... to rally for stadium legislation."

services, for the new $265 million retractable-roof stadium.[31] And Ken Lay would throw out the first pitch on opening day, April 7, 2000, a highlight of his life.

Figure 15.5 Enron Field was the capstone of Enron's national branding effort. The political fight to get new taxpayer-funded sports stadiums in Houston, shouldered by Ken Lay and Enron, was a come-from-behind victory. Beth Tilney (lower left), shaking hands with Astros owner Drayton McLane, was helped by Cindy Olson (center).

"Enron now joined dozens of companies that had their names on sports arenas, such as Qualcomm Stadium, Continental Airlines Arena, and Coors Field," noted author Loren Fox. The Enron logo was on tens of thousands of baseballs, caps, and bats, a nice accoutrement in many offices at 1400 Smith Street. Employees enjoyed their special access ("a lot of employees secured favorable seats at the field"), and staffers actually threw out the first pitch and sang the national anthem at games. Enron *was* a fun place to work. It would be a fun year and a

---

31. "We'll do what we do best, which is manage energy and facilities," Lay told reporters. "And we'll let the Astros do what they do best, which is winning baseball games."

half, ending when Enron's problems led McLane's Astros to buy naming rights back from Enron in 2002.[32]

The November 1996 affirmation led to a second vote to complete the three-stadium building plan: $286 million for baseball (Astros), $252 million for basketball (Rockets), and $500 million for football (Texans). "Few places have venues to match the billion-dollar collection of Minute Maid Park [formerly Enron Field], Reliant Stadium [now NRG Stadium], and the Toyota Center," the *Houston Chronicle* later noted.

Where did the public money come from? It was not property taxes but an increase in the hotel tax from 2 percent to 17 percent and a new 5 percent car rental tax. Ken Lay and Enron's decisive effort resulted in not only three stadiums but also the highest hotel tax rate in the country and a jolting car rental fee at the airports.

The Lay-Enron connection with Houston professional sports went beyond politics. In 1999, Bob McNair sold Cogen Technologies to Enron for $1.1 billion in Enron stock (and assumption of debt). Cashing out of ENE, he was ready to fund a National Football League franchise for Houston in 2001. (McNair's winning NFL bid was $700 million.) The next year, a new stadium next to the Astrodome brought the NFL back to Houston.

A third new stadium for the National Basketball Association's Houston Rockets followed a more complicated script.[33] A fourth facility, BBVA Compass Stadium, did not require voter approval. Built with city and county funding, the home for the Houston Dynamo soccer club broke ground in 2011 and opened the next year. Except for professional hockey (as in Dallas to the north), Houston was a professional sports town shaped by Ken Lay in the mid-1990s.

——

"We're just trying to do what is best for the city," Ken Lay told the *Houston Chronicle* as the vote neared. But what was good for Houston (Enron's headquarters) was good for Enron, for branding, for recruiting, and for employee morale. "Enron needs to have its headquarters in a world class city," Lay stated right after Enron Field opened four years later. "All world class cities have one thing in common: a world class downtown district, with an abundance of business and entertainment."

———

32. After Enron's bankruptcy, the Astros bought the naming rights back for $2.1 million to "start the season fresh," stated McLane. The briefly renamed Astros Field became Minute Maid Park in 2002 under similar terms as before: $100 million for 30 years. (Minute Maid was owned by the Coca-Cola Company.)

33. Originally rejected at referendum in 1999, a reworked deal was approved by voters in 2000. The Toyota Center opened in 2007.

The revitalization of downtown and Enron Field was a boon for Enron's cutting-edge recruitment. "It has been amazing," Enron recruiter Billy Lemmons stated in the summer of 2001. "Tomorrow afternoon, for example, I am taking a group of Analysts and Associates to a businessman's special, as they call it, for the afternoon game at 3:00." In addition, "We have a huge number of people in our program that are moving into these new condominiums and townhomes being developed around the perimeter of downtown." He added: "Some of them are walking to work now."

Indeed, "the house that Lay built" was a major factor in $1.6 billion in new downtown construction, with another billion dollars in projects under way or planned. Enron's gain was "much more than a management contract or marketing opportunity," an *Enron Business* retrospective stressed. "It is a chance to give something back to the community, and community efforts and charitable contributions are an important part of Enron's culture." Public purpose, private purpose: for Enron, it was one.

Acquiring Portland General Electric

Enron knew electricity as a cogenerator and as a marketer of natural gas to power plants. But Enron Capital & Trade Resources was well outside the fraternity represented by the Edison Electric Institute. Enron did not own transmission lines or have firm transmission contracts. Enron was not federally certified to buy or sell power—and certainly did not hold a franchise to deliver electricity at the local distribution level.

Still, Enron knew where it wanted to go. Mandated open access had helped to build the company on the natural gas side, and the same model awaited electricity with a change in federal and state law to enable, respectively, wholesale and retail marketing. Ken Lay's lobbying strength, in fact, got the ball rolling with Section 721 of the Energy Policy Act of 1992, which instructed FERC to issue wholesale transmission orders to parties seeking access to utility systems.[34]

Enron Power Marketing (EPM), formed in 1993, began buying and selling electricity the next year. But wholesale deals did not begin to bring in the margins that covered the start-up expenses of marketers, lobbyists, and public affairs specialists, not to mention support systems. A major scale-up was needed.

Skilling's original strategy was to confederate geographically dispersed utilities where, for a split of profits, Enron would market in each member's service area. EPM head Ken Rice pitched the North American Power Consortium (Power Con) idea to 25 or so companies and was able to meet with about 10. Those meetings were polite but tense; Enron was seen more as a threat than as

---

34. See p. 590; see also the Introduction, p. 44; and chapter 9, p. 415.

a business partner. Not one was interested, much less the six or so that Skilling wanted. It would take a special utility in the right locale with special incentive to get Enron into the electricity club, or at least to get, in Skilling's words, its "Good Housekeeping Seal of Approval."

___

PacifiCorp, based in Salt Lake City, was Enron's first target. Discussions collapsed, and Rice, along with merger and acquisitions specialist Cliff Baxter, focused on a smaller target, Portland General Electric.

PGE, which served most of Oregon, had prepared for the new regulatory environment. CEO Ken Harrison did not protest retail competition; his was a low-cost provider with a diverse resource mix, including hydropower. Having addressed cost recovery for its troubled Trojan Nuclear Plant, PGE was about to increase its dividend for the first time since 1986. Harrison was a director of the Edison Electric Institute too.

PGE described itself as "ahead of the industry in implementing strategies that bridge the old world of regulation and the new world of competition." Specifically, PGE was ahead of other electric utilities (but not Enron) when it came to trading. Because it employed a strategy of "staying short" on generation—that is, buying power at wholesale and limiting the amount of power it generated—PGE had a "fully integrated energy trading operations" tapping into the surplus western US power-generation market.

Thus, PGE was a premier wholesale power marketer in a premier market. In 1996, one of two delivery points chosen for electricity futures by the New York Mercantile Exchange (NYMEX) was a PGE interconnect at the California-Oregon border. The company's transmission accessed California, which had set rules for retail MOA. PGE's marketing push was not only for its 3,170-square-mile service territory but also in neighboring Oregon markets and in California.

More than electricity, PGE began selling home-safety products. For commercial and industrial users, PGE developed "a portfolio of energy and utility management services," including real-time pricing and storage, "to help manage power use and ultimately lower costs." Pilot programs were being introduced for residential users, offering new pricing and service options in anticipation of retail competition.

In mid-1994, Enron and PGE met. Serious discussions resumed in early 1996, whereupon the parties realized that the only path forward was a merger, not a complicated and possibly unworkable legal agreement, reminiscent of the ill-fated Enron–Bankers Trust partnership five years before.[35]

Enron offered PGE shareholders a 25 percent premium through a tax-free PGN-for-ENE exchange, fairly standard. PGE held out and got "an extraordinary

___

35. See chapter 8, pp. 367–68.

48 percent premium for shareholders," with a straight one-to-one swap of shares. This rich price for a set of highly regulated assets would result in a lower debt ratio for the combined company and help earnings too, Enron explained in an 18-page press release announcing the agreement, dated July 22, 1996. A ratings upgrade was even mentioned in the press.

The $3.2 billion acquisition, pending regulatory review, created a $12.5 billion gas and electric company "to provide integrated energy solutions for wholesale and retail natural gas and electricity customers in North America and internationally." The "strategic, not defensive" merger would not result in job losses, management changes, or a headquarters shift. The synergy was between Enron's *marketing* capabilities (national reach, risk management, and future branding) and PGE's *physical* delivery capabilities (generation; transmission; and metering, billing, and auditing for 658,000 retail customers).

The principal negotiators explained the rationale of Enron's gas-to-electric diversification. "At the retail level, our vision is to become the leading national brand-name total energy provider," Cliff Baxter of Enron stated. "Almost every other utility merger in the country has been about cost reductions, increased efficiency, and employee layoffs," stated Joe Hirko of PGE. "I think this is the first merger in this industry that is entirely focused on opportunity, strategic positions, and building markets."

Ken Lay was thinking bigger. "By leveraging the operating and engineering expertise of Portland General with Enron's worldwide asset base and experience, we will be able to expand domestic and international activities across multiple fuel lines, including gas, oil, coal, hydro, and renewables." PGE's Ken Harrison agreed. "This is going to be the most uniquely positioned company in our industry, period," he stated. "There is no one that will look like us or have the skills that we have."

"Overall, there will be a lot of rethinking as to what the competitive framework in this industry is going to be over the next two to three years," Lay told the press. He forecast more deals in which gas and electricity converged, as well as a quicker MOA for the $200 billion downstream electricity market. "They all want to be the Enron of the electric business," Lay stated in a hubristic moment. "But we're going to be the Enron of the electricity business."

July 22, 1996, was "a day that will be remembered as a new chapter in energy history," *Enron Business* stated. Ken Lay was quoted: "Just as coal was the primary energy source of the 19th century, and oil was the primary fuel of the 20th century, we believe natural gas and electricity will converge as the primary sources of energy in North America and many other markets around the world for the 21st century." For Enron investors, the article noted, the acquisition was "an outstanding opportunity for us to create the leading energy company of the future in the North American energy markets."

The buzz was all positive about a combination that remade Enron as the seventh-largest electric company (in kWh sales), ahead of hometown Houston Lighting & Power and even Southern California Edison. The merger was a "breakthrough," reported *Natural Gas Week*. "One plus one equals three," stated investment analyst Ron Barone of Paine Webber. For the industry, this was "the model for future [energy] combinations," reported the *Houston Chronicle*. "Once again, Enron is on the leading edge of the new world," stated another investment analyst in *Gas Daily*.

Other mergers in the period would give rise to the theory of a gas-electricity convergence.[36] But was there really a discontinuous jump in an MOA world? Electricity, after all, was a very different industry from natural gas. A plenty smart economist, seeing neither synergies nor scale economies, Robert Michaels, was saying *no*.

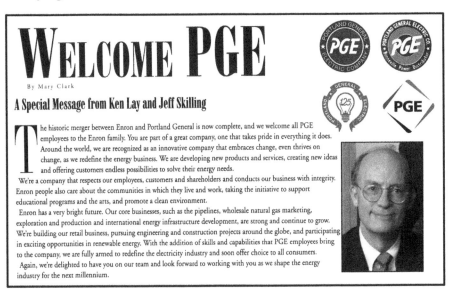

Figure 15.6 Enron heralded a new era of energy convergence in the energy industry by acquiring Portland General Electric in 1997. PGE's low-cost resource mix and open-mindedness toward retail wheeling were major attractions in the merger. Ken Harrison (right), CEO of PGE, became vice chairman of Enron.

———

The merger was *not* greeted enthusiastically by Enron investors. While PGN rose one-fourth to $28.125, ENE fell 5 percent to $39.75. It was reminiscent of the purchase of HNG by InterNorth back in 1985 when John Olson quipped: "It looks like a great business combination until you get to the terms."

———

36. In addition to Texas Utilities Company buying Enserch Corporation (April 1996: $1.7 billion), these included (right after Enron's announcement) Chevron buying a quarter interest in NGC (Dynegy) in August 1996; Houston Industries acquiring NorAm Energy Services (August 1996: $3.8 billion); and Duke Power acquiring PanEnergy (November 1996: $7.4 billion).

One concern was the role of the Oregon Public Utility Commission (OPUC) in trying to capture for ratepayers synergistic profits that otherwise would accrue to shareholders. The "pro-competition" merger would not create issues for the SEC, FERC, or the antitrust division of the Department of Justice. But OPUC's approval process could exploit Enron's eagerness to close the deal; after all, Oregon was not particularly friendly to business, much less to an interloper from Texas.

From the beginning, Enron stressed the consumer benefits for PGE, as well as each company's "strong traditions of active community involvement and support for a healthy environment." Enron's filing before OPUC in September 1996 included philanthropy of $10 million from each side, $20 million total. Still, opposition poured in from electric utilities in the Northwest and in California, civic groups, and environmental organizations.

OPUC set 23 conditions for approval.

Ken Lay and Jeff Skilling had more work to do to avoid an embarrassment. Doling out "a robust assortment" of benefits, Enron reached a memorandum of understanding with 13 civic and environmental groups (one, the Northwest Conservation Act Coalition, was an alliance of 80 subgroups). One provision of the understanding redounded to Enron's considerable benefit, however: a commitment by PGE to support 25 MW of wind power was a set-up for the just-purchased Zond Corporation (soon to be renamed Enron Wind Corporation).

The January 1997 agreement was hailed by Ralph Cavanagh, senior attorney with the Natural Resources Defense Council, as "a model for the industry as it evolves to greater competition." Cavanagh testified glowingly for the merger, citing Ken Lay's leadership on the climate-action and the renewable-energy fronts, including his ability to get Republican support for the environmentalists.[37]

Regarding a rate reduction for captive customers, the bidding began at a rate freeze from Enron versus a rate reduction of $190 million from OPUC, which Enron calculated to have a net present value of $141 million. OPUC staff held the cards, and the nonnegotiable offer led the merger partners to change their deal. A swap of 0.9825 ENE for PGN was favorably greeted by both companies' investors. OPUC approved the merger on June 4, the last such obstacle. (FERC had given expedited approval back in February.)

Effective July 1, 1997, the "stand-alone, fully integrated utility" became Enron's eighth business unit.[38] The acquisition price, with the assumption of

37. See chapter 7, pp. 332–34, 339.

38. PGE joined Enron Oil & Gas, Gas Pipeline Group, Enron Ventures (Engineering & Construction, Clean Fuels, EOTT), Enron Capital & Trade Resources, Enron International, Enron Global Power & Pipelines, and Enron Renewable Energy. Six months later, the business count had increased to 10, with the addition of Enron Energy Services, Enron Europe, and Enron Communications (split from PGE), and the subtraction of Enron Global Power & Pipelines.

$1.1 billion of debt, was just under $3 billion, a 42 percent premium for PGN in premerger terms.

"Welcome PGE," read the lead in *Enron Business*. "We're a company that respects our employees, customers, and shareholders and conducts our business with integrity," stated Ken Lay and Jeff Skilling. "Enron people also care about the communities in which they live and work, taking the initiative to support educational programs and the arts, and promote a clean environment." Lay and Skilling closed: "Again, we're delighted to have you on our team and look forward to working with you as we shape the energy industry in the next millennium."

A June 30 celebration at the Rose Garden Arena in Portland sported pennants, noisemakers, and prizes dropped from the sky. Big screens from Enron offices around the world welcomed PGE's 4,000. "We have created the single most strategically positioned energy company in the country, if not the world," said PGE's CEO—and new Enron vice chairman—Ken Harrison. "I firmly believe that three or four years from now, we will have people who are on career paths that were never dreamed or even conceived of years ago." (He could not have known how perversely true his words would become.)

In December, just five months into the merger, 20 ECT traders relocated to Portland to open Power Trading and Origination (Western Region), joining PGE's own traders. Some PGE employees transferred to Houston, such as Patrick Stupek, who joined Cindy Olson's branding effort as manager of community relations.

Another postmerger highlight was the Customer Choice Introductory Program, which allowed 50,000 PGE customers in four counties to select a new electricity provider as of December 1. With discounts of 10 percent off current rates offered by a dozen or more providers, the program was intended to prove the basic concept before beginning systemwide implementation in 1999. Enron had gladly offered retail wheeling as a part of its OPUC settlement; the idea was to model an "unflinching commitment to the principles of competition" (in Ken Harrison's words), what other utilities needed to do to implement national state-by-state MOA.

———

As it turned out, Enron's "entrée to California's power grid and a copy of the utility industry's secret playbook" was overstated—and increasingly costly. PGE earnings were predictable, nothing more. Other utility executives asked facetiously whether they too could get a 40–50 percent premium. (Enron's original offer of 25 percent was more normal.)

The upsides went away, one by one. With no stop to its regulating, OPUC rejected PGE's plan to spin off its generation units from its regulated (distribution) side. Trading synergies proved limited, with PGE's vaunted trading and transmission access reserved for its regulated side. PGE's subsidiary, FirstPoint

Communications, was not a golden extra but a temptation that would be taken much too far, contributing to Enron's ultimate fate.[39] PGE also created legacy problems for Enron when the Public Utility Holding Company Act of 1935 inspired financial shenanigans by Andy Fastow that would mark Enron's decline.

What was predicted to be either a home run or a long sacrifice fly turned out to be neither. While retaining the wholesale marketing and trading operation, as well as PGE's telecommunications unit, Enron would put the rest of PGE up for sale after two years. Enron not only needed the cash but also wanted to dislodge assets of Enron Wind from Fastow's special-purpose entity (RADR).

An announced sale to Sierra Pacific Power Company for $3.1 billion in 1999 (a $200 million loss) would fall through in the wake of the California and western US power crisis. A second sale announced in Spring 2001 to Northwest Natural Gas Company for $3.0 billion (a $300 million loss) was called off a year later.

At Enron's bankruptcy in December 2001, wholly owned PGE was not included in the parent's filing. But the woes of PGE employees' 401(k) accounts made national news as ENE fell from the $80s to several dollars per share and then to nothing.

(PGE would not separate from Enron until after the parent's bankruptcy. An agreement to be purchased by Texas Pacific Group in November 2003, approved by the bankruptcy court, was turned down by OPUC in April 2005. Still, for accounting purposes, Enron took a $1.8 billion write-off. Finally, a year later, with the 10th anniversary of the merger in sight, PGE would become a standalone company again via a stock distribution to Enron's creditors.)

"Like Dabhol," Malcolm Salter concluded, "the Portland General affair cost Enron shareholders hundreds of millions of dollars." It was errant entrepreneurship from those who thought they knew the most about the future of electricity. The gas-electric convergence for Enron, as for other such combinations, proved elusive. Trading "optionality" and a "spark spread" (Btu comparison of gas versus electricity prices) were more sound bites than economic opportunities, as it would turn out.

Pilot Programs

Enron participated in several pilot programs during 1996–98 to put ideas into action. Not only would Enron learn about selling gas and power to the home, observing state regulators could also decide whether to take MOA statewide. Only California was committed to statewide retail access, so it was important for Enron to show up, be competitive, and inspire wider markets.

---

39. "In their hubris," one account concluded, "Lay, Skilling, and other executives at Enron's broadband unit believed they didn't need to know how the telecom industry really worked."

Enron's major pilot for natural gas was in Toledo, Ohio, beginning March 1997. The other pilots involved electricity. Beginning in May 1996, Enron's national branding effort was focused on Peterborough, New Hampshire. Portland General Electric's program—effective December 1, 1997—found Enron competing against itself as the new owner of PGE. Although not a pilot, Enron's daring proposal in October 1997 to assume the service territory of Pennsylvania's PECO Energy Company for commodity sales created a skirmish that made headlines nationally.

Bellwether California's announced opening inspired Enron's most extensive effort of 1996–97. Southern and Northern California were huge markets, and Enron had a West Coast plan with the acquisition of PGE in mid-1997.

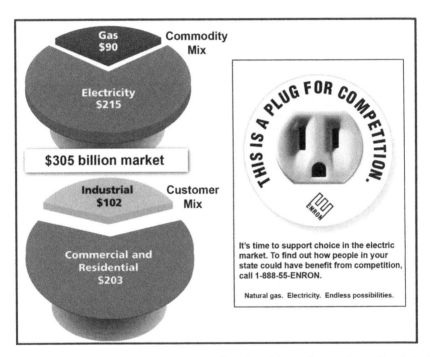

Figure 15.7 Enron's Big Enchilada was retailing electricity and natural gas directly to the home, not only to places of business. The estimated $305 billion market required a simultaneous lobbying and branding effort, which began with pilot programs in several states beginning in 1996.

Enron's early-in, all-in effort, conducted within ECT's consumer division of the Retail Group, was not expected to make money in part or whole. The loss leaders were intended to prove the concept for a growing market in which scale economies could emerge. "Now we are taking the lead in moving for deregulation of the retail electricity and natural gas markets," Ken Lay and Jeff Skilling told investors in the first quarter of 1997, "to become the largest provider of electricity and natural gas in the U.S."

Would enough customers respond to economic incentives to switch from a trusted supplier? Would a national market open rapidly enough to stem the losses? Would the rules be strict enough to neuter the advantage of incumbent utilities? Ken Lay and Jeff Skilling were betting yes all around—and hired a new leader to make it happen.

The new—and fourth—head of Retail Group (following Andy Fastow, Rick Causey, and Ray Bowen) was an experienced outsider. K. Ashok Rao had previously fought against incumbent AT&T with his own start-up, Midcom Communications, formed in 1990. With $250 million in revenues, Midcom was a top-10 long-distance carrier when taken public in 1995.[40]

An engineer by training, Rao had no energy experience when he joined ECT as managing director. But he did not want for enthusiasm and purpose. "Just like [Christopher] Columbus, we've got a vision that has taken us westward, and we've met a few challenges along the way," he told 1,100 employees just months after taking over Enron's residential effort in 1997 as president and COO of Enron Energy Services. "It's our vision that unites and drives us as we forge ahead to open up a new world of competition where every consumer has a choice."

Rao said all the right things. "We have to pay attention to a thousand details," he explained in *ENside ECT*, and "do everything a little better than the other guy in order to be successful." But was there a viable market? If there was, could Enron execute profitably? The pilots would provide the answer for the renamed Retail Group, Enron Energy Services.

Peterborough (Electricity)

In May 1996, a first-in-the-nation pilot program began for 17,000 customers of Public Service of New Hampshire (PSNH), representing 3 percent of the state's electricity users. The program was to prepare the statewide opening set for early 1998, a legislative initiative inspired by an average statewide rate of $0.15 per kWh, one of the highest in the country.

Enron dispatched 30 employees to New Hampshire, more than any other of the two dozen independents vying for the same business. Of particular interest was Peterborough (population 5,300), which bundled its business for bid. In June, Enron's offer of 2.3 cents per kWh was chosen, a one-third savings from the prior utility's commodity rate. To widen this pilot program, Enron secured other customers by offering a bonus of $50 for new signees, among other

---

40. A profile of Rao for ECT employees said: "A native of India who speaks seven languages, he was part of the telecommunications industry's restructuring effort, working for ITT, Extel, and ALC Communications before assuming the presidency of Ameritech Audiotext Services, the regional Bell for the midwestern states."

promotional packages. Overall, Enron advertised saving consumers about 20 percent.

The March 1997 *Enron Business* described the "big success" of Peterborough. Happy faces, from Jeff Skilling on down, adorned the story. But this was "a piddling conquest for a $13.2 billion energy company," noted a summary in the *New York Times*. The township's "preferred" provider (Enron) had spent six figures on advertising, promotions, donations, and a grand town party, not counting employee costs.[41]

Enron's "rock bottom" rates left little or no margin for the seller. What Peterborough did provide was the centerpiece of Enron's national branding campaign. "In a state whose motto is Live Free or Die, people didn't like paying some of the highest energy rates in America," the ad line went. "Now, their newfound freedom of choice is yielding lower rates, better service, and a likeminded partner in energy." The pitch closed: "What's on your energy wish list?" with a toll-free number.

As it turned out, New Hampshire would not open up to statewide competition until well after Enron's solvent lifetime. Enron exited the pilot in September 1998, about the time it pulled up stakes in California and elsewhere. Several hundred remaining customers in the state would be transferred back to PSNH.

Toledo (Natural Gas)

Enron's big try with natural gas concerned a retail pilot in Toledo, Ohio, in early 1997. Enron's *Clean Start* program offered 15 percent off each customer's previous-year average gas price. A media campaign and local sponsorships were undertaken to build brand and goodwill for the eligible market of 160,000 residentials and 12,000 small businesses.

Each customer offered only a few dollars of profit per month, a pittance compared to cost. The lure was learning-by-doing, in preparation for the big time. "If we can win first in Toledo and then in big states, such as California, we believe the momentum will carry through to a national victory," stated Enron's program head, Stuart Rexrode.

Enron cited its 15-year history in the state (via Access Energy, purchased 4 years before). Its book of 500 commercial customers demonstrated the company's "proven track record of providing reliable service and savings." The strategy incorporated lessons from Peterborough.

"Market softening" television commercials by Enron were followed by print ads featuring residents and local celebrities in the *Toledo Blade*. Direct advertising followed with specifics about Clean Start. An Energy Rewards program was set up, under which residents could get free electricity from Enron should that market open. An 800 number was set up, and plans for a local retail office were

---

41. The "marketing free-for-all" left many targets "overwhelmed," and most residents never switched from PSNH, indicating the power of incumbency.

readied. Sponsorships were bought for the zoo and the Mud Hens minor league baseball team. It was like a "political campaign," noted Rexrode.

Enron's sign-up exceeded 10,000 customers. But a single-digit switch rate from the eligible population reconfirmed the value of incumbency. For most customers, the promised savings were not worth the study, paperwork, and uncertainty of leaving mainstay Columbia Gas Company for an upstart headquartered 1,200 miles away.

Figure 15.8 Toledo, Ohio, was Enron's laboratory for retailing natural gas directly to residential users. Ray Bowen oversaw this and other pilot programs as vice president of Enron Energy Services. Despite an all-in effort, low margins and a lack of scale would doom the retail efforts with gas—and with electricity.

(Enron would quit and return its customers to Columbia Gas the next year. Also in 1998, Enron passed on a far bigger gas program with 1.4 million customers of Atlanta Gas Light Company, stating a need to wait until the market matured. By this time, Enron had made the painful decision to deemphasize commodity retailing in favor of having Enron Energy Services offer large organizations *total energy outsourcing*, discussed below.)

California (Electricity)

California's "Blue Book" proposal in 1994 triggered a national debate about moving from wholesale wheeling to retail access. Two proposals later, enough of a "California Consensus" emerged to put Enron in full deployment. But while "a clear and virtually irreversible choice to embrace retail wheeling" had been made, there was still a lot of politics ahead—enough, even, to sink Enron's effort.

In early 1997, Enron began a 400-strong deployment to the Golden State. "Major opportunities await in California, which will be the first state to open the electric power industry to full competition on January 1, 1998," stated Ashok Rao, president of the new subsidiary, Enron Energy Services. "EES has already launched a comprehensive public relations, advertising and direct marketing campaign there, where employees are working hard to sign up customers in this $10 billion market."

In October, with the market-opening a few months away, Enron offered "an eye catching" two-year deal of 10 percent off existing rates, plus two weeks of free electricity. "We are here to do business," EES's Chairman and CEO Lou Pai stated in a press release announcing the California blitz. "Enron has been fighting for energy deregulation for over a decade and now we're offering low rates and more innovative products to as many Californians as possible." Enron pitched green, too, citing its solar and wind power investments. But environmentalists were nonplussed over Enron's price emphasis, preferring conservation(ist) measures instead.[42]

Five marketing offices were opened: in San Diego, Long Beach, and Costa Mesa for the southern part of the state, and in San Francisco and Walnut Creek for the north. Direct mail and general advertising, as well as a technology bet on a new generation of meters, were part of Enron's $20–$25 million effort covering the state.

Six months in, this "Olympics of deregulation" yielded 50,000 households—*1 percent of the market*. "All that grassroots outrage about monopoly power than Lay talked about, the pent-up rage at the utilities—it simply didn't exist," one assessment concluded.

The failure of EES in California had several fathers. The politics of retail access cut against Enron, reflecting the clout of utilities. There was a three-month delay in the start date (to March 31, 1998). The California legislature mandated a residential rate cut of 10 percent by utilities, which diminished the incentive to switch. An unspecified transition-cost surcharge on retail rates charged by independents, intended to pay off the utility's uneconomic generation (stranded costs), also muddied Enron's value proposition.

---

42. "Unfortunately, environmental considerations such as energy efficiency are getting lost in the scramble for cheaper rates," the head of Friends of the Earth complained in the *Wall Street Journal*. "For example, Enron, a large utility marketer in California, offers two weeks of 'free electricity' for those customers who switch companies." These companies "would service consumers better by offering energy-efficient light bulbs, water-heater insulation blankets and tips."

Then there was competition. PG&E Energy Services (Pacific Gas & Electric, not Enron's Portland General Electric) set up 5 marketing offices in the state and another 15 elsewhere in the country. California-born New Energy Ventures secured a low-cost supply source to sign up retail groups. This was a tough game to play from all sides.

Oregon (PGE and Customer Choice)

Enron's purchase of Portland General Electric in mid-1997 was conditioned on a 60-day requirement that PGE implement a customer choice (customer disaggregation) plan for its 680,000 residential users. This requirement from the Oregon Public Utility Commission (OPUC) was exactly what Enron itself wanted when it joined the electricity club. PGE was already going there, a reason for the merger.

"We've been saying for several years that our customers should have a choice of energy suppliers," CEO Ken Harrison stated. "I foresee many of its central elements being adopted in customer choice plans around the nation."

In October 1997, OPUC approved a pilot choice plan for 50,000 customers in four cities beginning December 1. Harrison's number two, Peggy Fowler, called the program a "ground-breaking experience" to "ensure PGE makes a smooth transition to a future with customer choice ... to help customers and utilities throughout the nation realize the benefits only a competitive market can provide."

PGE's Customer Choice Introductory Program attracted only two competitors, ECT (Enron) and Electric Lite. Both independents ceased operations in July 1998, whereupon the participating residentials (8,700, or 17 percent of those eligible) were returned to PGE (the regulated side of Enron). The primary reason for the failure was familiar: high transaction (hassle) costs, that is, customers disliked spending the time and effort needed to switch more than they liked the savings that switching purported to offer.

PECO Energy (Electricity)

Restless Enron attempted to create its own sizeable market in a bold competitive skirmish against PECO Energy, the largest electric utility in Pennsylvania. PECO was well along in restructuring talks with the Pennsylvania Public Utility Commission (PPUC) when Enron nosed in. With a retail power rate of $0.14/kWh, double the national average, reflecting its high-cost nuclear fleet, PECO had hammered out a settlement that traded a 10 percent rate cut for postponed retail access. Enron had negotiated for a very different outcome and found itself on the outside. It was the classic just-say-no utility dodging retail competition.

Enron took matters in its own hands after PECO refused to meet again. With just days to go before the PECO/PPUC et al. settlement was approved, Ken Lay arrived in Philadelphia on October 7, 1997, with a bold proposal to lower rates by 20 percent, while assuming $5.4 billion in PECO's stranded (noneconomic) generation costs, which according to PPUC, would be fully recovered in rates.

With a national movement to precipitate and branding to do, an Enron-hired plane buzzed PECO's 29-story building with the banner "Enron Choice Plan Saves 20%."

Nothing like this had ever happened in the electricity industry in almost a century of public-utility regulation, when franchise protection and cost-based rates took firm-to-firm rivalry out of the picture.

PECO's CEO Corbin McNeill took it personally, comparing his background (a nuclear submarine commander) to that of "policy man" Lay. "He counts beans and bullets, and I launch torpedoes." But just the opposite had happened. Skilling and Lay took to radio and ran media ads in PECO's territory to sell their offer. Enron lobbyists worked the state legislature, and Christian Coalition leader Ralph Reed was hired to help with a grassroots strategy. "It's like a political campaign," Lay noted.

A press release from PECO and McNeill was blunt. Defending its all-but-approved settlement that "has already extracted the maximum value that our Company can give without financially damaging PECO Energy," McNeil directed his ire toward the uninvited party. "Enron, a Texas company often accused of less than forthright business dealings, is attempting to prostitute the regulatory process in Pennsylvania to attain for itself illegitimate business gain and advantage."

To the national press, Enron was rather ingeniously "seeking to take over the Pennsylvania service area." To McNeill, Enron's play was "nothing other than a 'hostile takeover' of a significant part of your local utility."

In a tight spot, regulators renegotiated their deal. Rates were cut 15 percent, midway between the original amount and Enron's offer. Wheeling was scheduled for 2000. Ken Lay's company, however, gained nothing.

"Enron did not win," summarized Loren Fox. "But its interference caused a different outcome." What Enron called "a win for consumers" was expensive publicity and a moral victory only.

Disengagement, Re-engagement
Andy Fastow, Rick Causey, Ray Bowen, Ashok Rao—the business plan and path to profitability for residentials was under severe strain. It had been a tough 18 months, costing some $20 million. The end came when a newly hired consumer marketer with experience at Pepsi and Taco Bell, Jim Badum, went (with Lou Pai at his side) to present his findings to Ken Lay.

Enron needed "to slow things down," Badum stated. Enron was not a prototype marketing company. There were simply not enough customers now or in the near term to bring revenues toward the level of cost.

"This is the last thing I expected from this meeting," Lay told Badum. Heady thoughts about half the national retail market being open by 2001 and Enron being an energy retailer on par with a major oil company were off the table. Securing as many as 20 million electricity customers to complement Enron's wholesale dominance would cease at less than 50,000, and they would need to be returned to their utilities.

Announcing "our decision to suspend our residential efforts in California" before the Western Economic Association in mid-1998, Lay complained about a wayward reform process that threatened to leave everyone worse off. Consumer welfare and supply-side innovation were being sacrificed to placate utility managers and shareholders, Lay explained. A combination of full stranded-cost recovery and incumbency advantage (leaving utilities as default providers) was akin to "trading in a regulated monopoly for an unregulated one."

But some of the blame was on Enron. "We're not a marketing company," Lou Pai would confess. "That's not our expertise." Boiler-room sales using Enron employees was a cultural mismatch, not only a financial one. And if the utility remained the default supplier, customers would rarely switch—with reason, as it turned out.

———

Lesson learned, the plan was now to wait until more markets opened—and to relaunch with partners who could cheapen and thus enlarge the needed customer base. That would come 2½ years later. In May 2000, Enron-led New Power Company went public at $21 per share, retailing electricity and "complementary products" to homeowners and small businesses. Capitalized "in excess of $120 million" and with in-kind service agreements with IBM and AOL for Internet marketing, New Power saw its valuation rise.

"We've studied the residential and small business market for several years and believe this is the optimal way to provide value to these customers," Lay stated at the rollout. "By assisting in setting up an independent company, Enron is able to leverage its core competencies of energy and risk management, while partnering with other industry leaders to give the New Power Company extraordinary and immediate depth and capability." The result, however, would not prove to be substantially different from what had occurred several years before.

Headed by H. Eugene Lockhart, New Power's promising beginning would stall. As before, there was tepid customer interest in expending effort and shouldering uncertainty to save a few dollars per month. Also halting progress was the California electricity crisis of 2000–2001, which had been set up by regulation but exacerbated by Enron's gaming, a story told in other books.[43] And as New Power's stock lost value from its early peak, Enron's hedging strategies (Raptor III) designed to lock in high profits and cash flows for year-2000 backfired.

With Enron's collapse, interest in retail wheeling waned in many states. (Texas was another story, with Enron's model law enacted in 1999.) New Power itself would enter bankruptcy in 2003.

———

43. See, for example, James Sweeney, *The California Electricity Crisis* (Stanford, CA: Hoover Institution Press, 2002).

Enron Energy Services

In February 1997, with residential dreams big, Jeff Skilling announced the formation of a "distinct, free-standing operating company" within ECT to pursue
retailing. Replacing the 10-month-old Retail Group, Enron Energy Services
(EES) would be led by Lou Pai, the erstwhile second to Skilling as COO and
president of ECT.[44] Pai, like Skilling, received phantom EES equity that would
become very valuable in just a year's time.

What Skilling called a "massive managerial and business development
challenge" was also the responsibility of recent hire Ashok Rao, who as COO
and president was managing the residential pilots. Rao reported to Pai, Pai to
Skilling, and Skilling to Lay in the corporate structure.

As a company within a company, EES had to hire whole divisions in
accounting, finance, legal, marketing, information technology, and human
resources. This was the job of managing director Rick Causey, who had been
with ECT in a variety of positions during the previous six years. The 400
employees at year-end 1996 would surge past 1,000 the next year. The goal was
to spin off at least part of the unit to cope with EES's mounting losses and help
a languishing ENE.

EES would serve a $300 billion market "by customizing innovative energy
products and services to meet the distinct retail customer needs." In addition to
the household market, the new front was *total energy outsourcing* (TEO) to large
commercial and to industrial customers. This new emphasis, championed by
Pai, was developed by Marty Sunde and Dan Leff. The former had been with
the business-to-business outsourcer IBM; the latter had had an energy equipment and engineering background before joining Enron. Enron's top strategic
thinker, Bruce Stram, also sold Pai on TEO's business viability.[45]

"With a 10-year agreement to manage value chains, we would start with
capital projects," remembered Sunde. "Then as the states deregulated, we
would migrate toward price savings and the commodity." In unbundled states,
he added, the approach would be from business-to-business to
business-to-household.

As energy manager, Enron would not only "get a commodity play" but also
"a demand-side management play" and "a labor play," as well as "bring capital
and do lighting retrofits in a broadly structured product." For the customer, the

---

44. With Pai's transfer, Ken Rice (North America), Kevin Hannon (Commodity and Trade
Services), and Mark Frevert (Enron Europe) reported directly to Jeff Skilling and joined the
Enron Management Committee and the Enron Operating Committee.

45. "I persuaded Lou [Pai], I think, that ESCO type activity for the commercial sector was
the way to go, because there were margins to be had as demonstrated by the existing small
scale ESCO business, and it was not dependent on regulation."

Commodity	Equipment Services
Natural Gas	Metering
Electricity	Surge Protection Equipment
	Carbon Monoxide Protectors
	Hearting & Cooling Systems
Services	Energy Information Systems
Capital	Safety Lighting
Energy	
Energy Audits	
Appliance Repair Program	**Billing Services**
Energy Efficiency Program	Levelized Payment Plan
Construction & Maintenance	Automatic Payments
Environmental Solutions	Credit Card Payments
Operations Training	High Bill Inquiry
Power Quality	Deferred Agreement Plan
Load Management	Double Notice Plan

Figure 15.9 Total energy outsourcing became the focus of Enron Energy Services. The range of services bundled together by Enron was assumed to multiply the opportunities to make margins. The premise that EES would achieve scale economies in centralizing such services for business would not be borne out in fact.

value added was lower overall costs from Enron's ability to cheapen energy-related expenses, whether buying the commodity, installing new equipment, scheduling energy usage, complying with regulations, even changing light bulbs. That was the theory, anyway.

The modification by Sunde, Leff, Stram, and Pai came at a "do that or die" moment, remembered Thomas White, the Teesside builder and infrastructure specialist who would soon replace the terminated Rao at EES. Commodity retailing was failing, and *total energy outsourcing* was the midcourse correction. What became known as the *energy service company* (ESCO) originated with Enron's 1997 unveiling of "one stop shopping" or "total solution" with energy services.

Enron "would make the running of a consumer's energy needs seem invisible." After all, in Skilling's words, "Customers want some function … [and] don't care if it comes from natural gas or electricity or petroleum." And why not Enron? Kinder had outsourced its information technology function to Ross Perot's EDS back in 1988.[46] Like many other companies, Enron had turned over to outside specialists its cafeteria (to Marriott), copiers (to IBM), and travel arrangements (to Travel Agency in the Park), as well as its graphics, health facility, and mailroom. Now energy-specialist Enron would offer *total energy outsourcing* to large energy users.

---

46. See chapter 6, pp. 260–61.

There were questions, though. The whole idea of *profitable* untapped energy-management opportunities assumed that self-interested enterprises were somehow unmotivated. Furthermore, local, state, and federal programs were already subsidizing less energy usage for its own sake (conservationism). Too, keeping electricity rates artificially high arguably *overencouraged* demand-side management. And nowhere was this truer than in California, which had the most subsidies and mandates for energy reduction of any state in the Union.

Total energy outsourcing was not a proven concept, and Enron was an unproven provider. A measured scale-up, not full-bore implementation, seemed prudent to deal with a number of questions.

- Did EES really know more about energy engineering than the companies' on-the-spot energy managers?

- Could Enron cost-effectively hire and centralize the expertise that otherwise was operating in a fragmented way (in Enron's view)?

- Could long-term contracts, many for 10 years and some as long as 15 years, incorporate all the contingencies to have stable, mutually beneficial relationships?

- Would the chosen accounting method provide reliable feedback for economic calculation?

- Did Enron have the balance sheet to afford up-front capital in order to win contracts (install new equipment that would save energy over the longer term)?

- Did Lou Pai know how to run a large business, and could Skilling (now without Kinder) provide tough oversight to Pai and EES?

Economies of scale, economies of scope, managerial competence: EES was going to be a no-expense-spared, rush effort, with investor expectations riding on the outcome.

———

Lou Pai described EES's scale-up at Enron's November 1997 management conference. The "huge market opportunity" was now estimated at $400 billion: $200 billion in "existing retail market" and $200 billion in "related energy services/equipment."[47] Amid losses that would within a month cumulatively reach $142 million ($35 million in 1996; $107 million in 1997), Rao spoke about a

———

47. Enron's market estimates varied. Enron's 1998 annual report read: "The 'private utility' … the boilers, chillers, lighting, and controls—are valued at approximately $450 billion, and the services—commodity, heating/ventilation/air conditioning and facilities management—represent an annual market of more than $240 billion, which represents twice the value of the electricity consumed annually by these customers."

"first mover advantage" whereby Enron could "define the market" from a "large number of customers wanting alternatives to their utilities."

"Margins will increase over time," he promised, and more services would expand profits more. "Bundling of products and services ... will increase margins" in eight "packaging" areas: "consolidated billing, financing, operation and maintenance, process enhancement, energy efficiency, distributed generation, power quality, distribution."[48] The thought was that the 1–2 percent retail margins for gas or electricity could expand to 10–15 percent via TEO.

Ken Lay and Jeff Skilling had a *new* pitch to skeptical investors. "Enron's success in this growing business is not dependent on the continued pace of deregulation," the 1997 annual report read. "Throughout the U.S., Enron has the freedom to offer customers innovative energy services that represent better value and higher quality than traditional services of the past."

EES's "energy buffet" needed much external help. Outside talent by the score was being hired. The energy software and billing company OmniCorp was acquired. A stake was taken in Statordyne, a power-quality company in the business of ensuring the continuous, uninterrupted flow of electricity for the Internet era. "As ECT enters into a competitive retail energy market," stated Jeff Skilling, "we must be able to deliver consistently pure power to our ... most demanding energy customers."

The Bentley Company, a California energy engineering and construction firm, was acquired in mid-1997. Located in the state that was mandating energy efficiency the most aggressively, Bentley's major asset was a new $5 billion contract to modernize the state's federal buildings. EES set up a "war room" at Bentley's Walnut Creek headquarters before moving California headquarters to San Ramon the next year.

Many more acquisitions were ahead, rolling up disparate heating, ventilation, and air conditioning (HVAC) companies in pursuit of scale economies and national reach. All this was up-front expenditure in the expectation of future revenue and, eventually, double-digit earnings.

———

EES was "bleeding to death," remembered Tom White. Yearly losses exceeding $100 million were forecast. The solution was to sell a piece of the company (really, whatever could be sold at a high value) to prove the concept—at least in terms of image. Turning to an old investment partner, and with extra help from Andy Fastow, EES would receive new life.

In January 1998, Enron completed its announced sale of 7 percent of EES to the new special-purpose entity that Enron had set up with CalPERS (JEDI II) and to the Ontario Teachers' Pension Union. "Two investors paid $130 million,"

---

48. Enron was thinking more broadly about "'horizontal bundling' gas, electricity, finance, telecom, etc."

Enron reported, "establishing an enterprise value of approximately $1.9 billion, equivalent to $5.50 per Enron share." But this placement hardly represented the value of the whole company. Skilling, in fact, had hoped for 10 percent, $230 million, and a wider placement. Enron had certainly been looking for more in troubled 1997,[49] and investors shrugged at the somewhat contrived placement.

Some lipstick had been put on a pig. EES was not expected to go IBIT-positive until late 2000, and the market had not given value to EES prior to or even after the announcement. There was disappointment inside Enron that "CalPERS came to the rescue." Worse: Fastow's machinations to get CalPERS out of JEDI I and into JEDI II had represented "the first instance in which Enron used Special-Purpose Entities (SPEs) run by company employees to engage in questionable accounting, starting the trend that eventually led to Enron's collapse."[50]

The new owners forced out Ashok Rao, whose bluster did not inspire confidence. (Tom White remembered: "We didn't do a lot of homework on Ashok and later found out he left his previous employment on rather unfortunate circumstances.") Household retailing had claimed its fourth executive, joining Fastow, Causey, and Bowen. But unlike these three, Rao left Enron.

The partial sale of EES bought time amid mounting losses. Compared to a $107 million deficit in its first full year of operation, losses widened to $119 million in 1998 before falling to $68 million the next year. Fourth-quarter 1999's net income before interest and taxes (IBIT) went positive, "marking the end of our start-up phase" to set up (per Enron) "exponential growth and sharply increased profitability." EES recorded IBIT in 2000 of $103 million, its first annual profit.

But the revenue side was tainted. Narrowing losses and recorded profit reflected an accounting method at odds with the cash-in, cash-out accrual method. Specifically, EES's dozens of major deals, representing tens of billions of dollars in "Total Contract Value" (the estimated total energy expenditure by the customers) was nothing but "a PR message embedded in a financial disclosure."[51] The contracts were marked to market, with subjective guesstimates

---

49. Enron would book the entire $61 million profit in 1997, although two of the three payments were scheduled for the next year. The contrivance accounted for more than half of Enron's total profit, "keeping the 1997 results ... from being even more dismal than they already were."

50. Enron had to buy out CalPERS' 50 percent stake in JEDI I before it would invest in JEDI II. Fastow arranged the buyout by forming the notorious Chewco Investments, described in Internet appendix 15.1, "From JEDI to Chewco," at www.politicalcapitalism.org/Book3/Chapter15/Appendix1.html.

51. The TCV of executed deals would increase from just more than $1 billion in 1997 to $3.8 billion in 1998, $8.5 billion in 1999, and $16.1 billion in 2000. Reported revenues were $1.1 billion in 1998, $1.8 billion in 1999, and $4.6 billion in 2000.

of future costs and revenues over the life of the contract collapsed into a present value and taken as profit in the current quarter. Without liquidity, mark-to-market was really mark-to-*model* accounting.

Real costs could not be masked by fictitious revenue forever. Enron's "expert-based, turnkey packaged solutions," as described by one EES principal, caused a cash drain that would metastasize into far greater problems that came to a head in 2001.[52]

———

"With the strengths and systems previously developed in Enron's wholesale market and its investments and talent specific to this new market," investors were told, "Enron is well prepared to execute its game plan to become the retail provider of choice." But Enron was *not* the right company to execute the energy-outsourcing model, even if the model itself was valid (which it did not prove to be).

Enron never had a core competency regarding the *usage* of energy, just buying and selling energy commodities. The minutiae of energy engineering, the on-the-spot knowledge of the energy managers of commercial and industrial establishments, was outside Enron's expertise. Even putting these engineers in EES uniform did not create the economies of scale and of scope.

EES's "long and tortured history" was a predictable outcome of a faulty business model and subpar execution working under the pretense of subjective accounting. This division was deceptive from virtually the beginning, with *philosophic fraud* turning into legal (prosecutable) fraud. Midcourse corrections were not made; near the end, Enron tried to hide a half-billion EES loss by combining the whole unit with ECT's profitable side. EES would become a core target for the federal prosecution to come.

Still, Enron excited environmentalists who were critical of the market.[53] EES was the first (and largest-ever) *energy service company* (ESCO). Who could complain about private-sector strategies that saved money and reduced energy usage and emissions at the same time—and profitably, it appeared?

EES advertised a 5–15 percent savings for large commercial and industrial users over the term of their contracts, which went as long as 15 years. Ken Lay

———

52. "If you tell all your highly aggressive deal makers that the only thing that matters is total contract value *and* add to that horrible controls and an extreme urgency to get things done quickly *and* a compensation system based on the projected profitability of long-term deals," summarized Bethany McLean and Peter Elkind, "you're inevitably going to get an awful lot of bad contracts."

53. Conservationism, the doctrine that energy consumption is a per se bad, supports any or all government intervention to reduce usage. This doctrine is different from increased energy efficiency or reduced consumption from free-market incentives. See Bradley, *Capitalism at Work*, pp. 187–88, 218, 242, 245, 251, 284, 311–12.

put the energy-use savings near 10 percent, which inspired some within the company to advocate certifying customers as "Kyoto compliant." EES cochairman Tom White estimated the customer cost savings at 20 percent.

But such reductions were only the beginning, according to energy conservationists who posited a profitable level of energy savings and greenhouse-gas emission reductions that made compliance with international climate-change agreements possible, even easy. "ESCOs are DEFINITELY the future," Joe Romm wrote Enron. In *Cool Companies: How the Best Businesses Boost Profits and Productivity by Cutting Greenhouse Gas Emissions* (1999), Romm wrote how "cool buildings" could "cut energy use—and hence greenhouse gas emissions—*in half.*" EES purchased 200 copies of Romm's book for existing and potential customers. Enron is "a company I greatly respect," Romm told Enron.

To Amory Lovins et al., ESCOs were part of "the new era of natural capitalism," only the beginning of what was still there to be had. "Something like 80% or 90% of the electricity now sold is uncompetitive with electricity-saving technologies," Lovins told *BusinessWeek* in 1984. Falling demand would mean the end of new power plants, he predicted.

Even with EES kaput, Lovins continued to opine about the endless opportunities for energy efficiency that could cut the nation's electricity bill in half. "That's not a free lunch," Lovins proclaimed. "It's a lunch you're paid to eat." But Enron's experience suggested otherwise, as did the failed ESCO ventures of PG&E and of Duke Energy. EES fooled conservationists with a whole division predicated on deceit, accounting and otherwise.[54] But hardly deterred, environmental activists continued to advocate government intervention to correct a believed-to-be systemic inability of business to recognize and implement energy savings.

In fact, *economic* energy savings is a subset of physical, technical energy savings. Accordingly, there can be *too much* energy conservation, not only too little, either from government subsidies or from entrepreneurial error (such as EES).

Ken Lay believed that business executives were not sufficiently attuned to energy savings and efficiency in-house, thus needing total energy outsourcing (TEO). But energy had a much larger, transparent cost than most other goods that attracted profitable outsourcing providers. In-house management, using outside services short of TEO, proved more sustainable than Enron Energy Services.

---

54. Enron's deceit included creating a "little Potemkin Village" that became "the perfect metaphor for EES." In January 1998, Enron drafted employees to set up shop on a different floor to pretend to be an EES war room for visiting financial analysts. "EES executives reasoned that this deception wasn't a problem" because "eventually, EES really would use all that space."

Conclusion

"There's no question the lobbying war is being won by the Edison Electric Institute and others aligned with the investor-owned utilities," a participant noted in March 1997. Possessing enough national political clout to block a federal-level MOA at the retail level, utilities were able to slow the process with sympathetic state legislatures and commissions.

"Endowed with a resource war chest for public relations, advertising, and lobbying, they can afford a long fight," Jeff Skilling lamented in 1996. "And a long fight is what they are looking for [by] ... delaying choice long enough to recover non-economic costs from consumers and lock-up markets under long-term contracts." In fact, 35 different lobbying coalitions were fighting for a particular form of electric restructuring, a constellation of which Enron was just a part.

Enron would not get its true contestable markets, replete with rules to neuter the utilities' incumbency advantage. But investors, at least as far as keeping ENE as a momentum stock, entertained the story that this setback was fortuitous because it led Enron to the lucrative TEO market. As it turned out, neither proved profitable, although the latter was masked by trickery under which accounting profits were reported, not economic profits as measured by positive cash flow.

Energy retailing was one of Enron's notable misjudgments, joining the company's failed ventures into MTBE and, later, water (Azurix) and high-bandwidth Internet (Enron Broadband Services). The Retail Group's bad bet began in 1995–96, raising the interesting question about whether Rich Kinder as CEO would have stopped the music, really the siren song, that was the basis of Enron 2000.

Epilogue
Dangerous Ambitions

Enron needed to reinvent itself—again. Ken Lay and Richard Kinder's 1995 promise to investors to double the size and profitability of Enron in five years was in keeping with the (nominally) torrid pace of the previous eight. By 2000, Enron was supposed to be valued at $20 billion, with annual profits of $1 billion and cash flow double that.

New profit centers would be necessary. Enron Oil & Gas was being sold down. Gas margins at Enron Capital & Trade Resources had narrowed. The interstate pipelines were rate regulated and otherwise market constrained. International was listing. And a major entry into the reformulated-gasoline market had soured.

Enron 2000, as the financial plan was called, was a way station toward achieving the new corporate vision. The self-declared *world's first natural gas major* was going to become the *world's leading energy company*, the fourth company reorientation under Ken Lay.

Three Eras

The decade prior to 1995 had been long and eventful. In 1984, the new chairman and CEO of Houston Natural Gas Corporation (HNG) transformed the Texas-centered company by purchasing two interstate pipelines: Transwestern Pipeline and Florida Gas Transmission. HNG's previous management had rejected a lucrative takeover, and some investors were suing. Lay's pricey acquisitions were no cure for that problem, however. Though doubled in size, the reconstituted company had *less* market valuation at the end of 1984 than the year before.[1]

---

1. See Introduction, p. 11; and chapter 1, pp. 95, 97.

Lay ended his inherited fiduciary problem in 1985 when HNG stockholders handsomely cashed out thanks to a merger with InterNorth Inc.[2] Lay's second revamping, which more than doubled the size of HNG once again, yielded a geographically diversified, integrated US natural gas company. But HNG/InterNorth had massive debt in unforgiving markets. A long slog seemed inevitable, with the company's engineers, accountants, and a few lawyers doing what energy firms traditionally did.

Ken Lay was not an engineer, accountant, or lawyer. He was a big-picture economist with a skill set tending toward the political in an inherited mixed economy. Impatient, energized, and überconfident, Lay—with many favors to give and conflicts of interest to create—was out to do things grandly and to shoulder large risks. Exxon, where he had once worked, was the tortoise; Enron would be the hare in a newly created energy industry.

Enron's third era was empowered by government policy. A regulatory restructuring by the Federal Energy Regulatory Commission (FERC) created a fourth industry segment—wholesale natural gas marketing—to join exploration and production, transmission, and local distribution. With its two predecessor gas-trading units already ahead, Enron became the national leader in 1985–86 and remained so until late 2001.

Enron Three also included high-risk international projects enabled by government-related financing. Another government-created opportunity was mandatory open access (MOA) for wholesale electricity, the product that joined Enron's portfolio in 1994.

Enron's next remake, the new frontier for Enron 2000, rested on a major public policy strategy. Wholesale MOA for gas and electricity, mastered by Enron, would be joined by *retail MOA* whereby both energies would be profitably sold to millions of homes and tens of thousands of businesses across the United States. Short of long-shot federal legislation opening up the retail market nationally, state legislatures and utility commissions stood between the third and fourth Enrons.

———

Energy, government, and smarts: Lay assembled brainy talent for the new competitive arena, quite unlike what HNG and InterNorth, and most any other energy firm, had ever seen. Enron's chief PhD had first learned about regulated markets as an economist at the Federal Power Commission (FPC, 1971–72) and the Department of the Interior (1972–74). He learned more when he worked among the regulated at Florida Gas Transmission (1974–81) and Transcontinental Gas Pipe Line Company (1981–84). Moreover, while in Washington, Lay had taught the topic in graduate-level courses in microeconomics, macroeconomics, and business-government relations.

———

2. See chapter 2, pp. 120–21.

From the get-go, Lay jumped at new profit centers enabled by federal regulations and subsidies. He hired John Wing away from General Electric to form a leading gas-fired cogeneration business, a division enabled by a 1978 federal law requiring electric utilities to buy power from qualifying facilities at a (generously determined) avoided cost. The iconoclastic Wing would have a series of hits that expanded Enron domestically and defined Enron internationally.[3]

Early Enron also began buying and selling natural gas in interstate markets, an area created by new rules from FERC (the successor to FPC). Both HNG and InterNorth had skill and experience when MOA opened up dozens of major interstate transmission systems across the country beginning in 1985–86.

For the first time since 1938, (unregulated) marketers could profitably buy and sell natural gas in interstate markets, replacing the hitherto bundled sales handled by regulated interstate pipelines wherein no margin was allowed for the gas itself. (It was only a cost passthrough.) The result was Enron Gas Marketing—renamed Enron Gas Services in 1991 and then Enron Capital & Trade Resources in 1994—which commoditized natural gas in the United States, Canada, and then Europe. Next up for commoditization would be electricity, first at wholesale and then retail.

Another defining change was the 1987 relaunching of Enron Oil & Gas under newly hired Forrest Hoglund. A PURPA-enabled contract from Wing's side and federal tight-sands tax credits propelled EOG in the late 1980s and early 1990s.[4] By using a different business model from that of Ken Lay, Hoglund created real marketplace value in his company-within-a-company—one that would gradually divorce from Enron. A fishes-and-loaves story for its parent, EOG generated more than $2 billion from profits, lucrative tax credits to shelter Enron's company-wide earnings, and stock sales in the period under review.

Internationally, Enron began with triumph: a megaproject in Margaret Thatcher's UK privatization push and dash-for-gas enabled by North Sea production. John Wing's Teesside, the world's largest cogeneration plant at 1,875 MW, beat strict deadlines to become an important profit center for Enron.

With international credentials, Enron leveraged government funding and lobbying to target high-risk/high-return projects in underdeveloped countries. Particularly during the Clinton administration, the United States put its full weight behind Enron's bold pursuits with loans, loan guarantees, trade missions, and government-to-government pressure in dozens of countries that were traditionally inhospitable to capitalist institutions, including the rule of law.

---

3. See chapter 1, pp. 96–97, 100–102; chapter 3, pp. 165–69; chapter 4, pp. 203–6; chapter 5, pp. 220–25; and chapter 6, pp. 269–71.

4. See chapter 5, pp. 218–19; and chapter 6, pp. 285–88, 290–91.

Electric restructuring was launched with an Enron-sponsored provision in the Energy Policy Act of 1992 (1992 EPAct), which led to MOA rules for the interstate (wholesale) market via FERC Orders No. 888 and No. 889 in 1996. The same George H. W. Bush legislation stipulated a lucrative tax break for qualifying renewable-energy generation, which would underlie Enron's entrance into solar power in 1995 and into wind generation two years later. (Enron did not lobby for this provision, however.)

PURPA projects; FERC Orders No. 436, No. 497, and No. 636 (wholesale gas MOA rules); Section 29 of the Omnibus Reconciliation Act of 1990 (tight-sands tax credit); OPIC and Ex-Im financing (for developing-country projects); Section 721 of 1992 EPAct (wholesale power wheeling); Section 1212 of 1992 EPAct (a renewable-production tax credit); and FERC Orders No. 888 and No. 889 (MOA for wholesale power): politically opportunistic Ken Lay was moving in directions far different from those of the traditional energy major.

———

Enron's unprecedented political orientation was part of something bigger. Lay's management strategy did not have a name, only such descriptions as *hyper-aggressive* and *rule breaking*. Part of the strategy was using public relations in ways that made the business seem bigger than it really was. Another part was gaming the rules legally to create a desired result or image despite the purpose and intent of those rules.

Enron's strategy also had other defining aspects: using government as an enabler or counterparty; building widespread faith in a grand corporate narrative; persuading itself that the ends justified the means; treating the promise of future profits as a form of current income. In the most general terms, then, the strategy comprised rent-seeking, philosophic fraud, and strategic deviations from bourgeois virtue: But these terms were not used or even considered. Without thinking about it or even realizing it, Ken Lay was pioneering a new management philosophy: *contra-capitalism*.[5]

Circa 1996

Thrice revamped, Enron in 1996 stood in stark contrast to the Houston Natural Gas that Ken Lay found in mid-1984. Assets and revenues in 12 years had grown sixfold, to $16 billion and $13 billion respectively. Reported net income had increased almost fivefold to $584 million. And the market value of the enterprise was three to four times greater than 1984's $3.7 billion.

Enron's 38 percent debt-to-total-capital ratio at the close of 1996 compared to 1984's 59 percent—and was a vast improvement from 1985's postmerger peak of 73 percent. But there was a back story. Off the balance sheet, Enron had $5.2 billion of debt (versus $3.3 billion reported on the balance sheet). This represented

———

5. See the Preface, pp. xi–xii; the Introduction, pp. 3–6, 59–64; and below, 671–74.

a 63 percent debt ratio, which could have reduced Enron's BBB+ (strong investment grade) rating to B (junk) according to John Bilardello, an analyst for Standard & Poor's Corp.

In fact, as reported at the time in *CFO* magazine, Enron's "ingenious structure" of off-balance-sheet entities allowed the company to report profits without the associated assets and liabilities. To the naked eye, it was as if the reported assets were generating all the profit.

And this too was during the Richard Kinder era.

At least on Enron's balance sheet and income statement, the trend lines were positive. ENE's appreciation increased capitalization to help bolster Enron's all-important credit ratings. But as detailed elsewhere, Enron was borrowing from the future in every way it could without setting off alarms, a practice that began in 1989.[6] Off-balance-sheet financing was increasing and about to skyrocket too.

Houston Natural Gas and InterNorth each had an international side, but major foreign divisions were divested or eliminated after the merger. Thus, Teesside began a new era for Enron, whose international units would involve some 30 nations by 1996.

Enron's employee count went down—then back up. The newly merged HNG/InterNorth had 8,800 employees. Asset sales and layoffs, as well as increasing efficiencies (including pipeline automation), reduced the headcount by one-third. From this 1988 low, new businesses brought the workforce to an all-time high of 11,000 at the end of 1996.

The company's composition had changed too. HNG at the end of 1984 was centered on natural gas transmission (mostly FERC regulated), representing 60 percent of assets and 80 percent of profits. Enron circa 1996 had gas marketing and international divisions accounting for nearly one-third of the parent's total earnings before interest and taxes. The new-business headcount, which was less than 200 through 1991, reached 1,500 by 1995 and more than doubled that the next year.

Enron's focus was still natural gas. In 1984, the front cover of Lay's first annual report stated: "We're going to stay with our knitting and do what we do best." This was reconfirmed with the purchase of two interstate gas pipelines that year, and it remained unchanged with the 1985 merger. (Petroleum was secondary to InterNorth's operations as well.)

In 1996, Enron was still oriented to natural gas except in those developing countries where a lack of indigenous gas supply made oil more affordable than imported LNG for power plants. Renewable energy, which competed against

---

6. See Introduction, pp. 24–28. The artificial nature of Enron's profitability could be traced to the very beginning of HNG/InterNorth, with the many frauds committed by Enron Oil Company (chapter 4).

natural gas in electrical generation, was a new emphasis for Enron as a "green" provider for the retail marketplace. It was also a pure political profit play, as detailed in chapter 13.

Enron's common stock was a growth story with high expectations built in. ENE's total return to shareholders was 234 percent between 1990 and 1996, out-distancing Standard and Poor's 135 percent as well as Enron's peer group (mostly natural gas firms), which recorded 43 percent growth. A $0.90/share dividend, though being raised approximately 5 percent annually, represented a 2 percent return. ENE was a growth stock, not a yield stock.

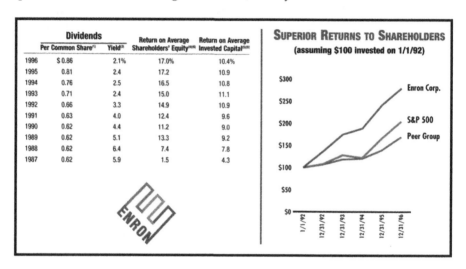

Figure E.1 Enron was a momentum stock on the way up, beginning in the late 1980s. The ENE pitch in 1996 was that the past was prologue, despite the challenges presented by start-up businesses.

ENE had a relatively high price/earnings ratio of 19 to 1, based on 1996's closing stock price. (Peer companies were lower, with Williams Company tops at 17 to 1.) Optimism abounded. Chief of staff Ed Segner spoke of the need to increase Enron's BBB credit rating from S&P and Baa1 credit rating from Moody's, as "a first step towards the A rating that we want to obtain." S&P did upgrade Enron to BBB+, but Moody's left Enron unchanged. The new goal of A−, set in 1997, would never be reached.

A Changing Company

Each of Enron's four major businesses could scarcely expect double-digit annual earnings growth. Enron's fifth division, renewable energy, was a start-up in a traditionally money-losing business. A new growth story was required to effec-tuate Enron 2000.

Out with the old; in with the new: Enron was cashing out of EOG to reduce debt and finance its new ventures. The third selldown in 1995, to 61 percent, included an agreement to reduce ownership to 54 percent three years later. Enron would do this and more, with a complete divestment of Enron Oil & Gas Company in 1999.

The interstate pipelines, although a model of entrepreneurship within their FERC-set rate ceilings, could not expect double-digit earnings growth, except in a rare year when major expansions came on stream. Five percent growth was good. But far from expendable, the interstates gave Enron a predictable earnings base and a high cash flow. The humming interstates would go down with the ship and be the most valuable assets sold by a bankrupt Enron.

International's touted $20 billion in potential projects was long on negotiations and short on signings, not to mention operational success. The counterparties—poor, unstable governments—were not prone to execution. The Dabhol power project in India, although back under construction in 1996, was not generating revenue to offset its snowballing costs, now in the hundreds of millions of dollars. Competition was also intensifying for the most viable projects, with host countries turning from negotiated deals to bids that narrowed returns.[7]

The coming of a new year at ECT did not bring new increments of earnings from previously executed multiyear deals. All the profit had been marked-to-market; changing circumstances might increase anticipated revenues, but change might also bring decreases, something Enron did not like to think about, as the Sithe deal showed.

Competition from Dynegy, El Paso, Coastal, and Transco—and other marketers in a field estimated at 200—were normalizing profits too. Earnings growth required new divisions and novel ways of doing business. Said Jeff Skilling in 1994: "The things we are doing are the things that our competition will be doing two or three years from now." But maintaining first-mover status by constant innovation had risks, and other firms were hiring away Skilling's talent, in order to emulate Enron's best.

Traditional Enron had annual earnings growth of 5 to 10 percent at best, particularly considering some postponed and looming write-offs, two of which neutered Enron 2000 in 1997.[8] New businesses, none greater than in electricity, had to come on as strong as natural gas had earlier in the decade, but electricity was an unknown despite Enron's confident proclamations. In addition, leading the fourth and most ambitious reinvention would be an untested new president—the new heir apparent to Ken Lay.

---

7. See Introduction, p. 22.

8. See Introduction, p. 17. Double-digit earnings growth from continuing operations remained a goal, however, even without the aspiration for multiyear averages.

New Leadership

Ken Lay was Enron's constant from start to the finish. But a number of other executives were noteworthy in the overall progression of the company during the pre-1997 era. The most notable was Rich Kinder, who ran Enron alongside Lay for almost the entire period. Kinder was a real chief operating officer and, with good reason, was poised to become CEO in the mid-1990s.

Jeffrey Skilling built a company on the gas-marketing side. Another company builder was Forrest Hoglund, whose EOG exercised autonomy from the parent. John Wing, in fits and starts, was a third division builder for Ken Lay, first with domestic cogeneration plants and then with Teesside.

Rebecca Mark erected a major division, Enron Development, that would benefit Enron far less than the other three. In terms of opportunity cost, Mark's developing-country investments equated to a major domestic gas pipeline acquisition, perhaps one to the (missing) Northeast, to achieve lasting asset value and cash flow for the corporation.

Enron's honor role on the pipeline side in the 1984–96 era would include Jim Rogers in the 1980s and Stan Horton thereafter. In the midstream and wholesale gas businesses, Ron Burns was a top executive who would be missed after leaving Enron in 1995.

Michael Muckleroy, who crucially limited the damage from Enron's oil-trading scandal in 1987, ably ran gas liquids until departing in 1993. John Esslinger led physical trading at Enron Gas Marketing, under its various names, until his departure by early 1997. And at EOG, Mark Papa was on the rise under Forrest Hoglund.

Richard Kinder Departs. There was much to like about Ken Lay's longtime number two. President and COO Richard Dan Kinder was a keen operations manager and an able strategist. He performed the hard jobs for Lay after joining HNG in January 1985, none greater than rectifying underperformance. In the early years, he was number three in the corporate division, behind president and COO Mick Seidl, and served as Lay's hammer.

As senior vice president and general counsel, Kinder chaired a cost-containment committee in the dark days of 1986 to learn all about the company. Promoted the next year to executive vice president and chief of staff, Kinder was breathing down the neck of Seidl before replacing him as Enron's number two in 1989. It was during this time that Kinder shepherded Jeff Skilling through a gauntlet of doubters—and drained the swamp of alligators in the transition away from bundled sales and transportation by pipelines.

Kinder confronted Enron's issues. His "brutal" executive staff meetings got problems solved. Accountability? Kinder got that from everyone except, perhaps, from his boss.

"I believe my expertise lies in analyzing complicated problems and situations, formulating several workable solutions, and with the aid of other talented people, reassembling them into a strategy," Kinder stated. This was good enough for growth of 5 to 10 percent. But when Ken Lay's zeal and permissiveness got Enron into new fields too quickly or dangerously, it ended up on Kinder's top-10 list of problems, which he carried in his pocket for action. The "roving Mr. Fixit," however, having signed off on such aggressiveness, even if reluctantly, had some items of his own making too.

Kinder's was a voice of humility and caution, at least compared to the CEO. "I believe in the old saying that 'pride goeth before the fall'," he wrote employees after a strong year. "We must continue to pay attention to detail and hard work and stay ahead of our competition if we want to remain the industry leader." Kinder warned against "drinking our own whiskey" or "smoking our own dope" in matters Enron, earning him a nickname, "Dr. Discipline."

Rich Kinder was detail oriented and stayed inside Enron's walls, two reasons why Lay increasingly relied on him. But Rich dutifully did the external tasks as well, such as chair the pipeline trade group Interstate Natural Gas Association of America (INGAA) in the mid-1990s.

With Kinder taking over, Lay gravitated to his first love: government affairs, public relations, and any outside-the-walls effort that would promote him as a Great Man—and ENE as a momentum stock. Lay and Kinder worked well as a team, although Lay thought himself far less replaceable than the COO, as did Enron's board of directors.

Kinder doggedly worked, cajoled, and browbeat to make the fat numbers promised to the Street. But this went from being a strength (when based on reality) to a major weakness (when based on manipulation), and he got Enron into a bad habit that would infect, and eventually take over, its corporate culture and business model. The post-Kinder Enron derided in books about the company's collapse was nurtured in the Lay-Kinder era.

———

Rich Kinder had been number three at Enron since 1987 and number two since 1989. In early 1994, the board debated elevating Kinder to CEO with Lay remaining as chairman. The directors were not quite ready for that, but the number two's new five-year employment contract, effective February 1, 1994, set up the changeover.

Kinder's new deal contained a trigger date of February 8, 1997, at which time Kinder could exit with full benefits "if mutually satisfactory terms pertaining to his future employment with Enron have not been agreed to by Mr. Kinder and Enron." Lay's new contract provided for an early termination on this same date.

Come 1996, Kinder was ready. The changeover might have happened already had the elder Bush been reelected and tapped his friend Ken Lay for a plum appointment, perhaps as Chief of Staff or Secretary of the Treasury. (Lay had reputedly turned down the lesser position of Secretary of Commerce, previously held by his own friend Robert Mosbacher.) Or, the change might have taken place had the mighty AT&T, faring poorly under CEO Robert Allen in the MOA telecommunications era, persuaded the 54-year-old Lay to come its way.[9]

During Lay's AT&T negotiation, Enron's board thought hard about Kinder as Mr. Enron. He was not as polished, diplomatic, or politically adept as Lay, they concluded. Neither was Kinder as visionary as Lay or, for that matter, Jeff Skilling—so the thinking went.

Lay, meanwhile, was enjoying Enron, with ever more reason to be Mr. Outside. The political and public sides of the company, Lay's playground, were more important than ever. The national effort to market gas and electricity to homes and businesses, after all, was a *crusade* for lower prices and competition in place of franchised monopoly. Mr. Enron could now become Mr. Economist to make this case to millions.

The branding challenge for customers to trust and choose Enron required Ken Lay to become nearly as well known as the company. Opening markets meant a lot of work in Washington and in dozens of state capitals. There was local work as well, such as securing public financing for new professional sports stadiums in Houston, to enhance Enron in direct and indirect ways.

Being the progenitor of energy retailing would be a step up for Mr. Natural Gas and the industry's provocateur on global warming. There was also congruency. Lay liked the applause from mainstream environmentalists, and renewable ("green") energy was now a means to differentiate retail Enron to create a "new energy major."

––––

As the date for management succession neared, something else became crucial in the decision that would mark Enron for the rest of its life. Drama in the executive suite created a divide between Kinder and Lay, which sealed the fate of the man who had been positioned to become Enron's new chief executive officer, effective January 1, 1997.

By mid-1996, it became known that Kinder was romantically involved with Nancy McNeil, Ken Lay's top assistant, who had risen to become the vice president of corporate affairs. "The little general," as she was known, was attractive, smart, tactful, and orderly. Along with Lay's wife, Linda, Nancy was Ken's confidante and liaison. McNeil had ended her marriage, and Kinder was about to end his when the rumors broke. Kinder did not admit to anything when directly asked by his boss, but the evidence was there.

Ken Lay informed his board of the facts. Personally, he felt doubly double-crossed. Had he not done more favors for Nancy and for Rich than could ever be known? The board voted not to promote Kinder, knowing the likely result.

––––

9. Unable to respond to regulatory change in telecommunications in ways that Lay had mastered with natural gas, AT&T was looking for new leadership. The September 1996 negotiation ended when Lay found out that the plan for him was not to become CEO immediately but to serve as president for two years under Allen.

Kinder immediately tendered his resignation, and Lay entered into a new five-year contract as chairman, CEO, and president. The November 1996 announcement surprised just about everyone.

"I want to do more than be No. 2," Kinder told the *Wall Street Journal*. "They offered me the chance to stay on, but it was sort of like 'Been there, done that'," Kinder told the *Houston Chronicle*.

ENE dropped less than 2 percent, hardly alarming but indicative of some pullout. Kinder had been the real Mr. Enron to the banks, the rating agencies, the whole investment community. "I view this as a loss to Enron," stated Carol Coale, energy analyst with Prudential Securities Research. PaineWebber's Ronald Barone was less concerned: "This is a company with great depth of management."

Rich Kinder left with a package exceeding $6 million. In short order, he sold his ENE cache for several times more and married Nancy McNeil. Enron's PR department presented Rich with a huge banner signed by thousands of employees. A lot of inside drama was forgotten at the instruction of smooth-things-over, friend-of-everyone Ken Lay.

What now? Though rich, Kinder had no thought of retirement. Instead, he approached William "Bill" Morgan, an old college and law school friend, as well as former colleague at Florida Gas and HNG/InterNorth. His idea was to start a midstream energy company. In fact, Kinder had laid the groundwork by acquiring the very assets that he had helped Enron spin off several years before: Enron Liquids Pipeline Company (ELPC).

Kinder Morgan Energy Partners was established in February 1997 upon the purchase of Enron's general-partner interest in ELPC. For $40 million, Kinder Morgan assumed two liquids plants, a carbon dioxide pipeline, and a coal-transfer terminal. By using a master limited partnership to buy assets with a lower rate of return than was acceptable to corporations paying income taxes, and by cutting costs in a way he could not at Enron, Kinder launched a midstream play that would achieve a billion-dollar valuation by 1998.[10]

When Enron was liquidated several years later, Kinder presided over a company worth $7 billion. His company's 200-page notebook for the 2003 analyst meeting was titled: "Same Old Boring Stuff: Real Assets, Real Earning, Real Cash." Kinder would take no questions about Enron, despite the obvious differentiation he was making from a company that, two years before, Jeff Skilling had claimed to be worth $126 per share (at a time when ENE was at $82). Just four months after that pitch, Skilling would resign from Enron, and four months later, Enron would declare bankruptcy, and ENE soon became worthless.

---

10. "When I was president of Enron, I would throw people out of the room if they came in with a proposal that had anything less than a 15% aftertax return," Kinder stated in 1998. But with the MLP tax advantage, "We can make acquisitions all day as long as we're over 8.5% pretax."

Jeff Skilling: President and COO. Who would be the new number two at Enron? Ken Lay, now chairman, CEO, and president for the first time since 1990, told his top operation officers—Jeff Skilling, Stan Horton, Rebecca Mark, and Forrest Hoglund—that no replacement would be named for the time being. The press, meanwhile, mentioned Horton, Enron's Kinder-like disciplinarian over the pipelines, and Ed Segner, Enron's brainy, finance-savvy chief of staff.

Lay wanted a number two with commercial experience. Forrest Hoglund was approached by the board but immediately declined, and Rebecca Mark, though a Lay favorite, was not considered ripe for the position. The frontrunner was wunderkind Jeffrey K. Skilling—who told Lay that he was ready for this promotion and was prepared to leave Enron if he did not get it.

On December 12, just one month after Kinder's resignation, the 43-year-old Jeff Skilling was named, effective January 1, 1997, Enron's president and chief operating officer, while remaining chairman and CEO of Enron Capital & Trade Resources. Lay and the board had wasted little time in choosing the new direction of Enron, which was already embarking on a growth path right up Skilling's alley. But to some near the top, "Jeff basically blackmailed Ken."

There was now a visionary at number one *and* number two, which Lay and the board felt was fine, as long as Horton and Hoglund were still in place. But Horton and Hoglund were Old Enron; the new businesses were another story. With Skilling's attention now divided, he had to turn the baton at ECT over to the talented but erratic Lou Pai. (John Esslinger, a mainstay on the physical side of ECT's business, had just retired.) Internationally, Lay was confident about Rebecca Mark, although Jeff Skilling (like Kinder) was not.

Wall Street liked Rich Kinder, but Skilling had never disappointed either. The father of commoditized natural gas at the center of a restructured industry was being compared to Clark Kent himself. "Don't ever think that Jeff doesn't have a big red S under his dress shirt," stated Steve Parla of Credit Suisse First Boston. "He was so far ahead that it took us a while to figure out what he was trying to do," stated another top Wall Street analyst, Kurt Launer of Donaldson, Lufkin & Jenrette. (Both bulls, incidentally, worked for investment banking firms that benefitted from Enron equity issues and were little inclined to peek too far under the hood.)

And wasn't Jeff Skilling the value creator who turned the 2-person Enron Finance Group and the 140-strong gas-marketing group into a 2,000-person behemoth, increasing revenues from $10 million in 1990 to $300 million? In thought and practice, there was virtually no blemish on his record.

But there were doubts. John Wing, for one, cashed out of ENE upon hearing of the change at the top. Investment analyst John Olson at Merrill Lynch had a furrowed brow. As it would turn out, Skilling-for-Kinder proved calamitous. Skilling was not skilled at setting and enforcing divisional budgets. Though Skilling engineered current-period profits, he was not managing costs. Enron's head of administration, Jim Barnhart, remembers Skilling saying "on several occasions, 'I don't care what you spend as long as you make your numbers'."

Richard Kinder, by contrast, would say: "'Jim, even when times are good, we want to be counting heads and looking at money.... You are going to have to justify everything you do'."[11]

The new COO was a big-concept guy, a 15-percent-growth thinker, who needed a disciplinarian. Skilling could certainly read financials and get to the essence of things, but Enron had many parts outside of the new COO's expertise. Perhaps most important, Skilling was a proven corner cutter, a deceiver in the cause of making the numbers to reach personal and corporate goals.

Skilling's dual titles with corporate and ECT were complicated. Citing burnout, he had almost quit Enron before hatching a plan to work half-time, although the plan was abandoned at the last minute. In 1994, Ron Burns had joined ECT with a title coequal to Skilling's (and Esslinger's), in order to deal with the Skilling uncertainty, but neither Burns nor Esslinger was still at the company.

Kenneth L. Lay
Chairman and CEO

Jeffrey K. Skilling
President and COO

March 4, 1997

Figure E.2 Post-Kinder, the new leadership team atop Enron was Ken Lay and Jeff Skilling. President and COO Skilling would soon join Enron's 14-person board of directors, which was led by John Duncan (bottom right).

11. One anecdote illustrates Kinder's "very intense" monthly meetings to go over budgeted costs and revenues in each division. "You could always tell if [Mike] Muckleroy's numbers were good because he would show up at the meeting!" remembered one participant. "If they were bad, he would send all his deputies to get beat up by Kinder."

Enron would now increasingly become Jeff's company with an (MOA-enabled) asset-light strategy. But could he run the entire enterprise? Ken Lay was not Richard Kinder, and there was really no one else, certainly not the vice chairmen, who had narrow roles.[12] Ron Burns, chairman of Enron Pipeline and Liquids Group before cochairing ECT, had left the year before to become president of Union Pacific Railroad.

But prior to Skilling's appointment, Burns was suddenly available to rejoin Enron after a rocky 15 months at Union Pacific Corporation. Lay invited him to do so, but Ron wanted to be number two (COO and president) with authority over both Skilling and Mark, who were sideways with each other. This was more than what Lay had in mind. The idea was to add Burns, not risk losing Skilling and upsetting Mark.

Ken Lay: Going Outside. Ken Lay had been Mr. Inside after joining HNG in mid-1984. With a bulging lawyer's briefcase, the workaholic tackled all things HNG, HNG/InterNorth, and Enron. This began to change in the late 1980s when it increasingly became Lay as "Enron's Mr. Outside and Kinder as Mr. Inside."

It was not that Lay was incapable of handling intricate detail, and a lot of it. His Pentagon research, turned into a doctoral dissertation, showed his technical proficiency in mathematics and statistics. And Lay always did what needed to be done at his previous corporate stops.

With Kinder et al. inside the walls back home, Lay's mission went international: first to put Teesside into play with the UK authorities and thereafter to court foreign dignitaries for Enron's developing-country projects. There was increasing work in Washington. And also beyond 1400 Smith Street in Houston, Lay's busy itinerary included state capitals, including Austin, Texas.

By the time Kinder left, Mr. Outside had become "the imperial chairman" who was not inclined to revert to his former hands-on life. This board director of Texas Commerce Bank (joined 1985), Compaq Computers (joined 1987), Trust Company of the West (joined 1992), and Eli Lilly Company (joined 1993) had responsibilities with dozens of other organizations, such as the President's Council on Sustainable Development, the Business Council, the National Petroleum Council, the American Enterprise Institute, and the H. John Heinz III Center (an environmental think tank). Past chairmanships included the Greater Houston Partnership, the University of Houston Board of Regents, and the

12. John Urquhart, vice chairman since 1990, helping Lay on assignments involving electricity technology, would become senior advisor under a consulting contract in 1998. Ken Harrison became vice chairman of Enron in 1997 with the purchase of Portland General Electric (PGE).

Houston Host Committee for the Republican National Convention, as well as his cochairmanship of the 1990 Houston Economic Summit.

Hosting events for important people and for philanthropic causes made for busy evenings. There was active grant making by the Linda and Ken Lay Family Foundation. Being everyone's friend—all in the service of branding Enron and widening the market for ENE—would increase Lay's association count to 76 by 2000. The question became: "When did Ken Lay even have the *time* to run Enron?"

Into 1997, Lay was the face of Enron to external constituencies and to employees, now a major investor group in the company. "Ken will spend much of his time on international projects, business development, government, customer, and employee relations," *Enron Business* explained in early 1997. "Both Ken and Jeff will continue to focus a lot of their time on strategy, including new energy-related business areas which will further accelerate Enron's growth."

But who would veto expediency that endangered financial sustainability? And who would dig deep into budgets to question and cajole the unit heads—and follow up weekly on the difference between what was promised and delivered? That would not be Skilling, and Kinder was doing it at his own company two blocks away—and with just-purchased Enron assets.

The New Enron

Old Enron was in the background by 1996. Interstate gas transmission remained at the core, and talent infusions would try to "Enronize" the pipelines in the face of regulatory constraints. But Enron was monetizing its traditional assets almost everywhere with selldowns and public offerings.[13] International was slowing: although Dabhol's construction was restarted in December 1996, most other projects were only inching ahead.

New Enron was centered on Jeff Skilling and Enron Capital & Trade Resources. Enron had mass customized (commodified) natural gas at wholesale in terms of price, term, location, and reliability. ECT, which between 1990 and 1996 increased its gas-product slate to more than 200, was moving more quickly on the power side. Enron's North American electricity unit (wholesale only) listed some 250 different products in 1996, whereas none had existed several years before. Europe, too, was offering an energy-product slate in excess of 250 by 1996, versus zero in 1994.

This was prologue to Enron's new big bet. The basis of Enron 2000's aggressive, even audacious, goal was *natural gas and electricity retailing*.

---

13. Enron was selling down Teesside and EOG. Public offerings included Enron Liquids Pipeline (1992), Northern Border Partners (1993), EOTT Partners (1994), and Enron Global Power & Pipelines (1994).

"We have started a new stand-alone retail business that five years from now will, we believe, generate revenues equal to or greater than our total 1996 net income of $584 million," Enron's *1996 Annual Report* informed investors. This would make Enron an *energy major*, on a par with the integrated oil majors. Assuming a 10 percent share of the $207 billion US retail electricity market (a figure considered conservative, given Enron's one-third share of the wholesale market), Ken Lay hypothesized that Enron's retail revenues would exceed those of the oil giants. Part of this was size: electricity's $207 billion market compared to gasoline and diesel's $107 billion market at the service station. Mobil, Shell, Exxon, Texaco—Enron would outsize them all.

The goal was to secure as many as 20 million households. The national effort would lead with pilot programs and a campaign to brand Enron. In addition to New Hampshire, where the major pilot program was under way, the first state-wide push would be in California, which had set dates for a retail phase-in program for electricity.

As detailed in chapter 15, Enron was working on five fronts to become a mass retailer of gas and electricity to homes and businesses:

- A business plan and product development to offer end users an alternative to utility service;

- Advocacy and lobbying for federal and state initiatives to open markets via mandatory open access on the retail level;

- Advertising and outreach ("branding") so customers would be comfortable in switching from their utility to Enron;[14]

- Pilot programs to prove the concept of signing up retail customers;

- Purchasing Portland General Electric (PGE) to learn the distribution business and set up a pilot program in the Northwest.

No other company was doing this. It was no small experiment. In relation to the rest of Enron, mass retailing was a *bet the company* strategy for keeping ENE's momentum. But electric utilities with decades of incumbency and political power stood between Enron and Enron 2000. It would not turn out as expected by the upstart.

1996 Annual Report. Enron's first branded annual report—dated March 4, 1997—described the company's storied past and transformative future. Lay's 14th annual report was different from Enron's previous 11, HNG/InterNorth's 1,

---

14. This effort arguably began in late 1994 with Enron's entry into rooftop solar, which was joined by wind power two years later. "In addition to monetary incentives," Enron would note in early 1997, "Enron's market research shows that most people prefer to do business with a company that is environmentally responsible."

and Houston Natural Gas's 2. The change was not only in the office of chairman, where a new number two executive was pictured. It was also the exuberant story of a Horatio Alger–like business poised to monetize a reinvented future.

The *who we are* section of the "Letter to Shareholders and Customers" (Letter) had several self-descriptions, such as:

- "one of the largest integrated natural gas and electricity companies in the world"
- "the top natural gas and electricity wholesale marketer in North America"
- "the most successful developer of energy infrastructure in the world"

Looking ahead: "We're also becoming one of the largest international suppliers of wind and solar renewable energy."

"We are proud to be a leader in a great industry," Lay and Skilling wrote. "But we believe our achievements so far are just a prologue to a new and enormously exciting story that is unfolding on the energy landscape."

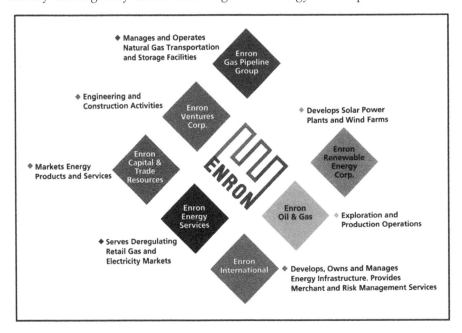

Figure E.3 Into 1997, Enron had seven divisions, the newest being Enron Renewable Energy and Enron Energy Services. Within a year, Enron would divide itself into core (interstate pipelines, exploration and production, wholesale energy services) and non-core (international, retail energy services, renewables).

Specifically, the deregulation of gas and electricity (translation: retail MOA for gas and electricity in North America) was creating *"a huge new $300 billion* *a year market."* And in other Western industrialized countries: *"State owned and private monopolies are giving way to private competition."* In the developing world, *"new markets are emerging as governments turn toward privatization, especially in the areas of telecommunications, transportation—and energy."*

Enron was in the middle of all three new energy plays, the Letter emphasized. The plan was to "become the largest provider of electricity and gas in the U.S."—and in Europe, in 5 to 10 years. LNG projects, not only electricity marketing, were "off to a tremendous start." Add renewables, and three new businesses were "on track" to deliver "a net present value of at least $1 billion or more by early in the next decade." Spin-offs were envisioned, such as EOG (but not ECT).

Buzz terms in the annual report included "extraordinary change" … "extraordinary promise and potential" … "accelerating convergence of the natural gas and electricity markets" … "the new world of energy" … "reinventing the energy business."

Live-for-the-moment Enron—which used and abused mark-to-market accounting and sold assets (future profit streams) in order to record extraordinary profit—publicly declared itself living for the future. "Enron is convinced the correct view is the long view," the 1996 Letter stated. "Invest time and resources now, plant seeds that will bear fruit, bolster market development efforts, cultivate change, grow the company."

———

This exuberance left many important underlying issues unmentioned, ones that the (conflicted) investment analysts were slow to uncover, much less highlight. They were:

- The challenge of earnings growth in rate-of-return regulated businesses, not only for the interstate pipelines but also for the pending acquisition, Portland General Electric.

- Normalizing margins in ECT, as well as the each-new-year burden from mark-to-market accounting.

- The trade-off (double counting) between prospective retail market share and already held wholesale market share.

- The lack of international deal closings and, in particular, the remaining counterparty problem of the Dabhol power plant that was back under construction.

- The prospect of imminent write-offs. (Teesside II's J-Block liability was discussed in the back of the annual report; the soured MTBE investment not at all.)[15]

———

15. Enron would take a $675 million charge to earnings three months later, stating that J-Block "will not have a materially adverse effect on its financial position."

- The November 21, 1996, propane explosion in San Juan, Puerto Rico, that left 33 dead, 80 injured. (Immediate suspicions would be confirmed, and Enron's San Juan Gas Company would conclude settlements in 2000.)

Half-truths were resorted to. The highlight of Enron's new growth story was the "very successful" retail pilot projects, led by electricity in New Hampshire. True, Enron was retailing as no independent company ever had with gas and electricity. But the economics were not working, just as rival Chuck Watson at NGC (later Dynegy) had predicted. By Enron's own math, the loss per customer at retail could not be made up on volume; the more the customers, the greater the overall deficit.

After changing out management several times, in fact, ECT was bailing out of the residential market in 1996. (The new model, total energy outsourcing for large commercial and industrial customers, led to the reorganization of Enron Energy Services in first-quarter 1997.) Talk in the annual report about serving "up to 1 million [retail] customers by year-end 1997" would not be repeated.[16]

The Letter contained another half-truth, even mistruth. Although not mentioned by name, Enron 2000's pledge was reiterated: *"We expect to achieve compound annual growth in earnings per share of at least 15 percent from 1996 through the year the year 2000. We expect minimum double-digit earnings per share growth every year during that time."* Yet several months later, write-offs were announced that would make 1997's earnings growth rate a *negative* 18 percent. The half-truth? Year-to-year net income growth *excluding* the special charges was 18 percent.

By all appearances, Enron was entering its new phase strongly. Financial engineering, as well as postponed write-offs, kept 1996's profit growth at double digits, a promise of Enron 2000. ENE was a momentum stock, not a yield stock as it had been a decade before. The optimism, the *shared narrative*, had to go on in order to preserve, if not upgrade, the credit ratings so crucial to Enron's large trading operation.

———

Enron's *1996 Annual Report* had special help. In search of a memorable Letter, not unlike that of Jack Welch at GE, Ken Lay and Jeff Skilling turned to Peggy Noonan, the White House speechwriter who had churned out memorable phrases for Ronald Reagan and then George H. W. Bush.

---

16. As described in chapter 15, Enron halted its 18-month, $20 million effort with only 46,000 customers.

Noonan spent two days touring Enron to learn about the company and its ambitions. She noted the "cavernous rooms," "omnipresent computer screens," and "future Masters of the Universe." She met individually with Ken Lay, Jeff Skilling, and Rebecca Mark. Was this the New Age corporate world, she wondered, or an outlier?

Everything went according to plan, but Noonan had trouble finding special prose for what "seemed to depend on things that were provisional." "They were building this and tearing down that, they were, they told me, talking to legislators in various state houses, lobbying to get deregulation bills passed," all of which "seemed expensive, labor-intensive, time-intensive."

"My contributions were not helpful," she admitted, even after spending between 100 and 200 hours of billable time, at $250 per. "I didn't fully understand what their mission was." It was something different from selling a ware in a store, she later explained. There was something else: "a sort of corporate monomania at the top—if you can't understand what we are doing then maybe you're not too bright."

In particular, Noonan found Skilling's retail pitch less than convincing. It was "too complicated," she told Jeff. In a busy world, choosing an electricity provider "just might be one item too many on the average consumer's Daily Decision List."

Noonan sensed what economists called *high transaction costs*. Sure enough, without a consumer uprising for change, Enron was spending a lot of money in multiple directions to attract what turned out to be few customers. Business from retail MOA was a breed apart from wholesale MOA, as Enron would painfully discover.

"An Empire Built on Ifs," certainly benefitting from hindsight, was published in the *Wall Street Journal* the month after Enron's bankruptcy. Noonan described greed in the abstract, recounted her Enron story, and then turned to public policy. Conservatives and Republicans, such as herself, had a "special responsibility … to come down hard on people who cheat their shareholders and their employees," especially since Enron's debacle was "damaging to faith in free markets."

But like other conservatives, she did not grasp Enron as a uniquely *contra-capitalist* company, practicing rent-seeking and dealing in omission, half-truths, and misdirection, not to mentioned imprudent behaviors.

Roaring Ahead. Into 1997, Kinder forgotten, the outside world was buying the story of a company in the sweet spot of four energy megatrends: *deregulation*, as defined by Enron (MOA); *privatization*; *demand growth*, mostly in natural gas and renewables; and *environmentalism*, the movement away from coal in particular. Enron was playing both Bootlegger and Baptist. "We're on the side of angels," Jeff Skilling stated. "We're making the environment cleaner, reducing costs for consumers, and disciplining the monopolies of 100 years."

The media found Enron compelling. News organizations certainly received a lot more press releases from Ken Lay's enterprise than from any other energy company. And Enron's public and government affairs departments, outsized by industry standards, would only get bigger as Enron took on the energy establishment in the political arena.

Enron was a world-class natural gas firm entering into new and existing fields. A business feature in early 1996 in the *Washington Post* was titled: "You've Heard of Big Oil. This is the Story of Big Gas ... And It Begins with Enron Corp., Which Wants to be No. 1 In World." Catch phrases, such as "integrated energy solutions" and "energy merchant," described a new kind of energy enterprise.

More differentiations were coming from the media and particularly from Enron. The "border-to-border, coast-to-coast" pipeline company of the 1980s was now a "new energy major" offering "energy management" and "green BTUs."

Enron was capitalizing on "major industry discontinuities," including a "convergence" of gas and electricity.[17] "First-mover advantage" and "strategic regulatory approaches" had produced, by 1997, an "incomparable North American competitive advantage," what two years later would be self-described as an "unassailable competitive advantage." The same model for Europe and South America was creating a "global energy franchise," Enron would tell investors in the 1998 annual report.

Enron was turning creative destruction into a profitable cornucopia, the message became, despite misses in the trial-and-error process. "Creativity is a fragile commodity," Enron's *1999 Annual Report* would state. "We support employees with the most innovative culture possible, where people are measured not by how many mistakes they make but how often they try."

In 1996, Enron had been recognized by *Fortune* magazine as America's most innovative company, the first of six consecutive adulations. "Most grateful," Enron responded in a full-page ad, thanking customers for envisioning change and employees for effectuating it. (See p. 662.)

Business Week named Lay as one of the nation's top 25 executives; *World Cogeneration* magazine named him its Executive of the Year. "Keen familiarity with the political landscape has been at the heart of Ken Lay's and Enron's success in the restructured energy business," the latter profile read.

Awards were also collected from outside the business community. For the company's green-energy initiatives, the left-of-center Council on Economic Priorities awarded Enron its Corporate Conscience Award for Environmental

---

17. The "economies of scope" between gas and electricity would lead to wider commodity trading and intermediation, so that Enron described itself in its last annual report (2000) as "a marketing and logistics company."

AS APPEARED IN **THE WALL STREET JOURNAL** MONDAY, MARCH 10, 1997

FORTUNE® MAGAZINE
KEEPS CALLING US NAMES.

"Most Innovative"
1. Enron
March 4, 1996

"Most Innovative"
1. Enron
March 3, 1997

We think they forgot one: **"Most Grateful."** The thanks here go to our customers and our employees. Our customers came with a vision of how things could be different. Our employees came back with ideas to make those things happen. For both, we're most grateful.

Natural gas. Electricity. Endless possibilities.™

© 1997. This copyrighted work, the logo and other marks are property of Enron Corp.

Figure E.4 By the mid-1990s, Enron was riding an innovation and reinvention wave, led by a wholesale-to-retail marketing push with natural gas and electricity. This *Wall Street Journal* advertisement by Enron touted its growing fame.

Leadership for 1996. Much more recognition and several awards came the next year in conjunction with the international climate conference in Kyoto, Japan.

How did Ken Lay see himself and business? The answer was provided in his life history, prepared in nomination for the Horatio Alger Award (which he would receive in 1998). The Enron-prepared 12-page biography contained these highlights:

- "Much of Ken's career has evolved around opening up regulated markets for competition and preparing whatever companies he has been involved with to win in the new competitive environment."

- "Ken also has led Enron to become a global powerhouse in energy."

- "He flattened the organization, reduced costs, established totally new incentive systems and, in the process, created centers of entrepreneurship throughout the company."

- "Extending his strong belief in markets and competition, Ken and his organization have been at the forefront of a number of the economic liberalization efforts in the developing world."

In the 10 years ending 1996, the profile detailed, Enron's market value increased from $2 billion to $11 billion, with a total return to shareholders of 408 percent, a multiple of that of Enron's peers and more than one-third above the average appreciation of the S&P 500.

"Ken Lay has been a strong proponent throughout his life of giving back to his community and nation," the primer added. "He is fond of a quote that he believes is from Bruce H. Wilkinson that says, 'You make a living from what you get, you make a life from what you give'."

The personal-philosophy section of Lay's application reproduced Ken's story as published in Michael Novak's *Business as a Calling*. "I grew up the son of a Baptist minister," it began.

> From this background, I was fully exposed to not only legal behavior but moral and ethical behavior and what that means from the standpoint of leading organizations and people. I was, and am, a strong believer that one of the most satisfying things in life is to create a highly moral and ethical environment in which every individual is allowed and encouraged to realize their God-given potential.

Novak resided at the American Enterprise Institute, and his book was published by AEI, a conservative, centrist public-policy foundation (think tank) where Lay was a board director. Enron's CEO was here, there, and everywhere.

Ken Lay was an inveterate optimist. He had never failed, only exceeded expectations. "Lay displays an unshakable confidence tempered by more than a decade of taking big risks and winning," read a mid-1997 *BusinessWeek* article, "The Quiet Man Who's Jolting Utilities." Enron versus the Edison Electric Institute was Lay's biggest political battle yet, the article noted, and the prize was MOA as a precondition to retailing gas and electricity profitably.

———

Golden Enron had a few critics. In a 1993 *Forbes* piece by Toni Mack, Enron's mark-to-market accounting was criticized as a short-run expedient. In a 1995 *Fortune* feature on Enron, Harry Hurt III identified an unhealthy short-term bias. From time to time, John Olson in the investment community expressed doubts.

But four years after her 1993 criticism, Mack wrote glowingly about Enron as a mass energy retailer in an opening market. "The numbers are awesome," she began her *Forbes* piece, pegging the contestable market for retail electricity at $215 billion and for retail gas at $90 billion. Representing a bigger market than long-distance telephony ($170 billion) and airlines ($100 billion), innumerable gas and electricity customers were in play.

"California, New York, Pennsylvania, Illinois, and some New England states are moving quickly toward deregulation," she wrote. Federal legislation was introduced to open the whole market nationally, and states would have to move fast to forestall federalization. Enron's branding was bold and prescient. She closed: "Enron Corp. President Jeffrey Skilling sums up the future of the electricity business when he says: 'It's going to be an absolute competitive battlefield.'"

Still, questions were raised about Enron's near-term profitability from mass retailing. Branding was a $100 million job, Mack estimated. And regarding Enron's touted $20 billion in international projects, another (otherwise laudatory) article noted: "Critics say that some of these projects are relatively small and that it's too soon to tell whether others will be completed." In addition: "The fate of the company's largest international project, the planned $2.5 billion naphtha and natural gas–fueled Dabhol plant in India, they say, remains uncertain."

In 1996, Prudential Securities and Dean Witter Reynolds downgraded ENE from a buy to a hold on profit concerns. ENE would slump after first-quarter 1997 as write-offs and retail's start-up costs kicked in. (Enron's negative return to shareholders in 1997 was "unacceptable," Lay would tell investors.) In fact, ENE was in a two-year slump, and, by late 1997, Enron a rumored takeover target. "Year-Long Slide in Stock Price May Put Giant Enron on Hit List," a *Natural Gas Week* headline read.

Skilling's Company. In mid-1996, when Kinder was presiding, Enron had four units: Enron Operations (housing the interstate pipelines, gas liquids, and construction services); Enron Capital & Trade Resources; Enron International; and Enron Oil & Gas Company.

A year later, when Skilling was presiding, there were seven units: Enron Oil & Gas; Gas Pipeline Group; Enron Ventures (Engineering & Construction; Clean Fuels; EOTT); Enron Capital & Trade Resources; Enron International; Enron Global Power & Pipelines; and Enron Renewable Energy.

By the end of 1997, the count was nine, with the addition of Enron Energy Services, Enron Europe, and Enron Communications (split from PGE), and the subtraction of Enron Global Power & Pipelines.

It was Jeff Skilling's company, with Ken Lay increasingly occupied with speeches, lobbying, and foreign projects. Skilling, with full support from Lay and Enron's board, put all of Enron's money on the table (and some under it). In 1997 alone, capital expenditure doubled to $1.4 billion, debt nearly doubled to $6.25 billion, and interest expense increased by almost half.

Skilling-side talent would rise too. "By the end of Skilling's first year, Skillingites filled 11 of the 26 slots on Enron's management committee, including such disparate positions as finance and government affairs."

A key early initiative to speed the company was Enron Capital Management (ECM), a corporate-level group that assumed the finance and risk functions for both the corporate division and within ECT. Headed by Andy Fastow, ECM's 100 staffers were responsible for pending projects cumulatively exceeding $15 billion with a potential for $40 billion more.

In addition to the traditional function of managing Enron's funds flow and cash balance, ECM pledged to give all business units a lower cost of capital, so that they could increase their flow of projects. "We want the commercial teams to have capital as a weapon in their arsenal that will allow them to do deals that other companies can't," explained Enron's new senior vice president. There would be no argument from Ken Lay about what his new number two was doing for Enron's quest to get to the top—ASAP.

Figure E.5 Heavy capital requirements from Enron's new businesses, coupled with the need to protect the corporation's creditworthiness, inspired a reorganization. Enron Capital Management under Andy Fastow (right) was composed of a finance unit under Bill Gathmann (left) and a risk-management unit under Rick Buy (center).

ECM quantified all of Enron's financing risks in one pool, not unlike what ECT did with its deal book. Fastow had already executed on-the-edge deals to

help Enron make its 1995 numbers and then its 1996 numbers. But there would
be some dramatic aggressiveness, even illegality, in 1997—and much more
ahead, resulting in Andy Fastow's becoming the most infamous figure in
Enron's eventual collapse.

Righting Misinterpretations

The rise and fall of Enron Corp. stands as one of the most astounding and con-
founding episodes in business history and in the annals of American capitalism.
Its interpretation involves the morality and efficacy of markets—and the legiti-
macy of commercial capitalism itself. Among political-economic narratives,
that of Enron rivals the stories of John D. Rockefeller's Standard Oil and of
America's Great Depression in terms of molding opinion and testing worldviews. Samuel Insull's rise and fall, the subject of *Edison to Enron* (Book 2 in this
series), was in its own day an opinion-forming event of comparable magnitude,
and one with many parallels to Ken Lay's rise and fall.

Yet through its many tellings, the Enron story has remained fundamentally
misinterpreted. As presented in the company's aftermath (2001–3)—and
repeated on the 5th, 10th, and 15th anniversaries of Enron's bankruptcy—the
mainstream view has been that flawed character traits were enabled by deregulation and that underregulation caused the artificial boom and decisive bust
called Enron. Capitalism's "infectious greed" and "irrational exuberance" were
the essence of Enron, it was said. Ayn Rand and free-market economists were
held intellectually culpable.

These takeaways must be thoroughly and wholly reconsidered, as this book
series has tried to do.[18] Enron manifested *contra-capitalistic* tendencies, virtually
from its beginning. These deviations from best-practices capitalism grew from
molehills to mounds to mountains, eventually bringing down the company in
complete and startling fashion.

———

Enron is the story of corporate decision making in action. "Ultimately," as one
Enron book concluded, "this is a story about people." Those people were *motivated* decision makers, responding to inducements and opportunities that had
much more to do with *political* capitalism and a postmodernist mentality than
with classical liberalism.[19]

———

18. See, particularly, Bradley, *Capitalism at Work* (Part I); and Bradley, *Edison to Enron*, pp.
2–3, 13–16, 479–80.

19. A sister term to political capitalism is *crony capitalism*. However, cronyism can occur
within the market itself, one major manifestation being a board of directors compliant to
senior management (a form of the principal-agent problem).

This book's review and reinterpretation of Enron's formative era reaches two major conclusions. First, Enron was not a free-market company; nor was Ken Lay a true free-market advocate. Just the opposite: Enron was a *contra-capitalist* company, and though Lay was procapitalist in his mind, he was contra-capitalist in action.

Second, Enron came to practice the incoherent philosophy of postmodernism, whereby thinking and wanting and expecting a state of affairs substituted for taking the hard, patient steps to create it—or the studied decision not to create it. Overambition, overconfidence, misplaced hope, and outright hubris were evident in the scary triumphs, major setbacks, and public relations highlighted in this book.

Enron as a Process

Enron was not a thing or a place. Enron was *a process of business decisions* with action leading to result, and result inspiring new action. This book's chronology of cause and effect by division, and for the corporate whole, has attempted to present Enron in you-were-there fashion, with the reader asking: *What would I have done? What would I have warned Enron's leadership about?* Such realism humanizes a story that in a simplified, storytelling, *nonprocess* form can appear peculiar, even inexplicable.[20]

Subtle and evolutionary, process analysis is key to understanding how Ken Lay's company morphed into something quite different from what even he and Enron's board of directors could have imagined. This is why the Enron story contains multiple tipping points, even a tipping point within tipping points.

"It seemed like a small leap to make from bending the rules to breaking them," one Enron chronology concluded. Author Loren Fox continued: "There was no single moment when Enron transgressed from rule bender to rule breaker: Rather, the transformation resulted from the gradual accretion of offenses, encouraged by a corporate culture that valued aggression."

Similarly, Harvard's Malcolm Salter described a "pattern of deceptive behavior that unfolded in incremental steps over time, as a result of pride and hubris, a host of unprofitable new ventures, a culture of deceit, and breakdowns in performance measurement and control systems at a time when Enron had trouble meeting its aggressive targets."

Best-practice business consultants, drawing upon field research, have also emphasized *process*. In *Good to Great: Why Some Companies Make the Leap and*

---

20. The change-always approach to Enron has been identified as *neo-Austrian economics*, incorporating the real-world variables of "time, knowledge, and market processes" in place of static, beginning-end points, the trade of neoclassical economics. See also Internet appendix I.1, "Business History Scholarship: Some Methodological Notes," at www.politicalcapitalism .org/Book3/Introduction/Appendix1.html.

Others Don't, Jim Collins showed how improvement "never happened in one fell swoop" but "by a cumulative process—step by step, action by action, decision by decision, turn by turn ... that adds up to sustained and spectacular results."

The "organic evolutionary" process identified by Collins can also work in reverse, with a great company deteriorating to merely good or a good company falling to bad—and worse. Enron, more than any other, demonstrated the good-to-bad sequence as the company's defective divisions overwhelmed the good, while the corporate center fell prey to behaviors opposite from those identified in a science of success.

In sum, Enron was a for-profit commercial enterprise in the mixed economy, where pecuniary incentives emanated from a jumble of consumer-led free markets and government-driven political markets. Taking into account personalities and incentives, the elusive *why* behind the why of Enron's classic saga emerges. This did not begin in the Lay-Skilling era, although it accelerated and became entrenched in 1997. Rather, this *why* was characteristic of the Kinder-Lay era, which closed in 1996.

The Richard Kinder Question

"Tempt not a desperate man." Enron was at a crossroads when it entered the Jeff Skilling era, and a year of hard reckoning lay ahead. Either the company needed to restructure and get back to the basics—as it had done a decade before—or accelerate with chancy bets. Already, some tipping points had been reached; now Enron was at a new crossroad, a big one.

The contra-capitalist course was chosen, in keeping with the still-fresh promises of Enron 2000 and the charge to become *the world's leading energy company*. Ken Lay knew only one speed—and Skilling liked that pace too. With two rock-solid physical-asset divisions (interstate pipelines and EOG), and a world-class energy trading division, Enron had a base from which to dive into the new.

As it turned out, monumental hype in wholly new areas (renewables, energy outsourcing, broadband, water, online trading); new heights of financial engineering (mark-to-model accounting, RADR, Chewco, LJM I, LJM II); Ken Lay's mighty persona; and political correctness would keep Enron's narrative going until 2001, when a harsh and irreversible reality set in. In retrospect, the end had been postponed by scurrilously deft work done by an empowered, conflicted, criminal CFO.

Most historians placed the beginning of the end, the "tipping point," in 1997, when Jeff Skilling took over as Ken Lay's second in command. Big losses were taken in that year to clear the decks for a robust future. That was the message, anyway. Appearances winning out, ENE fell only 4 percent that year, and the all-important credit ratings were maintained. Crisis averted. But behind the scenes, a very different Enron was being put into hiding.

———

Next to Valhalla, which nearly reached the point of bringing down Enron, the company's greatest what-if story is: *What would have happened if Richard Kinder had become chief executive officer as originally planned, with Lay as chairman of the board?*

The new CEO would have certainly been in a tight spot. Enron 2000 was Kinder's promise too, and he had signed off on a number of undertakings that became company problems. "To view Kinder simply as the white knight who got away is to ignore a more complicated reality," noted Bethany McLean and Peter Elkind. "In truth, some of the seeds of Enron's downfall were sown on Kinder's watch."

True—but more so.

A Kinder era at Enron would have been more painful and the pitfalls greater than could have been realized (even by Kinder at the time). Given the fate of top Enron executives who stayed until the end, Kinder's clean break in 1997 to build Kinder-Morgan made him very fortunate.

A counterfactual history of a post-1996 Kinder-Lay era can be surmised, however. First, Enron would have taken the same two write-offs that were taken in 1997. (Dabhol as a third write-down would probably not have been taken by Kinder—no change there.) But the year's net loss would have been *greater* under a Kinder-approved CFO than under Skilling's Andy Fastow, who got busy cooking the books.

A major cost-cutting campaign would have been necessary, not unlike the downsizing in 1988—when consolidation and layoffs were taken to reposition Enron "as one of the least-cost providers of natural gas in the country." Corporate expense, an overhead charge to the various business units, would have been slashed. Rich Kinder certainly would not have been Mr. Houston or a political dynamo or serial speech giver and image maker like the prior CEO—just an inside-the-walls chief executive getting back to basics, before enlarging the company.

Kinder's Enron would have been much closer to Forrest Hoglund's EOG and Stan Horton's interstate pipelines—and less like that which was taking shape by 1997–98: "a new type of company representing the next stage of U.S. capitalism." The new ventures that redefined Enron would have not been undertaken by Kinder. Or they would have been started as smaller experiments, perhaps to be abandoned or maybe even sold rather than developed at scale as they were.

ENE's stature as a momentum stock would have suffered with a full true-up. ENE likely would have dropped by double digits, with Kinder's tough reform being appreciated by some investors as necessary to dodge even further decline.

What about the narrative and the excessive hyperbole related to mass retailing? Bringing Enron's Star of Hope down to Earth would have been Kinder's real test as CEO. Would he have (painfully) demoted what he had spoken about so optimistically before? Second, would he have done it in such a way as not to deflate Enron's bubble, lower its credit rating, and put ECT in a downward spiral?

As in 1996, Kinder would have worked from a very sober—and not encouraging—assessment of retail. The pilots were losing big money, and the market was not opening in a way that would allow profitability. Skilling and Lay tiptoed out of this quandary by repositioning retail as *total energy outsourcing* (TEO) to commercial and industrial users within Enron Energy Services (established March 1997). The narrative to investors was that Enron, learning and correcting, had identified a new niche, even a mother lode.

As it was, this (artificial) energy-efficiency play nicely complemented Enron's renewable-energy push in the global-warming era. The media and environmentalists praised Enron, which became a reason for taking the easy way out.

TEO was *not* a proven concept, quite the opposite. The business depended on a host of engineering issues with which Enron had little experience and on long-term projections far beyond Enron's ability to know. Lou Pai's lawyers struggled to cover all the contingencies in the 5-, 10-, and 20-year contracts, and revenue reporting used mark-to-market (really mark-to-model) accounting to mitigate losses and eventually eke out (paper) profits.

Kinder, it can be surmised (but never known), would not have acquiesced to a full-bore TEO effort as was undertaken by Pai, Skilling, and Lay. Kinder, it can be only hoped, would have relied on better accounting methods and insisted on more accurate model assumptions to get better feedback from profit and loss—and reposition accordingly.

————

With retail off the table and true-ups elsewhere, Enron would have been humbled, ENE deflated. Slippery slopes would have given way to a long march up the hill. Enron 2000? Gone. World's leading energy company—forgotten. Revolutionary change? Replaced by incremental improvement. Extraordinary earnings? Not in every year, much less every quarter.

Ken Lay? Off to another business challenge—perhaps as a rainmaker for a major investment firm or perhaps to front the to-be-launched New Power Company. Perhaps even to Washington politics. Skilling, Pai, and Fastow might have not survived ECT's exit from retail, leaving wholesale at Rich Kinder's Enron.

Such a scenario is a best case. But even then, Kinder's Enron would not have been as valuable as Kinder Morgan, given the former's sunk investments and cost structures, and given the MLP business model of Kinder Morgan. But Kinder would surely have tapped the rich midstream asset market for Enron's growth, perhaps even restructuring much of Enron as a giant MLP. In any case, Lay's largesse and vision would have been relinquished and an annual earnings growth rate of 5 to 10 percent found quite acceptable.[21]

————

21. Already, Enron was missing opportunities at the core by not aggressively bidding for strategic midstream assets. Missing a pipeline to the Northeast, Enron's bid lost to Williams Company for distressed Transco Energy in 1994 and to El Paso Energy Corporation for

"Had he stayed, Enron's highs would never have been as high," McLean and Elkind surmised. "But the lows would never have been as low." This would have been a best case, however, not a worst case for a Kinder-led Enron given the need to reverse some mighty engines started in 1995–96.

Contra-Capitalist Enron

"The Enron case is arguably the most important meltdown in the modern history of American capitalism," noted Douglas Rae, the Richard Ely Professor of Political Science and Management at Yale University. Interpreting Enron may begin with Ken Lay's being an "incompetent CEO, whether or not he was guilty of criminal behavior," and continue by tying the company's ultimate fate to "a combination of bad business decisions," worsened by secret dealings and false accounting. But the reasons for death require a coherent motivational explanation.

Business diagnostics aside, what was the why behind the why? Why Ken Lay? Why Enron? Why in energy?

And why in America's mixed economy where investor protection had a half-century-plus regulatory tradition?

As posited in the Introduction and documented in the rest of the book, the answer was *contra-capitalist management*, growing out of a competitive business world in which prevailing philosophies, business fads, and the socioeconomic system itself worked against best practices, as classically defined.

Ken Lay the chameleon; Enron the unfocused. The hitherto Great Man of Natural Gas, of Houston, and of the New Energy Economy was enabled by the philosophies and opportunities of *political capitalism*, not of market capitalism as understood in law, philosophy, and political economy by classical liberals.

Political capitalism was defined in *Capitalism at Work* (Book 1 of this series) as "a variant of the mixed economy in which business interests routinely seek, obtain, and use government intervention for their own advantage, at the expense of consumers, taxpayers, and/or competitors." By 1996, Ken Lay's Enron certainly fit the bill—and it would become more political in the years ahead. Infamous Enron did not refute the free market in either practice or theory. Invisible-hand economics, after all, does not apply to the heavy hand of business-government cronyism.

––––

Enron brings into question the socioeconomic system whereby special government favor drives profit centers and can even define a whole company—and a

––––

Tennessee Gas Transmission Company in mid-1996. El Paso, in fact, eclipsed Enron as the nation's largest gas-transmission operator, boasting (Enron-like) of its ability "to move gas from Bakersfield (California) to Boston."

regulatory approach to business governance under which gaming and moral hazard occur. "Rather than viewing Enron as a market failure," Fred Smith cautioned, "we should consider whether political controls might have blocked competitive forces, which would have identified and addressed the problem earlier."

Erstwhile market critics who praised (politically correct) Enron on the way up, feeling betrayed, lowered the boom upon Enron's fall. Their wrath included doubling down with "grandiose hierarchic political regulatory schemes"—or laying more bricks on "the road to serfdom" (as Fred Smith put it, invoking F. A. Hayek). Progressivist post-Enron reforms would constrain good entrepreneurship in the quest to prevent bad. Laws such as the Sarbanes-Oxley Corporate Reform Act of 2002, the Bipartisan Campaign Reform Act of 2002, and the Energy Policy Act of 2005 created their own problems, some unintended and some predictable (a subject of Book 4).

"Heroic Capitalism" (Part I of *Capitalism at Work*) developed the theory of commercial success—and failure—from classical-liberal teachings. Centuries apart, Adam Smith, Samuel Smiles, Ayn Rand, and Charles Koch not only advocated economic freedom but also explicated the preconditions of marketplace success. Looking beyond the rule of law and market freedom, these intellectuals championed prudence, authenticity, wealth creation, and course correction—in place of negligence, mistruth, cronyism, and evasion.

Capitalism at Work chronicled how capitalist philosophers long warned against the sort of practices that consumed and ultimately conquered Enron. Adam Smith's 18th-century insights about "a sacred regard for general rules," "self-command," and "prudence," as well as his warnings about "self-deceit" and "over-weening conceit," presciently apply to Ken Lay's organization. "Smith would have been disappointed—but hardly surprised—by the systemic failure that characterized Enron," *Capitalism at Work* concluded.

A century after Adam Smith, Victorian moralist and self-help maestro Samuel Smiles tied commercial success to attention to detail, common sense, and integrity. He warned: "How many tricks are resorted to—in which honesty forms no part—for making money faster than others!" To Smiles, CFO Andy Fastow et al. would have been old vinegar in a new bottle.

A century later, and two centuries after Smith, Ayn Rand's philosophy of Objectivism explained how Enron's subjectivism and layers of deceits were a recipe for failure. Decades before Ken Lay's implosion, Rand warned against the corner-cutting business leader: "An attempt to gain a value by deceiving the mind of others is an act of raising your victim to a position higher than reality, where you become a pawn of their blindness, a slave to their non-thinking and their evasions, while their intelligence, their rationality, their perceptiveness become the enemies you have to dread."

Enron was a politically correct, *postmodern* company. Ken Lay "came to believe that wanting, believing, and saying something to be true could make it so." But external reality is not shaped by personal consciousness. Enron repeatedly and increasingly committed *philosophic fraud* by substituting fakery and fogginess for actuality and sobriety. (Prosecutable fraud was not an issue for the company circa 1996, but it would be later.) The company survived close calls in the 1980s, oversold itself in the early-to-mid 1990s, and charged into a highly speculative revamping in 1996–97. Its corporate culture never really changed until the company went insolvent.

———

How ironic, then, that free-market capitalism took the fall for Enron. Ken Lay was a well-schooled, indefatigable rent-seeker, scarcely differentiating strategies to remove unfavorable regulation to level the playing field from strategies imposing government intervention to benefit Enron at the expense of consumers, taxpayers, and/or competitors. Lay did posit public policy rationales at every turn, and his nonmarket activism was not beyond what his rival CEOs could, would, or did do, at least on a smaller scale. But Lay's political business model, and Enron itself, exemplified a paragon of political capitalism (or cronyism).

Smith, Smiles, and Rand, in their different centuries, criticized rent-seeking and pointed the way to *heroic capitalism*, defined in our day as "maximizing long-term profitability for the business by creating real value in society while always acting lawfully and with integrity."[22]

Charles Koch defended consumer-driven profit making against politically imbued profits: "Good profit comes from making a contribution in society—not from corporate welfare or other ways of taking advantage of people."[23] The virus of cronyism grows and corrupts. "Far too many businesses have been all too eager to lobby for maintaining and increasing subsidies and mandates paid by taxpayers and consumers," he noted. "This growing partnership between business and government is a destructive force, undermining not just our economy and our political system, but the very foundations of our culture."

From Adam Smith in the 18th century to Charles Koch in the 21st century, time-honored capitalist philosophers were anti-Enron intellectuals who (as concluded in *Capitalism at Work*) "elucidated the character traits, mental models, and interpersonal conditions behind success and failure, while differentiating sharply between free-market entrepreneurship and political rent-seeking. Their concern was less the material outputs of capitalism, however substantial, than the moral inputs of capitalism."

———

22. See Bradley, *Capitalism at Work*, pp. 9–11, 18, 24, 79, 89, 314–19.

23. In the words of his management philosophy: "Market-Based Management emphasizes Principled Entrepreneurship over corporate welfare, virtue over talent, challenge over hierarchy, comparative advantage over job title, and rewards for long-term value creation over managing to budgets."

The fundamental lesson from Enron is this: Capitalism did not fail. The mixed economy failed. The capitalist worldview is stronger, not weaker, post-Enron. But there is another, deeper lesson that explains Enron and the mistakes of the intellectual mainstream before, during, and after Enron's active life. It is that arrogant behaviors, or what in the Enron vernacular is called the *smartest-guys-in-the-room problem,* can strike anytime and anywhere. Whether in business or academia—or any profession or association—conceit, deceit, and dogmatism are the bane of personal, intellectual, and organizational success.

A reinterpretation of Enron, in short, has public policy implications quite different from what actually occurred in the wake of Enron's bankruptcy, a subject for this series' finale.

Final Thoughts

Former Enron executive Mike McConnell attempted to reconcile the company he thought he knew with the harsh reality that befell him and thousands of other Enron employees. "I watched a company that won 'Most Innovative' in the country five straight years move into bankruptcy, scandal and total chaos, literally overnight," he wrote in his autobiography.

> Why? I believe the truth is that it was coming to an end for a long time. We just didn't see it.... I recognized, in retrospect, the warning signs all around us. They were important items like culture, values, the way many leaders or groups treated customers and employees; situations that should have been noted and corrected.

McConnell's autopsy of Enron concluded: "If we paused to contemplate 'could' versus 'should,' I am convinced Enron would be a solid and growing company today."

The process of Enron harked all the way back to 1984–85. The common denominator was one unique, empowered, brilliant, soulful chief executive officer. Anointed a titan of industry, Ken Lay had never failed, only progressed, and he was determined that Enron would be his crowning glory. It was this hyperambition that led him down a contra-capitalist road in a politicized industry within America's mixed economy. If Lay did not recognize the treacherous path he was travelling, perhaps it was simply that no term existed to offer recognition of and thus caution against the Pragmatist-Progressivist management strategy producing his company's artificial boom and complete bust.

Ken Lay's enterprise would come to conflict and overtake the checks and balances of the world's largest and most sophisticated economy. Externally, Enron was able to conflict and fool bankers, investors, security analysts, regulators, intellectuals, and the press. Internally, Enron finagled its own lawyers, accountants, auditors, board of directors, and employees.

"One wonders," concluded one study, "whether Enron's senior management may have misled themselves by the combined effects of all the financial manipulation that they invited and approved." Jeff Skilling, not fooled, jumped ship. But Ken Lay, fooled, went down with his ship. More tragically, Lay stuck to a false narrative post-Enron to lose devastatingly at trial and died a broken man, awaiting what would have been a life sentence. Charlatan and criminal to the world, a greater fall of a once titan, Insull-like, could almost not be imagined. He deserved better, far better, if he could only have seen at Enron, even post-Enron, what he did not see.

———

"Something called 'capitalism' has long been held responsible for all sorts of supposed evils," noted the business philosopher Elaine Sternberg. Much more than a "supposed evil," Enron was a "systemic failure of American capitalism." But it was not capitalism as classically understood and defined.

Enron defined *contra-capitalism*: political capitalism, political correctness, regulatory gaming, and other crony sports of the mixed economy. In broad terms, Enron was about postmodernist philosophy and the unintended consequences of government interventionism that allowed the worst to get on top.

Enron's lessons are many, subtle, and profound. Regarding business management: Reality, not illusionism. Incrementalism, not only revolution. Win-win, not win-lose. And just doing the right thing.

Regarding political economy: Wealth creation, not rent-seeking. Simple rules for a complex world. Good profit, not bad.

Best-practices management in a free society, codified as Market-Based Management by classical-liberal entrepreneur Charles Koch, rests on the social philosophy that gave rise to capitalism just several centuries ago. This tradition lauds the epistemological virtues of reality-based thinking, trial-and-error testing from small beginnings, midcourse correction, simplicity, and, above all, humility in the face of creative destruction in the marketplace.

At the interpersonal level, classical-liberal business theorists and practitioners have embraced honesty, frankness, respect, openness, plain dealing, politeness, and promise keeping. Morally, they stand for prudence, caution, probity, character, and balance.

Enron, contrarily, absorbed a belief in image over reality, pretense over proof, feelings over facts, groupthink over independent analysis, and fads over fundamentals. Ethically, Ken Lay made room for new behaviors that came to be practiced by the smartest guys in the room. Politically, Enron embraced cronyism, whereby special public-sector favor propelled new profit centers.

True lessons must reflect what Enron did right and what it did wrong. But as G. K. Chesterton wrote, though there are an infinity of angles at which a man falls, there is only one at which he remains upright. So, too, the many negative lessons of Enron can be reduced to one positive: Truth matters—discovering it, remembering it, reporting it, practicing it. Thus, this revisionist history of Enron.

Kenneth L. Lay: A Chronology

The most reliable genealogies of Kenneth Lee Lay trace his ancestry back to a Jesse Lay, born about 1744 in Halifax County, Virginia. Jesse Lay may have been the son or grandson of David Lay from Wiltshire, England.

Prior to the Revolutionary War, Jesse Lay of Halifax County, VA, moves to Caswell County, North Carolina, in the north-central part of the colony. His son, Jesse Duncan Lay (b. 1766), moves farther west, to Wilkes County, NC, where his son John Michael Lay is born in 1790. John Michael Lay moves to Campbell County in northeastern Tennessee, where his son Thomas Lay is born in 1832.

After the death of his wife, Delilah Croley Lay, Thomas Lay remarries and moves with his son John Croley Lay, to Missouri. John Croley Lay, born circa 1850, is Ken Lay's great-grandfather.

1874   Andrew Jackson Lay, Ken Lay's grandfather, is born in Texas County, MO, in the heart of the Ozarks. (The county seat is Houston.) Andrew Jackson Lay will die in 1949 (when Ken Lay is seven) on the farm where he spent his entire life.

1895   Andrew Jackson Lay marries Matilda Ellen Owens (b. 1876).

1914   *October 3.* Omer Lay, father of Ken Lay, is born to Andrew Jackson Lay and his wife in Solo, Texas County, MO. Omer (1914–99) is the 10th of their 11 children, of whom 7 boys survive into adulthood: Clarence Otto (1896–1975), Luther Henry (1898–1984), John Shelby (1899–1980),

Ira (1901–73), Vester Euel (1907–1993), Omer, and Robert (1918–74). These will be Ken Lay's 6 paternal uncles, and their children will be his first cousins on his father's side.

1916   *October 23*. Ruth Ester Rees, mother of Ken Lay, is born to Joe Sievus Rees (also spelled Reese and Reece) and Rachel (née Ice) Rees in Tyrone, MO. Ruth (1916–1995) is the fifth of their six children: Ada (1903–97), Myrtle (1905–93), Virgil (1906–78), Bertha (1908–97), Ruth, and Ruby (1918–2005). These will be Ken Lay's four aunts (five, counting their half-sister Ethel Ice [1898–1991]) and one maternal uncle. Their children will be his first cousins on his mother's side.

1937   *May 22*. Omer Lay marries Ruth Ester Rees in Houston, Texas County, MO. The local newspaper calls their wedding the culmination of a childhood romance.

1939   *May 9*. Omer and Ruth Lay have their first child: a daughter, Bonnie Jean.

1941   *June 20*. FBI Special Agent Rowen Ayers, stationed in Jefferson City, MO, marries FBI clerk Eleanor Byarlay. They will be Ken Lay's first father- and mother-in-law.

1942   *April 15*. Kenneth Lee Lay is born at home to Omer and Ruth (Rees) Lay in Tyrone, Texas County, MO. In the first six years of Ken's life, the family lived in four small Missouri towns within 15 miles of each other: Tyrone, Cabool, Houston, and Raymondville.

1945   *October 8*. Ken Lay's younger sister, Sharon Sue Lay, is born to Omer and Ruth Lay; Sharon, their second daughter, is their third and last child.

1947   Omer Lay settles his family in Raymondville, MO (a Texas County village of fewer than 200 residents), where Ruth's older brother Virgil also lives. Omer Lay operates a feedstore but also buys farmers' chickens and sells them to stores in nearby towns. He is wiped out financially when a truck crashes while carrying a load of his chickens. He then takes a job as a traveling salesman in Mississippi for the Home Comfort Stove Co., moving his family from town to town.

1948   Omer Lay and his family move to Rush Hill, MO, where he works in sales for Montgomery Ward in the nearby town of Mexico. (He also works on the farm of his brother-in-law, Othel L. Hobbs, husband to his wife Ruth's older sister Bertha Ellen.)

Rush Hill, where the Lays would live for almost 10 years, is smaller than Raymondville, with about 120 residents, but it is outside the Ozarks.

1950   *Circa.* Ken Lay works three newspaper routes, mows lawns, shovels snow, and stacks hay bales to help out his family. He attends the three-room Rush Hill elementary school, which has one teacher for first and second grades; one for third, fourth, and fifth; and one for sixth, seventh, and eighth.

Omer Lay answers a call to preach at the nondenominational Rush Hill Community Church, which he continues doing until leaving the community in 1958.

1954   *Circa.* Ken Lay (age 12) gets a full-time summer job at 25¢ an hour, working 16 hours a day on a farm. From age 12 on, Ken Lay's jobs cover his personal expenses, apart from room and board. Also in 1954, Omer Lay's house gets indoor plumbing.

1956   Ken Lay (age 14) enters the Audrain County high school, the Community R-6 School.

1957   *June.* Ken Lay's older sister, Bonnie Jean, graduates from the Community R-6 School of Audrain County and prepares to enter Christian College, a conservative women's school in Columbia, MO. Omer Lay moves his family from Rush Hill to Columbia so that Bonnie Jean can save money by living at home while she attends college and so that his younger children can attend a better high school. Omer Lay becomes a security guard at the University of Missouri; Ruth Lay works in its bookstore. Omer also sells farm machinery on the side and serves as a preacher and Sunday school teacher at Bethel Baptist Church in Columbia.

September. Ken Lay (age 15) enters David H. Hickman High School in Columbia, where he sings in the choirs, plays in a trombone quartet, serves as Homecoming Chairman, is elected to the National Honor Society, and receives the American History Award.

1959   *June 6.* Bonnie Jean Lay marries James Richard Bourne, a senior at the University of Missouri. The wedding announcement states that, in September, the couple will enroll at Southern Methodist University, in Dallas, TX, where she will work toward a BS in music, and he will study for the ministry.

1960   *May.* Ken Lay graduates from Hickman High School. His grades place him 10th in a class of 276.

September. Ken enters the University of Missouri in Columbia. Attending college is a family first (shared with his two sisters) in relation to his 4 grandparents, both parents, 12 aunts and uncles, and 40 first cousins.

While school is paid for from scholarships, Ken works full time during the summer and part time (15–20 hours per week) during the school year to meet his personal expenses.

1962   Lay, though only a junior, is elected president of the Zeta Phi chapter of Beta Theta Pi fraternity at the University of Missouri, the largest fraternity on campus and a noted "dry" fraternity.

1963   Lay receives his BA in economics, with a GPA over 3.6, graduating Phi Beta Kappa. His college mentor is economics professor Pinkney Walker.

Sharon Lay marries Charles Edward Powers; both are 18 years old and just graduated from high school. Later in life, she will marry Joe Ellis, a prominent cosmetic dentist in the Houston area.

1965   *June.* Lay joins Humble Oil & Refining (now part of ExxonMobil) as an economist in the corporate planning department.

After seven years, Omer Lay (age 51) resigns his role as preacher at the Bethel Baptist Church in Columbia.

August. Ken Lay receives his MA in economics (with honors), also from the University of Missouri. His GPA is over 3.8.

September. Lay begins the PhD program in economics at the University of Houston.

1966   *January.* Linda Phillips (who would later marry Ken Lay) marries Robert F. Herrold. In September, Robert and Linda Herrold have their first child, a daughter, Robyn Anne, in Washington, DC.

June 18. In Jefferson City, MO, Ken Lay marries Judith Ayers, who graduated in 1966 from the University of Missouri as a journalism major and who had earlier sat in front of Ken Lay in the college's French class. Her bridesmaids include Mrs. William Morgan (Anne Lamkin) and

Mrs. Richard Kinder (Sara Lu Scholes), sorority sisters from Kappa Alpha Theta. Ken Lay's ushers are his brother-in-law Edward Powers (husband of Sharon Sue Lay) and the bride's brother, USN Lt. James Ayers, a 1964 graduate of the US Naval Academy in Annapolis. His best man is fraternity brother Robert Healy, who will go on to spend his entire career as a chemical engineer at ExxonMobil in Houston, TX, specializing in enhanced oil recovery.

1967   A collection of speeches by Humble Oil CEO Mike Wright, mostly ghostwritten by Ken Lay, is published as *The Business of Business* by McGraw-Hill.

1968   *January.* Facing conscription, Ken Lay enlists in the US Navy Officer Candidate School in Newport, RI. In May, he is commissioned as a naval officer. In June, on the recommendation of Pinkney Walker, he is transferred to the Pentagon to work with the assistant secretary of the Navy for financial management, and there he devises an improved military-purchasing system.

        August 15. Mark Kenneth Lay is born to Ken and Judie Lay in Arlington, VA.

        November 21. A Texas County newspaper's description of a Lay family gathering mentions Mr. and Mrs. Omer Lay, Miss Sharon Powers of Columbia, and Mrs. Bonnie Bourne and children of St. Joseph. Bonnie Bourne ultimately gets her PhD in education from the University of Missouri.

1970   *June.* Lay receives a PhD in economics from the University of Houston. His dissertation is "The Measurement of the Timing of the Economic Impact of Defense Procurement Activity: An Analysis of the Vietnam Buildup."

1970–73 Lay teaches night classes as a lecturer and then as an assistant professor at George Washington University, in Washington, DC. Among his favorite books is Peter Drucker's *The Age of Discontinuity.*

1971   *January 3.* Ken and Judie Lay have their second child, Elizabeth Ayers Lay, in Bethesda, MD.

        April. Lieutenant Ken Lay is honorably discharged from the Navy after 39 months of service.

May. Lay joins the Federal Power Commission (now the Federal Energy Regulatory Commission) as technical assistant to the vice chairman, Pinkney Walker, his mentor in economics at the University of Missouri. Lay becomes a de facto commissioner, with Walker absent to care for his ailing wife.

1972   *October.* Lay joins the Department of the Interior as deputy undersecretary of energy, a new position charged with overseeing energy policy across federal departments. He takes the lead in drafting President Richard Nixon's first presidential message on energy, delivered April 18, 1973. Lay also works on petroleum-allocation issues with the White House.

1973   Ken Lay meets Jack Bowen, CEO of Florida Gas, while moderating a meeting on oil and gas drilling in the Gulf of Mexico, near Florida. A few months later, he will write to Bowen about the possibility of getting a private-sector job with Florida Gas. Lay's job search would result in 15 offers.

1974   *January.* Lay joins Jack Bowen's Florida Gas Company in Winter Park, FL, as director of corporate planning. The unit is later called *corporate development*. CEO Jack Bowen advocates for his hiring; COO Shelby Sullivan is less enthusiastic. After Lay receives promotions, he and Judie will buy a house in the exclusive Via Lugano neighborhood and a condo at Melbourne Beach, FL. They attend Asbury United Methodist Church. For relaxation, Ken Lay jogs, plays tennis, golfs, and reads thrillers by John D. MacDonald, a Harvard MBA author whose Florida-based stories often include elaborate business swindles.

September. Lay is named vice president of Transgulf Pipeline Company.

1975   *May.* Lay is named vice president of corporate development at Florida Gas.

October. Lay is named senior vice president of Florida Gas Transmission Company, with responsibility for supply and engineering.

1976   *September.* Lay is named president of Florida Gas Transmission Company and executive vice president of its parent, Florida Gas Company.

1978   *March.* Lay is named board director of the Gas Research Institute, a position he holds until August 1986.

1979   *May.* Lay is named president of Florida Gas Company.

August. Continental Group buys Florida Gas Company and renames it Continental Resources Company. Lay is named president.

November. Lay is named to the additional post of corporate vice president for Continental Group.

Lay is named chairman of the Slurry Transport Association.

1980   *July.* Lay is named board director of the Interstate Natural Gas Association of America, where he would serve as chairman in 1989.

October. Lay is named board director of the American Gas Association, a position he would hold until September 1986.

1981   *April.* Lay resigns from Continental Resources Company. Bill Morgan becomes the company's senior executive in Winter Park.

April. Ken Lay files for a divorce from Judie Lay.

May 1. Lay joins Transco Companies Inc. as president and chief operating officer, under chairman and CEO Jack Bowen, the man who hired Lay to join Florida Gas.

June. Judie Lay suffers a nervous breakdown and is committed to a psychiatric hospital. The Lays' divorce trial is postponed.

July. Lay is named president and COO of Transcontinental Gas Pipe Line Company, an interim position he holds until April 30, 1982.

1982   *February.* Lay is named board director of the National Energy Foundation, a position he would hold until February 1988. Lay also joins the board of directors of First City National Bank of Houston.

May. Lay is named interim President and CEO of Transco Exploration Company (TXC), in addition to other titles.

June. With their divorce trial scheduled to begin in one week, Ken and Judie Lay reach a settlement.

July. Ken Lay marries his former secretary, Linda Phillips Herrold, in Houston. Linda has three children from her first marriage: Robyn Anne (b. 1965), Todd David (b. 1969), and Robert Ray "Beau" (b. 1971).

1983   *July.* A feature in the *Houston Chronicle* business section, "Transco's Ken Lay Credited as Natural Gas Innovator," would be the first of many positive business articles written on him in the next years.

November. Lay joins the board of directors of the American Council for Capital Formation.

1984   *June 6.* Houston Natural Gas announces the election of Ken Lay as chairman, president, and CEO, effective June 8 (Friday), the day Lay's resignation from Transco is effective.

June 8. Ken Lay enters into a five-year employment contract with HNG providing a minimum salary of $510,000 per annum, increasing at 10 percent per year. Lay will void the agreement in February 1986 and enter into a new five-year agreement three months later.

December 30. Ken Lay is featured (with picture) in a *New York Times* business story: "The Maverick Who Transformed an Industry."

1985   Lay is elected a board member of Texas Commerce Bank.

January. Lay is named a director of the American Petroleum Institute, a position he would resign from in December 1987.

July 16. Ken Lay is named president and chief operating officer of HNG/InterNorth.

November 12. Lay is named president and chief executive officer of HNG/InterNorth, following Sam Segnar's dismissal. Bill Strauss becomes chairman.

1986   *February.* Ken Lay voids his (1984) employment contract. He later turns down his $187,500 bonus award for 1986.

February 11. Lay is named president, chairman, and chief executive officer of HNG/InterNorth, following Bill Strauss's resignation.

April 10. HNG/InterNorth becomes Enron; Lay is named chairman and chief executive officer.

May. Ken Lay enters into a new contract with Enron providing for compensation in the event of an involuntary termination resulting from a change of control.

1987   *May.* Ken Lay enters into a four-year employment contract with Enron providing a minimum salary of $625,000 per annum, a loan commitment of $1,500,000, and other provisions.

Lay is elected a board director of Compaq Computers.

1988   Ken Lay joins the board of regents of the University of Houston System. He would later donate monies to fund two (Ken Lay) chairs in the political science and the economics departments. In 1995, he would receive UH's outstanding-alumni award.

Lay is named Houston Finance Chairman for George Bush for President.

1989   *September.* Ken Lay enters into a five-year employment contract with Enron providing a minimum salary of $750,000 per annum, stock option grants of 250,000 shares, and other provisions and financial incentives.

1990   Ken Lay is named cochair of the Economic Summit of Industrialized Nations–Houston Host Committee.

April. Lay is named to the 28-member Secretary of Energy Advisory Board, one of two representatives from the oil and gas industry. (He is already a member of the National Petroleum Council.)

1991   *October.* An in-depth business feature in the business section of the *Houston Chronicle,* "What Makes Kenneth Lay Run?" identifies the subject as multifaceted and enigmatic.

December. Lay rules out taking a cabinet-secretary position in the Bush administration after meeting with the president.

1992   Ken Lay receives an honorary LLD from the University of Missouri.

Lay is elected a board director of Trust Company of the West.

Lay is named chairman of the Host Committee for the 1992 Republican National Convention.

1993   *June.* Ken Lay is named to the 25-person President's Council on Sustainable Development in a White House ceremony in Washington, DC.

Lay is elected a board director of Eli Lilly Company.

1994   *February.* Ken Lay enters into a new five-year employment contract with Enron providing a minimum salary of $990,000 per annum, stock option grants of 1,200,000 shares, and other provisions. Lay has the option to terminate the agreement as of February 8, 1997.

1995   *March 10.* Ken Lay's mother, Ruth Rees Lay, dies at 79 in Columbia, MO.

1996   *November 26.* Lay agrees to a new five-year contract extension as chairman and chief executive officer. Rich Kinder resigns as president of Enron, effective January 1, 1997. Lay announces that he will take on the post of president.

December. Jeff Skilling is named to be president and chief operating officer, effective January 1, 1997.

Lay's new five-year employment contract with Enron provides for a minimum annual salary of $1,200,000 and stock options of 1,275,000 shares, among other provisions and financial incentives.

Business Week names Ken Lay as one of America's top 25 managers for 1996.

1997   Ken Lay receives four major recognitions: Ben K. Miller Memorial International Business Award (University of Colorado), Private Sector Council Leadership Award, Rotary Club Distinguished Citizen of the Year, and election to the Texas Business Hall of Fame.

October. Ken Lay presents the Enron Prize for Distinguished Public Service to Mikhail Gorbachev at Rice University's James A. Baker III Institute for Public Policy in Houston, TX.

1998 Ken Lay is elected into the membership of the Horatio Alger Society. He would join the board and serve as executive vice president from May 2000 until April 2002.

Ken Lay receives an honorary doctor of humane letters degree from the University of Houston.

1999 *February 12.* Omer Lay, Ken Lay's father, dies at age 84. He is buried in the Bethel Baptist Church of Columbia, MO, where he had preached.

Ken Lay receives two honorary degrees: doctor of social sciences from Brunel University (London) and doctor of humane letters from Oswego (NY) State University.

2000 *April 7.* Ken Lay throws out the ceremonial first pitch to begin the Houston Astros season at the new $265 million Enron Field. Lay, in fact, is credited with the referendum vote for the stadium that would retain the Houston Astros.

2001 *February.* Skilling becomes Enron's CEO; Lay remains as its chairman.

2002 *January 23.* Ken Lay resigns from Enron Corp., which had declared bankruptcy the month before.

February. Called to testify before Congress, Lay pleads the Fifth Amendment, although Skilling does not.

2004 *July 8.* Ken Lay is indicted by a grand jury on multiple counts of deceiving the SEC and the investing public about the true performance of Enron's businesses.

2005 *December 13.* With his trial set to begin the next month, Ken Lay delivers a speech to the Houston Forum: "Guilty, Until Proven Innocent."

2006 *January 30.* The trial of Lay and Skilling begins in Houston. US Supreme Court Justice Sotomayer later writes (in *Skilling v. United States* [2010]) that she is "doubtful that [the] jury was indeed free from the deep-seated animosity that pervaded the community." But the Court's majority rejects Skilling's claim that the trial should have been held outside Houston.

July 5. A biblical 40 days and 40 nights after his conviction, Ken Lay dies, at age 64, in the night, at a friend's vacation home in Aspen, CO, of a heart ailment that he has long kept secret. Judge Simeon Lake rules that, under the doctrine of *abatement ab initio*, not only is Lay's conviction voided but also the legal standing of his case is as though he had never been charged. Long-time Enron executive Mark Frevert calls it a pardon from God.

July 9. A Sunday memorial service for Ken Lay is held in Aspen, CO, where he died on vacation. Only 200 people, all family and friends, are permitted to attend.

July 12. A memorial service for Ken Lay is held in Houston. The service is attended by former President George H. W. Bush and former Secretary of State James Baker III. Lay's stepson David Herrold reads a passage from Psalms (New International Version, 18: 3, 19) that he said was among the last entries Ken Lay wrote in a notebook he carried with him: "I called to the Lord who is worthy of praise and I am saved from my enemies. ... He brought me out into a spacious place. He rescued me because He delighted in me." Lay's body is cremated and his ashes spread in the Aspen countryside.

2011   The Enron Creditors Recovery Corp. settles its suit against Linda Lay and Ken Lay's estate because Linda Lay has "extremely limited" assets and the estate is insolvent (Reuters, June 20, 2011).

Selected Bibliography

(A complete bibliography is available at www.politicalcapitalism.org/Book3
/Fullbibliography.html.)

Abbott, Catherine. "The Expanding Domain of the Nonjurisdictional Gas Industry." In
New Horizons in Natural Gas Deregulation, edited by Jerry Ellig and Joseph Kalt, 187–
94. Westport, CT: Praeger, 1996.

"Abolish FERC." Editorial, *Wall Street Journal*, September 18, 1985.

*Accounting Reform and Investor Protection Issues Raised by Enron and Other Public Compa-
nies: Oversight of the Accounting Profession, Audit Quality and Independence, and Formu-
lation of Accounting Principles: Hearings Before the Senate Committee on Banking, Housing,
and Urban Affairs*, 107th Cong., 2nd sess. (2002) (statement of Walter P. Schuetze),
235–38.

Alger, Dan. "The Scope of Deregulation for Natural Gas Pipelines and the 'Workable
Competition' Standard." In *New Horizons in Natural Gas Deregulation,* edited by Jerry
Ellig and Joseph Kalt, 85–106. Westport, CT: Praeger, 1996.

Alger, Dan, and Michael A. Toman. "Market-Based Regulation of Natural Gas Pipelines." *Journal of Regulatory Economics* 2, no. 3 (1990): 262–80.

American Wind Energy Association. "Enron Acquires Zond, Launches Enron Renewable Energy Corp." Press release, January 6, 1997.

"America's Most Admired Companies." *Fortune*, March 3, 1997, 73.

Amoco/Enron Solar. "Amoco Corporation and Enron Corporation Form Joint Venture to
Provide Missing Link in Solar Energy Industry." PR Newswire, December 19, 1994.

Anderson, Terry, and Donald Leal. *Free Market Environmentalism*. San Francisco: Pacific
Research Institute for Public Policy, 1991.

Angrist, Stanley. "Natural Gas Futures Are a Big Success." *Wall Street Journal*, September
17, 1990.

Arbogast, Stephen. *Resisting Corporate Corruption: Lessons in Practical Ethics from the Enron
Wreckage*. Salem, MA: M & M Scrivener Press, 2008.

Arthur Andersen. "Annual Energy Symposium: 1980–1999 Highlights." Houston, TX: 2000.

Babineck, Mark. "Enron Spins Off Oil, Asian Subsidiaries." Associated Press, July 21, 1999.

Ball, Ian, and Gary Pflugrath. "Government Accounting: Making Enron Look Good." *World Economics*, January–March 2012, 1–18.

Banerjee, Neela. "At Enron, Lavish Excess Often Came Before Success." *New York Times*, February 26, 2002, sec. C.

Barrett, William P. "Bargain Hunter." *Forbes*, May 4, 1998, 92.

Bartlett, Christopher A., and Meg Wozny. "Enron's Transformation: From Gas Pipelines to New Economy Powerhouse." Harvard Business School Case No. 9-301-064. Boston: Harvard Business School Press, 2001.

Bast, Joseph. "Enron Proves Capitalism Works." Heartland Institute, September 1, 2002. https://www.heartland.org/publications-resources/publications/september-2002-enron-proves-capitalism-works.

Baumol, William, and J. Gregory Sidak. *Transmission Pricing and Stranded Costs in the Electric Power Industry*. Washington, DC: American Enterprise Institute, 1995.

Beazley, J. Earnest. "USX's Hoglund Resigns to Take Post at Enron." *Wall Street Journal*, September 2, 1987.

Behr, Peter, and April Witt. "The Fall of Enron: Dream Job Turns into Nightmare." *Washington Post*, July 28, 2002, sec. A.

Benedict, Roger. "Analyst Backs Hedging as Alternative to Import Fee, Cartel." *Oil Daily*, December 28, 1992, 2.

Benston, George. "Fair-Value Accounting: A Cautionary Tale from Enron." *Journal of Accounting and Public Policy* 25 (2006): 465–84.

Bhatnagar, Sanjay, and Peter Tufano. "Enron Gas Services." Harvard Business School Case No. 9-294-076. Boston: Harvard Business School Press, 1995.

Binswanger, Harry, ed. *The Ayn Rand Lexicon: Objectivism from A to Z*. New York: Meridian, 1982.

Blauvelt, Randal. "Enron Corp. Purchases Shares, Establishes Employee Stock Ownership Plan and Authorizes Open Market Share Repurchase Program." Press release, October 20, 1986.

Bradley, Robert, Jr. "California DSM: A Pyrrhic Victory for Energy Efficiency?" *Public Utilities Fortnightly*, October 1, 1995, 41–47.

———. *Capitalism at Work: Business, Government, and Energy*. Salem, MA: M & M Scrivener Press, 2009.

———. *Climate Alarmism Reconsidered*. London: Institute of Economic Affairs, 2003.

———. "The Distortions and Dynamics of Gas Regulation." In *New Horizons in Natural Gas Deregulation*, edited by Jerry Ellig and Joseph Kalt, 1–29. Westport, CT: Praeger, 1996.

———. *Edison to Enron: Energy Markets and Political Strategies*. Hoboken, NJ: John Wiley & Sons; Salem, MA: Scrivener Publishing, 2011.

———. "Enron Wind Decision." Memorandum to Ken Lay, October 28, 1998.

———. Foreword to *New Horizons in Natural Gas Deregulation*, edited by Jerry Ellig and Joseph Kalt, ix–x. Westport, CT: Praeger, 1996.

———. *The Mirage of Oil Protection*. Lanham, MD: University Press of America, 1989.

———. "Natural Gas, Electricity, and the Environment." Presentation, various locales, 1998.

————. "New Energy Ideas at Enron." Presentation at Texas A&M University, October 14, 1999.

————. *Oil, Gas & Government: The U.S. Experience.* 2 vols. Lanham, MD: Rowman & Littlefield, 1996.

————. "Potential Enron Windpower Investment." Memorandum to Terry Thorn, November 25, 1996.

————. "Power Politics: Enron Lives!" Commentary. *POWER,* December 1, 2009. www .powermag.com/power-politics-enron-lives/.

————. "Renewable Energy: Not Cheap, Not 'Green'." Cato Institute Policy Analysis No. 280, August 27, 1997.

Brenner, Marie. "The Enron Wars." *Vanity Fair,* April 2002, 181–209.

Brewer, Lynn. *Confessions of an Enron Executive: A Whistleblower's Story.* College Station, TX: VirtualBookworm.com Publishing, 1992.

"Broad Use of Order 436 Seen Reducing Gas Prices 30¢/Mcf." *Oil & Gas Journal,* April 21, 1986, 33.

"Brooklyn Union and Enron Sign Gas Sales Agreement." *Business Wire,* January 14, 1987.

Brough, Wayne. "Market Structure, Measurements, and Deregulation." In *New Horizons in Natural Gas Deregulation,* edited by Jerry Ellig and Joseph Kalt, 107–20. Westport, CT: Praeger, 1996.

Brown, Lester, and Jennifer Mitchell. "Building a New Economy." In *State of the World 1998,* produced by the Worldwatch Institute. New York: W. W. Norton, 1998.

Browne, John. "Climate Change: The New Agenda." Address at Stanford University, May 19, 1997. Reprinted in *Global Climate Change: A Senior-Level Debate at the Intersection of Economics, Strategy, Technology, Science, Politics, and International Negotiation,* edited by Andrew Hoffman, 53–62. San Francisco: New Lexington Press, 1998.

Bryce, Robert. *Cronies: Oil, the Bushes, and the Rise of Texas, America's Superstate.* New York: PublicAffairs, 2004.

————. "King Kinder." *Houston Press.* March 6, 2003. http://www.houstonpress.com /news/king-kinder-6556981.

————. *Pipe Dreams: Greed, Ego, and the Death of Enron.* New York: PublicAffairs, 2002.

Bryson, Reid. Preface to *The Cooling: Has the Next Ice Age Already Begun?* by Lowell Ponte, xi–xii. Englewood Cliffs, NJ: Prentice Hall, 1976.

Burns, Ron. "Enron Pipeline & Liquids Group." *Enron Business,* January 1993, 7.

————. "FACTS ARE FRIENDLY." Memorandum to GPG Employees, October 2, 1991.

Burrough, Bryan. "Houston Natural Gas Chairman Quits; Transco Energy President Is Successor." *Wall Street Journal,* June 7, 1984.

Bush, George H. W. "Remarks on the National Energy Strategy." July 24, 1991. Available at American Presidency Project, http://www.presidency.ucsb.edu/ws/?pid=19827.

California Public Utilities Commission. "CPUC Offers Electric Restructuring Proposals for Comment." Press release, May 24, 1995.

————. *Order Instituting Rulemaking and Order Instituting Investigation on the Commission's Proposed Policies Governing Restructuring California's Electric Services Industry and Reforming Regulation.* Case Nos. R.94-04-031 and I.94-04-032, April 20, 1994.

————. "Proposed Policy Decision Adopting a Preferred Industry Structure." *Order Instituting Rulemaking and Order Instituting Investigation on the Commission's Proposed*

Policies Governing Restructuring California's Electric Services Industry and Reforming Regulation. Case Nos. R.94-04-031 and I.94-04-032, May 24, 1995.

Cano, Craig. "Feds Have No Taste for Retail Wheeling, but Hunger Grows in States." *Inside FERC*, January 25, 1993, 1, 8–10.

Castaneda, Christopher, and Joseph Pratt. *From Texas to the East: A Strategic History of Texas Eastern Corporation*. College Station: Texas A&M University Press, 1993.

Castaneda, Christopher, and Clarance Smith. *Gas Pipelines and the Emergence of America's Regulatory State: A History of Panhandle Eastern Corporation, 1928–1993*. New York: Cambridge University Press, 1996.

"Cato Institute Chair Criticizes Mandatory Open Access." *Megawatt Daily*, January 31, 1997.

Caudill, Mark D. "Competition in Natural Gas." Presentation to the NARUC Committee on Gas, Austin, TX, November 9, 2015.

Chui, Glennda. "BP Official Takes Global Warming Seriously." *San Jose Mercury News*, May 20, 1997, sec. A.

Citizens for a Sound Economy. "Typical Household Would Save $216 a Year if Consumers Had Choice in Electric Provider." Press release, May 30, 1996.

Clark, Mary. "Electricity Ruling Clears Path for Wholesale Wheeling." *Enron Business*, June 1996, 3, 8.

———. "Enron Ranks Among the Top 25 Most Admired Companies in America." *Enron Business*, April 1996, 2, 8.

———. "Enron's Board of Directors Sets the Standard in Corporate Leadership." *Enron Business*, June 1994, 2–3.

———. "Enron's New Vision and Values Set a Course for Success." *Enron Business*, June/July 1995, 2, 7.

———. "From a Fossil Fuel to a Commodity, Natural Gas Comes of Age with the Latest in Financial Marketing Tools." *Enron Business*, July 1993, 4.

———. Numerous articles, *Enron Business*, 1993–97.

Clark, Mary, and Carol Hensley. "Enron Gas Services and Enron International—United in the Global Marketplace." *Enron Business*, September 1994, 2–3.

Clark, Wilson. *Energy for Survival: The Alternative to Extinction*. Garden City, NY: Anchor Books, 1974.

Clayton, Gary. *Economics: Principles and Practices*. New York: McGraw-Hill, 2008.

Clean Air Act Reauthorization: Hearings Before the Subcommittee on Energy and Power, House Committee on Energy and Commerce, 101st Cong., 1st sess. (1989) (statement and testimony of Ken Lay, chairman of Enron Corp., appearing on behalf of the INGAA and the AGA), 471–90, 516–17; (statement and testimony of James Rogers, chairman of the Public Service Company of Indiana, appearing on behalf of the Indiana Coalition for Acid Rain Equity), 48–53, 70–86; (statement of Richard E. Ayers, senior attorney for the Natural Resources Defense Council), 467–71.

"Coal—the Latest Addition to ECT's Energy Portfolio." *Enside ECT*, May/June 1998, 3–4.

Collingwood, R. J. *The Idea of History*. Oxford: Clarendon Press, 1946.

Collins, Jim. *Good to Great: Why Some Companies Make the Leap ... and Others Don't*. New York: HarperBusiness, 2001.

Competitive Enterprise Institute. "CEI Statement Opposing 'Stranded Cost' Recovery." Press release, August 7, 1997.

Corporate Fraud Task Force. *Second Year Report to the President*. Washington, DC: Government Printing Office, July 20, 2004.

Costello, Kenneth, and J. Rodney Lemon. *Unbundling the Retail Gas Market: Current Activities and Guidance for Serving Residential and Small Customers*. Columbus, OH: National Regulatory Research Institute, May 1996.

"Court Confirms Enron Bankruptcy Plan." *USA Today*, wire reports, July 15, 2004.

Crandall, Robert, and Jerry Ellig. "Economic Deregulation and Customer Choice: Lessons for the Electric Industry." Center for Market Processes, 1997. https://www.mercatus.org /publication/economic-deregulation-and-customer-choice-lessons-electric-industry.

Crawford, Mark. "White House Takes a Shine to Solar Power." *Energy Daily*, July 2, 1997, 3.

"Creative Idea from Enron: Enron Promoting Demand Charge for Producers." *Gas Daily*, June 4, 1986, 3–4.

Creswell, Julie. "The Anti-Enron: In 1996, Rich Kinder lost out on the CEO job at Enron. So he left to start his own energy firm. Now he's a billionaire. Take that, Ken Lay!" *Fortune*, November 24, 2003, 178–84.

Crow, Patrick. "FERC Control of Gas Gathering at Issue Among U.S. Industry." *Oil and Gas Journal*, March 7, 1994, 23–25.

Crowley, Lawrence. "Enron Corporation." Rauscher Pierce Refsnes. March 5, 1993.

Culp, Christopher, and Steve Hanke. "Empire of the Sun." In *Corporate Aftershock*, edited by Christopher Culp and William Niskanen, 3–27. Hoboken, NJ: John Wiley & Sons, 2005.

Dar, Vinod. "'Dream Team' or MTV?" Letter to the editor, *Natural Gas Week*, October 5, 1992, 3.

Davidson, Mark. "Always-Confident Enron Aims to Grab 10% of Retail Energy Market by 2001." *Inside FERC's Gas Market Report*, Week of March 7, 1997.

Davies, Karin. "Texas Intrastates Chase After Falling Prices with Spot Sales." *Natural Gas Week*, January 21, 1985, 1, 3

Davis, Jo Ellen. "Enron's Pipeline Is Filled with Problems," *Business Week,* November 16, 1987, 156F, 156H.

———. "A Mega-Pipeline with a Massive Identity Crisis." *Business Week,* April 14, 1986, 65–66.

Davis, Michael. "Lay Staying, So Kinder Will Leave." *Houston Chronicle*, November 26, 1996.

DeMuth, Christopher (American Enterprise Institute). Letter to Ken Lay (Enron). June 10, 1996.

Dent, Gregory. "Enron Asks Oklahoma Regulators to Cut Back on Gas Production." *Natural Gas Week*, May 8, 1995, 6.

De Rouffignac, Ann. "Enron Pulls the Plug on Solar Power Operation." *Houston Business Journal*, Week of April 16–22, 1999, 44.

———. "Enron Ready to Retail Electric Power." *Houston Business Journal*, Week of May 10–16, 1996, sec. A.

———. "Enron Wins Bid to Supply Electric Power in New Hampshire Town." *Houston Business Journal*, June 23, 1996. https://www.bizjournals.com/houston/stories /1996/06/24/story8.html.

———. "Visions of Power." *Houston Business Journal*, Week of March 7–16, 1997, sec. A.

Deudney, Daniel, and Christopher Flavin. *Renewable Energy: The Power to Choose*. New York: W. W. Norton, 1983.

Doehne, Gaynell. "Backstage at the Northern Border Pipeline Project." *Enron Business,* October 1996, 8–9.

———. "Venezuela Fits EOG's Niche." *Enron Business,* September 1996, 8, 11.

Dolbee, Sandi. "Prophet or Profit? Energy Chief, Religious Leaders Dispute God's Role in Utility Price Spiral." *San Diego Union-Tribune,* February 2, 2001.

Donnelly, Ann. "Executive of the Year." *World Cogeneration,* November/December 1996, 1, 20.

Donway, Roger. "The Collapse of a Postmodern Corporation." *Navigator,* May 2002. https://atlassociety.org/commentary/commentary-blog/3846-the-collapse -of-a-postmodern-corporation.

Drummond, Jim. "Enron Sees Hubs Cutting U.S. Spot Gas Sales More Than Half." *Oil Daily,* April 18, 1990.

Durgin, Hillary. "Enron Taps Skilling for No. 2 Job." *Houston Chronicle,* December 11, 1996.

Ebdon, J. Fred. "Transwestern Builds an 'Advanced Inch.'" *Gas,* May 1960, 1–20.

"EES Employees Make a Powerful Stand for Electricity Competition." *Enron Business* 9 (1997): 6–7.

"EGS Takes on Some Powerful Business." *Enron Business,* February 1993, 7.

Ehrlich, Paul, and John Holdren. "Impact of Population Growth." *Science* 171 (1971): 1212–17.

Eichenwald, Kurt. *Conspiracy of Fools: A True Story.* New York: Broadway Books, 2005.

———. "Enron's Many Strands: The Partnerships; for Enron Executive, Big Profit on a Bad Deal." *New York Times,* February 26, 2002, sec. C.

"An Electric Combination: The Portland General Merger." *Enside ECT,* September/October 1996, 1.

Ellig, Jerry. "The Consumer Impact of Federal Natural Gas Regulation." *Transportation Practitioners Journal* 60, no. 3 (Spring 1993): 270–85.

———. "Why Do Regulators Regulate? The Case of the Southern California Gas Market." *Journal of Regulatory Economics* 7, no. 3 (1995): 293–308.

Ellig, Jerry, and Joseph P. Kalt, eds. *New Horizons in Natural Gas Deregulation.* Westport, CT: Praeger, 1996.

Ellig, Jerry, and Daniel Lin. "A Taxonomy of Dynamic Competition Theories." In *Dynamic Competition and Public Policy,* edited by Jerry Ellig, 16–44. Cambridge: Cambridge University Press, 2001.

"El Paso." In *Pacific Coast Gas Association: A Century of Excellence,* edited by Gordon Blackley, 70–71. Portland, OR: PCGA, 1993.

Energy Daily. Various issues.

Energy Information Administration. Annual energy review, monthly reviews, historical data.

———. *Distribution of Natural Gas.* Washington, DC: Department of Energy, 2008.

———. "Oregon Restructuring Active," updated April 2007. https://www.eia.gov /electricity/state/archive/062907.pdf.

———. *U.S. Crude Oil, Natural Gas, and Natural Gas Liquids Reserves 1990 Annual Report.* DOE/EIA-0216(90). Washington, DC: Department of Energy, 1991.

Enfuels. NGV Update. November 1992–January 1993.

Enron Business. 1993–98.

"Enron Buys Louisiana Resources." *Gas Processors Report,* April 26, 1993, 6–8.

"Enron Buys Stake in 'Pure Power' Firm." *Energy Daily,* December 23, 1996, 3.

Enron Capital & Trade Resources. "Beaver Creek, 1995." Enron Analyst Conference, Beaver Creek, CO, February 2–4, 1995.

———. *Understanding Risk Management.* 1994.

"Enron Casts Its Energy Reach to Wind with Purchase of Zond." *Energy Reports,* January 13, 1997.

"Enron CEO Boosts Gas-Fired Generator." *Natural Gas Week,* February 22, 1988, 7.

"Enron CEO Kenneth Lay Says Gas Industry Should Not Rule Out Full Deregulation After Stabilization in Post-636 Era; Berkeley Professor and FERC Director O'Neill Disagree on Open Access Impact." *Foster Report,* no. 1918 (March 11, 1993): 26–29.

"Enron CEO Lay Says NAFTA Will Help Improve U.S.-Mexico Business Climate, Development." *Oil Daily,* September 24, 1993.

Enron Corp. "The Clinton/Gore Administration: What's It Mean to Enron?" *To the Point,* November 1992.

———. Company documents, including annual reports, with statistical supplements; Form 10-Ks, Form 10-Qs, press releases, proxy statements, conference brochures.

———. "Enron Corp. Chairman Kenneth Lay Cites Means by Which to Rebuild U.S. Energy Infrastructure, Create New Jobs and U.S. Investment." Press release, January 21, 1993.

———. *Enron Corp.'s Outlook for Natural Gas,* 1989–1991, 1993.

———. *The 1995 Enron Outlook.*

———. *1997 Enron Energy Outlook.*

———. "Enron 2000 Work Plan," n.d.

———. "Federal Issues Panel Discussion." Handout at the Enron Federal Government Affairs meeting, Houston, TX, November 19–21, 1997.

———. "Motion for Leave to Intervene of Northern Natural Gas Company, Transwestern Pipeline Company, Florida Gas Transmission Company, and Enron Gas Marketing and Enron Gas Marketing Inc." *Long Island Lighting Company v. Federal Energy Regulatory Commission,* 11th Circuit US Court of Appeals, February 5, 1993.

———. "The Natural Gas Advantage: Strategies for Electric Utilities in the 1990s." Houston, TX: 1992.

———. *Transportadora de Gas del Sur S.A. 2000.*

———. "Visions and Values." Handout, 1995.

Enron Corp. and Portland General Electric. "Enron and Portland General Announce Pro-Competitive Merger." PR Newswire, July 22, 1996.

Enron Development. "Energy Systems to Meet the World's Power Demand." Company brochure, 1994.

"Enron Energy Services." *ENside ECT,* November/December 1996, 2.

Enron Finance Corp. "Innovative Financial Services for America's Natural Gas Industry." Company booklet, 1992.

———. "Is Funding the Future for Natural Gas." *EnSIDE EGS,* June 1993, 2.

Enron Gas Services. "Comments Before the Public Utilities Commission of the State of California Regarding Natural Gas Procurement." February 27, 1992 (Paul Wielgus, EGS, 1992 CPUC Comments).

———. "Comments Before the U.S. Department of Energy, Notice of Inquiry and Request for Public Comments: State Policies Affecting Natural Gas Consumption." November 18, 1992 (Leslie Lawner, EGS, 1992 DOE Comments).

Enron Global Power & Pipelines. Annual reports, various years.

Enron Interstates and Enron Gas Services. "Comments of the Enron Interstate Pipelines to Notice of Proposed Policy Statement on Incentive Regulation." Federal Energy Regulation Commission, Docket No. PL92-1-000, April 27, 1992.

———. Letter to FERC: "Response to Notice of Public [Gathering Policy] Conference." January 14, 1994.

"Enron Is Pitching a 'Gas Standard' for Electric Utilities." *Inside FERC*, March 16, 1992.

Enron Liquid Pipelines. Annual reports, various years.

Enron Oil & Gas Company. Company documents, including annual reports, Form 10-Ks, proxy statements.

———. Presentation at Enron Management Conference. Woodlands, TX. November 15–17, 1995.

Enron Oil Trading and Transportation Company. Annual reports, Form 10-Ks.

Enron Operations Corp. Presentation at Enron Analyst Conference, Beaver Creek, CO, February 2–4, 1995.

Enron People. 1986–92.

Enron Power Marketing. SEC No-Action Letter. January 5, 1994 (Ref. No. 94-1-OPUR).

"Enron Power Services Is Firing Up the Power Market." *EnSIDE EGS*, April 1993, 1–2.

Enron Power Services. *Natural Gas: The Power Generation Fuel for the 1990s* (prepared by ICF Resources Incorporated), 1992.

"Enron Pulls Out of New Hampshire Retail Pilot." *Megawatt Daily*, September 22, 1998.

Enron Renewable Energy Corp. "Reducing Greenhouse Gas Emissions in the Electricity Sector in China: A U.S. Policy Initiative." Internal presentation, December 1996.

"Enron Signs Definitive Agreement to Acquire Natural Gas Liquids Operations from Tenneco." PR Newswire, November 25, 1991.

"Enron's Lay Sees Third Summer Selling Below Cost." *Gas Daily*, April 4, 1988, 3–4.

"Enron's Sins." Editorial, *Wall Street Journal*, January 12, 2002.

"Enron Sweetens Long-Term Contracts with Offer to Market SO_2 Credits." *Inside FERC's Gas Market Report*, January 29, 1993, 2–3.

Enron v. Borget, 90-cv-1952-DNE-NRB.

EnSIDE EGS. Various issues.

Environmental Defense Fund. "Acid Rain: The Power of Markets to Help the Planet." Available at https://archive.fo/iN1V1#selection-1543.0-1543.230.

"Environmental Experts Consider New Task Force on Economic Links." *INSIDE EPA*, September 13, 1996, 10.

Environmental Protection Agency. *Regulation of Fuels and Fuel Additives: Standards for Reformulated and Conventional Gasoline*, 59 Fed. Reg. 7629 (February 16, 1994).

EOG Resources. *1999 Annual Report*.

Epstein, Richard. *Simple Rules for a Complex World*. Cambridge, MA: Harvard University Press, 1995.

Executive Office of the President. *The National Energy Plan*. Washington, DC: Government Printing Office, 1977.

"Expand 636 to States?" *Natural Gas Intelligence*, June 7, 1993, 3.

Federal Energy Regulatory Commission. Annual reports. Washington, DC: Government Printing Office, various years.

Fellows, Kenneth. *Houston Natural Gas Corporation: Its First Fifty Years, 1925–1975*. Houston, TX: Houston Natural Gas, 1976.

FERC Contract Carriage Proposal: Hearings Before the Subcommittee on Fossil and Synthetic Fuels, House Committee on Energy and Commerce, 99th Cong., 1st sess. (1985) (statement of Robert Loch), 510–15.

"FERC Ends Gathering Debate, to Keep Watchful Eye." *Gas Daily,* May 26, 1994, 1.

"FERC Needs to 'Let the Market Be Creative' in the Future." *Inside FERC,* February 1, 1988, 12.

"FERC Orders on Gathering Issues Clarify Jurisdictional Boundaries." *Inside FERC's Gas Market Report,* June 3, 1994, 13–14.

FERC's Mega-NOPR and Construction Rule: Hearing Before the Senate Committee on Energy and Natural Resources, 102nd Cong., 2nd sess. (1992) (statement of Ronald Kuehn), 7–12.

Fernando, Chitru, et al. "Unbundling the U.S. Electric Power Industry: A Blueprint for Change." Philadelphia: The Wharton School, March 1995.

Financial Oversight of Enron: The SEC and Private-Sector Watchdogs: Hearings Before the Senate Committee on Governmental Affairs, 107th Congress, 2nd sess. (2002) (staff report), 107–75.

Fink, Ronald. "On Again, Off Again," *CFO Magazine,* July 1, 1997, Available at: http:// ww2.cfo.com/accounting-tax/1997/07/off-again-on-again-fasb/.

Fisher, Daniel. "Sweet Consolation." *Forbes,* September 21, 1998, 144, 146.

Fitzgerald, Jay, and Joseph Pokalsky. "The Natural Gas Market." In *Managing Energy Price Risk.* London: Risk Publications, 1995, 189–211.

Flavin, Christopher. "The Bridge to Clean Energy." *World Watch,* July/August 1992, 10–18.

———. *Electricity for a Developing World: New Directions.* Worldwatch Paper 70. Washington, DC: Worldwatch Institute, June 1986.

———. *Nuclear Power: The Market Test.* Worldwatch Paper 57. Washington, DC: Worldwatch Institute, December 1983.

———. "Power Shock: The Next Energy Revolution." *World Watch,* January/February 1996, 10–19.

———. *Wind Power: A Turning Point.* Worldwatch Paper 45. Washington, DC: Worldwatch Institute, July 1981.

Flavin, Christopher, and Nicholas Lenssen. *Powering the Future: Blueprint for a Sustainable Electricity Industry.* Worldwatch Paper 119. Washington, DC: Worldwatch Institute, June 1994.

———. *Power Surge: Guide to the Coming Energy Revolution.* New York: W. W. Norton, 1994.

Fletcher, Sam. "Enron's International Projects Carry $19 Billion Price Tag." *Natural Gas Week International,* March 4, 1996, 1, 10–11.

———. "Lay Creates Stir in Industry with Frank Talk on Gas Issues." *Natural Gas Week,* March 11, 1991, 5.

———. "Lay Says Enron Plans to Target Less-Regulated Side of Business." *Natural Gas Week,* January 13, 1992, 1, 4.

———. "Majors' 'Predatory' Prices Hurt Small Producers, Lay Says." *Natural Gas Week,* February 11, 1991, 3–4.

———. "Merger to Form Largest U.S. Pipeline." *Houston Post,* May 3, 1985, sec. H.

———. "Phillips Digs in Its Heels in UK Gas Dispute with Enron." *Natural Gas Week International,* October 2, 1995, 1, 6.

"Florida Gas Proposes Freely Negotiated Service, No Release Limits." *Inside FERC,* January 9, 1995.

"Forrest Hoglund and 650 Employees Vie for Happiest Shareholder Title as EOG's Market Value Hits $4 Billion." *Enron Business* 1, no. 6 (1993): 4–5.

Foster, Richard, and Sarah Kaplan. *Creative Destruction.* New York: Currency, 2001.

Fox, Loren. *Enron: The Rise and Fall.* Hoboken, NJ: John Wiley & Sons, 2003.

Frank, Peter. "Enron to Close Unit After Costly Trades." *New York Times,* October 23, 1987, sec. D.

Frank, Thomas. "Ayn Rand's Libertarian 'Groundhog Day': Billionaire Greed, Deregulation and the Myth that Markets Aren't Free Enough." *Salon,* August 3, 2014. http://www.salon .com/2014/08/03/ayn_rands_libertarian_groundhog_day_billionaire _greed_deregulation_and_the_myth_that_markets_arent_free_enough/.

Fraser, K. Michael. "Is This Gas Bubble About to Pop?" *Business Week,* May 21, 1990, 132D.

Freeman, Beverly. "Enron Capital & Trade Resources Sets the Hurdle Higher for 1995." *Enron Business,* February/March 1995, 4, 10.

———. "Mark-to-Market Accounting: Endorsed for Risk Management Activities." *Enron Business,* May 1994, 8–9.

Fritsch, Peter. "Enron's President, Kinder, Will Leave at End of the Year." *Wall Street Journal,* November 26, 1996.

Fusaro, Peter. "The New Millennium in Energy Trading." In *Energy Convergence: The Beginnings of the Multi-Commodity Market,* by Peter Fusaro, 1–4. New York: John Wiley & Sons, 2002.

Fusaro, Peter, and Ross Miller. *What Went Wrong at Enron.* Hoboken, NJ: John Wiley & Sons, 2002.

Galbraith, Kate, and Asher Price. *The Great Texas Wind Rush.* Austin: University of Texas Press, 2013.

Garner, W. Lynn. "Enron Invests in Argentina; Nova Corp. Also Wins Gas Bid." *Natural Gas Week,* December 7, 1992, 3.

———. "Fall of Gas Threatens Independents." *Oil Daily,* July 8, 1991, 1, 8.

———. "Lay Calls for Toe-to-Toe Battle by Gas for Electricity Market." *Natural Gas Week,* May 18, 1992, 3.

———. "Passage of Natural Gas Tax Credit Turns into Hollow Victory." *Oil Daily,* August 19, 1991, 1, back page.

Gas Daily. 1986–97.

General Accounting Office. *Natural Gas Regulation: Little Opposition to FERC's Recent Policies on Transportation-Related Services.* December 1994. https://www.gpo.gov/fdsys /pkg/GAOREPORTS-RCED-95-39/html/GAOREPORTS-RCED-95-39.htm.

Gipe, Paul. *Wind Energy Comes of Age.* New York: John Wiley & Sons, 1995.

Givens, David. "CFTC Approves Options on Gas Futures." *Gas Daily,* March 6, 1992, 1–2.

Goldstein, Bill. "'Greenspan Shrugged': When Greed Was a Virtue and Regulation the Enemy." *New York Times,* July 21, 2002.

Gordon, Richard L. "Don't Restructure Electricity; Deregulate." *Cato Journal* 20, no. 3 (Winter 2001): 327–58.

Gore, Al. *Earth in the Balance: Ecology and the Human Spirit.* New York: Plume/Penguin, 1992, 1993.

Gott, Stephanie, and Mike Rieke. "Enron Gas Services Set to Buy Access Energy." *Gas Daily*, August 28, 1992, 1.

Graves, Cody, and Maria Seidler. "The Regulation of Gathering in a Federal System." *Energy Law Journal* 15 (1994): 405–25.

Graves, Joseph S., William W. Hogan, and Robert T. McWhinney Jr. *Mandatory Contract Carriage: An Essential Condition for Natural Gas Wellhead Competition and Least Consumer Cost.* Boston: Putnam, Hayes & Bartlett, September 1984.

Greenpeace International. *Plugging into the Sun—Kickstarting the Solar Age in Crete.* June 1997. http://www.skeptictank.org/treasure/GP4/PLUGTOT.TXT.

Griffin, James, and Henry Steele. *Energy Economics and Policy.* 2nd ed. New York: Academic Press College Division, 1986.

Grossman, Peter. *U.S. Energy Policy and the Pursuit of Failure.* New York: Cambridge University Press, 2013.

Gruley, Bryan, and Rebecca Smith. "Anatomy of a Fall: Keys to Success Left Kenneth Lay Open to Disaster." *Wall Street Journal*, April 26, 2002, sec. A.

Hagar, Rick, and Bob Williams. "Cogeneration Thrives in U.S. Despite Lower Oil, Gas Prices." *Oil & Gas Journal*, January 19, 1987, 15.

Hahn, Robert, and Robert Stavins. "Trading in Greenhouse Permits: A Critical Examination of Design and Implementation Issues." In *Shaping National Responses to Climate Change*, edited by Henry Lee, 177–217. Washington, DC: Island Press, 1995.

Hamel, Gary. *Leading the Revolution.* Boston: Harvard Business School Press, 2000.

———. *Leading the Revolution*, rev. ed. Boston: Harvard Business School Press, 2002.

———. "Strategy as Revolution" (discussion draft, 1995). Published in *Harvard Business Review* 74, no. 4 (July/August 1996): 69–82.

Hamel, Gary, and C. K. Prahalad. *Competing for the Future.* Boston: Harvard Business School Press, 1994; reprinted 1996.

Hammond, Allen, William D. Metz, and Thomas H. Maugh. *Energy and the Future.* Washington, DC: American Association for the Advancement of Science, 1973.

Hansard, Sara. "Environmentalists Favor Gas Use on Road to Energy Conservation." *Natural Gas Week*, August 7, 1989, 1, 6–8.

———. "INGAA Opposes Carbon Tax but Lay 'Not Quite as Negative'." *Natural Gas Week*, June 25, 1990, 1, 4.

———. "Treasury Favors Production Aid, Rips 'Unconventional' Subsidy." *Natural Gas Week*, March 12, 1990, 11.

Hansard, Sara, and John Jennrich. "Transwestern Seeks Pipeline from San Juan for 1991–92." *Natural Gas Week*, October 1, 1990, 10.

Hayden, Howard. *The Solar Fraud: Why Solar Energy Won't Run the World.* Pueblo West, CO: Vales Lake Publishing, 2004.

Hayek, F. A. "The Use of Knowledge in Society" (1945). Reprinted in Hayek, *Individualism and Economic Order*, 77–91. Chicago: Henry Regnery, 1972.

Hays, Kristen. "Enron Sells Last Major Assets to Private Equity Firm for $2.9 Billion." Associated Press, September 8, 2006.

Hefner, Robert, III. "Democrats Clinton, Gore Are Gas Industry's Dream Team." Letter to the editor, *Natural Gas Week*, August 17, 1992.

———. "Dream Team Will End 'Read My Lips.'" Letter to the editor, *Natural Gas Week*, October 12, 1992.

———. "Unconventional Gas Tax Credit Is Boondoggle." *Natural Gas Week*, October 22, 1990, 3.

Henney, Alex. "Poolco, Bilateral Trading, and Technology." *Public Utilities Fortnightly*, March 15, 1995, 25–27.

Hensley, Carol. "Enron and Portland General Set to Become Nation's 21st Century Natural Gas and Electricity Leader." *Enron Business*, September 1996, 2–3.

———. "Enron International Stakes Its Claim in the Growing Global Market." *Enron Business*, January 1994, 7.

———. "EOG Outlasts Low Prices with Aggressive Marketing and Cost Cutting." *Enron Business*, January/February 1996, 7, 9.

———. Numerous articles, *Enron Business*, 1994–97.

Hershey, Robert, Jr. "The Maverick Who Transformed an Industry." *New York Times*, December 30, 1984, sec. F.

Hesse, Martha. "Incentive-Based Regulation Targets Increased Efficiency by Gas Pipelines." *Oil Daily*, October 5, 1988, 4.

"HNG Decides to Concentrate on Oil & Gas Activities." *HNG Magazine*, Spring 1984, 7.

HNG/InterNorth Corp. *America's Premier Energy Company*. Company booklet, 1985.

———. *1985 Annual Report*.

———. *Year-End Report: Pulling Together in '86*. Company brochure, 1986.

"HNG/InterNorth Forms Premier Energy Network." *HNG/InterNorth* 1, no. 1 (July 1985).

"HNG/InterNorth to Become Enron Corp." *Houston Chronicle*, April 11, 1986.

"HNG to Buy Transwestern Pipeline Co." *Houston Chronicle*, November 6, 1984, sec. 3.

Hoekstra, Aldyn, and Gary Simon. "Making a Choice: California's New Move to Retail Wheeling." Cambridge, MA: Cambridge Energy Research Associates, 1996.

Hogan, Rick. "Energy Companies Eye Chance to Put Tags on Sports Palaces." *Natural Gas Week*, October 20, 1997, 10.

Holden, Benjamin. "Enron Agrees to Buy Portland General." *Wall Street Journal*, July 22, 1996, sec. A.

Houston Advanced Research Center. "Kenneth Lay: Guiding a Sustainable Energy Future." Interview, *Woodlands Forum* 10, no. 1 (1992): 1–4.

Houston Chronicle. 1985–2004.

Houston Economic Summit Host Committee. *The Economic Summit: A Pictorial History of the Economic Summit of Industrialized Nations, 1975–1990*. Charlottesville, VA: Thomasson-Grant, 1990.

Houston Natural Gas Corp (HNG). Company documents, including annual reports, Form 10-Ks, proxy statements.

"Houston Natural Submits Legal Memorandum Supporting 'Negotiated Rate' Proposal for Establishing Interruptible Transportation Rates within Zone of Reasonableness," *Foster Report*, April 18, 1985, 2–3.

Houston Post. 1985–88.

Huey, John. "Waking Up to the New Economy." *Fortune*, June 27, 1994, 36–38, 40, 44, 46.

Hurst, Teresa. "Amoco/Enron Solar Brings Solar Power Down to Earth." *Enron Business*, March 1996, 2–3.

———. "Enron Speaks Out in Antidumping Debate." *Enron Business*, June 1996, 4.

———. "Enron Takes Bold Steps into the Community Spotlight." *Enron Business,* November/December 1996, 8–9.

———. Numerous articles, *Enron Business,* 1994–97.

Hurt, Harry, III. "Power Players." *Fortune,* August 5, 1996, 94–97.

Hylton, Hilary. "Lawmakers Tepid About NGVs; Say Safety Concerns Remain." *Natural Gas Week,* May 8, 1995, 8.

INGAA Foundation. "Natural Gas for Electric Generation: Realizing the Potential." Washington, DC: Washington International Energy Group, 1994.

Ingersoll, John. *Natural Gas Vehicles.* Lilburn, GA: Fairmont Press, 1996.

"InterNorth, HNG Plan Merger to Form 'Premier' U.S. Pipeline." *Natural Gas Week,* May 6, 1985, 1, 8.

InterNorth Inc. Annual reports, business and financial profiles, and Form 10-Ks.

———. *Overview.* Company brochure, May 8, 1985.

"Introducing The New Power Company." *Business Wire,* May 16, 2000. http://boards.fool.com/investment-in-the-new-power-company-12575950.aspx.

Isser, Steve. *Electricity Restructuring in the United States: Markets and Policy from the 1978 Energy Act to the Present.* New York: Cambridge University Press, 2015.

James, Terrie. "1995 Prepares ECT for the Challenges and Opportunities of a Changing Marketplace." *Enron Business,* January/February 1996, 5.

Jennrich, John. "Creeping Capitalism Slithers Out of California." *Natural Gas Week,* May 2, 1994, 2.

———. "Enron's Lay Touts Deregulation, Calls Gas 'Winner' with BTU Tax." *Natural Gas Week,* March 8, 1993, 1, 18, 19.

———. "Gas Needs More Business, Less Politicking." *Natural Gas Week,* December 21, 1987, 2.

———. "Hanzlik to Recruit 'Competitive' Executives." *Natural Gas Week,* September 30, 1985, 2.

———. "It's a Great Time to Be in the Gas Business." *Natural Gas Week,* May 6, 1996, 2.

———. "NGVs: Much Ado About 0.005% of Gas Demand." *Natural Gas Week,* May 8, 1995, 2.

———. Numerous articles, *Natural Gas Week,* 1985–1996.

———. "Order 436 Produces Confusion and Caution." *Natural Gas Week,* October 21, 1985, 2.

———. "Some Overseas Gas 'Opportunities' Illusory." *Natural Gas Week,* November 13, 1995, 2.

———. "Survival in Gas Belongs to Most Adaptable." *Natural Gas Week,* June 9, 1986, 2.

Jensen, Carl. *20 Years of Censored News.* New York: Seven Stories Press, 1997.

Jevons, W. S. *The Coal Question: An Inquiry Concerning the Progress of the Nation and the Probable Exhaustion of our Coal Mines.* London: Macmillan, 1865.

Joint Committee on Taxation. *Report of Investigation of Enron Corporation and Related Entities Regarding Federal Tax and Compensation Issues, and Policy Recommendations.* Volume I: Report, February 2003.

Jones, Del. "Enron Chief: Energy Spending Generates Real Savings." *USA Today,* November 27, 2000.

Jones, Don. "T&E." *Northern Natural Gas News,* 1985, 3.

Jordon, Steve. "HNG, InterNorth Held Secret Courtship." *Omaha World-Herald,* May 19, 1985, sec. M.

———. "Segnar to Guide Joint Venture Until '87." *Omaha World-Herald*, May 3, 1985.

Jost, Kenneth. "Restructuring the Electric Industry." *CQ Researcher*, January 17, 1997, 25–48.

"Just the Boost Downtown Houston Needed." *Enron Business*, 2 (2000): 9, 11.

Kaminski, Vincent, and Stinson Gibner. "Exotic Options." In *Managing Energy Price Risk*, edited by Kaminski, 117–48. London: Risk Publications, 1995.

Kelly, Marjorie. "Waving Goodbye to the Invisible Hand: How the Enron Mess Grew and Grew." *San Francisco Chronicle*, February 24, 2002.

Kelly, Robert. "The Outlook for Renewable Energy in the 21st Century." Presentation to Yale Center for Environmental Law and Policy, New Haven, CT, May 1, 1996.

Kelly, Robert, with Mary Clark. "Enron International." *Enron Business*, March 1993, 8.

Kemezis, Paul. "SoCal Gas Turns Environmentalist to Fight Rival Pipeline Companies." *Energy Daily*, May 9, 1988, 3.

Kendall, Henry, and Steven Nadis, eds. *Energy Strategies: Toward a Solar Future*. A report by the Union of Concerned Scientists. Cambridge, MA: Ballinger, 1980.

"Kenetech Files for Bankruptcy Protection." *Wind Power Monthly*, June 1, 1996. http://www.windpowermonthly.com/article/953448/kenetech-files-bankruptcy-protection-meantime-corporation-stands-firm-hopes-clemency.

"Kern River." In *Pacific Coast Gas Association: A Century of Excellence*, edited by Gordon Blackley, 135. Portland, OR: PCGA, 1993.

Kerr, Richard. "Hansen vs. the World on the Greenhouse Threat." *Science* 244, no. 4908 (1989): 1041–43.

Kinder, Richard. "Argentina Pipeline Project." Memorandum to All Employees, from the Office of the Chairman, December 3, 1992.

———. "Customer Choice with Gas and Electricity: The Future Is Now." Presentation to the Mid-American Regulatory Commissioners Conference, Chicago, June 17, 1996.

———. "Letter from the President." *Enron Business*, January 1993, 3.

Klebnikov, Paul. "Power Plays." *Forbes*, December 21, 1992, 277.

Klempin, Ray. "Texas Utility Displaces Coal with Gas." *Gas Daily*, June 21, 1991, 2.

Knight, Jessie. Public Utilities Commission, State of California. Letter to the Honorable Elizabeth Moler, chairwoman of the Federal Energy Regulatory Commission. June 5, 1995.

Koch, Charles. "Corporate Cronyism Harms America." *Wall Street Journal*, September 9, 2012.

———. *Good Profit: How Creating Value for Others Built One of the World's Most Successful Companies*. New York: Crown Business, 2015.

———. *The Science of Success*. Hoboken, NJ: John Wiley & Sons, 2007.

Koch Industries. "The Challenge of Success." *Discovery*, January 2012, 1.

Koen, A. D. "U.S. Gas Industry Sees Signs of End to Lengthy Downturn." *Oil & Gas Journal*, January 13, 1993, 15.

———. "U.S. Gas Pipelines Preparing for Life under FERC Order 636." *Oil & Gas Journal*, July 6, 1992, 21–26.

Krugman, Paul. "The Great Divide." *New York Times*, January 29, 2002.

Kunen, James. "Enron's Vision (and Values) Thing." *New York Times*, January 19, 2002.

Kuttner, Robert. "Enron: A Powerful Blow to Market Fundamentalists." *BusinessWeek*, February 4, 2002, 20.

Lambert, Jeremiah. *The Power Brokers*. London: MIT Press, 2015.

Langlois, Richard. "Do Firms Plan?" *Constitutional Political Economy* 6, no. 3 (Fall 1995): 247–61.

Larson, Henrietta, Evelyn Knowlton, and Charles Popple. *New Horizons, 1927–1950: History of Standard Oil Company (New Jersey)*. New York: Harper & Row, 1971.

Lawton, George. "Fuel Cells Prepare for Prime Time." *Power*, May/June 2001, 86–88.

Lay, Ken. "Coming Soon to Your Home and Business: The New Energy Majors." In *Straight from the CEO*, edited by G. William Dauphinais and Colin Price, 250–56. New York: Simon & Schuster, 1998.

———. "Corporate Citizenship: A Priority in the Enron Workplace." *Enron Business*, July/August 1996, 2, 8.

———. "Deregulation of Gas and Electricity." Presentation to the Japan-US Southern Conference. New Orleans, October 1, 1998.

———. "Don't Drop the Ball." Memorandum to Houston-Based Employees, May 20, 1997.

———. "The Energy Company of the 21st Century." In *The Global Energy Company of the 21st Century*, edited by James Rosenfield and Penny Janeway, 33–41. Cambridge, MA: Cambridge Energy Research Associates, 1996.

———. "The Energy Industry in the Next Century: Opportunities and Constraints." In *Energy After 2000*, edited by Irwin Stelzer, 13–26. VIII Repsol-Harvard Seminar, June 1997.

———. Enron Corp Comments to FERC on Issues and Priorities for the Natural Gas Industry. FERC Docket No. PL 97-1. April 29, 1997.

———. "Enron in the New Economy." Presentation to a Harvard Business School conference, Boston, January 25, 2000.

———. "Enron in the 21st Century." Presentation to the 15th Annual CERA Executive Conference, Houston, TX, February 14, 1996.

———. "Enron New Hire Orientation." Speech in Houston, TX, September 14, 1999.

———. *The Enron Story*. Pamphlet. New York: Newcomen Society for the United States, 1990.

———. "From the Chairman," *HNG Annual Report for Employees*, 1984.

———. "Give All Customers the Right to Choose, Immediately." In *Customer Choice: Finding Value in Retail Electricity Markets*, edited by Ahmad Faruqui and J. Robert Malko, 291–96. Vienna, VA: Public Utility Reports, 1999.

———. "Give Bush Credit, He Is the 'Energy President'." *Houston Chronicle*, October 13, 1992, sec. A.

———. "Greenpeace Wrong in Attacking Natural Gas." Letter to the editor. *Natural Gas Week*, February 28, 1994, 3.

———. "Houston Outlook '86: Energy & Manufacturing Panel," Houston, TX, January 1986.

———. "If Natural Gas Is the Fuel of the Future, When Does the Future Start?" Presentation to the Independent Petroleum Association of America, Santa Fe, NM, May 7, 1992; Fifth Annual Natural Gas Marketing Conference, Santa Fe, New Mexico, May 11, 1992.

———. "The Importance of Vision." Text of speech to Enron employees, 1995.

————. "In the Middle of One of the Greatest 'Energy Plays' in History." *World Gas Yearbook 1996*.

————. "Investment Agency Helps US Companies." *Journal of Commerce*, September 10, 1996. Available at: http://www.joc.com/opic-does-nation-still-need-it -investment-agency-helps-us-companies_19960910.html.

————. "Kenneth L. Lay." Required Biographical Information: Part B. Career/Current Position. Nominee to the Horatio Alger Society, 1997.

————. "Lay Rips Hefner's 'Dream Team,' Favors GOP." Letter to the editor, *Natural Gas Week*, September 21, 1992, 3.

————. Letter to Christopher C. DeMuth, President, American Enterprise Institute, June 6, 1996.

————. Letter to Enron's business partners, November 30, 1995.

————. Letter to Martin Allday, chairman, FERC, March 12, 1992.

————. Letter to T. Boone Pickens, Jr., October 24, 1986.

————. "The Measurement of the Timing of the Economic Impact of Defense Procurement Activity: An Analysis of the Vietnam Buildup." Abstract of a Dissertation Submitted to the Faculty of the Graduate School, University of Houston. August 1970.

————. "Natural Gas and America's Energy Future: Beyond Compliance." Presentation to the National Clean Air Conference, Houston, TX, May 20, 1992.

————. "Natural Gas and Global Energy Challenges." Speech to Florida Natural Gas Association's 1998 Annual Convention, Naples, FL, June 19, 1998.

————. "Natural Gas: The Cost-Effective Link Between Robust Economic Growth and Aggressive Environmental Protection." Presentation to a conference of the Alliance to Save Energy, "Global Warming and the Earth Summit," Washington, DC, June 23, 1992.

————. "Natural Gas: The Power Fuel for the 1990s." Presentation to the Institute of Gas Technology, Chicago, March 9, 1992.

————. *Natural Gas Wellhead Decontrol. Hearing Before the Committee on Energy and Natural Resources, United States Senate*, 101st Cong., 1st sess., 1989, 99–104.

————. "New Energy Visions: Enron Corp." Presentation in the Profiles in American Enterprise Series, University of Colorado–Boulder, March 11, 1997.

————. "A New Vision." In *The Oil Makers: Insiders Look at the Petroleum Industry*, edited by Jeff Share, 351–65. Houston, TX: Rice University Press, 1995.

————. "The New Worlds of Natural Gas." Presentation to the Pacific Coast Gas Association's annual business meeting, Houston, TX, September 13, 1995.

————. "A North American Perspective." *Gascope*, Winter 1991/92, 11–15.

————. Presentation to the Houston Outlook '86 Conference: Energy & Manufacturing Panel, January 1986.

————. "Rebuilding the US Oil and Gas Industry." *Petroleum Economist*, March 1993, 8–9.

————. "Take It to the Top." *Enron People*, various issues, 1992.

————. "Talking Points." Aspen Institute Energy Policy Forum, July 13, 1991.

————. "The $30 Billion Corner Store." In *Lessons from the Top*, edited by Thomas Neff and James Citrin, with Paul Brown, 215–19. New York: Currency Doubleday, 1999.

————. "Toward the 'Heroic Enterprise'." *Dilemma*, Spring 1997, 1–3.

————. Transmittal note to Jack Bowen, Letter to T. Boone Pickens, Jr., October 24, 1986.

———. "Tuesday's Vote for Proposition 1." Memorandum to Houston-Based Employees, November 7, 1996.

———. "A Vision for the 21st Century Asia." Speech given at China, the United States, and Asia: Challenges for United States Policy and Business, an Asia Society/Baker Institute Conference, Houston, TX, February 9, 1996.

———. "White Paper: Electric Deregulation and Enron." *American Oil and Gas Reporter*, December 23, 1995.

Lay, Ken, and Rich Kinder. "Interview: 1996 Goals and Enron 2000." Typescript, January 17, 1996.

Lay, Ken, and Jim McIngvale. "Downtown's a Natural for Sports Arenas." *Houston Chronicle*, September 1, 1996.

Lay, Ken, et al. "Transcribed Interviews." 2000 Enron Management Conference, November 17, 2000.

"Lay Sees Cogeneration Plants Boosting Natural Gas Demand." *Oil & Gas Journal*, June 25, 1984, 33.

Lee, Amy. "Peterborough Electricity Pilot: Where Customers Come First." *Enron Business*, March 1997, 2–3.

Leggett, Jeremy. *The Carbon War: Global Warming and the End of the Oil Era*. London: Penguin Books, 1999.

Lenzner, Robert. "Let's Talk Business." *Forbes*, December 5, 1994, 161–62.

Levin, Yuval. "Recovering the Case for Capitalism." *National Affairs*, Spring 2010, 123–36.

Lovins, Amory. "Energy Strategy: The Road Not Taken?" *Foreign Affairs* 55, no. 1 (October 1976): 65–96.

———. "Saving Gigabucks with Negawatts." *Public Utility Fortnightly* 115, no. 6 (March 21, 1985): 19–26.

Lovins, Amory, et al. *Natural Capitalism*. New York: Little, Brown and Company, 1999.

Lowenstein, Roger. *When Genius Failed: The Rise and Fall of Long-Term Capital Management*. New York: Random House, 2000.

Macey, Daniel. "Gas and Environmentalism: Strange Bedfellows?" *NG Magazine*, Summer 1993, 24–27.

———. "Lay Backs Import Fee as Way to Promote Gas." *Gas Daily*, January 22, 1993, 1, 4.

———. "Lay Encourages Gas as Standard for New Plants." *Gas Daily*, March 10, 1992, 1, 4.

———. Numerous articles, *Gas Daily*, 1988–93.

Mack, Toni. "Hidden Risks." *Forbes*, May 24, 1993, 54–55.

———. "Orderly Mind in a Disorderly Market." *Forbes*, September 21, 1987, 62–64.

———. "The Other Enron Story." *Forbes*, October 14, 2002, 63–65.

———. "Power Players." *Forbes*, May 19, 1997, 114, 118, 120, 122.

———. "Prices Down, Supply Up." *Forbes*, December 19, 1994, 47–48.

———. "This Is Deregulation?" *Forbes*, January 2, 1984.

Mahoney, Peggy. "Kyoto Compliant." Memorandum to Robert Bradley Jr., May 11, 2000.

Maloney, Michael, and Robert McCormick, with Raymond Sauer. *Customer Choice, Consumer Value: An Analysis of Retail Competition in America's Electric Industry*. Washington, DC: Citizens for a Sound Economy Foundation, May 1996.

"Managers to Watch in 1997." *BusinessWeek*, January 13, 1997, 67.

Mark, Rebecca. "Testimony Before the Senate Committee on Foreign Relations." March 7, 1995, 76–78. Available at: https://energy.gov/sites/prod/files/maprod/documents /enron1995.pdf.

Markham, Jerry. *A Financial History of Modern U.S. Corporate Scandals: From Enron to Reform.* London: M. E. Sharpe, 2006.

Marshall, Jonathan. "Big Power Play: Enron Poised to Challenge PG&E in State." *San Francisco Chronicle*, August 26, 1997.

Martin, Douglas. "Environmental Risk from 'Renewable' Energy Sources?" *Wall Street Journal*, June 9, 1978.

Marxsen, Craig. "MTBE Latest Victim of US Environmental Overregulation?" *Oil & Gas Journal*, February 26, 2001, 20–24.

Mayhew, Robert. *Ayn Rand Answers.* New York: Centennial, 2005.

McCasland, Elaine. "Enron's Argentine Pipeline Expands to Meet Increased Demand." *Enron Business*, November/December 1993, 3.

———. Numerous articles, *Enron Business*, 1993–96.

McCloskey, Deirdre. *The Bourgeois Virtues: Ethics for an Age of Commerce.* Chicago: University of Chicago Press, 2006.

McConnell, Mike. *Just Because You Can Doesn't Mean You Should: Keys to a Successful Life.* New York: iUniverse, 2008.

McDonald, Forrest. *Insull.* Chicago: University of Chicago, 1962. Reprinted as *Insull: The Rise and Fall of a Billionaire Utility Tycoon.* Washington, DC: BeardBooks, 2004.

McKnight, John. "Enron, IBM, AOL Form 'The New Power Company.'" *ElectricNet*, May 17, 2000. https://www.electricnet.com/doc/enron-ibm-aol-form-the-new-power -company-0001.

McLean, Bethany, and Peter Elkind. *The Smartest Guys in the Room: The Amazing Rise and Scandalous Fall of Enron.* New York: Portfolio, 2003.

McNamar, R. T. "Bankers as Corporate Monitors." In *After Enron: Lessons for Public Policy*, edited by William Niskanen, 198–217. Lanham, MD: Rowman & Littlefield, 2005.

Mehta, Abhay. *Power Play: A Study of the Enron Project.* Telangana, India: Orient Longman, 1999.

Michaels, Patrick. *Sound and Fury: The Science and Politics of Global Warming.* Washington, DC: Cato Institute, 1992.

Michaels, Robert. "Preparing for Gas/Electric Convergence: Mergers or Alliances." In *Customer Choice: Finding Value in Retail Electricity Markets*, edited by Ahmad Faruqui and J. Robert Malko, 79–94. Vienna, VA: Public Utility Reports, 1999.

———. "Reducing Risk, Shifting Risk, and Concealing Risk: Why Are There Long-Term Gas Contracts?" In *New Horizons in Natural Gas Deregulation*, edited by Jerry Ellig and Joseph Kalt, 195–208. Westport, CT: Praeger, 1996.

———. "Wholesale Pooling: The Monopolist's New Clothes." *Electricity Journal*, December 1994, 64–76.

Miller, Mark. "Tough Calls." *American Journalism Review*, December 2002, 43–47.

Moffett, Matt. "HNG/InterNorth Goes to Pros in Bid to Get New Name." *Wall Street Journal*, February 20, 1986.

———. "Lay Doubles Houston Natural Gas's Size in Only 6 Months as Chairman and Chief." *Wall Street Journal*, December 4, 1984.

Montgomery, John. "Gas Dies with 'Greener' Fuels as Fossil Bridge." *Gas Daily*, December 14, 1992, 1, 3.

Moody, Rush, and Allan Garten. "The Natural Gas Policy Act of 1978: Analysis and Overview." *Rocky Mountain Institute* 25, no 2 (1979): 1–93.

Morriss, Andrew, et al. *The False Promise of Green Energy*. Washington, DC: Cato Institute, 2011.

Murray, Susan. "Tight-Gas Sand Credits." EOG Memorandum to Rob Bradley, February 19, 1998.

Myerson, Allen. "Solar Power, for Earthly Prices." *New York Times*, November 15, 1994, sec. D.

NAFTA: Energy Provisions and Environmental Implications: Hearings Before the Subcommittee on Energy and Power, House Committee on Energy and Commerce. 103rd Cong., 1st sess. (1993) (Ken Lay, testimony submitted for the record), 187–95.

National Energy Plan. Executive Office of the President, Energy Policy and Planning. Washington, DC: Government Printing Office, 1977.

National Energy Strategy (Part 1): Hearings Before the Subcommittee on Energy and Power, House Committee on Energy and Commerce, 102nd Cong., 1st sess. (1991) (statement of Arlon Tussing), 157–59.

National Independent Energy Producers. *Independent Energy Producers: The New Electric Generating Sector*. Washington, DC: NIEP, 1989.

National Transportation Safety Board. "San Juan Gas Company, Inc./Enron Corp. Propane Gas Explosion in San Juan, Puerto Rico, on November 21, 1996." Accident report. Washington, DC: December 1997.

———. "San Juan Gas Company's Inadequate Training of Employees and Government Deficiencies Led to Building Explosion." Press release, December 16, 1997.

Natural Coal Association. *Coal Background*, March 11, 1993.

Natural Gas Clearinghouse. *A Decade of Excellence in Energy 1984–1994*. Houston, TX: NGC, 1994.

Natural Gas Contract Renegotiations and FERC Authorities: Hearings Before the Subcommittee on Fossil and Synthetic Fuels, House Committee on Energy and Commerce, 98th Cong., 1st sess. (1983) (Dan Dienstbier, "Letter to the Honorable Phil Sharp"), 397–99.

Natural Gas: Hearing Before a Subcommittee of the House Committee on Interstate and Foreign Commerce, 74th Cong., 2nd sess. (1936) (statement of Ralph W. Gallagher, Standard Oil of New Jersey), 139–50.

Natural Gas Ratepayers Relief Act of 1991: Hearings Before the Senate Subcommittee on Energy and Natural Resources, 102nd Cong., 1st sess., (1991) (statement of John E. Olson, Vice President, Equity Research, Goldman, Sachs & Co.), 33–35.

Natural Gas Utilization Act of 1987: Hearing Before the Subcommittee on Energy Regulation and Conservation, Senate Committee on Energy and Natural Resources, 100th Cong., 1st sess. (1987) (opening statement of Senator Howard Metzenbaum), 1–2; (statement by Kenneth L. Lay), 147–63.

Natural Gas Week. 1985–97.

Navarro, Mireya. "Enron's Collapse: Five Uncertain Years." *New York Times*, January 21, 2002.

Neal, Roger. "Why Merge if You Can Share?" *Forbes*, May 20, 1985, 150, 154.

"The New World of Natural Gas Pipelines." *Enron Business*, August/September 1993, 5–6.

New York Times. 1982–2008.

"NGSA Proclaims Section 29 a Tax Credit Whose Time Is Up." *Natural Gas Week*, May 25, 1992, 6.

Nielsen, John, and Andrew Serwer. "Take that, Belco." *Fortune*, February 3, 1986, 9.

"1997 Guidebook to the Federal Restructuring Debate" (Special Report). *Electric Power Alert*, January 29, 1997.

Niskanen, William. "A Crisis of Trust." In *After Enron: Lessons for Public Policy*, edited by William Niskanen, 1–10. Lanham, MD: Rowman & Littlefield, 2005.

———. "Don't Count Too Much on Financial Accounting." In *After Enron: Lessons for Public Policy*, edited by William Niskanen, 47–54. Lanham, MD: Rowman & Littlefield, 2005.

———. Introduction to *Corporate Aftershock: The Public Policy Lessons from the Collapse of Enron and Other Major Corporations*, edited by Christopher Culp and William Niskanen, xxvii–xxviii. Hoboken, NJ: John Wiley & Sons, 2003.

Nocera, Joseph. "Living in the Enron Dream World." *New York Times*, December 17, 2005.

Noland, Jude. "Portland General/Enron Commitments Lead to Public Interest Groups' Support for Merger." *California Energy Markets*, January 10, 1997, 14.

Noonan, Peggy. "An Empire Built on Ifs." *Wall Street Journal*, January 25, 2002.

Norman, James. "In Natural Gas, It's Buy or Be Bought." *Business Week*, May 20, 1985, 62–63.

Northern Border Partners. Annual reports, with Form 10-Ks.

Northern Gas Marketing. *The Natural Gas Spot Market: The Dawn of a New Era*. Booklet, n.d.

Northern Natural Gas Company. Annual reports, various years.

———. *Northern: The First Fifty Years*. Company brochure, 1980.

Novak, Michael. *Business as a Calling: Work and the Examined Life*. New York: The Free Press, 1996.

O'Connor, Philip, Robert Bussa, and Wayne Olson. "Competition, Financial Innovation, and Diversification in the Electric Industry." *Public Utilities Fortnightly*, February 20, 1986, 17–21.

O'Donnell, Arthur. "New Coalition Supports Poolco Approach." *California Energy Markets*, July 14, 1995, 13.

O'Driscoll, Mary. "Fuel Wars: NCA's Lawson Blasts Natural Gas Industry." *Energy Daily*, April 15, 1992, 1, 3.

———. "Skilling: Customized Gas Services Are the Key to Profitability." *Energy Daily*, May 13, 1992, 3.

O'Reilly, Brian. "New Ideas, New Products: The Secrets of America's Most Admired Corporations." *Fortune*, March 3, 1997, 60–66.

O'Reilly, Cary. "Hub Trading Poised to Expand; May Decide Fate of Gas Futures." *Natural Gas Week*, February 4, 1991, 9–10, 18–19.

Olson, Cindy. *The Whole Truth ... So Help Me God*. Mustang, OK: Tate Publishing, 2008.

Olson, John. "Defining Deviancy Down: Market Challenges (Enron and After)." Presentation to the Texas Investment Portfolio Symposium, Houston, TX, February 21, 2015.

———. "Enron and After: A Conversation." Presentation to A. B. Freeman School of Business, Tulane University, New Orleans, April 27, 2010.

———. "The Pandora's Box: Enron and Its Consequences." Presentation, Houston, TX, n.d.

Oppel, Richard, Jr., and Andrew Sorkin. "Enron's Collapse: The Overview; Enron Corp. Files Largest U.S. Claim for Bankruptcy." *New York Times*, December 3, 2001.

Pagel, Al. "He Started at $210 a Month." *Omaha Sunday World-Herald Magazine of the Midlands*, April 25, 1976, 28.

Pai, Lou. "Enron Energy Services, 1997–1998." Presentation at Enron Management Conference, San Antonio, TX, November 6–7, 1997.

Palmeri, Christopher. "At the Heart of a Revolution." *Forbes*, January 12, 1998, 48.

———. "This Is About Money." *Forbes*, February 27, 1995, 52.

Papayoti, Lee. "A Brief History of NGVs." Memorandum to Rob Bradley, January 22, 1998.

———. "Natural Gas Vehicles: An Overview." Enron presentation, November 17, 1999.

"Paper: InterNorth to Move in '87." *Omaha World-Herald*, May 3, 1985.

Parker, Susan. "Pipelines Poised to Dive into Gathering Melting Pot." *Natural Gas Intelligence*, June 6, 1994, 1–2.

PECO Energy. "There Will Be No Deal with Enron." Press release, October 9, 1997.

Pending Natural Gas Legislation: Hearing Before the Senate Committee on Energy and Natural Resources, 99th Cong., 2nd sess. (1986) (statement of Brian E. O'Neill, President, Transcontinental Gas Pipe Line Corp.), 129–48; (A. Denny Ellerman, "Statement on the Repeal of the Powerplant & Industrial Fuel Use Act"), 510–15.

Perlin, John. *From Space to Earth: The Story of Solar Electricity*. Ann Arbor, MI: AATEC Publications, 1999.

Perrot, Etienne. "An Ethical Diagnosis of the Enron Affair." In *Enron and World Finance: A Case Study in Ethics*, edited by Paul Dembinski, Carole Lager, Andrew Cornford, and Jean-Michel Bonvin, 103–16. New York: Palgrave, 2006.

Peters, Tom, and Robert Waterman Jr. *In Search of Excellence*. New York: Warner Books, 1982.

Pierobon, James. "Transco's Ken Lay Credited as Natural Gas Innovator." *Houston Chronicle*, July 17, 1983, sec. 4.

"Pipelines Girding to Lobby FERC for Changes in Rates, Certificates." *Inside FERC*, February 12, 1990, 3–4.

Pope, Kyle. "What Makes Kenneth Lay Run?" *Houston Chronicle*, October 13, 1991, sec. F.

Port, David. "Clinton Gives Energy a Strong Say on New Policy Group." *Natural Gas Intelligence*, June 21, 1993.

Portland General Electric. Annual reports, Form 10-Ks, Form 10-Qs.

"Portland General Electric: 1997 in Review." *Enron Business*, 1 (1998): 5, 14.

Prah, Pamela. "Ames Says IPAA Supports Extension of Section 29 Credit." *Natural Gas Week*, July 6, 1992, 7.

Prashad, Vijay. *Fat Cats & Running Dogs: The Enron Stage of Capitalism*. London: Zed Books, 2002.

Pratt, Joseph. *Prelude to Merger: A History of Amoco Corporation, 1973–1998*. Houston, TX: Hart Publications, 2000.

Pratt, Joseph, with William Hale. *Exxon: Transforming Energy, 1973–2005*. Austin, TX: Briscoe Center for American History, 2013.

President's Council on Sustainable Development. "U.S. Environmental and Business Leaders Agree Early Action Is Needed to Reduce Greenhouse Gas Emissions and Present Principles for Early Action to Vice President Gore." Press release, October 27, 1998.

———. *Sustainable America: A New Consensus*. Washington, DC: Government Printing Office, February 1996.

———. *Towards a Sustainable America*. Washington, DC: Government Printing Office, May 1999.

Proposed Changes to Natural Gas Laws: Hearings Before the Subcommittee on Fossil and Synthetic Fuels, House Committee on Energy and Commerce, 98th Cong., 1st sess. (1983) (statement by Gary Hancock), vol. 5, 285–97.

Public Utility Regulatory Policies Act Amendments: Hearing Before the Subcommittee on Energy Regulation. Senate Committee on Energy and Natural Resources, 97th Cong., 2nd sess. (1982) (testimony of Barrett Stambler and Sam Enfield), 370–87.

Rae, Douglas. Interview with Jim Alexander (former executive of Enron Global Power & Pipelines). Yale University School of Management. September 30, 2009.

Raghunathan, N. *Memories, Men, and Matters*. Mumbai, India: Bharatiya Vidya Bhavan, 1999.

Rand, Ayn. "The Objectivist Ethics." In *The Virtue of Selfishness*, by Rand et al, 13–35. New York: Signet, 1964.

Randall, Karl, and Rick Buy. "RARC/Risk Analytics Group." Memorandum to All ECT Employees, July 13, 1995.

Rankin, Kristin. "Enron and CalPERS Join Forces to Invest in Natural Gas." *Enron Business*, July 1993, 7.

———. "Enron Oil & Gas Company." *Enron Business*, January 1993, 6.

———. "Louisiana Resources Company Generates New Gas Markets for Enron Gas Services." *Enron Business*, May 1993, 2–3.

Rao, Ashok. "Presentation." Enron Management Conference, San Antonio, TX. November 6–7, 1997.

RECON Research Corporation. "The Impact of Coal Seam Production on the California Natural Gas Market." Los Angeles, December 13, 1990.

"Record Volumes Going to California; Oklahoma Prices Up." *Natural Gas Intelligence*, February 9, 1987, 2.

Rehm, Barbara. "Transwestern Pipeline Prepares Deal Leading to Open Carriage." *Natural Gas Week*, January 20, 1986, 1, 4.

Renewable Northwest Project. "Conservation, Renewable Energy, Consumer Protection Form Basis of Agreement Between Advocates and PGE on Enron Merger." Press release, January 8, 1997.

Request for Arbitration … Between the Government of the United States (Claimant) and the Government of India (Respondent), November 4, 2004. Available at: https://www.opic.gov/sites/default/files/docs/GOI110804.pdf.

Revsine, Lawrence. "Enron: Sad but Inevitable." *Journal of Accounting and Public Policy* 21 (2002): 137–45.

Rice, Kenneth. "Electric Power Marketers: What Is Their Role in the Evolution of the Electric Power Industry?" Cambridge Energy Forum, 1995, 95–108.

———. "Public Power: Creating Success in the Evolving Electricity Industry." *Electricity Journal*, November 1997, 68–71.

Richardson, Ted. "New Transportation System Opens Two-Way Street." *Intercom* (publication of InterNorth Inc.) no. 8 (1982): 10.

Rieke, Mike. "Enron Exec Blames Spot Market for Low Prices." *Gas Daily*, March 25, 1991, 1–2.

———. "Lay Faults 'Predatory Pricing' for Low Prices." *Gas Daily*, February 7, 1991, 1–2.

Roberts, Paul Craig, and Karen LaFollette Araujo. *The Capitalist Revolution in Latin America*. New York: Oxford University Press, 1997.

Romm, Joe. *Cool Companies: How the Best Businesses Boost Profits and Productivity by Cutting Greenhouse Gas Emissions*. Washington, DC: Island Press, 1999.

Rosenheim, Daniel. "InterNorth, Houston Natural Gas in $2.3 Billion Merger." *Chicago Tribune*, May 3, 1985, sec. B.

Rothschild, Edwin. "Bushmen Dropped Ball on Natural Gas." Letter to the editor, *Natural Gas Week*, October 5, 1992, 3.

Rudin, Brad. "Enron Fuels Investor Interest; Recapitalization Tops Busy List for Oil and Gas Firm." *Pensions & Investment Age*, September 21, 1987, 52.

Salpukas, Agis. "Has a State Tried Too Hard to Deregulate?" *New York Times*, February 1, 1997.

Salter, Malcolm. *Innovation Corrupted: The Origins and Legacy of Enron's Collapse*. Cambridge, MA: Harvard University Press, 2008.

Saunders, Barbara. "Arrival of Spot Market Clearinghouse Draws Cautious Reviews from Industry." *Natural Gas*, September 1984, 4–6.

"SCE's Solar Two Deemed Workable, but Not Economical" (staff article). *Electricity Journal*, November 1999, 6–7.

Schuman, Michael. "Power Hungry." *Forbes*, April 24, 1995, 162–63.

Schwartz, John. "An Enron Unit Chief Warned, and Was Rebuffed." *New York Times*, February 20, 2002.

Schweppe, Fred C., Michael C. Caramanis, Richard D. Tabors, and Roger E. Bohn. *Spot Pricing of Electricity*. Boston: Kluwer Academic Publishers, 1988.

Scott, Tom, and Barbara Shook. "Lay Move to HNG Sparks Top Reshuffling." *Houston Chronicle*, June 7, 1984, sec. 3.

Seay, Gregory. "Transco Executive Will Head HNG." *Houston Post*, June 7, 1984, sec. E.

Segnar, Sam. "All InterNorth Employees." InterNorth memorandum and attachment, July 10, 1985.

"Segnar Resignation Leaves Lay in Charge of HNG/InterNorth." *Natural Gas Week*, November 11, 1985, 3–4.

Seidl, John ("Mick"). "Pipelines Caught in 'Unraveling' of Cradle-to-Grave Regulatory Scheme." *Oil Daily*, February 4, 1988, 4.

Shabecoff, Philip. "Global Warming Has Begun, Expert Tells Senate." *New York Times*, June 24, 1988.

Shea, Cynthia. *Renewable Energy: Today's Contribution, Tomorrow's Promise*. Worldwatch Paper 81. Washington, DC: Worldwatch Institute, 1988.

Shook, Barbara. "Enron Seen Gearing Up for Fight as Regulators Snag Oregon Deal." *Natural Gas Week*, March 24, 1997, 1, 10–11.

———. "Exxon Oil Spill Breeds Good Will for Gas." *Natural Gas Intelligence*, April 17, 1989, 1–2.

———. "HNG, InterNorth Merger Begins Today." *Houston Chronicle*, May 3, 1985, sec. 3.

———. "NGC Reigns as Top Marketer, But Watson Strives for More." *Natural Gas Week*, October 11, 1996, 1, 11.

———. "The Shakeout at HNG/InterNorth." *Houston Chronicle*, February 23, 1986, sec. 5.

———. "Skilling Predicts End of Integrated Energy Companies." *Oil Daily*, November 30, 2000, 5–6.

Shook, Barbara, and Howard Buskirk. "Year-Long Slide in Stock Price May Put Giant Enron on Hit List." *Natural Gas Week*, November 24, 1997, 1, 11.

Simons, Arno, and Jan-Peter Voss. "Politics by Other Means: The Making of the Emissions Trading Instrument as a 'Pre-History' of Carbon Trading." In *The Politics of Carbon Markets*, edited by Benjamin Stephan and Richard Lane, 51–68. New York: Routledge, 2015.

Skilling, Jeff. "Customer Choice with Electricity Is Coming." 1996 draft for speech.

———. "Enron." Presentation to VEBA Corporate Conference, Düsseldorf, Germany, June 19, 1998.

———. *Testimony Before the Public Utilities Commission of the State of California*. Order Instituting Rulemaking and Order Instituting Investigation on the Commission's Proposed Policies Governing Restructuring California's Electric Services Industry and Reforming Regulation. Case Nos. R.94-04-031 and I.94-04-032, June 14, 1994, 268–80.

Smil, Vaclav. *Energy • Food • Environment: Realities • Myths • Options*. New York: Oxford University Press, 1987.

Smiles, Samuel. *Duty: With Illustrations of Courage, Patience, and Endurance*. New York: Harper & Brothers, 1881.

———. *Self-Help: With Illustrations of Character, Conduct, and Perseverance*. 1859, 2nd ed. 1866. Reprinted with editing by Peter Sinnema. Oxford: Oxford University Press, 2002.

———. *Thrift*. New York: A. L. Burt, 1875.

Smith, Adam. *The Theory of Moral Sentiments*. 1759. 6th ed., 1790. Reprinted with introduction and notes by D. D. Raphael and A. L. Mcfie. Indianapolis, IN: LibertyPress, 1984.

———. *The Wealth of Nations*. London: 1776. Reprinted with editing by R. H. Campbell and A. S. Skinner. Indianapolis, IN: LibertyPress, 1981.

Smith, Fred. "Cowboys versus Cattle Thieves." In *Corporate Aftershock*, edited by William Niskanen, 265–300. Hoboken, NJ: John Wiley & Sons, 2003.

———. "Unsustainable Policies." *CEI UpDate*. April 1996, 2.

Smith, Gene, and Kathleen Wood. "Sabine's Henry Hub Crowned as Gas Futures Delivery Site." *Natural Gas Week*, October 30, 1989, 1, 6.

Smith, Rebecca. "Enron's Lay Says 'Very Bad Investments,' Loss of Investor Confidence Led to Sale." *Wall Street Journal*, November 15, 2001, sec. A.

Sodamann, David. "Permian Basin Gas Producers Worry About HNG-InterNorth." *Natural Gas Week*, May 13, 1985, 3.

"The 'Soft' Path Solution for Hard-Pressed Utilities." Interview with Amory Lovins, *BusinessWeek*, July 23, 1984, 96L–96N.

Solarex. "Powerful Solutions." Company brochure. April 1995.

———. "Solarex/Japanese Partners Complete World's First 'Zero-Energy House.'" Press release, December 7, 1998.

Solomon, Caleb. "Enron Expects an $85 Million Charge Because of Secret Trading." *Wall Street Journal*, October 23, 1987.

Sombart, Werner. *The Quintessence of Capitalism*, trans. and ed. by M. Epstein. New York: E. P. Dutton & Company, 1915.

Southerland, Daniel. "You've Heard of Big Oil. This Is the Story of Big Gas … and It Begins with Enron Corp., Which Wants to be No. 1 in World." *Washington Post*, February 4, 1996.

St. Clair, Jeffrey. "Oil for One and One for Oil. In *Dime's Worth of Difference: Beyond the Lesser of Two Evils*," edited by Alexander Cockburn and Jeffrey St. Clair, 193–214. Petrolia, CA: CounterPunch; AK Press, 2004.

Stagliano, Vito. *A Policy of Discontent: The Making of a National Energy Strategy*. Tulsa, OK: PennWell Books, 2001.

Steffes, Dale. "The 'Seven Brothers' of Natural Gas: A Matter of Vision." *Journal of Commerce*, January 3, 1995.

Stelzer, Irwin. "Electric Utilities—Next Stop for Deregulators." *Regulation*, July/August 1982, 29–35.

———, ed. *Energy After 2000*. VIII Repsol-Harvard Seminar, June 1997.

Sternberg, Elaine. "Defining Capitalism." *Economic Affairs* 35, no. 3 (2015): 380–96.

Stevens, William. "Gore Promises U.S. Leadership on Sustainable Development." *New York Times*, June 15, 1993, sec. C.

Stewart, James. *Den of Thieves*. New York: Simon and Schuster, 1991.

Stewart-Gordon, Thomas. "One in Three Drilling Rigs Tapping into Section 29 Credits." *Natural Gas Week*, September 28, 1992, 8.

Stipp, David. "Can This Man Solve America's Energy Crisis?" *Fortune*, May 13, 2002, 100–108.

"Stop the Bailout" Coalition. "Don't Charge Consumers for Utilities' Past Mistakes." Press Release, August 1997.

Stram, Bruce, and Terry Thorn. "Beyond Regulation: A 'Social Compact' for Gas and Electricity." *Public Utilities Fortnightly*, March 1, 1993, 19–22.

Swartz, Mimi, with Sherron Watkins. *Power Failure: The Inside Story of the Collapse of Enron*. New York: Doubleday, 2003.

Szmrecsanyi, Stephen. "InterNorth: The First Fifty Years." Unpublished book manuscript, completed in 1981.

Tatge, Mark. "Irv the Operator." Forbes, November 29, 2004, 180.

"Tax Credits for Non-Conventional Gas Production Offer a Big Bang." *Inside FERC*, February 17, 1992, 7.

Taylor, Jerry, and Peter VanDoren, "California's Electricity Crisis: What's Going On, Who's to Blame, and What to Do." Cato Policy Analysis No. 406. Washington, DC: Cato Institute, 2001.

Tenaska Company. *2015 Annual Report*.

"Texas Commissioners Inquire About 'Shadow Pipeline' Impact." *Natural Gas Week*, April 1, 1985, 1, 4.

Thakar, Nidhi. "The Urge to Merge: A Look at the Repeal of the Public Utility Holding Company Act of 1935." *Lewis & Clark Law Review* 12, no. 3 (1998): 903–42.

Thierer, Adam, and Wayne Crews. *What's Yours Is Mine: Open Access and the Rise of Infrastructure Socialism*. Washington, DC: Cato Institute, 2003.

Thomas, Elaine. "The Blending of Northern Natural Gas and Transwestern Pipeline." *Enron Business*, June 1996, 5.

Thomas, Evan, and Andrew Murr. "The Gambler Who Blew It All." *Newsweek*, February 4, 2002, 17, 20–24.

Thomas, Victoria. "Courts in England and Texas Caught Up in J-Block Battle." *Natural Gas Week International*, May 6, 1996, 3–4.

Thorp, Edward, and Sheen Kassouf. *Beat the Market: A Scientific Stock Market System*. New York: Random House, 1967.

Tiernan, Tom. "Johnston Floats Comprehensive Bill Mandating Retail Wheeling by 2010." *Inside FERC*, January 29, 1996, 5–7.

Tolson, Mike. "Skilling Energized Enron but Draws Suspicion After Its Fall." *Houston Chronicle*, February 10, 2002.

"The Top Managers of 1996." *BusinessWeek*. January 13, 1997, 58.

Transco Energy Company. Annual reports.

Transportadora de Gas del Sur, S.A. *Gas Stories in Argentina, 1823–1998*. Buenos Aires, Argentina: Artes Gráficas Corin Luna S.A., 1998.

"Transwestern Commences Pilot Program Relaxing Capacity Release Restrictions." *Foster Report*, January 9, 1997, 10–12.

"Transwestern Pipeline Company." In *Pacific Coast Gas Association: A Century of Excellence*, edited by Gordon Blackley, 209–10. Portland, OR: PCGA, 1993.

Transwestern Pipeline Company. *30 Year History*. Typescript. Internal company document, Summer 1990.

"Transwestern's Motion to Reopen Record for Additional Evidence on Rejected Direct Billing Mechanism for Recovery of Take-or-Pay Settlement Costs Opposed by FERC Staff, California Parties and Others." *Foster Report*, March 3, 1988, 18–19.

Tussing, Arlon, and Bob Tippee, *The Natural Gas Industry: Evolution, Structure, Performance*. Tulsa, OK: PennWell Books, 1995.

United Nations. *Agenda 21*. New York: United Nations, 1992.

"US Exim Bank Questioned Enron's Dabhol Project." Reuters, May 24, 2002.

Valdez, William. "Coal, Gas Holy War Spreads; Wednesday ERA Hearing Critical." *Natural Gas Week*, February 16, 1987, 1, 6.

———. "Pipeline Marketing Affiliates Rile Independent Gas Brokers." *Natural Gas Week*, September 8, 1986, 1, 4–5.

Vallette, Jim, and Daphne Wysham. *Enron's Pawns: How Public Institutions Bankrolled Enron's Globalization Game*. Washington, DC: Institute for Public Policy, 2002.

Wall Street Journal. 1984–2002.

Walsh, Campion. "Natural Gas Pipelines Push for Deregulation of Gathering Despite Producer Opposition." *Oil Daily*, February 25, 1994.

———. "3-D Seismic Changes Exploration by Shifting Spending to Computers from 'Dumb Iron.'" *Oil Daily*, January 23, 1995.

Wamsted, Dennis. "Michaels Dismisses Conventional Wisdom on Utility Mergers." *Energy Daily*, December 23, 1996, 3.

Washington Post. 1988–2005.

"Weak Demand, Supply Glut Crimping U.S. Gas Industry." *Oil & Gas Journal*, April 22, 1991, 25–28.

Weber, Joseph, with Gary McWilliams, "Cathy Abbott Is No Good Ol' Boy," *Business-Week*, February 12, 1996.

Weisman, Jonathan. "Congress Looks West for Lesson in Utility Deregulation." *Congressional Quarterly Weekly Report*, February 15, 1997, 712–19.

———. "Drive to Open Power Industry to Competition Gains Steam." *Congressional Quarterly Weekly Report*, October 12, 1996, 2911–17.

———. "An Energy Star Flames Out." *Congressional Quarterly Weekly Report*, October 12, 1996, 2916.

———. "Plea for Utility 'Bailout' May Spark Charges of Corporate Welfare." *Congressional Quarterly Weekly Report*, October 12, 1996, 2914–15.

———. "Utilities Hiring Former Members as They Gird for Battle." *Congressional Quarterly Weekly Report*, March 29, 1997, 742–45.

Wendt, Ed. "Black Consultants Shortchanged by Stadium PAC." *Forward Times*, November 6–12, 1996, sec. A.

White, Tom. "Enron Power Corp.," *Enron Business*, January 1993, 5.

———. "To All Enron Operations Corp. Customers and Vendors." Letter, August 2, 1994.

Will, George. "Events, Dear Boy, Events." *Newsweek*, January 28, 2002, 64.

Williams, Bob. "Struggle Develops Over Potential EOR Gas Market in California." *Oil & Gas Journal*, August 26, 1985, 25–30.

Williams, Gary. "The Quiet Man Who's Jolting Utilities." *BusinessWeek*, June 9, 1997, 84–88.

Williams, Stephen. *The Natural Gas Revolution of 1985*. Washington, DC: American Enterprise Institute, 1985.

Williams Company. Annual reports.

Wilson, Jane, and Rockford Meyer. "Comments of Transwestern Pipeline Company on Proposed Decision of [California Public Utilities Commission] ALJ Kim Malcolm Regarding the Application of California Gas Company for Authority to Implement Peaking Service Rates." May 18, 1995.

Wise, Donna. "Report of the WRI-Enron Working Group on a Fiscal Policy and Subsidy Commission." December 9, 1996, 1–5. Available at US Department of Energy, Enron Document, 107–12.

Wood, Kathleen. "Enron Crosses Gas Futures with 4-Hub Trading Program." *Natural Gas Week*, April 16, 1990, 1, 4.

———. "Enron Rejects E&P Unit Bids; Still Needs to Reduce Debt." *Natural Gas Week*, July 25, 1988, 5.

World Commission on Environment and Development. "Towards Sustainable Development." In *Our Common Future*. Transmitted as an Annex to UN Doc. A/42/427 (1987).

Yandle, Bruce. "Bootleggers and Baptists in Retrospect." *Regulation*. October 1999, 5–7.

———. "Bootleggers and Baptists—The Education of a Regulatory Economist." *Regulation*. May/June 1983, 12–16.

Yardley, Jim. "Enron's Many Strands: The Former Chairman; His Influence Lost, Lay Prepares to Answer Questions in Washington." *New York Times*, February 3, 2002.

Yergin, Daniel. *The Prize: The Epic Quest for Oil, Money, and Power*. New York: Simon & Schuster, 1991.

———. *The Quest: Energy, Security, and the Remaking of the Modern World*. New York: Penguin Press, 2011.

Yergin, Daniel, and Joseph Stanislaw. *The Commanding Heights: The Battle Between Government and the Marketplace That Is Remaking the Modern World*. New York: Simon & Schuster, 1998.

Zastudil, Michael. "Enron Launches Its Game Plan; Brand Identification Is Goal. *Natural Gas Week*, January 27, 1997, 2.

Zieman, Mark, Jonathan Cavanagh, and Brenton Schlender. "Peruvian Unit of U.S. Firm Is Nationalized." *Wall Street Journal*, December 30, 1985.

Zimmermann, Erich. *World Resources and Industries*. New York: Harper & Brothers, 1951.

Interviews

Allison, Robert. Interview by Robert Bradley Jr., Houston, TX, January 15, 2007.

Barnhart, Jim. Interview by Robert Bradley Jr., Houston, TX, July 31, 2002.

Beard, John. Interview by Robert Bradley Jr., Houston, TX, December 9, 2007.

Belfer, Robert. Interview by Robert Bradley Jr. and Ursula Brenner, Houston, TX, April 30, 2001.

Bennett, Gerald. Interview by Robert Bradley Jr., Houston, TX, May 13, 2006.

Berriman, Jay. Interview notes by Robert Bradley Jr., n.d.

———. Telephone conversation with Robert Bradley Jr., Houston, TX, n.d.

Beyer, Michael, and George McClellan. Interview by Robert Bradley Jr., Houston, TX, April 10, 2001.

Bhatnagar, Sanjay. Interview by Robert Bradley Jr., Houston, TX, January 17, 2001.

Boatwright, John. Interview by Robert Bradley Jr., Houston, TX, July 25, 2001.

Borget, Lou. Interview notes by Robert Bradley Jr., January 5, 2007.

Burns, Ron. Telephone interviews by Robert Bradley Jr., August 16, 2000, and December 6, 2006.

Collins, Ted. Telephone interviews by Robert Bradley Jr., October 2 and 9, 2006.

Cordes, William. Interview by Robert Bradley Jr. and Joseph Pratt on airplane flight between Houston, TX, and Omaha, NE, August 16, 2000.

Corman, Shelley. Interview by Robert Bradley Jr., Houston, TX, June 8, 2001.

Dienstbier, Dan. Interview by Robert Bradley Jr., Houston, TX, July 17, 2000.

———. Telephone interview by Robert Bradley Jr., July 17, 2006.

Doan, David, Philip Marston, and Ken Malloy. Interview by Robert Bradley Jr., Washington, DC, March 1, 2001.

Duncan, John. Interview by Robert Bradley Jr., Houston, TX, February 26, 2001.

———. Meeting notes by Robert Bradley Jr., Houston, TX, February 19, 2007.

Esslinger, John. Interview by Hamad Alkayhat, London, February 26, 2001 (Esslinger 1).

———. Interview by Robert Bradley Jr., Houston, TX, May 8, 2006 (Esslinger 2).

Frevert, Mark. Interview by Robert Bradley Jr. and Hamad Alkayhat, Houston, TX, February 20, 2001.

Gold, Joe. Interview by Robert Bradley Jr., Houston, TX, June 19, 2001.

Gomez, Julie. Interview by Robert Bradley Jr., Houston, TX, June 29, 2001.

Gullquist, Ronald. Interview by Robert Bradley Jr., Houston, TX, October 11, 2006.

Haug, David. Interview by Hamad Alkayhat and Ursula Brenner, Houston, TX, May 16, 2001.

Hawks, Harold. Telephone interview by Robert Bradley Jr., Houston, TX, and Omaha, NE, May 31, 2007.

———. Telephone conversation notes by Robert Bradley Jr., April 17, 2007.

Hendricks, Tom. Conversation with Robert Bradley Jr., Houston, TX, April 5, 2007.

Herring, Joanne. Interview by Robert Bradley Jr., Houston, TX, May 5, 2003.

Hillings, Joseph. Interview by Robert Bradley Jr., Washington, DC, March 2, 2001.

Hoglund, Forrest. Interview by Robert Bradley Jr., Houston, TX, June 21, 2006.

Horton, Stan. Interview by Robert Bradley Jr., Houston, TX, February 21, 2001 (Horton 1).

———. Interview by Robert Bradley Jr., Houston, TX, August 22, 2001 (Horton 2).

Horvath, Skip. Interview by Robert Bradley Jr., Washington, DC, March 2, 2001.

Hughes, Jim. Interview by Hamad Alkayhat, Houston, TX, April 2001.

Humphrey, Gene. Interview by Robert Bradley Jr., Houston, TX, August 28, 2006.

January, Steve. Interview by Robert Bradley Jr., Houston, TX, July 26, 2001.

Jennrich, John. Interview by Robert Bradley Jr., Washington, DC, October 17, 2001.

Kaminski, Vince. Interview by Robert Bradley Jr., Houston, TX, July 24, 2001.

Kelly, Robert. Interview by Robert Bradley Jr., Houston, TX, February 20, 2001.

Lanier, Bob. Interview by Robert Bradley Jr., Houston, TX, March 20, 2001.

Lay, Ken. Interview by Robert Bradley Jr. Houston, TX, November 10, 2003 (Lay 1).

———. Interview by Robert Bradley Jr., Houston, TX, April 28, 2005 (Lay 2).

———. Interview by Robert Bradley Jr., Houston, TX, August 2, 2005 (Lay 3).

Lemmons, Billy, and Paul Treischman. Interview by Robert Bradley Jr., Houston, TX, August 29, 2001.

Levin, Robert. Interview by Robert Bradley Jr., Houston, TX, August 1, 2001.

LoChiano, Rocco. Telephone interview by Robert Bradley Jr., June 13, 2006.

Love, Ben. Interview by Robert Bradley Jr., Houston, TX, March 13, 2001.

Malloy, Ken. Interview by Robert Bradley Jr., Washington, DC, March 1, 2001.

Mark, Rebecca. Interview notes by Robert Bradley Jr., November 4, 2015.

Marston, Philip. Interview by Robert Bradley Jr., Washington, DC, March 1, 2001.

McCarty, Dan. Interview by Robert Bradley Jr., Houston, TX, January 23, 2001.

McNair, Bob. Interview by Robert Bradley Jr., Houston, TX, August 16, 2006.

Menchaca, Peggy. Interview by Robert Bradley Jr., Houston, TX, August 21, 2001.

Meyer, Rockford. Interview by Robert Bradley Jr., Houston, TX, February 16, 2001.

Morgan, William. Interview by Robert Bradley Jr., Houston, TX, May 11, 2006.

Muckleroy, Mike. Interviews by Robert Bradley Jr., Winter Park, FL, June–October 2006.

Olson, John. Interview by Robert Bradley Jr., Houston, TX, December 16, 2006.

Piper, Greg. Interview by Robert Bradley Jr., Houston, TX, March 6, 2001.

Potempa, Lou. Interview by Robert Bradley Jr., Houston, TX, April 27, 2001 (Potempa 1).

———. Interview by Robert Bradley Jr., Houston, TX, September 8–9, 27, 2006 (Potempa 2).

Schroeder, Mark. Interview by Robert Bradley Jr. and Ursula Brenner, Houston, TX, June 13, 2001.

Segnar, Sam. Interview by Robert Bradley Jr., The Woodlands, TX, October 10, 2001.

Seidl, Mick. Interviews by Robert Bradley Jr., Houston, TX, September–October 2006.

Shapiro, Rick. Interview by Robert Bradley Jr., Houston, TX, February 12, 2001.

Sherriff, John. Interview by Hamad Alkayhat, London, February 26, 2001.

Skilling, Jeff. Interview by Robert Bradley Jr. and Joseph Pratt, Houston, TX, October 4, 2000.

Smith, Clark. Interview by Robert Bradley Jr., Houston, TX, May 3, 2006.

Stram, Bruce. Interview by Robert Bradley Jr., Houston, TX, May 3, 2001.

Strauss, Bill. Interview by Robert Bradley Jr. and Joseph Pratt, Omaha, NE, August 17, 2000.

Sunde, Marty. Interview by Robert Bradley Jr., Houston, TX, July 10, 2001.

Sutton, Joe. Interview by Robert Bradley Jr., Houston, TX, October 13, 2000.

Thompson, John. Interview by Robert Bradley Jr., London, June 20, 2001.

Thorn, Terence. Interview by Robert Bradley Jr., Houston, TX, June 6, 2001.

Wakeham, John. Interview by Robert Bradley Jr., Houston, TX, April 30, 2001.

Walzel, Jim. Interview by Robert Bradley Jr., Houston, TX, March 14, 2006.

Wasaff, George. Interview by Robert Bradley Jr., Houston, TX, March 7, 2001.

———. Interview notes by Robert Bradley Jr., February 5, 2014.

White, Tom. Interview by Robert Bradley Jr., Houston, TX, March 19, 2001.

Wing, John. Interviews by Robert Bradley Jr., The Woodlands, TX, and Houston, TX, June and October 2006.

———. Telephone interview by Robert Bradley Jr., The Woodlands, TX, and Houston, TX, December 6, 2006.

Woytek, David. Interview by Robert Bradley Jr., Houston, TX, January 10, 2007.

Illustration Credits

Figure I.1 Courtesy of Enron Corp. **Figure I.2** Courtesy of Enron Corp.
Figure I.3 Courtesy of Enron Corp. **Figure I.4** Courtesy of Enron Corp.
Figure I.6 Courtesy of Enron Corp. **Figure 1.1** *Annual Report and illustration:*
Courtesy of Enron Corp.; *book cover:* Courtesy of Warner Books. **Figure 1.2**
Courtesy of Enron Corp. **Figure 1.3** *Map and pictures*: Courtesy of SoCalGas.
Figure 1.4 Courtesy of Enron Corp. **Figure 1.5** Courtesy of Enron Corp.
Figure 1.6 *Photograph and logos:* Courtesy of Enron Corp. **Figure 2.1** Courtesy
of Enron Corp. **Figure 2.2** *Jacobs photograph*, Courtesy of Irwin Jacobs; *other
photographs, map, and logo:* Courtesy of Enron Corp. **Figure 2.3** Courtesy of
Enron Corp. **Figure 2.4** Courtesy of Enron Corp. **Figure 2.5** *Book cover and
contents:* Courtesy of Energy, Economics & Environmental Institute; *photograph:*
Courtesy of Oliver Richard III. **Figure 2.6** Courtesy of Enron Corp. **Figure 3.1**
Top photographs: Courtesy of Enron Corp.; *bottom photographs*: Courtesy of *The
Vandalia Leader.* **Figure 3.2** *Photographs and text:* Courtesy of Enron Corp.,
Houston Chronicle. **Figure 3.4** Courtesy of Enron Corp. **Figure 3.5** Courtesy of
Enron Corp. **Figure 3.6** *Photographs and text*: Courtesy of Enron Corp.
Figure 4.1 *Photographs:* Courtesy of Enron Corp.; *memo:* courtesy of Mike
Muckleroy. **Figure 4.2** Courtesy of Enron Corp. **Figure 5.1** *Photograph and
documents:* Courtesy of John Olson. **Figure 5.2** Courtesy of Enron Corp.
Figure 5.3 *Photographs and logo:* Courtesy of Robert McNair. **Figure 5.4** Cour-
tesy of Enron Corp. **Figure 6.1** Courtesy of Enron Corp. **Figure 6.2** *Photographs
and text*: Courtesy of Greater Houston Partnership. **Figure 6.3** Courtesy of
Enron Corp. **Figure 6.4** Courtesy of Enron Corp. **Figure 6.5** Courtesy of Enron
Corp. **Figure 6.6** Courtesy of Enron Corp. **Figure 6.7** Courtesy of Enron Corp.
Figure 6.8 Courtesy of Enron Corp. **Figure 6.9** Courtesy of Enron Corp.
Figure 7.1 Courtesy of Enron Corp. **Figure 7.2** Courtesy of Enron Corp.

Figure 7.3 *Illustration:* Courtesy of Enron Corp. **Figure 7.4** Courtesy of Enron Corp. **Figure 7.5** *Issue reproductions:* Courtesy of *Natural Gas Week.*
Figure 8.1 Courtesy of Enron Corp. **Figure 8.2** Courtesy of Enron Corp.
Figure 8.3 Courtesy of Enron Corp. **Figure 8.4** Courtesy of Enron Corp.
Figure 8.5 Courtesy of Enron Corp. **Figure 8.6** Courtesy of Enron Corp.
Figure 8.7 Courtesy of Enron Corp. **Figure 9.1** Courtesy of Enron Corp.
Figure 9.2 Courtesy of Enron Corp. **Figure 9.3** Courtesy of Enron Corp.
Figure 9.4 Courtesy of Enron Corp. **Figure 9.5** Courtesy of Enron Corp.
Figure 9.6 Courtesy of Enron Corp. **Figure 10.1** Courtesy of Enron Corp.
Figure 10.2 Courtesy of Enron Corp. **Figure 10.3** Courtesy of Enron Corp.
Figure 10.4 Courtesy of Enron Corp. **Figure 10.5** Courtesy of Enron Corp.
Figure 10.6 Courtesy of Enron Corp. **Figure 11.1** Courtesy of Enron Corp.
Figure 11.2 Courtesy of Enron Corp. **Figure 11.3** Courtesy of Enron Corp.
Figure 11.4 Courtesy of Enron Corp. **Figure 11.5** Courtesy of Enron Corp.
Figure 12.1 Courtesy of Enron Corp. **Figure 12.2** Courtesy of Enron Corp.
Figure 12.3 Courtesy of Enron Corp. **Figure 12.4** Courtesy of Enron Corp.
Figure 12.5 Courtesy of Enron Corp. **Figure 13.1** Courtesy of Enron Corp.
Figure 13.2 Courtesy of Enron Corp. **Figure 13.3** Courtesy of Enron Corp.
Figure 13.4 Courtesy of Enron Corp. **Figure 14.1** Courtesy of Enron Corp.
Figure 14.2 Courtesy of Enron Corp. **Figure 14.3** Courtesy of Enron Corp.
Figure 14.4 Courtesy of Enron Corp. **Figure 14.5** Courtesy of Enron Corp.
Figure 14.6 Courtesy of Enron Corp. **Figure 14.7** Courtesy of Enron Corp.
Figure 15.1 *Study covers:* Courtesy of Americans for Prosperity; Mercatus Center
Figure 15.2 Courtesy of Enron Corp. **Figure 15.3** Courtesy of Enron Corp.
Figure 15.4 Courtesy of Enron Corp. **Figure 15.5** Courtesy of Enron Corp.
Figure 15.6 Courtesy of Enron Corp. **Figure 15.7** Courtesy of Enron Corp.
Figure 15.8 Courtesy of Enron Corp. **Figure 15.9** Courtesy of Enron Corp.
Figure E.1 Courtesy of Enron Corp. **Figure E.2** Courtesy of Enron Corp.
Figure E.3 Courtesy of Enron Corp. **Figure E.4** Courtesy of Enron Corp.
Figure E.5 Courtesy of Enron Corp.

Name Index

An online version of the Name Index is available at: www.politicalcapitalism .org/Book3/Nameindex.html.

Note: A page number followed by "n" and a number refers to a footnote on that page. A page number followed by "fig." and a number refers to the contents of a figure on that page.

Jordan, Don, 323–24, 341, 598
Joshi, Manohar, 501
Joy, Corwin, 480

Kaminski, Vince, xviii, 28, 264, 350,
    395–96, 461, 473, 480–84,
    488, 498
Karas, Kenneth "Ken," 544–47
Kaskel, Ray, 280
Kean, Steve, 488, 603–4
Kee, Carolyn, 193
Kellstrom, Bill, 113–14, 129
Kelly, Robert "Bob," 96, 100, 101–2,
    129, 165, 168–69, 194, 203,
    205, 220, 222–24, 269, 270n24,
    272, 276–78, 280, 284n41, 495,
    506, 526–39, 543–47, 549, 560
Kelly, Thomas, 279, 341
Kennedy, John, 615
Kennedy, Joseph, 138
Kern, Keith D., 100, 126n19, 135,
    151–52, 173, 192, 202,
    206, 246
Kerr, Richard, 241, 328
Keynes, John Maynard, 67, 572n14
Kilmer, Rob, 90
Kinder, Darrell, 295–96, 509
Kinder, Richard Dan "Rich." See
    Business Index
Kinneman, Jeff, 480–81, 487
Kirby, John Henry, xv, 38n46
Kissinger, Henry, 280, 611
Klein, Barry, 614
Knight, Jesse, 605
Knorpp, Ron, 89, 100, 152
Knudsen, Sheila, 370 fig. 8.4, 405
Koch, Charles, x, xv, xviii, 5, 6n6,
    60–64, 672–73, 675
Koenig, Mark, 304n64
Kolko, Gabriel, 60
Kopper, Michael, 548
Krenz, Doug, 409, 412, 413 fig. 9.6
Krugman, Paul, 3

Krupp, Fred, 338
Kuehn, Ron, 163

Langdon, Jerry, 307
Lanier, Bob, 612–14
Larson, Elwin, 180
Larson, Henrietta, xvii
Lash, Jonathan, 554
Laughman, Bob, 399–400
Launer, Curt, 119, 121, 652
Lavoie, Don, v
Lavorato, John, 400n7, 478
Lawner, Leslie, 392, 416
Lawson, Richard, 179, 241, 326
Lawson, William, 614
Lay, Elizabeth, 583
Lay, Kenneth Lee "Ken." See Business
    Index; Political Economy
    Index
Lay, Linda Phillips Herrold, 17, 74,
    137, 650, 655, 680, 684
Lay, Mark K., 583–86, 681
Lay, Omer, 94, 149, 259, 361, 563,
    677–80, 687
Lay, Sharon, 80, 583–84, 680–81
Lay family. See Kenneth L. Lay: A
    Chronology, 677–88
Leal, Donald, 408
Leff, Dan, 633–34
LeMaistre, Charles A., 121n15, 152n5
Lenssen, Nicholas, 539
Levin, Robert, 359
Levine, Dennis, 120n14
Lewis, Richard, 476
Leworthy, Roger, 196, 198
Linder, P. Scott, 137, 152n5
LoChiano, Rocco "Rocky," 109, 116,
    118–20, 122, 125, 134, 151
Lockhart, H. Eugene, 632
Long, Sue (Mrs. Jeff Skilling), 361
Lovins, Amory, 528, 597, 639
Lowenstein, Andy, 474
Lowenstein, Roger, 481n24

Business Index

This index focuses principally on commercial, financial, and technological elements in *Enron Ascending*, along with relevant name entries. A more analytical, three-level Business Index can be found online at www.politicalcapitalism.org/Book3/Businessindex.html.

Note: A page number followed by "n" and a number refers to a footnote on that page. A page number followed by "fig." and a number refers to the contents of a figure on that page.

Accounting, financial
  conflicts of interest, 8, 27, 135, 383, 414, 483–84, 613n28
  earnings manipulation, xii, 1, 6, 18, 25, 27, 49, 51, 62, 187, 191, 246, 252, 299, 350, 372, 380, 383, 387, 413–14, 577
  gaming of ("engineering"), iii, ix, xii, xiv, 4, 28, 49–50, 60, 62–63, 65, 286n44, 381, 413, 485, 578, 600n14, 632, 644, 672, 675
  generally accepted accounting principles (GAAP), 246, 413
  mark-to-market, xii, 8, 18–19, 24–25, 27–28, 49–51, 62, 246, 252, 264, 288, 294, 299, 305, 350, 364, 368, 372, 377–85, 387, 391–92, 404, 413–14, 421, 462–63, 465, 477, 479, 481, 483, 488, 490, 492, 513, 520, 569, 591, 638, 658, 663, 670

"mark-to-model," xii, 23–24, 27, 62, 382, 638, 670
tax strategies, xii, xiv, 7, 14, 26, 38, 44, 47, 64, 170, 172n25, 222, 240, 252, 262, 285–88, 290–94, 310, 313–17, 369, 402, 429, 439, 446–48, 451, 454, 525, 529, 540, 543–46, 560n37, 574, 578, 643–44
write-offs, xiii, 6, 11, 18–22, 25, 27, 86, 92, 105, 125, 128n22, 143, 253, 257, 264n14, 350, 458, 462, 484, 498, 502–3, 520, 526n7, 624, 647, 658–59, 664, 669
See also Enron Corp.: accounting subjectivism
Alaska Natural Gas Transportation System (ANGTS), 86, 105n1, 109
American Natural Resources Co. (ANR), 88, 102, 103, 105, 116, 118, 265, 439, 463

and Lay (Ken), 60, 209, 378
and off-balance-sheet ventures, 28,
    377, 410, 464 fig. 11.2,
    465, 644
and Skilling (Jeff), 664
and Valhalla scandal, 203
See also Houston Natural Gas: and
    debt; HNG/InterNorth: and
    debt; Lay, Kenneth Lee: and
    debt dependence
Dienstbier, Dan L.
on Brooklyn Union contract, 180
departure from Enron, 213, 230
at Enron (head), natural gas
    operations, 126n19
vs. Enron's corporate culture, 213
on gas marketing benefits, 114
on gas-transportation profits, 114
at HNG/InterNorth (head), natural
    gas operations, 152
as HNG/InterNorth leader, 130,
    152n5
at HNG/InterNorth merger
    meeting (Granby ranch), 129
Natural Gas Clearinghouse,
    InterNorth declines
    participation, 114
and Northern Cogeneration One,
    165–66 (later, Texas City
    Plant)
at Northern Natural Gas
    (president), 114, 128
at Northern Natural Gas Pipeline
    (president), 106
as operations focused, 193n5
relocation to Houston, 128
on responsibility lines, pipelines vs.
    marketing, 140n35
subordinates of, at Enron, 180
Dominion Resources Inc., 25,
    210–11, 223
Dow Chemical Co., 107
DuPont, 107

Earnings, 17–28
acceleration of, xii, 24–26,
    245–46, 383
and asset sales, 19n23, 50, 155, 206,
    209, 439, 456, 475, 510, 515
cogen as source of, 50–51, 271, 476
Enron International, 278, 280, 283,
    427, 489, 515, 569, 645
and Enron Oil Corp., 11, 13, 156,
    188–94, 203
EOG as source of, 50, 447–53,
    492, 643
gas marketing as source of, 243,
    350, 356, 385, 404, 462, 466,
    479, 482, 484, 645, 647
imprudent marketing and, 22–23
Kinder (Rich) and, xii, 24, 246, 256,
    351, 426
liquids as source of, 50, 293, 455–59
"making the numbers," xii, 1, 6,
    27–28, 577
mark-to-market accounting, 27,
    49–51, 299, 350, 372,
    378–81, 385–87, 413–14,
    488, 569, 647
pipelines as source of, 43, 50, 53,
    225, 227, 257, 259, 273, 278,
    305, 429–33, 438, 647, 658
price/earnings ratio, 48–49, 62,
    482, 646
and retail marketing, 590, 646
streak in growth of, 13, 22–27, 50,
    252, 303, 566. *See also* Fraud,
    philosophic
subquality income, 23–24, 185, 187,
    247, 256
targets for, 60, 62, 246–48, 298,
    316, 426, 439, 462, 497,
    512, 519–20, 569–72, 576,
    589, 636, 646, 659. *See also*
    Enron 2000
and write-offs postponed, 20–22,
    493, 502

Enron Power Corp., chairman,
    224, 248
at GE, 100–101
at HNG, 100–103
at HNG/InterNorth, 133, 165
and HNG/InterNorth merger,
    118–19, 121, 151
HNG Interstate, head, 129; rejects,
    133, 431
and Lay (Ken), 260
and Mark (Rebecca), 271n25, 509
risk taking, 21
Teesside I, 269–72
Teesside II, 495
Wing Group, 223, 277
Wing-Merrill Group, 280
"World's First Natural Gas Major"
    (Enron vision), xv, 30, 244,

254, 256, 267, 271, 273,
275, 277, 297, 300, 302,
304, 349, 378, 426, 429–30,
451, 456, 489, 490, 520,
524, 564 fig. 14.1, 564–67,
587, 610
"World's Leading Company" (Enron
    vision), xiv, xv, xvii, 570
"World's Leading Energy Company"
    (Enron vision), xiv, xv, 24, 31,
    61, 514, 519, 567–70, 587, 589,
    620, 641, 668, 670

Zapata Gulf Marine Corp., 92, 93 fig.
    1.5, 247
Zilkha Energy Co., 371, 397
Zond Corp., 541, 541–48, 559,
    581, 622

Political Economy Index

This index focuses on political, legal, and regulatory elements in *Enron Ascending*, along with relevant name entries. A more analytical, three-level Political Economy Index can be found online at www.politicalcapitalism.org/Book3/Politicaleconomyindex.html.

Note: A page number followed by "n" and a number refers to a footnote on that page. A page number followed by "fig." and a number refers to the contents of a figure on that page.

Process analysis. *See also*
Historiographic method
Enron and, xvi, 2–3, 7, 59–60, 667–68
primrose paths and slippery slopes,
6–8, 670
Progressivism, xi, xiii, xiv, 3–6,
64–65, 332, 341, 540, 576, 598,
672, 674
Protectionism. *See* Tariffs
(international)
Public Choice economics. *See also*
Government failure
and CO_2 regulation, 556
market vs. government failure,
318–19, 382, 443, 556
Public-interest theory of regulation/
government/politics, 228,
265, 597
Public Power Corporation (Greece),
538
Public Utility Holding Company Act
of 1935, 38, 107n5, 243, 254,
341, 624
Enron Gas Marketing, exemption
from, 415
Enron opposition to, 342, 415
Public-utility regulation, 34, 47, 86,
101, 235
"beating the rate case," 257, 431
coal-plant bias under, 30n38, 58,
179, 218, 323, 366, 373
costs and, 257, 433–34
interstate gas-gathering lines and,
445–46
methodology of, 255, 257
Natural Gas Act and, 254
natural gas pipelines, 38, 155, 257,
352, 431–34, 438
natural gas utilities, 115
and nonintegrated gas industry,
254 55, 355
rate-base incentives, 30n38, 58, 179,
218, 323, 366, 432

rate-base maintenance, 38, 99,
110–11, 115, 257, 259, 431,
433, 514, 559
and stranded-cost recovery
(electricity), 37n44, 601–2
three-year rate cases (FERC), 432
vanishing rate-base problem,
115, 431
Public Utility Regulatory Policies Act
of 1978, 40, 97, 164n19, 173,
177, 204n20, 219, 224, 240,
251, 290n48, 310, 373, 422, 461
"avoided cost," 14, 41, 218,
525–26
Independent Power Producers,
373n21
"qualifying facilities," 525–26
solar lobby and, 525
Wheelabrator-Frye Corp. and, 525

Railroads
as coal lobby, 26, 106, 320–21
deregulation of, 596, 601
Rate liberalization. *See* Enron Corp.:
interstate pipeline regulation
Regulation. *See also* "Bootleggers and
Baptists"; Climate change;
Conservationism; Energy
crisis of 1970s; Lay, Ken, and
politics; Mandatory open
access; Rent-seeking
advantages to Enron of, xiv, 10–11,
13–14, 36–45, 422, 644
of banking and drilling capital, 364,
391, 422
vs. "by contract," 435
cost-benefit analysis of, 340, 556
as cumulative process, 234–35
gaming of, xiv, 5, 25–28, 50, 65, 650.
See also Philosophic fraud
gaps in, 234–35
precautionary principle and,
538, 556

The previous 2 books in the tetralogy still available

Book 2: Edison to Enron: Energy Markets and Political Strategies

Published 2011, 600 pages, ISBN 978-0-470-91736-7

During the last 150 years, the United States has been at the forefront of energy development. Robert L. Bradley Jr.'s *Edison to Enron* chronicles important swaths of this history by focusing on the great entrepreneurs of electricity and natural gas: their lives and labors, their faults and failures, their mortal enemies, and their sometimes more deadly friends.

Samuel Insull transformed the inventions of Thomas Edison into the modern electricity industry—only to have an Enron/Ken Lay-like fall late in his career. John Henry Kirby helped Texas enter the big leagues with timber, oil, and gas between his two bankruptcies. And Clint Murchison, Ray Fish, Robert Herring, and Jack Bowen, among others chronicled in the book, went through ups and downs in their quest to displace manufactured (coal) gas with cheaper, cleaner natural gas across the United States and in Canada.

Bradley's book covers market entrepreneurship, especially resourceship in regard to energy minerals. Yet there are also significant instances in which the energy creators engaged in political entrepreneurship, or rent-seeking, by extracting special government favor for pecuniary advantage. The waste and perils of the latter provide a stark contrast to the benefits and prudence of free-market enterprise.

Edison to Enron also tracks the career of Kenneth L. Lay, from a minor government bureaucrat to the heir apparent at Transco Energy Company to the wunderkind CEO of Houston Natural Gas Corporation. As a rare broad-based history of the American energy industry, *Edison to Enron* fills a critical gap in the historiography and takes its place as a classic account of the energy nation *par excellence* during its most dynamic century.

"This is a powerful story, brilliantly told." **Forrest McDonald,** Historian

"This scholarly work fills in much missing history about two of America's most important industries, electricity and natural gas." **Joseph A. Pratt**, *NEH-Cullen Professor of History and Business, University of Houston*

"... a remarkable book on the political inner workings of the U.S. energy industry." **Robert Peltier**, PE, Editor-in-Chief, *POWER Magazine*

"*Edison to Enron* synthesizes business history, economic history, biography, and political economy to tell a compelling tale of innovation and new value creation in two energy industries, as well as increasing regulation and political capitalism in them." **Lynne Kiesling** *Knowledgeproblem.com*

"This readable work offers great, interesting coverage of personalities and politics, with little economic analysis." Summing Up: Highly recommended."
Choice Magazine

Book 1: Capitalism at Work: Business, Government, and Energy

Published 2009, 498 pages, ISBN 978-0-9764041-7-0

Capitalism took the blame for Enron although the company was anything but a free-market enterprise, and company architect was hardly a principled capitalist. On the contrary, Enron was a politically dependent company and, in the end, a grotesque outcome of America's mixed economy.

That is the central finding of Robert L. Bradley's *Capitalism at Work*: The blame for Enron rests squarely with "political capitalism"--a system in which business firms routinely obtain government intervention to further their own interests at the expense of consumers, taxpayers, and competitors. Although Ken Lay professed allegiance to free markets, he was in fact a consummate politician. Only by manipulating the levers of government was he able to transform Enron from a $3 billion natural gas company to a $100 billion chimera, one that went in a matter of months from seventh place on Fortune's 500 list to bankruptcy.

But *Capitalism at Work* goes beyond unmasking Enron's sophisticated foray into political capitalism. Employing the timeless insights of Adam Smith, Samuel Smiles, and Ayn Rand, among others, Bradley shows how fashionable anti-capitalist doctrines set the stage for the ultimate business debacle. Those errant theories, like Enron itself, elevated form over substance, ignored legitimate criticism, and bypassed midcourse correction. Political capitalism was thus more than the handiwork of profit-hungry businessmen and power-hungry politicians. It was a legacy of failed scholarship.

Capitalism at Work's penetrating, multidisciplinary explanation of the demise of Enron breaks new ground regarding business history, business ethics, business best practices, and public policies toward business. As Bradley concludes: The fundamental lesson from Enron is this: Capitalism did not fail. The mixed economy failed. The capitalist worldview is stronger, not weaker, post-Enron. But there is another, deeper lesson that explains Enron and the mistakes of the intellectual mainstream before, during, and after Enron's active life: What in the Enron vernacular is called the "smartest guys-in-the-room problem" can strike at anytime and anywhere. Whether in business or academic – or a professional or an association – conceit, deceit, and dogmatism are the bane of personal, intellectual, and organizational success.

"Fascinating, comprehensive... far surpassing my own history of political capitalism done in the 1960s." **Gabriel Kolko**, *Historian*

"Bradley's book is especially timely and it raises fundamental questions about the business of competition. Given the author's documentation a wide audience might be served by reading *Capitalism at Work*." **William A. Mogel,** *Energy Law Journal*

"He (Bradley) has succeeded in his effort to show that Enron was guided by faulty premises well-refuted in the economics literature. A definitive study." **Richard L. Gordon,** *Cato Journal*

"Businesses succeed by creating real, long-term value for their owners, customers, and society. On the other hand, as *Capitalism at Work* shows, companies that resort to political profiteering and public grandstanding can fail spectacularly. Bradley's defense of economic freedom provides new insight for business ethics, business best practices, and public policy." **Charles Koch,** *Chairman of Koch Industries*

"Recommended for public and academic library collections, lower-division undergraduate and up." **Choice Magazine**

More information is available from
www.politicalcapitalism.org
www.scrivenerpublishing.com

Printed and bound by CPI Group (UK) Ltd, Croydon, CR0 4YY

23/04/2025

14660904-0004